THE POEM

DON PATERSON

THE POEM

Lyric, Sign, Metre

ff

FABER & FABER

First published in 2018
by Faber & Faber Ltd
Bloomsbury House
74–77 Great Russell Street
London WC1B 3DA

Typeset by Donald Sommerville
Printed and bound by CPI Group (UK) Ltd, Croydon, CR0 4YY

A CIP record for this book
is available from the British Library

ISBN 978–0–571–20662–9

2 4 6 8 10 9 7 5 3 1

for Douglas Dunn

CONTENTS

_____

CONTENTS

PART III – Metre: The Rhythm of the Poem

Qué te he dado, lo sé. Qué has recibido, no lo sé.

— ANTONIO PORCHIA

I know what I have given you
I do not know what you have received

PREFACE

'This is not for you', runs the dedication of Mark Z. Danielewski's unreadably distressing *The House of Leaves*, a book I finally abandoned after three nights of waking up to my own screams. I toyed with borrowing it here, but I have no real excuse for adopting such a minatory tone — however accurate the statement might be, or similar the effects this book produces. A few years ago I wrote a chatty and informal reader's guide to Shakespeare's *Sonnets*; I knew exactly who the book was for and for whom it was not. The former group received it in the spirit in which it was intended, but not every member of the latter got the memo, despite my careful explanation in a long preface. I don't blame them for one second. The clue here is 'long preface'. If you want to circulate instructions for a home-made ricin bomb with absolute discretion, I strongly suggest you stick it in a long preface. I'd prefer this one to be read, hence its brevity.

I *hope*, of course, that this book is for you, but the reason it might not be is that was written primarily for me, in an attempt to explain a couple of things to myself. Firstly, does the existence of the poem point to a basic poetic function of speech, and, if so, what is its purpose? Secondly, what *is* a poem? The first question is not very original, though I've attempted to answer it from an 'insider's perspective', so however misguided my conclusions are, some may at least have the merit of novelty. We usually answer the second question by separately addressing the business of the poem's creation and the poem's reception; the first we might call *ars poetica*, the second poetic analysis. It has long been my conviction that they are two aspects of the same thing, and can be fruitfully discussed together. This is the approach I have taken here. So if these questions also interest you

– welcome. However, this book is *not* a primer, a how-to guide, or a handbook of forms: there are plenty of those out there already. (Despite the fact I tend to write what others call 'formal' poetry, I should confess that I have little interest in 'poetic form', which I consider a finite and relatively unimportant subject.) Nor is this a book for 'poetry readers', the literate constituency for whom I have the most respect, and who will find it dull. These good people already know exactly what they're doing. I am less convinced that my own constituency do.

As for that constituency . . . Perhaps I just mean 'all those with a professional interest in poetry'. I am a poet, though this should always be a reluctant declaration, as poets spend far more of their time being not-poets. I also work as an editor, and I teach poetic composition to apprentice poets. And while I did not train as an academic, as a long-standing member of that dubious cohort, 'writers who work in the academy', I have morphed into something that can occasionally pass for one in a bad light, and I teach poetry and poetics as literary subjects to undergraduate students, and supervise postgraduate research. My interest in the subject of poetic composition is therefore formed by three perspectives: the practice of writing verse, and my knowledge of that procedure from first-hand experience; my work with other poets in the role of editor or mentor; and such scholarly and scientific theory as relates to my discipline.

Each perspective addresses a separate part of the process. The perils of that process are summed up by this book's epigraph, a beautiful line from Antonio Porchia's *Voces*: '*I know what I have given you. I do not know what you have received.*' Poets give the poem; editors and mentors are concerned with its careful transmission; scholars study the poem as it is received by a community of readers. Because I address all these constituencies simultaneously in this book, I may also have simultaneously alienated them all with what amounts to a wilful inconsistency of tone. They may find themselves suddenly addressed by a pronoun, or in a manner or in jargon with which they are uncomfortable. Academics mostly hate being called 'we', but when I use that word I'm usually referring to my own deranged community of fellow poets. We are a fractious community – 'when the stakes are low, tempers run high', to quote the late Joseph Chassler – but we *are* a community. When I talk as a poet, I know I can sometimes sound impatient, biased, overzealous and occasionally chippy (as has been pointed out to me, poets have a reputation for 'sensitivity', but mostly we're just touchy). However, suppressing that tone would also have meant me denying how strongly I feel about a discipline I've given up many years of my life to study and practise. Poets often hate reductive linguistic or scientific explanations for what they would prefer to think of as an inscrutable or mysterious procedure; but many academics expect that they at least be attempted. Editors hate everything. For them, all poems are bad until they prove themselves otherwise (they have the stats on their side, unfortunately), and that voice will again distinguish itself by its lousy attitude. But since I could find no middle ground, my most honest instinct led me to write from all three perspectives simultaneously, in the hope that the narrowness of any single one might be corrected by the others.

(I've had, and continue to indulge, another career in music – where I've worked as a guitarist and composer drifting between jazz, electronic, computer-based music and 'straight' composition. I mention this only to explain the excessive number of musical analogies employed here.)

I have done my best to curb my footnote addiction and have completely failed. I like footnotes. You may not. But I often get distracted by something that interests me, and can see no good reason not to pursue it some small way. Other writers put all this stuff in the back, but as a reader I dislike having to leave my place every five minutes to go rummaging in the basement for something I could have found in the kitchen drawer. However, I have placed the longer excursions as endnotes, so the reader might have some control over the frequency and length of these interruptions. I have used these notes to bury a long or particularly dry technical definition, address some analytical crux, relieve myself of some anecdote, or write a micro-essay on a parallel subject. The reader is free to ignore these asides, safe in the knowledge that the broad argument should make as much sense with or without them; nonetheless, the material they contain is as important or unimportant as anything else in the text.

I apologise, too, for the bad jokes and occasional scurrilities strewn throughout, but this book is a demanding enough read without my resisting the opportunity to lighten things up where I could. Besides, I am convinced that literature is not a subject that should *ever* be taken entirely seriously. It is, at the end of the day, a form of conversation that takes place between two monkeys, not an attempt to measure gravitational waves. If we don't conduct our research in the spirit of its subject, we should probably distrust our own conclusions on principle. However, this is also the reason the text will occasionally take metaphysical and even ethical detours. The argument might be made that poetics should confine itself to the business of poetic language alone; but since I'd hold that poetry's very purpose is to stop us articulating false statements about the world, avoiding these digressions here seems a perverse compunction. Language circum-scribes the concepts through which we both apprehend and read the world. When that apprehension becomes inadequate, or the reading self-evidently false, the poetic function of language reflexively attempts to restore it to something capable of telling the truth. It's perhaps too much to claim that the self-correcting habit of language we call 'poetry' is evidence of an intrinsic morality; but it's hard to make a poem out of lies, couched as they so often are in tired, empty and clichéd speech. (Lies would rather not draw attention to themselves. Though political sloganeering often makes use of the *lyricised* cliché: banal evils are often delivered sing-song.)

*

The Poem is essentially a treatise, consisting of three long essays. Part I, 'Lyric', should be accessible to most lay readers with an interest in the subject of poetic composition, so long as they have no objection to a bit of phonetics. It is not a technically complex subject, so I have kept the tone reasonably informal. Its relative brevity reflects my belief that it is a finite area of study.

Part II, 'Sign', is longer, and mostly concerned with domain theory, ideas of poetic meaning, and what the structure of poetic language actually looks like if you accept that poetry is a neutral aspect of human speech, not a deviant form of communication. Several of its more theoretical excursions are necessarily and miserably dense. It also strays furthest from my own expertise: at times, I confess, I felt like one of those visitors to Scotland who every year attempt Jock's Road in April dressed in plimsolls and a T-shirt – and whom we discover iced to a boulder three weeks later, their own bewilderment flash-frozen to their faces. However, too little has been heard from poets themselves on the subject of poetic trope, and I hope the experts (metaphor studies has become the string theory of poetry, so there is no shortage of them) will tolerate my own naivety and occasionally grievous error in return from bringing a little practical experience to the table. The study of conceptual domains has revolutionised the way we think about metaphor, but some recent assertions vis-à-vis the operation of *poetic* metaphor are, I'm afraid, deeply flawed. (Cognitive poetics is very much in its youth, and like most new disciplines is dominated by bad taxonomies, so I feel far less cautious about steaming in there.)

The last and longest part, 'Metre', is almost entirely technical, and unlikely to be of interest to anyone but specialists and students. The first half is fairly straightforward and taken up with the definition of terms; the second will likely prove a frustrating read for all but those with a professional interest. (I can assure the reader that I am not slyly baiting the hook here, but merely offering fair warning.) However, I have been careful to build the argument slowly for anyone new to the subject who cares to pursue it to its end.

There's no doubt that I've also indulged myself, and backed into unscholarly and unscientific crankery too many times. Alas, I'm now of the age when I had to make a big mandala of everything I think I know in an attempt to bring some order to it, and articulate my own beliefs about language, poetry, and the means by which the poem maintains its central role in our cultural and spiritual life.

*

Too many people – friends, poets, scholars and editors – have helped me with this text and its ideas to thank, and certainly to thank adequately. I have resisted giving a full list, because far too much of your advice was not taken where it should have been. Either way, you know who you are, and that you have my deep gratitude. However, I must explicitly thank Matthew Hollis, Nick Laird, Tom Jones, Chris Jones, Neil Rhodes and Rebecca Stott for their generous and meticulous comments, and Sally Shuttleworth for her invaluable support. Without the magnificent assistance of my St Andrews research students Jennifer Baker, Katherine Bone and Patrick Errington, this book would have been far more error-strewn than it no doubt is.

I thank Nora Chassler, as ever, for her refusal to countenance the lie, the easy answer, the stupid question and received wisdom in all its forms – and for pushing me again and again to try to see things as they are, not how I would prefer them. I offer my especial gratitude to two people: Fiona Sampson, who edited much shorter versions of several of these essays when they first appeared in *Poetry Review*, and whose comments had a shaping influence on my approach to the whole; and Derek Attridge, whose terrifyingly exact and trenchant criticism led me to revise many passages extensively (if not, I suspect, entirely to his satisfaction), and on whose fatal encouragement the completion of this book can be partly blamed.

And if you've read this far, well, who knows. Maybe this book *is* for you. But it's dedicated to Douglas Dunn, one of the finest poets my country has ever produced, and my first mentor. I very much doubt this book is for Dougie, but I didn't give him much choice.

Edinburgh 2017

PART I

Lyric: The Sound of the Poem

POETRY AND MUSIC

Our dominance as a species can largely be blamed on our superior future-predicting capability. This capability is both derived from and reflected in the sophistication and length of our memories. Language put us at a terrifically unfair advantage in terms of both strategising and forward planning, as it allowed us to discuss things in their absence; the biped with a few free hands and the capacity for abstract thought probably wins out on most of the viable exoplanets. To pursue the 'roots of poetry' through evolutionary psychology leads us quickly into wilder conjecture than even that speculative discipline can accommodate; but based on what we know of its use in less complex societies, it seems safe enough to assume that poetry was at least partly compelled into being through the need for preliterate cultures to have a mnemonic storage-and-retrieval system to supplement the information the mind could comfortably retain. Even in its most primitive form, poetry was concerned with transcending a human limitation; it was a 'magical' discipline – one that could conjure from thin air the location of waterholes, hunting grounds and food stores, recall the sequenced appearance of plants and flowers, the cycles and lore of weather, season and animal husbandry – as well as the stories, histories and genealogies that served the evolutionarily advantageous purpose of strengthening the sense of community and tribe. It would have immediately acquired a reputation as a mantic art, based on its ability to predict the future through its memory of the past. Long before the book, poetry was the brain's first 'external storage', our first 'mnemotechnology'.

Poetry, in its ur-form of easily memorisable speech, would have been deeply implicated in both our survival and sense of identity: little wonder that it quickly invested *itself* with those magical properties, and also took the form of spell, riddle, curse, blessing, incantation and prayer. For those atavistic reasons, poetry remains an invocatory form. Prose evokes; the well-chosen word describes the thing as if it were present. But poetry persists in its attempt to *invoke*, to call down its subject from above, as if there were no 'as if' at all. Of course, poetry can't literally conjure things from thin air, but one unique condition obtains here: artist and audience collude. Poet and reader enter a bizarre cultural contract where they *agree* to create the poem through the investment of an excess of imaginative energy; the poem is then subject to a kind of double reification. This convergence of minds adds a holographic dimension to the poem, one denied to other modes of human speech. A poem's elements can sometimes *appear* to have been summoned into existence with enough potency to engage our physical senses.

'Magical' practices naturally intermarry, and poetry has long been closely allied with music and song. *Lyric* is derived from *lyre*, and *music* from *muse*; for the Greeks, *mousike* was a general term that could cover any of the muse-ruled arts or sciences, and united dance, song and poem.[1] In Rome, *ars musica* described and conflated both instrumental music and poetry. While the experience of those songs was supposed to be sensuously pleasurable, and their practical object the acquisition of knowledge (we can reasonably infer Homer's poetics from his portrayal of Odysseus and the Sirens – 'an erotic encounter which nonetheless promises the gaining of wisdom' summarises his position tolerably well), a premium was always placed on Art's memorability: Mnemosyne, the muse of memory, was the mother of all the other muses. According to Hesiod, both kings and poets

---

1 My definition of 'lyric' in this chapter stays close to its etymological root: I mean by it simply 'that aspect of poetry which concerns itself with musical property', and would ask the reader to put from their mind the other uses to which the word 'lyric' is commonly put in a poetic context – i.e. to denote first-person, 'emotional', non-narrative or non-dramatic poetry, and so on.

arrogated authority to their speech through seeking her inspiration; they still do.

Unlike poetry, the raw material of music occurs without humans, and needs only to be actively perceived by them to come into being. The wind will whistle up octaves, tonics, dominants and harmonic overtones; the birds, complex melody. Rainwater dripping from a leaf-tip into a pool will supply a rhythmic series of random intervals around a mean pitch-centre. Elsewhere, music seems waiting to be made: a cut reed or bamboo stem just needs us to breathe across it to propose a vertical flute; in some versions of the Greek myth, Hermes discovers the lyre – the very emblem of our guild – when he finds a rotten tortoise-shell, still strung with a few muscle tendons, which he idly twangs. A few years ago I stood in a cave system in Andalusia where stalactites had formed a massive floor-length stone drape, each fold of which gave a different gong-like tone when struck. Music has long supplied us with the paradoxical sense of a language that is humanly manipulable and emotionally articulate – and yet of non-human origin, and beyond human words.

Music seems somehow precise in its emotional meaning, yet, quite unlike our object-taking word-sense, also feels wholly intransitive and 'unparaphrasable'. When we seek to infuse our speech with a mood or emotion it cannot easily express, it's to music, to the patterning of sounds, that we instinctively reach. This happens long before we're moved to make a song or poem: in our spoken conversation, variations in rhythm, pitch and timbre are responsible for most of what we convey of our emotional tone, and much nuance and emphasis the mere word-sense of our speech cannot carry. This is why the Daleks have trouble conveying irony, but also why – as Frost pointed out – a great deal of sense can still be made of a conversation heard through a wall.[2] (Many of us will have had the experience of overhearing an

2 Robert Frost to John T. Bartlett, 4 July 1913, *Selected Letters of Robert Frost*, ed. Lawrence Thompson (New York: Holt, Rinehart and Winston, 1964), 79–80.

argument through the party wall of a hotel room. Walls act as low-pass filters and remove the high frequencies of most consonants; consonants provide us with the means to differentiate one word from another, so we're essentially listening to folk talk with their mouths closed. But we can follow the emotional shape of the whole conversation though its intonational contour alone, without having actually heard a word of it.)

While musical signs are often culture-specific – minor keys, for example, will connote different very moods in different cultures[3] – we have still managed to map the infinitely complex landscape of human emotion to music's rather weirdly discarnate medium. Even more strangely, music seems able to conjure the presence of emotions *we had not felt before*, which suggests that the emotional referents of its various signs can become well enough agreed and understood to allow the creation of entirely new feelings through their original blending and combination, much as we blend and combine concepts in language. (I believe poetry also exercises this extraordinary facility, albeit at a secondary and backgrounded level. In Part II, I'll mention my own 'candidate particle of musical sense', something I call a 'patheme'.)

Song, though, is a uniquely human business. As beautiful as they are – or rather 'as we find them' – whale-song and bird-song are largely concerned with territory and sexual selection, and are barely analogous to the signature twitter of our speech, never mind *Winterreise* or 'Woodstock'. Human song is double: it binds an exclusively human system that we have carefully developed to a universal one, based on

---

3 Consider, say, the delightful musical coincidence between the Western blues scale, and *raga jog* in classical Indian music – the first full of sadness, anger and dissatisfaction; the second, a late-evening raga of contemplative yearning, and no little romance. I often think of this example when I see poetic translations which have echoed the sound and prosodic effects of the original poem. The cultural gestures then created in the target language are often drastically or even calamitously different, just as the blues played on the sitar isn't the blues.

physical law, that we have merely learned to manipulate. Fused with music, our speech becomes self-transcending, immediately part of a primal and universal realm in which it can symbolically and literally participate.[4] Perhaps for that reason, its ability to unite our choppy and fragmented perception by singing across the gaps, song has long been our aspirational archetype.

A rather larger 'gap' also haunts us. As mammals with foreknowledge of our own deaths, we are in an unusual position. Knowing we will die means that, in a sense, we already *have*. Dying is something we do very well; it's an imaginative exercise we conduct so often, our own future deaths are generally inscribed in us by five or six years old. Compared with the squid's, the sparrow's and the squirrel's, our existential condition is closer to one of ghosthood. Given this predicament, it's understandable that we take our comfort where we can. What Piaget identified as 'object permanence' — the child's realisation that an object persists in its being, even when it disappears from their immediate sight — is a darned useful thing to learn: when you understand that your mother hasn't evaporated every time she leaves the room, you needn't always feel orphaned by the experience. Unfortunately, when your mother *does* leave the room for good, a part of the brain now regards her vanishing as a logical impossibility. Religion allows us to read the sleight-of-hand by which our loved ones are conjured to another place, albeit one inaccessible to us; these necessary myths allow us to be reconciled to what we experience as the paradox of their absence.[5] I would claim that music, too, offers a

---

4 I feel I should declare – if for no other reason than allowing the reader the opportunity to compensate for my own predilections – that I subscribe to a materialist definition of the aesthetic sublime: those moments we think of as 'transcendent' are bringing us close not to God but to the earth, to which we now have a rather distant relationship, and with which our moments of reunion are so infrequent that they strike us with the force of revelation.

5 We never quite get that we are not nouns but verbs, not things but 'beings', i.e. complex sites of fairly stable processes; it's the external consistency of those

kind of spiritual solace, but one more physically direct in its rejection of our sequential, quantised sense of time that, in the end, serves only to divide us from one another. Musical time is rhythmic, cyclical, non-linear; song takes the vowels of our language and lengthens them, in defiance of its categorising, sequencing engine. Orpheus used song to cross the ultimate dividing border, and defy death itself. Rilke saw the Orphic project as one that allows us to enter a 'double realm', unifying the domain of the temporal, the passing and the living with that of the atemporal, the eternal and the shade – and in doing so, reconciling us to the paradox of our twin citizenship.

Poetry introduces music into language through a simple procedure. Like the musical note, the word is an event in time; but despite this, words (to adapt an old formula of Hugh Kenner's) can be recalled into one another's presence and have their meanings yoked together by the careful repetition and arrangement of their sounds. The effect of this is twofold. Our long-term memory encodes information semantically, our short-term memory acoustically, and these rhythmic, parallel and repetitive sound-tricks simply give the line a better chance of 'hooking' on a single hearing; this way they can be later recalled, and their meaning more carefully dwelt upon. But these patterns also introduce a perceptual distortion: they offer a small stay against the *passage* of time and, in their Orphic way, cheat death a little too.

---

processes that forms the souls that we fall in love with, look to for protection, or feel instinctively protective towards. Only death renders us mere objects. The shock of that phase shift and change of word class, I am assured, is better dealt with by sitting at home awhile with the bodies of our dead, not spiriting them away.

MEMORY

———————————

Poetry, then, has always been an 'aspirant' form, one which seeks to transcend the limitations of human memory. For a long time it seems it was an art barely distinguishable from song. Until very recently, poetic performances were more or less sung – something we hear very clearly in recordings of Tennyson, Yeats and Pound, all of whom centred their recitals on a relatively high, fixed key, about a fourth or fifth above normal conversation pitch, and elongated their vowels. Their falling phrase-end cadences are all regular and liturgical, not varied and conversational. (Good Anglo-Saxon student that he was, Pound's immaculate Harry Lauder impersonation nonetheless remains something of a mystery, but it was clearly rooted in some sense of a bardic tradition in which poems were not 'spoken' so much as broadcast.) Why was this? Well, for one thing, fixing an already-patterned speech to a repeating pattern of set pitches (effectively a melodic refrain, albeit one of a fiercely unvarying kind) will further strengthen the mnemonic power of the poem. However, one can sense that even in Tennyson's era the conventions of poetic recital had already undergone much change. With the advent of mass literacy and the concomitant ability to transmit the poem in written form – where pitch and note-length can't be easily indicated – poetry naturally and very slowly began to coil back on itself. It pulled away from the intonational patterns of its lyric origins, made a reflexive turn, and started to mine its music more directly from its own medium – that of language.[1]

———————

[1] I confess that this is an account simplified to within an inch of an outright untruth. The real narrative would trace a complex dialectic between the literary and the lyric

However, poetry retained a unique and near-magical property. It remains the one art form where its memory and its acquisition are one and the same thing. The memory of the symphony, painting, film or novel, however vivid, is no more than that: just a memory, or at best a very partial recovery. (Although there are a few visual artists with near-eidetic recall, and composers who can hear seven independent and simultaneous voices.) A remembered story perhaps remains more closely the story – but only its structure remains intact, not its form of words. But if you can remember a poem, you possess it wholly. To recall a poem *is* the poem; the poem has become, quite literally, part of your being. Because of this unusual property, the poem has inevitably tended to valorise – even fetishise – those strategies and devices which make it *more* memorable, in the narrow sense of its 'ability to be memorised'. (Perhaps because it's so uniquely well-suited to the task, the little time-trap of the poem often takes for its subject matter that which we feel should be not only remembered, but also forcefully *memorialised*. It does this so frequently that, in English, at least, its elegiac tone is so pervasive as to be inaudible.)

----

functions of poetry, which I'll touch on when I discuss metre. The song-lyric itself, incidentally, has absolutely no requirement to be particularly musical in the way that the poem does. From the poet's point of view, the song-lyric can seem an almost negative discipline: there are so many musical and lexical effects that it must *avoid* if it isn't to intrude on its own setting. With the exception of Burns and a handful of others, poets are rarely selfless enough to suppress their own hard-won expertise in this way, and tend to make indifferent or bad lyricists. Nonetheless poetry remains closely linked to the performative physicality of song, and something of its primitive power ebbs away when that lyric connection becomes strained or broken. At the very least, poetry is always highly conscious of the noise it makes: this is one reason the musical setting of poems is almost invariably a redundant or destructive exercise, resulting in either the contradiction of the original poetic music, or its melodramatic duplication – an exercise akin, in Valéry's perfect and perfectly damning formulation, to 'looking at a painting through a stained glass window'. Composers would do better to find other ways of shaping the air. (The German Lieder tradition directly benefited from its habit of using rather duff texts, leaving the music with a great deal to enhance, and little to destroy with any regret.)

This is the case even in our post-Gutenberg, internet age, when its mnemotechnological role has been taken over by print and digitisation; the poem is still a little machine for remembering itself. Strictly speaking its 'memorisability' should no longer be so crucial a quality, now we've delegated the task of its storage to media other than our own neurons, axons and synapses. But it seems likely that if it ceased to place a premium on memorable speech, the poem will also lose its most characteristic feature, and find its very cultural identity under threat. Mnemosyne still sits at the head of our table.

The most powerful mnemonic devices are brief speech, patterned speech and original speech. Brevity of speech is the poem's most basic formal strategy; originality of speech, its most basic literary virtue; patterned speech, its most basic identifying feature. The mere act of making brief speech often produces both original and patterned speech, the former by expedient necessity, the latter through physical law. While, on the tiny planet of the poem itself, there may be all manner of artful excursions, diversions and 'dead lines', the better to disguise its artifice and time its effects – generally speaking, most poems are sworn to say what they have to say in as few words as possible.[2] Brief, original and patterned speech all naturally arise from the compositional process, but we can also employ them as conscious strategies. Brevity is achieved with the help of the various tropes of contraction; originality through the various tropes of comparison;

2 With the exception of the epic form (now rarely written, and read more rarely still) and the equally rare hybrid form of verse drama. Novels, TV, film and video games have all but done for those longer forms of poetry, which were designed for fireside entertainment, probably by being much better at it. (Television is now both the literal and metaphorical 'focus' [Latin *focus*: hearth], being the hub of most living rooms.) These were expressly recitative forms, in which figures of expansion such as auxesis and enumeratio had a far more important structural place – length, for once, being at a premium. We see their survival in oral storytelling, but those folk who could quote hundreds of lines of, say, Robert Service (my grandfather was one such) are now long gone. This has left the shorter lyric form worryingly close to being the *only* written poetic form for which our society can find much practical use.

patterning, through the parallel schemes of form, metre and lyric. The compositional reality will invariably find all three deeply interwoven.

I have long regarded poetry as a naturally occurring mode of human speech. The effects we call 'poetic' occur when speech is made under two conditions: urgency and shortness of time. When the former is 'inspiration' and the latter is 'form', the result is the cultural convention known as 'the poem'. The poem originates from an emotionally or intellectually urgent impulse in the mind of the poet, and simultaneously seeks out and is drawn to forms which reflect and facilitate that urgency. I would generally hold that poems written without feeling teach us very little about poetry, and that it's a bad idea to write a poem if you're not moved to do so. (Which is why I maintain the unfashionable opinion that writing workshops where poems are actually *written* amount to little more than pleasant ways of passing the afternoon.[3] The argument is that such workshops – where you write a poem whose topic is set by the person on your left, or in only monosyllables, or the voice of your socks – 'jump-start the imagination', but I confess that I've never been able to understand why merely living a reflective life shouldn't suffice. I also suspect that an imagination that *needs* to be jump-started might be happier left sleeping. The results might be competent, but they're rarely necessary.) Moreover, language that is not *excited* about itself is metrically and musically different from language that is. Language behaves in a curiously material-like way and, placed under the dual

---

3 My larger complaint is that they infantilise a perfectly grown-up subject. I have seen too many teaching exercises, ostensibly aimed at serious adults, which involved crayons, glue, postcards, random words, card tricks, fridge magnets, 'a close family member, something pink and something dead', and swapping coats with the person next to you. If you're stuck, go to the zoo with a book. My all-time favourite exercise was set by Donald Hall in response to a student who kept begging him for an assignment. In exasperation, Hall scribbled on a piece of paper, handed it over, then told him to go and get on with it. When the student unfolded it, he read: 'Be as good as George Herbert. Take as long as you like.'

pressures of emotional urgency and temporal constraint, it will reveal its crystalline structure and intimate grain; whether written or spoken, it becomes rhythmic, lyric and original. As I hope to show, language itself can be considered as a coherent poetic system. Poetry exaggerates or makes manifest features already present or latent in speech; it emerges naturally from our speech as the immediate consequence of emotional urgency, and our desire to communicate this urgency by organising and intensifying those natural features of language which best carry it. (Like most poets, year after year I'm asked about 'the death of poetry', usually by a journalist who actively desires it. The answer is simply that, as long as humans speak, poetry is going nowhere.)

Poetry reveals language's underlying metrical and intonational regularity, and its tendency to pattern its sounds; it reveals the metaphoric engine by which language revivifies itself, and the metonymic nature of all human naming (which represents things by foregrounding an aspect that humans find either useful or perceptually salient); it reveals the rhythms that dominate language's natural phrase- and sentence-lengths, its narrative and argumentative episodes. The sum total of poetry's forms and tropes are no more or less than the natural tendencies of emotional language made manifest, and then codified.

The poet is engaged in something closely analogous to trying to remember a poem they have forgotten. While all poetic devices serve to increase the memorability of the poem for the reader (they all play a mnemonic role in addition to any other they might have), for the poet, their function is weirdly inverted: they are the very means, the intuitive tools of retrieval, by which the poem itself is drawn forth from the mind. The 'little machine for remembering itself' is doing just that, and – if the poet is working well – it can feel as if it is conjuring itself from nothing. All the tropes and schemes that help us achieve our brevity, originality and patterning are, in a sense, really as much aide-memoires to the poet as to the reader, and their experiences in writing and reading the poem can be strangely mirrored. These features, then, are not mere 'effects', but together form the engine of poetic composition itself. For many poets I know, the good poem has the certainty of a thing recalled as true, and they labour towards the final poem as towards a clear and indelible memory. A good poem often seems to arrive with an air of perfect inevitability – so much so we so often suspect our best lines of having already been written by someone else.[4]

Academic accounts of our subject are riddled with misconceptions, but the identification of so much intuitive, interwoven, contextually sensitive process as isolable extrinsic 'effect' is perhaps the most grievous. Many of these effects, as described, occur neither in the experience of the poet nor in that of the reader. The 'poetic effect' invariably sits at the convergence of twenty different technical and imaginative considerations – metrical, lyric, cultural, stylistic, thematic, deictic and so on – which construct between them a poetic Gestalt. Within this, much like a chess player, the poet will attempt to make their beautiful move – sometimes consciously, but just as often instinctively, guided by the shifting net of forces they perceive around them. We should be wary of all descriptions that *seek* to reduce the poem to a list of its effects; a good poem has a compositional integrity which cannot be addressed piecemeal. Any 'effect' that has emerged naturally from the compositional flux will also, to some degree, reflect the entire project. We should instead encourage the reader to think of each salient element as a means through which the sense of the whole poem can be experienced, much as a every part of a broken hologram contains the complete image.

---

4 I recall Michael Donaghy telling me that a friend of his, appalled and distressed by a short, blacker-than-black little ballad he'd written, had told him they couldn't believe that 'no one had put the words in that order before'. I think it was his most treasured compliment.

SILENCE

Poets often guarantee their own brief speech much as you would expect — by limiting the space they have to complete their work. This constitutes the most basic definition of 'form' and, as Raymond Chandler said, there can be no art without its resistance. The poem is shaped by a pressured silence. The vertical axis of poem- and stanza-length, and the horizontal axis of line-length create its rectilinear appearance on the page. This pressure compels the poet to make original speech simply through being forced to choose their words with total economy, since there is no room for redundant elaboration — of precisely the kind which would also destroy the unity they are trying to make of their material. Stanzas, for example, are a way of identifying the episodic rhythm of our poem; once this rough wavelength is established, a finite series of rooms can then be furnished appropriately, and redundancy and irrelevance will be far more quickly detected. Everything you *wanted* to put in now simply won't fit. What often looks merely like an episodic or visual division made for the reader's benefit is the most important editorial device the poet possesses. As Brodsky said, 'Poetry amounts to arranging words with the greatest specific gravity in the most effective and externally inevitable sequence.'[1] The common diagnosis that a poem is 'underpressured' usually means that its elements aren't unified by their theme, and their relationships are diffuse or underdeveloped; but many poems just leave the impression that their rooms are too empty. There are other content-addicted poets who clutter their

---

1   Joseph Brodsky, *Less Than One: Selected Essays* (London: Penguin Modern Classics, 2011), 186.

rooms with so many exquisite tallboys, escritoires and ottomans that the reader has no way of walking between them – and is left gawking at the doorway, like a man outside an antiques store he can't afford to enter. (The sense of cultural inferiority these poets often inspire sometimes leads us to be far too easy on them.)

In the course of its making, the poem becomes filled with its symptomatic artefacts. Brevity results in calculated elisions, contractions and discontinuities, and we rely on our reader, through active inference, to make up the gap between our carefully delineated contexts and the things we half-say within them.[2] Originality leaves its rhetorical and syntactic innovations, its tropes and its imaginative leaps. Patterning leaves its parallel effects of lineation, stanza, rhyme, metre, and consonantal and assonantal echoes. This leaves us, finally, with a piece of text often identifiable as a poem by its brazen lack of self-explanation, its original phrasemaking and its ostentatiously 'poem-like' shape. Were we to read this text as a 'normal' piece of prose, or within the frame of conversational speech, we would likely identify these features as respectively discontinuous, alien and artificial. The contract of poetry, however, is that we agree to see none of those things, but instead a wholly natural language-game in which poet and reader collude.

---

2   I'll speak about this at length in Part II, but a 'context' is coterminous with 'thematic domain', which provides the specific rules that allow for metonymic contraction and also explains 'peristatic focus' (otherwise known as 'the choice of details'). To take a trivial example – a couple making love is a couple making love; but establish that the context is 'car', and all you need to show is a steamed-up window and some lightly tested suspension. However, the calculation – that of generating maximal resonance with minimal information – is a vicious one, whose success depends on finding a sometimes agonisingly fine balance between context and content. This is made more complex by the formula being weirdly recursive: poetic information has to generate the context by which it is then understood. It is primarily this complication that makes reading and writing poetry the slow, dynamic process it is – and one reason why poetry books are so thin. The slim volume is usually less a sign of the author's lack of inspiration than the fact it just took them *ages*. As Pascal once wrote: 'I have made this letter longer than usual because I lack the time to make it short.'

All this generally leaves the reader with far more work to do than they would when faced with a piece of prose. (While patterning performs other functions too, it often seems to me a sort of sensual sweetener for the frequently challenging work the poem offers.) Poetry, by its very nature, has 'difficulty' built in. Half the poem is often missing, while the half we *do* write is often alarmingly unfamiliar in its diction: we will provide no more than metonymy and symbol, we will start our stories *in medias res*, we will make poems from fragments, we will introduce ellipses, lacunae, discontinuous leaps, and so on. We seem to have entered an age where our poets default to a strategy not unlike that of their old Celtic forebears: 'the half-said thing to them is dearest', as Kuno Meyer observed in his introduction to *Selections from Ancient Irish Poetry*.[3] Since each reader must meet the poem half-way, they will bring many different solutions to those inferential gaps between context and content. Poems therefore have an inbuilt flexibility of interpretation. Crucially, this interpretative freedom also permits *ownership* of the poem at a much deeper level, through the personalisation of its meaning. The poem, then, also works through a subtle appeal to the ego: the desirability of the well-made poem is, in part, the promise of its personal relevance, the poem's direct concern with the reader's own life. This aids its memorability as much as any of our mnemonic trickery.

However, the poem must be identifiable as such for the game to begin, since poetry is as much a mode of reading as writing. The reader must *know* they are reading a poem to actually do so, and apply all the human powers of signification and connection the poem asks of them. (Some of the most artful poems have the habit of disguising themselves as far simpler statements than they really are; any reader who *isn't* reading such a poem in an oversignifying mode will most

3   Kuno Meyer, *Selections from Ancient Irish Poetry* (London: Constable, 1911), xiii.

likely miss the best of it.[4]) Humans – no doubt in an act of vital compensation for their habit of hypercategorisation, and the fragmented perception it brings – are incorrigible dot-joiners, and will connect any two unrelated things you care to throw at them. Poets will often take advantage of this innate facility by prompting or initiating just such a game of 'connect', presenting the reader with elements that, on a first glance, seem only indirectly related – or not related at all.[5]

4 William Carlos Williams's 'This Is Just to Say' is easily read as a note left on a kitchen table, because it's written just as if it were one; but you'd be missing a fair bit. However, some 'touchstone poems' *are* simple. With poems which are really manifestos in disguise, there's often less than meets the eye: see Williams's 'The Red Wheelbarrow', or Pound's 'In a Station of the Metro', both of which have been the beneficiary of readings which projected sophistications far in excess than those actually introjected. (Everyone is or wants to be creative, and modernism essentially licensed 'the wholly creative reading' by making poetry that was frequently inscrutable. Alas, the proprieties of academic research insist that critics must talk as if they are 'doing science' rather than creative interpretation, i.e. they must (a) appear expert even when no special expertise is required, and (b) strive for a definitive and exclusive solution.) The cleverness of the gesture made by 'The Red Wheelbarrow' can only be understood contextually, i.e. by appreciating exactly what it is *not* (mainly, it is aggressively *not* T. S. Eliot); but what it actually *is* isn't much. This is, of course, blasphemous in those circles which regard it as a holy text. Michael Donaghy used to do an impersonation of WCW introducing 'The Red Wheelbarrow' in the windy style of a British poetry reading: 'This next poem is about a wheelbarrow I saw once . . . it was red, and it was wet, I recall – it'd been raining that afternoon – and there were some chickens. And I remember feeling at the time that – I don't know. Like a lot depended on it – do you folks ever get that? Anyway it goes like this . . .'

5 However, when the poem is *too* discontinuous, and insufficient context has been provided to link its elements, the reader compensates by sending their connecting faculty into overdrive, and starts finding connections and significances for which they were given no textual cue. (We are often too slow in diagnosing surrealism, incompetence, or a deliberately incoherent text.) The various types of confident misreading that can then result – for which the poet is often to blame – are aptly and neatly described in the terminology of clinical paranoia; but that's for later.

Our formal patterning often supplies a powerful typographical advertisement for the poem. What lineation advertises most conspicuously is that this piece of text has not taken up the whole page, and therefore considers itself rather important. The white space around the poem then becomes a potent symbol of the poem's signifying intent. Additionally, we tend to interpret white space as both literally and symbolically equivalent to 'silence', of the kind that connotes a respectful and hushed attention.

Silence is the poet's ground. Silence delineates the formal borders of the poem, and the formal arrangement of silences puts language under pressure. Silence – both invoked and symbolised by the white page, and specifically insisted upon by the gaps left by lineation, stanza and poem – underwrites the status of the poem as *significant mark*. This mark explicitly invites the reader to quietly attend to the poem in such a way as to release more of its resonant potential, both acoustically and semantically, as an important speaker within an auditorium. In doing so it also declares our master trope, the form of metonymy called 'synecdoche' – the business of representing a whole by the part, the generic truth by the specific evidence, the global principle by the local by-law. Almost all poetry operates under such an understanding, and even young children grasp it immediately: a poem is a small thing that stands for a larger thing. It has more *significance* than a piece of prose of the same length would have, simply because the reader has been directed to *find* more significance than its mere prose sense offers. (Though heaven help the poet if the reader invests their precious time in this way, and the poem then fails to reward them.) Silence is the space in which the poem makes its large echoes. If you want to test this, write a single noun on a blank sheet of paper and stare at it: note the superior attendance to the word that the blank space insists upon, and how it soon starts to draw out the word's ramifying sense-potential, its etymological story, its strange acoustic signature, its calligraphic mark: you are, effectively, reading the word as poetry.

Since it is silence that lends poems their significant look, and prompts the reader to begin their act of poetic signifying, poets go to great lengths to both summon and honour silence with bold and discrete sounds. Spoil it with extraneous chatter, inadvertent repetition, irrelevant information, superfluous qualifiers, nervous and unnecessary glosses, or, worst, with ugly accidental noise – and the ground of the silence is stained, the sense of the word as a distinct acoustic event is gone, and all subtle lyric patterning inaudible. (Whereas the transmissionary medium of the poem's semantic sense is language, the medium of its *lyric* sense is – just like music – motionless air, and we disturb it at our peril.) Worst of all, the spell of the poem, our small-thing-for-big synecdoche, is fatally weakened as the poem's own poem-status is undermined. We maintain the spell most effectively by balancing that unity of silence with a reciprocal singularity of utterance: the latter has the strange effect of raising the former.

A poetic form is essentially a codified pattern of silence. We have a little silence at the end of the line, a bigger one at the end of a stanza, and a huge one at the end of the poem. The semantic weight of the poem tends to naturally distribute itself according to that pattern, paying especial attention to the sounds and meanings of the words and phrases that resonate into the little empty stairwell of the line ending, the connecting hallway of the stanza-break, or the big church of the poem's end. These silences are where all the interesting things often tend to bunch up; they enjoy an acoustic salience in this position, with which the natural closures of phrase-length and episode tend to coincide. An ignorance of this tendency – and the subsequent inability to challenge it – can lead to tediously repetitive tics in some authors; they fail to naturalise the form. For example, most poets will instinctively use occasional enjambment; this helps avoid *always* promoting the most interesting word to the terminal position. (The last word or element in the line, incidentally, we call the 'teleuton'.) *What* patterns the silence will be the poet's choice of formal strategy. [I have in my head a cline of these strategies, derived from Vedantic logic; this is too crankish for a footnote, but see endnote 1.]

The white page is also a sign to the reader that poems were *won* from silence, drawn from it – when the poet was filled with the as-yet-unconsonated breath of their own inspiration, and began to try to articulate the inarticulable, those beyond-words relations, qualia, feelings, ideas . . . and were then granted a few strange words that seemed to adhere to them. Hence the strangeness of poetic speech: unable either to invent a new language or resort to a pure music or glossolalia, the words of poets are forced into original combinations. But they'd still perhaps appear too alien were they not unified through lyric strategies. Poets turn naturally towards music as an intercessory channel between the familiar and the strange, and use it to bind their 'weird meaning' with a pervasive strength that syntax alone cannot accomplish.

What, exactly, the silence invokes is a matter of individual conviction. For this author, silence seems to stand for a realm of perception where all things are connected as they were in our very early childhood, before the fall into time and category – a fall brutally reinforced by the acquisition of language. Without the clear differentiation of things – without making the distinction between self and other, mother and breast, sky and earth – there can be no proper experience of their temporal or causal sequence; as babies we had a different perception of passing time. I feel this place of atemporal and infinite connection still exists, like an operating system upon which the more recently acquired software of perceptual category and language sits. [This approach is derived, I should quickly confess, from the work of the Chilean psychoanalyst Ignacio Matte Blanco: see endnote 2.] Poetry is one means by which we can still access it. Our poetic meditations allow us to enter a space where new and original connections can be forged beyond language, and then find their linguistic incarnation at its very limits. However, the return to speech from silence is a fraught business – and echoes, perhaps, our original fall from pre-consciousness into consciousness, and from speechless consciousness into language acquisition itself. Much is left behind at the border or handed over at customs, and too many trips involve just as empty-handed a return as Orpheus himself suffered. Poets are therefore, paradoxically, experts in the failure of language; they tend to be disappointed souls, having had some tantalisingly direct experience of what *could* have been expressed, and little of what actually was. Their *medium* is failure. Words fail us continually, as we search for them beyond the borders of speech, push words to the limit of their meaning, and even drive them beyond it.

Something else lurks in this silence: Wittgenstein's that-of-which-we-cannot-speak, and must pass over. Many poets, I think, have a deep-seated worry about the extent to which the perceptual user-preferences of the human animal limit and distort its experience of reality, and the consequently unreliable nature of much of its thought. Poetry is the means by which we correct the main tool of that thought, language, for the worst of its anthropic distortions. Poetry is language's self-correcting function, and everywhere challenges our Adamite inheritance – the catastrophic, fragmenting design of our conceptualising machinery – through the insistence on a counter-balancing project: that of lyric and imaginative unity. (What we call 'poetry' is really only a cultural salience. Language has poetry wired through it, like the body has the endocrine system.) If we remember that all the light we shine on the universe is of a helplessly human shade, we can compensate for its narrow spectrum, and accept the partiality of what it reveals; one way of doing this is to sing of the larger unity of which we ourselves are merely a synecdochic, partial expression.[6]

---

6 It's amusing to think that if physics succeeds in its attempts to find some vibrational basis for the universe in the form of string or membrane – i.e. proves that difference itself is merely a manifestation of periodic frequencies – it will be consubstantial with the lyric project; that is to say it will show it to be non-symbolic.

To summarise: between the invisible master trope of synecdoche (although it's perhaps just as much 'symbol', as I'll later argue), the sworn oath of brevity and the project of honouring the silence, poets are subjecting their speech to a certain kind of pressure. This pressure requires the poem to unite its constituent elements at a far deeper and more integrated level than one would normally encounter in the (largely) linear narrative and argumentative structures of prose. To save space, we must introduce an additional dimensionality of meaning: we can't build out, so we must build up and dig down, and insist that our lines have harmonic depth as well as melodic interest.[7]

7 Most musicians, I am quite convinced, work within a deep and probably hard-wired psychological mapping that runs something like: melody = expressive sense; harmony = contextualised meaning.

THE PHONESTHEME

Creating the new out of the old means placing an accent on combination: a poet can only bring an unknown thing to light through the original combination of known things. Moreover, elements cannot deepen in their sophisticated relation and harmony while they continue to multiply. The more these thematic elements — the things the poem is 'about' — stack up, the less the poem will actually have to say. Most apprentice poems are bad because they are about four or five things, not one or two, and the poet has refused to cut them out. Early in the poem's composition, an experienced poet sets about *reducing* the thematic elements to an optimal minimum, so they can maximise the resonant potential of the very context these elements will create.

Having learned the trick of murdering of one's darlings early in the poem's draft (slitting their throats with Occam's razor, I guess), a more sophisticated project then emerges. In pursuit of the default goal of 'a unified statement composed of interlocking elements', the poetic line will instinctively avoid both understatement and overstatement: we try to say each necessary thing just once, and then run away. I often sense that poetry is the art of saying things once. (I exclude, obviously, those tricks and schemes of refrain and *deliberate* repetition.) For a decent poet, the sin is not saying a thing twice, or failing to say a thing at all; these are beginner's errors. The problem is saying things 0.8 or 1.3 times. (Crudely rewriting a couple of random phrases from Seamus Heaney's 'Making Strange' will illustrate the point: 'his speech like the twang of a bowstring' could easily have appeared in workshop poem as 'his speech was like a bowstring', with the student, having failed to win any editorial distance, assuming that the 'twang' was understood. 'A chaffinch flicked from an ash . . .' on the other hand, might be rendered as 'A chaffinch flicked quickly from an ash' – which adds a wholly redundant adverb, one already present as an aspect of 'flicked'.) A poem which makes the reader work unnecessarily hard for nothing more mind-blowing than its literal sense will soon become deeply irritating. Readers have a limited supply of energy, and expect commensurate reward for its investment. At the same time, what counts as a helpful gloss or expansion in a prose paragraph is often intolerably pleonastic in a poem; and the adduction of three pieces of evidence where one would have sufficed (the reader is already *looking* for evidence) tends to be counterproductive and weaken the poem's case considerably. The reader will then feel strong-armed into agreement rather than being allowed to discover the truth for themselves.

Most of my time editing is spent asking poets to clarify their meaning. A confusing or obscure passage is often just the result of the poet either saying something they did not intend, or *not* saying the thing that they did – and they are often mortified when the extent of the omission or miscalculation becomes clear. (I'm certainly as guilty of this as the next poet. But that's why editors exist: they contribute a pair of eyes which aren't tear-blinded by any emotional attachment to the text.) These miscalculations arise for two reasons. The first is that the poem is close-in work: however much editorial distance the poet *thinks* they have gained, they are often too close to the material – both in the sense of their focus on detail, and their personal investment – to see where basic and necessary information has been omitted. Overfamiliarity with the material, material often revised for months or years, can lead them to confuse the wholly obscure with the screamingly obvious. Perhaps they think that, say, their recovery from a long grief is clearly implicit in the extended analogy of a thawing lake, and needs no additional text-presence; but the reader is well within their rights to see nothing but a poem about a lake, unless otherwise prompted. The second reason is more sinister. The modernist project has bequeathed a state of affairs where the reader has come to *expect* a degree of obscurity; as a result, they are often far too tolerant of the unproductively or wilfully obscure, and treat poetry as having some kind of special exemption, rarely holding its muddy and misleading lines to proper account. (Eliot's gleefully de-contextualised 'genuine poetry can communicate before it is understood'[1] has a lot to answer for.) Poets are readers of their own poems too, and are just as unconsciously inclined to grant themselves this latitude – often allowing their triumphs of sound, rhythm and trope to circularly justify the very pointless darkenings of sense they have produced. As I'll discuss elsewhere, 'difficulty' is all too quickly thrown up by the compositional process itself, and by its pursuit of original speech; but it needs to be vigilantly mitigated, not cheerfully encouraged. In a good poem, there will be legitimate difficulties aplenty, and these will be the sites of our differences of interpretation. Those very ambiguities often grant the reader the freedom and interpretative slippage to win the poem some emotional resonance within their own life-experience. But for poets, all 'difficulty' should be first acknowledged, and then justified to oneself – and if it cannot be, removed. Trust me: I've been on the front line of this particular battle for almost two decades, and there has been a huge conspiracy of silence over the matter. I am certainly not making an argument for simplicity: complex subjects demand complex responses. But I am making an argument for 'attempting clear articulation' as default, because the things poets are trying to say will *never* be entirely clear.

To return to the business of poetic economy: having minimised our elements, the most efficient and natural way to accomplish this desired sophistication and complexity is through a shift in emphasis from denotative to connotative meaning. (This is something demonstrated by all poems which ally themselves with the lyric tradition, which

1 T. S. Eliot, *Dante* (London: Faber & Faber, 1929).

is to say all poems which do not deliberately reject it.) Since poems have to say a lot in a short space, connotation is at a premium, as it multiplies relations, not terms. In poetry, it functions as a subtle and pervasive unifying force, whose operation I'll describe in Part II. This relational sophistication is greatly enhanced by the poem's patterning of sound. Too often this is taken to mean strong, salient effects like rhyme or alliteration, but it's more often developed through far quieter patterns, often arrived at intuitively by the poet and registered subliminally by the reader. Behind this instinctive patterning lies the famous formula of Roman Jakobson (almost poetry's version of $E = mc^2$): 'the poetic function projects the principle of equivalence from the axis of selection into the axis of combination'. I'll unpack – and question – this assertion more fully elsewhere, as it requires a more technical approach than I can accommodate here. In the context of the present discussion, we can think of it as the broad principle that lyric poetry unifies its sense through the use of 'equivalent', parallel sounds along the line of its syntax.

Compare

> I caught this morning morning's minion, king-
> dom of daylight's dauphin, dapple-dawn-drawn Falcon,
>   in his riding . . .

> (G. M. HOPKINS, 'The Windhover')[2]

with

> I caught this daybreak morning's footman, king-
> dom of sunlight's princeling, mottle-dawn-pulled goshawk,
>   in his riding . . .

2 Gerard Manley Hopkins, *The Major Works*, ed. Catherine Phillips (Oxford: Oxford University Press, 2002).

The latter example may present roughly the same semantic information as the former, but its wretched and unpatterned music has pulled its sense apart.

The denotative sense of a word is singular; the connotative meaning of a word is potentially infinite and contains all possible terms. However, those terms are organised by their proximity to its principal referent (i.e. the animal 'horse' for the word 'horse'), and to those core properties without which this referent is impossible to conceive of. These are things we never think about – the 'hypernymic' sets to which we agree 'apple' must probably belong ('a fruit'; 'a thing grown', 'an edible food', etc.), but also those physical or categorical properties *without* which the thing becomes unthinkable as itself. It's impossible, for example, to write 'ping-pong ball' and communicate the idea of something with a wholly solid interior. (If we wanted to suggest such a thing, we would have to do so by unambiguous qualification.)

Beyond that core we find a penumbra of secondary aspects; these are less strongly fixed than those attributes at the centre. These secondary aspects radiate out, their bonds weakening as they pass from rigid designation, through consensual agreement, to the random associations of personal association and memory.

So as well as its solidity, fruitiness, edibility and so on, we tend to also think of 'apple' as having the qualities of being round, tree-grown, red, green or brown in colour, and sweet and sharp to the taste. Unlike the more difficult-to-conceive-of non-fruit apple – we *can* conceive, at a pinch, of a square apple, or even a blue one. But where does this leave the wax or wooden apple, whose only 'appleness' is its shape – the very aspect our 'square apple' demonstrated as non-essential? The truth is that what we think of as 'apple' is really a knot of consensually agreed aspects and connotations, *any* of which might find themselves individually expendable, and at whose centre there is a strange emptiness. 'Apple' is less a thing than a mere index, whose strength is variable; it's most potent when it points to the apple-fruit, the real-world object that oversees the domain, and possesses the highest number of our 'apple-ish properties' – but we also cheerfully use the word to point to a thing which might contain an alarmingly *minimal* number of those properties.

A word's strong connotations – its immediate circle of strong aspects, relations and associations – is what gives it its 'feel', but not its dictionary definition. Dictionaries are concerned only with the necessary fiction of denotation, and since direct denotation – that is, pointing at an apple and yelling *'that's* an apple!' – obviously isn't possible, the dictionary has to coyly circle around the referents of words by naming the fewest strong aspects and connotations required to narrow the possibilities to one. It's no use looking up 'apple', and finding 'it's an *apple!* Idiot.'[3] But it's the 'feel' of words, the *larger* circle of connotations they invoke, that concerns the poet at least as much as their dictionary meaning.

Unlike its single and often unique denotation, the set of any word's immediate connotations will contain many terms which overlap with those possessed by many other words. 'Beds' share their common associations with a thousand other things: we find their quality of

---

3 This offers a rather large clue to the nature of the onomastic process itself; it's often a metonymic or a metaphorical one. We can't call things the name God gave them, so we tend to represent things either by declaring a culturally salient aspect or relation of the thing itself, or what the thing itself reminds us of. Clocks used to ring bells, so we called them 'clocks', from the German *Glocke*; if we had to name them now, we'd likely call them hands, numbers, wakers, moons, faces, or the like. (In the pre-digital age we called them 'tickers'; a metonym now metaphorically transferred by to mean 'the heart' in colloquial English – where the 'ground' is not just that both clock and heart 'tick', but also 'run down time'.) 'Fool' goes back to Latin *follis*, bellows. Why? Because a fool is a windbag. We would no longer compare a fool to a bellows, as we no longer use bellows; so if our newly coined word for 'fool' were to represent the aspect 'full of empty talk' we would reach for another metaphor entirely. (I might propose something like 'the guy's squirty cream' or 'she's a total facebook'.) A study of etymology will remind us that our cultural vocabulary is in constant flux; by way of proof, I invite the reader to pursue the common Indo-European root of the words 'fierce' and 'treacle'.

'flatness' in plains, paper and floors; their 'softness' in feathers, skin and wool; their 'peacefulness' in church, narcotics and the grave. (Taken together, this nexus of qualities forms a 'conceptual domain', whose operation within poetic practice I'll describe in Part II.)

Words, then, will often have shared 'qualia' – i.e. they will overlap in 'feel', and share qualities of roundness, shortness, sharpness, bluntness, brevity, lightness, brightness. These shared qualities are *often betrayed by a common sound*, regardless of the sense-realm to which the word belongs: 'softness' or 'harshness', say, may be a quality of touch, sound, smell, emotional tone, and so on. This statement continues to be borderline heretical among certain diehard Saussurians, but one encounters them less and less frequently; most theorists accept that 'sound symbolism' is a far more important aspect of language than we once thought. It lies behind the poet's operational conceit and fundamental article of faith, which is that sound and sense are aspects of the same thing. In the poem's composition, we often allow sound to guide us to sense, and vice versa: the ear can be trusted to think, and the mind to hear. We make our decisions within a 'phonosemantic' system, where the 'rightness' of a word or line is verified as much by its sound as by its meaning, and within which we are never forced to choose one over the other; logically, such a contradiction cannot arise, as the two are merely manifest aspects of a same thing. If we get the sound wrong, the sense is also askew.

Whenever we encounter two things in nature which share a form – a brain and a cauliflower, the sea and a windy cornfield, an ear and a kidney bean, a kidney bean and a foetus, a tree and a nerve, a nerve and a tributary system, a tributary system and a pattern of electrical discharge . . . we unthinkingly assume some kind of analogous relation between the natural, dynamic forces that produced them. (Once, standing on top of Pen y Fan in the Brecons, I found ice clinging to some grass stalks that had been blown to immaculate, perfect bird-feathers, the wind and water between them having whistled up a form in a few hours that had taken several million years to evolve.)

By and large, such instinctive assumptions turn out to be reasonable and well founded. But somehow we have come to think of language as a special case, and we have been instructed to take many of its sound-symmetries as accidental. This, despite the fact that language *also* naturally arose – just like everything else in this place, from the paperclip and the bomb to the tulip and the Cepheid variable – and should therefore be governed by the same rules as everything else: the domain of 'the human' has to be understood as just another part of the natural process, not some kind of unnatural exception. But when we first encounter those symmetries, we have no inhibitions in identifying not just an acoustic relation, but a shared sense: when you're three years old, and you go *mum – tum – thumb – bum!* for the first time, your delight is not just in their sounding similar, but because they all have the same soft and rounded and warm *feel* about them.

One might go as far as to suggest that while the semantic unit in denotative speech is the morpheme, the semantic unit in poetic, connotative speech is the phoneme. (One would certainly have gone *too* far, but for our corrective purposes it's worth indulging the idea for a while.) That 'words seem to sound like the thing they mean' is something long understood instinctively, and the matter has been chewed over since Plato raised it in the Cratylus dialogue, where Socrates considered the relationship between things and the sound of their 'true natural names'. Yet it's difficult to prove: because we're dealing with inarticulable qualities of shared 'feel', we can only point to tendencies, not rules. As a result, even this late in the day, we still have to listen to the odd theorist insisting on the 'arbitrariness of the sign', something poets know to be sheer madness. The sounds by which we represent things cannot, we sense, have been randomly selected. (Actually Saussure wasn't quite so sure as he is often made out to be.[4] Nonetheless the 'arbitrariness'

---

4 Folk know themselves in strange ways, and Saussure had a good idea, I think, of the monstrous dogma he had proposed. Towards the end of his life – in what I like

line is maintained through Chomsky, and while it's satisfying to see a Chomsky-influenced linguist like Steven Pinker now give iconicity some serious attention, the idea has persisted much too long, despite brilliant corrective interventions, by Roman Jakobson in particular.)

The idea of the word as 'arbitrary sign' seems to holds up well for merely denotative speech – and indeed *were* language a matter of simple designation, then if, say, we all agreed to call a cup a 'banana', a banana it would be. But I propose that it would *feel* wrong, and for deeper reasons than just our cultural acclimation to the cuppiness of 'cup'. Scientific speech is, of necessity, almost wholly denotative, and free of the productive ambiguities poets love; it's also, alas, the sort of speech most linguisticians use, and still instinctively privilege. The speech we use in conversation, literature and especially poetry is a very different matter.

A number of good thought experiments seem to demonstrate the presence of a synaesthetic overlap between sound and sense. Consider this example from David Crystal: 'You're in a spaceship approaching a planet. You've been told there are two races on it, one beautiful and friendly to humans, the other unfriendly, ugly and mean-spirited. You also know that one of these groups is called the Lamonians; the other is called the Grataks. Which is which?'[5] Of course, most people posed this question take their chances with the soft-sounding, nasal-heavy Lamonians, not those guttural, harsh-sounding Grataks. (Think how

---

to think of as a unconscious act of guilty compensation – he was tormented by an unusual demon: his Kabbalistic and obsessive hobby was to search texts for anagrams, which, once uncovered, would reveal their hidden sense and their authors' true intentions. Of course this practice involved looking for specific repeated *sounds*, the pattern of which would reveal deeper meaning than any conventional analysis of lexemes and morphemes alone could permit; forty years later he'd have been playing Beatles records backwards. He really would have been better off writing a poem instead.

5   David Crystal, 'The Ugliest Words', *Guardian*, 18 July 2009.

much easier life would have been for the Klingons if they'd merely dropped the 'K'; no one would've seen them coming.)

The term 'iconicity' refers to the phenomenon where the sound of a word seems to enact its referent. Until fairly recently, it was primarily used to refer to onomatopoeia, where 'thump' sounds like a thump, 'clatter' like a clatter, and 'bark' like a bark. Understandably, given this narrow interpretation, it has been easy to dismiss as the relatively trivial effect of 'sound symbolism'. This is changing, and linguistics is slowly catching up with our poetic intuitions, especially in the field of phonosemantics, which attends to how the sounds of words carry meaning in and of themselves. Much of this is taken up with the study of 'phonesthemes'. A phonestheme is a point of sound-sense coincidence.[6] A standard example is the sound-cluster *gl-*, which occurs in a disproportionately high number of words related to 'reflected light', 'sight' and 'slide-iness' to be mere chance: *glisten, glare, glow, glower, glint, gleam, glaze, gloss, glance, glitter, glide, glass, gliss*. Many words which contain the sound 'unk' – *bunk, sunk, puncture, dunk, lunk, trunk, funk* – all have a low, sunken, heavy, concave 'feel' to them, even though most are etymologically unrelated. Some think the number of such phonesthemes is finite; it seems clear to me – and I suspect to most poets – that the phonestheme is merely the most obvious symptom of a fundamental and wholly pervasive rule of language.[7]

6   J. R. Firth coined the term in the 1930s (from *phone*, 'sound', and *aisthema*, 'perception') as a means of indicating the way in which linguistic form and meaning can be paired. Firth's linguistic approach, which emphasised context and relation over discrete phonemic category, can be summed up in one beautiful quotation: 'You shall know a word by the company it keeps.' J. R. Firth, *Papers in Linguistics 1934–1951* (London: Oxford University Press, 1957).

7   There are words (more easily identified in other languages than English) that explicitly use sound-symbolism to imitate things which have or make no sound. These are known as known as 'phenomimes' and 'psychomimes'; the former are used to describe external phenomena, the latter inner states. While they clearly exist, I'm personally queasy about invoking them as a category of 'in-between' words as

Counterexamples are easy to supply – e.g. phonemes whose onset is *gl*- but whose sense has nothing to do with light or sight (*glee*, *gland*, *glean*) – but prove nothing. This is because language works on a *diffuse* synaesthetic principle, a broad iconicity. The 'definition' of a phonestheme doesn't describe a rigid designation but a mere statistical tendency, and its sound denotes nothing but an area of overlapping connotative sense between several different words. The word 'meaning' can't honestly be used of a phonestheme either, since 'meaning' implies a clear denotation; it has *no* meaning, only a consensual 'feel', and is merely a point upon which words that host this 'feel' as part of their larger set of connotations will tend to converge.

One still occasionally meets the objection that a thing or event which makes no sound cannot possibly be *summoned* by a sound. But sounds can invoke *any* aspect of a thing: its visual appearance, its movement, shape, feel, smell, or function. We hear, somehow, the roundness of *moon*, the ruminativeness of *memory*, the hiss of *sea*, the thinness of *needle*, the littleness of *pin*, the lumpiness of *hump*, the speed of *quick*, the warmth of *mum*. (The last is an example of how words can arise through simple expediency. The word for 'mother' in most languages contains the *m*- sound, the only noise the child can make at the breast. 'Mum' was crowdsourced from babies.)[8] Language works in part by sensory analogue: through the brain's automatic habit of synaesthetic mapping, 'brightness' is a property of not only light, but also sound, shape, taste, emotional mood – and this habit is naturally reflected in our speech.

Poetry takes this passive linguistic tendency and turns it into an active strategy through its amplification. What we're seeing here,

---

evidence of a cline which runs from pure onomatopoeia to arbitrary naming, which seems merely a way of saving a bad idea.

8 There is a well-known and bizarre exception: in Georgian, mother is *deda*. This is only partly explained by the obvious choice being already taken by the Georgian word for father, *mama*.

I think, is a linguistic version of 'peak shift', where something we perceive in a natural context as an attractive salience – in this case, the phonosemantic aspect of language – is greatly exaggerated, this exaggeration being an important component of what we experience as aesthetic effect. Peak shift tends to be discussed in terms of single instantiations, but I think it also operates in a more diffuse way, as a complex shift of governing tendencies across entire sign-systems. In poetry, the privileging of the phonosemantic principle (i.e. sound being permitted much more sense-carrying power that we would normally allow) is only one aspect of a more global reprioritisation.[9] Others would include the sharpening of vague isochronic tendencies into perceptible rhythm, and the deployment of far stranger and more original metaphor and metonymy than our normal conversation would usually admit.

One reason phonesthemes arise must be simply the clustering of sounds around semi-arbitrary, tongue-specific conventions of usage. If a very common term for x starts with the sound y, other terms related in sense to x are more likely to contain y. Margaret Magnus, the author of a remarkable dictionary of phonesthemes, gives the example of the word *house*. Through this clustering effect, we see that a disproportionate number of the words that are concerned with the idea of 'shelter' also begin with /h/: hovel, hut, home, hutch, hangar, hall, hostel and so on.[10]

Elsewhere, though, phonesthemes seem to suggest that the shapes of word-sounds in the mouth formed naturally, as physical analogues

9 A decent metaphor for the process of peak shift might be drawn from music production; here, one might analyse a musical sound or extract, isolate its most characteristic frequencies, and then apply a parametric equaliser, which can both sharply narrow and exaggerate them. The sound remains 'characteristic' – only somehow *more* so. (However, this only works when the sound is heard in the context of others; in isolation, the effect is one of ugly caricature.)

10 Margaret Magnus, *Gods of the Word: Archetypes in the Consonants* (Kirksville, MO: Thomas Jefferson University Press, 1999), 121.

of the things, processes and concepts they indicated. (Crucially, this is borne out by interlingual studies – the short /ɪ/ phonestheme, for example, is pretty much universally associated with lightness, brevity, smallness.) The two forces of synaesthetic echoing and arbitrary clustering are probably impossible to separate out. It's hard to establish whether the many English words that begin with the sound *gl-* carry the connotations 'reflected light' because there is something in this human sound that mimics a reality, or because they have helplessly converged on an arbitrary English convention. As ever, the truth is likely somewhere in between.[11]

As is easy to demonstrate, new coinages will naturally and unconsciously gravitate towards the attracting nodes of certain phonesthemes as a way of deepening their own sense. This means that iconicity is 'strong' as well as broad. For example: the word 'blog' is felicitous not just because it's a contraction of 'weblog'; it carries the echoes of the *bl-* and *-og* phonesthemes. There's more than one *bl-* phonestheme ('bloom or spurt' is one, 'glow, blaze, redden' is another), but around the 'speechiness' *bl-* we find clustered *blather*, *blabber*, *blow*, *blame*, *blah*, *blurt*, *blurb*, *blub*, *bluster*, *bless*, *blether*, *blag*, *blast*, *bleat*; also present in 'blog', albeit more weakly, is the *bl-* of 'bluntness', as in *blunt*, *block*, *bluff*, *blur*, *blunder*, *blow*. The *-og* phonestheme has a low, crude, blunt, blocked feel found in too many *-og* and *-g* words to list. (Remember, it is almost impossible for a phonestheme to have a handy one-word definition: it has instead a quale – which is something we

---

11   Our habit of synaesthetic representation may have been a product of crossed wires. V. S. Ramachandran has argued that it has its origins in crosstalk between various collateral sense-centres in the modular architecture of the brain, and in exaptation – its taking expedient advantage of neural pathways that evolution had opened up for other purposes. Language *itself* may have come about through just such a synaesthetic transfer: a hand-signal, shaped in imitation of a real form, could be instinctively doubled by an analogous mouth-shape – especially when a cry was also being made to reinforce the gesture. (This effect is seen in our occasional habit of clenching and unclenching our teeth when we cut with scissors.)

can talk *about*, but not *of*.) This latter echo is probably semi-knowingly facetious, as in the unappetising contraction 'spag bol'. You can see how quickly all this can descend into idle – if enjoyable – speculation, and how important corpora studies will be in lending the subject any academic legitimacy.

In language, 'phonosemantic felicity' is closely analogous to evolutionary fitness, and gives a new word a better chance of survival within its linguistic biosphere. The poem works much the same way, and the words which closely honour the sound-rules of its little mad dialect tend to be the ones which survive the evolutionary culls of successive drafts. As the neologism is to the consistent phonosemantic system of the language, so the word is to the consistent musico-semantic idiom of the poetic line. (Poets will often find themselves with a poem which is finished, but for one missing word: what the word is, they cannot say – but by looking at what's going on either side of the gap, they can intuit that it probably goes duh-DAH, has a long *O* in it somewhere, and maybe also a sibilant or a liquid, and a *p* or a *b*, and has something to do with breakfast. On those occasions poems can feel like crosswords – albeit crosswords we have compiled ourselves and whose answers we've permanently forgotten.)

I strongly suspect that, as language developed, the emergent property of a broad and systematic iconicity began to exert, through a process of downward causality, a supervenient influence on language itself. When this sign-system was positively charged with 'iconic intent', the phonestheme – instead of being just a passively arising index of shared aspect – could then start to exert a genuinely active, gravitational pull. Words which shared a phoneme would now forge a real, if thin, semantic connection *regardless* of their initial distance. (That such a sense is merely 'apparitional' is a meaningless accusation in the already apparitional world of the closed sign-system). As this iconic effect became increasingly pervasive, *any* word, however 'arbitrary' in its sound-sense relation, would have its own gravitational field, and exert some tiny influence on the geometry of the whole system. 'Apple' starts to *sound* like an apple, and contributes its own micro-phonestheme, however weakly, to *all other occurrences* of the same phonemes in the language, which will all then carry the ghost of 'appleness'. The valency between two same-phonestheme-bearing words would be actively primed to increase in strength with their increase in spoken proximity.[12]

Read this way, the phonestheme becomes a mere salience in a disease-of-degree game, and words themselves sit at the convergence of many more sonic influences than their most obvious governing phonesthemes. Who can say if 'glue' has *not* taken on a little sheen from its 'unrelated' *gl*-bearing 'bright' words, or 'sneak' a little nasality from *sn*-bearing 'nosy' words – or indeed if 'apple' has borrowed from the *p*- phonesthemes related to 'pulling', 'stealing', 'picking' and 'quiet noise'? Forgive this lurch into what will be an unfamiliar metaphor for many readers, but were we able to submit words to the same spectral analysis we can the sounds of a musical instrument, we would see an extremely complex additive pattern of semantic overtone, from the 'fundamental' tone of denotative sense, through strong and weaker partials, all the way up to almost

12   It's interesting to speculate whether synaesthetically 'unseeded' artificial systems, like John Wilkins's philosophical language, could ever enjoy even a weak emergent iconicity. One feels that they inevitably would: within any system based on a principle of connection, no concept can have *any* kind of material representation that will not immediately be mapped to other material representations, whether phonetic, typographic or ideographic. The whole system is already primed, and overwired for semic conduction. This is a practical refutation of Wittgenstein's 'beetle-in-a-box' private language argument: as soon as any private language is publicly expressed in any way, it becomes to some degree interpretable, as (a) the speaker will have alighted upon his nonsensical expression for non-nonsensical reasons, since genuinely random expressions are *impossible* for humans to arrive at unaided; and (b) the listener interprets non-lexical nonsense as a signs whose meaning is defined by what they already know about the phonosemantic rules of the language they regard as 'host'. (The positing of context- and content-free expression is really an argument about intentionalist theories of perception.)

impossibly weak and almost inaudible upper harmonics. The picture is further complicated because language is a dynamic system, and each word changes according to its contextual deployment, that is to say its 'site-specific sense', and its 'semantic infection' from its near neighbours. This is *particularly* true in the poem, where context is rigged, individual word-senses are brought together through an overdetermining 'thematic domain' – and just such 'infection' is actively encouraged by its obsessive phonic patterning. Put 'pale' and 'apple' in the same line, and they conjure a ghost-phonestheme between them, and their senses are a little interfused; put them next to each other, and their iconising valencies almost allow them to form a new word. Thus my mythical semantic spectrograph would show words remaining fairly constant in the fundamentals of their denotative sense, but also register *constant*, flickering change in their upper partials, their 'shades of meaning'. We can muddy the waters further by introducing other parameters, like dialectal variation or personal association, but the picture is already complex and dynamic enough. It's clear that no sense can step into the same word twice.

One other odd corollary of the phonosemantic rule (there are many) is that when words have come to be represented by very similar sounds, semantic blurring is something of an inevitability, especially in the case of homophones – regardless of the very different etymological routes those sounds have taken into the phoneme itself. This is a largely unconscious dimension of language, since most conscious processes in our daily conversation strive to keep the words usefully distinct by focusing on their denotative function. Nonetheless, a synaesthetic conduit is opened between such words, rupturing their domain-boundaries and creating a kind of micro-intertextuality, where 'mum' as in 'mother' is also 'mum' as in 'keep mum', as well as 'mummer' (an imitative root meaning 'to mime, mumble, or to act without words') and 'mummy' (as in 'embalmed body'; a word we can trace back to the Persian *mūm*, meaning 'wax', one of the important components of the embalming process). This inevitably gives rise to metaphorical blends, leading to a very unfortunate – if vestigial – association between mothers, smothering, muteness and embalmed corpses, creating a kind of 'potentialised phonesthemic cluster', ready to be activated by the unconscious or the imagination. Our dreams love this sort of thing, and will make great Freudian play with phrases like 'unwrapping the mummy'. (And Lord knows how the Elizabethans felt sucking on their 'mum', as in 'German beer'; a word which may have has its roots in a hypocoristic Italian word for 'drink', *momma*, suggesting a breastfeeding connection at the root of it all.) Similarly, auto-antonyms such as 'cleave' – meaning to both 'to split' and 'to unite' (the words can be traced to entirely different Indo-European roots: 'to cut' and 'to stick' respectively) – will inevitably leave, in the mouth of the sensitive English speaker, the strange aftertaste of paradox.

To return to our phonestheme, and address a standard objection which probably goes back to Locke: one might reasonably assert that the world *can't* be said to imprint itself on speech, because it's not universally consistent: a dog and a tree are pretty much a dog and a tree wherever you go, but the sounds we make to indicate 'dog' and 'tree' are completely different in different languages – therefore the process must be arbitrary. But this gets it wrong in two ways. Firstly, to get the 'feel' of a phonestheme, we look at common *tendencies* in the *set* of words in which the sound occurs, not in any single word. (Again, as we're talking about an extra-linguistic quale, its 'primary denotation' doesn't really exist, and therefore cannot reside in any single word, or indeed anywhere.) Secondly, human designation is aspectual and synecdochic. Take the word *tree* in different sign languages: in American, you shape the wind in the branches; in Chinese, you shape the trunk. In both cases, the form of the tree has clearly imprinted itself on the language – but it has done so *aspectually*. The aspect is soon forgotten and overtaken by its referent; both signs simply mean 'tree', though remain infected by the different connotations of their form. Spoken language works in the same way. We may well make a-noise-like-the-thing by instinctively forming a shape in the mouth, tongue, teeth, palate and lips to make a synaesthetic echo of something in the real world; but because that thing is so complex in its aspectual properties, the chances are that we'll often get a very different-sounding sign, depending on which aspect we're imitating. Aspect is immediately overtaken by referent through sheer sociocultural necessity, and what may have began life as a word with a dominant phonestheme bearing the connotation 'shiny' or 'round' or 'white' or 'light' or 'seeing' or 'hunt', is suddenly, and exclusively, the word for 'moon' — albeit one that can remain strongly coloured by that original aspect. This again illustrates the primacy of metonymic process. None of this means the sign is less beautifully fit, and arguments over which tongue has the loveliest word for 'love' or 'moon' are silly: their referent might be the same — but their phonosemantic priorities, and the various connotations which their phonesthemes have generated, will differ wildly.

If you take together the fact that words in different languages can have the same referent but very different connotations, and the fact that poetry operates on a phonosemantic principle expressly *designed* to take advantage of those connotations within its own language — you have perhaps the most concise explanation for the sheer 'impossibility' of poetic translation. How can one hope to render the poetic beauty, for example, of *cipőfűző* ('shoelaces', in case you were wondering), the word voted the most beautiful in the Hungarian language? New words will often get their start in life by 'naming a connotation', as no denotation yet exists: denotations are forged, whereas connotations naturally arise through our porous receptive senses.[13]

---

13   I have deliberately and mendaciously avoided a huge complicating factor: most words sit at the top of a huge pile of dead metonyms and metaphors thousands of years old. Our lexeme may have fallen very far from the tree indeed. Although . . . sometimes an enquiry into a word's history seems to reveal what you half-knew all along. Take the Indo-European *kerd-* root, from which we derive all our 'heart' words ('cardiac', 'core', 'cordial'; 'courageous' [Germanic for *heartful*], 'concord', 'record',

The iconising engine – which declares a kinship of sense between words through shared features of their sounds – is deeply embedded in the structure of language. But iconicity is an active as well as a passive principle: words are so *indivisibly* part sound and part sense that the patterning of sound alone can generate sense as if it constituted a syntactic relation. In our speech, we naturally pattern sound to unite and strengthen sense all the time, forging ghost-phonesthemes from the air. The chalkboard outside the pub in Dundee train station reads 'FINE WINES GREAT BEERS', not 'GREAT WINES FINE BEERS'. Not only is the latter less euphonious – its meaning is simply less integrated. The words we choose to convey the most urgent and convincing senses tend to exhibit a higher level of musical organisation. As Bill Clinton said so movingly of his personal shame: 'Painful as the condemnation of the Congress would be, it would pale in comparison to the consequences of the pain I have caused my family. There is no greater agony.' I won't pull the cheap stunt of lineating this to reinforce the point, but his words are fairly astonishing in the coherence of their patterning, and riff virtuosically around the guttural stops /k/ and /g/, the labials /p/ and /b/, and a couple of whimpering nasals. His speech was not composed this way, we may be certain, merely to impress us with his lyric prowess. (Sloganeers would do well to consider the various forces at play in the relative success of Republican and Democrat slogans in the 2016 presidential election campaign. Compare 'Make America Great Again' – which is

---

'accord', 'accordion' and – via Grimm's law – 'heart'); is there not a *little* throb of the original word still in left in our hunted 'quarry', so named because the heart of the slain beast was thrown to the dogs? At the spoken end of the etymological tree is a word defined not just by its genealogy, but by the peculiar angle and particular attitude it now bears towards every other term in the entire *parole* – an attitude that can be partly explained by the long, strange etymological shadow it casts. Such features are almost homeopathically vestigial, but I'm convinced those ancient connotations are still embedded or encoded in the word's sense, via its odd, unique and unfathomably complex co-ordinate within the entire sign-system.

(a) euphonious, (b) already familiar, (c) rhythmic, (d) consonantally patterned, (e) assonantally symmetrical (its stressed vowels go ay–eh / ay–eh), (f) imperative and (g) unselfconscious – with something like 'Trumped-up Trickle-down Economics' – which is (a) 'innovative', (b) pleased with its own 'scintillating wordplay', (c) hard to say, (d) unrhythmic, (e) saliently alliterative, rather than consonantally woven, (f) random in its vowel-pattern and (g) largely meaningless.)

Because language is fundamentally *constituted* as an iconic system, when words which share sounds are brought into close proximity they will appear to be united in their sense, regardless of whether they conjure an existing phonestheme or not. Indeed sentences which exhibit a strong sound-pattern will appear to have some semantic coherence, even if they're sheer nonsense. This is why poetry deliberately integrates its music. It accomplishes more than just making a pretty sound; it consolidates poetic sense. Next to the synecdochic conceit that rules most poems, lyric is our most powerful tool of semantic contraction, integration and emphasis. If you want to trick a reader into thinking your terrible, mad poem actually makes sense: rhyme it. (Or to put it another way – imagine what a horror an unrhymed Edward Lear would be.[14])

To tie a few points together: denotative sense is generally capable of paraphrase. Connotative sense is not; it isn't cleanly articulable, because it has no synonyms; instead it has shared qualia and unique patterns of relations. The degree of semantic bleed between words in strongly denotative speech is far lower, as its aim is one of differentiation, not connection; poetry, though, is concerned with both. In poetry, semantic blurring is encouraged partly by its tactical

---

14 For example: There was a young man from Dundee
who was stung in the arm by a wasp.
When asked 'Does it hurt?'
He said 'No not particularly,
it can do it again if it feels like it.'

elisions, which force the collusion of the reader in the sense-making project, and ask them to leap the gaps by forging connections based on shared properties of sound and sense; but this blurring is largely *conducted* by the patterned phoneme, leaving a poetic statement which, while still paraphrasable in its denotative sense, also has a highly complex connotative sense, wholly tied to its site-specific acoustic expression. Poetic meaning pours across word-boundaries carried by the patterning of sounds, which often unites poetic lines as if they were a single word.[15] Because of this, poetic form and content have something of the same inseparability we find in a piece of music.

Cleanth Brooks's 'heresy of paraphrase' may be one of the few useful ideas to survive from New Criticism, and of course no great poem is reducible to another form of words. The poem exists precisely because its sentiments couldn't have been rendered any other way. However, to say a poem can have *no* paraphrase is to credit it *only* with connotation, which is plain crazy. (This, however, is precisely the position I've often seen students adopt when asked what their poem actually means. Mostly I get variations on Eliot's dodgy come-back, along the lines of 'It means what it means, Mr Paterson; had I meant something different I would have said so just as obscurely', etc. Which at least indicates the source of the problem: the sloppy mis-construction of modernist procedure.) While no poet should know what they intend to say before they begin – if writing a poem isn't a way of working out *what* you mean, then I don't know what it is[16] –

---

15 I strongly suspect that some degree of lexicalisation – where a phrase gets stored in the left brain as a word, a consolidated, single-sense chunk – affects the poetic phrase, via phonosemantic binding and various other 'memorability-enhancing' strategies. Lyric patterning can be seen as a strong feature of the lexicalised phraseme in normal speech, so once again it seems as if poetry is merely taking advantage of a naturally arising tendency, and turning it into deliberate strategy.

16 Though sometimes it can feel like an act of recovery: 'For me the initial delight is in the surprise of remembering something I didn't know I knew' – Robert Frost, 'The

they mostly know by the end. If they genuinely still haven't a clue, it's likely that the poem means little. No one is pretending for a moment that a paraphrase or an abstract *is* the poem, any more than a synopsis is a novel: it merely articulates or adumbrates the ideas that the poem, singularly and inimitably, has bodied forth. The 'idea' alone has no intrinsic poetic value (and indeed if you 'get a good idea for a poem', I'd suggest you run a mile, as this generally isn't the way poems make themselves known). In my own experience, while students often genuinely don't know what their poems mean – all experienced and serious poets can at least tell you what theirs are *about*. They just don't want to. (A poem with no denotative, paraphrasable sense is called a sound poem, and it is the only legitimate exception I can think of.[17])

The patterning of sound is a necessity in *any* short speech which seeks to integrate its elements at the deepest level, and maximise its

---

Figure a Poem Makes', *Collected Prose*, ed. Mark Richardson (Cambridge, MA: The Belknap Press of Harvard University Press, 2007), 132.

17   I exaggerate. I once made a phonetic analysis of a few of J. H. Prynne's later poems, and the results were interesting: while early and mid-period Prynne is often lyrically patterned and lightened with the language of grammatical function, Prynne's late default music runs directly counter to most of the norms of the English lyric tradition. In every aspect we find him doing what we might caricature as 'the opposite of Heaney': lots of *schwa* – partly a result of his use of jargon and polysyllabic words; lots of 'bound' words, with the vowel firmly opened and closed, often by unrelated plosives; and so on. However, the impressive thing was that these features occurred with far more frequency than they would in any random snatch of conversational speech; in other words, the verse appeared to have been designed on a deliberately *anti*-lyric principle. It was interesting to discover a project so rigorously defined in the negative. Which made me think better of it, as (a) this lent it a clear signature music, however hispid and angular I might have found it, and (b) its blanket rejection of even the most casual lyric patterning made the poem's sense (following the phonosemantic rule) even *more* jaggedly discontinuous that it would otherwise have been; and as we all know, Prynne's poetry is notoriously discontinuous. I refuse to use the word 'difficult', which implies a frustrated search for a certain kind of poetic meaning; this, I think, is to get Prynne and those more sincere members of his tribe all wrong, something I will address later.

connotative power. Since the writing of a poem often consists in an attempt to unify elements we had previously thought of as contradictory, contrasting, unrelated or mutually exclusive, the lyric weave is of crucial importance. Most poets are trying to make one big, musically coherent unit, in order to conjure up a thing, a state or relation that is new to language, but whose lyric integrity makes it verifiably *true* in the heart and mind of the reader. The resulting poem will have far more semantic coherence than the *refusal* of this lyric strategy could possibly allow. Perhaps we really are just trying to make one big word out of everything. We can trust our ears to do much of the thinking: if we can tie a word into its lyric context, its borders have been opened, and its meaning is now added to the poem as much through a kind of 'semic ambience' as its denotative sense. That meaning can then seep into the entire poem, and serve to unify its theme.

To summarise the argument so far:

1. Language is a poetic system. When language is subjected to emotional heat and formal pressure (which is to say formal limits placed on the time and space in which it can be spoken) the natural result is what we call 'poetic'.

2. Language consists of sound-signs, and while their acoustic and semantic aspects may be separately described, they are not actually separable.

3. The immediate corollary of their interdependence is that language operates on a principle of iconicity, which is to say *words sound like the things they mean*. They do this through a deep rule of synaesthetic representation, one that tends not to be consciously registered. The mechanism of this iconic system is complex.

4. Poetry is a mode of speech which, along with other deviations from prose and conversational norms, sees a natural shift from the denotative towards the connotative.

This is mainly driven by its pursuit of brief expression: in a constrained space, connotative speech is far more effective than denotative speech in expressing the complex relations that unify poetry's often disparate and contradictory materials. (It's in the imaginative connection of apparently contrary, unrelated or incompatible thematic elements that poetry often finds its 'epiphanies'.)

5. As a result of this connotative shift, poetry instinctively reaches towards the deliberate manipulation and intensification of language's iconic or 'phonosemantic' aspect, where phonesthemes represent shared connotations. As a result, poets are more likely to trust their ears in decisions of word-choice; ideally, no compromise between sound and sense need be negotiated, as they are understood as aspects of the same thing.

6. Within these special rules, unified sound becomes a literal, non-symbolic means of unifying sense. (This has many strange corollaries: for example, a poem that deliberately sought to exhibit *no* lyric patterning would also be engaged in a simultaneous project of dismantling its own sense.)

NOISE

Poetry, I'd like to think, proceeds from a generous instinct, not a selfish one. Whatever private torments might have been assuaged in our writing, we want to give these damn things away in the end. To have someone else want your poem for themselves, it must be desirable; to be desirable, it must be beautiful, or interesting, or both; and for a reader to find it so, it must exhibit some of the symmetry of form and organisation we find in the natural world. This last statement might sound a bit of a reactionary leap, and of course it's as old-school as it comes: it's been a cliché since Plato and Aristotle to say that the reason we find a piece of art satisfying is because it is 'imitative of nature'. However, I persist in thinking of the poem as kind of a human-made natural object, our 'best effort' that we quietly slip back into the world, and against which the world can raise no serious objection.[1] I appreciate, however, that I'm circularly justifying the kind of lyric poetry I myself want to write and read, not the non-lyric kind I do not.

---

1   The occasional use of the phrase 'organic poetry' for 'free verse' is just substituting an error – and a pretty stupid one – for a misnomer. In the organic, symmetry is *everywhere*. Once wholly 'freed' from every aspect of formal patterning, a poem may indeed be 'organic', but only like some kind of diseased amoeba. A better defence of the kind of free verse practice that abjures *all* formal patterning is the Lawrentian argument that it more closely represents the dynamic shape of spontaneous thought; but even this tends to ignore the fact that thought itself is highly rhythmic, and that spontaneous thought is often the least original we have. The 'flash of inspiration', welcome as it is, has given spontaneity an undeservedly good name. First thought = worst thought, speaking personally.

Poetry is often compared to music, but most of the comparisons tend to be facile, and many are plain false. In one important way, however, I think they're closely analogous. We might define music as 'those noises that we agree constitute satisfying or emotionally meaningful arrangements of sound'. When we examine such noises, and look at the way that one note-event follows another, we find that their sequenced patterns converge on the same fractal statistic (the $1/f$ ratio of spectral density) that we find in natural dynamic systems, in everything from quasar emissions to river discharge, traffic flow, sunspot activity and DNA sequences. This pattern is often referred to as 'pink noise'. It lies somewhere between 'white noise', where the relation between one note and the next is uncorrelated and completely random – in acoustics, it's that *shhhh* sound where all frequencies are heard simultaneously, at equal power – and correlated 'brown' or 'Brownian noise' (after Robert Brown, who discovered Brownian motion), where the pitch of the next note is wholly dependent on the position of the previous one, through the application of an inflexible rule. Music generated on a white noise algorithm is ugly in its unpredictability, and Brownian music is just as ugly *in* its predictability. But if we hit upon something in between, something 'pink', we tend to find it beautiful: we sense that it corresponds to an ideal balance of predictable regularity and surprise. [See endnote 3 for connections between white and brown noise and the paradigm/syntagm distinction.]

Analyses of static forms in nature – the outline of a landscape, for example – reveal correlated 'Brownian' patterns. Perhaps this explains why we find Brownian noise acceptable in static visual art, but not in a dynamic, time-based art like music. (The non-dynamic, static and visual aspect of poetry – its typographic arrangement on the page – is often tellingly 'correlated' in its stanzaic and lineated symmetries.) However, when it comes to natural *dynamic* processes, we find pink noise dominating. It appears to be the characteristic signature of complex systems, i.e. those which display non-random variation. The changing content of our sensory experience seems to hover around the pink noise mark. This sensory music is as much a product of the nervous system as of nature: the input received at our physical extremities can be near-chaotic white noise, but our brains, through the application of arbitrary but evolved 'rules', filter it down to pink – screening out the irrelevant noisy data and leaving only those patterns of change which have become useful to our specific evolved intelligence. The wholly dynamic, time-based medium of music is dominated by such a rule; the pattern of regularity and variation in its pitch and volume (just like human speech, incidentally) matches, perhaps more perfectly than any other kind of art, the spectral density of our flickering perception of the world.

It seems reasonable to assume that our brains also perceive the dynamic system of the successful poem as similarly balanced. (The poem itself can be thought of as operating, in its way, like a miniature nervous system, filtering the pink noise of our own perception even further, leaving only a pattern of locally significant data.) The best poetry has nothing so easily quantifiable as note pitch and length, but I'd suggest that *were* we able to measure accurately the ratios of its concrete and abstract speech, its light and its dense lines, the pattern of its metrical agreement and disagreement, we would see something identical emerge: a fair echo of nature, of its balance of correlated and uncorrelated, randomness and self-similarity. And, perhaps, a more crucial equilibrium: that of predictability and surprise, pattern and variation, familiar and unfamiliar, known and unknown.

Wholly familiar 'Brownian' poetry consists in the mere rehearsal of what the reader already knows to be the case, and it unfolds in a wholly predictable manner. It fails because it doesn't surprise. The brain hears nothing but its dull coincidence with rules it already knows too well. 'White' poetry is all unfamiliarity and novelty and discontinuity, and fails because it does nothing *but* surprise. (This sounds just dandy; but there is nothing so predictable as an infinite series of exceptions – nor, as most readers correctly sense, is there anything so easy to create.) All its elements, moreover, are sounded at equal power, and with no sense of a background against which a salience might appear. If our aim really *is* epiphany, the poem must demonstrate a move from the known to the unknown, which we might define here as making an uncorrelated leap from a correlated position. But it can only do so by actually *making* it – and therein lies the risk and seriousness of our word-game.

The suggestion remains controversial, but were we able to measure and quantify these things in an accurate way, there would be nothing to stop us automating the process. While I believe that one day it will be entirely possible to write a great poem with a computer, we will probably have 'gone biotech' by then anyway – and in making the smart move from carbon to silicon, also quit all the pointless fear, sweating and coughing, and limited our orifices to an optimal minimum. Generative poetry is unlikely to seem such a big deal to our bionic scions. (Indeed such an elusive poetic algorithm already seems to exist in the parallel-networked meat-machine of our brains, and it doesn't seem miraculous or impossible to us. It probably should.) We are far closer to devising such a successful generative process for music, though, and the fact that poetry and music are in many ways comparable systems might suggest that poets lack only a full description of their own compositional process. The perennial worry is that poetry written in this way would shed its 'humanity' – but you only have to look at the way traditional music skills have been ported over to programming to realise that those fears are quite unfounded. On the contrary: programmers invest their music with as much humanity and human expression as any other language, and the laptop turns out to be as humanly responsive as any other instrument. Our fear is just the standard human wariness over new means of production. Similar misgivings were initially voiced over cameras, typewriters, the pianoforte – and the printing of books themselves. Even if we are many decades from our robot Emily Dickinson, there is no good reason why computers should not be at least a little useful to the poetic art fairly soon. [For a note on poetry, computers and 'humanisation', see endnote 4.]

While we may be almost as many years from a comprehensive model of the poem as we are for one of the brain, certain aspects of the poetic art are more easily described than others. Just as music is amenable to fairly systematic description, so is the music of poetry. It's in lyric that we can most clearly see our 'pink' balance: poetry naturally refines the music of language to something close to the 'pink' ideal – something correlated, modulated by something variable – and it's that rule that I'll spend the rest of this essay discussing. In its lyric aspect, poetry displays the most instantly recognisable emblem of its art. This takes the form of a strange default: a balance of variation and repetition, composed of shifting vowel and patterned consonant, of both an airy and a stop-heavy music.

LYRIC, VOWEL AND CONSONANT

One of the grim things you learn after many years working as an editor – I hardly dare confess this – is that you can hold a poem at arm's length and, without having read a word, know there's a 90 per cent chance that it's bad. Most often this is because any random two- or three-line passage appears to contain all the letters of the alphabet. (Centred text, coloured ink, copperplate fonts, falling potpourri, money and photos of babies, dogs and naked poets are also reliable pointers.) This means the poem is unlikely to have any music. The phenomenon of 'music' in poetry is often spoken about as if it were a mysterious quality; but if we mean 'music' as in 'music', rather than 'some ineffable thing which my poetic intuition can subjectively divine but is beyond human articulation', it's very simply characterised. With few exceptions, it means that the poem displays deliberate organisation and some form of parallelism in its arrangement of sound. If a 'music' is ascribed to a poem, but cannot be described through pointing to some salient or parallel phonic effect (or – stretching the definition to its limit – a patterned silence), the only 'music' the listener has identified is that which resides naturally in the language itself.

The error is often made because this language-music is not inconsiderable. But nor is the poetic music we superimpose upon it a rare occurrence: even in everyday speech, given a choice of synonyms, we will express an unconscious preference for the more harmonious, contextually lyric sound when we need to make strong sense. Think of just about any phrase that strikes you as a memorable or felicitous – a proverb, a cliché, an advertising slogan – and you'll almost invariably find some patterning in its sounds.[1] The more considered our speech, the more this effect is naturally strengthened, and speech-writers alliterate and assonate almost helplessly. Written prose shows a higher degree of lyric patterning again, and poetry even more so. (The self-conscious foregrounding of this patterning in prose – along with an excessive lingering over concrete description – is what most often leads to that equivocal diagnosis, 'poetic' writing.) But even a random series of words will appear to demonstrate a musical coherence by virtue of any one language being a closed phonemic system, and having a finite set of sounds it can combine. This is the 'musicality' we quickly divine in languages or dialects we have trouble understanding, but are slow to acknowledge in our own: left to focus on the sound alone, we can attend to their distinct and often alien music (hence the apparently infinite suggestiveness of song-lyrics in languages we don't know). Each language uses only a fraction of the possible sounds that the human voice can produce. English is a musically versatile tongue: of the 200-odd phonemes in global employment, it manages to use around 50. We might pity the native Hawaiian speaker with their mere 13, but a poet would sensibly envy them: it must be an effort to speak a sentence in Hawaiian that is *not* lyrically coherent.[2] I was

1 Patterning seems exceptionally important in the formation of the lexicalised phrase or 'phraseme', which takes the forms of idiom, cliché and collocation. We don't hear 'below the belt' as anything to do with belts or punches, since we have learned it as a fixed phrase meaning 'unfair' or 'underhand' – i.e. it has effectively been learned as a word like 'house' or 'faith', for which an approximate synonym (there is no other kind) can be readily provided. A phrase seems to have a better chance of becoming a phraseme when its sounds observe some assonantal or consonantal patterning; this clearly aids the left brain's memorisation and storage of the term along the axis of selection.

2 Though this is nothing compared to Pirahã, the language of Pirahãn Amazons, which has around 10. '*Xigihai xoi kapioxiai. Xigioawaxai? xai xigiai xaaga. Ti gaisai. Xigiaixaaga. Xaooii xoai?*' – seems a typical sample, as far as I can tell. They compensate for their limited sound-palette in the most beautiful way, however, with an intonational prosody so complex that their whole language can be encoded in music,

once asked to comment on that automatically generated collage-text you sometimes get with your spam-mail; the journalist remarked on how beautiful and poetic it could sound. The trouble is that *any* old random garbage often strikes us as beautiful and poetic – but this pays a compliment to language itself, not to the 'poem'. In such circumstances, having little in the way of actual meaning to distract us, we can attend to the sound alone, and enjoy the distinctive gabble of the Anglophone.[3]

Nonetheless, even without salient sound effects like rhyme, assonance or alliteration to point to, we often have the strong sense that something else is going on beside the intrinsic musicality of the language; and indeed there is. In English poetry, the feeling that a piece of writing is 'musical' usually means that it also exhibits two kinds of phonetic bias. Between them, they effect a pattern of repetition and variation, similarity and difference – the motif the human brain craves in everything it perceives, if it is simultaneously to make both connection and distinction. The first is the deliberate variation of

---

and whistled or hummed instead of spoken. Note that this might appear directly to contradict my later assertion in this essay that music cannot be denotative; but this is less 'music' than a tonally encoded sign-system. If a language had a single phoneme, it would have to delegate its sign-making capability to intonational and qualitative manipulations of its one vowel, and such 'music' as it produced would be the mere byproduct of its sign-system (though this would, I suppose, provide one theory for the evolution of song in an 'oligophonemic' ur-language).

Much controversy surrounds Pirahã, and the linguist Daniel Everett has claimed that the apparent absence of recursion in Pirahã contradicts a fundamental tenet of the Chomskyan model – Daniel L. Everett, 'Cultural Constraints on Grammar and Cognition in Pirahã: Another Look at the Design Features of Human Language', *Current Anthropology* 76 (2005): 621–46. This claim has been widely discredited: Pirahã does indeed demonstrate recursive features; and besides, its speakers have no trouble learning a normal recursive language like Portuguese, for which it seems their brains are as just as grammatically well-equipped as those of any other human.

3 Spam text is produced using Markov chains, a stochastic algorithm which spits out a sequence of random variables; these can be used to generate 'plausible' fake texts from a series of real ones. I'll say more on this later.

stressed vowels; the second is the quiet, generally backgrounded patterning of consonants.

Between them, these two tendencies have come to represent an unconscious 'lyric ideal' in English. Importantly, they must be *no more* than tendencies. Generally speaking, if sound-patterning is too strong and too conspicuous, it will be perceived as contrived and will distract from the sense (open Robert Bridges's *Collected Poems* at random, if you want to see what I mean: *'Alone, aloud in the raptured ear of men / We pour our dark nocturnal secret; and then, / As night is withdrawn / From these sweet-springing meads and bursting boughs of May, Dream, while the innumerable choir of day / Welcome the dawn . . .'*[4]) unless it performs some explicit mnemonic or structural function, such as Anglo-Saxon alliteration, or terminal rhyme.[5]

A shift towards vowel heterophony and consonantal homophony creates the unconsciously experienced 'lyric ground' upon which the more consciously registered saliences of rhyme, assonance, alliteration and anomalous consonant can cleanly stand. Just as we see a global shift from denotative to connotative speech, so the phono-semantic principle ensures a concomitant global shift from an inchoate language-music to an explicit poetry-music. Nearly all poets with half an ear default to this lyric ground most of the time. It is, in effect, the poet's working medium, the canvas, clay or stone from which they make the poem.

In the human voice, the vowel carries the bulk of our 'feeling' in its complex tonal and quantitative discriminations; the consonants which interrupt that breath create the bulk of the semantic sense. The

---

4 Robert Bridges, 'Nightingales', *The Humours of the Court, and Other Poems* (London: George Bell and Sons, 1893).

5 Of course, the formal conventions of Anglo-Saxon verse *are* perceived as contrivance nowadays, but they would have been passed over as unremarkable by the Anglo-Saxon ear as the culturally agreed mode of poetic artifice, the invisible fashion of the day. Some US readers feel that full rhyme is just as much of a glaring anachronism, a fact that causes me some misery.

consonant, in making the distinction between *blue* and *shoe* and *true*, gives the phonetic differentiation we need for a sign-system capable of carrying distinct meanings. The envelopes with which it shapes the vowel allow for discrete words to be cut from the air, in much the same way that physical borders allow us to perceive discrete objects. The material basis of that sign-system, though, is the voiced breath, which we use to sing the language. Vowel fills the word with its fairly uniform stuff, while the consonant carves it into a recognisable shape. Consider, say, a mother's frustrated, third-attempt demand to her child, 'Put down the *cup!*' It's easy to separate out the four vowels [ʊ] – [aʊ] – [ɪ] – [ʌ] ('oo – ow – ih – uh'), then imagine the first vowel pitched high to indicate urgency; the second dipping down an interval of a fifth or so to reinforce the impression of sane control; the third pitched identically to the first to reinforce the imperative, and the fact of the demand's repetition; and the last rising another fifth – and increased in loudness – to convey both the anger and non-negotiability of the request. The emotional if not the literal sense would be clear from such a performed sequence of tones; whereas the consonants *pt dn th cp* alone will give us a fair stab at the semantic content, but would provide very few clues to the emotional context. (Note that with the consonants removed, speech suddenly becomes an extremely complex kind of singing – a kind of 'jazz ballad for human horn', full of emotional articulacy, but with no referential content.)

In the non-performative context of written language, however, things are trickier. If you want to demonstrate the hopelessly attenuated emotional palette of written speech, try all the different ways you can pitch and shape the vowels of 'I love you'. Spoken, it's easy to draw out shades of meaning that are alternately questioning, pleading, heartfelt, insecure, angry, desperate, tender, insincere, placatory and so on, just by modifying the song of the vowels. None of those things can be represented by the written phrase; the performative cues have to be figured out through interpreted context alone. At the level of word, meaning is something delegated largely to the consonant – and its emotional aspect is catastrophically attenuated in the process. Because written words can't represent the pitches and lengths that give them their spoken expressive range, it's easy for the vowel to become devalued, to the extent that some graphic systems, like Ancient Hebrew and Vedic Sanskrit, did without it altogether. (Writing systems have their left-brain, denotative bias built in; never forget that the original purpose of our immortal inscription was the recording of debt and the issuing of receipts.) In declaring itself as emotional, urgent speech, and in signalling its kinship with song, poetry must find a way to put the vowel back centre-stage.

Because vowels have perceptible duration, they are easy to hear. You can test this by trying to repeat the vowel sounds in the previous sentence. You should be able to do so almost without thinking about it, and just say the words as a form of de-consonated baby talk. *Because vowels have duration, they are easy to hear*: [ə 'ɔ] ['aʊ ə] [æ] [ʊ 'a ə] [eɪ][æ] ['i: ə][ʊ] [ɪə] – or something like it. Now try and do the same with the consonants. You'll find it almost impossible without thinking about it very carefully and consciously; this is because the vowel is the main durational component of the word, and the consonant is often experienced as temporally negligible.

From 'temporally negligible' it's a short imaginative leap to 'timeless', and it's interesting to note that those languages whose writing systems omit vowels – Egyptian hieroglyphs, Hebrew and Classical Arabic – have found it easy to sustain the idea of a holy book that had existed before the dawn of time, and then 'fell to earth' as a block of eternal and monolithic consonant, into which the impure, sour, time-bound breath of the human had not yet been introduced. Both the Torah and early versions of the Quran were written without vowels or diacritical marks, and both the Kabbalists and Sufis were engaged in the mystical project of re-envowelling their holy books in order to come up with alternative, deeper interpretations to set alongside the 'standard' reading; in this way, they could intuit the secret intentions of the Divine.

The researches of those early mystics are almost procedurally identical, incidentally, to what we call 'pararhyme' or 'consonantal' rhyme, where words with the same consonantal structure are sought out by choosing a word, removing the vowels, and then re-envowelling the consonantal string to generate a secret cognate, or a whole series of them. If we take 'green', we might produce *groin, Egraine, groan, girn, garni, Goran, grown, migraine, agrin*; 'press' gives *Parisi, peruse, disperse, prissy, purse, Paris, Percy, oppress*; 'table' — *tableau, tibial, eatable, unstable, taboulleh, pitbull, beatable, tubule*; 'cut' — *cat, acute, Cato, kite, quite, Hecate, acquit, Kyoto, predicate, kumquat, coot*. 'Consonance' is a global phonestheme whose semantic aspect is something like 'formal or structural equivalence' or 'isomorphism', and I'll expand on this as we go — but if you recall my earlier remark: the way consonants shape the air to allow us to hear discrete words is deeply analogous to the way that physical borders allow us to perceive discrete objects. I strongly suspect that the concepts indicated by words connected by pararhyme and consonance are often regarded, in some unconscious and synaesthetic way, as also somehow *related in their form*;[6] there is, I think, some unconsciously perceived formal equivalence or symmetry declared between *Caesar* and *scissor* and *seizure*, *brick* and *barrack* and *bark*, *rubble* and *rebel* and *terrible*, however nonsensical our conscious mind might find the idea. (Because they also have a visual presence, consonantal symmetries in written language are far more obvious than in spoken.)

One sensible use of this phenomenon is to use the generated word-series as a means of interrogating the unconscious, the memory and the imagination by asking that they link the words up as stations in an

6 Hence, I suspect, our stubborn superstition that an anagram of someone's name reveals something of their inner character. (Florence Nightingale = *angel of the reclining*, etc. Although my favourite is Elvis = *lives*.) I also have some strong anecdotal evidence that editors are peculiarly susceptible to submissions made by authors whose names are anagrams of their own; we are all our own blind spots.

intelligible narrative. Essentially, this procedure treats the mind as if it were itself a holy book.

> A mink escaped from a mink-farm
> in South Armagh
> is led to the grave of Robert Nairac
> by the fur-lined hood of his anorak.

(PAUL MULDOON, 'Mink')[7]

Here, the use of pararhyme less 'echoes' Paul Muldoon's larger artistic project of unexpected connection than facilitates it at every turn. Nairac was a rogue British Army officer who went missing while working undercover, and was killed by the IRA; his body was never found. He *is* found in this poem, however – by his rogue analogue, a freelance mink whose form is twinned in his army-issue anorak. I have no idea how this poem was composed; but I know that consonantal rhymes must be built far earlier into the compositional process than other kinds of rhyme. A poem does not just 'accommodate' them; it allows itself to be partly dictated by them.

Incidentally, Kabbalistic exegesis is not quite as crazy as it sounds. Semitic languages like Arabic and Hebrew work by using vowel-sounds to systematically modify a root group of consonants called a 'triliteral', or triconsonantal root. For example, in Arabic 'k-t-b' is the 'write' group, and yields *kataba*, to write; *yaktubu*, he writes; *kitab*, book; *maktaba*, library; and so on. Hebrew does something very similar with the same triliteral. Pararhyme, if you like, is built into their structure: the Kabbalists and Sufis were really just imaginatively extending the rules of their own morphology. English has no such excuse, and pararhymes generally sound a bit perverse if they're not concealed a little. Wilfred Owen's 'Strange Meeting' is a notable exception, though here the rhymes brilliantly enact the

---

7 Paul Muldoon, *Poems 1968–1998* (London: Faber & Faber, 2011).

subject. Paul Muldoon conceals his rhymes through a mixture of wide separation and variable line length; a uniform line would foreground them uncomfortably. Alas, Muldoon has virtually copyrighted the procedure in English poetry, making it almost impossible for anyone else to employ it in a way that doesn't simply sound imitative of him – although he uses pararhyme more and more as a deep compositional procedure, and less and less as a way of unifying the music simply for the reader's enjoyment. This is seen in the distance placed between his rhymes, which are often many lines and pages apart – and sometimes separated by entire *books*.[8] Nonetheless, the rhymes in his poetry, no matter how distant from each other they find themselves, seem bound by a kind of quantum entanglement.

Though it cheers me to think that poetry takes the opposite approach from that of religion: we have long thought of ourselves as starting not with the *logos* but the *pneuma*, not with those Platonic consonantal forms, but with the ether that encloses and unites them, the inspiration, the afflatus, the breath – the breath being that infinite possibility into which *consonant*, not vowel, must be driven to have it make any sense in the currency of our human speech. This strikes me as a far more serious kind of word-game than the Kabbalists ever played (and, of course, it's the one Muldoon and Owen are *principally* playing, like all lyric poets). Poets from Tennyson to Antonio Machado have alighted on 'wind' as the idealised inspirational source – shaping its one long vowel around every object it meets, making the unity we pursue through our articulation of the specific less an impossible

---

8 Note that, if we're using pararhyme purely as a compositional aid, we can bury the rhymes by simply not placing them in a terminal position. You'll lose the reader's applause, as they'll likely be none the wiser; but it's a legitimate use of a technique that, like syllabics, really has nothing to do with the reader at all. (Though I confess I was once reduced to the pathetic move of pointing out that a poem of mine was based on twenty-eight variations on the same consonantal string, as ten years had passed without anyone noticing – something a less insecure ego might have been *pleased* about.)

contradiction than a paradox to be dwelt within. And the wind brings weather, words, voices, scents from afar, from impossible elsewheres.[9]

Song works by 'unnaturally' elongating the vowel and diminishing the prominence of the consonant. This can be seen in its treatment of end-rhymes; when sung, the words *soon*, *room*, *cool*, *roof* will be perceived as close-to-full rhymes, and the longer the note, the fuller they sound. For lyricists, assonantal rhymes are often effectively full rhymes: when Bob Dylan sings 'Let me sleep in your meadows with the green grassy *leaves* / Let me walk down the highway with my brother in *peace*', we're quite untroubled by the 'inaccuracy' of the rhyme. And as you'd expect, in exaggerating the vowel, singing will often strongly foreground the emotional sense at the expense of the denotative. This is why great songs can survive awful lyrics, and what lies behind statements like 'She could break your heart singing the phonebook'.[10]

Instrumental music may be usefully considered as an unbroken vowel, a kind of pure tonal and quantitative speech whose sole purpose is to carry emotion – akin to the spoken vowel, but vastly more supple and articulate. However the absence of consonantal stops in music means that we are left with something possessive of

9 It seems to me that this universe operates on a principle of rapid alternation between 'pneuma and logos', duration and event, syntagm and paradigm, function and content – a pattern clearly imprinted in the basic linguistic phenomenon of metre. It is also realised in the vowel-consonant-vowel-consonant pattern of our speech, and further reflected in our unconscious mapping of consonants to 'contentual' qualities of physical boundary, and of vowels to 'functional' qualities of spatiotemporal relation.

10 Vowel-mangling can happen in other ways too. Most librettists will have had the miserable experience of hearing their best line rendered unintelligible by its being set for long notes in the upper register of the soprano voice, which has the vowel /i/, and no other. In their defence, though, composers have devised a million other ways to destroy a good line. This is one reason the librettist–composer relationship should sensibly be considered a co-operative rather than collaborative one. Hand it over, walk away and let them do their worst.

emotional articulacy, but with no differentiating ability, and so no way of constructing a sign-system; it can therefore have no denotative power.[11] When Richard Strauss said, 'I look forward to the day I can describe a teaspoon accurately in music', everyone was justifiably sceptical – and indeed Strauss's teaspoon has remained wholly elusive. In a good jazz ballad solo – especially played on an instrument close in timbre to the human voice, like a tenor saxophone – the timing and pitch of the notes are so closely mapped to the rhythms and cadences of plaintive speech and articulate argument, you can easily imagine 'enconsonating' the notes to give a clear denotative sense. Indeed, some 'vocalese' artists couldn't resist doing exactly that with a number of famous jazz solos, with predictably underwhelming results. In a sense, however, that's just the solution poetry arrives at, albeit from the other direction: in making a shift towards the privileging of the vowel, we restore some of the quantitative length absent from speech; poetry then becomes a kind of transitive, articulate music. In doing so, it leaves the door open to the reader to make their own highly personal intonational interpretation, i.e. the superimposition of subjective, performed sense on its stressed vowels. (But fix those vowels as a melodic series of pitches, and in a sense you *destroy* the possibility of a wholly personal reading; the poem may now be a serviceable lyric, but it has ceased to be a poem. A 'set poem', in a sense, nails its emotional sense to a single interpretation. Of course, singers have found a thousand ways to get round this limitation, even if composers would often rather they didn't. Since consonant is the tool of differentiation, of denotative meaning, a solid block of consonant like the Torah seems to propose a monosemic source. This is perhaps why the multiple interpretations proposed by Kabbalistic re-envowelling of the Pentateuch struck many as heretical. A block

---

11 'Denotative' in the normal sense of a sign indicating a concept. However, I believe there *is* a seme at work in music that corresponds to what I call the 'patheme'. I'll discuss this in Part II.

of uninterrupted vowel such as music represents, on the other hand, seems to imply a *polysemic* source, which is why a single interpretation often seems equally heretical in its 'precision' – as well as reductive and redundant.[12])

It's primarily the exaggerated prominence given to the vowel that distinguishes the characteristic noise of the poem from that of prose or conversational speech, though the effect can be a subtle one. It's also what opens up the poem's interpretative potential at the level of performance, since the vowel is also where the personality, geographical origin, age, social class, health, size and present mood of the reader find their tonal expression. There is an unconsciously received ideal of 'beautiful' English lyric. If we closely examine some representatively 'beautiful' texts, we find a backgrounded default where stressed vowels are arranged by careful contrast and variation. Each word retains its distinct spirit, and the reader has the vague sense of it standing in a clearly stated, discrete spatial and temporal relation to the words on either side. Against this varied ground, we also see occasional stark and consciously perceived *deviation*, which is to say assonance and rhyme. Assonance doesn't have any effect *unless* the vowel-changes are continually being rung elsewhere, and is a way of foregrounding important detail:

> . . .You can see how it was:
> Look at the pictures and the cutlery.
> The music in the piano stool. That vase.

> (PHILIP LARKIN, 'Home is So Sad')[13]

---

12 As anyone who has suffered Eddie Jefferson's miserable enconsonation of Coleman Hawkins's immortal solo on 'Body and Soul' will testify with alacrity: 'Don't you know he was the king of the saxophone – yes indeed he was, talkin' 'bout the guy who made it sound so good, some people knew him as The Bean but Hawkins was his name. He sure could swing,' etc.

13 Philip Larkin, *Collected Poems*, ed. Anthony Thwaite (London: Faber & Faber, 2003).

My 'place of clear water,'
the <u>first hill</u> in the world
where springs washed into
the shiny grass

(SEAMUS HEANEY, 'Anahorish')[14]

. . . I remember no <u>ship</u>
<u>slipping</u> from the dock –
no <u>cluster</u> of <u>hurt</u>, proud family . . .
. . . but we have surely gone,
and must knock with brass
kilted pipers
<u>doors</u> to the <u>old</u> land;
we emigrants of no farewell
who keep our bit language
in <u>jokes</u> and <u>quotes</u>;
our working knowledge
of coal-pits, fevers . . .

(KATHLEEN JAMIE, 'The Graduates')[15]

Some poets use assonance far more than others – but even then it's rare that you'll find a long run of similar vowels or assonantal pairs, as anything approaching vowel homophony will diminish assonance's foregrounding power. However, the 'varied vowel rule' may be arguably less a conscious strategy and more a matter of the unconscious avoidance of similarity.

Varied vowels also reinforce the impression that we are indeed saying things once, with especial clarity, just as our 'invoked hush' demands. Vowel-variation is a natural feature of both prose and spoken English too, but since they are generally conducted in rapidly delivered

---

14   Seamus Heaney, *New Selected Poems 1966–1987* (London: Faber & Faber, 1990).
15   Kathleen Jamie, *Jizzen* (London: Picador, 1999).

phrases, many stressed vowels on content-words are demoted to something approaching 'schwa', which I'll explain shortly. By contrast, lineation slows speech, restores the vowel to its full value and makes us conscious of the tonal quality of its various formants; it means we can then deliberately exaggerate the vowel-varying *tendency* of spoken English. This is yet another 'peak shift' strategy. Try slowly mouthing only the vowel-sounds in the following passages (you might also find it useful to compare them with a random chunk of good journalistic prose as a 'control'):

> I caught a tremendous fish
> and held him beside the boat
> half out of water, with my hook
> fast in a corner of its mouth
>
> (ELIZABETH BISHOP, 'The Fish')[16]

> 'This man can't bear our life here and will drown,'
> The abbot said, 'unless we help him.' So
> They did, the freed ship sailed, and the man climbed back
> Out of the marvellous as he had known it.
>
> (SEAMUS HEANEY, 'Lightenings: viii')[17]

> I would spread the cloths under your feet:
> But I, being poor, have only my dreams;
> I have spread my dreams under your feet;
> Tread softly, because you tread on my dreams.
>
> (W. B. YEATS, 'He Wishes for the Cloths of Heaven')[18]

---

16 Elizabeth Bishop, *Poems* (New York: Farrar, Straus & Giroux, 2011), 43.
17 Seamus Heaney, *Seeing Things* (London: Faber & Faber, 1991).
18 W. B. Yeats, *The Collected Poems of W. B. Yeats* (Ware: Wordsworth Editions, 1994), 59.

In each case you should have felt like you were trying to deal with a gigantic, intractable and invisible toffee. Upping the stressed vowel count has the effect of lengthening the line, and is actively achieved by deliberate word-choice, and passively aided by lessening the occurrence of thin or weak vowels. This means, essentially, keeping 'schwa' down to a minimum. *Schwa* is the short neutral vowel sound that occurs in most unstressed syllables, and is represented by the /ə/ symbol in the IPA. Schwa has its roots in the word for 'nought' in Hebrew, and its nondescript little grunt can be substituted for any written vowel, if it occurs in an unstressed position: the 'a' in 'abet' and 'petal'; the 'e' in 'bagel'; the 'i' in stencil; the 'o' in 'arrogant' or 'condition'; the 'u' in 'crocus' and the 'y' in 'satyr', and so on. In rapid speech, their numbers multiply. Schwa by *definition* can't be stressed or sustained; it's no more possible to sing a long schwa than it is to play Gregorian chant on the banjo.

One way of de-schwa-ing the line is to avoid too many polysyllabic words drawn from a classical word-base. Though Latin pronunciation was a very different matter, the way the vowels in polysyllabic Latin words come out in Germanic speech collapses them around a dominant stress. (Listen to how short most of the vowels are in words like *authoritative*, *intermittently*, *inimical* and so on.) There's a marked tendency in the English lyric tradition to just avoid them, and poetry often defaults to the mono- and disyllabic Anglo-Saxon, Norman or Norse word-hoard. However, there's a more important way of lengthening and aerating the line: through metre. One immediate consequence of writing in metre is that the unstressed syllable count falls dramatically in comparison with a prose passage of equal length. Whatever other purposes it might serve, metrical writing is also a fine way of increasing the relative number of big vowels per sentence, because it insists that every second syllable (in duple metres) or every third (in triple) must take a strong stress. (This is a shocking oversimplification, but by the time we get to 'Metre' you'll be thanking me for it. However, the broad principle holds.) This automatically lowers the schwa-count just by making it harder for unstressed vowels to squeeze in; it insists on an unusually high number of content words to take up those strong stresses, since function words are generally demoted to unstressed vowels in speech; and it even tricks the brain into processing some function words as content words when we drop them into a strong-stress position. (Note that if free verse is going to subscribe to the same lyric ideal, it must supply its large stressed vowels by more deliberate means, and its expert practitioners do precisely this.) This leaves the poetic line unusually information-rich. However, as I've mentioned, the act of lineation *itself* compels a slower spoken delivery, metred or not – and this often results in the re-emergence of our gobbled conversational schwas as full vowels. Contemporary poetry may indeed sound close to 'chopped-up prose' at times, but we use a magic knife – one it takes a fairly long apprenticeship to learn how to wield. It allows silence to take up residence between the stanzas, lines and words, and for the breath *within* words to expand. Or, to lineate the words of a certain disgraced US comedian:

> Always end
> the name
> of your child
> with a vowel
> so when
> you yell
> the name
> will carry

Here, what would be schwa or near-schwa when spoken rapidly in a joke – 'your', 'with', 'so', 'you' and 'will' – move towards full vowels. This is because short lines tend to be read very slowly with long gaps between them. This alone seems enough to confer a little 'poetry' on the statement; while it remains funny, we're also forced into a slower meditation of its wider resonance. This increase in vowel-presence forms half our 'lyric ground'. The effect is subtle, and the reader is mostly unconscious of it – but they experience it as sense of deepened length, space, breath, musicality and tonal (and hence emotional) differentiation.

The other half of the lyric ground is formed by the patterning of consonants. Simply put: if we employ consonants as the tool of semantic differentiation, the project of unifying the sense of our material will be broadly aided by our patterning them. This is, in effect, another global application of the phonosemantic principle described in the first part of this essay. Since consonants take up little space, their musical effect only really becomes audible through either their proximate repetition or their bold deviation from a repetitive ground. (Sound-linked but distant words – like pararhymed pairs – have to be processed consciously, and therefore highly salient, i.e. placed in prominent terminal, initial or caesural positions, or lyrically or semantically 'deviant'. Some critics have the unfortunate habit of identifying *non*-salient lyric effect in words separated by many lines, and then claiming that the poet had intended some semantic echo. 'In "Ground Beef"' by Terence Unthank, for example, we see how the idea of the death of the parent is pursued through the repetition of the *fa*- sounds in 'fatal' and 'father' in lines 3 and 29 . . .' and so on. This is popular criticism of the paranoiac school; these effects are nearly always accidental, and indeed imperceptible, unless you go hunting for them.) What we tend to find, just as we did with the variation of vowel-sound, is that in 'musical' writing there are almost always subtle patterns of consonantal echo. Here's an unsubtle example, where the English lyric default has been turned up to 11:

> Glory be to God for dappled things
> For skies of couple-colour as a brinded cow;
> For rose-moles all in stipple upon trout that swim;

Fresh-firecoal chestnut-falls; finches' wings;
Landscape plotted and pieced – fold, fallow, and plough . . .

(GERARD MANLEY HOPKINS, 'God's Glory')[19]

Though it can hold an underrated appeal for the eye, spelling is irrelevant to the ear; a poet who has learned to hear and recognise close phonetic relatives is at a distinct advantage when it comes to their fluent patterning. For compositional purposes, they can often be freely substituted for one another, and the difference between, say, a voiced and unvoiced consonant is relatively slight. I'll list the most common English sounds here. (I appreciate this book is not a primer, but a few poets may still be reading, and there is no earthly excuse for poets not to know them.) The unvoiced consonant is the first of each pair.

The unvoiced and voiced plosives:
     labial: p/b;
     dental: t/d;
     guttural: k/g

The unvoiced and voiced fricatives:
     the labiodentals: f/v;
     the dentals: th/TH [θ/ ð];

---

19 As well as all its bonkers staple-gun consonants, there are a few too many assonantal pairs in this poem for my taste too. Hopkins is a fine poet, of course – but he also holds a perennial appeal for the tone deaf, as even they cannot fail to hear his glorious racket. Many of Hopkins's effects are spectacular, but are sometimes achieved at the expense of his quieter ones; he can wander rather too cheerfully over the line between baroque lyricism and demented echolalia, and the result is language that can sound – to me at least – unrelated to anything we ever experience as natural human speech. Nonetheless, no poet better trains the apprentice lug, and neither Seamus Heaney nor George Mackay Brown (to name two marvellously attuned poets) would have grown the ears they had without him.

the sibilants: s/z, sh/zh [ʃ/ʒ]
the glottal: h

The unvoiced and voiced affricates:
ch/j [tʃ / dʒ]

And then we have three related groups:[20]
the nasals: m/n/ng [m/n/ŋ]
the glides: w/wh/y [w/ʍ/ j]
the liquids: l/r [l/ɹ]

(As a Scot I am obliged to add the rolled 'r' or alveolar tap [r], as well as the 'ch' of loch, or voiceless velar fricative [x].)

Most of these pairs or groups are close enough to function as interchangeable allophones in one language or another, *l* and *r* in Japanese being maybe the most famous example. [See endnote 5 for more on allophones and their role in shibboleths.] This is a very rough list, and the phonic relations between these sounds are far deeper and more interesting than just the voiced/unvoiced pairs, the nasal group, and so on. However, most of the closer cousins will already be familiar through various speech phenomena:

a) Grimm's law of consonant shift, which showed, amongst other things, how the classical unvoiced *p*/ *t*/ *k* stops morph into the Germanic unvoiced *f* / *th* / *h*; (see also Verner's Law).

b) Foreign allophones: Spanish betacism, where /b/ and /v/ are blurred; also Spanish /d/ and /r/; Japanese lambdacism, where /l/ and /r/ are blurred; the Filipino /p/ and /f/, as well as differences in pronunciation like French /R/ for /r/.

20 The last two categories are more properly 'approximants', but old habits die hard. 'Glides' and 'liquids' are nicer and more expressive names.

c) Dialectal pronunciation, as in the Cockney /f/ and /v/ for
/θ/ and /ð/ ('first' for 'thirst' and 'vose' for 'those'); the
Scots /x/ for /h/ ('daachter' and 'wecht' for 'daughter'
and 'weight'; and so on. This is less a dialectal variant than
a retention from an earlier Germanic speech – it was the
English 'gh' that became silent). Also /r/ for /ɹ/ or /ɾ/,
the burr of Scottish rhotacism; the Scouse /χ/ for final
/k/; the almost universal Estuary English droppin' of
/ŋ/ for /n/; the Devon /z/ for /s/ ('zider' for 'cider');
the Shetland /d/ for /ð/ ('da' for 'the'); the US /d/ for
/t/ (as in 'Creadive Wriding'); the Irish /t/ for /θ/ (as
in 'tree fellers' for 'three fellers'); the Gaelic /tʃ/ for /
dʒ/) ('Chudge Chudy' for 'Judge Judy'). One could easily
construct a map of the UK where every vaguely proximate
consonant had been reversed *somewhere*; indeed you soon
find bizarre examples like the Fife shibboleth /ʃ/ for / θ /
('shree' for 'three') or the Aberdonian /f/ for /ʍ/ ('fit' for
'what', 'fun-bus' for 'whin-bush'), or the Doric /r/ which
becomes a rather French /x/.[21]

d) Speech impediments: lisping, where /s/ becomes /θ/ (long
a source of scurrilous Carry On-style British humour); the
childish (or Cockney) /w/ for /r/ ('weadin', wi'in' an'

---

21   It's off the chart in more ways than one, but I do want to mention my favourite
substitution – the Dundee dialectal swapping of nearly everything for the voiceless
glottal plosive, leaving us with a phonemic palette as impoverished as something you'd
find up a mountain in Papua New Guinea. Thus a statement like *I ate all of it, didn't I* –
a common response to most food-related enquiries in Tayside – becomes *Eh ay' aa' o' i'
dih' uh*. (In an even more brutal linguistic economy, the negative affix is also dropped
entirely: 'did' means both 'did' *and* 'didn't'. Thus *Eh dih' dae i', dih' uh* is 'I didn't do
it, did I'. An *extra* glottal stop standing in as the *–n't* affix *–dih'* /'/ *uh* – would be
regarded as an effete refinement.) As the joke goes round here – Q: 'And how many
*t*s in *Paterson*, sir?' A: 'Nane'. The *aleph* of the Hebrew alphabet, incidentally, used to
represent the sacred ur-consonant of the glottal stop, from which we can reasonably
surmise that God talks with a Dundee accent.

awiffma'ic'); 'talking through a cold', where the nasals /m/, /n/ and /ŋ/ become /b/, /d/ and /g/, the dose being bugged up with bucus.

While a thorough study of these connections can provide poets with some invaluable ear-training, the practical method of achieving a unified consonantal music in the poetic line is simple: one must be alive to the music each line *itself* suggests in the initial stages of its composition. The poet must divine its consonantal signature, then tighten and sharpen it, vary the vowels, foreground important detail through assonance and anomalous consonants – and eliminate all unproductive, loud sound effects that enhance no sense. It *isn't* quite matter of looking at something like . . .

> But when your fine fizzog filled up his verse,
> Then lacked I theme; that really weakened mine.

and thinking – 'OK, *fine fizzog filled . . . verse* is a pointless and gratuitous alliteration; but I can pick up on the 'k' of *lacked* if I change *features* to *countenance*, and *enfeebled* will chime better with *filled*, and while *theme* keeps the nasal music going nicely, *matter* does the same – and also solves the problem of that metre-padding *really*, as well as keeping these nice clipped plosives going . . . Let's try

> But when your countenance filled up his line,
> Then lacked I matter; that enfeebled mine.

. . . Nailed it!' No, few poets would come from so far behind in a first draft. But almost every line will contain *some* revisions of this sort – and even if these decisions are rarely consciously articulated, a good ear, allied to some intuitive reasoning, will allow us make them by a pretty similar process.

The poet's almost pathological sensitivity to the weight and texture of words is a faculty that tends, I suspect, to get burned into the circuits in the age of lyric innocence, during one's early adventures in 'voice-finding' – Pound claimed this occurs between the ages of seventeen and twenty-two – but it could surely be learned by anyone prepared to cultivate the necessary obsession.[22] It leaves us with an odd skill: we can often identify, in the 'given' line or phrase, a kind of phonosemantic DNA, a generative proposition that, we feel, somehow prefigures the whole poem. The search for 'what it is we mean' is then conducted through that narrowed lyric-semantic channel, whose musical colour shifts from line to line, like another twist of the kaleidoscope. The compositional unit of the poetic line will display more and more of this memorable, unifying, song-like, phrase-creating patterning as the poet drafts and redrafts.

First lines are often good places to study such propositions. Take 'Throw all your stagey chandeliers in wheelbarrows and move them north' (Robert Crawford, 'Opera').[23] Besides the surreal drama of the line, look at the assonantal and consonantal echo between 'throw' and 'north'; the sibilants and liquids uniting 'chandeliers' and 'wheelbarrows'; the tonal antithesis of the high-society 'chandeliers' and the labouring-class signifier of 'wheelbarrows' made all the more palpable

22 Perhaps 'poet' can be simply defined as 'anyone prepared to cultivate the necessary obsession with writing poems'. Indulged for long enough, we now know that just about any obsessive practice will effect physical change in the corresponding part of the brain, making it in turn easier to indulge and perfect the practice itself. Einstein's brain turned out to be just as anomalous as we'd hoped – he was missing a bit of his lateral sulcus, which may or may not have helped with neuronal communication; but there was also a statistical bump in the glial cell count in the left inferior parietal region, a part of the associative cortex – which is where we synthesise information from other areas of the brain. It's speculated that this may have been the product of a lifetime spent in the environment of scientific problem-solving. Perhaps most geniuses 'mutantise' themselves; it would surely be weirder to find that Shakespeare's brain had *not* grown a little distorted in its language and empathy centres.
23 Robert Crawford, 'Opera', *Selected Poems* (London: Jonathan Cape, 2005).

through their assonantal connection, and their being both saliently polysyllabic;[24] the insistent (Glaswegian) nasals of 'and move them north'; 'stagey chandeliers' presents the line's most memorable phrase, with the two words close enough in sound that we vaguely sense the 'pale apple' effect, that of a phonestheme being conjured from the air.

I'll cover this in a more technical way when I discuss metre, but it's important to mention for now that poetic lines tend to something around three seconds in duration. This is the length of the human 'moment', and corresponds to what our brains can experience as an unbroken, living instant – an instant whose auditory contents we can then mentally replay, then either choose to remember or not, depending on their salience and importance.[25] (Although our brains can perform fairly accurate chronoceptions, our hearing is the only traditional sense which measures time with much accuracy.) The three-second rule has a powerful influence on the form and delivery of the poetic line, which – unsurprisingly, for an art whose cultural function has long been associated with memory and the memorable – universally defaults to a frequency of about 0.3 Hz to form an ideal mnemonic unit. This is the frequency of the carrier-wave of poetic meaning. In English, it comes out as a line of between eight and twelve syllables; our most popular literary line, iambic pentameter, strongly reflects this tendency.

24 This is a very Shakespearian trick: the poet creates a kind of tonal oxymoron by uniting an antithesis or deepening a paradox through a bonding lyric effect. Look at this palindromic assonance from Sonnet 79: 'My verse alone had all thy gentle grace; / But now my *gracious* numbers are *decayed*.' The frisson will be registered, but the means by which it has been achieved will remain hidden.

25 The relevance to poetry of the 'auditory present' was first affirmed in Ernst Pöppel and Frederick Turner's famous paper 'The Neural Lyre' (1983); its research has been subsequently validated, and the 'three-second line' has become many a poet's favourite scientific factoid. However, I have grave reservations over the original paper's reactionary conclusions, which can be roughly summarised as 'formal verse is therefore better than free', a silly and unsupportable position. The three-second rule has implications that are, if anything, even *more* profound for free than formal verse.

This is also explains what we mean by 'short' and 'long' lines. Short and long compared with what? Well — with a line that takes around three seconds to deliver. Short lines tend to lengthen the gap between them, as the brain will unconsciously seek to establish a three-second rhythm; similarly, long lines are read more quickly with only brief interlineal pauses as we try to shrink them down to size. This is also the reason that weak vowels on function words are often promoted to something closer to strong in short lines, and strong vowels on content words demoted to schwa in longer ones. All this will receive careful defence and explanation later, but for now it's important to understand that the three-second rule also influences the lyric weave: a sound-event has about three seconds on either side in which it can be either prepared for, or have its use retrospectively sanctioned. Any further apart, and the reader is unlikely to perceive them as belonging to the same 'moment', and connect them. Therefore, as the poet instinctively pursues this strategy in their redrafting, working the line again and again through their lyric handloom, every two- or three-line passage will most often start to exhibit its own distinctive pattern and colour. As I've mentioned, most of the sound-correspondences that some commentators identify as working over the distance of several lines simply aren't. The exceptions are sounds that the poet has made deliberately salient: the sounds that land on internal or terminal rhyme or pararhyme, sounds attached to dramatic or significant sense, rogue and unusual phonemes, or indeed any noise which is prominent enough to allow it to enter the memory, and then be recalled when its strong echo occurs later in the text.

Here's a short passage from 'The Dry Salvages'. Look at the immensely deft way in which Eliot weaves a pattern of consonants through the vowel's warp:

> Also pray for those who were in ships, and
> Ended their voyage on the sand, in the sea's lips
> Or in the dark throat which will not reject them

Or wherever cannot reach them the sound of the sea bell's
Perpetual angelus.[26]

The *j* in 'reject' could have been left standing very lonely indeed, but has been anticipated by the affricate in 'voyage', and later consolidated by that of 'reach' and 'angelus'. Note too the guttural chime between 'dark' and 'reject'; the power of the two monosyllables of 'dark throat', and their repeated plosive closure; the 'ships' / 'lips' rhyme; the echoic sibilance of 'sound of the sea bell's / Perpetual angelus'; the heavily patterned r/l liquids in the last two lines; the assonance of 'bell's / Perpetual', doubly consolidated in sense by the alliterating labial plosives . . . and so on. These effects are, of course, not the only reason the passage works – but they're the principal reason the passage is experienced as sensually beautiful. All this is work completed best by the instinct (and I have little doubt that this is *mostly* the way Eliot went about it); but the instinct can be consciously trained into making better and more consistent decisions.

26 T. S. Eliot, 'The Dry Salvages', *Four Quartets* (London: Faber & Faber, 1979).

RHYME

Most poets weave almost *all* their poetic expression into a lyric form. (Since many do so unconsciously, a few may persist in claiming otherwise; but lyric's appeal — even to the most radical postmodernist — is largely irresistible.) This decision to 'make music at all costs' creates a low-level formal resistance, one to which the direction and content of our sense-making must adapt. This way, we end up saying something more convincing and more original than the thing we first intended to; not just because what sounds good tends to be experienced as making better sense, but because this formal resistance forces us to mine the imagination more deeply, where the ore also tends to be of better quality. (One of the first pieces of advice I give to students is this: write the poem you're writing, not the one you *want* to write. Chances are that we've heard that one already.) This idea can be better understood if we look at an easily isolable lyric effect: rhyme.

It would take another book to discuss the subject fully, so for now I'll confine myself to a few brief remarks on the use of rhyme from a compositional perspective. In contrast to the backgrounded effect of the lyric weave, rhyme is a point of *high*-level formal resistance. Bold rhyme improves the memorability of the poem for the reader, and when employed in regular manner sets up a pattern of expectation that the poet can creatively honour, subvert and occasionally thwart.[1]

---

[1] I won't discuss the 'merits' of rhymed over non-rhymed poetry (or vice versa), as the argument is too fatuous to engage with. Both can be wonderful; both can be dreadful. Both have unique points in their favour; both have their limitations. Many poets write both, though some have a temperamental inclination towards one or the other. Neither approach enjoys any intrinsic superiority, and since both emerge

Rhyme can be a handy tool of psychological manipulation; within the phonosemantic system, its declared symmetry implies a logic, often falsely. An outrageous or uncomfortable statement is a great deal more likely to be believed and accepted if it's couched in apparently fluent and effortless rhyme. However, from the poet's point of view, things are rather different; rhyme has little compositional value for the poet if it does *not* present them with a problem. This is because the search for a rhyme should not be a search for a synonym ('OK . . . what means "happy" and has one syllable and ends with -*ump*?' usually won't get you far), but for a solution to a far more vaguely articulated question: 'What *is* it that I want to say?' (It's in such distinctions, incidentally, that we tell can the serious poet from the mere versifier.) We've already seen how this can work with pararhyme, which works in a directly content-generating way: the rhyme-words must be generated independently of argument or narrative, and are then allowed to anticipate the poem, whose shape must partly be determined by them. Conventional terminal rhyme is more a process of content-modification. We know vaguely what we want to say, and we rely on the resistance of the rhyme scheme to adapt that vague thought, to clarify, reshape and redirect it. Rhyme also offers *editorial* resistance: to push an idea through a rhyme-pattern feels like straining fruit through muslin, and it often emerges refined, sharpened and about 50 per cent lighter.

Compared to, say, Russian or Italian, English is an alarmingly rhyme-poor tongue. The chances of us finding a rhyming word-pair in an uninflected language that has both the sound *and* the sense we require are effectively nil. The trick is to turn a problem into an opportunity: we search for rhymes in the *expectation* that our intended sense will change, since it's generally desirable that it do so. The poet is committed to a process, not an operation; the difficulty of finding a

---

naturally from speech, neither is ever 'dead' – and anyone who tells you differently is not to be trusted.

natural rhyme guarantees that it will take time – and in that enforced delay, we often find out what it is we think, and discover what we didn't know. (The temptation to merely write down what you *do* know is perhaps the greatest danger in writing free verse.)[2]

I think this is generally accomplished by holding sound and sense in one's head simultaneously. The 'sense' need be no more than an intuition of a general direction, one that we understand will adapt and change. Since the resistance of rhyme is far stronger than that of the loose patterning of the lyric weave, the content must have enough 'give' to accommodate it: if the poet sets off with their 'great idea' or their *idée fixe*, the result will likely be buckling lines, and disaster. This is why we bring *hunches* to poems – vague propositions, not fully formed theses. The symmetry of rhyme may reinforce a logic in the reader's mind, but for the poet it often proposes one; and where the function of regular rhyme is anticipatory for the reader, it is predictive for the poet.

If rhyme is going to be used at all, its sheer intractability insists that it *must* be the main formal consideration. The process of hunting and finding rhyme-pairs often inspires or dictates a large part of the content – Yeats famously claimed that if it wasn't for rhyme, he wouldn't know what the next line was going to be – but the larger part of rhyme's formal resistance is derived not from the rhyme itself, but from the business of devising a syntax which *prepares for its natural fall*. Poems where the poet has refused to negotiate, refused to allow the direction of their intended sense to alter by one degree, are marked by both unconvincing rhymes and unnatural syntax, where the words in the line have bunched, switched, tripped and stumbled

---

2 English poetry has some very odd constraints indeed, but some may have proven critically useful: 'The crucial thing about English as a language for poetry is that you cannot rhyme the subject with the verb, because either "the cat distracts" and "the nerves swerve" or "the cats distract" and "the nerve swerves"; this bit of grammar has been enormously helpful to English poetry by forcing it away from platitude.' William Empson, *Argufying* (London: Chatto & Windus, 1987), 134.

so they can shunt the rhyme-word to the end. For the poet, 'rhyme' is a verb, not a noun, and implies a procedure where sense and content are kept in dynamic flux.

The unspoken 'rule of rhyme' demands that we balance similarity with difference. Like the joke, the rhyme represents a small and surprising collision of cognitive frames, and the ear delights in the way that two dissimilar items are shown to be related. Indeed 'small jokes for the ear' isn't such a bad definition of rhyme: too much difference in the sound, and the effect falls as flat as a contrived punchline. One winces at the memory of *Educating Rita*'s 'assonance is when you get the rhyme wrong' — but we all knew what she meant. Too much similarity, though, and the effect is more like a punchline everyone saw coming.[3] (*Rime riche* — 'mat' and 'matte'; 'die' and 'dye' — smacks of a fix, to the Anglo-Saxon ear. The coincidence of both sound *and* strong stress in an alternate-stressed language is just too much to buy; whereas in French the stresses are relatively even, meaning that while there's just as much similarity, there's less perceived 'implausible co-incidence'.) The most 'successful' rhymes are generally those which incarnate the same/different motif, and further enhance the vague sense of paradox we feel on encountering semantically opposed words or different parts of speech joined by similar sounds; this creates a kind of 'phonosemantic chiasmus', something Wimsatt alludes to when he claims that rhyme 'impose[s] upon the logical pattern of expressed argument a kind of fixative counterpattern of alogical

---

3 Classic examples of this are those wretched limericks of Lear's which repeat the first line in the last, here immaculately parodied by John Clarke:

> There was an old man with a beard,
> A funny old man with a beard
> He had a big beard
> A great big old beard
> That amusing old man with a beard.

implication',[4] i.e. the rational logic of the semantic is balanced by an 'irrational' rhyme scheme (although it strikes me that one can invert the statement just as successfully). I am not convinced this is a sensible way to think of it; the prospect of consciously constructing such an effect would be a miserable one for a poet, and the critic seems to have mistaken effect for conscious intention. However, no one would deny the aesthetic success of what often feels like a 'contrapuntal' effect between semantic and lyric 'logic'.

Often one element of the rhyme-pair will be a word we did not expect to use; but the feeling that we *could* perhaps use it will immediately find us ransacking mind, memory and imagination to make up the gap in its contextual or thematic sense, altering the poem's direction in the process – sometimes radically so. Even where we don't require an 'imaginative leap' or a change of direction to weave in the rhyme-word, we usually demand that the syntax appears to accommodate it effortlessly. Making natural syntax the aim of most of our formal struggles in the composition of rhymed verses is a new development, one for which we can thank modernism – and warmly, for once. After poetic diction was essentially placed under a cultural ban, poets were not only debarred from using happy little metre-making syncopes like *o'er* and *e'er*, but also required to write with the same syntax with which they naturally spoke. This means that we lost syntactic hyperbaton, the ability to arrange words in a non-standard order, and we soon found that we no longer had the freedom to arbitrarily shunt the word we needed for the rhyme to the end of the line. Hyperbatonic mangling used to be a fine, quick way of fixing the metre too: it really is impossible to convey how easy the Elizabethans had it. How easy the Elizabethans had it, it is impossible to convey. To convey how easy they had it? It is impossible:

---

4 W. K. Wimsatt, *The Verbal Icon: Studies in the Meaning of Poetry* (Lexington, KY: University of Kentucky Press, 1954), 165.

For nothing this wide universe I call,
Save thou, my rose; in it thou art my all.

(SHAKESPEARE, Sonnet 109)[5]

Yes, that line really *does* just mean 'for I call this wide universe "nothing"', a line which would have neither rhymed not scanned – but with one crazy switch, all is well. The unnaturalness of the syntax – and this is the cake-and-eat-it genius of it all – served only to *enhance* the rhetoric; switching the parts of speech out of their conventional position was merely perceived as a feature of heightened diction.[6]

The idea that poetry should reflect real speech and scale its heights by less convoluted means is hardly new: it was suggested in the *Preface to the Lyrical Ballads*, pursued vigorously in the practice of both palaeo- and neo-modernists, and more quietly developed by Frost, Thomas and others who sought to find a formal alternative to the fey and antique poetry of the Georgians and post-Victorians. By the 1930s, hyperbaton had all but disappeared. But faced with this new restriction, poets still inclined to use full rhyme suddenly found that

---

5 William Shakespeare, *Shakespeare's Sonnets*, ed. Katherine Duncan Jones (London: Arden Shakespeare, 2010), 329.

6 I'm aware that I'm about sound like a cross between Robert Bridges and Auberon Waugh, but I think poetic diction *will* make a comeback, if for no other reason than the fact people bought and read a lot more poetry when it *sounded* like poetry, i.e. a distinct and hieratic diction; market forces will eventually dictate we return to it. (And indeed already are, in the work of performance poets and rappers; 'page poets' are growing jealous of their audiences.) I would also argue that the syntactic and registral discontinuities of contemporary experimentalists amount to nothing more than an attempt to smuggle just such a poetic diction through the back door. However – a small but crucial point – their non-conventional syntax has been introduced voluntarily, *recreationally* – and not (like Augustan hyperbaton, for example) in answer to some genuine compositional exigency. All this is fine, of course, but strategies such as 'anti-closure' and the de-centred '*I*' start to look like smokescreens for plainly expressionist gestures. This is no surprise to those of us who (uncritically) regard the avant-garde and postmodernist movements as Late Romantic.

English really *was* just as short on rhymes as they'd been told; if they were to keep rhyming, other ways had to be found of increasing its combinatorial possibilities. One solution was the use of so-called 'half-rhyme'.

Half-rhyme is best considered a disease of degree: it should be defined by the ear, not the tone-deaf rule that says 'half rhyme keeps the final consonant the same, but changes the vowel'. 'Pour' is perceived by the ear as far closer to 'poor' and 'power' than it is to 'peer' or 'pair'; including a close vowel on either side of the rhyme-word vowel will produce three times the number of options, and still *sound* quite like a full rhyme. Some half-rhymes are obviously much closer than others, and a quick glance at a chart of the cardinal vowels will remind us in which directions our latitudes might be extended. There are, however, many other ways to improve our chances. There are no 'tired' rhymes or 'original' rhymes, only tired or original ways to use them. Words are given their meaning by context as much as received definition – and context is infinite. *Love* and *glove* are really no more worn than any other rhyme-pair.

A naive study of the process might conclude that the poet is essentially trying to find a rhyming match between two sets of roughly synonymized terms. If this was really the case, even English would prove mildly accommodating; but the reality is usually that one teleuton is already relatively fixed within its phrase – a phrase to which the poet has become attached – while another is sought to partner it. Rhyming dictionaries are perfectly legitimate resources, though will often do little more than confirm that the word the poet would love to use – the one that means '*tender*' and ends in '*-ubbish*' – does not exist. They also encourage the brief delusion that lines can be written by putting one word in front of another; whereas decent lines are far more often acts of original phrasemaking, where the words arrive in longer units. With that in mind, the huge flaw in most rhyming dictionaries is that they don't consider phrasemes and collocations, which effectively provide a second and much larger set of less-used lexical entries. Not just *love* and *glove*, then, but *cupboard love* and *rubber glove* too. It's one thing to reject the word 'heart' as unsuited to the line; but there's a good chance it will only have been considered in its monolexemic form – not *light heart, warm heart, broken heart, by heart, aching heart, lonely heart, in good heart, artichoke heart, harden the heart, with all your heart, artificial heart, be still my beating heart, have your best interests at heart, a man after your own heart*, and so on.

I tend to find that the best results come from getting rhyme-pairs nailed relatively early, and allowing them to dictate the sense around them; this way the syntax ends up affording them a more natural home, because the rhymes have built it themselves. There is far more combinatorial flexibility in English syntax than in English rhyme-pairs, and if a felicitous pair of rhymes have been found, it's almost always possible to naturalise them, if one is prepared to be open to both sense and content one did not anticipate. There is also decent argument for composing the lines *roughly* in order, whenever possible. The derivation of the second rhyme from the previous fixed teleuton is likely to advance a narrative or argument; but when the first line is derived from the *second* fixed rhyme-word, what happens is often a retrospective *interpolation* of sense – and there's always the chance such content is either redundant expansion or unwelcome addition, and will lose the poem some speed.

Since the work of preparing for the rhyme's natural fall is delegated to the syntax, the shorter the lines, the harder the trick is to pull off. Full-rhymed dimeter is no joke –

> Storm'd at with shot and shell,
> Boldly they rode and well,
> Into the jaws of Death,
> Into the mouth of Hell
> Rode the six hundred.
> Flash'd all their sabres bare,
> Flash'd as they turn'd in air

> Sabring the gunners there,
> Charging an army, while
> All the world wonder'd:

— and we can be sure Tennyson was intensely grateful for the couple of extra syllables the triple metre afforded him.

It's through formal resistance such as rhyme and metre that we're *forced* into rewriting, just to get the line to click into place; and of course no 'click' would be necessary without the 'place' constructed by formal template. Ideally one strives to compose in whole phrases, as they often have more semantic and tonal integrity; but that's not always the compositional reality. Personally speaking, I often feel like more of a safe-breaker, my ear to the door as I rotate this word or that word through half a degree, add or subtract a comma, exchange the position of two words, shift an emphasis here or there . . . Until eventually the words all line up straight and clear, I sense a dull *click*, and the door falls open on the goods. The words then seem to have found something I can subjectively verify as an integrated music, a natural syntax, and a necessary relevance to the theme. This is also why a demonic patience is at a premium: the difference between an average line and a good one often depends on the tiniest adjustments, and the better poet is often just the one prepared to stare at the line for an hour longer than anyone else. What's more astonishing is that lines composed in this fussy and meticulous manner can be our most surprising, strange, revelatory and uncomfortable: while we were busy with our little calculations, it often turns out that our unconscious had been muttering things we would have otherwise censored, had we not been so distracted. The rather uncanny mirror-arrangement we have with the reader obtains here too. While it is true, as Eliot said, that 'the chief use of the "meaning" of a poem, in the ordinary sense, may be . . . to satisfy one habit of the reader, to keep his mind diverted and quiet, while the poem does its work upon him: much as the imaginary burglar is always provided with a nice bit of meat for the house-dog',[7] the poet has consciously *constructed* those formal procedures by which the poem 'does its work', while he has raided his own distracted mind for the 'meaning'.

7 T. S. Eliot, *The Use of Poetry & The Use of Criticism* (London: Faber & Faber, 1933), 144.

THE LYRIC WEAVE

Backgrounded consonantal patterning can be considered a more diffuse version of the procedure of rhyme; it's way of burdening the language with more formal resistance than it would otherwise present. And just like rhyme, this lyric workflow – the dovetailing of sound and sense – is the humming engine of a heuristic method: the modification of one's *intended* sense in pursuit of a deeper truth or revelation.

To demonstrate how easily a natural consonantal patterning can be achieved, here's a little exercise. Take a noun and a random qualifier with different consonantal sounds in them, list those sounds separately, then try to compose a long sentence of words based on their permutations, with a few function words thrown in. Thus the words 'leaf mould' might produce something like:

> O deaf fellow, mellifluous loaf, my fallow muffin,
> dead failed mode of my dumb foal . . .
> deal me the foam, the old model of the fall,
> the leaf mould, the marvellous flume
> of my love's famed and larval veal!

Instant Hopkins. Absolute rubbish, of course, because the strictures are way too severe to admit much sensible possibility, but you get the idea. Left to its own devices, the ear will naturally permit other close consonants, as mine had instinctively started to do by the end. (Here, this would mean 't' for 'd', 'v' for 'f', the 'n' and 'ng' for 'm', and the liquid 'r' for 'l', and so on.) By doing so, we immediately win ourselves more musical latitude, and vastly increase our chances of writing an unforced, natural and non-crazy line; note, though, that this procedure is still likely to leave the line a *little* crazy. Which is, I suppose, what we want – and with any luck, it will at least be registered as 'originality'. (We should not forget the little function words in our musical calculations, however; schwa or no schwa, they also serve.)

When used instinctively, this method of free anagrammatising is not only an effective way of uniting the line's music, but also a local problem-solving tool. Later in the poem's composition, when we're so often left with blank spaces to fill, it's a useful trick just to take your musical bearings from the words two or three seconds either side of the gap, and see if their sounds alone will lead you to the answer. This is putting absolute trust in the phonosemantic principle. What's strange is how often it works; even when – and perhaps especially when – the sense is very different from that which you intended. Another instructive little game is to have someone remove a word from a lesser-known poem, and try to figure out what should go there from the sound-cues in the immediate vicinity. Take these lines of Emily Dickinson's:

> The daisy follows soft the sun,
> And when his ———— walk is done,
> Sits shyly at his feet.[1]

If we try to generate a bunch of trochaic words, taking our cue from the local consonantal music and allowing our choices to be *lightly* constrained by semantic context, we might get something like *lovely, soulful, daily, lighted, shallow, wakeful, shifting, coastal, kindled* – via what's essentially a diffuse version of the same process by which one might find a terminal rhyme. The key point is that all of these

[1] Emily Dickinson, 'The daisy follows soft the sun . . .', *The Collected Poems of Emily Dickinson*, ed. Rachel Wetzsteon (New York: Barnes & Noble, 2003).

words would more or less be 'allowed through' on the strength of their sound-fit, despite the sense being not quite right; whereas their non-lyric near-synonyms — *pretty*, *heartful*, *routine*, *radiant*, *surface*, *watchful*, *changing*, *shingly*, *burning* are clearly bad fits, whose clanging sounds would prompt the ear to alert the brain to their slightly alien or inappropriate sense, barring them at the gate. (The difference can be heard more starkly when we take two rough synonyms of a non-sensical replacement, one contextually euphonious, the other grating. Choosing between 'And when his knock-kneed walk is done' and 'And when his lurching walk is done' will be as easy for most readers as deciding whether to throw in their lot with the Lamonians or the Grataks; the knock-knees have it, surely.)

Tricking the reader into entertaining strange sense is precisely poetry's business. Even though the brain places roadblocks and armed guards along the border, lyric allows strangers to pass unchallenged, just in the way that Orpheus slipped into Hades past the lullabied Cerberus. By the time the strangeness has been registered, it's too late: the alien idea has been indulged, and the subversive work has been done. (The word Dickinson actually uses here is the relatively straightforward 'golden': the guttural 'g' picks up on the hard 'k' in 'walk', and '-den' echoes the consonants of 'done'; 'kindled' uses more or less identical consonants. The stressed first vowel in 'golden' also forms a fairly salient half-assonance with 'walked', and provides a lovely oh — aw — uh backwards progression of vowels in the three content words.)

Here's another fine example of consonantal weaving, from Douglas Dunn's *Elegies*:

> And fastened to a mourning blink
> Brought there by melanoma's
> Sun-coaxed horrific oncos,
> Leaving me to guess at

What mysteries you knew
Foretold by love or creatures.

('The Sundial')[2]

Look at that terrible, stunned line, 'Sun-coaxed horrific oncos'. 'Sun-coaxed' and 'oncos' are almost phonetic anagrams, and the assonantal *O*s stand in shocking, stark relief against Dunn's lovely variable-vowel default.

The road to the burn
is pails, gossip, grey linen.

The road to the shore
is salt and tar.

We call the track to the peats
the kestrel road.

The road to the kirk
is a road of silences.

(GEORGE MACKAY BROWN, 'Roads')[3]

The reader *knows* it sounds beautiful, but doesn't know why. Nor, ideally, should they. Though it's easily explained: in the first couplet, we find a salient alliteration in 'gossip, grey', but also the play of the *l* / *r* liquids, the *p* / *b* stops, and the nasal *n*; in the second, the sibilants *s* and *sh*, the plosive dentals *d* / *t*, and the liquids *l* / *r* again; in the third, the hard guttural *k*, the *l* / *r* pair and the *d* / *t* pair; and in the fourth, the exquisite, self-descriptive sibilant singularity of

2 Douglas Dunn, *Elegies* (London: Faber & Faber, 1985).
3 George Mackay Brown, *Selected Poems 1954–1992* (London: Hodder & Stoughton, 1996).

'silences', hushed even further in its plural, and its terminal position. All this is virtuosic, and I don't doubt largely written by instinct – but, again, it's an instinct trained by much practice. Ear-training can provide poets with the tools to correct bad lines: they can then say *why* they sound bad. Often the diagnosis is simply that the consonants are too disparate, and the vowels wholly unconsidered – which is to say they feel neither differentiated *nor* echoed. (A common error is to assume that vowels must inevitably be one or the other, even when left to their own devices; but what we get instead is a kind of soupy mess – lines full of whiney, moany, muttering or needling strings of vague half-assonance, echoing little sense; and worse, no strong contrast between the strategies of variation and repetition, without which assonance cannot function.) *The path to the stream / is buckets, conversation, filthy laundry. / The way to the beach* ... Alas, the bulk of poetry written sounds like this. A poem might be striking in its imagery and intelligently argued, but still sound like a bag of spanners thrown down a garbage chute. As predicted by our phonosemantic rule, such a poem has its poetic sense dismantled by its own incoherent music.

Poets should also be aware of articulatory gaps *between* words. For example, words where the coda and onset share an identical or close phone will blur on the ear, and are heard as forming a more tightly bound pair: *black cat, loose shirt, stiff feather, lost dime, hollow orb,* etc. Words which require more of an articulatory leap are, conversely, perceived to be less tightly bound: *black feather, lost cat, white shirt,* and so on. While the actual experience and importance of this kind of effect are also easy to overstate, it's nonetheless interesting to register the effect on the ear of delineating or daisy-chaining codas and onsets in this way. We might think of it as a kind of lexical staccato or legato, one that becomes more pronounced when it's sustained as a lineal strategy: contrast *The black cat tiptoed down the stairs so lightly* ... with *the big dog barked and whined right through the night.*

Let me finish by proposing an analogy: consonant is to vowel as noun is to verb. Consonant is all bounded form, atemporality, instantaneity and instantiation, like the static object. Vowel is spatially free, durational, temporal and relational, like the dynamic process. Consonant makes clean divisions of form, as do instance and boundary. (As I'll show in a moment, consonants which let the air pass *blur* border and boundary.) Vowel associates or contrasts one form with another, as do space and time. Somewhere in the mind, echoed consonants imply similarities of form, whereas singular arrangements of consonants imply singularity of form. Varied vowels imply spatial and temporal separation and discrete relation, while echoed vowels imply simultaneity, parallelism, proximity and similarities of interior spirit.

THING AND THOUGHT

I've mentioned already that some rough conclusions can be drawn about a poem's music merely by looking at the poem from a distance. Held at arm's length, poems can reveal themselves as compositionally askew in another way: the lack of balance between content and function words. Linguistic biases one way or the other are, unsurprisingly, often symptomatic of a predilection for either the more concrete language of physical description or the more abstract language of function and thought. (Not, I should make clear, 'a preference for either thinking or description'; plenty of thought can be conducted through descriptive language.) This is neither here nor there in a *single* poem, and one poet will often demonstrate a strong preference one way or the other (Bishop's language is generally more 'contentual' than Hardy's, for example); but it is not properly appreciated that a *generalised* addiction to concrete description and expression can have serious musical consequences. The problem lies with consonants.

The more physically descriptive language becomes in non-Latinate English, the more plosive-heavy and consonantal it becomes. The more functional, abstract and ratiocinative it becomes, the more plosive-light, and the higher the incidence of passages formed from 'open ended' words, where one or both ends of the vowel's envelope will be shaped not by stops, but by another vowel, a nasal stop, a fricative, an affricate, a glide or liquid. These interrupt the breath and voice far less frequently, keep the air flowing from one word to the next, and can give the impression of a single breath moving through the whole line. This is the result of the unusually heavy use of the small part of the English lexis that performs grammatical function — that Anglo-Saxon word-base of articles, connectives, prepositions, interrogative and relative adverbs, with all their *shs* and *whs* and *ths* and *ys* and *hs* and *ws* and *fs* – which necessarily forms the bulk of passages concerned primarily with 'reasoning things out'; and secondly, abstractions drawn from the Anglo-Saxon/Norse (and to a lesser extent Norman) word-pool, which – to a less obvious degree, but nonetheless a significant one – show a plosive-light bias: *life*, *weight*, *fulfil*, *hurt*, *wrong*, *thought*, *death*, *future*, *move*, *anger*, *high*, *less*. As ever, counterexamples abound, so it's important to reiterate that these are broad phonosemantic *tendencies*, and no more. (The more abstract language of reasoning only becomes plosive-heavy when it gets polysyllabic and classical; here, the sense of our intellectual precision, of our clear comparison of abstract forms, is reinforced by an act of lyric reification, the 'concretisation' of the music. However, because Latinate and polysyllabic vocabulary is schwa-heavy in English, it is often as carefully avoided in lyric poetry as it is in song.[1])

The airiness we find in passages which pursue a thought, and the plosive weight we find in passages of physical description, have iconic functions. They point to a kind of globally diffuse phonestheme, where light stops and air-flow equal insubstantiality, lightness, and abstraction, while heavy stops equal substantiality, weight, and the delineated borders of the physical object. By applying the law of phonosemantic reciprocity, we can predict that the 'de-reification' of concrete expression might be effected by a shift away from a stop-based music, and it's easy to find evidence that this is so. In concrete nouns, a move towards physical insubstantiality is often signed by the passage of air: *shift*, *chiffon*, *space*, *sheer*, *fluff*, *feather*, *whisper*, *see-through*, *mist*,

---

[1]   Latinate English tends to be used for 'the language of authority', in all its dialects – but even when it isn't, it still connotes 'authority' and 'officialdom'. Predictably, the democratisation of poetic speech saw its use even further diminished. Greek-derived words are mainly used for the scientific register, and even where they are not, carry the connotation of 'dispassionate intellectual precision'; its word-base seems therefore less inimical to contemporary practice. (Greek music in English is heavily rhotic and guttural, and reminds me strongly of Scots.)

haze, fog, haar, diaphanous, ether, veil, flower, thin, negligée, breath, and of course *air.*

Listen to the relatively breathy and plosive-light music of the following passages, all of which shift towards the abstract consideration of their themes:

> And since the whole thing's imagined anyhow,
> Imagine being Kevin. Which is he?
>
> (SEAMUS HEANEY, 'St Kevin and the Blackbird')[2]

> [. . .] Waking at times in the night she found assurance
> Due to his regular breathing but wondered whether
> It was really worth it and where
> The river had flowed away
> And where were the white flowers.
>
> (LOUIS MACNEICE, 'Les Sylphides')[3]

> So was I once myself a swinger of birches.
> And so I dream of going back to be.
> It's when I'm weary of considerations [. . .]
>
> (ROBERT FROST, 'Birches')[4]

The English speech of summary and descriptive adumbration produces a very similar effect:

> . . . my mother, all through my childhood,
> when I was saying something to her, something important,

---

2 Seamus Heaney, *New Selected Poems 1988–2013* (London: Faber & Faber, 2014).

3 Louis MacNeice, *Collected Poems*, ed. Peter Macdonald (London: Faber & Faber, 2007).

4 Robert Frost, *The Poetry of Robert Frost: The Collected Poems, Complete and Unabridged*, ed. Edward Connery Lathem (New York: Henry Holt, 2002).

would move her lips as I was speaking
so that she seemed to be saying under her breath the very
  words I was saying as I was saying them. [. . .]
  [. . .] I wonder what finally made me take umbrage enough,
    or heart enough, to confront her?

(C. K. WILLIAMS, 'My Mother's Lips')[5]

Often the balance between the language of thought and that of physical description is most effectively achieved when the two approaches are tightly interwoven, as in these lines from Kathleen Jamie's 'The Tree House':

> [. . .] we bemoan
> our families, our difficult
> chthonic anchorage
> in the apple-sweetened earth,
>   without whom we might have lived
> the long ebb of our mid-decades
> alone in sheds and attic rooms,
> awake in the moonlit soutterains
>   of our own minds; without whom
> we might have lived
> a hundred other lives [. . .]

At the end of a poem, the move from concrete to abstract or vice versa can form an effective deictic shift, which the change in consonantal music enhances dramatically:

5   C. K. Williams, *Collected Poems* (New York: Farrar, Straus & Giroux, 2006), 160–61.

he hanged himself from a lamp-post
with a length of chain, which made me think
of something else, then something else again.[6]

(PAUL MULDOON, 'Something Else')[7]

These days, the language of interior reflection requires a little more bravery than it used to. A quick dip into Tennyson's *In Memoriam* —

> I cannot love thee as I ought,
> For love reflects the thing beloved;
> My words are only words, and moved
> Upon the topmost froth of thought.
> 'Yet blame not thou thy plaintive song,'
> The Spirit of true love replied;
> 'Thou canst not move me from thy side,
> Nor human frailty do me wrong.'[8]

— serves to remind us that it was once standard practice to locate the poem largely in the realm of reasoned discussion, and dive into the world of concrete description only to plunder it for illustrative exempla, metaphor and anecdotal evidence. As a result, for all its argumentative strength, *In Memoriam* sounds light as a feather. 'Show-not-tell' is merely the dumb war-cry at the head of a more insidious movement which appears to be seeking the total concretisation of the poetic line. It is, I think, a neurotic response to the otherwise reasonable observation that no one is listening. We have correctly perceived a bored and dwindling audience, but have instituted a manic and cheap attempt to keep them awake with the brain-candies of image,

---

6 Paul Muldoon, *Poems 1968–1998* (London: Faber & Faber, 2011).

7 Kathleen Jamie, *The Tree House* (London: Picador, 2004), 41–2.

8 Alfred Lord Tennyson, *In Memoriam*, ed. Eric Irving Gray (New York: W. W. Norton, 2004).

anecdote and metaphor. (Postmodern poetry mostly avoids this, but its addiction to the language of content is even worse than that of the mainstream.) To get the air flowing through the poem again, we require the bravery of showing ourselves to be engaged in thought *while* in the act of writing: our abstract consideration of a subject immediately rebalances the function-to-content ratio in favour of the former. A poem is a lyric process through which we work out what we think. If our arguments are worked out *before* we write the poem, it's too easy to make the poem a mere receptacle for their concrete evidence. Indeed, an over-concrete poem can often tell us that its composition involved little intellectual struggle, all sign of it being suspiciously absent. (One must respect those poets whose stylistic preference is to remove it, of course, and let thing stand for thought.)

This approach might be a little controversial among those of our number who still claim that poetry is no place for notions, and effortlessly succeed in their attempts to write poetry entirely free of them. William Carlos Williams's 'No ideas but in things' was bad enough, but at least it was clearly articulated so you could scream at it. (The phrase, of course, is its own refutation, being an idea so patently false it could only have taken root through its own elegant, musical, abstract expression.) The weirdly persistent assumption that poetic speech is more effective when it is concrete and direct has been a musical disaster for the art form; worse, it has infantilised poetry by legislating against intelligent speech. 'Keep it direct' is often interpreted as an instruction to keep the syntax paratactic and straightforward. This advice would not have sat well with Yeats, Donne or Shakespeare, and the best poems of a contemporary poet like C. K. Williams show it up for the nonsense it is. (Indeed Williams's signature long line affords him the space to indulge all sorts of discursive and indirect strategies – in particular exquisitely long delays in the arrival of the main verb.) The subtlety and sophistication of a poet's thought is most often evidenced by its complex, qualified, nuanced and dynamic unfolding, something which must be bodied forth in a varied, hypotactic syntax; but this needn't mean 'a lack of clarity' or anything like it. A complex, nuanced thought forced to express itself too simply will betray itself. I sense intelligent readers are becoming bored senseless with poem after poem full of expository, paratactic syntax: *I saw this / then I saw that / and I had a think about this / and I felt this about that / and then this happened.* It patronises readers, and all but accuses them of being unable to follow the kind of mature argument only sophisticated hypotaxis can honour. Moreover, it declares that the poet has little *interest* in the kind of reasoning by which we make sense of the world and of our own experience: the poet becomes a mere camera, or at best (as in, say, the scrupulously idea-free poetry of the so-called 'Martian school') a camera with some trick filters. To put it in Piagetian terms, the results sound like the work of a mind stuck in the 'concrete operational' stage, as it appears to demonstrate no capacity for the abstract thought we associate with the later, 'functional operational' stage of development. In short, too many contemporary poems read as if they were written by unusually bright seven-year-olds.

All this may offer us another way to approach the issue of 'closed' and 'open' texts, an apparently inexhaustible source of tribal conflict, one largely preoccupied with closural strategy and ideological grandstanding. The perceptible flow of air is a phonetic artefact of our having thought aloud. It's here we see another aspect of poetry's weirdly reflexive nature: just as the memory of the poem *is* the poem, so poems *are* the epiphany, not its documentary evidence. (Robert Lowell: 'Poetry is not the record of an event: it is an event.') They show the writer in the *process* of making their discovery, so that the reader can re-enact and reactivate it – not merely feel its after-effects, or learn the poet's wise conclusions. The poem is open for the reader to extend its meaning. The absence of all language which indicates argument, reflection, meditation, interrogation, conditionality, consideration and equivocation is often a sign that the poem is being written 'after the event' – and out of what the poet already knows.

This is usually identical to what the reader already knows; the poem is closed to them, because they have nothing to contribute. An increase in air-flow is a sign that the poet, in the act of writing, has been detained in figuring out the how, the who, the where, the what, the when and the why of it all. Through this mouth-to-mouth resuscitation, the reader's own mind is revived – and they can then share in the living surprise of the poem's own arrival.

PART II

Sign: The Domain of the Poem

INTRODUCTION

This essay is concerned with what I'll call 'the poetic trope', and, by extension, poetic meaning. It attempts to frame a discussion of the linguistic and conceptual phenomenon of trope within the art of poetic composition, and the culturally distinct activity of 'reading a poem'. While it also draws on and adapts some recent ideas in conceptual metaphor and blending theory, it was prompted mainly by my growing conviction that while these theories give a far more reliable account of how metaphor and metonymy operate in our brains and in the patterns of our speech than those which preceded them, descriptions of how they actually work within the art of poetry fall badly short. Current theorists generally don't take into account the unique rules of poetic form, and the dynamic frame that makes both the composition and reading of a poem a distinct cultural experience. This essay offers itself up as a footnote (albeit, admittedly, an interminable one) to that larger discussion, though its primary aim is to propose a working definition of trope that will explain not only how it works on the page, but also ways in which it may develop in the future. Unlike lyric, whose rules alter at a glacial pace, trope is more directly reflective of technological change and paradigm shift in the information-processing part of the culture: it reflects 'how we think' at any one point in our history, and is itself capable of technical innovation. Finally, I hope to show that an analysis of trope is broadly consubstantial with the analysis of poetic meaning.[1] The argument

1 As before, the reader will notice a bias towards cognitive and semiotic explanations, as well as the odd ill-qualified excursion into that area some of my colleagues dismiss – perhaps with some justification – as 'neurobollocks'. However,

is not a linear one, nor could it be — and I apologise in advance for the many backtrackings, recapitulations, summings-up and advance warnings that I have inserted so I could avoid the overwhelming repetition of key points.

Trope comes from the Greek *tropos*, a 'turn'. We commonly use the word to mean a figurative or metaphorical expression; in traditional rhetoric, it describes a word or phrase that 'turns' from its normal use. Here I'll use it to describe the way in which one idea turns towards or into another — and in doing so, creates an original expression to reflect this new or composite thought. 'Trope' is the natural procedure whereby we give new ideas new expression in the language. We do this by using the things we already have in novel combinations and substitutions. In a time-constrained form like poetry, trope's ability to double semantic weight means that its effective use is less advantageous for the poet than it is wholly essential.

This essay addresses the creation and interpretation of the poem's strangest, most unstable and ambiguous effects, and how they sit within an understanding of poetic 'meaning'. In line with most contemporary theorists, I believe poetic 'meaning' to be an emergent and dynamic phenomenon. This essay is an attempt to create a framework where the evolving complexity of these effects might be analysed and understood, and will argue against forcing them towards premature closure through the practice of making fixed interpretations.

---

my strong preference is for *any* material explanation, no matter how outlandish or 'reductive', in preference to one predicated on fairies, pixies, God, inscrutable intercessors, sympathetic magic, or dark and unseen forces. In its dogged refusal to supply adequate descriptions of intermediary mechanism, critical theory can sound as much of a mysterian cult as theology, and so will mostly be avoided here. (I tend to think of it purely as a branch of literature, on the grounds that it has provided us with many indispensable insights, despite the self-justifying pseudoscience of much of its methodology.)

A note on trust

Much contemporary thought — literary analysis included — is still in the grip of a poorly interrogated, post-religious paradigm. It suffers from a logical error that goes by various names, but which I tend to think of as the 'theistic fallacy'. For millennia, religion allowed us to posit a distant parental overseer when we found ourselves unable to cope with the reality of our own cosmic orphanhood. Things have changed, at least in parts of the West. I suspect many if not most people reading this will have 'gotten over it', and regard themselves as atheist or agnostic; some, like this author, will have additionally recovered as best they could from a childhood warped by the pernicious lie of a caring god — as well as the pain of being later disabused of it. Nonetheless we still allow our thinking to be shaped by an idea just as perverse, one that I strongly suspect has its origins in our earlier theism: that 'things mean something', and that there is some natural mechanism by which things are 'lent meaning'. The idea that material objects, processes or events can somehow possess immaterial truths is, I suspect, a candidate for mankind's greatest error — and the reason we cannot free ourselves from the iniquitous and inequitable laws we believe ourselves ruled by. (I will return to the point frequently but should state my position now: what we call 'meaning' in the West is really the epistemic corollary of a power structure, and the result of the subservience of one frame of reference to another.)

In poetry, this is manifested in the oddly persistent belief that there is a meaning or interpretation which is *intrinsically* 'right', or at least 'more correct' than another. All this is derived, I sense, from our long habit of religious faith. Too often our interpretations are unconsciously predicated on the real-world existence of a truth, albeit a truth conveniently veiled or missing. Given its demonstrable absence, this truth must reside (we unconsciously presume) in the mind of some remote third party, who either can or will confirm the accuracy of our brilliant exegeses at some point in the future, possibly come the

Rapture. It doesn't; they won't; there's nobody here but us chickens, and for that reason no human can ever know what *anything* means – least of all a poem, whose sign is deliberately and necessarily unstable. 'Meaning' just isn't in residence anywhere. All the meaning we ever have is decided by context and consensus. Therefore we shouldn't talk about what the poem or line or metaphor or image *means* so much as what meaning it *generates*: the truest value of 'poetic meaning' accrues within the dynamic flux of our reading and rereading. This is true of *every* aspect of the poem – even prosody, whose nature is performative, and whose performance changes radically as our understanding of the poem changes and deepens.

The grim reality is that very little of *anything* inheres in a 'form of words', which – as far as their 'meaning' is concerned – often turns out to be just a locus of optimistic and mostly untested consensus. The more unusual the form of words, the more the consensus regarding their meaning is weakened; and as that consensus weakens, interpretations multiply. Poetry is built from 'unusual forms of words', and therefore by definition is open to varying interpretations.

For the poem to 'work' for the individual, however, they must commit to a single interpretation – which may be complex, broad, richly ambiguous, and capable of undergoing radical change . . . But must have a fair degree of integrity and consistency, if the poem is to move and enlighten them. For anyone playing the game of poetry with the serious personal commitment it asks of them, there can only be *one* true interpretation: their own. More disinterested critical and academic interpretations may state, with absolute correctness, that a poem may mean this and may mean that; but in at least one crucial sense, these readings are far *less* trustworthy, as they declare their own emotional detachment. That our feelings are engaged is the first thing the poem requests of the reader. As brilliant, necessary and enlightening as many scholarly 'thick descriptions' of poems can be, they are straightforwardly defective in this regard: they are not playing the one game the poem was written to initiate, in whose deeply felt and singular shape, unexpected turns and unpredictable outcome lie the most profound definition of its 'meaning'.

My belief is that such generated meaning can't be properly rich and *instrumental* without engaging the full range of our readerly sympathies: this extends from speculating on the psychology and motivation of the author, through our close reading and consideration of the text, to our reflection on what light the poem might shed on our own lives, thoughts and actions. The poem is *not* primarily a disinterested and ahistorical artefact, although reading it that way can often be extremely useful. Most fundamentally, as I've said before – the poem is just a couple of monkeys talking to each other. It's about us and it's about the poet, as much as it's about itself. And since we are more verb than noun, we change – and so will our interpretations. The text is always airborne, and any interpretation is a mere snapshot of that flight.

Readers might also detect here another attempt to rebalance the consciously rejected but unconsciously perpetuated model of New Critical 'close reading'. I propose we do this by restoring the catastrophically misnamed 'affective and intentional fallacies' to their rightful place as legitimate approaches to the text. (I would be inclined to replace 'fallacy' with 'force'.) This need not undermine or contradict the practice of good close reading, or anything like it. But it would, ideally, leave us with a kind of interpersonal version of thick description, or an entirely serious take on Frank O'Hara's beautiful joke-school, 'Personism': 'It puts the poem squarely between the poet and the person, Lucky Pierre style, and the poem is correspondingly gratified. The poem is at last between two persons instead of two pages.'[2]

This is pretty much the way most people read poetry before we told them they were doing it all wrong. I think their instincts were sound. Ideally, interpretation should emerge from the process of

---

2   Frank O'Hara, 'Personism: A Manifesto', *The Collected Poems of Frank O'Hara*, ed. Donald Allen (Oakland, CA: University of California Press, 1995).

simple, sensitive, innocent, intelligent and engaged *rereading*. My own definition of overinterpretation is the avowal of the presence of effects which you neither felt nor intellectually registered in the course of your open and direct engagement with the poem – but instead discovered in your post-reading critical vivisection. Despite the fact that this approach now forms the backbone of contemporary critical practice, I think it's to be strongly suspected. Such critical methods are often driven by intellectually insecurity, and unconsciously predicated on the existence of a brilliant, polymathic reader (or indeed god) who will casually register and enjoy these ineffably subtle and clever allusions, symbols and correspondences in the course of their reading. This ideal reader is nowhere to be found in the world.[3] We really have only one alternative: to replace our faith, which requires three terms, with trust, which requires only two – if rather more bravery. We have to learn to trust the poet, trust ourselves, and trust that the poet has trusted us.

The human trope

We tend to over-romanticise our infant perception of the world: though it may have been blissfully free of the labelling machine of human language, it still presented us with a deeply false impression. Incarnated selves all get off to variations on much the same bad start, and are given the perceptual equivalent of a pinhole camera through which they are obliged to experience the universe. Through the narrow perceptual aperture of their eyes, ears, noses, skin and brains, they perceive a world as only a tiny part of what our scientific instruments have now shown it to be: firstly, a place which broadcasts its existence in a way that is mostly inaccessible to the narrow spectrum of human sense; and secondly, a place that is not only mostly unknown, but

---

3 All the different forms that misreading can take are so accurately described by various types of clinical paranoia, one is forced to conclude that they're really just localised versions of an identical pathology. I'll expand on this later.

possibly unknowable. (At the time of writing, 96 per cent of matter and energy in the cosmos is still 'dark' and wholly unaccounted for.) Even the way we process that little information we *are* able to receive should hardly fill us with confidence. At the extremities of our senses, this sensory information is virtually white noise; our nervous systems have evolved to filter it down to something intelligible and useful – but useful only to humans. Who knows what madness is *really* out there, beyond our fingertips and retinas?

And even those sense-receptors themselves are scarily approximate and vague. All the retina does is register colour, intensity, patches of light and dark. After that – everything from our sensing of edge and border to the discrimination of objects is pure neural computation. We are walking trope-generators, which is to say that we must somehow generate wider meaning from such little information as we can gather in our perceptually reduced circumstances. As Philippe Jaccottet says, 'This world is just the tip / of an infinite conflagration'.[4] We're thrown at birth, then, into some kind of existential trope – one you'll read as a metaphor or a metonym, depending on whether you regard your experience of the world as false or as partial. But to see it as 'accurate' is staggeringly naive. (One definition of the human tragedy might run as follows: we are born into a wholly symbolic realm, and forever obliged to defend it as a reality.)

We are attuned to only a small part of the electromagnetic spectrum, and whatever universe our senses are conjuring up is patently *not* the universe. This epistemic asymmetry between the inner and outer realms – very much like those between the first- and third-person accounts of the world that dog all descriptions of consciousness – has to be leapt somehow. This is accomplished by the human trope, which we can think of as a kind of symbolic accommodation. This more or less defines the human dream we wake to each morning, and even

---

4 Philippe Jaccottet, *Selected Poems*, trans. Derek Mahon (London: Penguin, 1988).

dream within.[5] The strange rules of this realm, conjured up between evolutionary expedience and the more clearly arbitrary forces of culture, leave us seeing almost everything in terms of its human utility; this vision is fixed and reinforced by language. However, many of us have an inkling that this dream, too, is also false or partial, and take steps to correct it. This is the position occupied by human art, whose principal function is to join us to what we are not, and in doing so accomplish two beautifully contrastive things: restore something of the mystery of the wider world to our narrow human perception, and bring some of its hidden connections to light.

Either way, we have become creatures for whom things must connect, must 'mean'. This astonishing capacity for oversignifying, for 'reading in', is just what poets draw upon – both in their own practice, and in the lover's knot of the poem that they give to the reader, and trust them to unfold carefully. The poetic function is a reflexive turn language makes against its own project of conceptual division; it helps language both to heal itself and articulate new concepts it can't yet accommodate. Even though I'd maintain it's their ultimate result, the *immediate* effect of these poetic statements (whether conjured in conversation, or formalised as poems) cannot always be described as 'healing', or anything like it. Indeed they are often highly disruptive, and can send violent ripples across the serene surface of our human dreaming, much like the rock that throws the stream backwards against itself in Frost's 'West-Running Brook'. Nonetheless it's in this 'backward motion towards the source, / Against the stream, that most we see ourselves in'.[6] What follows is heavily braced on these few introductory remarks: I believe the motifs of conceptual and

5   In this case, a classical category formed of a giant, crazy collection of arbitrary syntagmatic rules. The confusion over their status as 'reality' results from the fact they do not necessarily *look* arbitrary from the human standpoint (take the phenomenon of iconicity, for example), but from the larger perspective of blind, non-teleological evolution, most of them certainly will.

6   Robert Frost, *The Collected Poems* (London: Vintage Classics, 2013).

literary trope are merely melodies that are already being played in parallel, down in the lower octaves of our gross physical existence.

Some cultural dangers

I use 'trope' as a name for the means by which one concept's rules and definitions finds fluid connection with, or within another concept's rules and definitions, and so produces *meaning*.[7] 'Meaning', in my own scheme, is a wholly relativistic procedure whereby one thing is wilfully read in terms of another thing; it is simultaneously illusory and necessary to our survival. However, in the West, what we mean by 'meaning' is a worryingly unchallenged metaphor in itself: one which entails the *subservience* of one frame to another, an arrangement that seems to have aided and driven the dominant patriarchal and capitalist structures within which we presently live. Suffice to say I think we can deal with meaning *itself* as just a form of trope, and the form and nature of that trope will dictate both the shape and quality of meaning we produce. It then follows that when we work within a

---

7 Increasingly, it seems worth thinking of these two aspects in terms of left- and right-brain tendencies. The old idea that the left brain is rational and logical while the right is creative was kicked into touch a long time ago; most kinds of thinking, whether logical or creative, reasoned or intuitive, involve both hemispheres. However, as Iain McGilchrist has argued in *The Master and his Emissary: The Divided Brain and the Making of the Western World* (New Haven, CT: Yale University Press, 2009), nor is it true to say there's no difference. The difference lies in the way they do things: the left hemisphere does definition, denotation, fixity, narrowly focused attention, the specific; the right does flow, connection, connotation, broad context, and the holistic. (We know this already from the right / left brain divisions of speech-functions into lexis and grammar, paradigm and syntagm.) When the left brain gains the upper hand in a culture, we die through an excess of law and logic and divisive definition and border, as well as the distance from our own environment that then results. The connotative shift we see in poetry – concerned, as it is, with the *feel* of things as much as their meaning – seeks a more harmonious balance and more truthful reflection of the interconnected nature of the world than our too denotation-heavy, conceptually fragmented and rule-bound speech can accomplish alone.

false cultural metaphor, the meaning that subsequently arises (usually as an unsuspected emergent property) is often a total lie, and can do tremendous damage.

Some of the worst metaphors are merely prepositional. Take 'the environment is around us'. The truth – as every other animal seems to know instinctively – is that we are continuous *with* our environment, and cannot exclude ourselves from the set of natural objects. But if we cannot see ourselves *as* our own environment, we cease to identify with it, and then recreationally destroy our own home. Or take 'the future is ahead of us'; this makes us think the future is something we can see and anticipate, and has led to astonishing hubris and misplaced self-confidence. Yet the Greeks saw the future as *behind* them and the past ahead of them, remaining sensibly fearful of that which they could not know.[8] This seems by far the more sane configuration – and certainly the more appropriately humble. 'Heaven is up' tends to mean that we disregard what is below us on the basis that it is non-transcendent, and seek redemption in an element we cannot inhabit. (This comes from a weirdly persistent 'flat earth' perspective, which says that 'the stars are up'. But the stars are *under* us too, which is why it's best to look at stars while lying on your back, so you have a truer sense of where they are: all around you, not 'up above'.)

Other metaphors are plain and pernicious untruths. Take 'life is a journey'. Well – if it *is* a journey, every journey has an identically disappointing destination. Life is not a hero's tale, or a novel or a film: it's a biological process characterised by a finite period of negative entropy. But from our knowledge of its certain end, we have foolishly backformed a dream of narrative progress – one our lives don't necessarily benefit from, and very often do not achieve; besides, our narrative addictions, the time we spend 'shaping our futures' or (God

---

8 For an overview of spatial time metaphors, see Lera Boroditsky, 'How Languages Construct Time', in *Space, Time and Number in the Brain*, ed. Stanislas Dehaene and Elizabeth Brannon (New York: Academic Press, 2011), 333–41.

help us) 'creating memories', can often deny us the opportunity to live in the present moment. Or take 'death is an adversary'. Death is most certainly not, and indeed is not anything; but from this idea we derive our 'battles with illness' and such daft advice as 'Do not go gentle into that good night'. (For heaven's sake, go gentle: the night's coming for you either way).

And finally, the worst one of them all. 'Things possess meaning' is a belief so all-pervasive it doesn't even sound like a metaphor. But things do *not* possess meaning; they have meaning conferred upon them. Meaning is never 'within', never intrinsic. Meaning usually relies on one frame lording it over another, the most tyrannical frame of all being that arbitrary set of rules known as 'human utility'. If meaning *were* intrinsic and could be discovered, one would have to presuppose a heavenly archive or a god in which it could eternally reside.[9]

When we insist that things possess meaning, we are subscribing blindly to the rules of our own human dream, our own unique set of lies, and are tuning out the fact of their species-specific (and often West-specific) arbitrariness. But the very fact that we write poetry is

---

9 Physical law doesn't fall within the categories of inter-domain meaning or intra-domain arbitrary rule, being a set of absolutes and non-negotiable constants. If we are merely an isolated part of a multiverse (arguably this is the *final* paradox), one might be inclined to say that *this* set of cosmic laws came about 'arbitrarily', and in a sense they are just an arbitrary metonymic aspect of a whole; but this would be a grave mischaracterisation, since for the concept of 'arbitrariness' to have any meaning, it must be predicated on the simultaneous existence of 'intention', not merely other instances of arbitrariness. Nor should we forget that the luck we sometimes feel in finding ourselves in a habitable universe is a bit circular, given we could find ourselves in no other; the 'meaningfulness' of our being here assumes that a perspective exists *outside* that which we currently define as our absolute limitary border, since meaning is non-intrinsic and only the product of one frame's enclosure within another (a point that will be laboured throughout this chapter). Until we find a wormhole into another universe with which we have been secretly interacting or within which secretly enclosed, the 'meaning' of our existence is nil, and the physical laws which govern that existence – terrifyingly and incomprehensibly – neither arbitrary *nor* deliberately framed. Stuff just happened, and we're in it.

a sign that we doubt the adequacy of our everyday language to reality; the poetic function in language is the principal means by which we try to make it fit for the purpose.

THE CONCEPTUAL DOMAIN

To give it something like its standard technical definition, 'a conceptual domain is a coherent area of conceptualisation relative to which semantic units may be characterised';[1] or 'a conceptual domain is any coherent organisation of human experience'.[2] Slightly breezier is my own definition: 'a conceptual domain is a bunch of stuff'. The conceptual domain can be 'things-associated-with-an-idea', i.e. whatever pops into your head as closely connected with 'life', 'time' or 'travel', 'refrigeration', 'bunnies', 'neo-liberalism' or 'proton acceleration'; it can be 'things-associated-with-a-locus', such as 'in the restaurant' or 'on the train' or 'in a lecture room'; it can be a conceptual set, such as 'regular verbs in English' or 'kinds of insect'. It can be pretty much what you like – so long as its constituents can be said to have some direct association with a central idea (either name-bearing or unnamed), this being the source of the rules which sustain the cohesion, coherence and integrity of the domain itself. These rules answer such questions as 'What qualities, aspects and constituent parts does this domain possess?', 'In what sequence should things occur within this domain?', 'Which qualities are more important that others in this domain?', and so on.

Words can also designate conceptual domains. We tend to think of words as having a denotative sense, but (to gloss cheerfully over a central controversy in the philosophy of language) a concrete noun,

1 Ronald Langacker, *Foundations of Cognitive Grammar*, vol. 1: *Theoretical Prerequisites* (Stanford, CA: Stanford University Press, 1987), 488.
2 Zoltán Kövecses, *Metaphor: A Practical Introduction* (Oxford: Oxford University Press, 2002), 4.

for example, really just designates a concept – one enclosing a bunch of attributes that we agree are most typical of the thing the word *would* designate, if that thing were actually present. Behind the concrete substantive lies a cluster of attributes, associations and consequences with a little black hole at its centre, a point of semic attraction where the referent should be. When we were small, we'd point at a sheep and say *sheep!* and that was all fine. After the acquisition of 'object permanence', language also enhanced our ability to think about stuff when it wasn't there; but what we lost was the *directly* referential core of the word. Now the actual sheep is gone, the referent of the word 'sheep' is really the concept of that sheep; and that turns out to be less a sheep than the 'conceptual domain of sheepness'. The slow intonation of the word may summon its icon – that's to say you might almost *see* a zebra when you say 'zebra' – but it's not actually the way you *use* the word. When we use it, it's mostly a brief index to jab towards a zebra-concept, but when we consciously *inspect* the word 'zebra', that zebra turns out to be less of a zebra than a hunch about what 'zebrahood' is. Which is to say that a word's denotation of a concrete thing is in many ways a happy fiction.

Mostly we don't have to think beyond using the word as a fleeting and weightless sign, juggled in the larger intent-driven performance of our sentences. When we *are* forced to think about it, and asked to define what is meant, exactly, by 'zebra' (in making what is sometimes known as the 'use–mention' distinction) – we're back to listing all its core attributes. *None* of which turns out to be essential: not its stripiness, nor its horsiness, its quadrupedalness, its African-ness, its mammalness, its aliveness, its solidity. A zebra can be albino, a stuffed pyjama case, or a ghost; it can be a headless, legless, Arctic, inflatable, invisible zebra; but generally speaking, so long as it ticks just enough of our core, dictionary-definition zebra-attributes to form a quorum, we'll agree to call it a damn zebra. [See endnote 6 for some idle speculation on whether the actual presence or absence of the zebra makes any difference.]

While all the attributes of a domain are individually negotiable and dispensable, we can nonetheless make a sensible if not a definitive distinction between which are 'core', primary attributes, and which are secondary connotations. Its unique combination of core attributes are not perhaps what *makes* a thing unique or individually discernible – but it is what underwrites its status as a 'thing worth naming'. The word 'bedroom' might designate a concept having the central attributes of 'room', 'bed', 'house' and maybe 'sleep', all of which we would tend to accept as legitimate components of the dictionary definition of 'bedroom'. But all a dictionary does is list enough core attributes to establish the smallest unique set that will indicate one thing and one thing alone, and this rarely needs to extend beyond five or six terms. (The game of 'twenty questions' performs the exercise negatively, via a subtractive process: all known terms are reduced to one candidate through the removal of large sets which, for the first ten questions or so, generally have too many members to be of use in the dictionary-style 'additive' process; of course the dictionary doesn't say '*carburettor*: mineral; a form of non-decorative inanimate object made from metal . . .' etc. The game is played devastatingly well by computers using neural networks, and several internet versions exist.) However, when we start to dwell upon the wider *domain* 'bedroom' indicates, we might also find the secondary terms *dark*, *dream*, *sex*, *dressing*, *mirror*, *pyjamas*, *quiet*, and so on. We might not consider these terms *essential* to our definition, but they can still fall naturally within the domain we indicate by the word. The constituent elements of a domain are bound by a kind of nuclear force, and are strongly consensual at its core; however these characteristic associations and qualities loosen as the domain expands, and become increasingly contingent, casual and subjective.

I should mention that while I'll use the words 'connotation' and 'attribute' to mean roughly the same thing, the nuance is still useful, since an attribute can be thought of as something 'possessed by' and intrinsic to a core, where a connotation is generated by its core – i.e.

the former has arisen via a process that is more passively definitional, and the latter through one more actively propositional. You can't have a system formed of nothing but passive semic co-ordinates and the summed difference between them; the entire *parole* would just shrug. Language is fundamentally motivated. [For some curious analogies with Fourier analysis, see endnote 7.]

A domain forms a unique set, but can be defined by no single attribute: every term within it will be shared with many other domains. It has a strong epicentre, to which certain terms gravitate or are magnetised; this creates a kind of force-field, resulting in a little semic solar-system of more- and less-tightly bound elements. The domains indicated by words can alter, expand, contract, weaken or strengthen depending on the enclosing domains of context, performance, discourse group, etc. within which they occur.[3]

Generic and specific domains

I'll now make a distinction between generic and specific conceptual domains, and look at how they operate within the literary trope.

As Wittgenstein observed, words are just the way we use them.[4] A language, or more accurately the Saussurian *langue*, is the *way* we use all its words and all its idiomatic phrases. It is a snapshot of the generic space in which we do the bulk of our thinking. The dictionary is just a guide to this generic space. It works by naming the core connotations each 'thing' possesses for a particular group consensus; for it to be

3 Something necessarily omitted from this description but worth mentioning briefly is the way the very *sound* of the word itself also functions as a further property of the word-invoked domain; this forges connections with other similar-sounding words (which may not, at first glance, be semantically related in any way) according to both globally diffuse and locally specific phonesthemic principles. I'd argue that these were derived from the iconic basis of language itself, and have pursued this in the essay on lyric.

4 Ludwig Wittgenstein, *Philosophical Investigations*, trans. G. E. M. Anscombe (Boston, MA: Blackwell, 1973).

useful, it has to be circular, which is to say it must reflect the culture, beliefs, knowledge and prejudices already held by the English/ French/specialist/eighteenth-century/Western/capitalist/colonial etc. class who consult it. It doesn't really tell you what a zebra *is* – one might argue that only a zebra *could* tell you – but it'll say what zebra-attributes we consider culturally or anthropocentrically salient within the conceptual domain we have come to accept as coincident with the real zebra.[5] Poets cannot trust the dictionary if their use of language is to be subversive. Indeed – to anticipate my conclusion – we might say that poetry fights the tyranny of unchallenged generic domains with its use of subversive specific domains.

A word is just a gravitational point in the phase space of language-as-a-whole towards which certain attributes are attracted. It holds itself apart from other words through those attributes it most repels, i.e. those it is least likely to share with them. The lexeme is, in this sense, just a complex semic co-ordinate. The semic attraction of this point radiates out to infinity: to use the better gravitational metaphor, it continues to subtly restructure semic space at a great distance from its own position (i.e. all words, to *some* degree, affect the whole

---

5 This process isn't quite enough, however. If language *could* offer a full description of our experience, we wouldn't need poetry. Poetry is just language's self-corrective function, kicking in whenever the human encounters a reality it can't properly articulate by the usual means. Technically, it's really no more than a recentring of language's performative norm; it moves towards an *explicit* patterning, a 'peak shift' of its salient formal features of rhythm, sound, syntactic construction, address and trope that define a *specific* language's characteristic structure, and thus simultaneously allow it to exaggerate those things, events and ideas that a language represents. As I've said, all you need is the pressure of time, the heat of emotion and the urge to speak – then the shift is made, and something identifiable to humans as 'poetic' will often be the natural result. However, this feature of 'peak shift' is something poetry probably shares with all art. As Thomas Hardy said long before V. S. Ramachandran, 'Art is a disproportioning – (i.e. distorting, throwing out of proportion) – of realities, to show more clearly the features that matter in those realities . . . Hence, "realism" is not Art.' Quoted in Florence Emily Hardy, *The Life of Thomas Hardy* (London: Wordsworth Editions, 2007), 235.

language, since language is predicated – at least in our necessarily ideal descriptions of it – on its being a closed sign-system). It can conceivably take *any* other term or attribute as a connotation. The reason, as we'll see, is that this semic co-ordinate, besides the attributes it possesses in the generic space of language-as-a-whole, is also subject to its 'context', the unique by-laws of its local universe, and this often mean that unexpected elements will fall under its influence. Furthermore, to repeat the Heraclitean point: because language flows and context constantly changes, no word ever really means the same thing twice.

The trope of metonymy, which substitutes a related term for 'the thing itself', proves this neatly. You can *always* construct a context or a circumstance to justify anything being called by an associated term (and since the conceptual domain is potentially infinite, *any* term at all; though the further the term is from the semic centre, the more unusual or contrived will be the circumstances which justify its substitutive use). The literary theorist Hugh Bredin seems to be arguing for a relatively finite and exclusive set of substitutive formulae that determine what we can accept as a well-formed metonym: 'Take the expression "publishing company": its semic field includes such concepts as book, distribution, and profit; yet it is impossible to employ the name of any of these as a metonymical replacement for "publishing company".'[6] This statement is quite false: I've *heard* publishing companies described as both a 'profit' and a 'book': the former in the context of a publishing house being part of a larger, financially motivated conglomerate, within which some subsidiary publishers were failing and others succeeding – 'profitable business' had been metonymised as 'profit'; the latter, in the phrase 'when your book goes against our book', which was uttered in the 'domain' of a conversation notionally 'about' two rival publishers' big books in the

6 Hugh Bredin, 'Metonymy', *Poetics Today* 5, no. 1 (1984): 45–58, at 52; http://www.jstor.org/stable/1772425.

pre-Christmas non-fiction sales charts, but which was actually – and quite openly – about inter-publisher competition. The speaker wholly intended 'when Bloomsbury goes against Penguin'. *Any* connotation can be used as a metonym. It's entirely to do with the way the relation between 'thing' and aspect is strengthened and legitimised by context, i.e. by the rules of its specific domain; and since rules are arbitrary, they can be constructed to emphasise any relation.

Within the domain of 'restaurant', contextually relevant things like table numbers, food orders, credit cards, and dietary requirements are tagged 'important restaurant stuff'. However, the sock-colour, the size of the stamp collection and the criminal history of the customers will *not* be tagged 'restaurant stuff' – though might well be in the specific domain of a clothing catalogue shoot, philately conference or county court. It's just our habitual way of reading our reality – which would be overwhelming, were it not for our ability to frame contexts and decide what was important on given occasions, 'given occasions' being the things that make up our entire lives. This is the basis of metonymy, and, as we'll see, the means by which (in the famous textbook example) a man can be transformed into a ham sandwich. If the peculiar rules of the specific domain insist upon it, anything can be related to anything else – and if that relation is made sufficiently strong, anything can *substitute* for anything else. The poem, I'll argue, is the specific domain *par excellence* – and if its strange by-laws are strictly applied, all manner of new, unnatural and miraculous transformations are possible.

Conceptual metaphor

If we accept (perhaps on trust, for now) that the conceptual domain is the only game in town, we can quickly see that there are two principal mental operations available to us: *intra-domain*, where we link things within a domain by the rules by which it is constituted; and *inter-domain*, where connections are made between two different conceptual domains. The first we often associate with metonymy; the second with metaphor. These terms, while cheerily familiar, are much too narrow, and really only describe single operations within a far larger set of tropes. The first set of intra-domain tropes I call *tropes of relation*; the second set of inter-domain tropes, *tropes of correspondence*.

This insight first became common intellectual currency in the 1980s, when George Lakoff explained it in the context of his theory of cognitive linguistics;[7] the more sophisticated model of conceptual blending – the combination of mental spaces, from which often unexpected third terms emerge – was later developed by Gilles Fauconnier and Mark Turner.[8] These theories also accord with an old insight of Roman Jakobson's, which I'll discuss briefly (it's of great historical importance, since it's where the old model of the trope was first booted into touch, and where it should have stayed).

Lakoff's idea was that most of our thought is guided by underlying conceptual mappings within one domain, or between two domains that share some content and overlap in the sets of their attributes. The theory holds incredibly well – up to a point. We know that the conceptual mapping LOVE IS A JOURNEY TO A DESTINATION is widely employed, and lies behind phrases such as *We had a bumpy start / We lost our way / We took a wrong turning / You and I have a hill to climb*, and so on. Occasionally someone might draw attention to this largely unconscious metaphor – and *make* it conscious and manipulable by phrasing it in a textually salient way: saying, poetically, *I feel like we've been freewheeling down a sunlit avenue this last year*; or comedically – *maybe we should pull over at the next services and take a break*; or nonsensically, *I think our glove-compartment's full*. (Such deliberate innovations, of

7   George Lakoff and Mark Johnson, *Metaphors We Live By* (London: University of Chicago Press, 1980).

8   Gilles Fauconnier and Mark Turner, *The Way We Think: Conceptual Blending and the Mind's Hidden Capacities* (New York: Basic Books, 2002).

what Arthur Koestler used to call the 'bisociative' kind,[9] tend to result in either poetry, comedy, surrealism, or nonsense.)

However, experimental psychology has shown that deep conceptual metaphors such as TIME IS SPACE – the one we use when we say 'I'll see you IN a moment' or 'I'll see you ON the twenty-fifth' – have been made almost wholly abstract. For example, spatial 'at' (I'll meet you AT the corner) and temporal 'at' (I'll see you AT eleven) have, effectively, entirely different senses. (One must always bear in mind that words are signifiers, not referents: they mean what they mean, not what they are.) Steven Pinker has pointed out that patients who have sustained brain damage can lose the ability to use spatial prepositions, while retaining the ability to use temporal, and vice versa, i.e. they will retain one use of 'at' while losing the other.[10] This indicates not only that time- and space-perception run on different neural circuits, but that at this *deep* level, the conceptual metaphor operates with far less force. [For some more careful qualification and discussion of 'embodied' aspects of metaphor, see endnote 8.]

Contrary to the assertions of Lakoff and others, Pinker demonstrates that we tend to read through to an underlying mapping only when the surface metaphor is new to us. The invention of new metaphors (and the resuscitation of dead ones) is one aspect of language's natural poetic function; the rest of the time, however, we are using less actual metaphor than we are petrified metaphoric clichés – as 'phrasemes' that represent an underlying abstraction. Phrasemes work just like single words; we memorise them as lexical items, and think of them as having synonyms. For example: through repeated usage, 'just park it' or 'just drop it' will eventually become wholly synonymous with 'just set aside your complaint for now' or even just 'shut up'; little conscious thought will be conjured of parking cars or dropping

9 Arthur Koestler, *The Act of Creation* (London: Hutchinson, 1964).
10 Steven Pinker, *The Stuff of Thought: Language as a Window into Human Nature* (London: Penguin, 2008).

anything. (Though it seems some vague sensorimotor twinge will still be activated, since wholly disembodied language is probably an impossibility.) But it's fundamentally the *abstraction* behind the words that's doing the work, not the metaphor – which is now pretty much 'dead', or at least cryogenically suspended, and just a phrasemic idiom.

A 'new metaphor' will usually do one of two things. Its innovations can make us conscious of the underlying mapping behind a virtually 'dead' conceptual metaphor: take the latent IDEAS ARE FOOD mapping behind 'I can't believe he swallowed that story whole' or 'He just regurgitated the same old stuff we always hear' or 'This is pretty indigestible news' or 'I'm still chewing it over'. This can be reactivated and more consciously embodied via the use of a new cliché, like, 'Your plan for the takeover made my mouth water'; or, more strongly, by the original extension of an existing phrase, like, 'I chewed it over, but in the end it was so tough I spat it out'; or, most powerfully and poetically, by original improvisation within the mapping itself: 'Did I like your idea? Hell, I swilled it round my head like a fine Bordeaux.' Poetic examples would include Shakespeare's constant riffing on CHILDREN ARE PLANTS, the mapping we find behind 'sowing your wild oats', 'spilling his seed', 'she's barren' and 'she's blossoming' (most iterations of this mapping are curiously sexist). Shakespeare deploys the metaphor in phrases like 'For where is she so fair whose unear'd womb / Disdains the tillage of thy husbandry?' (Sonnet 3). A better example is Eliot's comprehensive dismantling of LIFE IS A JOURNEY in Part III of 'The Dry Salvages': 'You are not the same people who left that station / Or who will arrive at any terminus, / While the narrowing rails slide together behind you [. . .]'[11]

Alternatively, a poetic phrase may innovate a *new* conceptual mapping. Its expression in the text is usually more or less coterminous

11 T. S. Eliot, *Collected Poems 1909–1962* (London: Faber & Faber, 2002).

with its deeper mapping, which is merely to say original poetic metaphors tend to openly state their own formulae, because they have no pre-existent mapping to activate. A new metaphor usually has to be clearly presented because the reader hasn't encountered it before. 'She is as in a field a silken tent' declares the rather charmless mapping THE WOMAN IS A TENT.[12] In Keats's 'On First Looking into Chapman's Homer', 'Then felt I like some watcher of the skies / When a new planet swims into his ken' appears to state explicitly the mapping A READER IS AN ASTRONOMER, an idea most readers will vaguely derive while also simply enjoying their more specific understanding of the lines as 'this reader of Chapman's translation of Homer felt like an astronomer discovering a new planet'.[13] A full engagement with a metaphor will and allow us to perceive both the depth and surface, the strangeness and accuracy of the comparison simultaneously; it's this paradox that gives metaphors their frisson. It will quickly abstract and simplify the metaphor to a conceptual mapping, as it's there that the striking originality of the comparison is best appreciated; and it will pursue the complexities of its textual articulation, as it's there the rich appositeness of the comparison is best indulged. (In Keats's metaphor we are *specifically* invited to map 'planet' to the new world Chapman has revealed, the alert stargazer to the assiduous reader, and so on; these aspects are largely missing from the mere formulaic mapping, and other realisations of the same mapping would produce very different takes on it.)

But often the metaphors are delivered so fast, we are only really asked to parse them for sense:

[. . .] the old claims
of soul leaving the body in a powdery

---

12   Robert Frost, *The Collected Poems* (London: Vintage Classics, 2013).
13   John Keats, 'On First Looking into Chapman's Homer', *The Complete Poems*, ed. John Barnard (London: Penguin, 1988), 72.

whoosh, an unwedging at the scapulas
scattering birds from belfry and roof,

a whir like radium half-lifing.

(DEAN YOUNG, 'Age of Discovery')[14]

Here, one *might* claim that we quickly make sense of these lines via unarticulated, on-the-hoof mappings like A WHOOSH IS POWDER EXPELLED, A SOUL FREEING ITSELF FROM THE BODY IS A THING SQUEEZING THROUGH A TIGHT SPACE BETWEEN THE SHOULDERBLADES and THE SOUND OF THE WINGS OF BIRDS SCARED FROM A ROOF IS THE RAPID CLICKING OF A GEIGER COUNTER IN THE PRESENCE OF A RADIOACTIVE SUBSTANCE; though you can immediately see the absurdity of calling these 'conceptual mappings' at all. The mapping is wholly coincident with its articulation.[15] All we are really doing is interpreting the lines by translating them from the (often codified, discontinuous and elliptical) language of poetry.

To sum up: one can innovate poetically within a well-established, deeply rooted mapping, like LIFE IS A JOURNEY or ARGUMENT IS WAR or HAPPINESS IS UP or PAST IS BEHIND; but if you want to create innovative or subversive mappings like ARGUMENT IS PASTA or that HAPPINESS IS DOWN or THE PAST IS UP, you'd best start by saying just that, and then elaborate on what the hell you mean —

14 Dean Young, *Design with X* (Middletown, CT: Wesleyan New Poets, 1988).
15 This shouldn't be interpreted as agreeing in any way with Donald Davidson's attractive 'brute force' argument: Davidson contended that metaphors have no meaning beyond what they say, and any paraphrase or abstracted truth they further prompt is a psychological act of interpretation, equivalent to 'dreamwork'. The theory is non-cognitivist, and based on a description of metaphor as a strongly linguistic phenomenon. I feel it holds little water these days. See Donald Davidson, 'What Metaphors Mean', *Critical Inquiry* 5, no. 1 (1978): 31–47.

and not just say 'I'm finding this conversation somewhat fusilli,' or 'Cheer down, that's all above us now.'

For the most part, though, in poetry conceptual mappings arise far more organically. To take a straightforward example, you look up, and you think: hey, a CLOUD IS A BOAT. As a rule, metaphors whose shared ground is a primary aspect of both tenor (the subject) and vehicle (that to which the subject is compared) can dispense with the textual presence of either vehicle, tenor or ground: boats and clouds both move slowly and smoothly, therefore 'the slow-sailing cloud', 'the tall white ships sailed overhead' and 'the cloud was a ship' are all just as comprehensible as 'the cloud sailed away like an ocean liner'. Metaphors which hinge on secondary connotations generally *have* to spell out their ground, however, as readers aren't psychic. Metaphors based on culturally familiar mappings can improvise within them; metaphors based on original mappings either have to declare them clearly, or at least explicitly declare those aspects which form the ground of the comparison.

As dull and dry as this point is, I really can't overemphasise its importance in poetic composition, where original mappings often contribute much confusion through the poet's failure to put themselves in the reader's position. 'The tall-sailed cloud' might make us think immediately of a masted ship; but 'the far-journeying cloud' doesn't, however much it may have put the *poet* in mind of it, and however much it was their *intention* to communicate the 'boatiness' of the cloud. In a metaphor which omits direct mention of the vehicle, the ground (here, the transferred epithet 'far-journeying'[16]) must

---

16 Let us hear no more of 'hypallage', another uselessly porous category from classical rhetoric. Note however that 'transferred epithet' describes a syntactic strategy, and need not result in an epithetic metaphor. It can occur in metonymy too. Suppose we have a bald man with a dog. If 'the bald dog' is merely intended – and taken – as a very peculiar way of designating 'the bald man's dog', then 'bald' is just a metonymic contraction. Often it's a little more confused: take Louis MacNeice's 'Suspended in a moving night / The face in the reflected train / Looks at first sight

function as its index. Alas, far too many other things besides boats are also 'far-journeying'. Half of poetic obscurity can be blamed on a tenor, ground or vehicle that has gone missing in action. If the ground is omitted, it must be able to be derived from the comparison alone. If tenor or vehicle are omitted, the ground must be explicitly stated, and contain a clear index to the missing component; which is to say the ground must contain an effective *metonym* of the absent vehicle or tenor.[17]

as self-assured / As your own face' – Louis MacNeice, 'Corner Seat', *Collected Poems*, ed. Peter Macdonald (London: Faber & Faber, 2007). The 'moving night', as figurative as it sounds, is in a sense just 'the night of the moving train'. If one expands the term and the result is a literally consistent peristasis – a mere descriptive phrase – then we're dealing with a metonym. However, it's clear that a metaphorical component is also generated in the process; indeed, the more unusual the syntactic expression of a metonym and the more the full expression behind it is contracted, the more we will be inclined to read in a blurring of domains. (Some might still say, 'No, it's just a metonym' – but since nothing is intrinsic, what we *read in* is all there is; if 'moving night' *feels* metaphorical, it is; and that dog was, in a way, a little bald too.)

17   (I will merely mention once again that, *pace* Jakobson, I am convinced that the poetic function *collapses* the principle of equivalence into the principle of selection, and this is another example of their poetic interdependence.) The following remark will be better understood once I've explained the relationship between peristasis and metonymy, where a descriptive detail is contracted to an index, but for now: if the ground is a core aspect of the tenor, it can act as an index to that tenor, which can then be metonymically omitted. If it's a core aspect of the vehicle, ditto. A TREE IS A BOAT is clear in the phrase 'tall-sailed tree', despite it having no text-present vehicle, and despite the attribute 'having tall things which catch the wind' being only a secondary and distant connotation of 'tree'; we can wing that, because it's explicitly stated. The point is that 'tall-sailed' provides a direct index to the missing vehicle. 'He heard the high rustling in the ship' (spoken of a tree) conversely deletes the tenor, though 'rustling' points to the tree well enough, and the secondary connotation 'having high things which rustle in the wind' is explicit enough to for us to quickly find 'sail' from the vehicle 'ship'. (Its 'success' as a metaphor is, conveniently, a separate question.) Given sufficient context, if we invoke aspects that are core to *both* tenor and vehicle ('he beheld the tall mast') or at least indexical of both ('he stared up into the crow's nest') we might arguably omit both tenor *and* vehicle, while still invoking them both. Vehicle and tenor can both be treated as peristases, and therefore

Lakoff, incidentally, has gone on to make something of a nuisance of himself by trying to turn conceptual metaphor into a one-size-fits-all solution to every dilemma ever posed by Western philosophy, linguistics and cognitive science. He even offered advice to the Democrats in a vaguely consultative capacity, claiming that their electoral chances would be improved by using the right conceptual metaphors. Taxes should not be called taxes but 'membership fees', since that phrase implies the underlying conceptual metaphor NATION IS A CLUB, and we'd all warm to that. It's not just that all this seems straightforwardly manipulative and sinister; Steven Pinker also points out that, come year-end, everyone is likely to feel just as brassed off about paying their exorbitant 'membership fees' as they did their 'taxes' the year before.[18] It's not long before the 'euphemistic treadmill'[19] completes its cycle, especially where the money, death and faeces are involved. [For connections to Whorfian theories, see endnote 9.]

But there's a 'referential treadmill' too: reality always catches up with *any* original metaphorical or metonymic representation in the end, and in most speech-act contexts turns it into an empty sign for the

---

a metonym can contact and substitute for either.

18   See George Lakoff, *Don't Think of an Elephant: Know Your Values and Frame the Debate* (White River Junction, VT: Chelsea Green Publishing Co., 1990) and *Whose Freedom? The Battle Over America's Most Important Idea* (New York: Farrar, Straus & Giroux, 2007); Steven Pinker, 'Block That Metaphor!' *New Republic* (9 October 2006), https://newrepublic.com/article/77730/block-metaphor-steven-pinker-whose-freedom-george-lakoff.

19   There's also a 'dysphemistic treadmill': see, for example, the urban Scots 'cunt' for 'person' (I have heard a female taxi driver describe her own father as 'basically a good cunt'.) 'Aa cunt' and 'nae cunt' are synonyms for 'everyone' and 'no one', as in 'I gave a poetry reading last week, and there was nae cunt there.' Unlike its offensive homonym, the word receives no stress emphasis. It is hard to convince outsiders that a term regarded in most other contexts as either sexually explicit, grossly sexist or deeply offensive carries little charge – but here, no offence is intended and none taken; the original meaning of the word has been emptied out, and its dialectal referent has taken over its sense.

most culturally banal, least contentious attributes of its referent. This is a phenomenon most sharply seen in the family trees that have grown from Indo-European roots, but traceable in just about any etymology. Randomly: *tunnel* is from the Medieval English *tonel*, a wide-mouthed net used to trap birds, so its first application to 'subterranean passage' will have been metaphorical — and would inevitably have carried the connotation 'trap' for a little while; *urn* is derived from the Latin *urere*, to burn, bake, so 'urn' was originally a metonym for 'baked [clay pot]', so would have carried overtones of 'heat' and perhaps 'food' (and may still). Each new application of the word might be the result of either a metaphoric or metonymic process. In both these examples, the original neologists will have been aware of their relation to earlier terms, but this consciousness awareness can be lost very rapidly. How many of us *can* now remember that 'blog' is a contraction of 'web-log'? (Nonetheless I sense that these overtones are often retained in the complex co-ordinate whereby words differentiate themselves within the *parole*.)

TYPES OF TROPE

The myth of the four tropes

I'd like to take a moment to dismiss one of the most persistent schemes – one which has appeared in various forms over the decades, and which we might refer to as 'the myth of the four tropes'. Theorists from Giambattista Vico in the eighteenth century to the twentieth-century rhetoricians Kenneth Burke and Hayden White (and even as recently as Jonathan Culler) have claimed that metaphor, metonymy, synecdoche and irony are the four 'master' tropes, and constitute the most meaningful categorical distinctions. They are, in Vico's wonderful phrase, 'the corollaries of a poetic logic'.[1] The idea is that these four tropes describe the basic types of relations that can exist between two terms. Metaphor relates through similarity; metonymy relates through direct link; synecdoche relates via the part to the whole; and irony relates through inversion.

I'm afraid, as the scientists say, the idea is so bad it isn't even wrong. Synecdoche is a useful term, especially when extended to species-for-genus and vice versa; but it's merely a subset of metonymy. A thing's belonging to a larger or smaller categorical or hierarchical class is just another attribute in the set of its aspects and connotations; in the mind, 'parts' are just attributes of wholes, and set-membership is an attribute of a set-member.[2] (The entire mess, incidentally, has

1 Giambattista Vico, *New Science: Principles of New Science Concerning the Common Nature of Nations*, 3rd edn (London: Penguin, 1999), 404.
2 In the admirably sensible scheme used by the Princeton Wordnet, nouns can often be sensibly designated as either meronyms and holonyms in their relation to one another, i.e. part of a whole, or a whole which has parts. Meronyms report to

its origin in a failure to distinguish between the myriad *expressions* of trope and the deep conceptual mapping that often reveals them as very similar mental operations. This is the error that leads people to conceive, say, of 'metaphor' and 'simile' as *conceptual* distinctions, though in this regard they're virtually identical, and their difference, while not insignificant, is largely presentational.)

Irony presents a stranger problem. The key phrase here is 'relates through inversion', a nonsense that should have the alarm bells ringing. Yes, irony appears to subvert or invert the relation between a word or statement and its referent, between the signifier and its signified. But the inversion doesn't *create* the connection: something else does first. Irony serves only to pervert a pre-existing relation, not forge a primary one. Indeed, most of the stock examples of ironic trope – e.g. 'Gorgeous weather today!' when it's raining, and 'Working hard, are we?' when you're clearly not – reveal irony as little more than an presentational mode (and so does any study of its more sophisticated manifestations in literature, film or drama, where it may take structural, gestural and generic as well as expressive forms). The inversion takes place at a linguistic, structural or interpretative

───────────

a hypernym ('zipper' and 'turn-ups' are parts of 'trousers'), and holonyms are such if they have meronyms ('trousers' is the holonym of 'zipper'; it gets messy when things do not necessary entail a hypernym, i.e. 'trousers' *may* be the meronym of 'lounge suit', but mostly aren't). If words share the same hypernym they are 'co-ordinate terms', but note that this does not make them synonyms ('Chihuahua' is not a synonym of 'wolf'. If you believe that words are continuous with 'reality' then there *are* no true synonyms, of course; a different word insists on representing a different concept, however slight the difference is.) The equivalent of the meronym in verbs is the troponym, which means that troponym X is a manner of the hypernym X ('mumbling' and 'shouting' are 'kinds of speaking'); the causal equivalent of the meronym is 'entailment', meaning that activity X is unthinkable without Y ('whispering' necessarily entails 'speech'; 'dreaming' implies 'sleep'). See George A. Miller, Christiane Fellbaum, Randee Tengi, *WordNet: A Lexical Database for English* (Princeton, NJ: Princeton University Press, 2015), https://wordnet.princeton.edu/wordnet.

level, but not at a conceptual one. Absolutely no one is thinking, deep down, that 'YOU ARE NOT WORKING = YOU ARE WORKING'. Trope-types, if they're going to form a useful taxonomy, can really only refer to relations being made *within or between concepts*. The whole subject of irony is therefore far more appropriately discussed under the linguistic heading of pragmatics or stylistics, or in our case, poetic address.[3] Metonymy and metaphor, as we'll see, are certainly significant and central fixtures in our neural circuitry; but I doubt much evidence will ever be found for an important 'irony centre' in the brain where concepts are inverted in sense before they seek a linguistic representation, however strongly certain politicians and US states give the impression of a bypass operation being widely available.

The idea that there are only two trope-classes, metaphor and metonymy, has been around for some time now. It was given its most famous defence by Roman Jakobson in the 1950s, when he argued that they represent the two fundamental 'axes' of human communication: selection and combination.[4] There is a horizontal dimension of *syntagm* (here, something like 'a rule of syntactic series'), based on rule, combination and contiguity; and a vertical dimension of *paradigm*, based on selection, substitution and similarity. If you take a dinner menu, the syntagm is the part of the menu that goes *appetiser – main course – dessert*, and the paradigm is what allows you to select between cheesecake, gateaux and ice-cream, the last three sharing the property of 'sweetness' we consider appropriate for entry to the conceptual domain of 'dessert'. These days linguists tend to talk more

3 Any time spent in New York will reveal irony as a modality, not a trope. So fundamental is the ironical stance to the cultural life of that great city that it amounts to a *dialect*; within it one can still be moving, funny, open, generous, sincere, and – pricelessly – ironic. I confess this is one reason I love the place, as this elevation in the phatic irony-floor strikes me as real human progress.
4 Roman Jakobson, 'The Metaphoric and Metonymic Poles' (1956), in *Metaphor and Metonymy in Comparison and Contrast*, eds René Dirven and Ralf Pörings (New York: Mouton de Gruyter, 2003), 41–8.

about things like grammaticality and lexicality, but it's the same broad principle.

Metonymy and metaphor reflect the two most fundamental ways our brains make useful inferences about the world and connect the information they extract from it. I'll refer to the first type, the metonymic type, as *intra-domain*, and the second, the metaphoric, as *inter-domain*. Another way of thinking about it is 'classical category' and 'family resemblance'. Classical categories allow us to apply the same rule to many subjects in any arbitrarily law-governed context, while family resemblances allow us to see similarities between disparate subjects, and rely on our memory to compare and verify those similarities. The first works by relation, the second by correspondence. In the first case the rule is prime; in the second, the item; in the first, grammatical procedure; in the second, memorised lexis. (A wonderful demonstration of this has been given by Pinker and his team in their work on regular and irregular verbs.)[5]

Tropes of relation, like metonymy, allow us to 'decline the world regularly' and apply broad and often arbitrary rules in a given context, and eat the five courses of our meal in the culturally prescribed order. Tropes of correspondence, like metaphor, allow us to find *ad hoc* rules based on common resemblances between memorised items. Though the menu may only offer bream, turbot and rollmop herring for the fish course, this allows us to ask 'do you have any shrimp?' without sounding like a lunatic, whereas the request 'do you do chicken livers?' will convey the impression that you have a broken paradigm-axis.

The question of whether we might consider 'symbol' – where concrete detail stands for an abstract quality – a distinct third category is moot, and I will pursue the matter at length in another chapter. Symbol has often been regarded as a mere subset of metaphor where the tenor is text-absent. I believe this is a mistake, based on the

5 Steven Pinker, *Words and Rules: The Ingredients of Language* (London: HarperPerennial, 2011).

failure to see that the symbol combines elements of both metonymy *and* metaphor, and is also a formal expression of the unique tropic properties of the abstract realm. My strong feeling is that symbol *is* a third class of trope, though its uniqueness lies less in its being a composite sign (which it is) than in its being a sign of pure semantic projection; symbol is a tropic means of *assigning meaning to the world*. It seems plain to me that, while metaphor and metonymy are really just human reflections of the basic universal functions of paradigm and syntagm, 'symbol' is an entirely human contribution, and describes the unique process whereby we confer the quality of 'meaning' on things which do not intrinsically possess it (i.e. 'everything'). As all this rather flies in the face of accepted practice, the proof will be miserably long; I offer my apologies in advance for the abstruseness of the argument, discussed in the chapter 'Concrete, Abstract and Symbol'.

The later chapter on 'Four Semes, Four Tropes' points the way to an alternative scheme. Theorists have long made the distinction between the 'pure symbol' and the 'literary symbol'; 'symbol' here is a mere homonym. The pure symbol is the result of an arbitrarily forged connection, one which can arise through a cultural, social or wholly subjective process. It 'means' nothing but that which is arbitrarily ascribed to it. The so-called 'literary' symbol is almost precisely its opposite; it's formed through an entirely different conceptual procedure, and is less 'literary' than 'the trope which generates what we call meaning'. In my own scheme there are still four tropes, but they are rather different from our traditional candidates. I refer to them as *metaphor*, *metonymy*, *symbol* and *asymbol* (which connects to 'aseme', the anti-seme of arbitrary link; the word 'asymbolic' has some minor currency). They correspond to inter-domain, intra-domain, supra-domain and what we might call extra-domain processes. (One might visualise them respectively as a circle; two intersecting circles; one circle enclosed within another; and two circles whose edges touch.) They work, respectively, through the attributes one domain encloses, the attributes shared by two domains, the enclosure of one domain within another, and the arbitrary contiguity of two domains.

Peristasis and metonymy

Peristasis and metonymy are 'tropes of relation', and both concerned with registering contextual saliences, that is, 'relevant detail'. They are tropes which show we are aware of the rules of our immediate frame of reference, or which body those rules forth. They are both intra-domain tropes which essentially differ only in their formal expression: peristasis is additive, while metonymy is subtractive.

Let's begin with *peristasis* (*peri* – around; *stasis* – stand), a term which will be new to most readers: I've stolen it from a little-used rhetorical figure that refers to the 'description of attendant circumstances.'[6] It's the difference, if you like, between saying 'the woman' and 'the old woman'; between 'the boy' and 'the boy with the red setter'; 'the office' and 'the office we have in Reform St'; 'the takeaway' 'and 'the greasy takeaway', 'the sum' and 'the difficult sum'. Peristasis adds to the subject by declaring or implying some *significant* secondary attribute, that's to say one either relevant to the specific domain in which it passively finds itself, or (as is more usually the case in a poem) *propositional* of a specific domain in which it actively places itself.

Now you might think a mere casual expansion in the noun phrase is such a natural and basic feature of language it's barely worth identifying as a trope at all. Usually we'd just subsume such things under 'descriptive language' and the wretched category of 'image'. What a peristasis does, however, is declare an *additional* detail, usually in the form of qualification or predicate, that for contextual, specific-domain reasons we find relevant, important and worthy of our attention. As we'll see, it's really a kind of pre-metonymy

6 Gideon O. Burton, 'Silva Rhetoricae', http://humanities.byu.edu/rhetoric/Figures/P/peristasis.htm.

(cognitively, I think it functions specifically as a *potentiated metonym*), and shares its deep form. 'Peristasis' bears roughly the same relation to 'metonym' as 'metaphor' does to 'enigma' (my word for 'riddle'): metonym omits the 'subject', enigma the 'tenor'. I would also argue that this 'additional detail' may be unspoken, i.e. text-absent, and present only as an 'active connotation' drawn forth or implied by the context – or what I'll soon call the 'thematic domain' – in which it appears. Similarly, what looks like a simple subject is often a contextually identifiable salience, telling us we have a metonym: for example 'the woman' may indeed be metonymic if the person concerned is being pointed out as the only female member of a gang of male football hooligans; the full sense here is really 'that human in the group who is female', or 'the woman one'. Formally, this is arguably identical to pointing out someone as 'the spots' in the context of a series of otherwise immaculate mugshots; a peristatic expression of the same detail would be 'the spotty one'. Peristasis is a contextually relevant expansion; metonymy is an understood contraction of a peristasis. Their presence in any text is a matter of sensitive interpretation.

Since peristasis encloses the idea of the so-called 'poetic image', thinking of it as such will at least give us a conceptual handle on the subject. It's important to note, though, that calling things 'images' has generally been a disaster for sensible poetic analysis. It's a vague and outmoded category, which falsely privileges 'the visual' where it should receive no special treatment. In more enlightened uses of the word, 'the image' will be broadened to include 'the sensual' – though this still tends to exclude qualities like 'emotional tone' and 'abstract quality', which are just as important to literary description as any others. That's not to say the category of 'the visual' is unimportant; it's just one of several concerns in the context of any linguistic analysis.

(To air a further irritation: 'the image' has allowed people to talk about 'ekphrastic' poetry as if it constituted a meaningful literary genre. It's a cool-sounding word all right, and ekphrasis did indeed have a nobler role in classical verse – but in our own age, it's almost as arbitrary a genre as 'poems about animals', much as I love poems about animals. Poetics concerns itself most usefully with word-stuff, because poems are machines made of words and concepts; 'image-talk' is often a way of avoiding any more rigorous analysis. Since 'peristasis' is unlikely to take off – I propose that we might also adopt the neutral word 'detail' as a serviceable, catch-all alternative to 'poetic image'.[7] The word 'image' is fine, provided its use is confined to 'visual representation made of words'.)

In the generic space of our standard 'resting state' definitions, 'an old woman' is just 'an old woman'. However, additional knowledge of the specific domain in which the detail occurs can assist us in seeing why the speaker chose to name *that* attendant detail, and not another. This turns the detail into a peristasis. Indeed, the attribute will often be unusual, striking or odd enough to alert us to the fact that we actually *have* a significant peristasis – and that its full meaning must

7   Despite the fact that the category of 'the image' has been under assault for several decades (P. N. Furbank's 1970 *Reflections on the Word 'Image'* being one notable critical intervention) it retains a wholly underserved currency, and is as cheerfully thrown around in academic criticism as it is in the poetry workshop. It tends to forge a false link with the idea of 'the imagination', with which it had little connection even for the Romantics. Even its use in describing visual effect is hopelessly narrow, and it reflects neither how we now understand our brains to process visual stimuli (i.e. through a complex process of interpretation and symbolic distillation) nor the fact that in poetry, 'the visual' is a highly dynamic and sensually porous domain. Even though 'image' and 'metaphor' are often discussed as if they can be cleanly distinguished (the first is too poorly defined to be distinguished from anything), the hegemony of 'the image' has meant that too many poets conceive of metaphor *visually by default* – even though it is anything but. If you need a handy example of a perfect sonic metaphor – take the British jazz slang name for the vibraphone, 'the haunted milk-float'. Lychees taste like elderflower, gorse smells like coconut, and drizzle on our skin feels like pins-and-needles. Moreover – if more subjectively – being in love might feel like stigmata, and the airport check-in remind you of the Bardo states. Not only do the non-visual senses also have their own axes of selection, but those senses – including those which deal in 'tone' and 'abstract concept' – are all wildly interfused. The image not only lies about this fact; it has the habit of censoring it.

be derived from the rules of its specific domain, the very presence of which it may have alerted us to.

To take the examples I gave earlier: the woman I described as 'old' is also Irish, I happen to know – but since I was pointing her out at the back of the bus, her Irishness is pretty useless in her quick identification. The boy with the red setter has a blue jumper, but in the final of Crufts, he is most relevantly identified by his dog. The office in Reform St is very spacious, handles billing, and is painted yellow – but this firm has two offices like this, and I needed to direct you to *this* one, because I work there. You get the picture. Peristasis is at the heart of poetic description, where poets select their qualifiers and descriptive language with obsessive care: this sharpens and directs the way in which a particular detail is interpreted, and implies which rules may be governing the whole local domain of the poem. Simplistically: if a yew tree is described as 'a thousand-year-old yew', it is likely that the poem in which it appears is concerned in some way with 'eternity', 'history' or 'time'. (And even more so if the peristasis has been made even more salient by metonymy, and shrunk to its theme-indicating aspect, i.e. 'I sat below the thousand-year-old yew.') *No* detail can be arbitrary in a poem, which (unless it declares itself otherwise, through surrealism or some other explicit strategy) is almost invariably read as 'consciously composed'. As we'll see, the reader is even entitled to insist that within the context of the poem-reading contract, a detail can never be *merely* descriptive. Even if its deeper meaning isn't yet understood, they will proceed with their rereading on the assumption that it *has* one, and its symbolic or peristatic importance will gradually manifest.

The concept of peristasis is, I think, invaluable in understanding poetic metonymy. A metonym is just a peristasis with the subject removed. The metonym narrows the subject by referring to it only via a declared aspect, part, direct connotation, causal relation, 'feel' or quality. To put it more succinctly, a metonym 'caricatures something in context'. This saves time, which is why it's often called a 'trope of contraction' – and poets love metonymy, because in poetry, time is money. Compositionally, it's a two-part process: the first stage is the identification of a contextually relevant and salient feature of a subject; the second is the elision of the subject, leaving the related feature to stand for it, and point to it.

The text-present part of the metonym, the connotation/aspect/feature/part/consequence of the thing, is functionally identical to an 'index' in semiotics. A beeping smoke alarm indicates 'danger' in the generic domain. However, we also interpret indices contextually, and in the specific domain of my kitchen, it usually indicates 'toast'.[8] Often these indices are complex, and composed of a succession of relational links – one thing stands for another thing, which stands for another thing – each of which might be constrained by generic or specific frames. The noise of a smoke alarm may say 'danger'; but it does so through first indicating 'the presence of smoke', which generically indicates 'fire', which, in the context of 'the home', generally indicates 'get the hell out of here'. A smoke alarm would go off near an outdoor barbecue too, but could safely be ignored. (I'll refer to the relational aspect and the subject of the metonym as 'index' and 'subject'.)

In literary theory, a compound metonym or a chain of substitution is sometimes referred to as a 'metalepsis'. My alcoholic great-great-grandfather was known as 'Drink-the-Bible' from the way he disposed of the money he earned as a door-to-door book salesman. He drank neither bibles nor the money he earned from their sale, of course, but whisky: 'Bible' here is metaleptic. (Working backwards: he drank 'whisky'; this is short for 'whisky bought with money'; this is short

---

8 This is true of an 'asymbol', i.e. a pure symbol, too: the generic domain will generally leave 'red light' meaning 'warning' or 'danger' – but in the specific qualifying context (sometimes called the 'fondement' in semiotics) of traffic, of studio recording, of prostitution, of weather, etc., it will take on a narrower and sometimes different sense. Specific domains tend to narrow generic senses, but through cultural convention they often establish their own symbolical rules as well.

for 'whisky bought with money from bibles'; this is short for 'whisky bought with money from bibles which were representative of the books he sold'.) The fact that several terms in the metaleptic chain might be skipped means that it can play only with such conventional and idiomatic connections as can be easily elided – e.g. one might casually say my forebear 'drank all the proceeds of his bible-selling', without even being *aware* of the metonymic substitution 'proceeds' for 'booze he bought with the proceeds'. In Sonnet 10, Shakespeare refers to the aristocratic family of the Fair Youth as 'that beauteous roof'. The qualifier 'beauteous' directs the vector of sense back to the lovely boy himself, while 'roof' lies at the end of the metaleptic chain. 'Roof' is a synecdochic metonym for 'house', and 'house' is a metonym for the aristocratic family of which the Fair Youth is a member. If we take Shakespeare's performance to be rather disingenuous, and suspect him of being *really* more concerned with the youth's desirable beauty than with his ability to replicate that beauty through procreation, we might diagnose that *beauteous* is itself a metonym, and not only refers to the fine features of the Fair Youth's noble line, but also points back to the 'real subject' of Shakespeare's undeclared love. (It very much depends, as they say, on 'what you think he meant', but to refuse to speculate on his intentions is a failure of intelligent analysis. Compassion prevents me from making a further assault on the already whimpering 'intentional fallacy'.)

Many metonyms in the generic domain will be very familiar, and are based on standard formulae, themselves straightforwardly indicative of what we find important on this planet, and in this human life. These might be place-for-person-or-institution ('the White House' for the US presidency; 'Scotland' for the Scottish football team); part-for-whole (local-type synecdoche, 'wheels' for 'car'; 'ass' for 'whole body'); whole-for-part ('society' for 'the rich'); substance-for-whole ('lead' for 'bullet'); place or time-for-event (Waterloo; 9/11); symbol – in the Peircian sense of arbitrary signifier, what I call an 'asymbol' – for signified ('flag' for 'nationality'; 'rose' for 'love'). All these formulae are the *intra*-domain equivalent of the LOVE IS WAR-type mapping formulae employed in inter-domain conceptual metaphor; that's to say they indicate the broad conceptual operation behind the specific verbal expression. With intra-domain tropes these formulae are syntagmatic and rule-based; with inter-domain, paradigmatic and item-based. As we'll see, they are both infinite sets.

Metonymies of the effect-for-cause and cause-for-effect type are standard literary (and especially poetic) substitutions; a hoe-handle described as 'sweat-seasoned' likely means 'by work' not merely 'by sweatiness', and the reader is asked by the very salience of the image to 'read in' and look down the causal chain towards the full sense. In George Mackay Brown's 'Hamnavoe Market',[9] we find 'Johnston stood beside the barrel. / All day he stood there. / He woke in a ditch, his mouth full of ashes' – and infer the hideous, drunken end to Johnston's day through the evidence of the morning after. Elsewhere in the same poem, 'A gypsy saw in the hand of Halcro / Great strolling herds, harvests, a proud woman. / He wintered in the poorhouse' – and again, we interpolate the patent uselessness of the gypsy's predictions at the causal lacuna of the second and third lines. (An example of 'enthymeme', if anyone still cares.)[10] [For a short

---

9 George Mackay Brown, 'Hamnavoe Market', *The Collected Poems of George Mackay Brown* (London: John Murray, 2005).

10 For the most part, I have avoided making much reference to the 'tropes and schemes' of traditional rhetoric. In the vicious logical rigour of their various classes and divisions (I jest), they recall nothing so much as Borges's infamous 'certain Chinese encyclopaedia', the 'Celestial Emporium of Benevolent Knowledge' ('[. . .] (g) stray dogs, (h) those that are included in this classification, (i) those that tremble as if they were mad, (j) innumerable ones, (k) those drawn with a very fine camel's hair brush, (l) others [. . .]', etc.) – Jorge Luis Borges, 'The Analytical Language of John Wilkins', *Other Inquisitions (1937–1952)*, trans. Ruth L. C. Simms (Austin, TX: University of Texas Press, 1964). One might argue that the identification of such effects in one's own writing and in the work of others is the first step toward their effective use – but as far as poets are concerned, all techniques should be learned with a view to forgetting them. This is especially the case with the dreaded Figures

handbook of rhetorical figures still in use, see endnote 10.] In another stanza, Garson receives 'an eye loaded with thunder', after a fight in a boxing ring – but we don't need to see the thrown punch, only its effect.

Many metonymic contractions are so familiar you don't notice them. They're so culturally convenient that they have become unconscious, and index has become wholly conflated with subject. When a kid uses a container-for-contained metonymy and asks you to 'zip me up', they mean 'zip up the coat-of-me', of course. 'Name-for-person' is even weirder, but metonymy it is, somewhere; 'Don Paterson' is a linguistic sign arbitrarily attached to me, but it can also be seen as shorthand for 'he-who-goes-by-the-name-of-Don Paterson', and this convention is again born of the generic domain, where we regard 'names given by our parents' as important and useful designators. [This statement is hardly uncontroversial. See endnote 11 for a defence.]

My name is not 'Stevenage' – but it was recently, in a conversation between two ticket inspectors about how many taxis to order to replace a cancelled train. In A&E, the same person might be better described by the index 'the broken arm' – or in a café as 'the ham sandwich', as in the famous textbook metonym 'the ham sandwich wants his bill'. All these specific-domain contexts – café, train, A&E,

---

of Speech, as their self-conscious deployment tends to sounds stagy in the extreme. A 'reasonably comprehensive list' seems not to exist; just when you think you've covered one area and are leaning in more closely to confirm as much, its elements proliferate before your eyes like the Mandelbrot set. It's therefore difficult to draw the line, and decide when one has slipped from the identification of useful effect and into the geeky pleasures of pointless taxonomic distinction. (In his highly entertaining *60 Ways to Turn a Phrase* [New York: Routledge, 1995], Arthur Quinn deliciously lists *hypozeuxis*: 'the refusal to use a zeugma when you could have'.) Should anyone care to pursue this matter further, please consult endnote 10, where I have placed a list of most of the classical figures, schemes and tropes still in regular use; though the reader would be better turning to the standard contemporary reference, Richard A. Lanham's splendidly sane and useful *A Handlist of Rhetorical Terms* (San Francisco, CA: University of California Press, 2013).

the bookie's, church, Facebook, kitchen, confessional, bedroom, academic conference – have their predominant concerns, which then produce the rules by which their contents are usefully organised and prioritised. In other words, while we might repeat the textbook definition that metonymy consists in 'the substitution of a related term for the thing itself', in *non*-generic contexts, it's the rules of the frame or context that promote certain kinds of relation, and make the substitution both possible and meaningful. Most poetic peristases and metonymies are products of subject, index *and* frame; indeed without a clear frame, the indexicality of the attribute is weakened drastically. We can consider indexicality *itself* a product of an enclosing, rule-based domain; the effective power of an index reflects the strength of the local rule which governs it.

It's been particularly difficult to nail what kinds of relation are up for grabs; one would require a full description of all possible attributes of a thing, and various theorists have produced some clines and systems and taxonomies that make my own look like models of sober continence. I'll discuss these in due course, but as I've said, *any* aspect, connotation or relation can form either the shared ground between two domains, or the substituted term in an intra-domain metonymy. We tend to derive our metaphor mappings from category-type (e.g. 'argument is war') and metonymic formulae from rule-type (e.g. 'container-for-contained'), but these are *both* descriptive of instances, not categories. The two sets are symmetrically infinite. The first is obviously so; however some theorists have tried to establish a finite number of metonym-rules, mainly because they find the prospect of an infinite number depressing. But they are forgetting that the 'rule' is generated not between the index and subject, but via the local by-laws of the specific domains and 'given situations' which enclose them – of which there are, of course, an infinite number.

Incidentally, if one were to attempt a *true* categorical list of 'kinds of connotation', this would inevitably be derived from something like the ontological categories Ray Jackendoff devised in conceptual semantics, a finite list of nine possible schemata which each have infinite generative extensions.[11] These primitives are very clean and Aristotelian, and seem comprehensive: Thing, Event, State, Action, Place, Path, Property, Manner and Amount. They would generate broad categories for all possible attributes, simply because they cover everything that humans could possibly be interested in. (If you're susceptible to this sort of thing, I defy anyone to look at Jackendoff's conceptual-semantic parsing of a sentence and not weep at the beauty of it – and be astonished that no one had thought of doing this before.) Of course, it's important to remember that articulate bats – not to mention those silicon-based dogfish in the Beehive Cluster, and that intelligent gas-cloud floating off Betelgeuse – will doubtless have other categories too. Our own may well turn out to be universal, but they are unlikely to be any more *comprehensive* than are our perceptual faculties.

All it takes to form a specific domain is for it to recur – or merely *occur*, if its exigencies are clear and compelling enough to propose a set of rules. In life, we go . . . 'I've been here before, and I am now cognisant of what should be prioritised in this situation'. This is a dentist's surgery, where my dinner plans and choice of comedy underpants are largely irrelevant; if I stagger towards the reclining chair yelling 'I can't sleep!' I can assume my dentist will not ask me if my bed is lumpy, or if I'm worrying about my relationship. Or if your dog goes missing, the salient rules of 'I've-lost-my-dog-domain' establish themselves immediately: when you scream at your partner, 'We have to call everyone!' – you don't mean the priest, the bin-man and the Arts Minister. You mean 'We have to call the dog pound, the police, the vet's and the local radio station!' i.e. 'everyone related to dog-losing'. However, *any* recurrence of a situation will produce rules. Take Lautreamont's famous scenario, 'the chance meeting of a sewing machine and an umbrella on a dissecting table': it might be pure

---

11 Ray S. Jackendoff, *Semantic Structures* (Cambridge, MA: MIT Press, 1992).

surrealism to begin with, but stare at this little tableau every day for a month. If, two months later, you happen to chance on an old Singer, resting on an operating table or otherwise . . . Just try *not* thinking of an umbrella. Within the domain of Singer sewing machines, umbrellas have now assumed a particular, if arbitrary significance.

The act of reading and rereading a poem forms and then confirms a specific domain, ideally one close to that which the poet had devised. (The poem is too unstable a sign for it ever to be identical; however, many poets are in permanent denial of this fact. Poetry can never be a mode of clear communication – though if it doesn't *aspire* to be, the results are doubly confusing.) While an initial reading will begin to conjure up this space, rereading will confirm and solidify its governing laws and priorities. The *way* we describe things in poems – whether in the form of peristases or metonyms, metaphors or symbols – will depend on the nature of the poem's specific domain and how it has formed in the act of *rewriting*, a heuristic process reflected in that of the reader's rereading. I'll refer to the poem's domain as the 'thematic domain'. This is simply the domain of 'what the poem is about', and its 'aboutness' remains in flux until the poem is fully composed or fully understood. These states are never attained but essential to posit, so they can guide the consistent direction in which our composition or interpretation should be heading.

To give a rather facile example: suppose you are writing a poem about a beloved aunt's funeral. In it, you describe our old poetic stand-by, a tree. You will immediately, and probably unconsciously, start to look for aspectual details that support the thematic domain. (Indeed this specific domain radically reconfigures the core and secondary connotations of 'the tree' as it would normally appear in the generic domain of the *parole*, essentially operating as if it constituted a micro-language.) You might describe the tree's many rings, as a way of introducing the themes of age and the passing of time; or its place by the cemetery wall, or its turning leaves. You may reduce it to an attribute or connotation alone, and show the reader just the tree's shadow, or the ghostly whispering in its foliage. You may draw out an unspoken connotation by context ('peristasis by inference') — if you chuck a 'yew tree' into a funereal poem, it will be hard for many readers to stifle the mythical associations the yew has with death and rebirth; or to take a less 'symbolic' example, a 'willow' or a 'blackthorn' will have more 'tearful' and 'darker' qualities drawn from them in our funeral poem than they would if they appear innocuously in a poem about a children's picnic. And so on. At the very least, the peristasis you use is unlikely to include many positive and optimistic words, since they would contradict the core funereal attribute of 'sad'. All that said, the reality of poetic composition is that the coherence of the result rarely reflects a coherent process: because the poet usually brings little more than a hunch to the empty page, a vague intuition that a couple of things, events, feelings, ideas might somehow be connected, it could easily be that a free-floating attribute suggested the inclusion of the tree in the first place: we need a shadow in this poem, so what might cast it? Indeed it's just as likely that the lone peristasis that proposed the funereal theme itself; you had begun the poem as merely a note about a tree in shadow, but had identified some hidden proposition, slippage, play or give in the image that proposed the larger theme — one you had perhaps been unconsciously ducking.[12] (I am convinced that an ignorance of the messiness of the poetic process must account for about 50 per cent of errors in critical analysis, where the poet is credited with the deliberate creation and brilliant timing of an effect that was achieved through a mixture of luck, intuition, accident, error or unconscious gesture. Poets will rarely contradict a positive critic, though, no matter how misguided their praise.)

Once the specific domain of the theme has been established, the poet has the option of cutting peristasis down to metonym, if they feel the full detail can be readily derived from the thematic context.

12   One of the most difficult rules to follow as a poet is 'always be prepared go where you're least comfortable or most afraid'. There are always dragons in front of the good stuff.

So, in something which has established itself in the reader's mind as a 'post-funeral arboreal poem', a man standing below a mournful, whispering oak may simply 'stand in the shadow of a mournful whispering'. In Sonnet 122, Shakespeare riffs on the idea of a notebook (one he appears to have been given as gift, and subsequently lost; the poem feels like a guilty contrivance) as a memory-substitute. This he compares unfavourably to his own excellent memory, claiming that his beloved is, besides, much too memorable and precious to require such a lowly means of record. Nine lines in, he is able to shorten his reference to the notebook to 'that poor retention'. Without the carefully established thematic domain of 'notebooks as inferior means of remembering the beloved', the metonym would be impossible, and the phrase incomprehensible.

The employment of intra-domain device as default in poetry is a profound technique which forces the reader into an intimate relationship with the text, and so with the poet. The rules of poetry-rereading mean readers *must* construct the thematic domain by which the metonym or peristasis will be correctly interpreted. '*Why* is that tree so oddly described? Aha . . .' It's through this quiet pursuit of the half-said thing that the reader enters into a state of co-authorship – and what makes poetry a more interactive art form than just about every other, bar the videogame. Often working far more quietly than inter-domain tropes, peristasis and metonymy are the main strategies by which a space is made for the reader, into which they can bring their own interpretation, feeling, ideas and experience. (Their discreet operation is one reason it took a couple of thousand years for them to be properly acknowledged; Jakobson can be credited with restoring metonymy to its rightful place, though neuroscience would have taken care of it eventually.) The half of the poem the reader completes will *never* wholly coincide with the half the poet intended; the thematic domain they construct will never quite be the one whose spell the poet was under. But this interpretative slippage is necessary for ownership of the poem to be transferred, and its meaning personalised. What, and how much, we are left to deduce from a poem's metonymic or peristatic evidence is very a matter of style. All good poems supply enough evidence for a complete domain to be circumscribed, but some poets prefer the 'expert Sudoku' approach of leaving four clues from which a far larger, interlocked pattern can be deduced or a unifying tone intuited, while at the other extreme, others ask that — as complete and transparent as their poem may seem — it be regarded as a synecdoche of a larger experience. The intra-domain contraction of the poem accomplishes two of our main poetic goals, and makes its speech both brief and original — but it also leaves space for the reader to act as co-creator. Metonymy is a door held open at an inviting angle — showing the reader neither too little, where the poem closes the reader out, nor too much, where the reader can see no reason to enter.

Metaphor

To return to our bad funeral poem: summoning our miserable tree with a peristasis or a metonymy might be insufficient to our meaning. We might want to describe it *as if it were something else* — a bared nerve, a woman wild with grief, or some kind of negative, inverted lightning. This means that we have to go inter-domain.

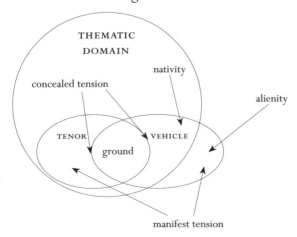

Metaphors are tropes of correspondence, and find family relationships between things. Taking our cue from I. A. Richards,[13] we generally term the literal subject the *tenor* (which I'll abbreviate to T), and the (most often) non-literal thing we compare it to the *vehicle* (V). Metaphors work through the shared content of T and V, which we call the metaphor's *ground*. The amount of this shared content determines the size of the ground, and the similarity of the thing compared. In semiotic terms, metaphors come somewhere between icons, or 'motivated signs' (which share so much content with the things they represent that they are instantly recognisable, e.g. a drawing of a sofa for the sofa itself), and true symbols, which share no content with their referents, and whose connection with them is completely arbitrary and learned.

In literature, metaphor is the act of connecting two apparently unconnected things. We say 'X is Y', and overcome the patent untruth of the statement by simultaneously demonstrating that X and Y are, at least, surprisingly alike; the metaphor is a lie that is then proven to be partly true. As usual, we naturally incline towards a 'pink noise' mean: if a metaphor is to be effective, it will usually steer a path between uncorrelated leap and overcorrelated connection. This means that we rarely make the mistake of creating a metaphor from two things that are either too close or too far apart. 'This table is a banana' is a pretty lousy metaphor, and could only be qualified into some sense by a very specific and accommodating context. The two things are too unlike, and the 'ground' is too thin; they don't share enough properties for the statement to declare anything but their difference. This, if you like, is a random, 'white-noise' metaphor. At the other extreme, a 'brown noise' metaphor is where tenor and vehicle are too close and predictable; it isn't worth the trouble of pointing out their similarity.[14]

13   I. A. Richards, *The Philosophy of Rhetoric* (Oxford: Oxford University Press, 1936).
14   I have just berated a student for describing three mojitos as being lined up 'like a row of shots', having refused to accept his defence of 'but they were'. I realised

To say an apple looks like a bit like a peach, or a can of *7-Up* looks a hell of a lot like a can of *Sprite* isn't making us see those things afresh, which is generally our aim: to have an opportunity to reconsider 'the known' via an unexpected correspondence. (For this reason, metaphor is one of the key ways in which language instinctively reinvents itself, and makes itself adequate to a changing reality; this is a point to which I'll return.)

I've mentioned that it's our instinct to connect any two things that happen to be thrown at us. Where we cannot forge a direct relation or a context (in poetry, a 'thematic domain'), we will resort to metaphor: if we can't connect by rule, we will do so by finding some family resemblance between things. This is neatly demonstrated in the workshop game where a noun is randomly given the definition of a completely different one. It can almost invariably be 'made to fit': we ransack the noun's internal properties, aspects and connotations until we have found several points of coincidence or imaginative correspondence – and it transpires that a keyhole *is*, in a sense, a square box in which one watches moving pictures, or that a TV *is* a hole into which one places a key that opens a room, or that a train *is* a small, quick-moving mammal of which some are irrationally

---

afterwards that I'd have been fine if, say, John Ashbery had written as much; but then I'd have assumed he was being funny, parading his awareness of the bad metaphor – and communicating a certain louche exhaustion in his indifference to the business of finding a better one, since his point was merely to indicate the speed at which he intended to down his cocktails. However, I decided those were *not* quite my student's intentions, and so felt justified in censuring him. An excellent parlour game to play among the poetically literate is to take a poem and pretend another poet wrote it, then watch how interpretations drastically change. (Some poems almost gain from the exercise – Frank O'Hara's 'Reasons for Attendance' is pretty storming, and Dickinson's 'The Jumblies' rounds out her personality delightfully. Eliot's 'maggie and milly and molly and may' is perhaps another matter.) The style of a famous poet constitutes a specific domain, one in which we learn to read everything they write, usually in a way that confirms – even by anomalous contradiction – what we already know about them. As readers we are very loath to allow poets to change their styles, much to their frustration.

frightened, or that a mouse *is* a fast kind of public transport that runs on rails . . . Or at least possibilities that can be entertained. (Most of us understand that in this life the imagination is not a negligible reality.) What's astonishing is the degree to which this process is instinctive and instantaneous – and the extent to which everything really *does* seem to be secretly related.

Metaphors can take many forms, and I'll explore some of these in due course. For now, keep in mind a couple of simple facts: there are an infinite number of ways metaphor can be presented in a text, and some of them (especially the 'simile', where one thing is compared to another, rather than claimed to *be* another) have traditionally been given undue prominence. These presentational differences are interesting: they will often imply alternative aspects of the same mapping and present different cognitive experiences, but they do not, I sense, represent important distinctions of formal structure. Far more crucial is the text-status of the vehicle and the tenor. For now: if V and T are both present in the text (and 'the moon's a balloon'), I'll refer to this as a 'metaphor'; if only V is text-present and the T is to be inferred (by 'the white balloon in the night sky'), I'll refer to this as an 'enigma' – Greek for 'riddle', which is all it is. Some authors refer to this formula as that of 'symbol'; however I use 'symbol' to refer to purely to a 'vehicle with an abstract tenor' (although I believe these are not tenors at all, since symbol is a wholly different tropic category).

There is a third category, which I refer to as the 'isologue', where V and T are text-present, but the dominant component (i.e. the tenor) cannot be established – usually because both are syntactically unconnected, and often both present in the literal frame of the poem. It may sound like a minor trope-type – but it is extremely common, if monumentally under-identified. (In the isologue, there really is no V or T, nor any limit on the number of mapped elements.) 'Tonal isologue' – details which overlap in shared tone – may be the most common trope of all. Isologues which share formal or dynamic properties are also common:

Someone mutters a flame from the lichen
and eats the red-and-white Fly Agaric
while the others hunker in the dark, taking it in turn
to drink his mind-expanding urine. [. . .]
At 2 a.m. I will clamber downstairs
to glimpse the red-and-white
up the chimney, my new rocking-horse
as yet unsteady on its legs.

(PAUL MULDOON, 'Trance')[15]

We'll now look at a metaphor 'in the field', and give it a more technical consideration.

I wandered lonely as a cloud
That floats on high o'er vales and hills,
When all at once I saw a crowd,
A host, of golden daffodils[16]

I think most readers would agree that Wordsworth's is a reasonably effective simile; at least it seems a uncontentious example to work with. A secondary connotation linking men (tenor) and clouds (vehicle), *lonely*, is declared in the text; as we've seen, original mappings have to be explicitly declared, and often these hinge on shared *secondary* connotations. Secondary connotations have a degree of subjectivity, are not central to the definition of either term, and are peripheral within their broad domains. Not that clouds are *really* lonely – this is just the poet's pathetic fallacy – but a core attribute of 'lonely' is 'isolated', which is surely the image we're presented with

15 Paul Muldoon, *Quoof* (London: Faber & Faber, 2001).
16 William Wordsworth, 'Daffodils', *The Collected Poems of William Wordsworth*, ed. Antonia Till (London: Wordsworth Editions, 1994).

here. By contrast, 'I wandered like a cloud' wouldn't narrow the sense in the way the author requires.

To assume a text-absent shared secondary attribute is self-evident or even 'obvious' is, one of the classic late-modernist and postmodern procedural errors in metaphor, and assumes that the connections between discontinuous statements can be clearly inferred.[17] The frequent claim is that such tactical elisions permit the reader a more democratic means of interpretation, or that the poet is graciously crediting the reader with the intelligence to divine these implicit connections. Too often this just overestimates the reader's powers of ESP, and results in 'reader's paranoia' (or more precisely a localised and temporary version of clinical 'cryptosemia', the identification of signs not perceptible to others). The situation has arisen because poets underestimate a sign's ability to generate a great many secondary attributes in the absence of any explicit narrowing context or *fondement* – here, a clear thematic domain of the kind often absent in the late modernist poem – and the results are invariably polysemy gone berserk. (Beware poets who, despite their having *intended* a specific meaning, will nonetheless justify the confusion their incompetence has generated by telling you that no interpretation can be 'wrong'.)[18]

Returning to our man-cloud: guided by the additional information provided by the text-present 'lonely', we can probably all agree to identify attributes of 'solitariness', 'freedom' and 'roaming' as the common ground in this metaphor. ('Lonely' is really a form of trans-ferred epithet from 'I wandered'; the cloud is not 'lonely', but we

---

17 Indeed, one might say enthymeme- and anapodoton-fail are the hallmark errors of neo-modernism; though one should probably decline to.

18 In a sense this statement is true, of course, but not when it's used to abdicate one's responsibly to 'as clear expression as one can manage', regardless of the complexity of the thing expressed. My own line is that all interpretations are valid, but some can sensibly be declared stupid, erroneous or mere projections on the reader's part: one can misread an obvious and plain sense, or narrow a sense without justification, or import a sense for which the text has given no cue.

reach a more cloud-native attribute – 'solitary' or 'single' – by the usual process of making rapid metaleptic links in the abstract domain, where we jump from concept to concept until we land on one closely linked to our target element.) But the ground tells us *nothing additional*, and in a sense merely focuses our minds on an attribute already present within either domain. A man and a cloud can both be, in their ways, solitary and alone. The real poignancy comes with something I call the 'concealed tension'.

The 'manifest tension' is that between the big central denotations, if you'll allow me that happy fiction, of 'cloud' and 'man'; a vaporous, floating rain-giving thing, and a solid, walking bloke. This gives us the requisite *difference* between T and V that we need to make the metaphor arresting and surprising: 'Wow! Who'd have thought that these two things were in some sense the *same?*' is the kind of reaction we often hope to provoke in the reader. However, the concealed tension resides in the attributes they either *almost* share but do not, or *do* share – but possess in a radically different quality, kind or degree. It's at the very *edge* of their overlap, in the fuzzy area between ground and tension, that we unconsciously sense them (hence 'concealed'). The man cannot quite rise, although the poet seems to express an abstract yearning to; a cloud is almost weightless; a man is not. The cloud is unconstrained in 3D space; a wandering man is confined by his plane-bound paths and routes, even though he might desire it otherwise. Poetic metaphor expresses a desire that *something were otherwise*, and gains its poignancy through the literal impossibility of that desire being realised – while still appearing to hold out the imaginative possibility that it *might* be. (In a sense, it is expressive of 'a rage against category'.) Isolated textbook examples won't help us here, since the concealed tension is often generated by the thematic domain. In 'the dinner plate is a moon' our manifest tension is, well, that plates are small and close-at-hand and ceramic, and the moon is huge and distant and rocky; it's hard to say what the concealed tension could be. But suppose that the poem is about dining alone after a failed marriage: the plate and moon are round and white; though the plate is *not* remote, isolated, freezing or barren, it conceivably *could* be – and these hidden poignancies are, to some degree, capable of being drawn forth by the miserable context. (The word 'lonely' in 'I wandered lonely as a cloud' accomplishes just that.) The concealed tension is an area of conceptual flux, one in which a core or secondary attribute of the V which is *not* shared by the T is vestigially transferred to it through a determined, context-directed act of the imaginative will. Rich thematic domains and contextually apposite metaphors generate these unstable and poignant associations; simplistic domains and inapposite metaphors do not.[19]

The ground is not just the place where V and T share attributes. The ground opens up a conduit whereby the tenor can be infected with aspects of the vehicle, and vice versa. It is therefore an *active field*, and directs sense from the V towards the T and the T towards the V, and is the emergent structure of an original and dynamic conceptual blend. Too often we forget that this dynamic is bidirectional. Let's flip our earlier example, and take 'the moon is a dinner plate'. The moon is round and white, and these qualities will have directed our choosing 'plate' as a vehicle; but via the ground, the plate returns its own connotations to reshape the idea of 'moon' itself, and might draw out quieter aspects of the T like 'something that comes out in the evening', as well as more secondary attributes such as 'shininess'. Releasing these possibilities is a matter of focusing the reader's attention and intrigue in the right way, but also encouraging them to treat the metaphor as a compound sign.

---

19   I am aware that in this attempt to explain the slippery effects that lie behind the poignancy of certain tropes I have been reduced to qualifying somewhat outmoded terms into some kind of accuracy. Literary terminology does not describe cognitive processes particularly well. Old-fashioned literary analysis may be in its last throes, but 'last throes' are an essential part of any process: they are, for one thing, a caution against the too-hasty adoption of fatally flawed new terminology (see my comments on *source* and *target*).

Such metaphors can be very rich, and form their own emergent domains. This is why the current use of the terms 'source and target' in semiotics to replace V and T respectively makes very little sense – and none at all in a poetic context: it's a lousy metaphor. Things just aren't that simple. In a compound sign, sense flows in both directions from either component, not in a simple vector from one to the other. (This can be most clearly seen in the sub-trope of isologue.) In Wordsworth's poem, 'man' is mapped to 'cloud', and 'cloud' to 'man'. However, whether man or cloud is tagged V or T is an issue of a context-dependent polarity, i.e. whether cloud or poet belongs to the 'literal domain' (this is a matter of deixis, discussed elsewhere). This is, of course, crucial, and the metaphor cannot be inverted without changing its sense; how we present a metaphor tells us which conceptual frame is dominant. Nonetheless, the various syntactic forms the metaphor might take don't eliminate the backwash and undertow of meaning running from V back to T. Each term colours the other. The overinterrogation of the sign implicit in the poetic 'reading contract' amplifies and complicates sense-flow massively, and the result is a conceptual blend.

However, I'd suggest that we have become inured to the effects of our presentational defaults and the power-relations they propose:

> When I poured it
> it had a cutting edge
> and flamed
> like Betelgeuse.

> (SEAMUS HEANEY, 'Sloe Gin')[20]

Here, the tenor of the sloe gin perhaps also contributes a little tipsiness and deliriousness to the vehicle of Betelgeuse – but primarily the old red giant is invoked just to lend its eerie colour, and perhaps

20 Seamus Heaney, *Station Island* (London: Faber & Faber, 1984).

a hint of its remote strangeness; it does so by seeing its *own* sense-potential dramatically constrained. (Heaney being Heaney, he may well have had the final raising of the glass in mind too: Betelgeuse means 'the hand of Orion'.) As superbly effective as I find this example, I do sometimes worry if we can persist *exclusively* with this kind of metaphor – the kind where we turn the world into a handy means of lending our human concerns some shape, flavour, colour, drama, dignity; at times it seems yet another way of indulging our own hegemonic delusions.

Nativity and alienity

Too often we fail to take account of the metaphor's place within the context of the poem itself. A metaphor's success depends on more than its originality; it must also be apposite, and like any other detail, serve the emergent, rule-based environment of the thematic domain. This all hinges on the *nativity* or *alienity* of its vehicle relative to that domain. As poets, we generally try to maximise the metaphor's effect by placing the vehicle at the optimal distance from the poem's thematic concerns. A vehicle imported from too distant a sphere relative to the thematic domain might be flashy and impressive – but there's a very good chance that, having nothing much to do with the poem, it will then rip it apart. The deliberate use of this practice was the aesthetic of 'Martian poetry', a movement associated with the literary critic Craig Raine.[21] The school only ever had a couple of adherents, but was briefly influential; this was a tribute not just to the moribund state of poetry in England at the time, but to the atrophying of its visual imagination, and 'Martianism' at least performed the service of reminding poets that part of their job was to look afresh at what was in front of them. The term 'Martian' is still a useful way of describing a flamboyant comparison, often in the

21 See Craig Raine, *A Martian Sends a Postcard Home* (Oxford: Oxford University Press, 1979).

form of a 'visual pun', that comes at the expense of the poem's larger integrity. To give an example from Raine's own writing: in 'In The Kalahari Desert', a poem about the fate of the English missionaries, we find the clever and striking image 'a glinting beetle on its back / struggled like an orchestra / with Beethoven'.[22] However, the fact that the image is strenuously justified by the lines that flank it only raises our doubts over its authenticity: the line is preceded by the rather nervous 'the wilderness was full of home', and then followed by the suspiciously well-timed corroboration, 'The Hallé, / Isabella thought and hummed'. Such rickety accommodations seem to point to the metaphor being hatched outside the poem's own thematic domain, and then let loose into the text. The missionaries may well have been lovers of classical music back in Blighty, but to claim that 'orchestra' is an indexically *representative* member of the conceptual domain 'English home' is stretching it. (This shoehorning is further given away by the partly transferred quality 'struggled', used here to increase the ground of the metaphor: the upturned beetle is not only like an orchestral violin section, but also even *more* like an incompetent one; in the larger context of the poem, this seems an odd thing to get nostalgic for.) The image would have been just as happy or unhappy in a thousand other poems, and the vehicle has been imported from too distant a domain; relative to the theme, it suffers an uncomfortable degree of 'alienity'. (Tonal dissonance between theme and tenor can be just as much of a problem, e.g. 'Roger spat into the fire, / leaned back and watched his phlegm / like a Welsh rarebit / bubbling on the brands . . .' Ah, home.) There is nothing intrinsically bad about Raine's poetic thesis here; indeed there is a decent point to be made about the colonial mindset and its imaginative hegemony — but because the thematic and tonal consistency of the images is disregarded, the evidence looks merely

22 Craig Raine, 'In the Kalahari Desert', *Collected Poems 1978–1998* (London: Picador, 2000).

'planted', and the argument can't build. With such effects, the reader must leave the spell of the poem in order to applaud them, and then somehow fight their way back in – which can be as difficult as finding your way back into a dream after the dog has woken you up.

The middle-way, similarity-and-difference rule says the comparison should be close enough to the poem's concerns to draw on its argumentative or thematic circuitry, and distant enough to arrest the reader with its felicity and originality. The following deliberately simplified example will illustrate the point. Let's propose a theme, and say . . . We have a poem in which a poor man who has just cleaned up his act – he's quit drinking, and saved a little money – is taking a holiday on a ferry with his kid; the tone of the poem is a happy and redemptive one. The guy is standing by the guard-rail, looking out to the horizon as his young child falls asleep on his shoulder. He is watching the sun go down. Now: suppose that you have decided to use a metaphor to describe the sun, and present it in the form of an enigma (i.e. where you omit the tenor and just state the vehicle). Which of the following fits the poem best? (a) 'Derek watched the great, suppurating, angry boil sink into the sea'; (b) 'Derek watched the plump satsuma sink into the sea'; (c) 'Derek watched the huge gold coin sink into the sea'; (d) 'Derek watched the giant happy beachball sink into the sea'.

Setting aside the fact that they're *all* pretty bad, this exercise will nonetheless supply us with a little cline for metaphor-fail. Example (a) clearly dissonates; it's wholly *alien* to the thematic domain, and imports a tone which clashes badly with the redemptive, serene one we've carefully established. Example (b) is better, but the tone and content of the vehicle is really *incidental* to the thematic domain, and does little to enhance or deepen it. Many poets know to avoid type (a) but cannot resist type (b) (see our 'Martians') because it forms a potentially rich category of striking and effective comparison – but *only* if no attention is paid to context; these tropes may not actually dissonate, but neither are they particularly apposite. Nonetheless, we might still argue that such a metaphor is effective: it gives local pleasure, it lightly disrupts the predictability of things, and it performs a decorative function. (This kind of trope is regularly favoured by ostentatiously clever novelists of the sub-Martin Amis school. Amis himself uses it skilfully.) Example (c) is our best bet; it is not only consonant with both the subject and tone of the thematic domain, it's quietly propositional of it. It certainly avoids the sin of example (d), a type of metaphor we see far more than we should. It is less supportive or propositional of the thematic domain than it is crudely directive of it: it lacks any naturalism and sounds implausibly 'convenient'; we might say that it was simply *too* native to the theme.

Staying with 'over-nativity': when the V of the metaphor is drawn from concerns very close to the poem's theme it runs the danger of being misread *as* a literal detail, especially in a symbolic construction. In a poem about 'fear in airports', 'I gripped my ticket like my boarding pass' is a catastrophic metaphor, but making it an enigma – 'I gripped my boarding pass' when you meant your ticket – is just idiotic. You might think this trope would never come up, but milder versions certainly do, and too regularly. I recall a poem describing someone having an epileptic fit on a boat. They were described as flopping around like a fish – but the metaphor was presented as an enigma, i.e. 'the landed fish flopped about the deck', by which the poet had intended 'the man'. But since the V was consistent with the scene's own literal domain, there was no cue to read it figuratively – and it was simply a line about a fish. However, though deictic clarity is crucially important, it's often *good* default practice to find our metaphors in the poem's own imaginative circumstances; this has the effect of deepening the idiom of its thematic domain, and plugging the V straight into the poem's own circuitry:

> It's his peculiar way of putting things
> That fills in the spaces of Tullabaun.

> The dregs stewed in the teapot remind me,
> And wind creaming rainwater off the butt.
>
> (MICHAEL LONGLEY, 'Brothers')[23]

In the last line Longley hints lightly at a beautiful metaphor, 'water is like cream', or more specifically something like 'water skimmed by the wind from a water-butt is like cream being skimmed from the top of the milk'; 'cream' is drawn from and consistent with the 'rural, farming community' aspect of the thematic domain. We may even vaguely sense 'water is like cream' is a symbol of something like 'the paradoxical richness that can be found in apparent poverty'.

> These stories must have been inside my head
> That day, falling in love, preparing this
> Good life; and this, this fly, verbosely buried
> In 'Bliss', one dry tear punctuating 'Bliss'.
>
> (DOUGLAS DUNN, 'Re-reading Katherine Mansfield's
> Bliss and Other Stories')[24]

In this poem from Douglas Dunn's book of elegies for his first wife, the astonishing appositeness and nativity of the vehicle 'dry tear' used to describe the wing of an accidentally 'pressed fly' hardly needs pointed out; and in the usual non-linear way, it's possible that this very association prompted the entire poem, or was at least a major factor in the development of its theme.

Incidentally, most poets – whether or not they are making a more specific thematic point – will stick to the safe, good practice of drawing on natural-world or domestic-world vehicles (moon, grass, rose, sunlight, table, lamp, door, etc.), whose presence will rarely

23 Michael Longley, *Collected Poems* (London: Jonathan Cape, 2007).
24 Douglas Dunn, *Elegies* (London: Faber & Faber, 2001).

clash with the thematic domain. Vehicle-raiding the natural and domestic domains is something of an undiagnosed default.

Poetic metaphors are more often complex than the ones I've adduced here, and don't compare substantives but peristases. They'll rarely compare the moon and a balloon; simple examples are often handy for analysing the structure of trope, and tend to be the kinds of metaphor discussed by theorists, but the compositional reality is vastly more complex, dynamic and chaotic. Metaphors will be spun by the poet within the nascent, inchoate thematic domain of a hunch, a feeling, a tone, a 'half an idea' – and elaborated through the exercise of what Jung used to call the 'active imagination'. In other words, that moon of ours will more likely be seen through scudding clouds while lodged in the branches of a bare elm, and be watched by a recently bereaved man who has lost his way home while taking a short-cut over the fields. If that image does not already constitute the poet's objective correlative – i.e. if it does not satisfactorily symbolise the emotion guiding the poem – we may well feel the need to elaborate its metaphor; balloons and plates will not suffice. The man will look at the tree-trapped, cloud-swept moon the way he once did that big silver coin he saw deep down in that murky stream when he was a child, knowing if he could only reach it . . . and so on. Moreover, peristases often have attributes that are *text-absent* and derived purely from context, an area often entirely ignored by textbook analysis.

The act of poetic composition is a messy process, the object of which is to find out 'the truth'; but, from a subjective perspective, 'poetic truth' is just the point at which the poet arrives at something they feel to be true. The method by which they get there is unique to the art of poetic composition. In poetry, language is placed under an excessive degree of formal pressure and emotional urgency, until it undergoes a kind of phase shift, as water does at freezing or boiling point. At that point of turning, the poet knows they 'have something'.[25] We pursue

25 Naturally, poems written 'from life' – from its immediate frustrations, angers,

that solvent truth, the sudden fusing of sense, music and measure, by necessarily chaotic means – means that our neat formulae and clean textbook examples inevitably betray. The final poem is usually the result of far more radical revisions, cuts, pastes and switches than the reader or critic could ever suspect. Since the good poet tends to work by vague hunch and process, not clear idea and operation, they will often allow the felicity of a comparison *itself* to propose a thematic domain very different to the one they may originally have had in mind. Actually: poets sometimes have very little in mind. They generally write to find out *what* they think, not to 'commit a thought to poetry'. This is because they know that the thoughts they have *outside* the discipline of poetry are pretty much the same as everyone else's, and poetry provides their one opportunity to have an original one. In poetic composition, all 'effects' are verbs. Metaphor and metonymy are how we write poems, not how we populate them.

------

joys and tragedies – will often have greater emotional urgency than those we merely 'make up'. Emotional speech has a different musical and rhythmic quality to non-emotional speech (and a quantifiable, characterisable one at that); there are, to be cold about it, some good technical reasons why 'the confessional mode' might sometimes make for a superior poem. Alas, 'life-poems' – however necessary they feel to the poet, or genuine the assuagement they bring – are often blighted by the tear-blinded distortions that accompany great emotion: an unconscious tendency to self-censorship, a coyness with the facts or the factual context that helps the reader makes sense of them, and a loss of editorial perspective. We often assume the events by which we have been most moved to have an intrinsic emotional resonance that requires only our plainest description, when in fact their intensity depended on the intricate harmonic circumstances of our lives. We either need to provide the reader with a little of that context (what we merely *remember* of a sad event, say, is generally not the best metonymic evidence of it; this must be sought out), or alter the facts to fit the truth. Writing *with* your genuine feeling but otherwise just 'making it all up' might often be the poet's best strategy.

THE POETIC CONTRACT

———————————

'The poetic' emerges naturally from the language under certain performance conditions; but when considered as a conceptual phenomenon, it is as much a mode of reading as it is of speaking or writing. This can be thought of in terms of three vaguely defined sub-modes. Any one of these activities can produce effects in the reader that might be called 'poetic' – by which is almost invariably meant a kind of 'meaning-infused aesthetic experience'; however these effects only arise through creative investment, not passive reception. The three modes also bleed rather seamlessly into one another, as they really represent points on a scale from the largely semantic appreciation of the text to a purely musical or aesthetic one.

Take our old standby, the word 'moon'. Give it some space, some page-silence, as we do words within a poem; stare at it for a minute.

moon

What kind of reading have we just made? Firstly, our reading has become an act of determined and wilful *oversignification* – of 'reading in' far more than we would in a simple monosemic interpretation: we might start to think of all connotations and alternative senses of the word 'moon' (at least one is rather unfortunate). Secondly, it's one of conscious *overattention* to the phonosemantic dimension of the language, that interfusion of sound and sense which produces synaesthetic effect. This might lead us to *hear* the nasal-rounded, empty white sphere of the moon. Thirdly, it's one of unconscious, receptive *oversensitivity* to its sensual physical properties, its acoustic mark, its music and rhythm. Here, we feel the shape of the word 'moon' in our mouth, its envelope of nasals and its long vowel, and experience it as a lyric effect.

(I've covered this at length in the first essay, but before we go on I should provide a quick recap. Poets have known for thousands of years that words are definitely not the kind of arbitrary signs Saussure claimed. The mere fact that 'moon' is represented by very different phonemes in other languages is no disproof of the existence of a broad iconic principle which underlies the structure of speech. It isn't the referent itself that imprints itself into the sound of speech, but – since the process is directed by the mind – *an aspect of the conceptual domain* of the referent. This aspect will be different, depending on cultural circumstances and environmental exigencies. These determine the salient quale the word will then iconically reflect, even thought the word-sound will also function indexically for its entire conceptual domain. So the word for the moon, in various languages, might phono-semantically connote 'light', or 'roundness', or 'distance', or 'the hunt', or 'tide-pulling', or 'menses', and so on; but there is *no* universal quale of 'moonness'. Phonesthemes have no 'dictionary definitions', but are mere phonemic nodes which indicate a quale capable of being shared across lexemes; and while I would maintain they are acutely 'felt', their actual presence in the language can be argued only by pointing to tendencies, not instantiations. I should admit that I have no particular evidence for all this, but speaking 'as a poet' – a dubious and narrow expertise one should rarely brandish – it strikes me as simple common sense.)

Any text can receive a 'hypersensitive' reading. Take the standard matchbox warning *Keep away from damp places and small children* – which, when you think about it for a moment, is excellent general advice. To supply this reading, you have to wilfully remove it from its specific domain, in this case 'safety instructions on matchboxes', and allow it its polysemy by releasing it back into its generic domain – in this case that of 'general advice', a possibility aided by its imperative mood. Note that for this domain-shift to happen, you need to *reread*. Your first reading will likely be made, quite unthinkingly, in the context of the specific domain, which is often established by straightforward cultural circumstance. Most so-called 'found poems' release a specific-domain sign into the generic domain (additionally rendered 'pregnant with significance' through its merely 'being a poem'), or into a different specific domain circumscribed by a title:

> I found a pigeon's skull on the machair,
> All the bones pure white and dry, and chalky,
> But perfect,
> Without a crack or flaw anywhere.
>
> (HUGH MACDIARMID, 'Perfect')[1]

The above, rendered immediately symbolic by its title, was originally liberated from the specific domain of a novel called *The Blue Bed*, by Glyn Jones (initially without acknowledgement).[2]

> One's a crown, two's a crown,
> three, four, five distal occlusal,
> six distal occlusal, seven occlusal.
> Upper left: one mesial incisal, [. . .]
>
> (PAUL FARLEY, 'Relic')[3]

---

1 Hugh MacDiarmid, *The Islands of Scotland* (London: Scribner, 1939).
2 MacDiarmid's defence of unconscious theft was not quite as ingenious as that of a talented former student of mine: when confronted with an essay he had cut and pasted from a news website, he held his head in his hands and moaned, 'I can't believe it's happened *again*.' He then went on to claim a rare and complex medical syndrome whose main symptoms were photographic memory, kleptomania and amnesia, an excuse so brilliant I felt I had no option but to pass him.
3 Paul Farley, *The Ice Age* (London: Picador, 2002).

Here the title reframes the material, and indicates that we might also read the author's own dental records as an alarming *memento mori*.

Many poetic effects that fall into the broad category of 'the play on words', e.g. paronomasia and punning, will domain-shift from the specific to the generic, or vice-versa. (Think of all actress-and-bishop jokes.) Clichéd and idiomatic phrasemes – which are learned by rote by the right brain as single lexicalised entries, as synonyms for other things – catch the strange light-angles characteristic of their new context and are considered afresh, as words heard as if for the first time, with all the double-take poignancy of them being additionally familiar. I tend to think of this 'reframing of the known' as the definition of poetic originality, as distinct from poetic 'novelty'. Look at the bolded phrases in this passage from 'Mules' by Paul Muldoon:

> Should they not have the **best of both worlds**?
> Her **feet of clay gave the lie**
> To the star burned in our mare's brow.
> Would Parsons' jackass not **rest more assured**
> That **cross wrenched from his shoulders**?
> We had loosed them into one field.
> I watched Sam Parsons and my quick father
> Tense for the **punch below their belts**,
> For what was **neither one thing or the other**.[4]

> (PAUL MULDOON, 'Mules')[5]

---

4 Paul Muldoon, *Mules* (London: Faber & Faber, 1977).

5 Novelty – which we can characterise by the reader's reaction of 'I didn't see that coming' – is no bad thing in the poem, and when experienced in contrast to the 'background default' of broadly 'received' speech can be thought of as the necessary pink-noise variation we need to keep ourselves and our readers awake. But poetry which consists of nothing but the relentless parade of novel effect is soon incapable of surprise.

In a sense, this is one cliché after another; but the poet requires us to reinterpret and renew each of those worn phrases in the new thematic domain, one which concerns sterile crossbreeds, sterility, the earthly and the divine, miscegenation, and otherworldliness in general. Therefore 'feet of clay' takes on qualities of 'the earthbound', in contrast to the divine star – a mark of pedigree – on the mare's brow; 'cross wrenched from his shoulders' manages to connote *both* Christ and the lifted burden of the donkey, who is delivered of the mule's unnatural crossbreed; the boxing-derived cliché 'punch below their belts' connotes both the 'wrongness' and illegitimacy of this breeding, and the genital seat of it all; and 'neither one thing or the other' dramatically literalises a phraseme so tired it is usually lexicalised with a single stress on 'other'.[6] (I'll explore the complex business of the subversion of phraseme and collocation in a more technical way in Part III on metre.)

Now if you turn *over* our box of matches, you might see *Strike softly away from the body* – which to my ear sounds rather lovely, when I 'overattend' to its lyric qualities, and suggestions of other meanings. As we've seen, ambiguity, polysemy and altered sense in poetry are

6 (Note that the instability of the phrase is further enhanced by its being deliberately ungrammatical; 'nor' is correct, but most folk say 'or', so it also has dialectal verisimilitude, but that's exactly half Muldoon's point.) The interpretation that the poem is 'really' about the English and Irish languages or cultures strikes me as fanciful, and a classic example of 'critic's projection' – even if one might reasonably claim that such a subject is, maybe, hovering in the wings as a 'resonance'. One can certainly *make* it 'about' this – but not without importing a frame the text does not supply, beyond the poem featuring Muldoon's father and the vaguely English surname 'Parsons'. The larger worry is why on earth you'd *want* to make such an interpretation, since (like most allegorical readings) it's just no fun: it diminishes the poem badly, and is not consonant with its other themes. The poets of 'the provinces' suffer greatly from this kind of thing. To a metropolitan reader or critic, their local history, culture and speech seem to be the most salient things about them – and are therefore often assumed to be the subjects the poets are themselves addressing. This rarely is the case. (I've lost count of the times I've been asked 'how it feels to be Scottish', which is like being asked how it feels to have toenails.)

achieved largely by domain-shift, where we choose to read a word, phrase or detail in either a larger, smaller or multiple frame. We can release it from its specific use into a wider generic domain, or take it from the generic domain to a specific one (both these moves are intra-domain; more precisely, 'synecdochic'); or we can reframe it within another specific domain (as in Farley's 'Relic', which uses an inter-domain strategy). This process draws out and makes salient alternative senses from the umbra of its central and secondary attributes. Although perhaps the most fundamental reframing is produced by the words simply being read within the larger domain of 'reading poetry', with all its unique protocols, oversignifyings and overattentions.[7]

Poets start with the assumption of an oversignifying reader. Those texts that appear to reward this reader for their additional investment – texts that we find unusually striking, apposite, or musical – are usually adjudged 'poetic', but this oversignifying faculty is anterior to the poem itself. The work of the poet is to contribute a text that will firstly invite such a reading, and secondly reward such a reading. What we're left with is a cultural contract between reader and writer, involving three identifiable and independent stages. A poem is usually (a) written as a poem; (b) presented as a poem; then (c) read as a poem. It is written as a poem, with the built-in polysemic density, lyric integration and originality we tend to require of it; it is then presented as a poem – conventionally through designation, lineation (whose most immediate visual consequence is to declare the self-importance of the text), and obvious, identifiable poetic 'effect'; then

---

7 Skipping ahead a little, my formula is that 'poetic meaning' is the complexity that results when an element is domain-shifted from a generic sense to a local, specific sense the generic encloses. Generic sense is the carrier wave of specific meaning. From this statement I'd extrapolate the general point that, while you may bend and twist them, if you *break* the conventions of syntax, grammar and interdependent, linked statement, you're in danger of destroying the transmissionary medium of *poetry* – and are effectively revving up a motorcycle in the concert hall. Any deeper 'meaning' is then largely confined to the iconoclastic gesture itself.

it is read as a poem, in that state of mild paranoia that more or less defines the poetry reader.[8]

One might say that in the act of 'over-reading', the reader has taken the poem as a synecdoche,[9] where the poem is a part that stands for a whole, a smaller thing which stands for a larger. This has led us to identify synecdoche as poetry's 'master trope'. A poem 'about' x is often read as being also 'about' the larger set of terms y to which x belongs, to a greater or lesser, more- or less-conscious degree. A poem concerning a couple's argument over a biscuit, then, will often and unthinkingly be seen as 'about' the entire failing relationship. Philip Larkin's 'Mr Bleaney' shows details of a disappointed life which is also 'about' that *entire* disappointed life (and, it emerges, that of the poem's speaker).[10] The larger x we are invited to ponder via representative member y can either be directly

---

8 I appreciate that this will soon become a tedious mantra, but words in poems are restored much of their own individual referentiality since their speed of delivery is no longer driven by that of conversational speech. In normal conversation the 'experienced referentiality' of the lexeme is attenuated to little more than a ghostly marker within the larger performance, argument or phatic exchange of the sentence itself. Under the usual somnambulant conditions, the brain tends to conceive of the phrase, not the word, as the semantic unit; while the *thought* it expresses may not be so, nearly every phrase we utter is unoriginal, and already part-way to phraseme and lexicalisation. (I know this sounds insulting to humans; but if you have ever experienced a panic attack involving severe disassociation, you will have been struck by the ease with which your brain produces perfectly coherent speech, entirely free from linguistic originality or innovation; it does so through a kind of zombie stock-phrase selection. I am always astonished by those who claim that speech is evidence of consciousness, let alone a higher consciousness. Speech is mostly human twitter and bark, and sometimes merely the rustle of leaves.) In poetry, lineation, metre and the cultural frame of 'important speech' guarantee this slower delivery, and our sense of semantic unit is shifted back a little towards the word.

9 As I discussed in the first part of this essay, synecdoche is just a sub-type of metonymy. The application of 'synecdoche' in this context is especially loose, since the relational mapping is less 'part for whole' than 'representative member for set'.

10 Philip Larkin, 'Mr Bleaney', *Collected Poems*, ed. Anthony Thwaite (London: Faber & Faber, 2003).

stated, implied by the poem itself (often through the anchorage of
its title), or invoked for no other reason than *y* is 'in a poem'; or
it can – as in the case of our couple arguing over the biscuit – be
declared via the *fondement* or tonal context, which directs us far more
emphatically to 'the set of failing relations' than it does to, say, the
poem's being a political allegory. Things get a little shakier when we
say that Burns's 'To a Mouse' is 'about' one little life's helplessness
before capricious fate, which represents the helpless fate of *all* things;
or that Frost's 'Design' is a little godless scenario he presents as a tea-
spoonful of our whole godless universe. I mentioned that we read
our existential trope – the living experience of our senses – as either
metaphor or a metonym of the universal set, depending on whether
we regard our experience of things as 'symbolic' or partial. I suspect
that poets, being the designing gods of their little universes, think
they are creating things that are as much symbol as synecdoche – and
that readers are only too happy to help them. Symbols are inter-
domain,[11] and therefore create meaning – of which there is none
in the real universe, unless some conscious creature is projecting
it; perhaps symbols are better at creating a 'momentary stay against
confusion'. By contrast, a synecdoche may 'stand for' a larger set,
but technically it *contributes* no more order or sense to that set than it
already possesses: we would perhaps prefer to see the fate of Burns's
mouse as symbolising a larger domain, that fatal zone where 'The
best-laid schemes o' mice and men / gang aft agley' – one which will
'make sense of things', not merely enclose representative members

---

11   I have conveniently elided a fundamental distinction as if it was a passing detail:
the difference between a symbol where the V stands for a text-absent concrete
tenor, and where V stands for a text-absent abstraction. They are, as far as I can
tell, conflated in most analyses. However they are conceptually so different they
should not share the same name. We'll get to it, but for now: our ideas of concrete
things are also polyadic specific domains, composed of aspects and components and
connotations; abstractions, on the other hand, are monadic and belong only to the
domain of abstractions.

within a larger set.[12] Nonetheless, even when a poet has merely revealed that a scenario, event, or detail is a representative part of a larger enclosing whole, it can be just as 'meaningful' as any symbol, if the larger domain comes as a surprise. Indeed, 'what but design of darkness to appal?' – Frost asks, chillingly – *could* possibly explain the hellish conjunction of the white spider, white moth and white heal-all tableaux in 'Design'?[13] [For a discussion of this kind of 'reveal' in the context of experimentalism, see endnote 12.] But in terms of hard analysis, the relation that the poem has to either its enclosing set or its allegorical abstraction is *both* symbol and synecdoche, and likely to go duck-rabbit on anyone trying to pin it down, for reasons I'll unpack. (It's largely to do with symbol belonging to distinct trope-type, one which collapses the intra-domain and inter-domain functions.)

To summarise: while the poem works in much the same way as prose, evoking its reality-states through the usual showing-and-telling, it also invokes and/or symbolises a larger state by positioning itself as interpretable object. Much of this depends on its relationship to silence. Silence is a universal signifier: to invoke it or arrange it is to prepare for important news, for music, for contemplative space. A poem is in one sense just a codified pattern of silence: this silence is advertised most prominently by the white page ('white/empty field = silence' seems to be our instinctive synaesthetic mapping); created by lineation and stanza; imposed by the pattern of temporal pause that line and stanza both propose; invoked by the pointedly musical manipulation of word-sound (against which we are asked to hear the silence as physically contrastive, very much like the dark outlines Dutch painters put around figures to give them more prominence); and flagged up by the practices of rhetorical omission or elision

12   Robert Burns, 'To a Mouse', *Collected Poems of Robert Burns* (London: Wordsworth Poetry Library, 1994).

13   Robert Frost, 'Design', *The Collected Poems* (London: Vintage Classics, 2013).

that in normal speech we might label obscure, perverse or discontinuous.

This collusion of writerly and readerly intent means the text is transformed into what we might call a 'supercharged semic field', where the mere salience of a detail is enough to declare it symbolic (if we read it as inter-domain) or evidential (if we read it as intra-domain). Readers just assume that if something occupies the state of being-in-a-poem, it must *mean* something beyond its local sense: those are the terms of the contract. A poem is generally assumed to be an artifice that takes the form of an unusually unified, meaningful speech act, and a 'poetic reading' is the brain's attempt to resolve it as such through the formation of an enclosing thematic domain.[14] In short, the poem has two authors hell-bent on expressing themselves – the poet and the reader; between them, poems are doubly charged. If this is always borne in mind, many of poetry's more mysterious phenomena can be more easily explained.

14 With the usual qualifications: there are poetries and reading-conventions where 'unified statement' is not automatically assumed to be the poem's ambition. Horses for courses.

CONCRETE, ABSTRACT AND SYMBOL

That there is any need for a poet to blunder into one of the more vexed areas in the philosophy of language is moot, to say the least. There are many experts already at work in the field, and considerable literature has been generated on the subject since Frege charted its horrors and abysses. Nonetheless, this key issue – the use of abstract speech and the poem's relationship to abstraction – is rarely discussed, despite it lying behind several of our most widely circulated diktats, from the idiot war-cry of 'show not tell', to Pound's patently unhelpful remark in *A Few Don'ts* that the 'natural object is always the adequate symbol',[1] as well as a fundamental confusion over the nature of 'the symbol' more generally. As far as possible, I'll attempt to confine my remarks to that aspect of the problem most relevant to our own art. Nonetheless, the reader should be warned that the next fifty or so pages wander deep into a jagged and gloomy thicket, one I would suggest they spare themselves (I will propose a short-cut in a moment). Finding an adequate description of a mental process in non-neurological terms will always mean writing metaphorically; and adequate metaphors will vary, depending on what we require them to be adequate *to*. This is an issue that has already been tackled via different expert methodologies and jargons. The only justification I have for the amateur contribution of one more is that I have found these approaches inadequate to the description of the phenomenon of symbol *in poetry*, or in language which operates under the poetic function. However, I think there is a way in which the business of abstraction and 'the symbolic' can be

---

[1] Ezra Pound, 'A Few Don'ts by an Imagiste', *Modernism: An Anthology*, ed. Lawrence Rainey (London: Blackwell, 2005).

described in terms of conceptual domain, and made relevant to the poetic art.

The argument reaches the difficult conclusion that 'symbol' is a distinct trope-type which performs a kind of reflexive collapse of the inter- and intra-domain functions of metonym and metaphor. It is the primary trope of meaning-generation. Symbol has long been discussed as a sub-type of metaphor, but I believe this to be false. The 'abstract' is a domain wholly distinct in its composition and its procedures; 'symbol', which provides a non-literal means of linking the abstract and the concrete realms, is also a necessarily distinct procedure, as well as a solely human one. Nature 'does metaphor', and generates things which share motifs and attributes through which they are sometimes directly connected. Only humans make symbols.

The following five sections – 'Definitions', 'Type and token', 'Differences of domain, 'Hypostasis and hyperstasis' and 'Some examples of the use of abstraction' – can and probably should be skipped by readers more interested in my conclusions on the nature and role of symbol than in the repetitious and agonised means of my arrival at them. There is no way to make this stuff any fun. (I apologise especially for the frequent recapitulation of key points, but often they have to be held in mind before the argument can advance.) The section on 'Symbolicity' and those which follow it are more approachable, summarise the argument, and should be broadly comprehensible without these earlier remarks, though will make assertions that might seem indefensible; I would plead with any reader who finds them so to then skim these preceding notes.

Definitions

Intra-domain and inter-domain tropes operate across two conceptual magisteria, the 'concrete' and the 'abstract'. We generally use these terms to distinguish between a set of words which refer to the tangible, physical plane, and a set which refer to the conceptual plane.

This sounds like a clear enough distinction; would that it were so. The division between the abstract and concrete is less a clean border than a mile-wide no-man's-land in which has been sown the perfect mine-field – and there is, as yet, no real agreement as to how the distinction should be broached, let alone drawn. Marking out the epistemological or ontological division between the material and immaterial is a difficult enough exercise; 'thing' is already a tricky enough concept to nail down, but both 'process' and 'quality' seem to belong to and defy either category. All this is massively complicated by the introduction of linguistic reference, the words and speech we use to communicate these ideas and name these 'things'.

Linguistic reference is, if not arbitrary, a crowdsourced business, and recruits both material and immaterial 'things' to the immaterial realm of its own sign-system. [Boldly setting aside arguments over the ontological status of 'the word' itself. For further discussion, see endnote 13.] This has a dramatic consequence. Language's already 'abstract' status means that it finds it easy to blur, blend, shade and scale the distinction between abstract and concrete, rather than clarify it; moreover, it is strongly in its interests to do so, as language's purpose is not just to 'name objects' but to represent the vast range of our almost-ineffable sensory, emotional and intellectual experience. Certainly, poetry's *explicit* purpose is to do so, and for that reason – nowhere is it harder to track the status of the abstractum. Furthermore, I strongly sense that language *itself* introduces a category of second-tier abstraction which cannot really be said to exist in the world at all without the kind of conceptual definition and formation that only the act of linguistic reference can provide. (I am proceeding on the assumption that this thought is a cliché in professional circles, though I have not found it expressed in quite this way.)

Either way, one soon begins to wonder if the problem is in declaring 'abstract' and 'concrete' a useful division in the first place; yet we persist in believing it so. As I've mentioned, even the simple question of 'what is a material thing?' is far from settled. To take just one example from the endless cycle of definitions and refutations: 'An object is abstract if and only if it is non-spatial and causally inefficacious'.[2] But where does that leave the quale? Certainly – for all it might *summon* a sensory experience, or the memory of one – 'redness' can have no causal effect. But what about that utterly specific, reliably replicable feeling that comes over me every time I hear the opening bars of Busoni's *Berceuse Élégiaque*? Morbid, beautiful, nightmarish, ritualistic, almost monstrously sad, with the heavy, sodden air of one of Corot's more drab landscapes – it is, for me, very far from 'abstract', yet for all its tangible 'thingness' it can hardly be said to be capable of any 'causal effect'. Clearly it is not an 'object' I can drop on my foot, but it has all the sensory richness of a 'real' piece of woven silk; and as for causality – if I play it in the morning, my day will go very differently as a result; but this is because of its concomitant qualia, and doesn't reside in its physical manifestation as a series of frequencies that shake the air, or in the CD or streaming service producing them. Possibly we might one day be able to point to the physical 'existence' of my feeling in the replicable precision of its neural correlates, in a way that distinguishes it from such un-sensual abstractions as, say, 'the concept of litigation' – but that seems a hopeless distinction. Perhaps its being a self-declared 'unnamable' state beyond the apprehension of language, and therefore by definition beyond the scope of this discussion, lets it off the hook here; but somewhat ironically so, given poetry's job is to conjure just such inarticulable states with new combinations of words. Of course, even if we succeed in partly 'reifying' the state by naming or describing it, we still don't actually substantialise it. Yet we feel instinctively that many qualia are, or at least should be, part-way 'things'.

The concept of hyponym and hypernym reveals another problem with language and concreta: the extent to which naming is just a matter

2 *Stanford Encyclopedia of Philosophy*, http://plato.stanford.edu/entries/abstract-objects.

of contextual specificity. My shoes are at once 'clothing', 'shoes', 'sports footwear', 'New Balance trainers', 'grey New Balance trainers with green piping' and 'that pair of grey New Balance trainers with the green piping I got cheap at TK Maxx because no one else would go near them'. Each successive category, while serving as a plausible or contextually useful index to these very shoes, is nonetheless also an abstraction – even if the last, most detailed hyponym appears to draw a set round a single member. Yet we cannot accept even this last designation as the final, fixed and monadic term for my concrete boots, since the circumstances of their purchase could plausibly arise again (though heaven forfend). The gap can never be closed, and while I indisputably have real shoes – what can we *really* call them, without the use of a demonstrative pronoun? And then there's the matter of agreement: one man's trainers are another man's sneakers (indeed there was a time in Scotland where they would have been designated 'sannies', a contraction of 'sandshoes'); the set of what the Princeton Wordnet sensibly calls 'co-ordinate terms' – synonyms which report to the same hypernym, and so are gathered along the same paradigmatic axis of selection – can add considerable cultural and subjective distortion to the process.

Then there's the issue of those abstracta which seem to have a certain real-world 'solidity' because we intuit they are patently *there*, having always existed – and which we have merely discovered and named (π, the speed of light, or the number 6), as opposed to those which have only come about through human activity or arbitrary distinction (the set of Munros, the rules of poker, or the concept of 'governance').[3]

---

3 An unfortunate downside to language is its habit of economising on terms through its use of the same word in both the concrete and abstract realms. These homophones – far more often than they should in an allegedly rational species – generate much confusion and pointless argument. The 'administration' of a medicine is a rather different and far more concrete business than that of 'government administration', being more closely connected to its verb 'administer', from which 'government administration' has largely floated free. This is an easy example, but many other

In ontological, never mind logical terms, this hardly seems a trivial distinction. But even then . . . Are we correct to deny the concrete 'reality' of poker rules and Munros just because we 'made them up'? They seem to enjoy at least as much reality as the illocutionary act, where a 'blessing' or 'curse' are unthinkable without both real-world intent and possible consequence (I tend to think of poker rules and Munros as 'performative concepts'). If we cannot even make the very category of the abstract cohere, any attempt to draw a clear line between abstract and concrete is bound to fail.

Our own situation is compounded by poetic theory – inasmuch as it exists as a proper subject – being positioned at the juncture between linguistic and philosophical discourse. Their respective accounts of the abstract and concrete realms are far from a neat match. In *An Essay Concerning Human Understanding* we find Locke's famous

---

apparently identical words display far finer degrees of material or non-material reference, and we should remember to treat each one like a different note on the piano of language. This is no trivial matter: 'The War on Terror' justified its existence by deliberately confusing the concrete and abstract. By taking a metonym – the abstractum 'terror', as in 'the terror that results from acts of so-called terrorism' – and using it as concrete synonym *for* 'terrorism', our leaders substantialised and isolated an effect, and were able to pretend it was something capable of being located and targeted. The phrase holds out the promise that one day we could be safely 'unterrified' – while leaving any actual cause or real enemy conveniently indeterminate. (Poetry is always important in sloganeering: the 'Axis of Evil' won out over 'Hinge of Bad' only because of its intrinsic lyricism.)

Homophones will kill us. Every year I find myself sitting on panels discussing this, that or the next thing – and the discussion almost invariably founders on disagreements over the definition of terms, where the mere agreement to use different words to mean different things, rather than the same damn word for both, would satisfy everyone. The real mystery is why two people will remain irrationally attached to their own definition and continue to fight over it as if it actually mattered, even when they are in mutual agreement in every other regard. As usual, it comes down to a perverse attachment to the idea of intrinsicality; but words only mean what we collectively decide they mean. Peirce was complaining about all this 130 years ago, which would suggest we have absolutely no intention of addressing an issue which generates so much fun for us, albeit fun of the most stupid and dangerous kind.

clarification that 'it is plain, that General and Universal, belong not to the real existence of things; but are Inventions and Creatures of the Understanding, made by it for its own use, and concern only signs, whether Words or Ideas'.[4] That still seems fair enough. But to adduce the key complicating factor of reference itself: one of the most destabilising aspects of our current understanding of how language works is that it's partly the very *business* of naming that turns a concrete thing into a conceptually discrete entity – i.e. effectively a concept – through a process of semantic circumscription. It is not a matter of simple denotation, because denotation is no simple matter. All named concrete things are abstractions, in that they consist of little but a definitional border enclosing a domain, whose limits and content have been decided by human evolution, accident and cultural necessity. Remove those, remove us – and the line between thing and environment is less blurred than elided; in our absence, the clock radio, the stone, the window and the dog are all returned to a kind of Nirvana, to the definitionally indeterminate flow of phenomena. One can hardly cite 'physical reference to a thing' as the test for concreta if the idea of both 'thing' and 'reference' are themselves so deeply unstable.

I mention all this to justify the simplifications which follow – or at least to indicate that I am aware they are such. We should perhaps take the common-sense position that all we can know of words lies in the manner in which we use them, and what it is we're *actually* thinking about when we use them. Nothing is going on other than whatever is going on; but setting aside more sensible ideas of 'symbolic mentalese', many theorists continue to posit a whole realm of non-verbal transaction below the surface of speech – in the absence of much evidence from neurology, linguistics or subjective experience that it's taking place at all. Sometimes whatever *is* clearly going on is

4   John Locke, *An Essay Concerning Human Understanding* (London: Prometheus Books, 1995).

problematic enough. Words are not used singly, but in combination and in context, where they perform very different functions from the ones they might appear to when considered in isolation. In isolation, things like their abstract or concrete status might be breezily decided – but often speciously so (not least because the so-called 'use-mention distinction' is still patchily applied; there is a great difference between what we mean by a word in the flow of a sentence, and what we mean by it when we isolate it so we can discuss it as a pure signifier, i.e. when we make the word its own subject). The glue of syntax, collocative expression and the phonosemantic rule means that 'things' are represented, summoned or invoked in our speech by phrase and phraseme just as often as the are by discrete lexeme (much in the way that the metaphors we *actually* coin in poems are often complex, tonal, multisensory and dynamic, and quite unlike the pretty 'Juliet is the sun' textbook examples we love to cite for our easy analysis). Within the flow of speech, the 'thing' a lexeme appears to represent is often dismissed from the word completely, as its function or sense is rapidly renegotiated according to larger phrasal, thematic or pragmatic contexts.

No doubt the wiser alternative for this writer might have been to shut up about the problem entirely until the experts had finally picked the bones out of it. My hunch is that it is a subject best and perhaps solely approached through the technical language of conceptual semantics, a task for which I am exquisitely unqualified. However, we may yet be here some time, and in poetic practice and trope analysis, the division between concrete and abstract throws up some very odd and crucially important problems; to have failed to address them at all would have been straightforwardly remiss. (The matter also has deep, parallel connections to central issues in both lyric and metre: in lyric, the balancing of closed-vowel concrete contentual and open-vowel abstract functional language – and more generally the language of physical description, and that of thought – can have very considerable musical consequences; in metre, the distribution of stress according to strong contentual or weak functional position is central to the entire field of study.)

I will attempt to lay out my position, then examine how this affects our ideas of the 'abstract', the 'concrete' and the 'symbolic' in the analysis and generation of trope. Since we are here dealing with manipulations of language, I will take 'concrete' and 'abstract' to refer to the conceptual world of tangible things, and the conceptual world of ideas, types and qualities. Concrete terms have physical, real-world referents; abstract terms do not. However, all terms are, in a sense, 'abstract'. We simply cannot attempt the clean ontological division between the sets of concrete and abstract terms that we do between the outer physical and the inner mental universes. As will now be obvious, my own position is that 'physical real-world reference' is very much a disease of degree, and a business of mode and manner, but that so long as we are discussing a spoken language predicated on reference (as opposed to the purely symbolic language of algebra, say, where monadic signs can be juggled freely) *all* terms, no matter how 'abstract', are by definition meaningfully engaged in some form of real-world reference, no matter how obliquely, vestigially, or at however many removes.[5]

Type and token

Some writers continue to apply and extend Peirce's useful 'type–token distinction'; here, 'type' is the abstract concept and 'token' is the real-world instantiation of that concept – or, if you like, the means

---

5   Again, this is not to say I regard the concepts they enclose as having any real-world, a priori existence in and of themselves. Some readers will be aware that I have skirted all the metaphysical controversy over competing realist, nominalist and conceptualist approaches to universals (i.e. whether 'common qualities' can be said to exist at all). Let me come out quickly as a full-blown conceptualist, and say that, without denying external reality, nothing *meaningfully* exists except degrees, forms and manners of real-world reference – all of which takes place in the mind, which is a thing-creating, pink-noise filter for the near-white noise of external phenomena.

by which the concept can be bodied forth.[6] So the word 'train' in 'the train is no longer a truly viable form of transport in the US' or 'you should take the train' (as in 'travel by rail') is a 'type'; its 'token' would be the specific, real-world train as in 'Quick – get on the train before it leaves!' 'The thrush', in the sense of the species 'thrush', is the 'type' of which the *occurrence* of the individual thrush in your garden right now is the token. (To employ the old 'ness-ity-hood' rule, 'the thrush' in this type-sense assumes we have a coherent concept of thrush-ness, thrush-ity, thrush-hood.)

Terms that we might consider more straightforwardly abstract don't appear to operate in quite the same way. We sense instinctively that 'thrush-hood' and 'parameter' are not the same kinds of abstraction – yet both are resolutely 'concepts'; however, 'thrush-hood' is unthinkable without a concrete world to host it, while 'parameter' seems to belong to a category of pure concepts which can be invoked without *immediate* reference to that world.

I would contend, firstly, that the difference between abstract and concrete is not categorical but a disease of degree, a scalar, not a binary distinction. Secondly, while the class of abstract types (like 'the train') are unthinkable without reference to concrete *rei*, others (like 'mercy') belong to a class of reified concepts, i.e. words we have come to treat as standing for 'a thing in itself'. These abstracta, while *predicated* on the existence of real-world, exemplary tokens – can function largely (if never quite entirely) in their absence; and while they might seem to enclose particular examples, these concrete exempla are consciously generated *from* the abstractum itself, or consciously identified because they share the concept as an attribute. It's a two-way street: abstract types are perceived to work bottom-up, and arise from tokens; abstract concepts are perceived to work top-down, and generate exempla.

6   C. S. Peirce, *The Collected Papers of Charles Sanders Peirce*, vol. 2, ed. C. Hartshorne and P. Weiss (Cambridge, MA: Harvard University Press, 1958).

So, while we may consciously decide in our interrogation of the abstractum 'justice' that it can only be *truly* defined by reference to an illustrative token of a 'just act', and is otherwise meaningless – generally speaking (the qualification is advised), our *performance* of the word breezily refers to a consensually agreed and broadly reified concept of justice, and not to 'the sum of just acts', nor to 'the average just act', whatever cognitive or cultural background role these things may play in its 'definition'. By contrast, the abstract type 'the thrush' refers only to the concept of 'thrushness' insofar as it has been directly formed through the sum and the mean of its tokens. Asked to explain 'justice', we must seek to actively and consciously source 'illustrative just acts' from our knowledge of the world, since we sense the thing we call 'justice' *already* exists, much as the real thrush does; these acts are not immediately invoked by the term. Conversely, with the abstractum 'the thrush', the type is a posteriori, and its sense clearly and immediately dependent on and derived from the thrush-tokens of the physical world.

I suspect this is partly because we create and learn what we *now* regard as a priori, second-level abstracta (such as concepts of 'justice', 'mercy', 'metaphor', 'bliss', 'synthesis' and 'governance') less through reference to the real-world tokens than to first-level abstracta of a posteriori types. For example, we do not tend to learn the concepts of 'administration', 'synthesis' or 'justice' from being told about illustrative acts, but derive them either intuitively from context (we posit its likely sense in advance, and then seek contextual evidence for the accuracy of the supposition), or through meta-statements such as: 'Justice? Justice, son, is when someone has done something wrong, and they get a punishment of about the same size as the bad thing they've done.' Here, the terms 'someone', 'wrong', 'punishment', 'roughly', 'size' and so on are likely perceived as semi-concrete type-terms that are strongly predicated on – and will have been most likely learned from – real-world encounters that have their root in early embodied experience. The concept of 'wrong' is learned from a series of clearly identified 'wrong things' far more powerfully than the concept of 'justice' is from 'just things'. Of course, this does not mean that 'punishment', say, will not also be employed as a reified concept like 'justice', but it would have attained that second-level usage via a similar route, or have assumed it via an 'abstractum treadmill' of repeated invocation. One thinks of these terms in a fundamentally different way, but both senses – i.e. *type-* 'punishment' and abstract *concept-* 'punishment' – are retained in our speech. However, when this use of an abstractum attains the status of reified concept, it is effectively *monadic*. We can throw the word 'justice' around as freely as we do words 'pavement' or 'trousers'.

To reinforce an earlier point: there are performance conditions, among which poetry is prime, where the slow speed and deliberate care of speech-performance makes it difficult for any monadic or near-monadic term to remain so. Poetry tends to pull all language one ladder-rung closer to the world and its tangled bank of associations, and hence one rung further from the isolable purity of abstract concept; partly through its insistence on the physical performance of the sign in its lyric context, poetry increases both connotation and referentiality. Concrete terms increase in their connotative richness (the thrush – who will inevitably make her appearance as 'the bright thrush trilling in the twisted hawthorn', say – seems full of lyric, phonosemantic and etymological possibility). First-level 'type' abstractions are partly concretised (the type 'train' will appear to summon its corresponding token of the real 'train' more forcefully). Second-level monadic abstracta are somewhat re-reified, and returned to their first-level referential state: they seem to invoke far more actively the concrete exempla from which they culturally arose,[7] or on

---

7 And from which they borrowed an aspect or quality, as a cursory investigation of the etymology of the great majority of abstract words will prove: for example 'great' probably goes back to Old Teutonic root concerning 'coarsely ground grain', which lent its 'large' quality to the word – and is therefore cognate with 'groats'. Most

which their definition ultimately depends: the reified concept 'justice' usually has no need to define itself any more than does 'thrush'— but in its invocation, its slowed and deliberately relished delivery – 'Though Justice against Fate complain, / And plead the ancient rights in vain – / But those do hold or break / As men are strong or weak . . .'[8] – it suddenly *does* feel derived from or indicative of the sum of just acts, far more than it does in 'we all feel that justice has not been served by this poor decision'.

Furthermore, poetry's rhetorical invocations and shifting forms of address will deliberately *blur* the difference between type and token; look at the apostrophised 'train' here, which is surely both:

> . . . The reader,
> Middle-aged now and knowing in detail
> What a disappointment looks like,
> Glimpses the shape of a roof, a lit window,
> A branch line the train never follows
> Through those woods and consequences . . .
>
> (SEAN O'BRIEN, 'Something to Read on the Train')[9]

To a certain extent all that's happening is what we already know: poetry erodes the division between abstract and concrete by allowing words fuller associative resonance. Under the poetic function, a word is a physical event as well as a signifier; but *what* it signifies changes too, and we become partly aware – just as we do when we analyse or meditate upon words individually – that its referent is also a *domain*. When we say 'bedroom' in a sentence, we generally tend

---

abstract concepts are built on roots which once referred to physical actions: 'idea' goes back to 'sight', 'concept' to 'taking', 'metaphor' to 'carrying', and so on.

8 Andrew Marvell, 'An Horatian Ode Upon Cromwell's Return from Ireland', *The Broadview Anthology of British Literature*, 2nd edn (London: Broadview Press, 2010), 967–9.

9 Sean O'Brien, *Collected Poems* (London: Picador, 2012).

to mean something like its monosemic denotation; but when we place 'bedroom' in a poem, we can also invoke 'bedroom-domain' to a greater or lesser degree by activating its connotative potential via its relative salience. It's now the *idea* of 'bedroom' as well as the mere room. While poetry pulls its abstracta a little closer to the real world, all concreta in poems are, contrastively, both a little 'typified' and a little conceptualised, and in the process gain a touch of both the universal and the abstract.

On the other hand – within the poem we may, of course, also choose to freely toss around, say, 'mercy' with no merciful act in mind, 'tokenising' or otherwise: when Blake says 'To Mercy Pity Peace and Love, / All pray in their distress', one could argue that 'mercy' here, slung in as part of an itemised list, should just be read as no more or less than its monadic concept.[10] Significantly, when these words are used in combination with others, we will take the same approach as with any other concrete term, and parse it literally or metaphorically depending on context – or, if no sense-making context can be easily found (as is often the case in poetry), we will use the expression itself to conjure an accommodating domain. 'A merciful judge' is just that; 'the merciful rain', on the other hand, is not immediately intelligible and requires us to read for context, and then interrogate both 'rain' and 'merciful' a little harder for coherent sense – to reach, say, the idea of 'rain as a merciful agency', or 'a merciful agency who sends rain after a long drought', depending on what we can establish of the thematic domain. 'The merciful carpet' sounds a bit crazier, but one might explain it – after the back-formation of sympathetic context – as 'a carpet yielding comfort to one who is footsore'. This appears to be just the kind of thinking we would do faced with concrete near-nonsensicals: 'the mossed rain', 'the wind hopped away' and 'the sticky snow' are confusing phrases, but we resolve them in the same way, through allowing them to form meaningful compounds

10 William Blake, *Songs of Innocence and Experience* (London: Filiquarian, 2007).

that we then read within appropriately accommodating contexts – which themselves often have to be *actively* sought within, if not wholly projected into, the text. Alternatively, we allow them to pass as surrealism.

A note: most striking poetic originality depends on a degree of semantic disjunction. But while disjunctive, knight's-move concreta tend to create new, complex peristases or 'images' – 'a sky / Palely and flamily / Igniting its carbon monoxides' (Sylvia Plath, 'Poppies in October')[11] – parts of speech derived from most second-level abstract concepts tend to lead to the attribution of agency, because they refer to modes of being (e.g. 'a sky / Fretfully and abstractly / Igniting its carbon monoxides'). The semantically disjunctive or verifiably original combination of abstract and concrete in poetry is pretty much a one-way ticket to the pathetic fallacy. This lies, I think, behind the perennial suspicion that this kind of language is potentially sentimental, pretentious or lazy; to return to Pound's famous complaint over 'dim lands of peace': 'It dulls the image. It mixes an abstraction with the concrete. It comes from the writer's not realising that the natural object is always the adequate symbol.'[12] This is nonsense, of course – there is nothing wrong with mixing the abstract and the concrete, nor is there any independent class of 'natural object' (all objects *are* natural), and nor is there any absolute or consensual measure of 'adequacy'. The real problem is the phrase's banality, but perhaps more crucially the casual, sentimental attribution of peace-giving *intention* to the lands – though, of course, these things are a matter of taste. (The phrase is just rather 'poetic' peristasis: it might be thought of as the mere detachment of the word 'peace' from the literal image or phrase 'peaceful lands'. Indeed, some would identify the rhetorical effect as an example of antiptosis, a form of

---

11 Sylvia Plath, 'Poppies in October', *Collected Poems* (London: Faber & Faber, 1998).

12 Ezra Pound, 'A Few Don'ts by an Imagiste', *Modernism: An Anthology*, ed. Lawrence Rainey (London: Blackwell, 2005).

hendiadys — with 'peaceful lands' separated into two nouns, then joined by a conjunction; the next step towards 'metonymising' the phrase would be to say something like 'he travelled across the great peace'.) Contrast, for example, Shakespeare's 'Nor that full star that ushers in the even, / Doth half that glory to the sober west, / As those two mourning eyes become thy face' (Sonnet 132); while we register the pathetic fallacy, we don't feel that the west's alleged sobriety is necessarily a sentimental affectation.

So we reach a miserably if predictably relativistic conclusion: there is a flexible distance both between token and type, and between monadic abstractum and the exempla it might actively conjure; this will vary from one word to another. Additionally, this word-specific co-ordinate will *itself* change under different contexts and performance conditions, poetry being one of the most radical. No distinctions can be clearly drawn. To look at the issue from the other side: when we analyse them closely, we can barely credit concrete terms with doing more than enclosing a concept for the purpose of denotative reference; and even when we lift it from the most crazy, freewheeling work of critical theory, it is difficult to say that an abstract term is *ever* used in a way that seems entirely free of the shadow of its real-world exemplum, something kept 'in the back of the mind' as a kind of experiential guarantor of the term's potential hypostatization. (Can we really focus on the word 'incomprehension' in an analytical context *without* conjuring an actual act of incomprehension, however shadowy or vestigial?) But mostly we do *not* analyse. Written or spoken, we throw words away within the larger units of our phrasal sense-making, in which we are no more conscious of the exempla that might accompany 'justice', 'parameter' or 'situation' than we are of the larger domains we invoke every time we say 'horse', 'kitchen' or 'president'. However, the one performance condition where we consistently refuse to do this is poetry. Here, all words flourish under our close attention: all concreta are a little conceptualised (things are rarely invoked as 'merely themselves' in poems; they always have a self-important touch of the 'type' or symbol about them), while all conceptual abstracta seem sufficiently charged with enough intent to invoke or realise their exempla, even vestigially. In a sense, the use-mention distinction is elided: one might say that while other kinds of speech merely 'use' words, poetry both 'uses' them *and* 'mentions' them. As others have previously remarked, poetry is also 'about' its own language.

Differences of domain

In agreeing on our definitions of words, we determine not the distances between the set of their 'qualities', but between the 'things' they designate. As a by-product of this definitional project, concrete words often appear monadic too, and in our rapid performance we certainly appear to use them that way; but we know that they are not, and we invoke the aspects and attributes their polyadic domains enclose whenever we need to. To crudely simplify, we might think of the set of concrete things as a circle representing 'the supra-domain of the concrete', containing many smaller circles, some of which are proximate, and some of which overlap because they share associated terms. The set of abstract concepts, on the other hand, can be visualised as a circle containing many dots, some of which can be directly connected through their contiguity. Within the concrete set, terms can be both directly connected and overlapping in their domains, i.e. they can interact via both relation and correspondence; within the abstract set, terms can only relate.

We may say things like '"mercy" and "joy" both have positive connotations', but 'connotation' here is not used in the usual sense. We mean something more akin to 'association', i.e. that 'the ideas of "mercy" and "joy" are both close to the idea of "positivity"'. They have the relative *proximity* of this abstraction in common, but it does not form any 'ground' between them. Within the abstract domain, no metaphorical constructions are possible, because the entire abstract domain acts like a single grammatical qualifier of 'being'. One abstract term can only qualify another into greater conceptual precision; it may *appear* compound, but is the expression of a monadic concept for which no single term exists. It functions as a giant qualifier to the giant noun of the concrete, the *how* to the *what*, the mind's epistemology to the world's ontology. 'Being' is an infinitely malleable noun. [For a defence of the role of jargon in the verbal apprehension of the abstract, see endnote 14.]

By contrast, the concrete realm is full of things which talk to one another either via rule or correspondence. Furthermore, these polyadic domains can also contain both concrete and abstract terms (e.g. 'kitchen' may connote 'food', 'pots', 'welcome' and 'comfort'). By contrast, the abstract realm functions like a *single* conceptual domain, the axiomatic proof of this being that fact that *inter*-domain operations are almost logically impossible within it. 'Mercy is like scandal', for example, is a pretty meaningless mapping. This is not to say that those terms might not somehow find themselves connected in sense, but most semantically close abstractions – say 'mercy' and 'love', 'cessation' and 'termineity', 'spiritual transport' and 'ecstasy' – are felt to 'relate', I would suggest, far more than they are to 'correspond'. 'Mercy is like forgiveness' is close to tautology; even connected terms that are clearly related, but at a greater remove – say 'spiritual transport is like ecstasy' – seems a little redundant, since 'spiritual transport', like every other conceptual abstractum, is 'like' nothing but itself; indeed one approach is to treat an abstractum as a 'quale with a name'. If we wish to demonstrate that it is 'like' ecstasy, we either qualify it directly to make it a compound abstraction ('ecstatic transport'), derive the same token or close tokens of either 'type', or simply call it 'ecstasy' instead.

For our purposes, a more interesting business lies with substitutions between more distant terms – and I'd argue that while they may *feel* so, they cannot be metaphorical. If we take two abstracta which are far apart, say 'ecstasy is death' – we can only make sense of the statement by searching for common associated terms, not overlapping shared properties, since there are none, unless our metalepsis makes a detour through concrete token (e.g. death = lifeless state → post-coital state = orgasm → ecstasy) and chaining them via a sort of metalepsis, where a common near-synonym does the job of a 'ground' by substituting a connecting link: death = ultimate state = absolute state = ecstasy, or by making a compound idea of it: 'ecstatic death', or 'deathly ecstasy'. *Any* abstractum can plausibly qualify any other – partly because the absence of physical referents mean nothing is impossible, and partly because they are *already* connected through their single-domain status, and both words together merely qualify 'being'. This means that even in the absence of a mutually proximate term, a statement involving distant or apparently randomly chosen elements like 'mercy is like bewilderment' still allows us to entertain the idea via either 'bewildered mercy' or 'merciful bewilderment' – neither of which is a condition beyond imagining, given a sympathetic or enabling context. Ingenuity might, however, *discover* that connecting third term, or some other means of creating a metalepsis, e.g. 'mercy' → 'selfless act' → 'capricious act' → 'illogical act' → 'bewilderment', or 'bewilderment' → 'guilelessness' → 'innocence' → 'moral purity' → 'mercy', though these connecting terms could be intuitively 'sensed' as easily as they were articulated.

I appreciate that this idea might strike some readers as unconvincing, so forgive me for developing it a little. It seems reasonable to assume that in concrete domains, the connotative elements within the domain are not 'little domains themselves' but – through a cognitive economy and to avoid any infinite regress – attenuated points of almost pure conceptual denotation. 'Bedroom' may 'include' sleep / bed / illness / dark, but these terms are contextually constrained and generate no further associations themselves; they are for the most part barely activated in *most* performances of the word 'bedroom', and neither the richly associative concrete domains nor the multivalent abstracta they are when we encounter them alone, in circumstances which allow or encourage their connotations and relations to resonate freely, i.e. contemplated in isolation, placed under our deliberate analysis, or encountered in a poem. These connotations have been reduced to monadic reference; if they had not been, we might be driven mad by endlessly multiplying associations. This follows my formula that a well-formed enclosing domain always drastically attenuates and concentrates the connotative power of the elements it encloses; this gives them a neutral rule-based 'sense'. (If that domain is itself enclosed by another, the domain and its elements additionally have what we perceive as 'meaning'.) Similarly, the abstract domain, consisting as it does of *one* domain, is also just a collection of monadic points; however, while they are distinct, their mono-domain status means they are also highly multivalent. (In a sense, the only pure denotation that language actually *manages* is its abstracta; which, irony of ironies, turns out to be close to 'articulated qualia'.) When two of these abstract points are close in their sense, we gain a strong impression of redundancy or tautology when we yoke them together. When they are distant in sense, they can link in one of two ways. The first is via a mutually contiguous term, which functions as a two-way index. (*Not* as a ground: note 'mutually contiguous', not 'shared'.) As monadic points, neither abstractum can 'contain' the linking term, but finds itself proximate to it within the abstract domain. For the link to 'make sense', the term must be consciously derived. Contrast how connections between concreta often work: 'a cloud is like a ship' is a statement we might corroborate thoughtlessly, via the shared connotation of 'a thing's smooth passage through a medium'. On the other hand, while we might get 'ecstasy is like death' to make sense through the shared link of 'ultimate state', such a link would have to be more consciously sought out. (Hence my calling such links 'meta-leptic', i.e. functioning via a metonymic chain.) Also, they can link through a kind of miraculous direct combination, where they leap across semantic space – a luxury the components of any single, well-defined domain can enjoy. (To remind ourselves: consider the terms 'dessert' and 'table number' in the domain of 'restaurant'; a man in a tall white hat holds a panna cotta – forgive my predilection – out to the waiter, says the word 'Three!', and is immediately understood. Now imagine the same exchange at a football game or in an operating theatre, where the man's actions would swiftly be designated as 'lunatic'.) Two terms I have just randomly generated, 'dispositional justice' and 'derivational contingency' – unlike 'milk shoes' or the 'tree dog', which require accommodating contexts to make sense – are credible non-imaginative, non-surreal propositions; like 'blue bedroom' or 'wooden floor', their component terms appear to operate within the same generic domain. However, our unusual willingness to both seek 'accommodating context' and to connect concepts through metaleptic link in a *poetic* context goes some way to explaining why Chomsky's allegedly nonsensical 'Colourless green ideas sleep furiously' is perfectly easy to wrap your head round, if you read it as a line of poetry. (Indeed, anyone who understands poetic speech knows that only an excessively logical mind would *declare* it meaningless, or declare that a 'poetic' accommodation of the statement was by definition a trivial one.) Poetry's semantic field is primed with connective and connotative intent, as well being synaesthetically overwired.

There is a route from the concrete realm to the abstract which links them directly: the abstract modifies states of being, and surrounds the concrete like a rarefied cloud of potential qualification; however, the only way an abstract concept can link to the concrete is via an 'imaginative leap', i.e. through some process of metaphorical correspondence. If I might quickly recap: unlike concrete words, abstract concepts do not designate domains, but monadic, semantically irreducible ideas, types and qualities. A conceptual abstractum doesn't have anything 'inside' it to form a correspondence or a ground with another abstract term. 'Mercy' does not connect to 'justice' through a 'shared aspect'. Abstracta relate to other abstracta through direct or indirect link, based on their relative semantic proximity or distance; if abstract subjects relate to concreta, it is via an inter-domain operation whereby the concretum is seen as a *token* of the abstractum's type, or as an exemplum produced to show how it embodies or exhibits its quality; or else the abstractum is linked to the concretum via a 'hinging' contiguous term or terms drawn from the abstract domain. ('Fiery passion' makes sense because 'passion' is directly linked to 'ardent' and 'impetuous', etc. – qualities to be found within the domain of 'fire', and with which it can therefore intersect. This does not make 'fire' a *symbol* of 'passion' in this construction; symbol requires a text-absent 'animus'. It's a mere unit metaphor.) Concreta relate to other concreta through both direct relation and correspondence; if a concrete subject relates to an abstractum, it is via an *intra*-domain operation which declares it an aspect or connotation of its domain, or encloses the abstract term within its own domain via a metaleptically linking term, closer to its denotative centre.

There is little difference in the way that concretum connects to abstractum or vice versa, except in the subtle shift of trope-type that occurs when one or the other is perceived to form the subject or the dominant frame.[13] Abstract terms qualified by distant (i.e. non-token/non-exemplum) concrete terms (e.g. 'lavender compassion') are intra-domain metaphors, and connected via an abstract term or terms contiguous to the abstractum which then *overlap* with a term found within the concrete domain, producing a ground. In the previous example, we might think of something like 'compassion'→ 'sweetness of disposition' → 'sweetness in general' ∩ ['sweetness' → 'fragrance']'lavender'. Formally, 'fiery passion' is identical to 'milky passion', or 'the passion of oatmeal', or a 'passion like a USB adaptor' – the only difference is the size of the tension. In such constructions, the metaleptic chain will have to be longer to find a common term within the domain of the concrete vehicle. In the last example we

---

13   In an isologic relationship – e.g. where both 'ice' and 'indifference' occur in a text in a salient but unconnected way – the trope is *both* intra- and inter-domain. (It is, actually, a form of animus-present symbol, and has 'meaningful intent'.)

might think something like 'passion' → 'energy'→ 'speed' ∩ ['speedy connection'] 'USB adaptor'. (I think we can all agree that I don't know how to write set algebra; this is my own shorthand. The square brackets enclose proximate attributes within the conceptual domain; as for the intersection ∩, while the abstract domain can qualify the concrete — it is primarily concerned with modality, with 'ways of being' — the concrete can only qualify the abstract indirectly, by crossing domains. Concrete domains can contain abstract terms, but monadic abstract concepts are never themselves directly contiguous with concrete terms. They can, however, form a ground through an overlap between their generic domain and the specific concrete domain, via a metaleptic chain directed by the specific abstractum, as above. [14])

If we look at a randomly chosen example of a disjunctive pairing, we see that there is only as a slightly greater glitch in the difference between resolving, say, the 'meaningless' phrases 'lustful glass' (a peristasis) and 'glass lust' (a metaphor). (These glitches I can almost distinguish by their particular shade of cognitive dissonance: I respond to the former phrase with a sceptical '*OK* . . .', and to the latter with more of a 'You *huh?*') In 'lustful glass' the quality must be metaleptically recruited to 'glass-domain' via a term closer to the denotative centre. Glass is generally thought of as 'breakable', so conceivably the elided terms could be 'lustful (emotionally unstable → fragile → frangible) glass'; or else it could be a means through which we behold things, so the chain might run 'lustful (desirous → acquisitive → all-containing → full-of-the-world) glass'. (Or else, stumped, we may posit a missing tenor and read the phrase as an enigma; but this would still entail identifying

14 Be reassured that I am at least as exasperated as the reader by my attempt to consciously explicate processes that are solved 'intuitively' by all readers of poetry. However, employing 'intuition' as a proper explanation is just a logical fallacy, and elides what I believe to be a consistent process. The actual value of this explication is, of course, another matter.

the source of 'lustful' from context, as the polysemy of the phrase would have to be narrowed for the game to be worth playing.) Actual poetic context invariably makes the analysis more complex: let's say the 'lustful glass' describes the bedroom window of a honeymooning couple; we then read 'lustful' as a transferred epithet, indicating 'the glass is in some way like a honeymooning couple'. However 'lustful glass' is still just a peristatic phrase that must be resolved *within* that metaphor, not the metaphor itself; we still need to figure out what the hell it means. Perhaps the glass is 'beholding the dawn, the whole new day ahead' with an acquisitive desire equivalent to that of the couple, etc. (The rule is that 'peristases can always expand to literal sense'.) We still have to resolve the sense of 'lustful' via exactly the same kind of metaleptic chain to have it link with 'glass-domain'.

In the case of the metaphor 'glass lust' (assuming we are not talking about such trivial elisions as 'a lust for glassware'), the conceptual domain of glass must be connected to the subject 'lust' *via* a shared lust-contiguous term, not linked *by* one. So we join them by experimenting with terms which could constitute a *ground* between glass-domain and abstract-domain lust-node: we might decide, perhaps, that 'glass' [friability → fragility] ∩ fragility → form of unstable emotion → 'lust'.

So how do these pointlessly nice distinctions apply to poetic trope? We can, I believe, take away some simple and useful rules here. While conceptual mapping between concrete terms is fairly straightforward, and formally reversible ('the sea' can be mapped onto 'the wheatfield' and vice versa, via the 'hinge' of the shared attribute 'water-carrying'), relationships between the concrete and abstract realms are one-way affairs; this is down to the single-domain status of the abstract realm. If we take the concretum 'a game of pool' and the abstractum 'karma', if feels that to say 'a game of pool is like karma' is very similar to saying 'karma is like a game of pool'. But the first is intra-domain (pool-domain has a 'karmic aspect' to it, being all about the knock-on consequences of one's own actions) and the second is inter-domain (pool is an *example* of something that has karma-like consequences, since exempla are a kind of top-down 'generated tokens', and are not 'connoted'). 'Karma' can be joined with 'a game of pool' and vice versa; but when we switch the dominant subject, it proposes a different conceptual operation. 'Perfect storm' is a mere peristasis (though I believe all abstract qualifiers carry a hint of pathetic fallacy), 'stormy perfection' a metaphor. The conceptual *directly* qualifies the concrete domain; the concrete *metaphorically* qualifies the conceptual domain. To take a nonsensical, where we can often sense these things more easily: an 'idea-like carpet' is a possible if implausible compound, and thus must be resolved as an intra-domain peristasis; and even without understanding it, we can see that a 'carpet-like idea' is inter-domain, and appears to present some kind of unit metaphor.

For this reason, an abstract attribute of a concrete thing can substitute for it in a standard metonymy – e.g. 'he lit a brilliance (instead of 'fire') in the grate'; or it can be represented by a more *distant* abstract quality, via a metaleptic link of its own. When we call fire 'passionate', 'crazy', or even 'merciful' (in the accommodating *fondement*, say, of 'purgatorial fire'), we are replacing the fire-domain attributes 'hot', 'unpredictable' and 'cleansing' with contiguous qualities – but *not* 'corresponding' ones. Extreme metalepsis sometimes looks and even feels as if a domain has been jumped; but it's a different cognitive operation, and is a form of extended metonym, because it's ultimately just derived from a peristasis. By contrast, an abstract quality can't be metonymically replaced by a concrete attribute, because the former is monadic, and therefore has no attributes. If an abstract quality is represented by a concrete thing – e.g. 'when he saw her, a great fire [i.e. 'a passion', derived from 'passion is like fire'] rose in him' – the relation is by definition inter-domain; the plainly figurative *concretum* 'fire' now symbolises the quality 'desire'. 'Fire' has been produced as an exemplum, a token of passion: within the abstract domain, the quality 'desire' is contiguous to the ideas of 'heat', 'agitation', 'self-consumption' and so on, all of which are aspects readily located within the domain of 'fire', providing an easy correspondence between the two domains. However, a trope is only 'symbol' if the abstract quality is text-absent.

Hypostasis and hyperstasis

I don't know if it's worth coining distinct names for these substitutive operations, but if you'll play along: *hypostasis* is a kind of metaphor where a concrete thing stands for an abstract quality, and basically a type of 'symbol'. If we take 'morning' for 'hope': 'something rose in his soul like a new morning'; 'this model represents the dawn of a new era in robotics'. *Hyperstasis* is a kind of metonym where a relational abstract quality stands for a concrete thing ('hope' for 'morning' – 'he arose and drew the curtains on the brilliant hope', or to give its full peristatic form, 'the morning arose like a great hope' – which only *sounds* like a simile (this kind of trope is distinguished by its conjunctions having atypical senses – effectively, by enallage or anthimeria); the trope here is not a metaphor 'morning is like hope', but the metonym 'hope' can be an aspect of morning (which like other forms of 'commencement', is associated with 'anticipation', which is close to 'hope'). Of course, we are barely aware of thinking any such thing: contiguous links between monadic points in the abstract domain need not be articulated, and perhaps not even consciously felt; we zip between them as quickly as our neurons and axons will allow. (I have the strong sense that this may be a huge cognitive advantage of monadicity; any domain can be reduced to a mere neural node, and employed as a stepping-stone in the hopping-race between one disparate concept and another.)

Note, however, that 'relational link' is not as clean an idea when we discuss abstract connotations of concrete domains; as I've said, it is perhaps just a little harder to *articulate* what connects 'dawn' and 'hope' than it is 'dawn' and 'commencement', but we can cheerfully hold such uncontroversial and directly linked qualities (i.e. 'commence-ment' → 'hope') within the 'secondary connotations' of a *concrete* domain, and see that they overlap with the abstract concept, or some quality contiguous to it (e.g. the abstractum 'wish' in 'he opened the curtains and beheld the wish of the day' might be resolved as 'hope' → 'wish'). 'He opened the curtains and beheld the crossed fingers of the day' shows how quickly the brain can derive a tropic equation to explain a substitution ('crossed fingers' for 'dawn') via a complex chain of metalepsis and inter-domain connection, here, something like: C 'dawn' ['commencement → 'hope'] ∩ A ['hope' → 'wish'] ∩ C (the hypostatic exemplum of 'wish') 'crossed fingers'. Complex tropes which mix abstract and concrete — whichever way round they run — often involve an element of *both* correspondence and relation, since the chain of substitution that produces the trope is often both metaleptic *and* symbolic, as well as bidirectional. All of this is directed and made vastly more efficient by a shaping, rule-defined context or thematic domain, which often provides a ready-made watercourse for such thought. (Again, I know common sense tells us we often resolve such tropes by 'fuzzy intuition', and that certainly accords with our conscious experience; but this cannot explain the decent sense we make of them.) It amounts to another way that language is rendered far more fluid under poetic conditions.

As previously stated, when a concrete thing links to an abstraction, in a sense it simultaneously connects to the *entire* abstract domain. The abstract domain cannot subdivide to form mutually exclusive subdomains in the way the realm of tangible things can; but the feel of some intra-domain abstract-concrete tropes with concrete subjects may *feel* very metaphor-like indeed. I'll now subject a poetic example to an excessive degree of scrutiny, and take Alice Oswald's line in which we meet 'a little random man, with his head in a bad / controversy of midges'. In the peristasis 'controversy of midges',[15] the abstract term 'controversy' is again at the end of a metaleptic

15 Alice Oswald, 'Bike Ride on a Roman Road', *The Thing in the Gap Stone Stile* (London: Faber & Faber, 2010).

chain of connotations, i.e. a series of intra-domain, contextually con-
strained, direct connections extended within the domain of 'midges'.
To take all the fun out of it: were one to *articulate* the intuitive
solving process our neurons execute on encountering this line, the
chain of contiguous terms might go something like 'controversy' →
'confused and fractious exchange' → 'a confusion of non-cooperating
independent agents' (encouraged by the contextualising proximity of
'random', and the word's own etymology, if known, i.e. 'a turning
against') → 'blurred commotion' (aha!) → 'midge-cloud'→ 'midges'.
Though everyone will have their own zippy way of getting there, this
perversity illustrates my earlier point that we might better think of
many concepts as 'articulated qualia': we *may* articulate them, but
such an act implies neither an articulable domain of attributes (the
problem with monadicity) nor a consensually agreed metaleptic
chain. Left blissfully unanalysed (*please, can we*, the poem seems to
beg), Oswald's use of the word 'controversy' is essentially a kind of
tonal, pathemic, 'qualial' modifier, which is how most critics would
probably discuss it. However, when the phrase is *considered*, our solving
process for it turns out to be far more than mere 'fuzzy intuition';
bear in mind, though, that poetic analysis of this sort can quickly turn
into a long-form essay on the dangers of ignoring the use-mention
distinction. (As a sidenote, one cannot stress enough the importance
of iconicity and the lyric weave in lending the illusion of symmetry,
plausibility and integrity to these more outlandish tropes.) But most
importantly – 'controversy of midges' is a startlingly original phrase,
and such abstract-concrete compound peristases are *far* too rarely seen;
as usual, we tend to think of the category of peristasis, that of 'literary
detail', as too-coincident with the visual 'image' – and unconsciously
rule out the possibility of such rich compound descriptions. (One
reason Oswald *is* such a fine poet is that she refuses to be bound by
such conventions.) Yet the tonal, conceptual and emotional are also
fair game for any conceptual domain, and I for one – Pound be damned
– would like to see fewer lambent or nacreous or high-sailed or slow-

moving or rain-freighted clouds, and a lot more perceptive, wealthy, amnesiac, astonished or indeed merciful ones, if only for the change.

As metaphorical as 'controversy of midges' sounds and feels, then, it's an intra-domain operation, and just a peristasis – albeit a highly original one. The poet is less comparing the midges to a controversy than saying that they posses the *quality* of controversy. We cannot say midges are 'like' controversy, since controversy cannot be 'like' any-thing, as abstractions have no qualities; but controversy is directly related to ideas that fall within the domain of midges. (Even if the midge-cloud were referred to *only* as 'a controversy' – e.g. 'a con-troversy buzzed around his head' – we would have a hyperstasis, i.e. a form of metonymy; however, the longer the metaleptic chain, the more indirect the route between the two terms; and the more indirect the connection, the more we will *perceive* it as metaphor-*like*, since 'gap and leap' is a feeling we associate with the inter-domain operation.) As discussed, when we say 'midges are like controversy' we are not using 'like' in the usual simple comparative sense, the one we use to indicate an inter-domain trope. We are aware of a glitch, a lacuna, a disjunction – because we know ourselves to be saying either 'midges have the quality of (something a few direct removes from) controversy' – or we are *indeed* using a kind of elliptical or enthymematic metaphor, and intend 'in this context, tenor-midges are like (a text-absent concrete vehicle that shares the quality of) controversy', i.e. the phrase is a hendiadic way of putting 'controversial midges', where 'controversial' is an epithet transferred from thematic context, or some other nearby concrete domain. (Here, the hinging ground-quality 'controversy' would, of course, still have to be metaleptically sought within the domain of 'midges'.)[16]

---

16 Shakespeare was very breezy about this sort of thing, and often regarded grammatical convention as an irritant that constrained the full expressive charge of a word. Insofar as they are amenable to analysis, this is pretty much the only sense (other than the subjectively associative or the clearly intertextual) that we can

bring to bear on the tropes of much postmodern verse, i.e. we can only posit either complex intra-domain metalepses, or enthymematic or lacunal metaphor:

> Partition blurred caloric engine his spiral transfusion
> playful to flex, inherent tuneful quantity. Both recessive
> to malabsorb, lapse of thought. Neither remembered this,
> neck flushed allumette profusion, caressment. Up through
> by a turn in apical thrill conveyed to famish, ingenious
> breast cured to breathe. [. . .]
>
> – J. H. Prynne, 'Blue Sides at Rest', *Poems*
> (Newcastle upon Tyne: Bloodaxe, 2005)

– though one feels one has laid the dining table with dental equipment. (Poetry written in this mode, incidentally, is frequently distinguished by its deliberate fusing of the abstract and concrete into a single word-hoard.) If it such poetry is to be enjoyed, it clearly must be 'by other means', and indeed Prynne himself has boldly suggested as much – another reason he should command our respect. Fine by me; but the fact that such techniques casually introduce massive semantic instability can only be dismissed by someone for whom 'meaning' is straightforwardly secondary to 'feeling', i.e. the effects induced by the peculiar scented candle such a poem lights in the room. For all the interesting 'research' one might conduct into the mass of index and intertext that composes such a poem, there is surely a limit to how much active 'thinking' one can do in the various cul-de-sacs and dark vennels that boldly diverge from 'the arduous royal road' to poetic meaning that Prynne has publicly abjured. However, the frequent claim that these poems are '*about* meaning more than they *possess* meaning' is about as disingenuous as our late Romantic critic gets, and I will leave the reader to pursue the circular meaninglessness of this formulation at their reflective leisure. Such remarks usually indicate the presence of a cult. Indeed the situation vis-à-vis the avant-garde and the question of 'meaning' is startlingly similar to that of the Gaelic Revivalists in Flann O'Brien's *An Béal Bocht*, where the elected President of a Gaelic *feis* addresses the crowd thus:

> If we're truly Gaelic, we must constantly discuss the question of the
> Gaelic revival and the question of Gaelicism. There is no use in having
> Gaelic, if we converse in it on non-Gaelic topics. He who speaks Gaelic
> but fails to discuss the language question is not truly Gaelic in his heart;
> such conduct is of no benefit to Gaelicism because he only jeers at Gaelic
> and reviles the Gaels. There is nothing in this life so nice and so Gaelic as
> truly true Gaelic Gaels who speak in true Gaelic Gaelic about the truly
> Gaelic language.
>
> – Flann O'Brien, *An Béal Bocht*, trans. Patrick C. Power
> (London: Grafton, 1973)

This assumes that we take 'midges' to be the subject in 'controversy of midges'. If we instead take 'controversy' to be the ruling subject, things change. The grammar of 'controversy of midges' pretty much prevents us from doing so (unless the 'midges' are clearly metaphorical); but if somehow 'controversy' is text-absent but yet forcefully *implied* by the usual means (salience, careful peristasis, thematic domain, title, etc.), we will read 'midges', whether presented literally or figuratively, as an inter-domain symbol.[17] Abstractions may have no qualities, but in symbolic constructions, their contiguous links to other abstractions function as the *equivalent* of a domain with which the concrete domain can intersect. The specific terms whereby they *do* intersect form a kind of ground.

It is *not* always clear whether the abstraction or the concrete detail forms the dominant frame; note that the trope is very different, depending on which the reader decides it to be. To look again at a substitutive operation: when 'honey' becomes 'sweetness' (as in the hyperstasis 'he spread the dark sweetness on his toast') it's intra-domain, because 'sweetness' is an attribute of honey. But when 'sweetness' becomes 'honey' (as in the symbol or hypostasis 'I love you, honey,' or the more literal 'We need to put some honey in the mix here' — uttered, say, by a studio engineer looking to add some pleasant sounds to an austere piece of techno) it's inter-domain, because 'honey' is not an attribute or aspect or relational property of sweetness, but something which possesses, embodies or symbolises it strongly enough for us to then see that property as a shared ground with the real subject (in the

---

17 E.g. 'The news of his betrayal had been broken to the press. Reading the papers that morning, he felt his head was in an angry cloud of midges,' or suchlike. When vehicles are literal details, the trope could be mistaken for one of isologue: 'The news of his betrayal had broken. By late afternoon he had read every furious leader and op-ed. He went for a walk. It felt somehow appropriate that he immediately found himself in an angry cloud of midges.' However, in this case the reader will sense that 'midges' and 'controversy' are *not* equal; 'controversy' is the ruling subject, and 'midges' a symbolic hypostasis, even though it occurs within the 'literal frame'.

above examples, one's beloved, or the engineer's 'ear-candy'). Or, in the absence of a tenor ('let us consider the innate quality of *honey* in the human soul'; here we intend the quality of 'sweetness', as in 'kind disposition') we recognise the abstraction as the tenor or subject itself, as is the case with the symbol. If we represent any abstractum by a concrete term, we are – by definition – *always* creating what we call 'a symbol', even when that symbol is couched within a further enclosing metaphor.[18] 'What is substituting for what, here?' is by no means always straightforwardly answered, but once we have *decided* on an answer we parse the phrase accordingly.[19]

To take a less cliché-bound example, a sugar-lover saying 'I don't want any of this fake sweetness!' when refusing saccharine is obviously using a simple metonym or hyperstasis. But suppose you heard someone call their insincerely charming boyfriend by the significantly salient nickname 'aspartame': you might understand the nickname by allowing context and logic to guide you the solution that while 'aspartame' likely symbolised 'fake sweetness', the aspartame-property 'fake sweetness' was furthermore the ground of a metaphor. We would then resolve the phrase by understanding an enclosing trope, where 'tenor-boyfriend' and 'vehicle-aspartame' share the ground 'fake sweetness', just as we understand 'Honey, I'm home' to refer to a substance and a person who share a sweet aspect. The

18 However, we need to be careful, especially over the business of literality. Imagine a cooking competition: the judge eats a piece of cake, and says 'you need some more honey in there', by which they seem to mean the quality of 'sweetness'. 'Honey' might then appear to substitute hypostatically for 'sweetness', making it a symbol; but the intention might actually be 'another physical ingredient which possesses the literal quality of sweetness, such as honey does'. 'Sweetness' is then only the ground of an inter-domain substitution (tenor = unnamed sweet ingredient, vehicle = honey), one which takes place solely on the concrete side of the equation.

19 When we suddenly perceive an element as text-absent we almost always assume it's constructing the dominant frame. This sounds axiomatic, but it's really a deeply rooted cultural metaphor, and I would guess most likely the consequence of our longstanding human assumption of an absent, invisible and yet all-powerful god.

difference is that the 'aspartame' example is 'poetic' on account of its originality and unfamiliarity, meaning there is a further step to complete where we must additionally decide *what* it is that the concrete vehicle is a symbol of.

So, one last time: whether we characterise a concrete-abstract trope as inter- or intra-domain is dependent on which element is regarded as the primary subject, and forms the ruling frame. This is often (though not always) a matter of what we take to be 'the real or the literal subject'.[20] A final example: 'apple', in the specific domain

---

20 I will explain the point more fully in due course, but it should be borne in mind that deixis in literature is not just a matter of location, tense and pronominal address. It also has a component of 'literality'. This is not a distinction we need to make in our daily lives, but in the merely *depicted* realities of literature it *must* be made, and the non-literal or the figurative very carefully indicated. It's instructive to look at the standard tropes that movies have developed to accomplish this: the protagonist will look up, or stare into the middle distance, and the frame will start to undulate to indicate the onset of the 'dream-sequence'; or there will be a wipe or dissolve into a scene whose 'unreality' is signed by its soft-focus, tilt-shift focus, slow motion, or surreal or improbable content.

A proper discussion of deixis would require another book, but my own take on it is basically a version of the analytical approach known as 'deictic shift theory'. I think the mind forms a fixed point-of-view (POV) locus, or origo, within a kind of deictic phase-space, derived from locational, temporal, personal and representational cues in the text. (In poetry, this last category is broadly consubstantial with that of 'the metapoetic', and subsumes indices of 'literality and non-literality', being analogues of 'the real and the imagined'.) It can then shift this single complex co-ordinate *relative* to this fixed point – changing, perhaps, location, tense, address, 'reality', etc. – *unless* the cues are strong enough, or sufficiently numerous, to indicate the permanent relocation of this deictic centre itself. Consider the difference between a movie which jumps ahead ten years in the narrative, and continues it in another country – and then *stays* there, against one in which we merely see a 'flash-forward' to that time ten years hence, which we watch with the expectation we will soon be returned to the origo of our old 'present'. Or a movie that suddenly does not follow the actions of our lead protagonist, but cuts instead those of a supporting character. Again, the expectation is that this second story will be revealed as little more than a narrative aside – but if after fifteen minutes we did *not* return to our hero's tale, our origo would then be shifted permanently. Deixis in literature operates in a more or less identical fashion.

of biblical context, has the connotation 'original sin'; so a Southern
Baptist holding up an apple in church and crying *sin*! is using metonymy
from the apple's perspective – and so it's a trope of relation, or hyper-
stasis; but seen from the *sin's* viewpoint, the apple is a poetic symbol,
a hypostasis, and a trope of correspondence. Whenever we feel the
abstract concept is the framing subject, the result is metaphor; if
we feel the concrete thing is the dominant subject, it's a peristasis.
If the concretum or abstractum is merely implied and text-absent,
we invariably assume it to be the dominant frame. (In 'she munched
the green sin', 'sin' is still just a metonymic contraction of 'sinful
apple';[21] in 'Eve munched ominously on the green apple' we have a
symbol for 'sin'.)

However, all this points to a persistent, fundamental and un-
addressed confusion: when a detail is text-literal, we cannot always
decide if it is symbolic *of* a larger subject, or whether that 'larger
subject' is a mere intra-domain connotation. To return to our honey:
let me posit another lousy imaginary poem. The poem is set after a
civil war has ended; a thaw is depicted between family members who
previously had found themselves on opposite sides. Things are tense,
however. There was also rationing, but this has now been relaxed, and
the mother is making toast for her two still-bitterly divided sons, and
spreading it thickly with honey. Now we are clearly meant to derive,
among other things, the connotation 'sweetness' here (remembering
that peristases can also carry undeclared connotations heavily implied
by context). But we may also now decide, given the emerging rules
of the thematic domain, and our desire – this is a poem, after all
– to *create* such a theme, and that perhaps '*honey*' invokes the larger

---

21 Which is itself a metonymic contraction of 'apple which in its irresistible
temptation caused the knowledge of good and evil, which constituted – within the
specific domain of God's law – a sinful act'. I expand the term just to make the point
that 'a culture elides its common knowledge'. Its tendency to do so often leaves that
knowledge conveniently unchallenged.

domain of sweetness, a sweetening of atmosphere, a détente, and all that. So 'honey' flips in function between the peristasis of 'sweetness-connoting honey' and 'honey as a means of symbolising the theme of sweetness'. (I will soon be throwing around the the symbol-specific terms 'totem' and 'animus', explained in due course.)

Symbolicity in literature is achieved by switching a trope from intra- to inter-domain, by mentally upgrading an abstract connotation of a concrete subject to the status of *an absent and ruling theme*, while changing the role of the original subject to that of the symbolising term. Symbol is *both* intra- and intra-domain, a kind of 'connoted theme'. In a poem, we have to decide whether that skull on the kitchen table merely connotes 'death', or *represents* 'death'; if the former, the deathly skull is a peristasis (whether we name the deathly connotation or not); if the latter, the skull is a symbol, and 'death' is a thematic subject – which will then have some degree of influence over the whole poem, and everything in it.

Some examples of the use of abstraction

Before we turn to the trope of symbol, let's look at a couple of real-world examples:

> The gill net of history will pluck us soon enough
>> From the cold waters of self-contentment we drift in
> One by one
>> into its suffocating light and air.
>>>> (CHARLES WRIGHT, 'Chickamauga')[22]

Here, 'the cold waters of self-contentment' has an abstract subject, but even though it's not so obviously inter-domain a construction as, say, 'he stared into the cold waters of his vodka glass', a metaphor

22 Charles Wright, *Chickamauga* (New York: Farrar, Straus & Giroux, 1996).

it nonetheless is. If 'self-contentment is cold waters' is to make sense as a metaphor, there must be a perceived overlap between the connotations included in the domain of 'cold waters' and the terms directly related to 'self-contentment'. Note that if the phrase had read 'the self-contented cold waters', the trope is now clearly *intra*-domain, with 'self-contented' merely an obscure but literal qualifier: for all its strangeness and anthropomorphism, it's as much a peristasis as 'the blue and cold waters'.[23] In real-life poetry, the difference between the intra- and the inter-domain in concrete-abstract tropes depends on whether the text presents us with an abstract-subject metaphor or a concrete-subject peristasis. Regardless of which it is, of far more importance is that pleasurable lacuna of understanding that opens up in such difficult phrases; this is our 'controversy of midges' all over again, and we sense we are saying 'cold waters have this quality of self-contentment via unspoken intermediary terms'. This type of trope is a minor stock-in-trade of most modernist and neo-modernist practice, and for me, one of its most attractive, boldly 'poetic', anti-Poundian aspects. Sensibly, no one bothers to analyse it much, and certainly not in the miserably boring way I've just outlined: critics prefer to wing it or 'vibe' it as much as readers do, and will ascribe its success or failure to vague tonal consonances or dissonances. But all language provokes thought, and while that thought is not obliged to articulate itself, we should avoid getting all mystical about it just to duck a conversation. My analysis just suggests a way we might describe the unconscious or intuitive process whereby such tropes will be found satisfying or wanting. (For the record, I find those 'cold waters', in Wright's larger allegorical space, both convincing and finely nuanced.)

23   . . . Even though it *appears* to ascribe a figurative quality to a real thing. The question of whether the pathetic fallacy is really metaphorical is a philosophical one: the ascription of practically *any* quality to anything, however apparently neutral, is arguably 'anthropomorphic', which as a conceptual domain shades seamlessly into the anthropocentric. 'A small animal' doesn't think of itself as small any more than you think of yourself as big, and 'a small chair' even less so.

Some writers seem to occupy a cognitive space — perhaps it's a uniquely poetic one — where the two realms are fused:

I write poems to untie myself, to do penance and disappear
Through the upper right-hand corner of things, to say grace.

(CHARLES WRIGHT, 'Reunion')[24]

the knowledge we kept in the bones
for wet afternoons,
the slink of tides, the absolutes of fog,

(JOHN BURNSIDE, 'Being and Time')[25]

To turn briefly to the use of the abstract as a global strategy: a few — regrettably, far too few — have made themselves expert in writing wholly *within* the abstract domain. It is another contemporary myth that poetry cannot be sustained in a mode of pure abstract 'telling'. Take, for example, C. K. Williams's description of a dying clerk, gunned down on CCTV during a hold-up at store:

Nothing of that: even torn by the flaws in the tape it was a voice
    that knew it was dying,
knew it was being — horrible — slaughtered, all that it knew and
    aspired to instantly voided;
such hopeless, astonished pleading, such overwhelmed,
    untempered pity for the self dying;
no indignation, no passion for justice, only woe, woe, woe, as he
    felt himself falling,
even falling knowing already he was dead, and how much I pray
    to myself I want not, ever,

24 Charles Wright, *Country Music: Selected Early Poems* (Middletown, CT: Wesleyan University Press, 1982).
25 John Burnside, *The Light Trap* (London: Jonathan Cape, 2002).

to know this, how much I want to ask why I must, with such
    perfect, detailed precision,
know this, this anguish, this agony for a self departing wishing
    only to stay, to endure,
knowing all the while that, having known, I always will know
    this torn, singular voice
of a soul calling 'God!' as it sinks back through the darkness it
    came from, cancelled, annulled.

C. K. WILLIAMS, ('Fragment')[26]

There are obvious technical reasons for the passage's dramatic success, especially the use of successive, short, racing phrases and the employment of a long line, apparently 'free' but metrically cognate with a fourteener, or Clough-like English hexameter. (These, as we'll see, lower the overall strong-stress count considerably, and accelerate the delivery of syllables – a great advantage when switching from the strong-stress content words of physical description to the more functional, weak-stress language of demotic abstraction.) However, the decision to write the *whole passage* as abstract diegesis goes strongly against the grain of contemporary practice; the poem is less the description of an event than its intellectual and emotional imprint, and the unifying coherence of the single abstract domain stands in powerful contrast to the image-carnival of the standard descriptive approach. This syntactically robust and musical passage of fairly pure 'telling' represents, if not quite the road not taken in the poetry of the age, one decidedly less travelled.

All this should, I hope, tool us up to tackle one of the most poorly described aspects of poetic function, that of 'the symbolic'.

26   C. K. Williams, *Selected Later Poems* (New York: Farrar, Straus & Giroux, 2015).

Symbolicity

If you're rejoining us having sensibly skipped the last couple of dozen pages: I've described how a specific domain can render its enclosed components denotative to the point of near-monadicity. Any detail analysed or meditated upon in isolation may appear to enclose a domain (let's say 'Christmas', with all its Santas and reindeer, tinsel and holidays, presents and snow); but if that detail is read within a *further* enclosing domain, it is either drastically attenuated in its connotative potential, or rendered monadic by the rules of that new frame ('We need the work on this project completed by Christmas' is not going to have you spinning off into a snowy, well-fed, tinselled reverie; the only aspect of 'Christmas' relevant to 'deadline domain' is its calendar date).

This is the reason that, when an abstract connotation is 'upgraded' to an enclosing idea (take, say, the notion that Dickinson's 'I started early, took my dog' is 'really about sex'), it renders the original details of the poem attenuated, with the abstract idea now serving to constrain the meaning of that detail within an emergent and rule-bound thematic domain. ('But no man moved me till the tide / Went past my simple shoe, / And past my apron and my belt, / And past my bodice too'[27] . . . 'Oh God – isn't that about sex and desire? sounds like it . . . perhaps this whole *poem* is about sex?') In a microcosm of concept-acquisition, the 'type' derived bottom-up from the detail's 'token' now forms a *second*-level conceptual abstractum; this now exercises a top-down influence on the material it encloses, where the original detail is now seen as an attenuated (and possibly near-monadic) 'exemplum', with its original salient *connotation* (in our example, its latent eroticism) now serving as a mere index to that larger idea ('Ah – that poem: it's really all about sexual desire'). This

27   Emily Dickinson, 'I Started Early – Took my Dog – (656)', *The Poems of Emily Dickinson*, ed. Thomas H. Johnson (Cambridge, MA: Harvard University Press, 1983).

– 215 –

idea now encloses far more than the original details which initially proposed it: its enclosure now 'makes sense of' and connects all *other* details by intra-domain rule ('Ah yes, that "past my bodice too" line is clearly a *symbol* of a sexual desire; but now that I look at "And he – he followed close behind – / I felt his silver heel / Upon my ankle, – then my shoes / Would overflow with pearl" . . . – Good Lord! It's . . . sexy everywhere.') This roughly describes the process of 'symbolicity'. A peristasis – a detail with a salient and active connotation or aspect – proposes a theme; upon rereading the poem, that detail is then *itself* identified as thetic or thematic within the enclosing thematic domain it helped form. The relationship between detail and theme then becomes circular and self-reinforcing. (Note that if Dickinson's poem had begun 'A sexy dream I had last night: / I stood upon the strand . . .' the poem would rapidly be demoted to the status of extended metaphor.)

Although it conventionally describes a concrete detail which 'stands for' a larger abstraction (X is a 'symbol of' something), 'symbol' should really refer to the *whole* relationship between a concrete detail which is adduced as evidence of a text-absent abstractum. I refer to the concrete, text-present component of the symbol as the *totem*, the abstract subject itself as the *animus*.[28] (In Plath's 'Balloons',[29] one might decide that 'balloon' represents something like 'vulnerable childlike

---

28 Not without some misgivings, but the alternatives were worse. 'Animus', primarily in its Latin sense, but with some degree of the contemporary definition 'actuating spirit'; 'totem', as in 'any species of living or inanimate thing regarded [. . .] as an outward symbol of an existing intimate unseen relation' (*Chambers Dictionary*, 2014).

I should confess to a certain queasiness over the entire business of symbol and symbolic process, and I read it as a fundamental sign that humans cannot leave things be. We are everywhere insistent on the significance of things, while rarely pausing to reflect on the anthropocentric nature of that significance. (I can see now that this has also unconsciously guided my preferring the word 'animus' to a more positive alternative like 'genius' or 'psyche'.)

29 Sylvia Plath, *The Collected Poems* (London: HarperPerennial, 2008).

hope'; here the totem is the balloon and 'vulnerable childlike hope' is the animus.[30]) If the animus is strong enough, it will enclose the domain of the totem, and attenuate its sense accordingly. (In a poem about conception, say – the bed is no longer a bed, but forms a symbol whose animus may be something like 'the creation of life through the action of love'.) If the animus is given minimal encouragement from other poetic elements, it will form part of the thematic domain; the original concrete detail still carries the animus as an attribute, to which it is now also indexical. As the animus grows and strengthens on rereading, it increasingly appears to have adduced the totem as an

30 We might be inclined to approach those rare metaphors of text-*present* abstract subject in the same way, and say that in 'the cold waters of self-contentment', 'self-contentment' is the animus and 'cold waters' the totem; the primary difference is that such tropes are, by definition, locally contained effects. Only the text-*absent* animus extends its influence over a wider field than its 'proposing detail', so I will persist in calling such tropes 'metaphors' for now.

Some housekeeping: if you recall, a text-present concrete thing which stands for an absent concrete thing I call an 'enigma' (everyone else calls it a 'riddle'); it differs radically in nature from the thing-for-abstraction trope of 'symbol'. Just as a concrete-term peristasis is a kind of pre-metonymy, so a concrete-term metaphor can be thought of as a pre-enigma; the first creates a metonym by making the subject text-absent, the second creates an enigma by making the tenor text-absent. Both concrete-abstract peristases and abstract-concrete metaphors are pre-symbolic forms; in the former, if the abstract attribute ('death' in 'deathly skull') is made text-absent, the concrete subject is left to symbolise it. In abstract-concrete metaphors (e.g. 'lion-like courage'), making the abstract tenor text-absent ('he released his inner lion on the pitch') results in what is also a symbol – with the crucial difference that symbolising detail is non-literal. With symbolic contractions of abstract-concrete metaphor, the relation is 'top-down': the abstraction comes first, and substituted out by a token (e.g. 'he received her news as a bucket of ice-water', but also the cultural clichés of fig leaves, banana skins and hair shirts). In symbols which originate in concrete-abstract peristases, things work 'bottom-up': the symbolic nature of the detail can 'emerge' or 'rise' from the detail. The non-literal and the literal are sub-classes of symbol which differ primarily in the vector of their own sense-making: the former are 'solvable', locally contained effects, and function like enigmata; the latter make their semic contribution to the whole field of the poem.

exemplum or token. Suppose we write a poem in which a rat appears, and suppose with some contextual encouragement we then make the poem about 'death and contagion'; the rat still bears its connotation 'deadly contagion', but the theme then additionally directs us as to how we should read the rat. (The totem then contains part of the animus much as a Christian might tell you that we 'carry a piece of God within us'. To say that the thematic animus works like 'the god of the poem' is not the worst analogy.)

To put it all in more straightforwardly tropic terms: the symbol is often described as 'metaphorical', but even in its isolated form (i.e. not enclosed by a thematic domain), it is *simultaneously* an intra-and inter-domain operation, and forms a unique and distinct category of trope. This is because (a) it involves the domain of the abstract and (b) between totem and animus there is an asymmetric, two-way flow of meaning. To recap for those who may have recently joined us: first, a concrete detail strongly proposes an unarticulated abstract aspect or connotation; to that end it is a kind of 'flipped metonymy', where the attribute (the salient quality we would usually see qualifying the subject in a peristasis) is *text-absent*: a skull on the kitchen table is just that, but we inevitably think of it as 'a *deathly* skull'. Usually metonymy consists of the deletion of the subject to leave only the attribute, which then functions as a index — as it would if we described our skull via the metonymic hyperstasis 'death lay on the kitchen table'; 'death' is the index to 'skull', derived from the peristasis '[deathly] skull'. However, symbol requires the deletion of the *attribute*; the significance of this is that the attribute must *then be found*. (As a gesture, its deletion by the symbol-creator and discovery by the symbol-finder is almost a metaphysical insistence that 'there is something *else* to all this'. Nowhere do we see the human rage against the intrinsic meaninglessness of things than in our projections of the symbolic.) In 'seeking out the meaning' of our totem we not only create but automatically *privilege* the animus; on the discovery of its meaning, it becomes our dominant subject, and further attenuates and sharpens the sense of the totem.

Were we to stop there, we would just have that weird anti-metonym we conventionally call 'a symbol'. However, we *rarely* stop there, and in the context of the closed system of the poem, where we have a finite number of semantic elements, we will often see the energy ploughed into the animus allow it to keep rising in 'semantic status' – and then either form the whole thematic domain, or contribute a key aspect of it, taking greater and greater control over the meaning of those elements under its jurisdiction.

The symbol is a double thought, and unless arbitrarily forged by convention is formed by an active and energetic process. The key thing to note is that the poet's *deletion* of the index, leaving us a peristasis with a text-absent attribute, means that a symbol is not a symbol unless it is *found*. A rose may be 'love'; but if it's left untroubled by an animus, a rose is a rose is a rose.[31] However, once the salient attribute is correctly inferred, the symbolic process seems inevitable: detail X actively implies quality Y; when quality Y is promoted to the 'real' subject, it forms an animus; this then 'rules' detail X, turning it into an attenuated totem.

Obvious, rigorous and overdetermined forms of this procedure we tend to call 'allegory'; in allegory, all details are subservient to the animus and *everything* is symbolic. For this reason allegories have a well-deserved reputation for being no fun whatsoever: the reader is obliged to stop before every detail to ask how it fits into the symbolic frame, and any naturalistic mimesis, any descriptive passage which may offer some recreational relief from the parade of deep significance, becomes impossible to sustain. Indeed, if one does find oneself merely

---

31 The terms I use to describe the imposition of a metrical template on a poetic line, 'introjection' and 'projection', would also describe the process by which a poet 'charges' a detail with symbolic intent, and by which the reader then discovers it. The communicative ideal is 'convergence', where introjection and projection match, or are at least commensurate; but poets often think they've implied much more than they actually have, while readers are equally capable of projecting any old rubbish – or, indeed, missing everything.

'enjoying the story', say – it has technically ceased to be an allegory. Allegory was a didactic tool, and its work long delegated to other literary forms. Movies and novels are far better at sustaining both naturalistic and allegorical conceits simultaneously.

I am attempting a correction to that standard formulation of the literary symbol as 'vehicle plus text-absent tenor'; this simplifies it into falsehood, and fails to take on board the implications of the 'abstract tenor', which does not really function like a tenor at all. As I've mentioned, I feel strongly that symbol is a product of our fundamental rage against the absence of instrinsic meaning in the universe, a rage against the curse of being born a sense-making creature into a place where nothing but neutral process is to be found. This rage takes the form of strenuous, unapologetic and highly energetic projection. It is on this primal *determination* to find meaning that the animus feeds, and sees it easily rise to swallow the other elements in its purlieu – and, if you like, 'bend them to its will'. Readers may reasonably reject the patriarchal form of my own metaphor here, with all its ruling and dominating and overpowering. But rule-making as a means of creating sense is a broad feature of the whole species, not just the minds of men; and the symbol is the natural corollary of a mind built, perhaps regrettably, on that principle. Whether it would be possible to write without them, who knows; but the author who makes too much deliberate use of the technique is certainly in danger of becoming 'superior', or a weaver of tedious allegories. The most effective symbols arrive organically in the creation of the poem's Gestalt. I might go further, and say that just as the abstraction is an 'articulated quale', the unspoken abstraction of the symbol's animus is often better *left* that way: experienced, but silent. The most powerfully affecting symbols are, for me, those which create a distinct animus – but one too nuanced or strange to be easily characterised by a few off-the-peg abstractions. We can have a consistent, tonal, qualial thematic domain enclose a poem's significant elements, and *feel* its symbolic importance without actually articulating it. This articulation seems an increasingly tedious game to me, and an occupation for the student and literary critic – whose demands, with respect, must always come second to those of the innocently, intelligently engaged reader. But a misunderstanding over the importance of the symbol's *deliberate* deployment has led to a rash of dire 'significant writing', from didactic allegories that are 600 years out of step with the age to, in narrative contexts, an explosion of symbolic 'foreshadowing'. (Thank you, Iowa Writers' Workshop and crappy readings of Flannery O'Connor.) For all it remains a valuable critical exercise, to see the exegesis of the symbol as the *purpose* of the symbol gets its cultural purpose completely backwards. This is because the exegesis of the symbol *is the poem*.

The symbol in poetic practice

When we analyse real-world examples, we must never forget the importance of shaping context. It's worth breaking the process down: suppose a poem contains 'a lost golf ball'. Let's say the poem presents it as a literal detail, not in a way that would mark it as figurative, e.g. 'the lost golf ball in the sky'. So, while we now know it's not the V of a metaphor describing, say, a new moon (which is to say that it's not an enigma), the detail nonetheless feels too salient and significant to be *merely* read literally. In this case, 'the lost golf ball' has occurred in the following frame: the poem recalls a sad solo game of pitch-and-putt, played by the poet back when they were a poor, friendless child who only owned one club and one ball – now lost. After a moment, we decide that this lost golf ball is *really* to be read as 'lost hope'. With 'the lost golf ball is lost hope', 'lost hope' is an attribute and a monadic abstraction, and part of the unspoken peristasis 'the lost golf ball of hope'. This abstract quality has been derived from 'the lost golf ball' via an intra-domain operation; though the animus 'lost hope' is plainly not an attribute of the domain of 'lost golf ball', but of the domain of 'the lost golf ball' *in context*, i.e. 'the lost golf ball of the poor and friendless child'. In poems, peristases are often much more than their mere verbal expression. (This gives further justification to the symbolic animus playing a ruling role in the whole thematic domain, since it was derived by *broad* contextual means in the first place.)

The symbol is rarely cleanly or clearly presented, and is a disease of degree. We feel instinctively that in Larkin's 'Mr Bleaney', the fact that Bleaney keeps on 'plugging at the four aways'[32] is not mere literal evidence of his dogged gambling, but a symbol of his doomed hope, while his annual 'Christmas at his sister's house in Stoke' merely speaks of (i.e. is a synecdochic metonym of) his lonely and friendless life. It is, of course, the mounting evidence of the latter and the thematic domain it generates that will help form the symbolicity of the former. And yet the formal difference between the synecdoche of 'Christmas at his sister's house in Stoke' and the totem of 'he kept on plugging at the four aways' lies in little more than the amount of energy we decide to invest in these peristases to draw out their fullest meaning. If we also sense, increasingly, an air of 'desperate lost hope' in 'Christmas at his sister's house in Stoke', then it has become infected with the ruling 'hopeless' animus of the poem, and will be to some degree 'totemised'.[33] The process is roughly as follows: we energetically

---

32 That is he kept filling in the same away-game bet on his weekly football coupons, a once universally popular form of gambling in the UK. And an exclusively British form, it would seem: there is a well-known French translation of 'Mr Bleaney' which renders the line as 'he took four holidays a year'. Philip Larkin, 'Mr Bleaney', *The Collected Poems*, ed. Anthony Thwaite (London: Faber & Faber, 2003).

33 Indeed I worry that – our pretty and precise theoretical distinctions apart – the most we can really say about the difference between metonym and symbol is that the first is likely to be naturally and readily understood, while the latter's sense tends to be 'won', invested, projected, or slowly discovered; the two may be divided by little more than, firstly, a vague distinction between direct and indirect connection, and secondly the inflated 'importance' we instinctively ascribe to the latter. However, I feel they belong to different trope classes: symbol involves the *generation* of meaning; metonymy, the derivation of meaning. Consider a poem about rain which states or implies its 'welcomeness', and a poem about rain which states or implies its

CONCRETE, ABSTRACT AND SYMBOL

'read in' to contextualised detail; this draws forth abstract attributes; these in turn become an animus; the animus forms the abstract part of the thematic domain; the animus then 'totemises' such detail as shares its abstract attribute; and the sense of that detail, when reread, focuses and narrows to a motivated index which continues to shape and qualify the thematic domain every time we reread the poem. What emerges from this process is the careful, nuanced qualification of the monadic global animus itself. 'Forlorn hope' does no justice to the complexity and nuance of Bleaney's or the speaker's tawdry anomie, their resigned despair, their fatalistic depression. The animus could only have been adequately articulated *by the poem*, which exists for precisely that purpose.

So in isolating and analysing the symbol we first need to acknowledge that it is a very dirty category. The point really is worth repeating that we should first be wary of the 'green light = go', 'pentacle = witchcraft' or 'rose = love' type of arbitrary cultural symbol, which is 'symbolic' only in the semiotic use of the word. This might seem an easy distinction to make; but one must remain alert to *poets*' own susceptibility to this sort of thing. (I subsume both cultural symbol and arbitrary connection under 'aseme', discussed in due course.) For example, I have no doubt that Yeats's '*nine* bean rows' in 'Inisfree' are no accident, and likely connected to some enneadic theosophical nonsense; what they are not, however, is a 'symbol' in

---

'capricious generosity'. This shows that the peristatic or symbol status of a detail is a disease of degree. It depends on the directness of the relation between subject and aspect (i.e. perhaps the 'welcomeness' is merely a conventional property of rain in certain contexts: our perennial intentional stance towards the world means that the pathetic fallacy is certainly not always enough to recruit every such human projection to the category of 'symbol'. However, 'capricious generosity' could be derived only via the usual symbolic procedure, where terms like 'changeable' and 'copious' are somehow actively sought within the domain of 'rain', and then metaleptically chained to the qualities of 'capriciousness' and 'generosity' within the abstract domain; given sufficient contextual encouragement, these might then form an animus to inversely supervene on 'rain', rendering it totem).

the literary sense.[34] Secondly, there is problem is with us thinking of the abstract animus as we do other abstractions, i.e. a 'quale with a name'. Through our fatal and persistent logocentricity, this had led us to privilege namable quale, and fail to recognise that the less articulable – but no less perceptible – tones, emotions, ambiences and complex abstractions that poetic details connote should have the same status. We have dismissed as so much vague feeling, as indefinable 'atmosphere', as accidentally consonant surrealism, that vast category of poetic effect which conducts its sense through *inarticulable* qualia. (I again refer the reader to my notes on the 'patheme', my 'seme of tone', which might explain why these qualia are *necessarily* inarticulable). It is therefore crucially important to remember that the function of symbol in a poem, as opposed to symbols which occur elsewhere, is that the totem (or indeed the entire poem, in the case of allegory) serves as a means *by which* the inarticulable animus can still be articulated at a distance, can be qualified, constrained, rendered nuanced and precise – even if never actually 'named'. The knight's-move articulation of the ineffable is one of poetry's principal cultural functions. While 'ineffable' by definition cannot be 'spoken', its complex symbolic avatar can be spun up. Frost's extended single metaphor 'The Silken Tent' opens with 'She is as in a field a silken tent';[35] this turns out to be roughly equivalent to something *like* 'this woman's inner moral uprightness and purity is like a well-erected silk tent in field', but it is the very inadequacy of this précis of the woman's inner quality that made the poem necessary in the first place, and Frost takes fourteen lines to explain what it is he finds so admirable. (I am setting the issue of the poem's period-piece sexism to one side, albeit with difficulty.) The poem itself goes to great pains to create a carefully considered domain of what that 'feminine spiritual compass' might be, by giving it aspect, quality, nuance (it has the qualities of

34 W. B. Yeats, *The Collected Poems of W. B. Yeats* (London: Scribner, 1996).
35 Robert Frost, *The Collected Poems* (London: Vintage Classics, 2013).

uprightness, responsiveness, delicacy, balance and so on). It does not render it non-monadic, because it remains an abstraction, but it becomes such a beautifully well-qualified and well-defined monad that the poet easily proves his point: whatever kind of transcendental and unique quality this woman possesses, there is no 'normal' human term even vaguely adequate to it.

Symbol as process: poetic meaning and the feedback loop

The symbol is a distinct tropic category whose function is the production of meaning. It achieves this by a two-way intra-domain and inter-domain process: a peristasis forms a ruling domain through an indexical procedure; the ruling domain then constrains and directs the sense of that detail through a metaphorical one.

This definition of symbol allows us not only to employ it as an analytical tool, but also to see that the whole business of poetic meaning is coterminous and possibly consubstantial with that of symbol-forming. It also explains how a staggering amount of information can be vertically encoded within the poem, and slowly unearthed through successive readings.

I appreciate these recapitulations are tiresome, but I can justify the inclusion of one more on the grounds that what it describes is, I believe, 'what makes poetry poetry'. So if the reader will permit me one final 'way of looking at it': the asymmetry of the sense-flow between the concrete totem and its abstract animus points to an inbuilt paradox within 'the poetic image', which in turn lays bare the process of 'poetic reading'. Usually the thematic domain (effectively the 'intentionality' of the poem, what the poem is 'about', 'saying', 'up to') is not explicitly given. It's rarely wholly revealed in, say, the title (which may even be deliberately misleading) or stated in neatly expository lines which 'tell not show'. Instead, it's usually developed by its own constituent material. The overdetermined semantic boundary of the poem, the closed semantic space it enjoys as a bounded text, results in something that to some extent operates as a microlanguage, and circularly forms its own definition of 'what it means'. Very often our poetic donnée is revealed *only* through such a self-reflexive procedure.

What happens, as we've seen, is that the members of a vaguely defined set 'stuff in the present poem titled *x*', the 'images' and details, attitudes and ideas, tones and formal gestures, are first carefully read. When some context is understood (context adds text-absent attributes to each peristasis), the reader makes an unconscious critical distinction between 'element' and mere passing detail. ('Elements' might be bodied forth as individual details or effects, or several details or effects bonded by a tonal isologue, explicit theme, and so on.) Through the reader's determined oversignifying, these elements begin to create the better-defined set 'what this poem is about', of which they are members. After a few readings, and once the thematic domain is established, two things happen: *all* details are now held within a thematic domain coterminous with the poem's boundary; and the original elements see the terms of their membership change as their relation toward the thematic animus switches from *evidential* of that thematic domain to actively *propositional* of it – and then, finally, *totemic* of a global animus that is coterminous with the theme, as the poem's symbols are formed. To put it in more fashionable terms, the thematic domain is akin to an emergent property in a complex physical system. ('Akin to an emergent property' only because emergent properties tend to be unforeseen; the poem's domain has been at least *partly* anticipated.[36]) Once formed, it exerts a downward causality,

---

36 I should express a misgiving over the too-casual use of the word 'emergent' in the context of domain theory; conceptual blends can sometimes be calculated for, while true 'emergence' cannot. It's better used to describe the tendency of this odd universe towards self-organised creativity, and as such, our use of it here is really metaphorical. Nonetheless, conceptual blending can produce new and unexpected concepts, a distinctly 'poetic' process that arises naturally from our speech. The inter-domain often recruits, synthesises or throws up unexpected elements in the

and alters the very nature and structure of the material by which it was originally constituted – as well as that by which it was not: not only does a thematic animus *doubly* charge those peristases which proposed it, it recruits to its cause other details besides, drawing from them hitherto unsuspected indices. It renders them 'meaningful'. This describes the dynamic process of 'reading a bounded text as poetry'.

---

composite ground created by the intersection of two 'mental spaces' (to use the favoured term of Fauconnier and Turner, and others). A toy dog is conceptually a toy and a dog; but if you believe these domains are held in the mind separately, try stabbing one in front of a child. More poetically, beer-froth in a half-empty glass looks like sea-spume, but the poet may have spun off into dreams of oceans of beer, drunk mermaids, or doubloons at the bottom of the glass before he knows it. The third mental space created in the intersection may be an 'impossible world', in the language of truth-conditional semantics, but is *also* one we can think within – and *what* we think will not necessarily be constrained by the mere impossibility of the space itself. (A trade secret: the most celebrated 'imaginative leaps' and original brilliancies in poetry are not the result of 'newly coined metaphors'; they are further thoughts that take place *within* the new mental space these metaphors create. A less expensive kind of innovation sees a familiar comparison enlivened by forming the ground through an original metonym, not off-the-peg index.) But the more complex the interrelations themselves, the less predicable the results, especially with metaleptic chains, or the intersection of wholly separate metaphors.

Let me give you an example drawn from life, and forgive my For Your Too Much Information. I have two miniature poodles, one ginger and saintly, the other black and insane. Because of Yentl's mischievous temperament, the conceit has arisen that she was born in hell, and that she is the devil's poodle. Additionally, she has the rather scary habit of suddenly stopping dead and staring at a wall, or at nothing at all for minutes at a time; this behaviour is uncannily reminiscent of a character left unattended in a video game, when the gamer has put down the controller to go and make tea, or answer the phone. Yentl is also given to bouts of excessive overfriendliness. During one of these love-bombings, and under the usual pressures of time and urgency that produce the poetic, my stepdaughter yelled: 'Satan's mashing the cuddle button!' Cute, huh? ('Button-mashing' is gamerspeak for mindlessly bashing away the same key during a dumb fight or similarly repetitive activity.) This collapses two inter-domain conceits – leaving a new conceptual blend that produces, 'emergently', not only the idea that Lucifer plays on an infernal Xbox that controls his minions, but – via the incorporation of another aspect of Yentl's behaviour into the third space – that he has an unexpectedly sweeter side to him.

A 'poem' is a text written to be read in this way; when 'read as poetry' it will 'form a poem in the mind' as sure a paper flower will unfold in water.

Because poems are semically overwired, *any* detail in a poem is already 'overconnoting' and charged with an extra, motivated valency: it is already seeking out a thematic domain to which it wants to connect, and from which it can draw power.[37] Where we sense the

37 Any unified field theory of poetry would, I believe, be based around the principle of a global shift from denotative to connotative speech. Reading 'the poetic' as a global move towards 'the connotative' dovetails with my own reading of 'the lyric principle', which is based on the idea that a distinctively connotative speech systematises its organisation around the nodes of (a) existing local phonesthemes, (b) the innovation of new local phonesthemes that the iconic system legitimates (as in poetry), and (c) more diffuse global phonesthemic shifts, involving the relocation of whole sound-groups in the language. These result in different musics, under different performance conditions.

Metaphor and metonymy are *invariably* interfused under the global shift towards the poetic function. Intra-domain operations are an aspect of all metaphor's careful linguistic construction, i.e. tenor and vehicle are often composed of careful peristases, and indicative and propositional of their enclosing specific domains. In contracted forms which omit the tenor, metonymy often is nested within the inter-domain metaphor, and appears as an index to the subject ('tall-sailed cloud' has an embedded metonym, i.e. sail = boat). Metonymy and peristases too have a habit of recruiting their qualifying index from a less-than-perfectly literal domain, thus ruining our pretty Venn diagrams; as we've seen, they also tend to undergo promotion from evidential to symbolic status as the thematic domain forms. Jakobson himself was reaching this conclusion towards the end: 'In poetry, where likeness is projected upon contiguity, every metonymy is slightly metaphorical and every metaphor contains a metonymic tinge.' However, he resists saying that in poetry, contiguity is *also* simultaneously projected upon likeness, which I am convinced it is. Under certain formal and rhetorical pressures, language undergoes a phase shift and enters a 'poetic state'. This state is characterised by the collapse of the paradigmatic and syntagmatic functions. (Nowhere is this clearer than in the work of Shakespeare, whose disregard for syntagmatic order and overdetermined, echolalic, thematically obsessive and involute style we read as a sign of his 'poetic genius', probably correctly. More recently the work of John Ashbery, Geoffrey Hill, J. H. Prynne and Alice Oswald shows similar symptoms – and similar diagnoses of 'genius' are frequently made. Who

connotations of salient elements converge, a set of shared abstract concerns is implied, which begins to form a conceptual integrity, a Gestalt. This comes to define the thematic domain of the poem. The thematic domain then becomes the abstract subject, the global animus, instead of the mere sum of the poem's detail; and in this way, we begin to move from surface sense to deeper meaning. The details, images and elements that constitute the material of the poem are now charged and recharged as poetic symbols, wired into the self-sustaining thematic and argumentative circuitry of the whole. The poem is now perceived less and less as a linear or narrative construction, and is more and more, as Paul Valéry said of the sonnet, 'a single cellular entity', with its own internal logic, economy and generative power. The complex meaning of a poem, the deep and interwoven harmony distinct to the form, is thus created through a kind of bootstrapping mechanism. All salient detail in a poem is propositional of a rule; through these rules, the thematic domain forms – but *slowly*, since this detail is relatively 'difficult' to parse because of its density and unfamiliarity; indeed, it arguably *must* be 'original' to propose any further significance. The thematic domain itself then becomes the subject of the poem, having been proposed by the sum of its constituent detail when considered as 'significant evidence'. The entire text of the poem, to some degree, stands in an indexical relation to this larger enclosing animus. Through rereading, the thematic domain is further confirmed by a self-strengthening agreement to understand those formerly propositional details as now symbolic of the poem's concerns. Hence the paradox of poetic detail: because it is the result of a dynamic process, it is simultaneously indexical of the thematic domain, and totemic of the global animus which is its own abstract aspect. It both predicts and is predicted by the thematic domain, and is both anterior and posterior to it.

---

knows; the myopia of the contemporary should mean that we should strenuously resist all such judgements as a matter of course, but 'geniuses' they may prove.)

Take 'Men at Forty' by Donald Justice:

> Men at forty
> Learn to close softly
> The doors to rooms they will not be
> Coming back to.
> At rest on a stair landing, They feel it
> Moving beneath them now like the deck of a ship,
> Though the swell is gentle.
> [. . .]
>
> They are more fathers than sons themselves now.
> Something is filling them, something
>
> That is like the twilight sound
> Of the crickets, immense,
> Filling the woods at the foot of the slope
> Behind their mortgaged houses.[38]

The poem is 'about' an unnamed force rising from the dark, 'about' a strange sense that comes over men in mid-life, which combines the spectre of death, finality, their wholly ceasing to be children in any sense, the point at which mortality becomes inescapable, and so on. Because 'at rest on a stair landing' is a casually delivered line with little textual or rhetorical salience, you might conceivably miss it on the very first reading; but on the second, the line starts to suggest its half-buried attribute of 'halfwayness' and 'ascending or descending', this quality being drawn forth by the gradually clarifying thematic domain (with its ghost-attributes of hell or heaven, perhaps, elicited by the rather eschatological feel of it all). On a first pass, it was a mere 'image' – but one which all poetry readers would reflexively read as potentially capable of implying a further meaning, within the supercharged field of the poem.

38 Donald Justice, *Collected Poems* (New York: Alfred A. Knopf, 2006).

As the thematic domain becomes better established on a second or third reading, 'stair landing' begins to be *overtaken* by its 'halfway, mid-point' attribute, and soon starts to look less like an 'image' and more what we'd call a 'symbol' of the poem's emerging concerns. Other details in the poem rise towards the totemic in much the same way, though often by different routes. For example, 'mortgaged houses' is already salient by its last-line position, and sounds creepy enough – though a rereading will leave the deadly '*mort*' in 'mortgaged' singing out loudly, and perhaps even send us back to the word's etymology, and its origins in the Old French for 'dead pledge'.

Note that a *bad* reading is one that reduces a detail wholly to its symbolic interpretation. Poems are twice-lit, as Antonio Machado said – 'once for the straight reading, once for the slant' – and it's the thematic domain that provides us with the sidelong reading, the new sun to which the details turn their head, and which casts new, longer and stranger shadows. But to take one reading over the other is to simplify and reduce the poem. One mustn't ever deny plain, literal sense in favour of that stranger meaning; the second braces itself on the first, and keeping *both* in play is the secret of rich, open-ended reading. To fail to do so is to deny the outward-facing world its own integrity, its *own* intrinsic depth; the last time poetry went down that route, Objectivism was invented as a necessary corrective, a situation we might try to avoid in the future. (I recall Jung points out somewhere that a native fertility ceremony involving a big hole in the ground may *indeed* invoke the archetypes of the vagina, of receptivity, of death, the void, and so on – but it's very much also a big hole in the ground.) A good reader will not have the poem's details rendered *wholly* narrow or monadic by its theme or 'definitive interpretation'. 'Literal sense' often stands as the door to that richer reading, and 'deeper meaning' approached via any *other* route risks being an invention of the reader's alone, its having been neither proposed from nor validated by the paraphrasable sense of the text.[39] But more fundamentally, readings which skip too quickly to 'interpretation' deny themselves the sensual pleasure of all the poem's native flora and fauna – all the immediate data of its image and music and anecdote and detail – that can reside nowhere *other* than the surface of the text.

The progression of a detail from peristasis to symbol is the result and the purpose of the dynamic process of rereading. This is why a decent poem can never be wholly appreciated in a single reading. Its simple commitment to original expression will leave it with built-in unfamiliarities that can only be naturalised by a second, third or tenth encounter – by which time the land that holds them native will have grown very strange. Symbolicity is an emergent condition not of reading a poem, *but of rereading a poem*.[40] The supercharged semic field of the thematic domain is, in a sense, self-sustaining, as it constitutes a semiotic feedback loop. It is intra-domain on the way out, with salient detail and image implying their shared abstract concerns; inter-domain on the way back, with those summed abstract concerns hypostatising the same detail as totem. There is a *net gain* in this loop, so it does not immediately settle into equilibrium, as long as it receives as input the reader's own interpretative energy, their own rereading. This is ploughed into the circuitry of the thematic domain, which can 'fully charge' the symbol like a battery cell, and allow for its widening,

39 We might anticipate another, more sinister, corollary: poems with *no* paraphrasable sense can neither confirm nor deny anything, and have infinite polysemy. Knock yourself out, by all means, but don't expect a word of agreement for your own interpretation – except from those folk you have spared the trouble of making a reading of their own.

40 Another thematic domain can also be formed by a reader's thorough familiarity with an entire oeuvre; in this way, we can be conditioned to respond to detail in a virtually Pavlovian way. The mention of 'rainbow' in Bishop is always a particularly joyous thing; the word 'yellow' in Plath always seems to connote death; the appearance of 'frost' in the poetry of John Burnside is often just 'frost', but also a Burnsidean symbol, a kind of magical or transforming patina that the immaterial leaves on the material when they brush against each other.

resonant interpretation within the simultaneously broadening range of the theme. I don't mean to imply that the reader need be wholly conscious of this mechanism at all, and indeed I suspect it might all grind to a halt if they were. But if poetry has any 'alchemical procedure' by which it magically transmutes its sometimes mundane materials, I suspect this is it.[41]

This loop reaches equilibrium only when the component signs have reached a stable orientation towards a thematic domain sophisticated enough in its animus to accommodate them all. If such a domain cannot be formed, this is usually a sign that the poem contains elements that legislate against its formation: it is 'about too many things'. (The global animus can be hugely 'sophisticated' but it cannot be polyadic.) This is what we mean, I think, when we talk about elements reaching their 'full resonant potential'. (Of course this is absurdly idealised; as the reader changes as an individual, so do those aspects of the poem open to subjective interpretation.) One might say that poetry is the only place we see this semiotic feedback loop in language; it would be truer to say, I think, that its presence constitutes the singularity of the poetic experience. A poem can't *be* a poem without an overdetermining thematic domain, the powerful sense that the poem is its own self-contained logical universe – inspissating its own idiom, within which individual gestures take on a more and more subtle significance; that the poem is more than its mere words.

As I've said, this self-feeding fire can't be ignited if the poem has too many salient elements which compete to form a consistent thematic domain; indeed, confronted with a bad apprentice poem, the most common diagnosis one makes is that there's too much

41   I'll throw this out here, since I suspect it to be the case: jumping down a couple of octaves, this procedure is identical in its dynamic form to that which shapes consciousness, and in relationship to which it stands as a kind of aliasing artefact, to draw an unforgivably obscure metaphor from signal processing. This accords with some recent theories of mind, especially those of Douglas Hofstadter. See his *I Am a Strange Loop* (New York: Basic Books, 2007).

stuff in it. (A poem which is a discontinuous cornucopia or ragbag may be perfectly enjoyable, but it can form no thematic domain; its elements will either be read much the same way the second time, or will have a false theme projected into them.) Those poems in the canon we tend to think of as 'great' generally work with an optimal minimum of theme-generating elements, as the thematic domain can be formed only by their complex agreement, and by their intricate and sophisticated interrelation. If these elements merely 'stack up', merely *accumulate* – no thematic domain ever arises in the reader's mind. (This is exactly what happens to poems under the extreme 'Martian' conditions I described earlier.) Many poets, worried about the reader falling asleep, nervously fill the poem with far too many interesting things, with the result that the poem never really forms at all. However, this default compositional practice is something all our great poets seem to share: the deep integration of two or three elements, whose connections continue to proliferate within the global animus they conspiratorially form.

I

FOUR SEMES, FOUR TROPES

The chapter which follows this makes some notes towards a working taxonomy of poetic metaphor, analysing it at the levels of conceptual form and textual expression. The scheme I'll initially present here is a rather anecdotal description of the 'character' of metaphoric ground (or 'isomorphism'), the underlying conceptual mapping. This is one I used for years when teaching; it is itself largely a metaphorical description, which all non-scientific accounts necessarily are, but the *ways* in which it was patently inadequate struck me as interesting. An examination of its flaws led me to propose a more fundamental revision: a new scheme of four tropes.

Metaphor depends on there existing a ground between (or blend constructed of) two domains. This takes the form of an *isomorphism*, a contentual overlap, which defines a set of shared properties. The character of the isomorphism will identify the *kind* of properties shared by the T and V. This is not really a poetic or even a linguistic issue, but a conceptual-semantic one. For years I taught – mainly because I had to teach *something* – the little mnemonic quintet of the 'five Fs', which essentially sketch in 'the nature of content': *form, function, flow, feel* and *free association*. As useful as I found these categories over the years, I always knew them to be completely flawed. I mention them here only to introduce a second and more conceptually precise scheme, which I believe may point the way not only to a clearer understanding of metaphor, but also – because they essentially describe not just the nature of passive isomorphic content but the active semic *means* by which one thing can join another – a new scheme which replaces our old 'four tropes'.

But let's begin with my five *f*s. As will be obvious, the categories are porous, and can't – and shouldn't – be kept distinct: the kind of instantiations we deal with in the real world, and which the best poetry reflects, are usually complex peristases with functional, dynamic and tonal qualities, not single aspects of single things.

Form: A list of formal properties might answer the question *What kind of thing is it?* With 'moon', we might note the properties of crescentness, brightness, whiteness, distance, etc. Using these as a ground, we might form a strong comparison with a toenail clipping (crescent, white), or a boomerang (crescent, kind-of-distant), and so on.

Function: A list of functional properties might answer the question *What does it do?* or *What is it for?* or (if we want to indulge the anthropomorphic conceit of 'the intentional stance') *What does it want to do?* To stick with 'moon' – it sheds light, it draws tides, it drives humans mad, it sometimes occludes the sun in an eclipse, and so on. So we might compare it to 'a strong lamp used in an interrogation', 'a hallucinogenic drug', 'a magnet' or 'a dark coin covering a bright coin'.

Flow: Though I really mean *dynamic*. A list of dynamic properties might answer the question *In what way does it move or change over time?* The moon floats, it follows an orbit, it librates, it waxes and wanes, etc. The slow rounds of a milk-float might coincide with the idea of lunar orbit; a dark mood might wax and wane like the moon. (Though note that things get messy immediately: in the first example, formal properties are borrowed – 'whiteness' – and in the second, tonal and lyric properties.)

Feel: Though 'tone' is the better word. A list of tonal properties might answer the question *What does it feel like?* This alludes to the more subtle and subjective tonal, emotional, sensual and aesthetic qualities of the T. The moon 'feels' cold, lifeless, distant (of course it literally *is* all of those things), but it also might remind us of death, of emotional sterility, of 'distant relationships'. Incidentally, the role of the object as cultural symbol – e.g. the red rose as a symbol of love – is also subsumed into this category.[1] These are sometimes claimed as pure Peircian symbols, or what I call 'asymbols' – meaning they have zero coincidence of attribute, zero ground, since the connection between signifier and signified is entirely arbitrary and learned. However, these symbols invariably turn out to have been formed, in part, by shared tonal concerns. To take a relatively recent example: in the allegedly pure 'symbol' the late musician Prince briefly adopted instead of his own name – ♀ – one is obliged to observe that Prince and 'the Prince symbol' *do* have certain shared tonal attributes. Both demonstrate a certain pomposity, pretentiousness and baroqueness, and the symbol itself has isomorphic similarities with everything from astrological symbols and male-female biological symbols, to Jimmy Page's old tag in Led Zeppelin – all of which were likely to be contributing factors in the new symbol's design, and all evidence of its patent non-arbitrariness; the symbol was symptomatic of many things in Prince's character, from his rock heritage and sexual identity to his mental state. Humans cannot select *anything* arbitrarily. Even an asymbol selected by an aleatoric process will immediately have some degree of iconicity as soon as it takes a form; the total infection of the human realm with a kind of primed, Higgs-field tonal ether means that *any* attempt at pure 'asymbolicity' is always doomed. However close it might approach it, the sign can never attain true independence from its referent.

Free association: A list of associative properties might answer the question *What does it put you in mind of?* This is a disease of degree, of course, the disease in question being unverifiable subjectivity, and

---

1 We seem to process these cultural asymbols in a way very close to reading. Danish researchers have recently shown that when the brain encounters items used in a 'pure-symbolic' manner – flowers left on a doorstep, say, as opposed to the same flowers growing wild – the left fusiform gyrus and the inferior frontal cortex light up, areas associated with reading and semantic meaning, respectively.

'free' connotations are the least-tightly bound to the semic core of the domain – at least as far as everyone else is concerned. The moon might remind you of a cold and unfeeling parent, and the reader might construct enough of a ground to make the trope work; but it might also remind you of Newcastle Brown Ale or blue sweatpants, for reasons which are wholly personal or random, and probably better kept to yourself. Vigilance is required on the poet's part; too often wholly subjective associations are presented as if they were widely shared, the poet having mistaken their apparent strength for currency.

That pretty much covers isomorphic 'character'. However, this account is really only useful as a handy little mnemonic. As I've mentioned, poetic metaphor in the field will often combine elements of any or all five categories, and even the illustrative examples I gave were helplessly and freely borrowing from those categories; additionally, the metaphor will likely have dynamic, causal and contextual dimensions too, as well as areas of lyric, rhythmic and phonesthemic overlap. We embroider peristases, not isolated substantives: the moon will rarely be alone, but part of a larger imagistic landscape – 'disappearing behind the rank clouds as a clear idea suddenly lost to confusion', say. Poetic metaphor is no different from the kind of complex metaphor we often innovate in real life. The other day I tried to pour from a bottle of wine upon which the top had been screwed back on. My partner observed, 'You've left the lens cap on.' The metaphor here is formal, dynamic *and* tonal in nature. Yes, the mapping is A LENS CAP IS A SCREW TOP based on the ground 'ABSOLUTE IMPEDIMENT TO AN ACTION WHICH REQUIRES UNIMPEDED FLOW', but that wouldn't have been as sharp a comparison unless it was understood with the dynamic and tonal isomorphism of 'an impeded intentional action involving a befuddled agent' and within the larger contextual domain of 'drunken occasion which legitimates the use of distant metaphors'. (These subtler connections and dynamic contexts are often missing from accounts of the operation of conceptual metaphor; our descriptions are often suspiciously oversimplified.)

For years, I found these rough-and-ready divisions a fairly useful way of interrogating the metaphoric potential of two interacting domains. However, I'd now like to propose a more serious scheme. It will be self-evident that the categorical division between 'functional' and 'dynamic' attributes is rather arbitrary; it will also be clear that the business of 'feel' is a laughably subjective one, and that 'free association' is off the scale. Therefore I'd suggest we might categorise the properties of a domain according to the following types:

Formeme: A seme which describes contentual, formal and spatial elements.

Aeteme: A seme which describes functional, causal, temporal and dynamic elements.[2]

Patheme: A seme which describes all elements which we identify as carrying an isolable and distinct feeling, emotion, tone or 'meaning'.

Aseme: An anti-seme of connection enforced by context or frame *alone*, i.e. between two elements via personal, culturally learned or arbitrary association. (Some will baulk at my conflation of these categories, but these associations are all 'forged' by outside forces, as opposed to the others, which are 'domain-emergent', and based on the intrinsic motivation of the sign.) Asemes are by definition content-less, empty, and mere vectors of connection.

The term 'aseme' reifies the unreifiable. An aseme carries a real connection for the author or a cultural group, but remains a nonsense for the reader, or a culturally excluded group. Old Betamax videotapes plunge me into the feeling of a very specific and miserable loss, for

2 I have made all the Mr T jokes in advance, so spare me. 'Ergeme' was one possibility, but the Greek root – *aitia*, 'cause' (as in 'aetiology'), seems both accurate and appropriately primal.

reasons too dull to explain; either way, I doubt you share my feelings for them. On the other hand, *I* know what you were trying to convey when you brought roses to the hospital bed of your new Amazonian girlfriend (who ignored a red traffic light while out riding her new bicycle, reasonably assuming it was some kind of street decoration), but being a newcomer to Europe, she is broadly confused by your gesture. *Either* personal or cultural aseme effectively operates as a Peircian symbol, i.e. it creates an 'asymbol'.

By contrast, as we'll see, we have evidence that we *share* pathemes, even if we cannot readily supply synonyms for them; we agree what things *feel* like. However, asemes are another matter. *Your* aseme, which, let's say, is a tone that will forever arrive only with *Après l'Ondée*, and is one of unbearably sweet melancholy – because she wore it *that* afternoon, the day she told you that what she felt for you was deep and true, but she was nonetheless running off with a Polish lawyer who owned a big house in Thetford Forest. But for *me*, your merely telling me how it makes you feel is an arbitrary connection, although it may well taint my experience of the scent in the future. On the other hand, those roses she left for you – on this we can both agree – seem a sure symbol of her strong feeling, although we might now question its sincerity. Although the first association has been forged in an arbitrarily and personal way, and the second by culture – *both* associations are learned, and both the perfume and the roses are asemic. (All metonyms are 'asymbols' until you own the rule-book.)

Now we can begin to see how these semes may also propose the new tropic scheme I mentioned earlier. *Formeme* and *aeteme* represent the universal principles of (contentual-paradigmatic) static correspondence and (functional-syntagmatic) dynamic link respectively. These are the means by which metaphoric inter-domain and metonymic intra-domain processes are driven. *Patheme* and *aseme* represent such human meaning as falls outside these two axes. The patheme is the seme of 'feeling', of which more shortly; and if you recall my definition of abstracta as 'qualia with names', its potential relation to 'the symbolic' is obvious: I will argue that the patheme is simultaneously *the seme of meaning*, and points to the deep consubstantiality of 'meaning' and 'feeling' in human experience. *Aseme* covers the business of arbitrarily forged connections I alluded to in 'free association', and creates the 'asymbol' (i.e. the Peircian arbitrary symbol).

We now have terms for what a thing *is* (if we can use 'is' in the limited sense of 'the sum of a thing's formal and contentual attributes'); what a thing *does*; what a thing makes you *feel*; and what you associate (or we associate) with that thing through *arbitrary and learned connection*. These terms seem to correspond to four distinct semiotic categories:

1. the formeme to the correspondence-function of the metaphoric (or 'semi-iconicity');
2. the aeteme to the directly relational function of index;
3. the patheme to the representational function of icon (this will take some explaining) and the animus/quale of the symbol, if we consider tone and abstract quale consubstantial categories;
4. the aseme to the function of the *asymbol*, the pure Peircian arbitrary symbol.

The patheme

What follows is a short discussion of the most controversial member of this group, the patheme, whose properties are difficult to think of as anything we might consider a seme at all. (The aseme, the anti-seme of 'meaninglessness', merely links the two categories of arbitrary personal association and semiotic 'asymbol', which are structurally identical.) I have long been plagued by the thought that much of what ties a poetic passage together and moves us is 'tonal' in nature, yet this goes largely unmentioned and unanalysed. By 'tonal', I mean communicated through its feel, tone, ambience, atmosphere, 'vibe'. The seme of 'tone', the patheme, is largely non-articulable;

it is, I am convinced, the dominant seme of music. (Its inarticulable nature, its coterminosity with 'feeling' itself, is the reason works on the aesthetics of music are in relatively short supply; indeed, the entire subject often strikes us as almost redundant or tautological.[3]) As the logical positivists and 'language school' of analytic philosophy were eventually forced to admit, there is a whole realm of human thinking and feeling that is resistant or alien to linguistic articulation; there are, it seems to me, an infinite number of discrete human moods whose transcendental qualities seem almost *defined* by their being inarticulable, by the fact no word can successfully adhere to them, despite their utter specificity. I would claim that these feelings, while they cannot be adequately 'described' in words, can nonetheless be *provoked* by words.

---

3 Roger Scruton has made one of the few meaningful contributions to the field – see *The Aesthetics of Music* (Oxford: Oxford University Press, 1997) – though his analysis of songs by Nirvana, R.E.M. and the like shows up a problem of methodology. For Scruton, beauty or meaning in music resides primarily in those aspects that can be adequately described by pitch, note-length and the Western conventions of expression and performance represented by the symbols and marks of traditional notation. (Where that would leave, say, that period of Aphex Twin's career when he decided not to use *notes* is anyone's guess.) However, traditional notation does not account even tolerably well for the subtleties of rhythmic displacement and emphasis, and it is especially poor at describing dynamic changes in timbre; since these are the *principal* means by which any sophisticated information is carried in folk, electronic, dance or experimental music – none of which tend to demonstrate very much in the way of traditional harmonic or melodic complexity – this is close to asserting the superiority of one musical genre over all others, which sounds like a form of codal interference or incompetence; although there are many like Scruton who articulately contend that the intrinsic superiority of Western classical music lies in the sophistication of its compositional method, I would still counter that this position is only really tenable if one either ignores or is simply repelled by other musics. (It seems a cultural prejudice one can immediately dismantle by merely listing those artists who move between culturally prestigious and 'lower' musics – say, Keith Jarrett, Chris Thile or Squarepusher.) However, we are all unconsciously drawn towards explanations which *least* challenge our own tastes and prejudices, and methodology can also produce a form of confirmation bias; I very much doubt this book has escaped that charge either.

To provide a means of entry into the idea, I offer this brief diversion into the sign-system of music, which is, I believe, entirely 'pathemic'. Music's signs are connected to its 'referents' neither by indexical nor by symbolic means, and they invoke neither formal nor causal attributes, but 'emotional states' – descriptively vague but experientially specific loci in the realm of feeling and the affections. The situation is complicated, however, by the fact that music has no referents in the linguistic sense at all, since it lacks anything like a denotative lexis. It creates its signs instead via a recursive process, wherein its isolable components are given meaning beyond their most generic associations only by *self*-contextualisation – i.e. the melodic, harmonic, rhythmic, timbral and thematic matrix which they simultaneously create and occur within.

For example: the 'emotional' function of the A note above middle C on the piano will change radically as another note is added to adapt the harmonic context, and provide a different emotional cue. Play the A, and the effect on the Western listener is approximately: *hmm* . . . (single note, no context, entirely neutral);[4] add the C above, and the result might be *mmm* . . . (the root note of a minor third, a little sad); add the F below and we might get an *awww* . . . (the major third of a major triad, the 'happy' effect considerably heightened by the fact that one had 'misinterpreted' the sadness of the minor third); add the B♭ below the F and we might get an *oh* . . . (the addition of the low B♭ turning it into a sweet, lounge-bar chord, but also one built on the subdominant relative to the F triad, the less stable and more bittersweet chord of the plagal cadence); and if we add a G♭ below *that*, we get *huh?* (the low note resulting in a tense, unsettling and

---

4 Unless the listener is a musical synaesthete and A has an 'asemic' link to the colour purple, the texture of cheesecloth, feelings of sexual inadequacy, or all three – 'A' can carry complex information only in its articulation and its timbral composition, not in its pitch. A single pitched note has few associations beyond the metaphorical mapping 'high' or low', and its corresponding place within the human vocal range, with its vague connotations of gender, age, body-size, etc.

dissonant chord only jazz musicians would bother to give a name: $Gb\Delta7\#9\#11$, for the record). I could describe its broad emotional effect of this last chord as before, but the point to note is that as harmony increases in complexity the number of words required to describe its effect will increase too, and *explicit* consensus regarding its emotional 'sense' is concomitantly harder to achieve. But the musical sign '440Hz' has no intrinsic musical 'meaning' whatsoever, despite what certain synaesthetes might try to tell you.[5] [For a note on music synaesthesia and how it might relate to poetry, see endnote 15.]

I realised recently that, for years, I have regarded the following explanation as something of a truism. After committing it to paper, it seems considerably weirder and more speculative than I had hitherto admitted to myself. As I discussed in the first essay, music has a miraculous ability to map itself to the landscape of human emotion and also to generate 'emotional sense'. Some semioticians claim music is polysemic, i.e. that its meanings are simultaneously multiple; but this is down, I think, to nothing but the text-centred life of the individuals attempting the description. My own experience has always been that music conjures something absolutely specific but self-evidently inarticulable, and that this belongs to a realm of feeling to which language has little direct access. For this reason we tend to characterise it as 'spiritual' as much as emotional, in recognition of its plainly transcendent – or at the very least language-transcending – qualities.[6]

---

5 We instinctively sense that music is structured by a directional metaphor. Harmony is gravitational or 'telluric', and works from the bottom up, not the top down: the lowest note in a chord gives it its fundamental colour. Ernst Levy in *A Theory of Harmony* (New York: SUNY Press, 1985), and others have posited the existence of alternative, *negative* harmonic structures based not on the overtone but the (largely unperceived) undertone series. If 'meaning is harmony' there may also be a telluric structure at play in language, with 'denotative centre' standing in for something like 'root note'; a 'negative semantics', where connotations would override and revise fundamental primary denotation, may also be possible through some mental training – but perhaps it already exists in the form of symbolic procedure, as outlined earlier.

6 Much of what follows was initially prompted by Susanne K. Langer, whose long-

Poetry enjoys something of the same 'spiritual' reputation, and for much the same reasons. It attempts to say things that language cannot usually contain, through increasing language's combinatorial, idea-blending power – which has the simultaneous effects of destabilising its consensual meaning and increasing its capacity for personal interpretation. The first essay described how poetry moves its whole internal value-system closer to that of music's, reinforcing the synaesthetic link between sound and sense through the strengthening of the iconic function already present in speech. I think the solution to the question *What kind of sign-system is music?* lies in that very approach. Semiotics struggles to shoehorn music into anything even vaguely resembling the standard terminology we use to describe the operation of the sign, and 'why stuff means other stuff'. The trouble is that music nonetheless *appears* to mean something, inasmuch as it produces effects that are clearly and directly related to our experience of it; it also appears – to judge by its replicable success, and our clumsy verbal adumbrations of our encounters with it – that we are experiencing roughly the *same* effects. The trouble is we can't decide *how* it achieves this connection.

If music works in a way that is neither indexical nor symbolic, then pretty much all that's left to us – without inventing another mysterious, etheric category of semiotic connection to accommodate the experience – is to claim that music is somehow *iconic*. As we've seen in the phenomenon of 'iconicity', an icon is a sign that shares enough of the content of its referent to be 'motivated', i.e. it is a sign so close in its attributes to the thing to which it refers that it immediately *invokes* that thing – as the imitative word 'thump' mirrors

---

neglected *Philosophy in a New Key* and *Form and Feeling* were both way ahead of their time. 'Because the forms of human feeling are much more congruent with musical forms than with the forms of language, music can reveal the nature of feelings with a detail and truth that language cannot approach.' Susanne K. Langer, *Philosophy in a New Key: A Study in the Symbolism of Reason, Rite, and Art*, 2nd edn (Cambridge, MA: Harvard University Press, 1951).

the sound of the action 'thump', or a picture of a chair immediately conjures up the chair itself.[7]

Here, we have a kind of empirical proof: the idea that the relationship between a musical passage and its emotional effect is iconic might chime deeply with our own experience. Where language refers to things and to concepts,[8] music appears to 'refer' to emotions and

[7] Iconicity is a business of degree, and the isomorphism linking the V and T of all 'X is Y' type metaphors is, in a straightforward sense, just its 'iconic' content. If the iconicity is high, then V and T can be merely stated for the connection to be obvious; if it is low, it will need to be established through further context – in other words, 'metaphors which depend on secondary connotations for their ground must articulate them'. However, the V-sign cannot be so motivated that its *uncontextualised* occurrence alone will be sufficient to invoke the T-signified, unlike the Peircian asymbol and its pre-established asemic link. (For example, in our hypothetical bad poem, let's say we just have the image of a lawn being mowed. We suspect this is a V representing 'genocide' by the anchorage of the title, 'The Aftermath', and the poet's having qualified the grass-blades as 'trembling multitudes'. But without those contextualising elements, the lawn is a mere detail; by contrast, there is no way the guy with the hood and sickle is merely in the poem to mow the grass.) The only aspect of language which is motivated is its mimetic function: we read descriptions of things and events as possessing sufficient iconicity to invoke those things and events themselves. This is only possible though the fundamental 'operative conceit' of the deep confusion of word and concept, via their quasi-asemic, semi-symbolic link. (The *part*-arbitrariness of this link I explored in Part I, arguing that it is strongly reinforced by an underlying non-arbitrary phonosemantic iconicity.)

[8] From Schopenhauer onwards, arguments have occasionally been advanced for the idea that music might have a semantic and referential function like that of language. I cannot take any of this seriously, and find no evidence whatsoever for such a position within my own direct experience. Supporters of the notion seem to argue only for its theoretical possibility. Other than its programmatic and onomatopoeic effects, music simply lacks a system of isolable signs and concomitant valencies to map itself to the realm of discrete concept. Besides, the most basic model of music as a denotatory sign-system would also have to assume things like universal perfect pitch, as well as a period of innocent language acquisition, where the function of the sign is primarily indexical until the links are forged. (See my earlier, admittedly contentious statements on presence and absence.) This would allow initial arbitrary connections to be made – between, say, the second inversion of the B♭ triad and that armchair, or the *tierce de picardie* in the key of D and an overweening self-confidence. However,

feelings – but with such immediacy, such speed, we can hardly get a cigarette-paper between the music and our emotional response to it. 'Refer' seems a bad verb: the presence of music and the arrival of our feelings 'about' it seem almost simultaneous, and to elide the 'about' itself. Our feelings are less evoked or invoked than *provoked*, and the usual sign-system of signifier – (contextually derived index) – signified has been short-circuited, with the 'feeling' arriving as a kind of inseparable daemon of the sound itself, in a way that could be described as *forcefully* motivated. Only an iconic procedure could account for the instantaneity of the experience (unless we are to claim that there is *no* semiosis involved, and that the response is as purely physical as the pain derived from hitting your thumb with a hammer). But given that music's 'referents', those provoked feelings of ours, are apparently so abstract *and* visceral . . . What on earth might that shared iconic content be? Where, in other words, is the sonic representation of our emotions that acts as just like the picture of our chair?

Despite the fact it has no isolable signs equivalent to the lexis of language, music comes on for all the world like a coherent sign-system. It has complex rules of pitch relation, of consonance and dissonance; it has something very close to a grammar and a syntax; and for centuries now theoreticians have explored parallels between the rhetorical structure of music and literature. Beginning with Joachim Burmeister's *Musica Poetica* in 1606, theorists of the baroque era were especially keen to pursue analogies between musical figure and rhetorical structure as a means of systematising the expression of an emotional state, or the way in which such an expression will imprint itself on the listener's affections. (Rhetorical terms would seek out their musical analogies: 'anabasis' might refer to an ascending passage which expresses rising spirits or heightened images; 'litotes',

this seems effectively no different from forging a sign-system based on, say, various patterns of fluff, paperclips or small change.

to musical understatement; 'aposiopesis' to a *tacet* in all voices that echoes the inability of an emotionally overcome speaker to proceed, and so on.) I am convinced that melody and harmony are mapped to surface sense and complex meaning respectively in a non-trivial way.

This sign-system, then, shares many of its characteristics with the sign-system of language, from its division into phrases to its argumentative structure. And while music has no equivalent to lexis, its various gestures nonetheless seem 'tied' to specific emotional states as effectively as lexis seems to refer to objects and to concepts. This has arisen, I suspect, from three convergent frames. The first is physical law; the second is a prelinguistic, learned association between vowel and human emotion; the third is language acquisition, in both its realised and potentiated state. In the first instance, music draws on the natural phenomena of isochrony and the harmonic series to organise its sonic material. In the second, it draws on strong prelinguistic, presymbolic and likely intrauterine connections between intonational vowel and human emotion. Finally, it arranges or maps that material to the recursive (and probably neurally embedded) syntactic structure of language itself.

In language, consonant is the means whereby we win the differentiating power to create a lexis capable of indicating a vast range of distinguishable referents. Without consonant, we can have no denotative system. I mentioned before that speech is a complex form of song; I strongly suspect music is, *in part*, both perceived and processed by the brain as a form of de-consonated speech, and can be considered as one long, infinitely differentiated and complex vowel-sound, carrying just the same kind of timbral, intonational and amplitudinal information as our speech-vowel.[9] While we know music

9 While I appreciate all arguments from experience should probably be disregarded, I should mention that I feel I instinctively know this from my own work as a jazz musician (one reason I have hitherto – and erroneously – regarded this as a commonplace). In the improvised ballad solo, especially, the rate of note-delivery is

engages many parts of the brain simultaneously, I feel that it is also understood as a linguistically processed intonational prosody, a speech-minus-lexis – and parsed as something incapable of denotation, but possessing the same potential for the carriage of *emotional* information as the vowel does in speech. Music *purely* connotes.

If vowel is the principal carrier of emotional content, and we do indeed process music as vowel-speech – this allows us our iconic operation. In the same way that we can closely follow the emotional contour of an argument on the other side of the hotel wall, so we heard vowels in the womb. Our intrauterine experience also contains the human voice, de-consonated by the wall of the womb – which acts as a low-pass filter, cutting out the higher frequencies of consonants. While the association between vowel and expression is, of course, complex and guided by the reinforcing contexts of facial expression, gesture, etc. (although some facial expression is innate), it seems entirely possible that iconic links between intonational contour and emotion could be forged there and then, possibly at the level of neurotransmitter. (Six-month-old babies respond to the beat of their mother's speech; emotions are shared via the hormones associated with them; certain feelings could then be firmly and viscerally associated with the cadences of a happy conversation, etc.) This is a material description of an idea that partly coincides with Kristeva's take on Plato's *chora*, by which he originally intended the matrical space in which The Forms were held. Kristeva sees this as an intrauterine presymbolic function, one which opposes the phallo-

---

often very close to that of conversational prosody, and my experience of improvising in these circumstances is entirely 'rhetorical'. To play a solo on a long-note, human-voice-range, monophonic instrument over, say, the melancholic, plaintive harmonic argument of Bill Evans's 'Time Remembered' feels more or less identical to the sensation of making a speech whose intention is to convince a listener of a *truth*; I feel my aim is to argue my point, articulate my emotional position, with as much nuance, conviction, reasoned debate and perhaps 'manipulative' tenderness as I can summon.

centric symbolicity of language itself.[10] Thus the patheme might be thought of as a 'choric' seme. By the time we are born the link is *effectively iconic*, because feeling and intonation are regarded as aspects of the same phenomenon, and one induces the other.

The patheme relies upon an immediate identification between sign and feeling. It has no 'verification process', whereby we might check the 'reasonableness' of our interpretation. In the case of a metaphor, our vehicle and tenor might share a formeme or aeteme; we inspect our ground for shared content to reassure ourselves that, say, the fluffy correspondence we noted between this cloud and that sheep was a sane one. However, the 'verification' of the patheme is consubstantial with its experienced effect. Its exchange can only take place in a less symbolic, less mediated sign-system, in a far purer medium that will afford a very high signal-to-noise ratio.

I suspect by the time we emerge – albeit born with grammar-capability and largely 'good to go' – we have *already* forged a direct, unmediated, iconic and motivated mapping between intonationally discriminated vowel and emotion. Our time spent as prelinguistic infants would further reinforce this; the phenomenon of both phono-logical contour and grammatical structure preceding the acquisition of lexis is well known. (YouTube has several delightful examples of infants communicating with the phrase-structures and intonational contours of speech without any lexis whatsoever – sometimes with each other, in vigorous debate.)

Just as language acquisition not only equips us with a bunch of handy signs to indicate stuff, but also provides us with a network structure along which abstract thought itself can take place (here, I'm more or less following Daniel Dennett), so the neural patterns laid down by grammar and recursive syntax might supply the carriage

---

10   Julia Kristeva, 'Motherhood According to Giovanni Bellini', *Desire in Language: A Semiotic Approach to Literature and Art*, ed. Leon S. Roudiez, trans. Thomas Gora and Alice A. Jardine (New York: Columbia University Press, 1980).

and combination of something other than lexis. Fill those channels, waterways and chambers with *motivated* vowel sounds which are perceived as partly consubstantial with the emotions they also invoke, and you have a system with the same properties of grammatical structure and recursive combination as language; it might have no denotative power, but it possesses the ability both to provoke and reflect feeling – *and to generate feelings previously unfelt*. Music has a generative power through its ability to develop context recursively; like syntax, these structures are infinite, and emotional analogues are automatically conjured for any combination of sounds, even those produced by aleatoric means. (Here the iconic nature of the sign forces us to make the interesting move of projecting not only our own feeling, but also the introjected feeling of a maker we know cannot exist.) This means we have access, in music, to a realm of *imaginative* feeling additional to that provided by our lived experience.

All this would leave us with a simple explanation: music *is* emotionally iconic. Music does not 'represent human emotions'; music is *exactly* what human emotions sound like, and when combined with the ratiocinative power of linguistic structure, can drive our human emotions into more and more complex and nuanced patterns, quite literally allying our emotion with our intelligence. (I can find only a very limited amount of scholarly literature on the subject, but I'm sure others will also have observed that the ability to appreciate and 'emotionally parse' harmonically complex music often – though not always – goes hand in hand with a high degree of literacy.)[11]

We know that 'poetry has a strong emotional effect' on its readers. Much of this is simply down to its emotionally charged subject matter, which, if the process of mimesis is transparent enough, inevitably

---

11 A further and necessary complication is the mapping between complex and nuanced meaning and musical harmony, which I suspect we perceive as directly analogous 'vertical' sophistications – one more example, if you like, of the projection of the axis of selection into the axis of combination, and a historically parallel development to poetry's use as a literary and not merely lyric form.

engages our own emotional memory in its powerful invocation and description of events, leaving our mirror neurons flashing like the lights on a Christmas tree; this relation between the depiction of 'moving events' and feeling seems straightforwardly iconic in its operation. However, it's worthwhile being pedantically clear on this point. I use the word 'depiction' advisedly. While a depiction of a chair summons the chair iconically, a 'depiction of an emotion' has no iconic force, since an emotion can only be summoned in words via hypostatic symbol. Naming the concept 'happy' or 'melancholic' makes us feel neither of those things. In other words, telling me *how* you feel makes me feel nothing (which is why one encourages all apprentice poets to write *with* but not *about* their feelings); what provokes the emotion is the depiction of a situation or event, or the making of a song or argument, which incarnates, realises or activates it – and likely has also provoked it in the poet. Frost's law of reciprocity, 'No tears in the writer, no tears in the reader; no surprise for the writer, no surprise for the reader', cannot be stated often enough, and is the fundamental rule of emotionally effective writing. The feelings which are provoked in the experience of the unsentimental reader are broadly those which mirror those the author felt during the process of composition itself.[12]

12 Sentimental readers move themselves. Nonetheless, there's a balance to strike here. Young poets are often encouraged to 'take risks', but by 'risk' what's often intended is 'experiment'. However, 'experiment' is mostly a pretty safe activity: the worst that can happen is the reader will get bored, confused or mildly offended. The most fruitful risks will often involve writing very simply, just before it shades into simple-mindedness; with prophetic force, just before it shades into pretentiousness; and at the extremes of feeling, just before it shades into sentimentality. I tend to be of the opinion that when you write, you should always risk looking like an idiot, a pretentious fool or a sap – or, indeed, a failure. Readers read poetry to take them closer to something they'd not usually be *prepared* let themselves feel: they 'gear up for it', and say – right: now I will read *a poem*.

In Japanese restaurants, great respect is accorded to those chefs who can prepare the puffer fish called the *fugu*. To qualify, you have to train for years; most candidates never even get to sit the exam – and even there, 90 per cent fail. The reason that it

I suspect only mutant geniuses like Bach and Shakespeare were spared suffering the emotions their art provokes.

Another obvious way of conducting the patheme is the one music employs. As I've already discussed (and will cover from another angle in Part III), the increase in the salience, number and length of strong stressed vowels through lineation, metre, lyric selection and the preference for content over function words has an immediate effect: it simultaneously increases the line's potential for the carriage of intonational information, and so emotional expression. Poetry cannot achieve the level of emotional iconicity music does; but it *attempts* to, and one aspect of the global shift from denotative to connotative function is to drag the stressed vowel centre-stage, so that the mind is primed for the reception and performance of just the kind of articulated feeling it associates with music. As we have seen, vowel is heavily exaggerated in poetry.

A crucially important aspect of this is the way rereading *fixes intonational pattern*, in a manner similar to the storage of prosodic pattern in the lexicalised phraseme. (This will be explored at length in the final essay. Lexis is stored along with its prosody; when a phrase become lexicalised, it undergoes the same intonational nailing-down as any other word. There are a thousand ways of stressing the phrase

---

takes so much training is not so the chef can avoid cutting into the fish's poison sac; that's easily learned. And certainly, if you cut it too close, you will kill the diner: but the reason the diner has ordered the fish is for the 'high' of the toxin. If the chef can cut it just close enough, a little of the toxin will seep into the flesh of the *fugu*, and give the diner the strange sensation they've paid so heavily to experience. So it is with the poetic art. One slip of the knife, and 'the reader will die on you', which is to say they will find you too stupid, or sentimental, or ridiculous to trouble themselves with, and close the book. But cut just close enough, and they'll be rewarded for their investment. So we should, by all means, *risk*: but it's our reputations that should be risked. And as for the reader – their mental health should be at risk, their sleep should be at risk, their unchallenged assumptions about the world should be at risk, just as the poet's will have been. But if the poet *isn't* walking the highest tightrope they dare . . . mediocrity is guaranteed.

'close the kitchen window', but barely more than one of 'go figure'.)
There is a rather astonishing psychological effect known as the 'speech-
to-song illusion', which works as follows: a recording of a piece of
conversational speech is played to a listener; then a random sentence or
phrase is then isolated, and played several times over. The effect of this
is to embed the intonational contour of the sentence as a memorised
series of tones. When the full passage is played back to the listener, and
the repeated phrase is heard again, the speaker appears to be clearly
singing the phrase, in a kind of auditory version of the 'persistence
of vision' effect.[13] Repetition — of both reading and recitation — can
also nail words to an intonational pattern closely resembling that of
memorised song. One can see that poetry, with its built-in emphasis on
song-like, strong-stressed vowels, is uniquely placed to take advantage
of this. When memorisation takes place, that aspect of music which
is non-sequential and atemporal (that part which, in the Rilkean

---

13   The effect reinforces the argument that a deep structural connection exists
between language and music:

> To conclude, this illusion is in line with what philosophers and musicians
> have been arguing for centuries, that strong linkages must exist between
> speech and music. We still need to determine the neural processes that
> are responsible for this striking perceptual transformation. However,
> the present experiments show that for a phrase to be heard as spoken
> or as sung, it does not need to have a set of physical properties that
> are unique to speech, or a different set of physical properties that are
> unique to song. Rather, we must conclude that, assuming the neural
> circuitries underlying speech and song are at some point distinct and
> separate, they can accept the same input, but process the information in
> different ways so as to produce different outputs. As a further point, this
> illusion demonstrates a striking example of very rapid and highly specific
> perceptual reorganisation, so showing an extreme form of short-term
> neural plasticity in the auditory system.
>
> > – Diana Deutsch, Rachael Lapidis and Trevor Henthorn, 'The Speech
> > to Song Illusion' (invited lay language paper presented at the
> > 156th meeting of the Acoustical Society of America, Miami, FL)
> > *Journal of the Acoustical Society of America*, 2008

conception, 'sings across the gaps') intrudes into the syntagm to make 'one big word of everything', rendering it simply song-like, with the nuanced and fixed prosody of a single word many syllables long. Song-poetry persists and exists in different parts of the brain from mere word-poetry. The auditory cortex is working a bit harder, the fun-centre of the nucleus accumbens is high on dopamine, and – if the poem is learned, say, while *in* love – the amygdala is meta-tagging the word-song as emotionally important, a feeling that will be recalled and revived when it is sung again. I have versions of Shakespeare's Sonnet 18 and Yeats's 'Inisfree' in my head that I can hum, and that exist separately as intonational contours, fixed patterns of semantic emphasis and emotional nuance; they feel to me as song-like as any songs I know.

This process will strongly reinforce the experience of the 'pathemic' through the codifying of emotional information – until, perhaps, it becomes a fixed performance; though in my own experience, inton-ational pattern just as often becomes a template to gently improvise within, and adapt to further performed interpretations. Add this to the mimetic power of vivid descriptive language, and we have, in effect, the definition of lyric potential – whose nature is fundamentally pathemic.

The details of a good poem are almost always bound by what I identify as the trope of 'tonal isologue', shared properties of 'feel' that overlap and create stylistic, emotional and tonal consistencies in any composition. Raising the stressed vowel-count is one direct means of permitting the carriage of emotional information in any spoken or internalised performance. The other has already been discussed at length: our examination of the phonestheme showed how shared con-notations are often indicated through the presence of shared sounds. The patheme extends this idea, and states that the phonestheme – whether in the form of pre-existing sound-nodes in the language, or local innovations within the poem – *conducts and activates* shared qualia between words.

However, there's more to the literary patheme than sound and vowel and consonant, and it may be transmitted by mimesis, semantic connotation, aesthetic feature, etc. – or any combination thereof. The point is that in every case the procedure will be, on closer inspection, iconic to some degree, i.e. carried via some form of direct representation. Whichever way we might analyse it, though, the fundamental characteristic of the patheme is that, like its musical equivalent: (a) it can only exist as a product of its context and not as an isolable sign; therefore (b) it can *only* connote; therefore (c) while it can be both indicated and conducted, it cannot be adequately paraphrased or have its complex, compound sense broken into constituents, and indeed often seems to resist linguistic description entirely. The patheme is the *tonal* aspect of sense. (At this point readers still sympathetic to my argument may see where this is all about to head: since the animus of the symbol is often indistinguishable from tone or feeling, the patheme is the semic means *by which the symbolic is conducted*.)

One might think of the denotation-free sign as a musical note shorn of its fundamental, leaving it with nothing but the higher partials of its distinct timbre – therefore unable to be woven into any harmonic or melodic structure, despite its possessing a clear timbral quality, one which other notes might share. It's as if we could hear every one of a series of notes as being produced by a viola – but couldn't clearly identify or name *which* notes they actually are. 'Semantic timbre' is excepted from both paradigmatic and syntagmatic (our harmonic and melodic, vertical and horizontal, if you will) analyses of texts. It can only be approached through retrospective verification, which is to say all we can do is make informal checks that two readers were indeed experiencing the same effects. The means of producing these effects is not mysterious. The means of defining them *is* mysterious, and not just hopelessly so: *precisely* so. The patheme is that very aspect of poetry that leads us still to proclaim the 'heresy of paraphrase'; it is the quality without which the poem would be mere verse.

Meaning and feeling

I will resist exploring the matter in any great depth, as there is a book to be written on the subject – but I will merely observe that the patheme may also be a way of explaining the semiosis of the kind of symbol whose abstract animus is left unarticulated or felt to be inarticulable, i.e. those symbols which merely leave an aura of significance around a 'totemised' concrete detail. It seems to me that the brain processes such vague aurae as qualial effect, and may effectively 'translate them into tone'. Suppose the patheme, our seme of feeling, is also the means by which we conduct *uninterrogated* meaning; inversely, this may propose that 'interrogated feeling' is therefore an alternative definition of 'meaning'. Merely saying that 'meaning is the epistemic corollary of the subservience of one domain to another' *describes* the process, but does not address the mechanism by which meaning is conferred; the process will have its irreducible seme like any other. My strong hunch is that the seme of meaning is *also* – or at least can very usefully be designated as – the patheme, which means that the human (i.e. non-syntagmatic or non-paradigmatic) processes of meaning and feeling are, at their deepest level, consubstantial. We may have confused 'meaning' with the verbal articulation of 'the feeling of meaning'.

The patheme is the seme of iconic function. But while music may be what our human feelings *sound* like, consider this for the last word in iconicity: 'feelings' are also simply what our feelings *feel* like. Antonio Damasio and others have provided plausible aetiologies of what we might call 'meaningfulness' through a description of the evolution of feeling: through the combination of learned cause-and-effect and memory (pain or pleasure centres are provoked by certain environmental conditions; these occasions are remembered; memory restimulates them), more complex emotions arise, with higher 'feelings' being the consequence of an *awareness* of those emotions. If one accepts that authentic 'feeling' might be a strong component of what we mean by 'meaningfulness', then you have something close to a proven link. This also points us back to the consciousness-creating feedback loop that I sense is also the key motif of meaning-creation. (Some current theorists in neuroscience feel that the only sensible measure of our 'unique human consciousness' is the extent of our *awareness* of our awareness; animals may be aware, but they seem not to be awake to the fact that they *are* so. For that same reason I very much doubt they 'mean' like us either.) So these feelings might be said to 'possess' meaning.[14]

However, I sense that what's being missed is the extent to which that mere ascription is misread as inscription: the wilful designation of 'feelings' as meaning*ful* is intrinsicality by the back door. This strikes me as axiomatic: one decides on the meaning of the word 'meaning' by applying it to something that strikes one as self-evidently meaningful. My preference is first to say that feelings may rather be the *means* by which meaning is created, and then to look for an explanation with some predictive capability: how might meaning be *created*, from scratch, from one moment to the next? The origin of the process may well lie in the mapping of a self-reflexive, self-aware emotional procedure onto a semantic one via some exaptive expediency, resulting in the symbolic procedure we see today. But no description frees us from the obligation to understand the intermediary mechanism. For this we would have to understand the currency, the seme, the method of its conduction, the structural basis of its exchange.

A poet's stake in all this is that it would make 'meaning' something capable of being consciously revised; poets sense intuitively that the dominant frames which govern received meaning can be switched, altered or subverted. If 'meaning' is an awareness of 'sense' that produces a conscious state (our use of the same word for 'lower' receptive faculties and basic understanding is no accident), then 'an awareness of meaning' may be the neutral definition of a 'higher consciousness'; if,

14 Antonio Damasio, *Looking for Spinoza: Joy, Sorrow, and the Feeling Brain* (London: Vintage, 2004).

FOUR SEMES, FOUR TROPES

furthermore, the terms 'feeling and meaning' and 'emotion and sense' are linked by the fact that the former are merely a consciously aware version of the latter, we then have a definition of a 'conscious emotional intelligence', one that is likely the aim of all artists who seek to make the structure of both meaning *and* emotion manipulable.

The four tropic categories

These reflect the four ways in which trope is generated; they consist of two universal categories and two human-specific categories. These categories have many other characteristic rules, operations, expressions and aspects, but these seem to me prime: (a) operative principle; (b) seme; (c) typical semiotic form; (d) operation; (e) domainial character; (f) principal trope-type; (g) generic role; (h) function; (i) metrical-prosodic role. Each function or aspect to a degree implies all the others in the same column; therefore when one role is altered, all associated roles are at least modified.[15]

1	2	3	4
(a) paradigm	(a) syntagm	(a) iconicity	(a) contingency
(b) formeme	(b) aeteme	(b) patheme	(b) aseme
(c) isomorphism	(c) index	(c) icon	(c) emblem
(d) correspondence	(d) relation	(d) representation	(d) arbitrary association
(e) inter-domain	(e) intra-domain	(e) supra-domain	(e) extra-domain
(f) metaphor	(f) metonymy	(f) symbol	(f) asymbol
(g) content	(g) function	(g) quale	(g) arbitrary association
(h) form	(h) cause	(h) meaning	(h) arbitrary link
(i) strong event/strong	(i) weak space/weak	(i) intonation/accent	(i) arbitrary stress

15 This table is ripe for crankish expansion: one could cheerfully start listing everything from the fundamental interactions (these fit rather well, alarmingly) to the Four Horsemen of the Apocalypse (ditto), but I have restrained myself. Nonetheless I am convinced that *some* kind of unified poetic field lurks behind it.

TOWARDS A TAXONOMY OF POETIC TROPE

Metaphor and symbol in aspect

In the analysis of the poetic metaphor and symbol we might consider a number of different variables. Some of them are scalar, and some are binary. Binary variables result in clean distinctions; scalar, in fuzzy ones or distinctions of degree. The following variables strike me as the most pertinent, though this list is far from exhaustive. (T = tenor; V = vehicle; TD = thematic domain. Symbol is mentioned here, though I consider it a separate tropic category.)

1. *The categorical distinction* between metaphor and symbol. Metaphor consists of V and T. T may be text-present or absent; T and V may be interchangeable, as in isologue (though the terms T and V are inappropriate where no dominant frame is implied). In metaphor, text-present T may be abstract or concrete. Text-absent T can only be concrete. A text-absent abstract T indicates a *symbol* (where T is instead 'animus') and is a different tropic class.

2. *The degree of text-presence of T or V.* In the case of metaphor, if T is concrete and text-absent, V is an 'enigma', in my terms. V cannot be wholly text-absent, but is often only vestigially suggested, via transferred epithet, etc.

3. *The literality or non-literality of the V.* 'Literality' refers only to the 'literal' within the mimetic conceit of the poem. 'She played a fiery trumpet' or 'She has a fiery passion' invokes but does not feature the V 'fire' as a literal element within

the poem's origo;[1] the V is non-literal. A poem which saliently features both a bonfire and a birthday cake ablaze with candles as salient details will draw them together in an isologue; both elements collapse the functions of T *and* V, and both occupy the literal frame. (However, in 'this bonfire we are building in our garden is our passion', 'bonfire' is a literal V, and therefore the sentence, while still a form of syntactically bound isologue, is a kind of metaphoric/ symbolic hybrid. If we are supposed to infer a text-absent 'passion' from 'in our garden the bonfire blazed', we have a symbol, not a metaphor. Generally speaking, symbol has no sub-types beyond the global/thematic literal-totem type, and the local figurative-totem type; the latter are often cultural clichés of the 'roaring lion' or 'fig leaf' kind.)

4. *The relative length of the comparison.* This determines whether the trope is local, extended or global. If T is text-present and abstract or concrete, it can form a local metaphor, or an extended metaphor (or 'conceit'). If T is text-absent and concrete, it can form a local enigma or global 'riddle'. (If T is text-absent and abstract, the result is local symbol or a global allegory.)

5. *The relative nativity of the V* (in the case of metaphor) or totem (in the case of symbol) to the thematic domain; the degree to which the reader will consider the V or totem 'native' or 'alien' to the poem's concerns. (The issue rarely arises with non-figurative totems, which are generally 'part of the furniture', but local symbols based on figurative or

---

1 An origo, for our purposes, is the POV in which the poem is based, i.e. the deictic field the text establishes by mimetic means. This locational, temporal, pronominal and literal /non-literal frame is the site of our imagined literary reality, and the 'home co-ordinate' from which it might be deictically shifted to *other* times, places, POVs and non-literal, figurative or metatextual spaces.

non-literal totems can be as alien as any metaphor if they are not merely phrasemic cultural idioms.)

6. *The relative degree of the isomorphism* (i.e. the size of the ground, which can be considered as a negative product of the size of the tension) in the case of metaphor; *the relative directness of the index*, in the case of the totem. This determines whether the metaphor is tenuous or broad, the symbol 'obvious' or buried – and plays a large role in the ease of interpretability of either trope-type. (In the case of metaphor: too broad, and the comparison is redundant; too tenuous, and it's simply unconvincing. Grounds which are composed of secondary connotations alone *must* be text-present to have any chance of being discovered, i.e. they must be *declared* as grounds.[2] The same applies to indirect indexical components of totems, whose animus might never be discovered without either the clear articulation of the index or the careful contextualisation of the totem to draw out the appropriate indexical, and aid its interpretability.)

7. *The abstract or concrete nature of either V or T.* This has been exhaustively covered elsewhere. The present/absent or concrete/abstract status of T and V will sometimes entail a change of tropic class:

    a) text-present concrete T, text-present concrete V: metaphor or isologue

---

2 To recap: in 'fiery passion' we don't need to be told why 'fire' is a good V for the T of 'passion', as the ground – which might contain 'hot', 'agitated', 'potentially destructive', 'dangerous' and 'easily out of control', etc. – is both broad, obvious and culturally accepted to the point of cliché. If we say, unironically, 'my passion for you is like a cup of tea', only 'hot' is shared, and the reader may feel the metaphor is a tenuous one. If we say 'my passion for you is a radio-mast', the ground is a mystery. If what we have in mind is that both are 'crackling with broadcasty intent', the poet must *declare* this secondary connotation, if the metaphor is not to remain wholly obscure.

  b) text-absent concrete T, text-present concrete V: enigma
  c) text-present abstract T, text-present concrete V:
     metaphor
  d) text-present abstract T (subject), text-present abstract V
     (attribute): abstract peristasis
  e) text-absent concrete T (subject), text-present abstract V
     (index): hyperstatic metonym
  f) text-absent abstract T (animus), text-present concrete V
     (totem): hypostatic symbol.

8. *The textual presentation of the trope.* In the case of metaphor,
   this refers to the strength of the expression of the copula,
   and generates most of the best-known textual sub-types of
   metaphor. Beyond those mentioned under 3, symbol has no
   sub-types.

9. *Text-salience of the V or totem*, i.e. the degree to which it will
   be consciously registered, something which has a major role
   in its ease of interpretability. Text-salience involves far too
   many stylistic, interpretative and practical factors to list.

It's a fact apparently underappreciated by several theorists that
when one looks at a phenomenon with many variables, *many* legiti-
mate taxonomies can be generated. Just as one might choose to
classify fruit according to its size and colour, or its taste and colour,
or its colour and origin, its origin and taste, and so on — a taxonomic
list is generated by selecting those variables most pertinent to one's
area of enquiry, and working out all possible permutations. While this
will present a true taxonomy, it will nonetheless be a highly partial
account of the complex phenomenon, overlap with other taxonomies
using one or more of the same variables, and create fuzzy categories,
which arise when at least one of those parameters is scalar. With
those caveats, there are, I think, several useful taxonomies that can by
derived from the variables above.

Conceptual modes of metaphor and symbol:
forms of isomorphism

These simply describe the nature of the V–T relationship. Here I've taken just the second and third variables in my earlier list: the degree of text-presence of T and the literality or non-literality of the V. From these, we can derive five useful modes of V–T relations.

(We should correct anyone who talks about the vehicle 'inhabiting a figurative realm'. Tenor, vehicle or indeed *both* can form literal elements in a poem. The most important aspect of the V–T relationship is simply that it's inter-domain. The 'literal and figurative' is a highly confused and confusing distinction, and lacks a clear definition. Their use should probably be limited to a deictic one.)

1) Independent subject: **literal mode**

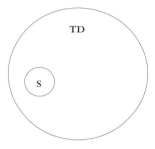

They sat by the calm sea.

This is essentially 'base mode', prior to any transformation of a detail into either a metaphoric, metonymic or symbolic type. Here 'calm sea' is just what it says, a simple substantive. Note however that the condition of *anything* being 'just what it says' doesn't exist in the poem, so this is a happy fiction. It will already be serving as some kind of intra-domain, evidential peristasis at the very least – and thereafter is potentiated as either metaphoric vehicle or symbolic totem, depending on what sense is then made of it in context.

2) T + V text-present, but both literal: **isologic mode**

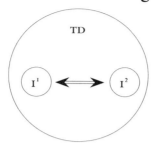

They sat by the calm sea. They opened the flask of tea. She felt her mind settle and still.

An *isologue* (a term I borrowed from chemistry) consists of two elements in relative proximity, which both take place in the same literal frame, and which clearly share attributes: in this case, 'calm sea' and 'her mind settle and still'. The distinguishing feature of the isologue is that is neither possible *nor desirable* to say which is tenor and which is vehicle and for that reason – the abscence of a dominant frame – we might do better to label its elements I^1, I^2, I^3, etc., and distance it from the power structure T and V imply. It's a favourite strategy of Paul Muldoon's, and chimes strongly with Muldoon's almost-philosophical stance that 'the conditional' often defines the most honest human response to the world and its bewilderments, and where a mere connection between things is often as much as we can meaningfully point out; this is *not* the kind of 'meaning' other kinds of metaphorical construction insist on.[3] The isologue is shockingly under-identified and under-analysed. (In Muldoon's 'Cuba', to take

3   I have already defined meaning as the product of the subservience of one conceptual domain to another. 'Meaning' requires one frame to be 'top' and one 'bottom', as in tenor and vehicle. Their elements cannot explain one another; 'explanation' demands reference to the laws of a single dominant frame. The mechanism by which meaning is generated is almost invariably political. Note that the isologue, in its radical democratic refusal of such conceptual hegemony or enslavement, resists siting its truth-value in 'meaning' and places it instead in 'contingency'. Isologues don't have 'meaning', but mutual sympathetic resonance.

one example, we find the twin literal themes of the sister's sexual near-encounter and the Cuban Missile Crisis carefully mapped to each another through the shared ground of something like 'close scrapes' or 'narrowly avoided catastrophes' – though that caricature completely betrays the subtlety of the poem's construction and other aspects of the thematic domain, primarily its various takes on 'patriarchy'.[4]) Isologues depend heavily on the poetry-reading contract, and only reveal themselves to a reader 'reading in', i.e. *looking* for connections between apparently disconnected elements, because one *knows* in a poem that nothing is mere chance, that nothing is unconnected – nor can be left so. (We except those poems derived, obviously, from aleatoric or surreal procedure.) The 'tonal isologue' – where what is shared between elements is pathemic in nature – is its most common form.

3) Text-present T + non-literal V: **metaphoric mode**

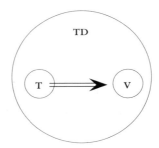

The sea at night looked like a black wheatfield.

This is our 'standard' metaphorical construction and covers the all the explicit metaphor types of simile ('like'-types), copular metaphor ('is'-types), genitive metaphor ('of'-types), unit metaphor (verb-metaphor, epithetic metaphors, modifier+noun-types, etc.) and so on.

---

4 Paul Muldoon, 'Cuba', *Poems 1968–2014* (London: Faber & Faber, 2016).

4) Literal V + text-absent literal T: **enigmatic mode**

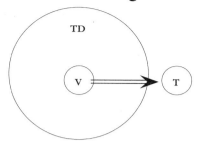

They sat by the calm sea . . .

. . . where what is intended by 'calm sea' is the basin of water placed before the kids on the kitchen floor in a poem about, say, not going on holiday but making the best of it. Enigmata are riddles; an enigma is just a text-present concrete vehicle that points to a text-absent concrete tenor.

> Grieve bought a balloon and a goldfish.
> He swung through the air,
> He fired shotguns, rolled pennies, ate sweet fog from a stick.
>
> (GEORGE MACKAY BROWN, 'Hamnavoe Market')[5]

The 'sweet fog from a stick' is, we can quickly see, candyfloss.[6] We reach this conclusion from the thematic domain, 'things that happen at a fair', and the transferred epithet 'sweet'. Enigmata are also beloved of the Martian school: 'And I am author / of this toga'd tribune / on

---

5 George Mackay Brown, *The Collected Poems of George Mackay Brown* (London: John Murray, 2005).

6 As opposed to, if you recall, the 'hyperstasis', a metonym where an abstract quality indicates a text-absent concrete tenor – e.g. 'the bitterness' for 'lemon juice'; and the 'hypostasis', a symbol where a concrete totem stands for and points to a text-absent abstract animus – e.g. in Blake's 'O Rose thou art sick', we are inclined to read the rose as 'love/beauty/the Edenic/, and the worm as 'contagion/evil/decay (as well as the enigma 'serpent').

my aproned lap' (Craig Raine, 'In Modern Dress').[7] Here, the 'toga'd tribune' is an infant child draped in a bath towel.

Most text-absent T 'Martianisms' and visual puns are enigmata. The V under this condition is, of course, *resolutely* non-literal.

5) Unalloyed V: **cryptic mode**

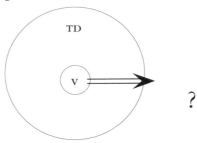

He opened a drawer. Inside was the calm sea.

V, by virtue of its salience (it often achieves this salience by being obviously non-literal or non-reality-consistent), indicates the presence of a text-absent T: however, no context or confirmation is provided by the thematic domain whatsoever. Since the mind always takes the shortest route to literal sense, it will attempt to resolve it as first an enigma (*Is it something else? Is it* acting *like something else?*), and then as a symbolic hypostasis, the animus of which proves not just inarticulable but wholly elusive; the reader might then posit a private meaning, making of it an arbitrary 'asymbol' – before they give up. I.e.: 'Perhaps the drawer is full of water? No. Or maybe it just reflective of his state of mind? Or . . . of *something*? Something about it makes me think of that idyllic lido from my childhood in Carnoustie. No: it's just weird.' A reflection you will find cool or not cool, depending on your taste for this kind of stuff. If the detail is consistent with the literal frame, the result is an obscure 'halo of significance'; if it is not, the diagnosis is often surrealism, magic

7   Craig Raine, *A Martian Sends a Postcard Home* (Oxford: Oxford University Press, 1979).

realism, or the school song of some other literary mode. In a decent poem, these 'surreal images' are generally saved from incoherent nonsense by some kind of pathemic overlap. (I strongly suspect that when presented with such an impossible crossword clue, the mind automatically tries to conduct its business as I've just described — through formeme, aeteme, patheme and then aseme, in that order. Having ransacked the V for some context-directed formeme or aeteme which might point to a tenor, the reader is likely then to try to 'vibe' some kind of a patheme, and read the image tonally and totemically, which might yield an animus; finally, they might posit an asemic link, and read it either subjectively and arbitrarily — or assume the poet's meaninglessly subjective or arbitrary intent.[8])

6) Totem + text-absent abstract animus: **symbolic mode**

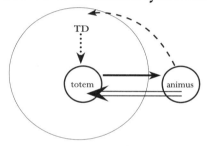

They sat by the calm sea . . .

(I regard the symbolic as a distinct tropic mode whose function is the production of meaning, something it accomplishes by simultaneous and reflexive intra-domain and inter-domain operation. A detail indicates a ruling abstraction; that animus then constrains and directs the sense of the original detail 'metaphorically'; 'meaning' is emergent from the process.)

---

8   Or they read it as surrealism, an anti-mode of deliberately strange juxtaposition. (Surrealism is a literary mode like any other. André Breton would redraft the poems written during his sessions of psychic automatism, if he adjudged them not automatic enough.)

This comes in two sub-types. (a) A symbol with a literal totem: in a poem in which a warring couple who have put their differences aside with a trip to the seaside – a poem 'about', it becomes clear, the idea of 'détente and peaceful resolution' – 'they sat by the calm sea' indicates and will be subsequently totemised by the emerging animus, i.e. 'it will come to mean' peaceful resolution, etc. This is far and away the most common type of symbol. (b) A symbol with a non-literal totem: in a poem in which a warring couple have put their differences aside, and are merely sitting on a sofa, the poet adds 'they sat by the calm sea'. (If they couple had just ran a bath, this statement is an enigma, as it merely stands in front of a literal statement; the enigma might *then* be subsequently totemised. Tropes can be complex.) This differs from type (a), as I've previously footnoted, in that it tends to localise its own contribution relative to the thematic domain, since its totem-status is more conferred 'top-down' than it is emergent. The abstract attribute 'peaceful resolution' comes first, and is substituted out by a representative example or token, 'calm sea'; I suppose 'symbolic enigma' would be accurate. Type b) is rare and when it occurs often does so in the form of a cultural cliché; generally, like the enigma, it's a trivially substitutive operation.

Textual modes of metaphor:
the expression of the isomorphism

This describes the nature of the metaphor's surface representation in the text. The types here are derived from the variable I earlier listed as 'the textual presentation of the trope', which essentially describes *the relative strength of the expression of the copula*. The metaphor has its frisson because it states a categorical impossibility, i.e. that something is that which it is clearly not. (As we've seen, this peculiar frisson is often the result of an antithesis softened by its binding lyric expression, whose sweetness tends to smuggle it past the sensors before the brain has acknowledged the heresy, controversy or insanity of the statement; singing can be a way of forcing the listener to entertain the impossible.)

> Type 1 sees two elements juxtaposed but not syntactically
> connected;
> Type 2 sees the V compared to the T;
> Type 3 sees the V identified with the T;
> Type 4 sees the V conflated with the T;
> Type 5 sees the V substituted for the T.

(All symbols take the form of type 5: concrete V is substituted for abstract T.)

All type-1 metaphors can again be covered by the term 'isologue'. This describes all the implicit inter-domain frisson between independent terms or elements in a single text; while it covers bold figures like the 'Muldoonian isologue', the effect is often very subtle, and can amount to little more than a shared ambience. Longley's 'Self-Heal', again: 'That day I pulled a cuckoo-pint apart / To release the giddy insects from their cell. / Gently he slipped his hand between my thighs.'[9] The two statements are not directly connected, but seem to be bound together through a vague tonal ground, one of languor, sexuality, 'things opened'; and while one can identify 'formemic' or 'aetemic' elements, the sense is carried here by the patheme as much as anything else. Since most elements in good poems float in a common tonal soup, the pathemic version of the trope can be almost wholly pervasive.

For this reason the 'tonal isologue' may be both the most prevalent trope in poetry – and the least-identified. Whenever we encounter images or lines we 'feel work' together or form a smooth segue despite having apparently little in the way of direct connection or clear correspondence, they tend to be connected through just this

---

9 Michael Longley, *Collected Poems* (London: Jonathan Cape, 2007).

kind of tonal, pathemic ambience: they are joined by a shared 'feeling'. This constitutes the ground between the two elements; we *sense* a connection – though not in a way amenable to easy analysis. That they 'feel connected', is, actually, the extent and the content of our knowledge of them, since the conduction of the patheme is iconic, i.e. a notoriously narrow space in which to interpolate anything like an articulation of its process. Still, 'tonal isomorphism' sounds like an oxymoron; how can something so unique *and* vaguely defined be shared between two elements? 'Subjective and intuitive verification', seems to be the answer. This consistent tonal ether forms the breathable weather of any great poem, and most or all of its elements will drawn on it and be connected by it to some degree. This is how a poem builds its most subtle and consistent expressions of languor, gloominess, confusion, cold, warmth, desperation or jouissance; not only does this tonal ether, our 'Higgs field of sense', mean that everything will gain semantic weight from it; its particular charge also means that any detail in the poem with *symbolic* intent will find the needle of its index swing round towards the condensing global animus all the more quickly.

While tonalities are the least paraphrasable kind of connotation, they should nonetheless be amenable to some description, even if it inevitably tends towards the vague and subjective. The trope operates across elements in a manner closely analogous to the phonestheme across lexemes; the more elements in which the patheme can be felt or shown to reside, the more clearly it is conjured up and bodied forth in a way that can be identified. It is not, however, 'magic' – though the way the tonal isologue does its work is *so* quiet, pervasive and inarticulably subtle, the casual reader or the poet with no interest in their own process (a stance I respect, if it works for them) might be forgiven for thinking it so.

Types 2, 3 and 4 give us the common, well-known forms of the V text-present types of metaphor: the comparative type yields simile and analogy; the copular, 'classic' metaphor and extended metaphor or conceit; the unit types conflating V and T in a single expression (e.g.

epithetic metaphors like 'the tall-sailed cloud', 'the boiling sea'), as well as 'interfused' or fabular metaphor over longer passages; finally, the type-5 substitutives, which are covered by (metaphorical) enigma and (symbolic) hypostasis, and their long forms of riddle and allegory.

Adding in local and global variables yields the following:

1. **Isologic type** (isologue: a trope of correspondence formed through the juxtaposition of literal-domain-consistent elements)

       Local – isologue at the level of detail

       Global – isologue at the level of passage

2. **Comparative type**

       Local – simile ('like' and 'as'-type)

       Global – analogy (simile at the level of passage), extended comparison

3. **Copular type**

       Local – ('is'-type) metaphor

       Global – extended metaphor or conceit

4. **Unit type**

       Local – unit metaphor types (epithetic metaphor, verbal metaphor, genitive metaphor, neologistic blends, etc.)

       Global – extended metaphor or conceit, 'interfused metaphor', myth

5. **Substitutive type**

       Local – (metaphoric) enigma; (symbolic) hypostasis

       Global – (metaphoric) riddle; (symbolic) allegory

A taxonomy of metonymy

We can spare ourselves this. If a culture can be isolated and defined, there probably *is* relatively finite list of generic-domain metonymic rules in any one culture, even if we know the specific-domain rules are necessarily infinite. The rough four divisions of the semes probably hold: formemic formal relations, aetemic causal relations, pathemic tonal relations and asemic, freely forged arbitrary relations. Behind this, however, will lurk something like the broad conceptual-semantic declension of Action, Place, Thing, Event, State, Path, Property, Manner and Amount, from which we might more carefully derive causal metonymies, topographical metonymies, formal metonymies, temporal metonymies, and so on. Although there would be nothing to stop someone working out the combinatorial possibilities, then seeing where a broad and representative range of exempla fitted into the scheme; discovering which formulae were the more favoured would give an indication of particular cultural or literary styles. Assuming Jackendoff is correct in his declension, the number of such metonymic categories would be:

$$9! / 2!(9 - 2)! = 36$$

– leaving us with, for example, PLACE FOR EVENT (e.g. 'Wembley' for 'Cup Final'), AMOUNT FOR THING ('11' for 'football team'), PROPERTY FOR THING ('lead' for 'bullet') PLACE FOR EVENT ('twin towers' for 'the events of 9/11') or synecdoches like THING FOR THING or PLACE FOR PLACE ('wheels' for 'car' or 'the Tower' for 'The Tower of London'), and so on. All of the other metonymic formulae one hears cheerfully kicked around are members of the infinite sub-sets of this finite set. ('Definitive lists' of such formulae are train-wrecks of false taxonomy.) If all isolable phenomena have, potentially, about nine isolable categories of aspects – under domain-determined contextual constraints, one side of the nonagon is going to be turned *most* outwardly (a guitar, say, will be present in a poem through its shape, or the music it makes, or its unmoving stillness, or its place in a room of other guitars, or its just being a guitar, and so on), and this aspect is likely to provide the metonymic attribute which will then perform an indexical function.

Form-types of metonymy are also simplified by the fact that direct indices can't, obviously, point outside the domain, and are therefore limited to peristasis and metonym. *Anything* identifiable as an element that appears in a poem, even an unalloyed noun, is arguably a peristasis, as the reader's awareness of its careful selection alone has rendered it – at the very least – contextually 'evidential'.

Expression-types might conceivably declare 'strength of relation', as they do with 'the copular conceit' – but what such a cline would look like, heaven knows. The two are not conceptually analogous. Again, they could only reflect two conceptual forms: (a) the Subject + Attribute of peristasis, and (b) the free Attribute + text-absent Subject of metonymy (i.e. the Attribute is now an Index; this might be a concrete attribute, or an abstract hyperstasis). Their textual forms are probably infinite; unlike copula-strength, nothing very meaningful is reflected in their syntactic presentation. The paradigmatic trope results in something that can be caricatured in terms of its syntagmatic form, while the syntagmatic trope results in something that generates nothing but a series of paradigmatic instances.

DEIXIS, PARANOIA AND
ERRORS IN TRANSMISSION

It is with some relief that we can now turn to an area only really approachable by anecdotal means. In 'Questions about Angels', Billy Collins addresses and solves the old scholastic chestnut, 'how many angels can dance of on the head of a pin?', concluding that

> perhaps the answer is simply one:
> one female angel dancing alone in her stocking feet,
> a small jazz combo working in the background.
> She sways like a branch in the wind, her beautiful
> eyes closed, and the tall thin bassist leans over
> to glance at his watch because she has been dancing
> forever, and now it is very late, even for musicians.[1]

As fine a solution as this is, it also reminds us that poems are not to be trusted, and their methods almost rigorously unscientific. This is not to say such conclusions are worthless: it just means that a poem's value tends to reside largely within its own instantiation, and – its use as 'wisdom literature' apart – poems have little 'general applicability' or predictive force. But this is art all over, of course. It's a bit like Pierre Wantzel proving that the trisection of the angle using a pair of compasses and a ruler is impossible, only to have some passing Giotto wander into his study, take up a pencil and execute it perfectly, freehand. While that might solve everything, it proves nothing. It's

---

1 Billy Collins, *Questions About Angels* (Pittsburgh, PA: University of Pittsburgh Press, 1991).

another trick, a brilliant, useless, one-off performance; but it's through such performances that poetry nonetheless allows us to glimpse those truths we might otherwise find impossible to apprehend.

Poetry is both trustworthy *and* untrustworthy: it is a truth-telling, but it often gets at the truth at the expense of the facts, facts being something most poets tend to regard as an inconvenience. However, this slipperiness means that they can sneak things past the real and psychological censors that otherwise would have to be declared: there is a secret lining in poetry's pack of lies in which it will smuggle in its truth, and the surreptitious methods by which poetry might declare love in peacetime are the same as those by which might inspire rebellion in a time of political oppression. Poetry often 'flies under the radar'. As Hardy once remarked, 'If Galileo had said in *verse* that the world moved, the Inquisition might have left him well alone.'[2]

The English version of that line of Antonio Porchia's I placed at the start of this book, and mentioned in the introduction – 'I know what I have given you; I do not know what you have received' – was made by W. S. Merwin, and appears in his translation of Porchia's *Voces*.[3] In my role as a publisher, I was once sent an alternative translation of Porchia's classic. The translator, a native Spanish speaker, had complained that Merwin had travestied Porchia's original. I turned to 'Qué te he dado, lo sé. Qué has recibido, no lo sé', and found: 'What I've given you, I know. What you've received, I don't know.'

One can see why the translator might have thought this superior: its syntax more accurately follows the Spanish. However, it's in poorer, less idiomatic and less rhetorically effective English.[4] The underlying

2 Thomas Hardy, quoted in Florence Hardy, *The Life of Thomas Hardy* (London: Studio Editions, 1994).

3 Antonio Porchia, *Voices*, trans. W. S. Merwin (Port Townsend, WA: Copper Canyon Press, 1994).

4 Its weakness is due, in part, to the position of the nuclear stress (NS) in each phrase. In English, NS – unless there's a overdetermining context involved – tends to land on the stressed vowel of the last content word of the phrase unit.

dynamic of mediocre translation is more clearly seen when you run the procedure continuously, in a game of what Americans call 'Telephone' and the British still unfortunately call 'Chinese Whispers'. I ran the Porchia quote through the (Douglas Adams-inspired) translation program 'Babelfish', or rather through its 'Improbability Translator'. This runs a text through every language in its database in alphabetical order – translating it into Afrikaans, back into English, into Armenian, back into English, and so on, all the way through to Yiddish. Via the likes of 'I know that I gave you, I do not know what you got'; 'I know what I want, I do not know what happened' – the Porchia lines were finally spat out the other end as 'I do not know what it is.' (Beginning instead with the Spanish original produced the delightful 'I think I know. You know, I do not.')

The process is fundamentally subtractive, and shrinks text. What's shed in each step is often little more than nuance, but nuance grows into lexical affix, affix into word, word into phrase, and phrase into everything. (Another pass gives 'I do not know what I was thinking', another 'I don't know what to say'.) Because it's automated and not human, the procedure also sheds any binding semantic context that

---

In Merwin's version, this gives us a rise on *given* and *received*; this additional stress makes the antithesis even more stark, and the fact that Merwin has made this already parallel structure heavily metrical (it's almost clean iambic tetrameter) means that the alternate stress rule (ASR) also comes strongly into play. The ASR works hierarchically over larger units too, but there it becomes an intonational phenomenon: this leaves a fall in pitch between the two nuclear stresses, *given* to *received*, which also – to my ear anyway – lightly enacts the giving-receiving synaesthetically. In the new translation, the speaker's *know* and *don't know* are promoted via NS to the salient rhetorical contrast. But the problem is that readers care about themselves, the *you*, not the poet; they are far more interested in what *they're* getting or not getting than they are the speaker's relative state of ignorance. Thus Merwin's translation holds our interest because it directly engages *us*. Rather ironically, the second translator probably knew what he had received, alright; but he didn't know what he *had* to give, and therefore ended up keeping it. After the simple error of unidiomatic 'translationese', this kind of codal incompetence is the most common hallmark of poor translation.

would have been maintained either by a sensitivity to meaning, or a commitment to making sense. And this is where the fun starts. Here are the first eight lines of Shakespeare's Sonnet 18 run through the Improbability Translator:

> Shall I compare thee to a summer's day?
> Thou art more lovely and more temperate.
> Rough winds do shake the darling buds of May,
> And summer's lease hath all too short a date.
> Sometime too hot the eye of heaven shines,
> And often is his gold complexion dimmed;
> And every fair from fair sometime declines,
> By chance, or nature's changing course, untrimmed . . .

> It takes a day in summer?
> You are more beautiful and more moderate
> winds shake the beloved buds of May,
> and summer is very short history of cycling
> in warm weather in the eyes of heaven, happy,
> and often the master of the skin gold
> and provide any equitable waste by accident of course,
> the nature of D. untrimmed 'to some extent'

> This should be the summer?
> They are beautiful,
> gentle breeze loved warm summer weather in May,
> click to see the sky,
> good fortune, often the skin
> 'was just a waste of an accident
> with a very brief historical cyclical nature of the process'

> It is hot?
> You gust of wind, and glory in the hot summer

weather and entertainment options for air crash in May,
the skin is often the economic nature
of the proposed process,
a brief history of the development of waste.

This is hot?
Yes, very quickly, because the story is the summer air,
and this step is in heaven,
and often sleep in the dim, hiding, and fortunately
it is very hot,
you need to change and metabolic disorders.

It hardly improves on the original, and in semantic terms it has
utterly discohered – but it *does* sound like poetry of a late modernist
sort, and indeed there are magazines which would happily publish
this stuff, especially with the additional *fondement* of the right name
attached. Codal incompetence, otherwise known as 'not getting it' –
is a big problem with any kind of speech act that tries to communicate
accurate information; but in poetry, we are *not* trying to communicate
accurate information. When you turn up the 'codal incompetence
knob', as we have through this automated procedure, the result can
often just produce *more poetry*. The reason this increasingly random
garbage still has the feel of the poetic is because we are used to meeting
poems halfway. Poems are half-said things, full of deliberate elisions
no normal conversation would countenance. The poet has held this
space open for the reader to enter – and *what* they enter into is an
act of co-authorship, in the course of which, if they find the poem
'meaningful', they make it their own. This is both the *point* of poetry,
but also why poetry is often 'difficult to understand'. It would not
be a poem if it did not stimulate our capacity for oversignifying and
overinterpretation (a capacity which derives from our evolutionarily
advantageous trick of reading 'meaning' into a universe that possesses
none, if you'll forgive me wheeling out my little hobbyhorse for one

more ride). Poetry readers are primed to 'read too much in' as part of the contract. Thus *any* random, unconnected input can send the reader's connective faculties into overdrive – and that's a feeling they associate with, and can mistake *for*, poetry. The domain of poetry is therefore what we might call a 'permissive context', unlike the heavily rule-constrained context of other domains like legalese, knitting patterns, or physics. Poetry will *legitimise* misreadings: the unexpected is expected of it.

To give an analogous example, take some common mishearings of The Beatles' lyric 'Lucy In the Sky with Diamonds'. 'Lucy in the Sky with Diamonds' has been variously misheard as 'Lucy and this guy are dying' / 'Lucy's getting high with Linus' / 'Lucy in disguise with lions' / 'Lick me in the sky with Brian', and so on. (Perhaps the best 'mondegreen' of this song renders 'the girl with kaleidoscope eyes' as 'the girl with colitis goes by'.) The listener already *knows* the song is surreal and drug-addled and half-crazy; therefore the context will mean their mishearings will be rather wild and unconstrained, when compared with those of, say, the less-bonkers domain of a country and western ballad.

I've heard several people remark on the 'poetry' of the mad spam text you sometimes get in your email inbox. Interestingly, this is *also* just a way of smuggling in hidden freight: not of declared love or the seeds of political foment – but a Viagra or Xanax advert, a Ponzi scheme, or a kind offer from a member of Nigerian royalty to rest £10 million in your bank account over the weekend. Here's an example from my own in-tray:

> . . . he had a kind of paternal muscular spasm
> about the mouth, which is capable
> of being developed. Life became
> like what the poet Johnnie says –
> one grand, sweet song. She made me feel
> as if I were a memorising freak at the halls.

> I hadn't been expecting her
> for days. Payable in advance?

A quick bit of judicious lineation creates something not half bad that, again, would be eminently publishable in certain quarterlies. But once again it's the *discontinuity* that's poetic — and the work we do in the gaps to forge original links and surprising ideas. As I've mentioned, this material is generated using Markov chains, a stochastic algorithm which spits out a sequence of random variables; these can be used to generate 'plausible' fake texts from a series of real texts. (The above example is garbled P. G. Wodehouse.) The 'Post-modern Essay Generator' uses just such a procedure, and so does the 'Surrealist Compliment Generator':

> You mutter such objects
> of equine delight
> that the mind's ability
> to sew slices of mordant ivory
> becomes tamed with visions
> of Tamils in Constantinople . . .

These have enough local coherence to fool most search-engine rankings, plagiarism software and spam filters, including the one in our temporal lobes — and enough local discontinuity to be found 'poetic', if you've a mind to. Since poetry is as much 'read in' by the reader as 'written out' by the poet, and since 'reading in' requires a gap in which to do so — the mere *presence* of that gap itself is often taken by the reader as a cue to make poetry.

The aim of much poetry is not to 'communicate clearly', but to communicate its ambiguous and original signs clearly. Its signs have to have enough silence, emptiness and connotative blur around them to allow the reader to adapt them to their own reading — but not so much that the reader has the sense that they could make *nothing* or indeed *anything* of them, which is a game most readers find not worth playing; it tends to just make them feel stupid or lonely. (For years what I enjoyed most in the poetry of Clark Coolidge was, I now realise, my own company.) However, 'clear ambiguity' is less a paradox than a balancing act, albeit one made more difficult by the stylistic tics of our late modernist style, which has made a virtue and sometimes a *fetish* of ellipsis, and only increased the potential for slippage between the poet's giving and the reader's reception; contemporary readers are also far too tolerant of the many errors of omission that poets commit in the name of this style. Nonetheless *without* the gap between giving and receiving, the poem cannot, of course, be given at all.

The 'Store of Signs' illustrated here[5] is a version of the kind of communication model originally proposed by Karl Bühler and Roman Jakobson.[6]

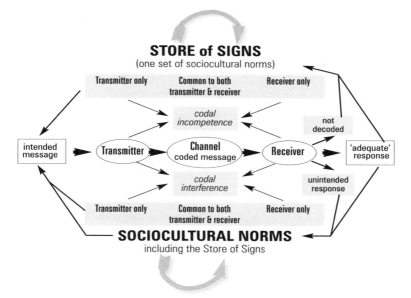

5 This is adapted from Philip Tagg, *Music's Meanings* (Larchmont, NY: The Mass Media Music Scholar's Press, 2012). Tagg's book is a fine introduction to the semiotics of music, and should be eagerly sought out by anyone interested in the subject.
6 Roman Jakobson, 'Linguistics and Poetics', in *Style in Language*, ed. T. Sebeok (Cambridge, MA: MIT Press, 1960), 350–77.

In the case of poetry, the main difference is that – unlike jazz or algebra or pig Latin – poetry's gappy communication means that the code that carries its symbols and signs can change frequently, from poem to poem, or within the poem itself. When the channel switches, new receiving equipment must be acquired; and *within* that channel itself, there's often a poor signal-to-noise ratio. Unlike algebra, it's not just a matter of understanding the conventions of symbolic representation: the reader has to be alert not *just* to the signs, but ready to learn the new code by which they are to be interpreted.[7] Every new thematic domain means a new code, a new set of rules and a new set of semantic priorities. If we were to design a model to reflect poetic communication, not only would our channel-box look like points control on the London Underground, the words *incompetence* and *interference* would also be considerably larger.

Codal incompetence is often just not *understanding* stuff. You don't enjoy Bartok, because you're trying to listen to him the way you do Mozart, or you're trying to read Eliot as you would Kipling. Codal interference is often just not *liking* stuff: you know *exactly* what Finnish death metal or abstract expressionism and postmodern verse are doing, but because your preference is for a different set of cultural rules and norms, you'd much rather they did something

---

7 A singular code is often, rightly or wrongly, taken as the hallmark of a great style or a great talent. See Wordsworth's 'Never forget what I believe was observed to you by Coleridge, that every great and original writer, in proportion as he is great and original, must himself create the taste by which he is to be relished.' (William Wordsworth, *The Letters of William Wordsworth*, ed. Alan G. Hill [Oxford: Oxford University Press, 1985].) This statement should perhaps be more notorious than it is, given the comfort it has provided those writers who read 'failure' as 'unjust neglect', and who hurl no larger criticism at themselves than being too louche to have gotten round to cultivating the means by which their greatness and originality can be appreciated. There *is* a small, horribly tormented cohort of the living and the dead who go by 'unjustly neglected', of course – and it is the responsibility of the community of readers, critics and successful writers to make sure it stays as small as possible.

else. However, a further delicious complication that we find within poetry's unstable and noisy code is that norm and sign are confused or transposed; the reader will muddle incompetence and interference, and think they don't get stuff when they just don't *like* it – and think they don't like stuff when they just don't *get* it.[8] This can produce a reader constantly worried about not getting it – or in the grip of a deeply misplaced confidence that they *do* get it. (Just check below the fold of any online poetry article, if you need proof that such readers are legion.) This is close to something like a paranoid condition, and indeed 'mild paranoia' is often the resting state of the contemporary poetry reader. They either worry they do not have the code, or the means to make sense of the detail it carries – or else they panic, and import the wrong code entirely.

One part-solution lies in clarity of deixis. I often find myself in the fortunate position of being able to simply ask poets what they *meant* by this or that line. Sometimes the shortfall between what they *think* they're giving and what is actually being traded on the page is remarkable. While 'eliminating ambiguity' cannot possibly be our reasonable aim, two conditions should nonetheless ideally obtain, unless there is a strong reason for them not to: firstly, the poet should be deictically explicit; secondly, the reader should feel able to take the shortest route to literal sense, i.e. the one for which the text gives clearest cue. If both sides stuck to this agreement, I swear we'd eliminate about 80 per cent of the accidental, pointless and unproductive confusion and difficulty that poems appear to introduce. By 'productive difficulty', I mean places where the reader will be rewarded for their interpretative investment – which is to say the very paradoxical, inarticulable, evanescent, obscure or ambiguous

---

8 It's possible to derive a little semiotic square here, which might be fun for someone to run with: this would add two terms to incompetence and interference: *delusion*, or 'thinking you get it when you don't'; and *denial*, or 'thinking you like it when you don't'.

things that the *poet* is wrestling with. By 'non-productive', I mean either detaining the reader in the meta-game of trying to work out the rules by which the poem is to be interpreted, or information the poet could easily have just *told* them. If the poet is trying to move or enlighten a reader, trying to propose an idea that can actually be *engaged* with, rather than just laboriously parsed, unpacked and then exhaustedly set aside, if they are determined to use the poem as more than an excuse to have a conversation *about poetry* . . . Then the poem's codal channels must be kept as noise-free as possible. Plenty of noise is already introduced by the procedure of poetic composition alone.

'The shortest route to literal sense' is generally indicated by deictic cue. In speech, we tend to think of deixis as a means of 'siting' a point of view via temporal, spatial and pronominal information: once we have the when, the where and the who of it all, we have constructed a mental space, an origo in which events and relations can be clearly imagined and described in an economical way. As I've mentioned, deixis in literature has an additional component, one of 'literality'. In our living day-to-day, we are aware of a broadly non-negotiable outer reality, and a configurable inner imaginative reality. These are, to all but the psychotic, self-evidently distinct. In the depicted reality of literature, the distinction is maintained – except *both* the 'real' and the 'unreal' have to be carefully signed to avoid confusion. The reader is perfectly aware of the mimetic convention that their disbelief should be suspended, and that events will be 'reported' by the text just as a speaker might relate a real event. However, this means that the *non-*literal – the figurative, imaginary, metatextual or metapoetic – must be very carefully indicated.

Too often, though, the poet has forgotten to say that the poem is (a) a conversation between two elephants (b) just after the battle of Jutland (c) in a raft in the middle of the North Sea and (d) that it's *really* about their abandonment issues. They have assumed these matters to be somehow self-evident. (I exaggerate, but only a little.[9]) Poetry is close-in work, and this often involves a considerable loss of perspective. Hence my second war cry: *anticipate the state of publication*. If a poet is doing this properly it will involve shudders, cold sweats and weeping jags: nothing sharpens our perspective more than the prospect of imminent public humiliation, and publication is primarily an exercise in shame. This allows the poet the editorial distance to see that they must return the crucial detail they had foolishly omitted, and to tell a creative gap from a simple lacuna; otherwise the reader will expend all their energy in establishing dumb stuff that the poet could have just *told* them, and will have none left for the poem's weightier or more interesting propositions. All the reader requests is a poem free from the kind of inadvertent obscurity which arises from a failure to provide clear context. Such omissions bump up the noise-to-signal

---

9 This is why God gave us the title. Western convention dictates that titles will be read, invariably, as 'what the thing under this is about', so we might as well use them that way. This not only offers a lot of opportunity for subversion, but also simple delegation. A poem called 'Death' which merely recounts a dull business lunch has no need to ever mention the morbidity it inspired in the poet. A simple, straightforward title often relieves the poem of the responsibility of having to mention the matter again – meaning that, say, six lines of clumsy deictic exposition about our seafaring Dumbos can be lifted clean from the poem 'The Insecure Pachyderm in Naval History'. Indeed, a well-chosen title can *halve* the length of some poems, as readers are more than happy to make up the distance between title and poem, and will more often than not treat it as a creative lacuna in which they can develop an inter-domain ground where they see a shared aspect or property, or an intra-domain link where they spot a direct relation. Another effective technique sees the promotion of a detail in the poem to title-status, leading to its immediate symbolicity and 'totemisation'; see, for example, Roger Mitchell's 'The White Cup' in *Lemon Peeled the Moment Before: New and Selected Poems, 1967–2008* (Port Townsend, WA: Ausable Press, 2008).

Incidentally, we do not need to understand the meaning of a symbol to know we're probably dealing with one. This technique often creates a kind of desire-vector where the sense of the poem is structured around the attractive force of one partially understood, semi-symbolic detail, one which overlaps with the concepts of both McGuffin and *objet petit a*.

ratio to deafening levels; and if we now add to the mix a bold reader who is prepared to make their interpretation *regardless* of barely being able to make out a word – the result will be a text which has vastly increased its accidental polysemy (or its 'entropy', in information theory terms). This is not the fun thing it sounds. With even the best poets, much of the poetic ambiguity and obscurity we routinely indulge turns out not to be deliberate literary tactic, not the snappy stylistic elisions of the late modernist style – but incompetence, in the form of poorly established deixis.

Problems arise most frequently when the poet changes from one deictic space to another. The pronominal, temporal, locational and 'reality' co-ordinates of any imaginative space *must* be clearly defined, unless there's a very decent reason not to.[10] We should, by default, be clear about dramatis personae, speakers and addressees, and consistent in our use of their pronouns; we need to be consistent in our tenses, and make the chronological order of events explicit; we need to show where things are, and where they are taking place, which means being clear about both location and prepositional relations; and we need to be clear about *whether* they are actually taking place or not. I have lost count of the number of workshops where all our energy has been spent in working out that the 'she' in stanza two now has a different antecedent from the earlier 'she', and now refers to the poet's grandmother; or that 'we' now refers to the married couple, and is no longer being used to address the reader; or where the road accident just described

10 It's poetry, so often there *is* a good reason. But the next time a workshop poem generates ten mutually exclusive interpretations, and I hear the poet pipe up with 'Oh – I *really* don't mind if this poem/line/detail is read both ways/different ways/ any old way' when it was perfectly clear that they wrote it with *one* specific intention, it will trigger my version of Cúchulainn's warp-spasm. One *should* mind. Judicious ambiguity or deliberate instability is one thing; self-delighted incompetence is another. The modernist aesthetic – whose elisions and discontinuities dramatically increased the expressive range of the poetic art – should never be the flag of convenience for these rudderless, leaky rustbuckets of poems.

is taking place *before* the event described in the first stanza; or that we are now no longer behind but *under* the desk, or indeed outdoors, underground, in twelfth-century Tibet, down among the quarks or in a fish-market in Victorian Hartlepool; or that the tea-shop described in the final stanza is not intended literally, but is, in fact, the tea-shop of the soul.[11] All this, the poet believes, is either self-evident, or will be picked up through some mysterious osmosis. They are too close to the poem to see that clear cues – or at least decent clues – have not been provided, or have, and are highly misleading. The muddle is often retrospectively justified by the silly assumption that a periphrastic or elliptical style is merely the neutral poetic *mode du jour*. Recent bad precedents – see the indulgence of Geoffrey Hill's later extempore and antic obnubilations – have done little to arrest this trend.

If it aims for concision and originality, poetic composition will produce metaphoric and metonymic difficulty *as a matter of course*. Any complex subject will request a complex response, but as complexity increases, so should our counterbalancing commitment to clarity of statement. Clarity need not mean laborious exposition, and is often just a matter of providing a single well-placed function word; if it costs the poet nothing, they should slap it in. (Traditionally, *metrical* exigency lay at the root of most dubious elisions, and this certainly drove the common poeticism of omitting grammatical articles; the result often sounds like 'content bingo'. Poets who work in metre

11 Billy Collins's 'Workshop' – a self-descriptive poem written in the voice of an exasperated poetry tutor – is a handy lexicon of deictic errors: 'First, we're in this big aerodrome / and the speaker is inspecting a row of dirigibles, / which makes me think this could be a dream. / Then he takes us into his garden, / the part with the dahlias and the coiling hose, / though that's nice, the coiling hose, / but then I'm not sure where we're supposed to be. / The rain and the mint green light, that makes it feel outdoors, but what about this wallpaper? / Or is it a kind of indoor cemetery? There's something about death going on here. / In fact, I start to wonder if what we have here is really two poems, or three, or four, / or possibly none.' Billy Collins, *The Art of Drowning* (Pittsburgh, PA: University of Pittsburgh Press, 1995).

should still be keenly aware of such temptations, and poets who do not should be aware they have lost their only excuse.) Also — by definition, poets are too close to their material. If you have spent a long afternoon agonising whether that en-dash should stay in or out, or weeping over the long-suppressed memory your sonnet has unearthed, or wrestling with some fine metaphysical nuance, or just firing the principle of equivalence into the syntagm until everything seems like one giant, meaningless word . . . You can quickly lose perspective. Our focal lengths are necessarily short. Obsession — and the overfamiliarity and exhaustion with one's material that it eventually brings — can lead to a total loss of overview, and great confusion over what is and isn't self-evident in the text.[12]

Denied a guiding deictic context, the reader gets lost. The phenomenon of the Lost Reader presents a little simulacrum of the kind of codal incompetence we see in clinical psychosis, and which we can discuss in almost exactly the same terms. While this taxonomy is rather

12 While I'd maintain that 'anticipating the state of publication' is a great cure for lack of editorial distance, there are others, too: the community of poets exists not just as support network for a calling whose principal rewards are mental illness, poverty, broken relationships and substance abuse, but as a ready source of honest editorial perspective. Poets dispense with that community — however late they are in their careers — at their own peril. Who knows how many bad poems or bad books we might have been spared if their authors had had one friend prepared to tell them the truth?

The most common mid-to-late career downturns — especially, one grimly notes, those of male poets — seem to involve either a glum segue from poetry into mere 'verse', a descent into unwitting self-impersonation, or some knock-on consequence of their total loss of libido. Many poets would be better shutting up until death is visible on the horizon, something which reliably triggers a late lyric efflorescence. But most poets go on repeating themselves, while seeing in every microscopic advance a radical new direction. (The most exquisite put-down I ever heard was from the mouth of the great Gael Sorley Maclean, a man of few words, but also one possessed of a dry, sly wit. I recall he was being interviewed in his garden on Raasay for a TV programme about George Mackay Brown. The interviewer asked him to give his estimation of Mackay Brown's literary merit. Sorley rested on his hoe a long while, and then said 'Lovely poem.' 'What do you mean?' said the interviewer. Sorley raised his eyes to the horizon. 'Oh; that poem he writes.')

obscure, the nature of these semiotic pathologies will be alarmingly familiar to most readers.[13] These states can arise through incompetence and interference on either one or both sides. 'Lostness' is a disease of degree: at its most extreme, the poet is essentially speaking Klingon while the reader nods in deep misunderstanding. More often, though, the rules have not been made clear on the writer's side, so another set of rules have been too-precipitately applied by the reader, and it all ends with one side playing checkers and the other chess. (The ability of humans to wilfully sustain such reciprocal misapprehension is a thing of wonder. I once had a ten-minute conversation on *The Prelude* with a composer friend of mine; we talked of its longueurs, its bright passages, its turgid lines, its pointless repetitions, its lyric grandeur, its overblown rhetoric. Had it not been for him whistling a passage by way of illustration, it's unlikely we'd ever have discovered that I'd been talking about Wordsworth's *Prelude* while he'd been talking about Wagner's.)

Given the central role that misreading has in poetry, it's perhaps surprising we have no working taxonomy to describe it. The following may serve as some notes towards a pathology of the lost reader.

Cryptosemia: identifying signs not apparent to others. One often encounters readers who believe poets have hidden messages in their poems. They have been taught in school that meaning is something poets deliberately and sadistically withhold, and that the poem is something you therefore must torture a confession out of. To give

---

13 Some of the terms I'll employ are borrowed from a paper on sign malfunction in psychotic reality. I don't pretend that this is a complete taxonomy, though I believe one could probably be derived from the four variables of transmissive and receptive codal interference, and transmissive and receptive codal incompetence. The result would be something like a contemporary version of I. A. Richard's list of the 'chief difficulties' of reading. (These – while still relevant – are anecdotal, unsystematic and pretty much useless from an analytical perspective.) Stepan Davtian and Tatyana Chernigovskaya, 'Psychiatry in Free Fall: In Pursuit of a Semiotic Foothold', *Sign Systems Studies* 31, no. 2 (2003): 533–46.

an extreme but well-known example: a great deal of numerological and Kabbalistic frenzy surrounds Shakespeare's *Sonnets*. (I recall one assiduous cryptographer uncovered a message in one of the sonnets, which reveals that KIT MARLOWE WROTE THIS. By more or less identical methods, I managed to derive the phrase PARIS HILTON WROTE THIS.) This utter nonsense is often fuelled and sanctioned by the genuine Elizabethan obsession with numerology and codes. But cryptosemia is also the classic hallmark of scholarly readings, where a text – however bad or indifferent – will be *obliged* to live up to the high expectations of the often superior intelligence reading it: this is the kind of thing Helen Vendler indulges in her theory of 'Key Words' and 'Couplet Ties' in her commentary on the *Sonnets* – phenomena which exist, alas, only in the capacious and restive mind of Helen Vendler. While there is often far more to poems than meets the eye, there is just as often far less. Indeed if you take the trouble to read a poem slowly enough and carefully enough, you will find many things that are not there. This is not to say that some poets do *not* weave hidden messages and infra-texts into their poems (barely a single poem by the late Michael Donaghy did not also have a secret life, and almost every poem – *maybe* every poem – contained a buried Fibonacci number); but when the reader finds one they must be certain, and the text must then clearly confirm that certainty. However, the principal danger of cryptosemia – especially in its academic flavours – is that the hunt for buried signs quickly overtakes any engagement with the poem itself, which has become a kind of textual inconvenience.

Parasemia: the perverse reading of signs through the invention of false contexts. If the thematic domain is not well formed or indicated, the reader will often just decide the poem is about something else, usually something they're more interested in; they will then make every detail fit this thesis. While many readers default to old standbys ('no – this poem about learning the piano is clearly *really* about death/love/God/the act of writing poetry' etc.) such projections are often wilfully neurotic or sexual in nature, which is to say there is little the poet can do to deflect them in advance. I once met an individual who was genuinely convinced that in Robert Frost's 'Stopping by Woods on a Snowy Evening', the poet was confessing to having interfered with his pony: 'He gives his harness bells a shake / to ask if there is some mistake', and so on.[14] An excessively fond little poem of my own, written to commemorate my then-baby son's first smile, was described by a *Daily Mail* journalist as 'a love poem from one gay man to another'. The trouble is that if *one* line seems to fit the hypothesis well – in this case 'how fine, I thought, this waking amongst men' – a slack reader will often issue themselves exceptional licence to make all the others fit too. (I admit that in their new thematic domain, certain lines in my poem took on a delightful new sense: 'his four-day-old smile dawned on him again', for example, seems to speak eloquently of the stamina of the author.[15])

Hypersemia: the foregrounding of some signs at the expense of others. Otherwise known as 'strenuous overinterpretation'. This frequently arises through the unconscious desire to apply a specialism (I have had reviews of my own work where the critic has identified nothing but the influence of poets I had barely read – poets on whom the critic was invariably expert). It's also often an error committed in an attempt to nail 'what a poem *really* means' as opposed to just 'means' or 'means to me'; the word '*really*' marks the speaker as an essentialist. Meaning is no more intrinsic to a poem than to a word; poems don't 'really' mean anything but what we make of them, exactly as words are no more or less than the way we use them. Poets who are more interested in paradox, tension, the freer play of meaning, or open-ended questions are especially badly served by this approach.

14 Robert Frost, 'Stopping by Woods on a Snowy Evening', *The Collected Poems* (London: Vintage Classics, 2013).
15 Don Paterson, 'Waking with Russell', *Landing Light* (London: Faber & Faber, 2003).

This is Paul Muldoon's 'Ireland' in its entirety:

> The Volkswagen parked in the gap,
> But gently ticking over.
> You wonder if it's lovers
> And not men hurrying back
> Across two fields and a river.[16]

This poem asks us to look at the same image – the parked car with the engine still running – in the two ways that we might think of 'Ireland' (the title doing a splendidly clear job of eliminating other frames of interpretation). The last two lines are metonymic and evidential, and supremely economical. They tell us there was something urgent and likely terrible to be done, quickly, at very a specific distance from the car; the map-like precision of 'two fields and a river' indicates that there had probably been some reconnaissance involved, meaning the men likely took the trouble to enter through the back door of the house rather than the front, for the sake of surprise; and even if that hypothesis is 'wrong', that car ticking like a bomb (an inevitable association, given the context of the title, and the historical period confirmed by the last detail) suggests that *whatever* it was these men were up to – the detonation of a roadside device also fits – it was the opposite of a young couple nipping into the wood or ducking into the back seat to make love. This seems to me the most sensible line to pursue, 'the most direct route to literal sense', given the information we have and the context (provided by the firm anchorage of the poem's title) which gives it its larger meaning. The poem itself forms a single coherent peristasis, from which the abstract qualities 'irresolvable doubleness', 'instability' and 'paradox' rise to indicate a rich animus, leaving the whole poem a symbol of 'Ireland in all its contradictory terror and romance'. However, encouraged by the

16 Paul Muldoon, *Poems 1968–2014* (London: Faber & Faber, 2016).

title, more than one person has told me that the 'two fields and a river' are 'symbolic' of Ireland, the Irish sea and the UK mainland, making the whole poem an allegory. But that's a wretchedly poor and totally unproductive reading: the poem is about *two* interpretations held in tension, a double-take, and such a reading leaves the poem overwhelmed by merely one – setting aside the fact of its making no sense of the poem's composite details. Overinterpretation can take many forms. Readerly incompetence can arise through excited, wilful projection, disproportionate to its textual cue; it can also be the product of overweening confidence, exhaustion, and what we are sometimes obliged to call stupidity.[17]

Hyposemia: diminishing the significance of important signs. In other words, *under*-interpretation. One classic example: those many readers who take Robert Frost's 'The Road Not Taken' as an inspirational tract, a poem of bold, inspired, against-the-grain individualism. 'The Road Not Taken' is quoted by self-help gurus, recited by high school valedictorians and cannibalised by car advertisements; in China, the poem is taught in schools as a political allegory about turning away from the path of Western capitalism. Heavens, do they all misread it. In their defence, Frost deliberately made a poem to trip the unwary. Yes, he says 'Two roads diverged in a wood, and I – / I took the one less traveled by, / And that has made all the difference.'[18] But *nowhere* does he say that the difference made was a positive one. Significantly, one often hears the title misquoted as the far bolder 'The Road Less Travelled'; but the correct title indicates the poem is about the path

---

17 I once judged a poetry competition back in the days when no one used sifters. I was totally page-blind after reading 5,000 entries, could not find a clear winner, and had almost given up. At 4 a.m. I came across a poem called 'To My Dog Benjy Who Died Under a Landrover Aged Three Years*'. The asterisk led me to a footnote which read 'Benjy was a cocker spaniel'. In the morning I found that I'd written the words 'harrowing' and 'top 3 at least' in the margin, before I'd fallen into a coma at the desk.
18 Robert Frost, 'The Road Not Taken', *The Collected Poems* (London: Vintage Classics, 2013).

Frost did *not* take. To my ear that makes the 'sigh' far less one of wistful self-congratulation, and (knowing 'the domain of Frost' as we do) likely one of exhaustion, nihilistic indifference, or even bleak regret. Another, equally plausible interpretation exists or co-exists, and it's just as miserable: the choice made no damn difference whatsoever. (The clue is 'And both that morning equally lay / In leaves no step had trodden black'.) In this reading, what Frost predicts he will be telling '. . . with a sigh / Somewhere ages and ages hence' is the self-deluded lie of old men: that their life was a noble journey in which they had been masters of their own destiny. Just read out the last stanza in a sarcastic voice, and you'll hear it. Either way, Frost knew all about the cheerful errors committed by the glass-half-fullers, and he toyed with them mercilessly.

Asemia: the inability to understand any signs at all. J. H. Prynne's poetry is either 'notoriously' or neutrally discontinuous, depending on your taste. Personally speaking, I now enjoy it rather more than I used to, mainly because I realised that it wasn't quite as hard as I thought. I used to call such poetry 'difficult', but these days tend to think of it as merely 'bracing'. The fault was both his and mine. Prynne has been notoriously silent on the subject of his own work, but recently more forthcoming:

> I am rather frequently accused of having more or less altogether taken leave of discernible sense. In fact I believe this accusation to be more or less *true*, and not to me alarmingly so, because what for so long has seemed the arduous royal road into the domain of poetry ('what does it mean?') seems less and less an unavoidably necessary precondition for successful reading.[19]

In short: if you give up on trying to find a paraphrasable meaning in Prynne's poetry, you can give yourself over to the freer play of

19 J. H. Prynne, 'Mental Ears and Poetic Work', *Chicago Review* 55, no. 1 (2010).

sense, sound, intertextual association, and so on; it is text written —
to use Louise M. Rosenblatt's distinction — for an 'aesthetic' not an
'efferent', information-extracting reading. At that point, I moved from
a self-diagnosis of codal incompetence (otherwise known as 'feeling
stupid') to codal interference, where I *was* in possession of the correct
code and therefore *could* understand what was going on — but was
not necessarily obliged to like it, although I found immediately that I
rather did. Admittedly, it might have helped if he'd said all this earlier.
(More telling, perhaps, is the total absence of hand-wringing from
Prynne scholars over what Prynne himself has apparently dismissed
as forty years of misguided and pointless exegesis. Perhaps they think
he was joking: I don't.) Then again there are many occasions when
we should merely blame the poet for holding out the *promise* of sense
or thematic coherence (a clear title, a clear initial proposition, a
handful of propositions that are obviously connected) and then not
making even 'tonal' sense, which is the last kind of coherence such a
poem can claim. (The habitual elisions, 'jargon collages' and hyper-
intertextuality of late modernism can easily create poetry that makes
intelligent people feel like idiots; if that is the intention, this is an aim
that can be sincerely pursued only by the intellectually insecure. Either
way, the situation would be improved by some in-house critique that
possessed something like a language of disapproval.)[20]

20 Occasionally one hears accusations of a failure to 'innovate'; though this is a non-
neutral criticism only if you feel that 'innovative verse' is a reasonable synonym for
avant-garde practice, in which case it amounts to the betrayal of the cause. However,
with the exception of a very few commentators – Peter Riley significant among them
in the UK – neo-modern or postmodern critics tend to restrict themselves to neutral
exegesis and extravagant praise. Anyone in the mood for a graceless, badly timed
and poorly judged rant on the subject might want to skim my introduction to *New
British Poetry*, which I edited jointly with Charles Simic (Minneapolis, MN: Graywolf
Press, 2004). It was a fractious time in UK poetry, and I was much too taken up with
what seemed the avant-garde's constant abuse of 'the mainstream'. (I was also too
influenced by the late Michael Donaghy, who had become morbidly obsessed with
the typographically challenged barbarians at the gate – while occasionally offering

Dysemia and *eusemia*: reading signs too negatively or positively; for our purposes, the unjustified projection of negative or positive qualities. These represent the two principal types of critical distortion: the negative assessment of work of self-evident literary merit (while you will never meet a poet who has not suffered as a result of this monstrous perversion, there are reasons to believe the disease is not as widespread as is claimed), and the cheerful projection of the quality of literary merit into work which appears to demonstrate no evidence of it. Both are impossible to prove, but no one doubts their existence. Eusemia is the most prevalent kind of contemporary misreading, and is probably less a reflection of the loss of shared literary values than it is of a politically intermediate age. As with dysemia, it can too easily be dismissed as 'all a matter of taste'. Nonetheless I have lost track of the number of times I have heard judges on literary panels declare that (what seems to me) self-evidently bad book X is intrinsically and yet inexpressibly superior to self-evidently good book Y, when it's clear that this assessment is the product of an extraliterary agenda, usually with its origins in a political or personal bias. If they are aware of this, the judges are corrupt. If, as is far more often the case, they are honest and unaware, they are merely hosting an opinion they *feel* they should have, and reading the book on behalf of an imaginary reader whose standards are superior to their own and to whose taste and judgement they unconsciously defer. There may be any number of factors at the root of this, from intellectual insecurity to tribal or

---

them poems for publication, by various alter egos. These heteronyms included the immaculately opaque *ampersandeuse* Helene-Marie Journod, who wrote acrostic sonnets spelling out things like THIS IS BULLSHIT, all composed with a egg-timer. It was no one's finest hour.) While it will always be fun to bait the humourless and the ideologues – one *should*, on principle – my own position is much more live-and-let-live these days; I sense a similar tolerance emerging from the left bank, and the general feeling is one of shaky rapprochement. This has been due largely to the wiser influence of a younger generation who had no idea what we were all fighting about, nor could care less.

sectional allegiance.[21] (The only unforgivable mistake is in declaring yourself free from all such bias, and wholly without blind spots; certainly, I could have been – and indeed may well have been – dead wrong in every case.) 'Literary merit', it should go without saying, is *never* intrinsic; we have nothing to work with but critical consensus and such expertise as we're inclined to grant one another. But any critic who declares a literary work self-evidently good or bad and yet cannot articulate *why*, beyond the adduction of their own strength of feeling – should never be conceded *any* expertise, however reliable their taste may later prove.

Often the easiest way for a poet to win a prize or an endorsement is for the poet to have already won a prize or an endorsement, since this provides the authoritative recommendation an unconfident judge needs to sway their vote; there's every chance that the earlier prize was secured in the same manner. (I can think of at least one occasion where a poetry prize was awarded to a book *no one on the panel had read*, simply on the basis that its author was 'a major figure'.) I don't doubt that I've personally been the beneficiary of such a chain of good fortune. And I suspect that many unaccountably fortunate careers can be traced back to a single favour or piece of luck, one which eventually led to the most advantageous situation a writer can enjoy: to have your book thought well of before the spine has been cracked. There are many more poets who never got the break they needed and deserved.

---

21 We must never lose sight of the fact that the great 'eusemic' problem over the last couple of thousand years has been the assumed natural superiority of a lot of dreadful white male writing. I think we should all be pretty breezy about the pendulum swinging in a different direction for a while; given that some mediocre poetry will always be unjustly overpraised – better, surely, that it's the poetry of a more diverse constituency; getting things wrong is all part of serious critical attention. While we should not imagine that historical injustices can be addressed through contemporary correctives, we can at least ask that where 'generosities are extended' it's towards those writers previously denied them.

THE INTERTEXTUAL

Poetry has always gained a disproportionate amount of its resonance and meaning from its rich fields of intertextual reference; given the fundamentally connotative and associative nature of the poetic mode, this is hardly surprising. Indeed this aspect of the art was once foregrounded to a far greater degree when *cento* was a competitive form, and performers tried to out-vie each other in feats of memory and skill through the seamless stitching-together of passages from classical authors (we see analogous developments today in hip-hop and rap poetry; not all 'freestyling' is as free as it seems, and performers adapt and quote liberally from the texts of their contemporaries). The poetry reader, too, encourages the poet's use of intertextuality: their being prepared to 'read in' and to oversignify is an ideally receptive and alert state in which to present them with clues, hints and cues which would otherwise go unnoticed in prose.

Poets are far more 'the product of their influences' than are other kinds of writer. Eliot was surely correct when he remarked, 'No poet, no artist of any art, has his complete meaning alone. His significance, his appreciation is the appreciation of his relation to the dead poets and artists' – and poets know as much, too. The originality of their appreciation is just as important: most writers establish a kind of bespoke retrospective genealogy, and sit at the end of a unique line of influence whose family connections are often known to them alone. But they also change the *meaning* of those texts that have produced them, and in their attempts at originality – to challenge Eliot's metaphor – often go further than merely modifying the 'ideal order' of the 'existing monuments'. (Here I like to quote Borges: 'the concept of a definitive text corresponds only to religion or fatigue'.)[1] For that reason a hidden genealogy can often be pursued in our reading, too; one reference leads to another, then another, then another, revealing a strange chain of influence and inspiration. The fact that the poet may not be fully aware of the length of this chain is irrelevant; all it proves is that poetry is a profoundly interconnected and overwired art form.

In Seamus Heaney's 'Station Island', for example, he refers to a 'familiar compound ghost'.[2] The identity of this ghost is clearly part-James Joyce; but the phrase also alludes to Eliot's 'Little Gidding' — from which cue we can quickly source aspects of the figure of Eliot too. Eliot himself identifies his own 'compound ghost' as at least part-Mallarmé (as well as more clearly Yeats and Dante), from the proximity of the phrase 'purify the dialect of the tribe',[3] a rough version of Mallarmé's line *donner un sens plus pur aux mots de la tribu* in 'Le Tombeau d'Edgar Poe'.[4] Wherein we find a buried allusion to Poe's deranged prose poem 'Eureka', which itself references Archimedes . . . And so on. One can easily to imagine an intertextual 'Kevin Bacon' parlour game where a random contemporary poem is selected, and the challenge is to make it back to Homer in five steps or less.

Intertextuality and allusion overlap, but they are fundamentally different terms — both, alas, poorly defined. 'Intertextuality' was coined by Julia Kristeva, who also gave it its most coherent and useful definition: to paraphrase, 'intertextuality' refers to the idea that meaning is *not* always created through the direct intersubjective transfer from author to reader, but is also conducted through the meanings of other texts, or codes the reader has learned from other

---

1   Jorge Luis Borges, 'Homeric Versions', *Selected Non-Fictions*, ed. Eliot Weinberger, trans. Esther Allen and Suzanne Jill Levine (London: Penguin, 2000).

2   Seamus Heaney, 'Station Island', *Station Island* (London: Faber & Faber, 1984).

3   T. S. Eliot, 'Little Gidding', *Collected Poems: 1909–1962* (London: Faber & Faber, 2002).

4   Stéphane Mallarmé, *Poésies complètes* (Paris: Éditions de Cluny, 1948).

SIGN: THE DOMAIN OF THE POEM

texts.[5] This insight represented a brilliant perspectival shift, allowing us to see how *any* text sits at the nexus of a thousand others, all simultaneously bringing themselves to bear upon it, and bodying it forth.

Alas — since then, intertextuality has become so variously and messily defined it seems to require careful qualification at its every appearance. The current use of the word to also describe relationships *within* texts seems calculated to render the term unfit for practical use, though it merely adds another complexity: if this means 'intertextuality' can now include self-reference, it's perhaps a worthwhile broadening of its definition. In the theory of poetic translation, we may also regard it as a useful term to describe the natural extension of the spectrum of interpretation that runs from 'strict translation' to 'free version', and into an ultraviolet range that accommodates such less easily visible categories as the interpenetration of texts — poems written 'after' other poets, 'homage', influence, and simple literary inspiration.[6]

'Allusion' is a loose but useful convention covering two distinct forms of deliberate reference, though it tends to except the self-referential. The simplest form of allusion is a sign that points to a text-absent domain of which it is also a part, and here it operates as the index of a metonym. In a sense, a siren 'alludes' to an emergency; though this misuse of the word allows us to see that 'allude', as we normally employ it, is devoid of any connotation of urgency, and,

---

5 Julia Kristeva, *Desire in Language: A Semiotic Approach to Literature and Art* (New York: Columbia University Press, 1980).

6 What it cannot accommodate is 'plagiarism'. Plagiarism seems to me a cut-and-dried affair; if a text is used verbatim or with minimal adaptation, without acknowledgement, and with no significant recontextualisation through which one could argue a change of sense – the poet can go hang. Stealing the work of others is stealing the time they spent making it, and adding it to the stock your own leisure. Recent attempts to justify this kind of staggeringly lazy activity under the cool, crit-theory-lite cover of 'intertextuality' are, I think, disgraceful. Plagiarism cannot be 'part of your process'. Get another process, or be sued, shamed and pulped. And if you cannot remember whether or not you wrote something, have your head checked.

indeed, any sense of the index having a *direct* or strongly motivated connection to its subject. An allusion needs 'getting'. (In semiotic terms, whether the domain that the index points to is a 'text' or any other kind of domain is neither here nor there. When we allude to other texts, we often use the informal qualification 'literary allusion'.)

However, there are complexities even here, especially when we introduce the warping effect of cultural perspective: one man's allusion is another man's datum. A poem which contained the line 'He was my first foot that year' might be said to 'allude' to the Scottish practice of visiting after midnight on Hogmanay, and thus 'indicate' Hogmanay as a whole — but only through a lack of familiarity with the tradition. For Scots, there is no distance to travel between index and subject; it's just a noun describing a well-known practice, and if one has to think 'Hogmanay' at all, it less 'alludes' to it than forms a neutral synecdoche. However, where it *is* felt to point to that larger domain, the allusion is really a motivated index[7] — and so the relationship is intra-domain, and to some extent just a form of synecdoche. If the allusion is 'literary' and refers to an *actual* text made of words, as opposed to, say, a cultural practice, news story or individual biography, the situation is no more complex. Allusion is just a qualified form of metonymy.

While in current use it blurs with the 'intertextual', allusion might nonetheless usefully be considered another word for the intertextual index. (The intertextual reference, which subsumes the concept of allusion, is a slightly more complex matter. However, it's important to stress again that these complexities don't *necessarily* derive from the linked domains having the status of 'texts', and this assumption is more to do with our unconscious privileging of the literary.)

---

7 By 'motivated index' here, I mean a salient feature regarded as sufficiently typical, characteristic, definitively representative or partially iconic of the domain to *immediately* bring it to mind, even in the absence of any shaping context. If these conditions obtain it is invariably also part of that domain, and can be regarded as a synecdoche.

Since it seems the simplest solution, I'll refer to the text we are reading as the present text or **p-text**, and the text we are not reading but to which to we have been directed, the absent text or **a-text.** ('Hypertext' and 'hypotext' strike me as predicated on an unhelpful prepositional metaphor.) Generally speaking, the intertextual allusion works as follows: one text-present detail (i.e. a peristasis) has the salience to be read as an index directing us to a text-absent domain (a cultural artefact, text or event), while itself remaining continuous with the origo and material of the entire p-text. (To this extent one can view the *whole* p-text as linking to the a-text via a metonymic index, a fascinating complication which partly explains the a-text often having a broad, animus-like influence over the whole p-text, not just a connection to the local allusion.) This motivated index to the absent-text *then* forms a ground, where the a-text is linked to the p-text through an inter-domain operation. In short, p-text will link to a-text via a metonym of the a-text, which forms part of the p-text or is the p-text itself.[8] This forms a textual ground between the whole a-text and the p-text, and – as is usual with inter-domain tropes – the flow of sense between them is bidirectional.

Their often perfect continuity with the p-text is why intertextual allusions are generally *optional*, unlike enigmata or 'riddles', which declare themselves such by their very non-literal strangeness or 'blatant lies'. Allusions can and often will be cheerfully missed. For the 'intertextual' to exist at all, the reader has to 'get it'. The motivated index of the allusion must point sufficiently clearly to the a-text for the reader to discover it, meaning that the a-text will generally be represented by one of its best- or better-known aspects, whether in the form of quotation or reference.

There is nonetheless something ineffably 'classy', I feel, about those poems which have the quality of 'optional depth' (an excellent phrase

---

8 This may sound like a purely theoretical situation, but cf. Borges, Jorge Luis. 'Pierre Menard, Author of the Quixote', in *Labyrinths*, trans. Donald A. Yates, James E. Irby (New York: New Directions, 1962).

I first heard used by Michael Alexander of *Four Quartets*, and which I have since used at every opportunity). Good examples abound, but the later Eliot's general approach, together with the contemporary practice of the likes of Michael Donaghy and Denise Riley, best represent what I mean by this. Take, for example, this passage from Riley's long poem of mourning, 'A Part Song':

> The flaws in suicide are clear
> Apart from causing bother
> To those alive who hold us dear
> We could miss one another
> We might be trapped eternally
> Oblivious to each other
> One crying *Where are you, my child*
> The other calling *Mother*.[9]

The passage is already almost intolerably moving. But if one additionally hears the echo of Herbert's 'The Collar' ('Methought I heard one calling, *Child!* / And I replied *My Lord*', the echo strengthened by the shared metrical form) our reading of the poem is further enriched. In providing this index to 'The Collar', Riley *offers* the reader the opportunity to map Herbert's poem to her own, through an ironic inversion. (There is, one should caution, no way of knowing an author has employed an allusion accidentally or unconsciously; a great many more are inventions of the reader alone.) Herbert rants at the constraints of his faith, describes his temptation to break free into a worldly existence – and is subsequently calmed through the restoration of a direct connection with God, who calls him back to the simple rule of religious submission. We might now contrast Herbert's position with that of the speaker in Riley's poem – her frustration with the *pain* of worldly existence, her temptation to break free of

9 Denise Riley, *Say Something Back* (London: Picador, 2016).

it, and the horror of the broken connection between mother and child that might then result. (Riley excels at this apparently effortless use of the intertextual, and her work is wholly free from any hint of a self-conscious desire to 'impress the reader': see, for example, 'Shantung', which seamlessly and invisibly recruits both Marvin Gaye and Macbeth to its lovelorn, exhausted lyric.)

Here's another straightforward example. It describes a snowglobe:

> Catch! This marvellous drop, like its own tear,
> has leaked for years. The tiny Ferris wheel
> has surfaced in an oval bubble where it never snows
> and little by little all is forgotten. Shhh!
>
> (MICHAEL DONAGHY, 'Our Life Stories')[10]

One might conceivably miss it, since its index is not *energetically* motivated – the author would have felt it gauche to make it any more obvious – but 'This marvellous drop, like its own tear' clearly refers to Marvell's 'On a Drop of Dew', where the line 'like its own tear' also occurs. While the 'alluding' indices 'marvellous' and 'like its own tear' are also details *within* the thematic domain and literal origo of the poem (and have been naturalised well enough for us to miss them, if we don't know the Marvell poem, or we're not paying attention) they are also signs which are *sufficiently* motivated to point outside it. (The punning word 'marvellous' – by which the author also means 'Marvellesque' – is *just* odd enough to pique our interest.) In doing so, they not only link p-text to a-text, but open a conduit where one may be read in the light of the other, creating a compound inter-domain sign; just like the copular metaphor, the flow of qualifying sense can go both ways. This conduit between texts is potentiated by the author, who 'planted' the allusion, but activated by the reader, who found it. And then the reader may decide – correctly reading,

---

10 Michael Donaghy, *Collected Poems* (London: Pan Macmillan, 2014).

I think, the author's intentions – that other aspects of Marvell's poem *also* comment on Donaghy's. After Marvell's beautiful description of the physical dewdrop, he makes a metaphor of it:

> So the soul, that drop, that ray
> Of the clear fountain of eternal day,
> (Could it within the human flower be seen,)
> Remembering still its former height,
> Shuns the sweet leaves, and blossoms green,
> And, recollecting its own light,
> Does, in its pure and circling thoughts, express
> The greater heaven in an heaven less.[11]

Into this meticulously developed comparison we might now read a metaphor analogous to Donaghy's own. Marvell's dewdrop was no mere dewdrop; and in the context of the poem 'Our Life Stories', Donaghy's snowglobes are no mere snowglobes either, but metaphors for the sealed, sentimentally precious memories by which we constitute our own sense of self. He suggests that new lovers, in their intimate exchange of 'our life stories', can let each other *forget* them, and by implication 'lose themselves':

> Let's hold the sad toy storms in which we're held,
> let's hold them gingerly above the bed,
> bubbles gulping contentedly, as we rock them to sleep,
> flurries aswim by our gentle skill,
> their names on the tips of our tongues.[12]

The relationship between the poem and the a-text to which the allusion refers is inter-domain, with the line 'like its own tear'

11 Andrew Marvell, *The Complete Poems*, ed. Elizabeth Donno and Jonathan Bate (London: Penguin, 2005).

12 Michael Donaghy, *Collected Poems* (London: Pan Macmillan, 2014).

constituting the shared ground between both texts. The 'motivation' of certain details to point beyond the text means two things: a connection close enough to the original to be synecdochic or partly iconic of it, in the way a picture of a few black and white keys implies a whole piano (Donaghy half-cites Marvell's title); and a further textual salience, one sufficient to *alert* the reader to this absent text. This textual salience often takes the form of a judicious degree of rhetorical or thematic alienity: our allusions often advertise themselves as such by sounding a little strange. 'Allusiveness' is a disease of degree, since its salience, and therefore strength, depends on the alienity of the index relative to the domain of the p-text. The more the allusion is 'buried' through its thematic-domain nativity, the less chance it will have of being identified as an a-text. index. 'This shiny drop' – an attempt to point the reader firmly towards the poem 'On a Fat Raindrop' by the none-too-famous minor Metaphysical, Sir Nathanial Shiny – would have likely failed as an allusion, having been too well 'nativised' to potentiate an index to an already obscure a-text.

Note the detail 'like its own tear' is also still a simple allusive index, which if it had been not been naturalised to form a seamless part of the p-text would have been a mere 'quotation'. If its *only* intention was to direct us to the Marvell poem of which it is part, this would have been just an unalloyed form of synecdoche. The *more* the allusion is alien to the text, the more salience it will have – but the less it will function in a genuinely intertextual way, and the more it will be perceived as simple reference and a mere peristasis. ('This blob of superglue / which reminds me / of the dewdrop in that Marvell poem'.) The point towards which I'm labouring is simply that the 'good default' of effective intertextual allusion involves steering a middle path between seamlessness and salience, exactly as the ground of an effective metaphor steers a path between proposing too close and too distant a comparison between tenor and vehicle. (Or indeed as a totem steers a path between thematic nativity and alienity; the totem-animus relationship of the symbol is structurally close to that of p- and a-text.) If we err too much on one side or the other, there is no inter-domain aspect to the reading at all: the result is either mere quotation, or it's nothing, because the reference is simply missed.

Again this is hardly a 'rule', but taking a balanced approach seems to be a commonsensical way to guard against the stylistic goofs that proceed from excessive self-consciousness; because allusion and the intertextual inevitably put one's reading and learning on display, the whole business is fraught like no other. Some authors are happy to keep the intertextual layer buried below the surface, accessible only to a select, super-alert and culturally hyperliterate few; one feels that in these cases, its primary intention is less a literary than a social one, and aimed at the formation of just such a *cognoscenti*. This is certainly not just a trait of the avant-garde; intellectual snobs have no genre. Intellectual insecurity can take the inverse shape, of course: I can think of one book where the poet *lists* his allusions in his introduction, lest we somehow miss them. For the most part, though, the middle way might be considered best practice.

Some complications

As we've discussed, the ground of most metaphors will be partly formed of indices to their vehicle or tenor. For example, in a unit metaphor, the qualifier in 'the writhing sea' might point vaguely to the vehicle 'great serpent', or something like it. The content of the ground of the metaphor often multitasks, being both a motivated index pointing to the vehicle or tenor, *and* a shared component of both tenor and vehicle, leaving much metaphor composed of a loud inter-domain component and quiet intra-domain component. 'The sprinter was revving up in the blocks' is a metaphor whose conceptual form is RUNNERS ARE CARS, but it depends on the metonymic index 'revving', short for 'the revving engine of a car', to point us to that vehicular domain. In terms of where our attention lies, we are more concerned with the metaphoric aspect than with the metonymic, which is usually processed quickly and half-consciously (unless the index is oblique or original, e.g. 'The sprinter knelt in the blocks and turned the key in his ignition'. (Original metaphors are often less to do with the novelty of the comparison than that of the indices forming the ground.)

The observation that all metaphor has an internal metonymic component isn't original, but it's worth pointing out that while the intertextual is also an inter-domain effect, it differs in that we are consciously *aware* of the index; indeed, it has sufficient salience to challenge the inter-domain function in its perceived strength. We experience intertextuality, effectively, as a double trope: once as a direct metonymy whose index points to the a-text – its 'allusive' aspect; and again 'metaphorically', as the ground which links *both* texts. This double-take gives intertextual device its 'postmodern', unstable and self-reflexive feel, and our sense of it as a complex compound effect. There are additional explanations for this complexity, principally the status of 'text', which I'll explore shortly. [For a note on other reasons we might sense a paradox here, see endnote 16.]

Though if the p-text accommodates the intertextual allusion fairly seamlessly, with all its indices 'nativised', the allusion may also be skipped: either through its too-effective camouflage, an ignorance of the reference, or deliberately simplified modes of reading – leaving a text with our desirable quality of 'optional depth'. (One can simplify texts retrospectively: personally, while I know 'All shall be well and / All manner of thing shall be well' is derived from Julian of Norwich, I usually choose to background the allusion when I reread *Four Quartets.*[13])

The calculation the poet must make is to what extent this inter-textual reference will be pursued by the reader – who, if they are not familiar with it, will either have to 'exit' the text to pursue the

13 T. S. Eliot, *Collected Poems: 1909–1962* (London: Faber & Faber, 1974).

reference, ignore it, 'not get it' (and possibly feel stupid for doing so) or miss it altogether. Missing or ignoring a reference need not be a bad thing: an allusion can simply provide a text with another level of richness which can either be accessed or not. Much enjoyment can still be had from, say, *The Pisan Cantos* without every allusion being actively pursued (arguably rather more than if you actually do). On the other hand, if the meaning of the text *rests* on an allusion – the poet had best be doubly secure in their own good judgement, and aware of the riskiness of the strategy.

The status of the text

If we interrogate the word 'intertextuality' we find two odd things. The first looks like a complexity, but is in fact a conceptual error; the second is a complicating product of the *kind* of reading the word proposes. 'Intertextuality', if we regard it 'as a real thing', *appears* predicated on the existence of two texts – and this entails an awareness of the p-text *as* text. However, the mimetic conceit of the primary text often requires of us a partial suspension of disbelief. As the native readers of poetry that we become, we are often just as disinclined to constantly keep in mind that 'I am reading a poem' as we might be 'I am watching a movie' in the cinema, and often the medium itself will have to remind us. (One thinks of the notorious scene in Michael Haneke's *Funny Games* where one of the young torturers, having been briefly outwitted, breaks the fourth wall by staring into the camera lens – then rewinds the film to replay the scene with his preferred outcome, restoring the narrative to its inevitable, horrible course.) Our awareness of the text-as-text, while always present, is often partial – and many of us might even claim that when our engagement with literature is deepest, it disappears altogether.

On those occasions where the mimetic conceit is strong, there is a cognitive fracture between the p-text we read, and the a-text to which it refers. We were, say, in the middle of a complex polemic on the nature of love, or on the 8-ball in a bad pool game, or sitting in a garden in Kent having lunch with our double-crossing business partner — and suddenly we are asked to think about the *Purgatorio*. These are not equivalent domains. Because of the textual manner of its indication, which requires that we self-consciously process the allusion in an extra-mimetic way (for one thing, it requires us to perform a feat of memory) — the a-text belongs less to the domain of literature than of 'the literary'. The p-text we're innocently reading was *not* 'text' in quite the same sense: it was experienced performatively, and (unless we're rereading it) both partially and locally. Therefore it cannot be said to form a domain equivalent in its integration and coherence to the a-text; rightly or wrongly, the a-text is always indicated as if it were something both known *and* complete. The p-text — if it's 'any good' or is not pursuing some self-reflexive strategy — has likely escaped that particular self-consciousness altogether, except in those readers either most keenly aware of artifice, or determined never to suspend their disbelief. (This is sometimes the case with readers of postmodern and avant-garde verse; the task of keeping the artifice of the poem constantly in mind is made easier by the deployment of a great deal of metatextual and self-reflexive device, as well as assaults upon the fourth wall so violent one suspects it of having ruined the poet's childhood.)

Here is that intractable complexity I referred to earlier: the mere presence of literary allusion may return us to *precisely* that self-conscious awareness of the text-as-text. For this reason, defining intertextuality in terms of the pretty interlocked circles of domain theory is impossible, since it very much depends *how* we experience the p-text in any given moment. It is not a *mise en abyme*, but it is a variable and shifting relationship, destabilising both the written passage and our emotional investment in it — which is likely to 'go text' on the reader at any moment, a little like a stereographic picture on which one fleetingly defocuses and loses the 3D image, finding it suddenly turned to a flat pattern. None of this should suggest that —

despite its only recently having been 'identified' — intertextuality is a modern or postmodern invention. Intertextuality has existed since there were two books. The book is both a mere 'thing', a sequence of dead signs, *and* an imaginative portal — and while the intertextual can't make these two incompatible states coexist, it is perfectly capable of making them go duck-rabbit on the reader.

Practice

The use of allusion and intertextuality is defined by all sorts of fraught calculation and second-guessing on the poet's side, and all sorts of fretting on the reader's. A proper study of intertextuality in the poem would have to plot out how it sits within the communication model, paying particular attention to the codal incompetence and inter-ference that can be contributed by both transmitter and receiver.

However, we can make an anecdotal simplification. Unless we require it to operate below the surface of conscious processing, or bury it so it can be found only by paranoiacs or initiates, the inter-textual allusion is a little like a riddle we would like to give the reader the opportunity and pleasure of answering. We just need to calculate how much grief we want to put them through before they arrive at the key, solving text. The process can be delayed by several codal factors, including the textual salience of the index, the strength of the motivation of the index (i.e. its degree of obliquity), the relative obscurity of the a-text, and so on. 'How much allusion can I get away with?' is something one often hears from younger poets, and the answer is: your question is naive. All one can ever do is put oneself in the place of the intended reader, and be honest about your own intentions, checking especially that your motivation for placing the allusion there in the first place is a pure one, and doesn't involve egotism, vanity or intellectual insecurity; check, too, that you are not deluding yourself as to the relative 'difficulty' of the allusion. I have already referred to the kind of poet who, despite their avowals to the contrary and their defence of the 'democracy of difficulty' (as if these planted mines and tripwires were somehow not their doing, but God's or nature's), take a perverse delight in making smart people feel dumb. Their excessive influence has probably lost more casual readers of poetry in the past hundred years than any other single factor. Impossible crosswords are, however, far easier to compile than to solve, and writing a difficult poem full of obscure allusions is quite the easiest thing in the world.

The poet, having posited an external eye, must then try to read the poem through it, checking that this ideal reader is not God, or some alien or super-genius somehow acquainted with the entire corpus of human literature, or indeed . . . The poet themselves. We all have our own unlikely or unusual expertise, our own intimate acquaintance with books outside the curriculum, and to pretend these things are widely shared is either delusional or vainly solipsistic. It seems to be no more complex than the poet asking themselves whether, placed in precisely *this* position, *they'd* 'get' their own allusion. No other question forces us to think so hard about who, exactly, this ideal reader of ours is, how this editorial distance can be constructed, and in what way we might correct for our blind spots and distortions. Nor do we want to be plunged into a self-conscious paroxysm of second-guessing either – and on those occasions we might fairly ask if the allusion is really worth the bother. If it *is* worth the bother, then 'How can I gloss, contextualise or clarify – without being too boring, clumsy or expository – this obscure but cool reference to Thomas Urquart *within* the poem?' is just the kind of mundane but testing question we should be tackling far more often. Too often we simply impose heavily on the reader's patience and goodwill – or use the strange reading-conventions of late modernism as an opportunity to shrug in indifference to their plight.

Assuming the poet would prefer the reader to 'get it' than not, the first rule of sane and sensible practice is that any allusion which refers to a circumstance or thing *unlikely* to have been encountered by the poet's 'average' reader should be identified as such by the poet. This way, at the very least, the reader can be alerted to their own ignorance. This seems a matter of courtesy: no literary work or historical event which is not held by common consensus to be 'canonical' or well-known should be represented by an allusion which does not provide *some* hint as to its provenance. (In this case, the rule is the exactly same for a metaphor whose ground is a secondary connotation: the connotation must be text-present.)

Secondly – if no gloss is possible or desirable – an allusion should be quietly advertised as such, *especially* in those circumstances where the word or phrase is unexotic, and a plausible literal interpretation is available. I recall a student poem which mentioned the 'second line'; this turned out to allude to an Acadian Mississippi funeral, something the poet was disinclined to spell out, for the simple reason he didn't want to give 'the funereal' disproportionate prominence in the poem; fair enough. Capitals or quote marks were far too disruptive. He solved the problem through relineation, and by placing the phrase at the end of the line he felt he had done enough to indicate that it *was* a cultural specificity, whose meaning the reader might want to pursue. The reader who had no clue what the allusion referred to is at least now broadly certain there *is* an allusion – and can either settle comfortably back into their own ignorance, start the hunt for contextualising clues, or just go look it up. Thirdly, the poet should not be so fond of the intertextual that they forget to *write the text*. Some poems are so heavily protected by their own allusive carapace they have either died inside it like an overwintering tortoise, or wandered off without anyone noticing.

To summarise, we may identify the main parameters as (a) *'canonicity'*, i.e. the extent to which the text or event alluded to is well known to the target readership; does it belong to 'the standard corpus' or the set of common knowledge? (b) the *salience* of the reference, i.e. the extent to which the reader will identify the p-text index *as* such; (c) the *directness* of the index, and the ease with which the a-text can be identified. Additionally there are intentional and affective issues – i.e. why is the poet risking this disruption, and what does the reader have to gain or lose by it?

Self-reflexivity

Self-reference, the declaration by the text that it *is* text, is a *mise en abyme* because the paradox of the feedback loop (i.e. that the p-text allusion is an intra-domain index which seeks out the a-text, which in turn changes the function of the allusion to that of a connecting ground, altering the perception of the p-text by inter-domain means) is usually elided under normal circumstances: it only operates as such from the alternate perspectives of the two texts, and thus the two functions are conceptually separated. When the reference is to the p-text itself, the indexical sign leaves the thematic domain in search of its a-text only to be immediately directed back to its own home; the effect is that of a Möbius strip, and the 'fourth wall' is breached as the text itself admits its own artifice. It's a little like when there's a power failure, or your water supply is cut, or a window falls out, or the boiler dies – and one is suddenly aware that 'home', that warm box for sheltering and feeding and sleeping safely in, is in reality a rather flimsy conceit. The self-reflexive move tends to leave the poem a less trustworthy and casually hospitable place, telling us an uncomfortable and sometimes valuable truth about the hollowness of its own mimetic conceit. The most explicit self-referencing often addresses exactly this:

> Close your eyes, yawn. It will be over soon.
> You will forge the poem, but not before
> It has forgotten you. And it does not matter.
> It has been most beautiful in its erasures.
>
> O bleached mirrors! Oceans of the drowned!
> Nor is one silence equal to another.

And it does not matter what you think.
This poem is not addressed to you.

(DONALD JUSTICE, 'Poem')[14]

Another frisson is produced by the fact that the self-reflexive allusion appears to predict its own future existence. The p-text is experienced in a state of *becoming*, linearly, partially and performatively – and within it, the alluding index refers to an a-text which, by contrast, is presumed to be extant, spatially integrated, whole, and fixed. If the p-text alludes to the p-text, it breaks an unspoken law based on common sense, which says that present text A cannot allude to future text B, which cannot have yet been read. If it does so the result feels almost 'magical'. (I recall the odd frisson of reading, as a young Christian believer, those accounts which appear to predict the coming of Christ in the Old Testament, in prophetic books written hundred of years before his appearance. Given that the Bible, as I then believed, was a single coherent text – this self-authentication seemed miraculous). Self-reflexion in a sense 'predicts' the existence of the text, which then gains in its 'presence' and inevitability as a coherent object.

Self-reflexive effect is always disruptive, but the effect of 'the text becoming aware of itself as text' need not be cheaply 'postmodern'. The effect can occasionally realise a comic tension, as the fourth wall can't break without a shared moment between performer and audience (see Roddy Lumsden's 'Poem Based on a Line of Roddy Lumsden'); but subtly handled, it can be as moving as any other effect. Take the last lines of Paul Muldoon's long elegy 'Incantata':

. . . than that Lugh of the Long Arm might have found
in the midst of *lus*
na leac or *lus na treatha* or *Frannc-lus*,

14 Donald Justice, *New and Selected Poems* (New York: Knopf, 1997)

in the midst of eyebright, or speedwell, or tansy,
    an antidote,
than that this *Incantata*
might have you look up from your plate of copper
    or zinc
on which you've etched the row upon row
of army-worms, than that you might reach out, arrah,
and take in your ink-stained hands my own hands
    stained with ink.[15]

Here, we experience an almost shocking coterminosity: we are brought face-to-face with the poet in the act of finishing the very furiously-written elegy we are now reading. Again, some frisson is derived from the impossibility of this situation.

Note that the self-reflexive is also a metapoetic form of the kind of deictic shift which frequently makes its first appearance at the end of the poem, and, indeed, that we associate with poetic closure. There is also the kind of *half* self-reflexive move that — through the familiar technique of closural shift — reframes what has gone previously; for example, in Richard Wilbur's 'The Mind Reader', the long soliloquy that constitutes the whole poem is revealed as having being conducted under interview. The verisimilitude is not disrupted, but we are made aware of another level of artifice, in this case the self-conscious performance of the speech itself.

The intertextual at work: Heaney's 'The Underground'

As I've said, a poem can work perfectly well without the reader being aware of its intertextual dimension. 'The Underground' by Seamus Heaney is written with the author's usual muscular naturalism (somehow, Heaney was not required to *resort* to poetic metaphor the way most other poets apparently have to); but one enriched by

15   Paul Muldoon, *The Annals of Chile* (New York: Farrar, Straus & Giroux, 1995).

his signature use of the intertexual, where a sign will reach deep into the culture to find its mythic or literary echo. Typically, 'The Underground' presents these allusions with the kind of natural grace and 'nativity' that can leave them undiscovered by the reader; again we might say the poem possesses the quality of 'optional depth'. But once they have picked up the clew, the reader might unravel an entire, partly hidden psychological narrative.

The Underground

There we were in the vaulted tunnel running,
You in your going-away coat speeding ahead
And me, me then like a fleet god gaining
Upon you before you turned to a reed

Or some new white flower japped with crimson
As the coat flapped wild and button after button
Sprang off and fell in a trail
Between the Underground and the Albert Hall.

Honeymooning, moonlighting, late for the Proms,
Our echoes die in that corridor and now
I come as Hansel came on the moonlit stones
Retracing the path back, lifting the buttons

To end up in a draughty lamplit station
After the trains have gone, the wet track
Bared and tensed as I am, all attention
For your step following and damned if I look back.[16]

On a first reading, the poem seems a reasonably straightforward affair. An older man – perhaps wiser, certainly more sad and fearful – remembers an episode from his earlier life. The younger man we see

16 Seamus Heaney, *Station Island* (London: Faber & Faber, 1984).

at the start of the poem is both in love and in lust, on his honeymoon, chasing his new bride on their way to a concert. In the second half of the poem he makes some kind of lonely return. The journey to the upper world seems broadly literal: he emerges from the London Underground to make an overground train connection. (The upper world is indicated by the simple deictic cue of 'wet track', a brilliant metonymic economy.) Identified by the clear allusion 'all attention / For your step following and damned if I look back', the older couple at the end become Orpheus and Eurydice. And, of course, Eurydice, the Schrödinger's girlfriend of classical myth, is either following him out or she isn't: Orpheus has no way of knowing but that which would definitely lose her. In the context of his marriage, we might even say that the speaker sounds uncertain if he and his wife are 'still together', in quite the same way. If we conclude no more, they are certainly not the same pair who entered the Underground, and their experience down there has changed them. However, let's take the poet's final injunction or warning literally. If we do look back – in the previous stanza, we find Hansel's return home: he picks up the moonlit coat-buttons, still magically silvered from the couple's earlier 'honeymooning, moonlighting', as if they were a way back to the old, true hearth. (This makes the 'Proms' sound like a symbol not only of cultural sophistication, but also of something like 'cultural aspiration'; it starts to look like a culprit here, an alienating zone.)

In the second stanza, there may be a lightly buried reference to Hades' pursuit and snatching of Persephone. When the gloomy god rose from the ground, the flowers Persephone was picking fell from her lap and were strewn behind her, like the coat-buttons in the poem; the strange japped flower might be the 'divine trap' placed by Zeus to trigger the alarm, mentioned in the Homeric *Hymn to Demeter* as 'a snare for the bloom-like girl, a marvellous, radiant flower'.[17] The

---

17   It was a thing of awe whether for deathless gods or mortal men to see: from
      its root grew a hundred blooms and it smelled most sweetly, so that all wide

salient word 'Sprang' begins to looks like a past tense of the season Persephone will take with her from the earth.

And now we return to where we came in. But in our rereading, things have changed considerably since we first encountered these lines. The lusty young honeymooner chasing after his young wife is compared to the goat-god Pan. Syrinx, pursued by Pan, turned herself into a reed to *escape* his attentions. (We might now look again at that 'white' and 'crimson', and detect a hint of 'hymeneal blood staining the nuptial sheet', if we know that in one version of the Syrinx myth the nymph was subjected to a virginity test; though the connotation is there anyway.[18]) At which point we may suddenly recall that Eurydice, in Ovid's telling, was herself set upon by a satyr: in her efforts to escape him, Eurydice fell into a nest of vipers and received a fatal bite on her heel. Her body was found by Orpheus – and in some ways, this was the making of him: he made such sad songs that the gods themselves wept.

It feels almost intrusive to dwell too long on the terrible note of self-accusation that now suffuses the poem, with the poet as satyr, Hades and grieving husband all at once, having brought about this state of affairs – a double death, and his own abandonment. It's presumably the death of earlier, younger selves that the poet is mourning; but the note of withering self-criticism and self-blame for the *possible* loss of his beloved, his 'soulmate' to Poetry is to my mind unmistakable.

---

heaven above and the whole earth and the sea's salt swell laughed for joy. And the girl was amazed and reached out with both hands to take the lovely toy; but the wide-pathed earth yawned there in the plain of Nysa, and the lord, Host of Many, with his immortal horses sprang out upon her – the Son of Cronos, He who has many names.

– *Hymn to Demeter*, trans. Hugh G. Evelyn-White
(Cambridge, MA: Harvard University Press, 1914)

18   I once asked Marie Heaney the origin of this image, and she replied 'we got beetroot on my coat in the pub'. Delacroix liked painting tigers, but he was too lazy to go to the zoo, so he just painted his cat and made it big and stripy. Genius tends to work with whatever is at hand.

In identifying himself as the source of his current misfortune, he is indeed 'damned if he looks back'. (All this is beautifully prefigured in the bride's 'going-away coat', a colloquialism for the good coat one might buy for one's honeymoon – though we can now see that Heaney also intended something more sadly literal by it.)

All this intertextual reference leaves the poem immeasurably rich, highly polysemic, doubled and trebled in the complexity of its signs (meaning everyone has the latitude to make their own interpretation; I have only made one to my own taste) and much too harmonically complex to suffer to easy paraphrase; certainly this little attempt still feels like whistling the top line of the St Matthew Passion. Heaney's 'tunes', like those of many preternaturally gifted poets, are often so good that readers get no further. The line that Heaney was a 'simple' poet – a 'stone, bone and bog man' who used plain and direct language to make musical, straight-talking poems that anyone could understand – was widely repeated after his death. This ignorant diagnosis is a great frustration to the rest of his readers, even though that mass appeal may have been precisely Heaney's intention. His intertextual complexities – like Frost's metaphysics, and Larkin's moral subtlety – were nothing if not exquisitely well disguised.

Etymological play

Another kind of intertextual technique is 'etymological play', through which the 'referential treadmill' is reversed. Besides a few tenacious roots, our language is built on almost nothing but dead metaphors and metonyms. A new thing will often be named according to the imaginative, trope-driven use of an old name: this is the poetic function of language that keeps it adequate to reality. But 'reality' always catches up in the end, and turns the rich new word into an empty sign for the most culturally non-contentious attributes of its referent. That white outcrop in the sky we named a 'cloud' after our word for 'hill' is soon just a cloud. Heaney — who, along with Geoffrey Hill, excelled in this area — often used etymology to create a kind of diachronic trope. When a word is salient in Heaney's verse, especially if it used in an unusual way or is polysyllabic (i.e. Latinate, and not drawn from his default Anglo-Saxon word-hoard), it's often an indication that the poet also means us to inspect the strange shape and length of the shadow it casts.

One might cut into Heaney anywhere and find evidence of this. Perhaps the most admirable aspect of his use of this technique is the extent to which it reinforces the thematic domain. Take the opening lines of 'The Harvest Bow':

> As you <u>plaited</u> the harvest bow
> You <u>implicated</u> the <u>mellowed</u> silence in you
> In wheat that does not rust
> But brightens as it tightens <u>twist</u> by <u>twist</u>
> Into a knowable corona,
> A throwaway love-knot of straw.
>
> Hands that aged round ashplants and <u>cane</u> sticks
> And <u>lapped</u> the spurs on a lifetime of game cocks
> Harked to their gift and worked with <u>fine intent</u> . . .'[19]

In this poem about a woven art, we find 'plait', from the Latin *plicare* to fold, via the French; this is placed close to 'implicated', from *implicare* — to fold in; these two now very different words are woven together again through Heaney's juxtaposition. (This kind of crypto-polyptoton is both common in Heaney and possibly unique to his work.) The odd use of 'mellowed' makes it salient, and alerts us to inspect it: we find it's derived from the Old English *melu*, or 'meal', the softness of the corn itself. 'Twist' has a weave-root too, and is Old

19   Seamus Heaney, *Field Work* (London: Faber & Faber, 1979).

English for 'rope'. The vague themes of 'finished, perfect artefact' and 'old age' present in the poem are lightly presented in the word 'fine', from the French *fin* – which is probably a back-formation from the Latin *finitus*, 'finished'. 'Cane' is hardly in disguise, but goes right back to the Sumerian *gin*, 'reed'. 'Lapped' is from the Old English for 'skirt', or a flap of woven cloth. 'Intent' is also implicated in all this, and is weave-stuff too, from the Latin *intendere*: *in-*, towards, and *-tendere*, to stretch . . . There are possibly other words I've missed in this wonderfully self-delighted use of word-lineage to weave language back into itself and into a new whole. Heaney appears to be claiming that words can be braided together not only with sound and syntax, but through the intertextual – and here we use the word with Heaneyesque precision – use of their own history.

An even more extraordinary example occurs towards the end of 'The Underground' (earlier in the poem, alert readers may have already have noticed the pursuit of the bride reflected in the word 'corridor', L. *corridorium*, 'running place', which echoes 'tunnel running' in the first line; 'vaulted' is a running word too, being derived from the Old French *volter*, 'leap' or 'gambol'):

> Sprang off and fell in a <u>trail</u> [. . .]
> [. . .] <u>Retracing</u> the path back, lifting the buttons
>
> To end up in a <u>draughty</u> lamplit station
> After the <u>trains</u> have gone, the wet <u>track</u>
> Bared and <u>tensed</u> as I am, all <u>attention</u>
> For your step following and damned if I look back.

If we inspect the etymologies of the underlined words, we find:

> trail – late Latin *tragulare*: to drag;
> retrace – Latin *trahere*: to draw out;
> draughty – Old English *dragan*: to draw, to draw out;

train — Old French *trahiner*: to drag;
track — via the Old Dutch *trek* and the Old High German
   trechan: to drag;
tense — Latin *tendere*: to stretch;
attention — Latin *adtendere*: to stretch.

While some of those words may conceivably have suggested themselves to the poet by their shared sounds as well as the clear operation of a [*dra-/tra-*] = 'slow drag/pull' phonestheme in English (*travail*, *travel*, *traverse*, *tramp*, *tram*, *traffic*, *trauchle* [Scots]), *draw*, *drail*, *drawl* all seem affected by it) — the chance of *all* this being intuitive or co-incidental is, I'd suggest, roughly nil. Heaney must have believed that the poem's half-buried theme of 'being dragged or drawn inevitably towards one's fate' was also being activated via those entangled roots, albeit at an almost subliminal level. Again, such a technique seems predicated on the belief that words still carry strong traces of their own history. In Heaney's poetry, this history is made audible through their suddenly proximate acoustic echoes, as long-lost cousins at a family wedding might be surprised to see their own faces reflected everywhere they looked. I suspect this tale is collapsed and inscribed in the complex co-ordinate of the lexeme itself, its specific collocative use within the entire *parole* — a station into which it drifts via a slow, historical process, and which is then reflected in its infinitely nuanced stance, being the sum of its specific valencies and attitudes towards every other word.

MEANING AND READING

I trust by now it will be clear that I believe not just poetic meaning but *all* meaning to be the consequence of a tropic process. Meaning is the epistemic corollary of a power structure, and is the consequence of the subordination of one conceptual domain to another.[1] A conceptual domain is a set of arbitrary rules. When one domain is enclosed by another, its contents are altered by the arbitrary rules of the enclosing domain, which narrows their sense, overdetermines the strength and direction of their valencies, and renegotiates their value. From the perspective of the subservient domain, the rules of the governing domain often do not *look* arbitrary, but this is the definition of a subservient relation. Furthermore, the components of the enclosed domain may now have the illusion of intrinsic meaning, but this is merely the apparitional result of the specific semantic attenuation, valencies and values dictated by the rules of the governing frame – as well as its frequent invisibility. Generally speaking, governing frames are not placed under scrutiny (though it is the work of poetry to see that they are). From the perspective of the governing domain, its own

[1] This description may seem to apply to meaning only in its semantic aspect; but even that primal 'emotional meaning' – which I have argued both underwrites and is, at a fundamental level, continuous with semantic meaning – can be thought of as 'feeling interpreted within the enclosing domain of conscious awareness'. Embodied theories of meaning, a topic I don't have space to pursue here, are in danger of providing merely circular definitions of meaning based on what we find 'meaningful' – or broadening the domain of meaning to include *all* emotional experience. They also have the habit of overstating the primacy of the physical over the cognitive, and for all their broad insights are currently of little use for analysis. Nonetheless they must *surely* be correct, in that the fundamental basis of human meaning-generation must be our embodied senses.

rules are either known to be just as arbitrary as those of the governed (a knowledge that, if withheld from the subservient domain, is equivalent to the exercise of tyrannical rule or divine whim); or they are taken for mere natural law or unchallengeable status quo.[2] So if we can accept that nothing is intrinsic, meaning is revealed as a form of metaphor: our meanings are really illusory, figurative vehicles, and when interrogated, will point to the ruling domain or 'tenor' which they serve – whether that frame is political, cultural, social, ideological, or just the 'generic frame' of the human dream. Poetry is a 'making conscious' of this semanticising process; it's the means by which dominant frames are held to account and their worst distortions corrected, semantic potential and polysemy restored to things, and new meanings generated.

I appreciate that I have described the way in which poetry generates its strange meanings rather idealistically. A poem in which every detail sought out and completed some ideal unity and achieved some perfect, self-supporting circularity would not, of course, be possible or desirable. I for one am a strong believer in 'the grit in the pearl', the *punctum*, the '. . . bump of clay / in the Navaho rug, / put there to mitigate / the too god-like perfection / of that merely human artifact' (Derek Mahon, 'Lives'),[3] and disruptive effect for its own sake. However, it's the formation of the thematic domain, even just the reader's *urge* to form it, that gives our deviations, fragments, surreal images

2   E.g. the British aristocracy were long keen to accept at face value Aristotle's assertion that 'Nature would like to distinguish between the bodies of freemen and slaves, making the one strong for servile labour, the other upright, and although useless for such services, useful for political life in the arts both of war and peace.' – Aristotle, *Politics*, ed. Benjamin Jowett Kitchener, ON: Batoche Books, 1999.) This nonetheless speaks of *some* kind of moral conscience that requires *some* kind of explanation for the superiority of an elite, however absurd; nonetheless you can see why Darwin was not popular among them. Real tyrants, on the other hand, have no need even for Aristotle, and are perfectly happy to declare *force majeure* as all the explanation required for their behaviour.

3   Derek Mahon, *Lives* (Oxford: Oxford University Press, 1972).

and blindsidings their contrary power in the first place. Words like 'unity' are used here only to describe the formation of the poetic Gestalt – which the vast majority of readers will attempt to form as a matter of course, and in which the poet might as well be complicit. This says nothing about the destabilising potential of the poems one might then *create* by these unifying means; all I've attempted is a neutral description of the symbolic mechanism. A poem composed in such a way might still be incendiary.

The reader's attempt to read the poem as an internally consistent domain isn't something that can be challenged without renegotiating the cultural sign of 'poem', which connotes – unrevisably, it seems to me – a semic space in which one may productively oversignify. Local instructions to read fragments *as* fragments would most likely be as counterproductive as asking readers 'not to think of an elephant'. The formation of this domain amounts to one of the basic *rights* of the discourse group of poetry-readers – along with being allowed always to take the most direct route to literal sense, unless the poem has explicitly indicated otherwise. A lot of effective experimental verse does precisely this, i.e. demonstrates its cognisance of this unrevisable convention; it subverts it but does not deny its existence. Poems can certainly play by special rules – but if they do so they had best make them explicitly known to the reader, otherwise they risk wasting the reader's time, and are essentially in the position of selling tickets for *Oklahoma* while intending to perform *Lulu*.

To repeat: consistency does *not* legislate against deviation and subversion, but actively prepares for it. Without consistency there can be no deviation. The best argument that those more extreme practitioners of fragmentalist or discontinuous approaches have at their disposal is that language and culture *themselves* form this background consistency, and the reader is therefore already well equipped to map the poem's deviations from its wholly arbitrary rules. Indeed, they might argue that such an approach is procedurally superior and more democratic: perhaps it actively *demonstrates* the extent to which cultural and linguistic norms are not the ineluctable results of historical and natural forces – but structures as arbitrary, in their own way, as the poems themselves. (Although why *poetry* is necessarily the best means of pursuing those politico-linguistic explorations has long been a mystery to me.)

The most direct challenge one can offer most radically alternative poetic manifestoes from Charles Olson onwards is just to say – and then prove – that this simply isn't how the human mind works. Its less subtle defenders might argue the discontinuous statement's case as an 'adequate symbol', based on the fact that it 'reflects' a society in fragments, or multitasking, or in chaos, or atomised, or minimally attentive, or deranged by multiple and simultaneous 'feeds'; but this reveals a naivety about the mechanism of representation in language. (This particular naivety is the hallmark of too much contemporary critical theory, which often finds itself in the grip of bad metaphors.) Language doesn't work like a mirror; it isn't a medium primarily governed by physical law; and its fragments aren't analogues of real-world broken shards, but disconnected units of speech. Which is to say that these discontinuities don't challenge the political status quo, or received cultural norms, or societal conformity – only the rules of syntax and logic, both of which are required to ask someone to change the toilet roll, never mind the social order. The leap that maps radical speech-gestures to radical political ones is purely romantic, and rarely comes with an explanation of the intermediary mechanism; the ground of these operative metaphors may apparently be filled with shared 'radical' attributes, but they are false cousins. Metaphor only affects the world when it challenges or replaces the dominant frame. Replace 'radical poetry' with 'radical painting' and you quickly understand why such art rarely rouses the masses to action. It's all so much sympathetic magic, like weeping in the hope that it'll rain.

This is the inverse of the 'free verse revolution' argument, where the changing cultural and social order mysteriously supervened on the poetic form: all this happens, one presumes, via the medium of some magical ether through which such cultural semiosis is conducted. But the irrelevance or moribundity of certain forms can be proven only by their general desuetude or disappearance; if you judge them on, say, their 'demonstrable failure to meet the demands of the times', you're making the sentimental error of thinking that the form has somehow *dictated* the (irrelevant, out of date, mediocre, etc.) content. But *no* mere form has that power. The most you might conclude is that perhaps the older forms are more popular with temperamental reactionaries or reactionary temperaments, who'll bring their conservative and retrograde imaginations to the show.

None of this is to say that you can't give a clear causal account of how these things come about, and how poetic and cultural forces are intertwined – as one must, if the argument is going to be taken any more seriously than, say, the near-psychotic claim that 'passive verbs deny female agency'. (Behind all these superstitions, behind all magical thinking, lies an inter-domain mapping that the speaker has mistaken for an intra-domain one, i.e. the old correlation-for-cause fallacy. We muddle metaphor and metonym at our peril.) One can always sensibly point to changes to the host language, when the old forms wake up one morning to find themselves out of step with the language's own prosodic structure, or no longer hewn along its natural fault lines, or working against its structural grain; that's how the 4-stress alliterative line died. In the case of free verse, we might look towards changes in rhetorical and performative aspects of the language to account for its success or linguistic 'fitness': the loss or concession of a distinct hieratic or poetic diction, the consequent difficulty of positioning natural-sounding full rhymes in the absence of a diction that permits hyperbaton, the social and cultural desirability of a more democratic and conversational tone . . . Whatever the proponents of free verse might have *thought* they were doing. But the false belief that it reflects or incarnates an idea of 'freedom' – as opposed to merely reflecting more general trends in the *parole*, within which poetry is only one mode of discourse – soon leads these natural and responsive procedures to harden into self-conscious ideology: formal features are self-consciously generated, new rules are made, in the hope that they'll hasten the revolution. Again, it's hard not to read this as pure superstition based on a failure to appreciate the nature of the causal chain, i.e. that while form might *reflect* cultural change, only content (or 'content' understood as continuous with form) can actually effect it. Evolutionarily 'fit' forms, if we're permitted that dodgy metaphor, might facilitate, speed and ease this, to be sure; but none of this ever relieves the poet of the task of actually just *saying* something that will make some damn difference. Radical forms will not always assist radical communication.

When many poets operating within the vaguely defined bandwidth of 'the mainstream' will employ the strategy of 'the fragment' in the free-standing phrase, the productive discontinuity, the surreal flourish, the romantic inclinations of the avant-garde sometimes lead them up the garden path, and they merely fail to identify the old tropes of local omission (of enthymeme, anapodoton, aporia, aposiopesis and praecisio) that they freely employ as global strategies. These are all logical procedures, all have a clear and articulable design on the reader, and the way they work isn't mysterious.[4] Pursued as an inflexible aesthetic *rule*, however, 'fragmentalism' — the wilful discontinuities of the schools of Olson, Hejinian and Prynne, if not necessarily those authors themselves — can have unproductive consequences. They are, at their most extreme, capable of destroying poetry's transmissionary medium. Poetry, unlike music, is a meta-art, and relies upon non-physical structures for the production of its effects. In poetry's case, the medium is syntax, grammar and logical continuity, which

---

4 There is more to be written on how textual lacunae perform an essentially grammatical function in 'weak' space, i.e. how they can indicate the *relationship* between fragments, and reveal them as juxtaposed, deleted, obliquely related, sequential, curtailed by ellipses or abbreviation, and so on. The Canadian poet Anne Carson strikes me as exemplary in this creative use of 'present space'.

together form the carrier-wave of plain sense within which its deeper meanings are broadcast.

They also conduct the subtle performative cues by which a nuanced and meaningful 'delivery' of the poem can be indicated. Unless the poem is being spoken aloud in real time, the performative dimension of the poem is dependent on the delicate consensus of coherent speech, its virtuosic moves within the language's vast pattern of idiom and collocation, its subtly implied sign-system of emphasis and de-emphasis, ambiguation and disambiguation – *all* of which rests heavily on syntactic convention. This is, of course, a huge subject in its own right. (A coherent description would have to start with mapping the surface structures of rhetorical figure to the deeper structures des-cribed in contemporary pragmatics.) But it's astonishing how much sense one can derive from listening to the poet's own performance of an avant-garde poem; to judge by all those the nicely weighted suprasegmentals, those shapely, muscular intonational contours – the *poet* clearly understands it, and much conventional, uncontroversial 'meaning' is suddenly revealed. I don't know how anyone could *not* enjoy Keston Sutherland performing 'Hot White Andy'[5] – by which, to paraphrase John Wilkinson, he appears to have been transformed into a kind of 'text-puppet'. This is no criticism of Sutherland, a bold and interesting poet for whom I have considerable respect. However, there's no doubt that his performance aids one's 'page' reading enormously. But many other 'difficult' poets and avant-gardistas often lose track of the extent to which the contextual, argumentative and dramatic cues that would allow the *reader* to perform a similarly nuanced stressing of the poem just haven't made it to the page (a far more serious omission, surely, than would be the case in 'easier' poetry) – to the extent that one wonders if the written word is *always* their natural element.[6]

5 Keston Sutherland, *Poetical Works 1999–2015* (London: Enitharmon Press, 2016).
6 It would be tempting to argue that any form which did not work with longer, parsable units or employed a strategy which disrupted their automatic connection

The transmissionary medium of grammatically well-formed sentences need not be rigorously 'honoured', any more than that of music — air and silence — need be rigorously observed: much fruitful tension (as well as subliminal effect) can be created in music by altering the background silence, with everything from room noise, tape hiss, vinyl scratches and radio-surfing, to the irruption of other musics. Similarly, grammar, logic and syntax can be bent, twisted and turned to make the reader conscious of the structure of language itself, not just the information and meaning it carries; employed with enough internal consistency and restraint (i.e. in a way that allows the reader to register not just the extent of the change, but its nature), these

---

is poorly geared up to project anything like a 'recognisable style'. Certainly such strategies do mean that the subtler means by which a style is forged are not open to the poet. Common sense should tell us that the consistency of certain tonal qualities, certain idiosyncratic habits of word choice, deixis and syntax, etc., are bound to be harder to establish over a discontinuous structure. The larger irony is that strategies of discontinuity often result in poetry that's really very conservative in *content*, as evidenced by the fact that – despite its perennial claims of linguistic innovation – experimental poetry hasn't changed much in a hundred years. A comparison with free improvisation in jazz is instructive. In its 'strict' form, this music has sounded stylistically consistent since the mid-sixties, being governed by a negatively defined aesthetic which eschews theme, excessive harmonic or rhythmic repetition, long melodic passages, and so on. (And even certain kinds of 'conversation'; I was once bawled out by the free improv drummer John Stevens for bouncing a saxophonist's phrase back to him, with the reprimand 'play your *own* f***ing licks!') Which is certainly not to say it cannot be beautiful and expressive; but despite the fact it's reasonably allowed to *think* of itself as radical, on account of 99 per cent of innocent listeners hating it on an accidental encounter – it remains a conservative, rule-bound music and virtually a classical form. So is the literary avant-garde, which also has much of the authorial anonymity one associates with classicism. Both would probably sleep better if they gave up on dreams of ever reaching a mass audience, or usurping that mainstream whose hidebound traditional practice is the very *means* by which their often startling, innovative, disruptive and catalytic gestures are given purpose. Given the great benefit they both gain through their mutual antagonism, neither traditionalism nor experimentalism should ever claim to be the intrinsically superior approach.

distortions can effectively form new rules, and propose alterations to the language-medium itself, which the reader can grow relaxed and comfortable enough with to accept uncritically. This might arguably permit the carriage of new tropes that conventional language-structure could not sustain.[7]

But this is a dangerous game, and what's at stake is not being too radical for one's own good (that just sounds sexy and attractive) – it's losing the reader; and not 'losing' as in 'disorienting'. These should be strategies of last resort, since they are the riskiest; the gesture is always likely to drown the sign. (Here I don't mean 'gesture' as 'illocutionary or performative act', but 'the line's hysterical attempt to get itself noticed'.) Their being strategies of *first* resort tends to be proof that the author is more concerned with the superficial gesture *than* the deep sign. Gesture-before-sign is one of the badges of the late neo-modern – and, diagnosed as a symptom of rampant expressionism, can fairly be seen as the flailing and twitching tail-end of the Romantic movement.[8] It's here we have to learn the mature art

7 In the analogy 'harmony is meaning' there may appear to be a save: harmony can either be functional (i.e. cadential, and based on patterns of tension and resolution) or non-functional (i.e. not seeking tonic resolution, but organised according to other rules, whether modal, mathematical, serial, aleatoric, etc.; its 'not going anywhere' does not limit its expressivity). Perhaps the mainstream compose within the poetic equivalent of functional harmony, and the avant-garde, those Elliot Carters and Brian Ferneyhoughs of the page, write within a non-functional system? There may be something in this, but the analogy quickly creaks. The question is: *can* meaning meaningfully survive when the normal sense-making mechanism of regular syntax is dismantled? Non-functional harmony still leaves the piano intact; it does not randomly detune it, or retune it, or take an axe to it, or suggest that we yell at it instead. And we have an additional asymmetry: some members of the 'listening public' find the music of Iannis Xenakis beautiful and compelling; mostly, only the avant-garde find the avant-garde beautiful and compelling, for reasons too abstruse or vaguely defined to enlist a general readership.

8 They might indeed ally themselves with the energetic spoken word scene, as they did in the sixties; this group of hugely popular and energetic performers have essentially revived the Romantic idea of the 'uniquely sensitive artist' in whom the

of what Cocteau called 'knowing how far to go too far'. (The poets
of the New York School have long seemed to me exemplary in their
understanding of this principle, in their striking a middle way between
saying something and providing enough disruption to make us think
about *how* they're saying it.) But to *break* things, to leave language in
pieces . . . Is no more than that: it's to smash the record, burn down
the gallery, shred the book. All of which can provide a temporary
relief, but while occasional, well-timed iconoclasm is one important
means by which the culture progresses – as a preferred artistic *mode*,
it strikes me as simply adolescent.

Our work is to place that received 'plain sense' under the *interrogation*
of poetic sense. 'Meaning', as the reader will be tired of me repeating,
I define as the product of the subservience of one conceptual domain
to another.[9] Again, the word 'subservience' is advised. Meaning

---

audience can *believe*, less as a desirable trait than a necessary condition, given that
much of their poetry is taken up with moral and political exhortation. That poet and
poem are largely conflated – and that few listeners bother to separate the word on the
page from its performance – is not a dereliction of tradition critical practice, but a
sign that they regard it as a different art form. This collapse of function can also has an
economic aspect, and performance poets are also their books' principal point of sale –
not the bookshop; social media does the work of reinforcing the intense biographical
or personal lens through which their work is read, and in a sense validated, another
aspect 'page poets' are inclined to reject as an irrelevant distraction. The complaint
that most of this stuff is 'no good on the page' will not wash, and critics would do
well to try to hold this poetry to its own aesthetic standards (often derived from rap's
ideal of smooth 'flow' and effective 'delivery', but also, crucially, the *authenticity* of the
whole; this last being a standard I am afraid many page poets would fail to meet).
9   If I may pedantically clarify: 'meaning' (the word considered as rhetic act, to
use Austin's term) as distinct from 'sense', its mere potential: essentially 'meaning'
with the idea of 'reference' subtracted – J. L. Austin, *How to Do Things With Words*
(Cambridge, MA: Harvard University Press, 1975). While such strategies as the
semiotic square can place the individual signs that compose the larger system of the
generic domain under useful scrutiny, these signs are almost never used (are, indeed,
almost impossible to use) in an unalloyed or decontextualised way. There is always
a 'given occasion' for any real speech or speech act; as Kristeva pointed out, all is
intertextual. Consider, for example, the word 'free', first as an unalloyed concept,

resides nowhere except in the agreed or enforced power-structure of conceptual relations. In the generic domain, it resides in the insistence of the authenticity of the human dream over all other domains (and how the world is suffering through its blind tyranny). Poetry goes some little way towards challenging the hegemony of that larger domain. But it can only do so coherently, polemically, effectively, through echoing the form of that larger power-structure, turning it against itself, and presenting *alternative* meanings through alternative frames. (Isologue is the exception. This strategy rejects 'meaning' in favour of motivic correspondence, i.e. the *ground* is the point, not the supremacy of one frame. The results are, depending on how you choose to see it, poignant but 'meaningless', or a radical critique of our received ideas of meaning in the form of an non-hegemonic structure. 'That many things are alike' is worth saying; the isologue is a way of forcing the universe to shed light on itself, as an alternative to yet another human explanation. Nonetheless isologue will normally occur within meaning-forming, conventional thematic domains; though some experimental practice seems to attempt to liberate it

---

and then in the contexts of poetry, jazz improvisation, and US political discourse. In the first instance, it has a 'sense', in the strict Saussurian sense of a term capable of distinguishing itself from other terms through differentiation and negation, but it does not yet have speech or speech-act status, and therefore no use-value. It might be compared to a tool whose purpose is known but for which one as yet has no specific need. In the second instance, its practical application is plainly dependent on the contextual constraint of its full sense-potential. The quasi-economic structure underlying these transactions can be more clearly seen in operations between specific domains. A painting-style described as 'free jazz' or 'free' (somehow metonymically proposing 'as in free jazz'; 'free' is used in jazz to refer to the genre in just that way) uses the word 'free' with clear connotations of spontaneous composition; without that domain-qualification, 'free' might mean anything from 'with a loose or easy brushstroke' to 'imaginatively unfettered'. The use-value of the original term (generic-domain 'free', uttered within the specific domain 'jazz') is replaced by the redetermined exchange-value of its meaning within the new dominant frame, 'painting'. (A hop and a skip to a Marxist theory of poetic meaning, I suppose; but as they say – let's not and say we did.)

into freer play.) If meaning is never intrinsic, if its locus never lies within one conceptual domain but the position that domain (or its sign) occupies within the laws of a larger dominant frame – without the formation of a new thematic domain under which old ideas are shown in a new light and there held to account, the epistemological corrective the poem can offer is weak and ineffectual. Whatever its 'difficulties', the poem will present no real challenge at all.[10]

Once again, consider the sort of talk such 'difficult' poetry generates. Mostly it pursues variants of 'what it might mean'; but this is a secondary, critical activity which elides the primary one of 'actually reading the poem'. This can be accomplished only by the unconscious delegation of that primary reading to a mysterious third-party – a reader whose enjoyment of this poem *is* transparent and unmediated, a reader who might react innocently and intelligently to those meanings we are now laboriously prising from the text, and who might engage directly with the ideas the poem proposes. If only such a wondrous creature existed! But if we did *not* posit this fabulous

10   Should a publisher ever publish a book they cannot edit? Among all the literary genres, only 'linguistically innovative' poetry is ring-fenced from editorial intervention; here, 'editing' is almost entirely limited to copy-editing, spellchecking and formatting. Elsewhere, the rules of the word-game are sufficiently well understood to be shared: this means that a line or stanza can be found wanting in the poem's own terms, and is capable of being effectively revised (or at least having such a revision proposed) by an editor. If you *cannot* edit a poem, you are confessing a codal incompetence, and are declaring that you can't understand the rules by which it has been composed, or the nature of its own ambitions – and that you have infinite faith in the author's good judgement. You are now the simply the publisher of the work. If a poem's rules and ambitions cannot be broadly articulated by its poet (and by 'rules' I don't mean mere algorithmic procedure), it has been composed either intuitively or naively, regardless of the intelligence of its author; and if they cannot be more generally intuited, the poem's 'success' is a purely subjective matter on which we may or may not agree, but either way cannot defend. I confess am rather bored of hearing about the self-evident greatness or x or y or z poet, and merely *neutral* qualities of their work – its allusiveness, playfulness, learning, experimentalism or novelty – being adduced as its great merits.

reader, we would be forced to admit than the mere extraction of parsable sense — of whatever a multiple, many-layered or rich nature — is the *primary* way in which we engage with this kind of poem. There is absolutely nothing wrong with any of this; but personally it strikes me as a gey lean form of entertainment.

To be taken as form of 'trustworthy human speech', as a domain in which the feelings it expresses are shared, in which its ideas are not merely extracted, but also discussed, challenged, modified, meditated upon, *acted* upon . . . Poetry has to make *some* degree of plain sense. When it ceases to, one must decide that — even if its unstable, shifting sense is *not* trustworthy — its interrogation still presents a game worth playing. Either that or one must do the decent thing, and make the argument that there are other games to be played under the heading of 'poetry' than the mere pursuit of meaning.

Too often we waste valuable time calling two mutually exclusive things by the same name, and we might save a great deal of it by agreeing to call them something different. Music and poetry long ago decided that one word could not accommodate them both; at some point 'the composition of verse' and 'short-form linguistic experiment' may be inclined to follow the same path. It would likely bring them closer together, as complementary, not competing art forms.

PART III

Metre: The Rhythm of the Poem

INTRODUCTION

I

Schopenhauer said that 'rhythm is to time as symmetry is to space'. Symmetry tends to be an overt or latent feature of most art which attempts to make an integrated unity of its material: as humans, it seems we can find no deeper sign of a thing's structural integrity than the doubling, reflection, repetition or self-similarity of its own form. Poetry's medium is time-based, being that of spoken or read language. The relatively recent innovation of representing it on the page has lent it very strong spatial features too, allowing us to not only sense but also *see* the poem as a 'single-celled entity', where its elements are related not just in syntagmatic series, but in paradigmatic parallel. Poets will now write directly for this spatialised medium; 'symmetry' can be formed through the kind of motivic, thematic and conceptual connections we looked at in the previous essay. But many of us feel that poetry is still written to be first read aloud – or at least 'aloud in one's head' – in that time-driven, gappy noise humans use for making sense. The principal way in which symmetry manifests itself in spoken language is rhythm.

Rhythm is an inevitable feature of poetic speech. As representative products of nature, everything we create is imprinted with the steady beats and cycles of which we are ourselves composed in time, and language is no exception. Language is hopelessly rhythmic because we are hopelessly rhythmic – in our circadian cycles, footsteps, heartbeats, breathing, in the oscillations of our brainwaves and the circulation of the blood. We are rhythmic because physical law has created a rhythmic universe, and settles everywhere into periodicity:

patterns of regular gravitational orbit, spin, electromagnetic pulse. (If there *was* a god or prime cause, they clearly had a hell of a groove on them.) The poet who would denounce all explicit rhythm in verse as so much artifice should affect the same distaste towards their own regular breathing and their habit of sleeping every night.

Furthermore, written and oral poetry is generally composed in lines or strophes, which not only constitute metrical units in themselves, but also draw forth, exaggerate and crystallise those rhythmic properties already latent in our speech. The poetic line pressurises language, which then reveals that which is most strongly characteristic of its structure and grain. ('Free verse' can never be 'free' in the sense of 'free from all rhythmic patterning', even if it wanted to be.) Rhythm is also the aspect of poetry which most directly declares its sisterhood with music – and through music, its connection to dance. Rhythm has the automatic effect of making our bodies dance, inwardly or outwardly: the metrical 'foot' is derived from the Latin *pes* or Greek πούς, in the sense of 'what you beat time or tap out a rhythm with'.

Compared to the subjects of sound-patterning and trope, metre has taken up a disproportionately large amount of theoretical discussion; it is an easy subject for any academic suffering from 'physics envy' to turn their attention to, and – allied with some basic arithmetic – generate insight after barren insight, each one full of more nuance and detail than the last.[1] However I believe the study of prosody to be a finite one, and hope to show why. Poetic prosody tends to be described in either a simple inaccurate way or a complex inaccurate

1 This is still preferable to the bewildering ignorance displayed by certain other experts in poetics, for whom the subject of prosody still appears to be something of a mystery. Here, for example, is Marjorie Perloff attempting to destroy a poem by the early twentieth-century African-American poet Georgia Douglas Johnson. She quotes the following:

> [. . .] The heart of a woman falls back with the night,
> And enters some alien cage in its plight,

way. The inaccuracies originate, straightforwardly, in a failure to accept its paradoxical nature: it is *both* a simple and a complex matter. As phonology has understood for many years, prosody is a rather broader project than one of merely describing 'the pattern of stress'. Prosody describes a relationship between metre and sense-making, one in which they are taken to be inextricably connected. This symbiosis has consequences: because sense is infinitely multiple, being non-intrinsic and residing nowhere, it is ultimately subjective; this means that in its real-world performance, stress is not accurately quantifiable, as its relative strength from one syllable to the next depends on the local, subjective interpretation of a fundamentally unstable sense. Quantifying the unquantifiable is an endless and pointless project which can nonetheless do a fine impersonation of a rich and insightful one, with the prosodist confirming his brilliant findings again and again – through what, on closer inspection, often turns out to be sheer subjective projection, and the circular confirmation of one's own discoveries. What is required is a description of the system which *includes* its subjectivity as integral to it, and does not try to eliminate it. It must also take into account the dynamic dimension of both the poet's rewriting and the reader's rereading, both of which further destabilise the stress pattern.

So, an early warning: while musical rhythm can be intelligently discussed in the abstract, poets and theorists of verse should not make the mistake of discussing poetic metre outside the context of the speech act to which it is inextricably bound. In poetry, as in speech, a metrical

---

And tries to forget it has dreamed of the stars
While it breaks, breaks, breaks, on the sheltering bars.
                                        – 'The Heart of a Woman' (1918)

And continues: 'These chug-chug *iambic pentameter* stanzas rhyming aabb remind one of a Hallmark card; indeed, so slack is the diction, so hackneyed the phraseology and sentiment . . .' – Marjorie Perloff, 'Janus-Faced Blockbuster', review of Cary Nelson (ed.), *Anthology of Modern American Poetry*, *Symploké* 8, nos. 1/2 (2000): 206.

event can't be properly understood unless one takes account of the music and the sense it marks. Both music and sense directly impact on the quality of syllabic stress itself, and our perception of it.

While this part of the book concerns itself with 'form', inasmuch as stanzas are metrical units too, it does not provide a 'handbook of forms'. The 'received forms' are a metrically trivial matter. Their interest lies in their literary-historical evolution, and in the kind of pressure their structures place upon language in every aspect, not just its rhythm. *Terza rima*, the standard habbie, the pantoum and especially the sonnet all have rich tales to tell, and there are many books which tell them. Other forms consist of little more than arbitrary rules and strategies. (For the life of me I have never understood how the rich interior tensions generated by the sonnet form can possibly be discussed in the same breath as the merely apparent sophistications of the villanelle and the sestina. [For a short rant on the frequent silliness of the troubadour forms, see endnote 17.]

The second half of this essay will not be easily accessible to the lay reader. While I'll endeavour to define the many technical terms as clearly as possible, they will soon have to be hurled around with a fair degree of abandon. For better or worse, this is a treatise, not a primer.[2] It is an essay on poetic form considered as temporal and rhythmic structure, and is an attempt to explain how and why we shape poems to templates of stanza, line and metrical rhythm, and how these templates might work in the mind and in the ear. As before, its sole novelty is that it is written with someone with a little experience of how such effects are generated from the inside out, and knows them as process rather than effect. I am nonetheless aware that I have occasionally strayed from my own very narrow expertise into fields of scholarly research in which I am barely more expert

2 Readers after a crash-course in metrics or a handbook of forms should turn to the excellent books for the general reader by Derek Attridge, James Fenton and John Hollander.

than any other reader. However, authorities in *those* fields have also blundered into mine for long enough. My hope is that we soon might meet in the middle, and in the meantime be tolerant of our respective ignorances.

II

The first thing we must address is *what* form actually does. We know versification is somehow at the heart of the enterprise, but have been pretty bad at articulating why this is so. In his influential paper 'A Disciplinary Map for Verse Study', Richard Cureton described three possible explanations of the function of verse-form and metre.[3] The first and the most commonly propounded is that it essentially performs a kind of rhetorical function or extends an existing one, and merely reinforces sense. This is predicated on the idea that poetry is primarily valued for its prose-like virtues, and that its value lies in its content (its physical descriptions, fictional speakers, speeches and verisimilitudes), the main difference from prose lying only in its aesthetic orientation, the intensity of its effects and the manner of its rhythmic organisation. One can see that such an approach would immediately trivialise the whole study of form and metre, or at least relegate it to a resolutely secondary and supporting role.

The second, favoured by more post-structural and critical-theoretical descriptions, is that verse form actually *disrupts* meaning, destabilising our interpretation of the text by providing a kind of playground of artificial effect that goes far beyond mere rhetoric, and declares an extraliterary agenda – deliberately drawing our attention to the very failure of normal language to provide adequate symbols for our contemporary experience. The first position is essentially that verse performs a merely rhetorical function; the second that it provides a disruptive one (or an aestheticising, ludic or empty one).

3   Richard D. Cureton, 'A Disciplinary Map for Verse Study', *Versification: An Electronic Journal of Literary Prosody* 1 (1997).

Cureton rejects these as alternately weak and inadequate, and posits a third approach, which he claims 'turns the standard view of verse function on its head', though I think this is a unnecessarily violent corrective. He says:

> The more productive alternative to these standard conceptions of verse function, I would maintain, are the claims (1) that poetry does indeed 'tell' us various complex and significant things about human sensibility and (2) that these things derive primarily from the verse form itself, not from the meanings arranged in these forms and the fictional representations that we infer from those meanings.

His first point seems to me unarguably true. His second is overstated to the point of absurdity. It is self-evident that 'the poetic experience' is derived from both form *and* semantic content, and indeed any quick poll of readers and poets − neither of whom have been especially mystified by poetry's effects, even if its machinery has remained obscure − at any point in the last 1,000 years would have established precisely that.

However, his statement that 'the major gesture in poetry, this theory of verse function claims, is to semanticise the temporal significances of its linguistic forms and to temporalise the spatial significances of its linguistic meanings and their fictional representations' seems far more nuanced and balanced, and is certainly close to my own experience of both reading and writing verse. My immediate instinct is to link this − yes, again − to Jakobson's notorious formula: 'the poetic function projects the principle of equivalence from the axis of selection into the axis of combination'. Once more, with feeling: what Jakobson means here is that the paradigmatic axis, the parallel rule of correspondence between things which governs our alternate choices, comparisons, lyric echoes, metaphors and so on, is developed along the axis of the syntagm, i.e. the serial rules whereby we combine words with other words along poetic sentences. In poetry we both find and 'project' a whole host of effects where the similarity *between* sequential elements is crucial to our experience of them as 'poetic'. These 'effects of equivalence' might include rhyme, consonance, metricality, syntactic parallelism, and so on. (As well as, I would argue, a fundamental increase in the connotative function of language, developed often by phonosemantic means, blurring the boundaries between words and so enhancing our sense of their semantic overlap.) In poetry we see a high degree of connection, integration and a consequent interchangeability of form and content, leaving us with a horizontal structure with vertical depth, where the melodies of surface-sense are underpinned by complex and shifting harmonies of semantic resonance, association and correspondence. And, if Jakobson's rule is true, it would certainly be no surprise to see an increase not only in the mere horizontal, tap-along presence of metrical rhythm, but also deep involvement of that rhythm in the vertical and recursive structuring of the very spaces it encloses. (I think the often-quoted statement that 'rhythm creates time' in the human experience is a little ambitious; we do not yet understand the nature of time well enough to assert anything of the sort. 'Rhythm structures time' seems the more defensible claim.)

III

Watching the lengths to which some authors go to maintain the integrity of their prosodic theory is like watching the last days of the Ptolemaic system, with more and more epicycles, adjustments, exceptions and retrograde motions being introduced in order to justify the one big error at the centre. I think their mistake is this: many theorists have completely lost track of the fact that this material has been produced by *poets*, whose relationship to the raw material of poetry – language itself – is of such a fundamentally strange nature I doubt they would quite believe it. Ignorance of the impulses and processes that have produced the work have led to a grave misreading of its intent; misreading of intent leads to misdiagnoses of function. There is still a fashion for the kind of pure-text readings inherited from the Leavisite, New Critical and post-structural schools (and, as I have occasionally discovered to my cost, from a certain breed of older scholar who continues to regard the poet as a bewildered naïf through which the work is channelled). However, such coldly forensic explorations – they remind one of a team of scientists gathered in bewilderment round a spade, wisely concluding that it is a giant teaspoon – are steadily losing their credibility. Unless each poem is used for the *rough* purpose for which its author intended it, its full power is unlikely to be released. Therefore any genuinely sensitive, useful reading must also posit what those authorial intentions actually *were*. Poetry is an act of communication; like any other, you misread the cues at your peril.

An effort to remove messy intent and affect from the study of metre has led to a failure to read stress and rhythm as a sufficiently complex and subjective phenomenon. This is compounded by attempts to notate it in binary or ternary forms nowhere near sophisticated enough to represent accurately either 'what's going on', or the variety of legitimate alternative scansions. Furthermore, while there is often great confusion about what is being measured, there is even more over *why* it is being measured.

It is, nonetheless, important for the prosodist to remember T. F. Brogan's wise warning:

> It is natural to want to enrich s[cansion] with other kinds of analyses which capture more of the phonological and syntactic structure of the line; Scott speaks of the 'real, and indefensible, coarseness' of s[cansion]. But all such efforts exceed the boundary of strict metrical analysis, moving into description of linguistic rhythm, and thus serve to blur or dissolve the distinction between meter and rhythm. Strictly speaking, s[cansion] marks

which syllables are metrically prominent – i.e. ictus . . . and non-ictus – not how much. Scansions which take account of more levels of metrical degree than two, or intonation, or the timing of syllables are all guilty of overspecification.[4]

This sounds unchallengeably wise, but the whispering goes on. While metre is binary, language is not. (There is also a specific technical objection to Brogan's statement: sometimes 'timing' syllables is a procedural necessity. This is discussed later under 'the displaced weak rule', and elsewhere.) As I'll show, mere 'metrical prominence' is not a phenomenon that can be successfully decoupled either from a qualitative and quantitative description of its nature, or from the semantic context that often produces it. As soon as one registers an agreement or disagreement between metrical position and syllable stress, one is *already* claiming a quality and meaning for that syllable. The problem is this: stress is an inseparable performative aspect of meaning; meaning is in flux, because words have no intrinsicality; and nothing, *no* other form of human discourse, undermines and revises the connection between a word and its meaning quite like a poem. Lexical stress is already highly destabilised in poetry, but if one also takes no account of the intonational properties of sense-*performance* – while they might still *claim* to be working with poetry, the theorist is treating it as mere versified language.

Ideally, poetry is radical thought expressed in appropriately radical language. It often finds this language directly *through* the attractions of an inflexible metrical frame. The frame additionally provides a safety-net, a set of co-ordinates, a zoo-cage, a musical structure, a matrix – that simultaneously licenses, contains, mitigates and encourages poetry's excesses. Metrical frame grants words a substitute structure

4 Alex Preminger and T. V. F. Brogan (eds), 'Scansion', in *The New Princeton Encyclopedia of Poetry and Poetics* (Princeton, NJ: Princeton University Press, 1993), 1118.

— a scaffold, an earth, a ground, a bearing — that emboldens them to take liberties with even such basic qualities as their own part of speech, and even to sever their link with their own primary denotation. But by the time the reader gets to it, it has also served to *arrange* these very words, which have been drawn into the pattern of the metre much in the way scattered iron filings are drawn into the nodal patterns of a vibrating membrane. The grievous mistake of many prosodic systems (of which I regard certain kinds of phrase rhythm analysis and generative metrics the worst culprits) is to treat poetic language as if it were *any* language that happened to find itself versified, and merely 'thrown up against' metre, rather than having been born directly from it.

Metre is *the* perfect minefield. However, we should be guided as far as possible by what it is, exactly, we want to achieve from this exercise, and my aim here is not to clear the minefield but to map it, so we can dance through it. I want to account for the interpretative and compositional possibilities of the metrical line in a dynamic frame, one which will see stress alter with interpreted and reinterpreted sense within a developing thematic domain. However, in attempting to give an account of such a rich field using only the meagre, binary tools of scansion, one is faced with a technical problem similar in nature to that of labanotation, or encountered by the narrator of 'Flatland'. I needed all the help I could get, and the approach taken here owes something — perhaps nearly everything — to those scholars of metre I've studied over the years, from Otto Jesperson and Paul Fussell to Richard Cureton and Nigel Fabb. Without their clear and insightful articulations to completely disagree with, there would be little to say.

However, for better or worse, I have written this chapter from scratch, from the ground up, without their books at my side — mainly to force myself to define every term and account for every step of a process whose integrity can lie only in the hideous interdependence of its parts. Where there are agreements between my system and another, I acknowledge them if I feel they are borrowed; if I don't,

I have probably arrived there by my own route. (A wholly original metrical theory should be treated with great suspicion.) The exception is Derek Attridge's method. Attridge has, in my opinion, come closest to a full explanation of 'what's going on exactly' in English metrical rhythm, but I hope the methods I use here sound more like broad concurrence than plagiarism. I often arrive at a similar conclusion by different means, though in several key regards our ideas appear to differ substantially. However, I still suspect that – since Attridge's perspective is that of a scholar, and mine that of a poet – we are merely looking at the same lumbering, asymmetrical mountain from different angles.

Poetry is just speech placed under a spatiotemporal constraint, behind which act lies an emotional impulse: to say something which will maximise language's power and density. No other poetic technique facilitates this more effectively than measure and number, and an understanding of metre's complexity is coterminous with an understanding of some of poetry's most challenging mysteries. We don't need to understand them to either write or read poetry, and I very much doubt they make much difference to the results either way. But there are, as they say, two kinds of people in the world – and personally, I find material explanations stranger, wilder and altogether far more slack-jawed amazing than those which invoke shadowy and invisible forces. If we learn nothing else, I believe it will be this: that there is little in the phenomenon of metre but our own determined dreaming, and the crystalline projection of the rhythmic structures of our own minds.

SOME BASIC TERMS

The terms which follow will receive more in-depth discussion, but it will be useful to define them briefly. Most are in general use, but I should emphasise that all glossaries and taxonomies are my own. I will often adapt or narrow a term to better suit my purpose, and occasionally introduce an entirely new one.

Isochrony is a widespread phenomenon, but refers here to the inherent rhythm of spoken language, and the tendency strong stresses have to distribute themselves at roughly even intervals. It is often alleged that English is a 'stress-timed language', where strongly stressed syllables are delivered at a more or less constant rate, with weakly stressed syllables bunching up or spreading out to accommodate and facilitate that regularity. However, the effect is significantly stronger (and perhaps only really perceptible) in 'urgent speech', i.e. speech delivered with a high degree of emotional or rhetorical emphasis.

A **word**, for our purposes, is the smallest unit of language used independently. Monosyllabic and disyllabic words take a single stress and – while their prosody may be complex – polysyllabic words take a single *principal* stress, regardless of how long they may be.[1]

Stress can be **strong** or **weak**, and serves to foreground or background a spoken syllable. Strong stress, salient stress, can be made by anything from typographical cue to facial expression. However

---

1 There exists some disagreement as to whether we should call neutrally performed syllables 'weak stresses' or 'unstressed syllables', as the terms have crucially different implications. For now, I'll simply state 'weak stress' as my preference. I will, however, address the consequences of this choice in the section on pentameter.

I try to use the word 'stress' with a determined neutrality, denoting a physical quality that is present simply by virtue of a speech-noise being made; but I do not intend by it 'a deliberate act'. In poetry, the definition is similar to that used in phonology, with 'stress' referring to a normative admixture of the **pitch, loudness** and **length** of the vowel, and 'weak' or 'strong' stress referring to generally predictable changes in that norm. Under certain conditions, one of those components may be more salient than others, and extend its effect over more than one syllable as a **suprasegmental**. 'Weak' and 'strong' are often abbreviated to **w** and **s**.

Forgive the re-emphasis, which may seem excessively punctilious – but it's important to establish that while stress has two principal qualities of w and s, *both* are nonetheless neutral, and s stresses are generally not *consciously* produced saliences. The w has a normative strength which reflects the average stress of spoken *function*; the s, one which reflects that of spoken *content*. (Strong stress is such because it asks that the listener 'consciously' process the words it makes salient; this does not mean that the *habitual act* of providing content-words with a strong stress, or indeed processing them in this way, is in itself 'conscious' in any sense of 'wakefully deliberate'.) The reason for holding on to the word 'stress' as a phenomenon which *all* speech realises is that, in performance, it is an absolutely fluid quality. Its w- and s-levels are in themselves no more than the mean-points of spoken function and content; but the fluid use that the brain makes of the *categories* of function, content and emotional expression are realised in our speech as infinitely gradated stresses.[2]

---

2 No doubt this potential confusion could have been alleviated by the creation
of different terms – which would have meant the word 'stress' did not have to
multitask quite so heavily. However, after explaining a couple of potentially confusing
shorthands, I will endeavour to qualify 'stress' consistently, as in '*weak* stress', 'strong
stress *position*', etc. My pernickety zealousness here probably betrays a metaphysical
position: some feel that when we speak, we stress against a river of unstressed
syllables. I think that when we speak, we stress against the void.

METRE: THE RHYTHM OF THE POEM

In the context of lines, I use a simple but potentially confusing shorthand. '4-strong' means a lineal template for a line with *four strong-stress positions* — not *only* four stresses, since weak stresses are, in my own scheme, kinds of stresses too.[3] Nor does 4-strong imply a line which can *realise* only four strong stresses, as many more stresses may occur within that template when the line is actually written or performed. It refers only to the number of strong positions in the metrical template.

Lexical stress refers to the w-s prosody of individual words, and is enforced by linguistic convention. 'Banana' is generally pronounced with a strong middle stress, where simultaneously the vowel is lengthened, its pitch raised and its loudness increased. If you speak any monosyllable on its own, it will *sound* like it takes a stress; but most of the worker ants — the legions of articles, prepositions, connectives, determiners, clitics and affixes that show how our verbs and nouns and qualifiers should relate to one another or be inflected — take a weak stress in the course of a normal sentence, and have near-schwas for vowels. Although we can check these conventions in the dictionary, lexical stress may also change according to syntactic context, and be different for the same word when used as different parts of speech. The word 'when', for example, will be conventionally stressed strong when used as an interrogative adverb; but in most other uses (as in the previous sentence) it will find itself receiving as weak a stress as would *a*, *the*, *but* or *to*; the light secondary s stress on the last syllable of the verb 'predicate' disappears when the word is employed as a noun, and so on. Lexical stress can also find itself modified through expressive contrast ('What he lacks in sensitivity he makes up for

---

3 'Unstressed syllable', for me, implies a certain non-existence. All syllables take a kind of stress, since the qualities of a strong stress are different from a weak one only in their intensity, not their nature. However, nor do I think that stress itself implies that a series of *any* old stresses has rhythm-carrying potential; this suggests 'syllabic rhythm' is a reality, and I hope to show that this is false.

in *IN*sensitivity'), and by the compound, alternate stress or nuclear stress rules, among others. Nonetheless, it should be thought of as a relatively fixed system. In the context of spoken phrases, the rule of thumb is that *function words tend to take weak stresses, content words take strong.*

Intonational accent is used to mark 'sense stress'. It also operates at the level of word, but is determined by semantic context, and provides a level of prosodic information distinct from and 'sitting above' w/s stress. It has a salient pitch component: it can be either high or low, and singles out a word to foreground its importance – or to background it because it's assumed to be already understood (or because the speaker desires it to go unnoticed).[4]

Metre is a finite, fixed, binary pattern of symbols representing strong- and weak-stress positions. It consists of **weak placeholders, which denote even durational gaps**, and **strong positions, which denote single transient events**. While it functions as a deeply embedded idea – one powerful enough in its habitual organisation of speech to be called a physical phenomenon – it is

---

4 Only the most salient accents and de-accents are worth marking in poetry, and these can be represented by a simple notational system. The real-world function of pitch and pitch contour is infinitely more subtle, and can communicate far more than mere informational contrast, or sad, happy, questioning, equivocal or sarcastic tones; the pitch contour and timbral character of the intonational phrase can encode a vast amount of complex tonal, emotional, physical, personal and straightforwardly semantic information, and almost operates as a sign-system-above-a-sign-system. However, this is only *implicitly* coded in the written language of poetry – in the form of interpretable sense, how that sense is indicated via textual cue (punctuation, line-break, etc.) and through its subsequent performance. Therefore only the most uncontroversial saliences are worth marking. In poetry there is far too much room for personal interpretation, and the complex symbolic notations of phonology are only good for recording *spoken* intonational and timbral nuance. To do the same for the written word would be largely pointless, and defeat our purpose, which is not to provide a full *description* of a line's performance as speech – this would be impossible – but to establish the performative potential of a written line. (One cannot *scan* the spoken word, only describe it.)

only perceptible when 'realised' in the physical form of alternately stressed material, whether in the form of percussive beats, musical notes, words, or other physical events. I try to use the word 'pattern' neutrally; 'pattern' only really becomes 'template' when it is cognitised. So these fixed-length metrical patterns that we hold in our heads as perceived repeated patterns and as rhythmic *expectations* I refer to as **templates**, and sometimes **frames**.

Scansion is the subjective description of the pattern of agreement and disagreement between a metrical template and written speech, the latter being analysed (in my system) as *both* lexical stress and sense stress. With tight and loose metres, I make two scansions: a primary scansion, which accounts for the relationship between lexical stress (and phrasemic prosody, to which it is related), and metrical position. This alerts readers to points of disagreement or tensions which the poet has introduced, usually for expressive reasons. Then I make a secondary scansion, which accounts for a more performative sense stress.

Sense stress is a prosody which – while it may often manifest as isolated word-stresses – operates at the level of phrase and sentence, and is performative: it describes the expressive way we stress written words while vocally performing them to make it clear to a listener that we have comprehended their full meaning, or that we wish to communicate a particular sense. It will also convey what we *feel* about what we are reading – in others words, it has an emotional as well as a semantic component. In the case of metred lines of verse, we must always aim at the most sensible consensual interpretation; however the business of sense-comprehension remains necessarily subjective. Therefore sense stress is also subjective. Sense stress is primarily intonational in its properties, and 'sits above' a basic metrical scansion. ('Definitive' scansions – especially those which make sense-stress analysis, or deal with light metres – can *never* be given. All scansions presented as definitive have misunderstood their project, which is an interpretative and not a proscriptive one.)

Versification refers to the rhythmic constraint of speech acts by an organised metrical pattern, the process whereby language 'becomes verse'.

Alternate stress, or **AS**, describes our human tendency to hear close, evenly distributed and identical sound-events as differentiated in strength, with the first or second beat stronger: it can be thought of as the 'tick-tock' effect, where the even 'tick-tick-tick-tick' of the clock is perceived as 'tick-tock, tick-tock'. This effect works hierarchically in doubling groups: we hear TICKtock ticktock, and then **TICK**tock ticktock TICKtock ticktock. The **alternate stress rule** or **ASR** refers to the strong tendency of AS to realise this pattern wherever the opportunity arises.

Nuclear stress is an intonational reflection of the fact that, statistically speaking, the prominent material in an English phrase tends to take up a syntactic position near the end; since lines are frequently phrase-coincident, this will often lead the last content word in a line to take a light intonational accent by default, though semantic and expressive circumstances will frequently see it fall on some other word instead. (Phrases or clauses which the speaker has *failed* to understand are often marked by the *inappropriate* use of the nuclear stress in this default final position; this is a common feature of 'actor's stress'.) Some kinds of line facilitate its easy positioning, while others do not.

Key is the initial height from which the phonological contour of the line begins, and which gives its overall higher or lower intonational (or musical, if you prefer) pitch.

A GLOSSARY OF TERMS
IN METRE AND SCANSION

_____

Although most of these terms are common and used in much the same way by other commentators, I should again emphasise that these particular definitions are my own.

Metre

ictus – a strong stressed event-position, or the realised stress itself

non-ictus – a position of weak durational 'placeholding', or the realised weak stress itself

s – strong

w – weak

/ – a notated strong-stress position

/ – a performed strong-stress syllable

x or **-x-** – a notated weak-stress placeholder

x – a performed weak-stress syllable

[x/] or **[x/ x/]** – this convention will indicate 'missing feet', or 'ghost metrons'

tactus – a regular ictic series, a 'pulse'

hiatus – a gap between a series of icti, here used to indicate the space or gap between lines

mora [:] – a very brief pause, notionally of about half a weak stress; here, I use it to describe a compensatory product of variation under certain metrical conditions. Its presence can often be heard (and so measured), but it can also be so vestigial that it exists only as a psychological effect.

Scansion

A few of these terms are mine alone. NB: at each level, a metrical unit will encounter a different order of linguistic boundary which, depending on its coincidence or non-coincidence *with* that unit, may provide either smoothly consistent or disruptive effect.

w – weak syllable

s – strong syllable

metron – a single 'measure' of the metrical template, taking one stress, roughly equivalent to the foot (coincident or non-coincident with the word/lexeme)

foot – a metron whose character is implied by the verse line itself, or any arbitrarily selected two- or three-syllable sequence (on rare occasions, four-syllable)

dimetron – a double metron (coincident or non-coincident with phrase unit)

stich – a line in the sense of a unit of *two or three dimetrons*; (coincident or non-coincident with intonation unit or syntactic phrase; the three-second 'auditory present' rule also influences it)

distich – a unit of two stichs; a couplet (coincident or non-coincident with sentence, clause or declination unit; also breath-capacity)

strophe – a verse of two distichs; a quatrain (coincident or non-coincident with the 'episodic' unit, i.e. one with stanzaic definition; larger declination units; the sung verse)

distrophe – a unit of two strophes (coincident or non-coincident with the 'episode' or the paragraph)

tetrastrophe – a unit of two distrophes[1]

---

1 Which is probably above the sensible hierarchical limit of alternate stress influence.

trimetron – a triple metron (coincident or non-coincident with syntactic phrase)

tristich – a tercet

ghost metron – one or more s stresses in the line or form implied by the metre but unrealised in the verse itself. Alternate stress compels even units; therefore 'ghost metron' [x/] = the missing foot at the end of odd-number-stressed lines. (This is sometimes referred to by others as a 'silent foot' or 'silent beat'; 'ghost' lends it the vestigial presence it commands, I think, and as hypercatalectic or anacrustic syllables are sometimes crammed into this measured hiatus – pushing, if you like, through the wall of the previous metron; it's often none-too-silent. Ghosts rustle and moan, and sometimes even make themselves known with a grunt.)

4-strong – the four-strong-stress metrical template, consisting of four weak placeholders and four strong-stress positions

4 × 4 – the universally influential template of the four-line, 4-strong stanza; it consists of four successive instances of a 4-strong metrical template

i.p. – iambic pentameter

metre-strong – the practice of imprinting performance with the metrical template, overriding more natural speech-performance

speech-strong – the practice of favouring natural speech-rhythm over a deliberately performed realisation of the metrical template

song-strong – the borrowing of the latitudes of sung performance through the metronomic spacing of strong stress, quantitative correction and the free population of weak placeholders (see 'light 4 × 4', 'Dolnik' and rap especially)

acatalexis (adj. *acatalectic***)** : the condition of a line having the exact (and minimum) number of syllables implied by its metrical template

catalexis (adj. *catalectic***)**: the omission in a line of one or more of the (usually strong-stressed) final syllables implied by the metrical template

hypercatalexis (adj. *hypercatalectic***)**: the addition of w syllables at the end of a line

anacrusis (adj. *anacrustic***)**: the addition of w syllables at the start of a line

acephalisis (adj. *acephalic***)**: the omission of w syllables at the start of a line

Feet

Feet are used to either characterise a rhythm, or describe an isolated short run of syllables. In the first instance they are useful to describe overdetermined patterns; in the second they are useful as a diagnostic or analytical tool. *Feet are a wholly abstract concept, and do not exist in the real world.* (In the way that, say, metrical pattern does; metrical pattern, when converted to a template, has a predictive and organising force. Feet do not.)

We have appropriated the following terms from classical prosody. There are four disyllabic feet:

iamb   x/   'defence'
trochee   /x   'butter'
spondee   //   'blue plate'
pyrrhic (or **dibrach**)   xx   'in a . . .'

and eight trisyllabic feet. We tend to use only three:

dactyl   /xx   'parable'
anapaest   xx/   'interrupt'
amphibrach   x/x   'initial'

and less commonly and usefully:

tribrach   xxx   'But in a . . .'
amphimacer   /x/   'silver spoon'
bacchius   x//   'defence cuts'
antibacchius   //x   'red terror'
molossus   ///   'Oh dear God'

Nearly all metrical writing in English realises a duple or triple rhythm. In light variations of 4-strong metres, though, we sometimes see quadruplet patterns emerge, which we might call 'paeonic', after the classical foot known as the paeon: one long syllable + three short, and known as first, second, third or fourth paeon depending on the position of the long syllable. So we might add:

(first) paeon   /xxx   'mystically'
(second) paeon   x/xx   'unbeatable'
(third) paeon   xx/x   'intonation'
(fourth) paeon   xxx/   'Azerbaijan'

PULSE

There are reliably recurring events which are nonetheless distributed within very rough cycles. Take the 'chrons' of a half-million years, give or take a few hundred thousand, between the earth's geomagnetic reversal, or the random but steady bursts of radioactive decay picked up by a Geiger counter. Then there are other events produced by stable systems which have regular periodicity. The even repetition of any time-based event of which we are consciously aware can be (but is certainly not always) perceived as a *pulse*. Two occurrences of identical or sufficiently similar things are all we need to raise our suspicions of the existence of a pulse: the brain goes 'I just heard/felt/saw one of those!' However, we need *three* occurrences to confirm it, since this creates two successive instances of an even-length gap. Despite the beat-event itself being the most consciously salient aspect of pulse, it's the evenness of the gaps *between* those beats that confirm its existence. The gaps can be automatically compared and found symmetrical, because they have duration; sometimes the material content of the beat itself – take a snare drum hit in a dead room, for example – has negligible length. Additionally, that content may vary considerably in nature: a snare drum followed by a duck quack followed by a lonesome whistle will still be perceived as a pulse, if the gaps between them are of even length. Through pulse is borne 'the passage of time' – time, in its perceptual incarnation,[1] being a phenomenon which is

---

[1] Some renegade physicists such as Julian Barbour feel this is time's *only* existence – and that its place within physical law is apparitional; it is merely an illusion created by change, and our ability to recall and predict it. It may indeed be that time is a mere structure born of human intelligence – like mathematics – that we use to measure, sequence and compare events. But Mark Tegmark and others have argued eloquently

structured by the measurement of constant lengths. Through these fixed durations we both count our years, weeks, minutes and seconds, and organise their content.

These repeated beats can be very close, like a ticks of a clock or the drilling of a woodpecker, or – given enough salience – separated by hundreds or thousands of years, like the perigees of a comet. The limit of our auditory perception of a pulse, however, is around 10Hz or 600bpm, above which the beats are not heard as discrete events but as a continuous drone. This can be tested by twanging a ruler at the edge of a table, and lengthening it until the sound is low enough to hear the individual beats of which the notes are composed. If you were to keep going, and your ruler was thirty feet long, you would hear a different effect: any beats slower than 0.5Hz or 30bpm are hard to experience as a pulse at all without great conscious attention. I have no idea if it indicates something more fundamentally literal, but 30bpm also happens to coincide with the slowest viable human heartbeat. (The cyclist Miguel Indurain seems to hold the record for the slowest healthy human heart – at 29bpm.) So while the phenomenon of pulse is vast and various, its perceived aural bandwidth is considerably smaller, and roughly between the frequencies of a tenth of a second and a couple of seconds.

---

that the external physical reality experienced by conscious beings in the cosmos rides on an underlying and verifiable mathematical reality; perhaps this place is similarly constituted by a temporal one. However, whether it is a 'dimension' or not (i.e. a thing 'in which' events can flow and things can move) it is patently unlike any other. Either way we appear to be too strongly composed of it to gain much perspective on its nature, deathbeds excepted. (The Zen Buddhist tradition of the 'death poem' explicitly takes advantage of this unique if fleeting prospect.)

ISOCHRONY

Isochrony is a natural expression of the phenomenon of pulse in speech, and describes the tendency for strong stresses to arrange themselves at roughly even intervals; it is the 'innate pulse' of spoken language. As I mentioned in my earlier definitions, English is often claimed to be a 'stress-timed language', i.e. one where strongly stressed syllables are perceived to be delivered at an approximately constant rate, and where weak syllables will bunch up or spread out to facilitate it. Vowels which land on strong stresses can either elongate or, through a kind of mutual repulsion, command space around them. Weak stresses tend to be treated as being of relatively negligible length, and converge on a broadly uniform, indeterminate short vowel (the 'schwa'); they are thus able to bunch up as tightly or loosely as they need to within the weak gap between the strong stresses, and so facilitate their relatively even placement.

Isochrony is most clearly heard when language is emotionally urgent. Its existence has been rather hard to prove in the lab, and one occasionally hears it written off by phonologists as a psychological projection, which is likely a part-truth. However, the studies I have looked at seem compromised by their not taking into account the regularising effect of high emotion and rhetorical pitch. Verse is generally 'urgent speech' of one sort or another, and tends to foreground isochrony even in its non-metrical forms. Crucially for poets, the connection also works inversely: the psychological association is so strong that language which displays isochronic pulse *sounds* emotionally urgent, regardless of its content.

Consider:

language which displays isochronic pulse sounds emotionally urgent.
/   /   /   /   /   /   /

versus the same line spoken as 'demagoguery' (imagine Hitler, or the Rev. Ian Paisley):

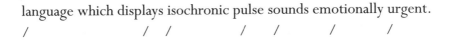

language which displays -x- iso chronic pulse -x- sounds emotionally urgent.
/   /   /   /   /   /   /   /   /

But while isochrony is a clear feature of brainwave, heartbeat, foot-step, breath, and so on, its presence in spoken language remains a mere tendency, and it is as much a psychological, listener-projected phenomenon as a feature upon which speech naturally converges. However, *all* heightened speech – from cries of terror to declarations of love, from barked instructions and political speeches to 'lecturer's stress' ('This SEEMingly iRRELevant POINT I am MAKing about BYron's HEADgear is VEry imPORtant') – will overdetermine the isochronic effect, and introject it heavily as a performative feature. Isochrony is not a *rule*, but just the linguistic expression of the physical *drift* towards periodicity that we find in any series of salient events, and a straightforward by-product of physical law.

Isochrony runs through time, but does not measure time. Many natural processes in this particular universe settle down into period-icity, with the same event recurring at even intervals; but this is not yet 'rhythm', which is a perceptual phenomenon – and one likely confined to humans, at least on this planet. Isochrony can, however, be considered the 'wallpaper' from which rhythmic, metrical template is cut. Like metre, it consists in the alternation of weak placeholders of even duration, and strong positions which mark single events. The passive character of this weak interstitial space is linguistically advantageous in that it allows grammatical function to be demoted to weakly stressed positions of cognitive non-salience, allowing the brain's live processing to concentrate on lexical content, where strong stress and strong position are aligned.

Presumably, however, the *ability* to make such differentiations, and perhaps even the very origin of the function-content distinction, derives from the condition of periodicity itself. In other words: what is also alternating in this continuous weak-strong flow is syntagmatic connection and paradigmatic instance – one connecting horizontally, one instantiating vertically. (The axial relationship is strikingly reminiscent of an electromagnetic wave, where two fields, one magnetic and one electrical, oscillate at right angles to one another, inducing each other perpetually through space-time. It could easily be where we 'got the idea.')

As urgency increases, the frequency of strong stress increases; at zero-degree, emotionally zombified rhetoric, there are close to no perceptible stresses at all. I overheard a conversation in a bus in Dundee recently of such informational non-import I could not identify a single s-stressed syllable. I believe the statement was to do with milk, and was delivered like a sewing machine. *Eh-dinna-ken-if-or-no'-there's-ony-left-in-the-hoose / Eh-hink-Eck-yased-the-last-o'-it-last-nicht-but-Ah'll-beh-some-the morn's-morn-tho'.*[1] It would scan as x x x x x x x x x x x x x x x x x x x x x. On the same bus a day later, I overheard a woman (of Indian ethnicity, for the record) deliver a far more urgent line to rein in her badly misbehaving child: *YOU-WEE-MINK-YOU-COME-OWR-HERE-RICHT-THIS-MEENIT*, which has ten consecutive s stresses.

The clear isochronic tendency of emotionally charged speech is one form of 'proof' that metrical poetry arises naturally from the

[1] 'I do not know whether or not there is any left in the house; I think Alex used the last of it last night, but I'll purchase some tomorrow morning.' My using an example drawn from dialectal speech may sound patronising, but dialect accommodates the merely phatic exchange (i.e. one whose purpose is more social than informational) far more cheerfully than formal English – hence, frankly, its superior warmth.

language, and merely foregrounds an ever-present pulse. Poetry is often written out of some emotional necessity anyway, and isochrony will be naturally 'imprinted' under such conditions. (This explains the identifiable presence of a strong isochronic pulse in free verse.)

Poetry gives explicit expression to this tendency when it makes use of a fixed metrical frame. Its ur-form, its primitive cognitive template, consists of a fixed series of strong positions separated by weak positions, and its subsequent realisation in the form of either light, loose or tight metres. While we generally mark weak and strong stress positions with an x or /, these marks do *not* 'represent spoken stresses'. (Metres can be realised by many other material phenomena besides speech.) The w position mark represents a placeholding *duration*, while the s position mark represents an *event*, and in poetry these positions are realised by syllables which carry the characteristic of a weak or strong stress. (The point will be developed, but bear in mind for now that a 'weak' stress entails a considerably diminished vowel length, 'strong' an increased one; for this reason, more than one weakly stressed vowel can inhabit a w placeholding duration, while only one s-stressed vowel can coincide with an s event position.)

Additionally, the kind of isochrony that all poetic lines draw forth – even those of 'free verse' – will increase the relative frequency of strong stresses. With an increase in the evenness, number and proximity of those strong stresses, we see an increase in the incidence of consciously processed content words, leading to an increased degree of referentiality in the language itself; this explains poetry's reputation as vivid, imagistic and 'invocatory' speech. No one ever *says* things quite like 'On the middle of that quiet floor / sits a fleet of small black ships, / square-rigged, sails furled, motionless, / their spars like burnt match-sticks'[2] except in poetic lines. Strong-stress frequency also increases the overall vowel-to-schwa ratio, and potentiates the

---

2 Elizabeth Bishop, 'Large Bad Picture', *Poems* (New York: Farrar, Straus & Giroux, 2011).

carriage of much tonal and therefore personal information: accent, origin, ethnicity, emotional state, age, sex, body-size and so on; this is no small factor in the reader's ability to 'make the poem their own'. It simply increases the poem's expressive potential, through expanding that component of speech capable of 'personalisation' in its vocal or internalised performance.

Metred verse, through its insistence on both a greater degree of regularity and a higher incidence of regular s-stress syllables than we might encounter in our natural speech, overdetermines all the iso-chronic effects mentioned earlier. It not only forcefully echoes the sound of urgent speech, regardless of its content, but simultaneously enforces a rhetorical or emotional urgency of delivery, and requests that the poet's words also 'step up to the mark': they had better have something urgent to *say* if they are to take such a tone with the reader.

The 'natural metre' of speech consists primarily (but not exclus-ively) in a combination of the isochronic rule and the alternate stress rule, discussed shortly. Language already exhibits a strong degree of metricality in its 'resting state'. Free verse relies only on language's natural metre, together with the intensified isochrony of heightened speech and the metricalising effects of lineation. Syllabic 'metres', while compositionally useful, are oxymorons in English; they do not compel a pulse, and are simple counting systems producing no more metre than, say, regular occurrences of the letter 'q', or the evenly spaced names of English regional cheeses. You will hear some individuals claim otherwise, but they are fooling themselves or their ears; Germanic syllables can only be counted consciously, not 'grooved along to' instinctively – and even then only by completely mangling the natural prosody of the language to flatten out the difference between weak and strong, so all syllables fall on evenly spaced event positions. Nonetheless I have heard people try to win this point by reading poems aloud in what sounds like an old beta for Stephen Hawking's voice software. (There *is* a better argument for the audible syllabic quality of iambic pentameter, but we'll get to that.)

STRESS

While some languages have prominent features of vowel length and of tone, the quality providing the most potential for linguistic contrast in English at the level of syllable is *stress*. While there are many other ways of looking at them, our sentences can be considered as arrangements of weak and strong stresses built up from a series of words, each of which has its own prosody: a 'lexical stress' that we learn simultaneously with its sense, and seem to store in the same location in the brain as a synaesthetic unit.

The complex phenomenon we breezily denote with the word 'stress' is an aspect of our speech composed of three constituent elements: loudness, pitch and length (which, within the flow of speech, can lead to a fourth: rhythmic displacement). When stress is salient, we call it 'strong'; when not, 'weak'. Sometimes only particular aspects of stress will be exaggerated, but we'll nonetheless still characterise them as 'strong' or 'weak'. Loudness is a common enough weak-strong-stress indicator in conversation, but both the yell for attention and the *sotto voce* euphemism are, through their shared quality of 'salience', both kinds of stress.[1] (Significant increases or decreases in loudness are very rarely used as a salient foregrounding device in poetry, and are only ever indicated by typographical cue: this usually involves the novel use of font size, type or colour. The convention, such as one exists, is that 'caps lock equals shouting'; far

---

[1] Another reason for my queasiness over the word 'unstressed': there are few words so apparently understressed as the soundless mouthing of the word 'cancer', but a form of stress it is.

less frequently we might see small or faintly printed fonts indicating whispers. This takes advantage of our instinctive SMALL IS QUIET / BIG IS LOUD or VISUALLY FAINT IS QUIET / VISUALLY INTENSE IS LOUD synaesthetic metaphors.[2])

However, in most English conversation, those small increases and decreases in loudness are accompanied by small rises and falls in pitch, and generally experienced as indistinguishable from them. In each strong stress, we see in the syllable a slight but perceptible rise in its loudness, a rise in its pitch and a slight lengthening of either its vowel or the temporal gap on either side of it. (Often when we detect such a space between words, we are actually hearing nothing of the sort; most speech blurs the sound of the last word into the next, and the definitional boundaries of each individual word are more psychological than physical, just as they are with the visual perception of discrete objects. Indeed, I suspect deliberate phonosemantic patterning has the effect of blurring discrete semantic boundary in a way directly analogous to the blurring of visual object-boundary in certain low-lit or painterly circumstances).

The classical iamb was measured as one short + one long vowel, equivalent in duration to a brach + two brachs: in musical terms, this is close to a single quaver triplet followed by two tied quaver triplets. The difference between the durations of the two syllables of our own stress-based iamb is nothing like so pronounced. The ratio is closer to 2/5ths to 3/5ths, and usually even subtler: it is more or less identical the so-called 'swing quaver' in jazz, where each alternate eighth-note is slightly delayed. And just like the swing quaver, it's a flexible ratio which can be 'heavy' or 'light' depending on a number

---

2 Mark Z. Danielewski's mind-crushingly disturbing *House of Leaves* provides one of the cleverest examples of this technique: the word 'house', wherever it appears, is printed slightly lighter and slightly askew (and blue, in the hardback version), a technique that seems innocuous enough – but as the house slowly gains in menace, the reader begins to actively dread its next appearance.

of variables – including dialect and emotional tone, both of which can also drastically affect the rate of syllabic delivery.[3]

This difference in vowel length would be noticed even less, were it not almost invariably emphasised by a slight rise in loudness (as in the jazz quaver) and in pitch. Pitch, in emotionally neutral and non-urgent conversation, is usually centred on a note in the lower third of the speaker's natural register, and rises somewhere between the interval of a minor second and a minor third on the s-stressed syllable. (In a few UK accents – in parts of Fife and Aberdeenshire, for example – the s-stressed syllable drops *below* the pitch of the weakly stressed syllables, lending a 'questioning' character to the speech; certain Scandinavian accents do much the same.) This means strongly stressed vowel-sounds have a distinctive formant and an identifiable character, in contrast to weakly stressed vowels, which have a short neutral sound often close to a schwa; these weak sounds are relatively characterless, regardless of how the vowel is represented by its spelling.[4]

In the context of a normal sentence most monosyllabic content words – nouns, verbs, adjectives, adverbs and proper nouns – will take a strong stress, and most monosyllabic function words a weak

3 The most important factor determining the degree of iambic 'swing', as we'll see, is whether the iamb occurs in a line derived from 4-strong, or in iambic pentameter; in the latter, the iamb can be flattened out to something close to the even jazz rhythm known as 'straight 8s'. Whether the jazz quaver developed in imitation of African-American English speech is moot, but it was likely influenced by it (although certain folk musics which fed into the mix have a strong swung quaver too: that heard in traditional Scottish music is often so pronounced it sounds like John Knox angrily stapling pamphlets together). The iamb surely does not originate, as certain authors still sweetly claim, in the flub-dub of the heartbeat. If it did, we would expect francophone hearts, in contrast to anglophone hearts, to deliver a nice, even 'boum-boum'.

4 However, I once met someone who pronounced *all* schwa with a touch of the vowel colour of their written form (i.e. they would say 'vowel colour' just a little like 'vow-ell cul-oor') – the result of a childhood spent largely in isolation with only books for company.

one. Function words indicate how content words should relate and orientate themselves to one another. In adult speakers, function is a learned and automated procedure, and function words rarely need to be consciously processed, unless you're reading Henry James. Their weak stress helps to 'background' them, and keep the brain's CPU focused on the content. New or especially important content is flagged by an additional, contrastive stress which is intonational in character, and usually involves a sharp rise in pitch.

We can immediately see that any prosodic analysis which treats stress as a fixed phenomenon is going to create a terrible over-simplification. Depending on what *kind* of stress we encounter, its constituents – loudness, pitch and rhythmic displacement – will be mixed in a very different way, and have a very different quality. Consider, for example, the stress I just asked you to put on the word 'kind': the use of italics implies a foregrounded rise in vocal pitch on the italicised vowel – perhaps as much as the interval of a sixth from the median pitch – and a short (mora-length) pause after it, before the next weak stress. The stress-shape of speech should really be analysed in terms of its suprasegmentals – the sound-qualities which extend beyond isolable phonemes, e.g. pitch, timbre and so on. Poetic prosody is just a useful, simplified and codified way of speaking about a phenomenon that has received a far better scientific description in the field of phonology. In poetry we focus on how written poetic cues are *translated* into real-world, spoken stress – but not on the precise nature of that spoken stress itself, since there can be no 'ideal performances' of the line, even though one performance may be strongly proposed.

For this reason, the way I'll represent sense-stress pattern in metrical analysis will be necessarily crude. Our metrical symbols are intended only to describe a strong-weak pattern; however, pitch – a crucial aspect of stress when we analyse sense – is not something that can be accurately indicated in this way; nor can vowel length. (Our Germanic speech-rhythm is *primarily* qualitative, but not wholly so; and there are metrical circumstances – such as very short lines – where quantity, in the form of vowel length, can become salient too.) However, the use of strong-weak symbol patterns is an extremely useful shorthand in determining underlying metrical templates, and noting which lexical stresses deviate from them; but since this doesn't tell us *why* they deviate, the symbols themselves should not be reified and then talked about as if they had any real-world existence. If we are interested in gaining an understanding of *real* stresses, we have to consider not only their strength but also their quality – and since that performed stress is intimately bound up in 'understood sense', our final prosodical analysis must never become divorced from a discussion of sense and contextual meaning.

Despite T. F. Brogan's earlier warning, I feel that adding an intonational aspect to notation is necessary if we are going to be true to that aim. Words spoken with no pitch accent or de-accent sound literally 'robotic'. They communicate *some* sense, but leave us unable to judge whether the speaker either understands or identifies with it. Our understanding and interpretation of a line is revealed and broadcast in our vocal performance. If we are to regard the poem as a speech act, we must make some account of this performance, or at least its sensible variables. As ever, the purpose of this approach is to restore some agency to the humans on either side of the poem, and their role in the production of its meaning. In a poetic context, 'stress' is *always* a performative and interpretative act.

METRE AND THE FOOT

A metrical template is a fixed, binary pattern of strong and weak positions. It consists of weak placeholders which denote even durational gaps, and strong positions which denote single transient events. It forms a 'cognitive frame' upon which the real syllables of our speech can converge. Thus, for example, the x/x/x/x/ template of iambic tetrameter or duple 4-strong is held in the mind as a duh-DAH-duh-DAH-duh-DAH-duh-DAH pattern, to which the poet's speech is magnetised to a greater or lesser degree. Lightly and very lightly convergent metres I call 'loose' and 'light' metres respectively; strongly convergent metres (which reinforce the metre through one-to-one correspondence between the single w-syllable and the w-position) I call 'tight' metre. These various degrees of convergence themselves form part of the cognitive metrical template.

When we conceive of metre as a series of repeated units, we often refer to them as 'feet'. We don't experience metre in this way at all, but as rhythmic flow; however this deliberate segmentation of metre has its analytical uses. (I tend to use the word 'metron' to describe a fixed unit of metre, measured non-inclusively from one strong-stress position to the next, and 'foot' to describe a verbal *instantiation* of that metre, which can have a far greater number of variables.) We've seen that 'foot' comes from the Greek πούς; our feet are what we use to beat out the time. We inherited our Greek foot-names from classical prosody. These metres were quantitative, and measured vowel length, length being as salient a feature in classical verse as stress is in our own.[1] We use the language of classical quantitative metrics to indicate patterns of *qualitative* metres, and in doing so have made things deeply confusing for ourselves. Most problematically, it has reified unimportant metrical phenomena by giving them pretty names: identifying something doesn't make it *worth* identifying. (Most poets will know the word 'dactyl', but rather fewer 'teleuton', 'the last word in the line' – despite it being a far more important compositional consideration.)

There is no such thing as the foot in the poet's compositional experience. Poets think and compose in units of lines, metrical or otherwise. Allowing spoken sentences to adhere to a metrical template is difficult for non-poets, but for fluent and experienced composers of verse it is practically a motor skill, and a conversation can be easily conducted in blank verse.[2] Indeed, learning to speak metrically is a far better and quicker way of learning how to think in metrical lines than is writing them; one gains a deep sense of the line as an indivisible unit, not merely a series of counted stresses. It also reminds us that anyone railing against the 'tyranny of the metre' is campaigning only against their own incompetence.

While largely useless in poetic composition, feet are a handy tool of retrospective analysis that allow the poet consciously to examine their instinctive metrical decisions, and make sure – in the way that a composer might check that a semiquaver had not suddenly been

1 I've heard classicists say that Latin church music can be understood better than English; extreme vowel lengthening doesn't have quite the catastrophic effect on intelligibility that it does on stress-based languages. Sung long-note English is mostly in code, and in the context of a choral *largo*, a shopping list would probably do just as well as John Donne, for all the sense anyone ever makes of it. The most sympathetic setting for English poetry is probably mid-tempo jazz singing, where the asymmetric jazz quaver coincides nicely with the iamb.

2 A fine parlour game of a drunken evening, especially when you switch to rhyme – at which point the infinite usefulness of hyperbaton and elision become immediately apparent, and you suddenly understand the practical exigencies that produced 'poetic diction'.

dropped during the calculation of a complex melody in a bar of 4/4 — that they've achieved the kind of metrical consistency they had desired for the line. They're also useful for the theorist in providing a handy shorthand for describing the fixed prosody of any word or phrase of two or three syllables; this comes up often enough to justify their continued use on the grounds of convenience. Feet are *not* equivalent to 'measures' in music; these have a real and perceptible existence, as they are often reinforced rigorously by even-length phrases. Feet cross word- and phrase-boundaries without a second thought or (*pace* certain theorists) perceptible disruption.

Feet are useful, too, for characterising certain rare metres: one might want to point out, say, that Dr Seuss's 'And, speaking of birds, there's the Russian Palooski, / Whose headski is redski and belly is blueski' is determinedly amphibrachic. Nonetheless there are basically only *two* kinds of metre type that 'naturally' arise in English: duple and triple, or binary and ternary. This is because any run of three weak syllables will usually see the middle weak attempt to turn itself into a strong, under the alternate stress rule. (The one exception is the occasional appearance of quadruple 'paeonic' metres in light 4 × 4 or 'Dolknik' forms.) All other metres, like Dr Seuss's above, have to be 'overdetermined', a process I'll explain in due course. Duple metre is a . . . w-s-w-s-w-s . . . pattern which can be cut into anywhere; similarly, triple metre runs . . . w-w-s-w-w-s-w-w-s-w-w-s . . . and can cheerfully start or end on the strong syllable, or on either weak syllable. (Both kinds of line are themselves just interpretations of the same weak placeholder/strong event template.) Absolutely regular iambs and trochees, anapaests and dactyls appear only in the very tightest, most formally overdetermined metres.[3] Despite the foot's usefulness in describing some poems by Dr Seuss, Longfellow and

3 We must dismiss earlier transitional practices: for example that fact that, while moving from Latin to English verse, the Tudor poets were to some extent still composing in the ghost of the classical foot – as (allegedly) verified by the degree of disyllabic segmentation we find in some of their iambic verse.

Edith Sitwell, to identify a 4-strong triple metre line as 'dactylic' or 'anapaestic', say, generally turns out to be a waste of time: most poets will freely vary the end- and start-points, and we usually have little sense of the line being clearly 'rising' or 'falling', in the way we can sometimes identify in duple metres. In the same way there is really little need for a distinction between iambic and trochaic duple metres – except, again, under formally overdetermined circumstances. Confusingly, we've come to use 'iambic' as a general shorthand for 'duple'. This unfortunate convention is now embedded too deeply to be worth the trouble of challenging: the problem has been compounded by the duple line we call 'iambic pentameter', which has reinforced the error in a way that seems culturally unrevisable. I'll continue to use them – albeit grudgingly – as synonyms, unless I specify otherwise.

Duple metre goes least against the grain of the natural rhythm, syntactic structure and delivery of the slow, deliberate, elegiac, lyric English that is currently our unconscious poetic default. (This is *not* true of medieval, conversational, jaunty, journalistic and some dialectal Englishes; the idea that iambic metre is 'the natural rhythm of English speech' is a myth.)

> Beyond our lives, they laugh, and drink their tea.
> We look at them just as the winter night
> With its vast empty spaces bends to see
> Our isolated little world of light,
> Covered with snow, and snow in clouds above it,
> And drifts and swirls too deep to understand.
> Still, I must try to think a little of it,
> With so much winter in my head and hand.
>
> (GJERTRUD SCHNACKENBERG, 'The Paperweight')[4]

---

4 Gjertrud Schnackenberg, *Supernatural Love: Poems 1976–2000* (Newcastle upon Tyne: Bloodaxe, 2001).

Triple metre has more speed: its two consecutive light, weak stresses mean it simply reads more quickly, and as a result it has often been used for light, popular or narrative verse. There is no real reason that this should be so other than convention; recently poets like Sean O'Brien have done a great deal to reclaim it for 'serious' poetry. In its composition, its galloping nature naturally leads not just to lists and litanies but to long sentences, and therefore frequent and frictionless enjambment. It remains a fine technical solution for the poet who can't get above sonnet length, or finds themselves so bogged down in preciously drawn imagery and costive little arguments that they daren't break out into something more freely associative; in its tendency to produce racing chains of phrases, it actively facilitates the 'imaginative leap' by fuelling the headlong run that prepares for it.

> It is Londesborough Street with the roof gone—
> That smell as the wallpaper goes, as it rains
> On the landing, on pot dogs and photos
> And ancient assumptions of upright servility.
> Nothing is dry. The pillow-tick shivers
>
> And water comes up through the scullery tiles
> And as steam from the grate. There are funerals
> Backed up the street for a mile
> As the gravediggers wrestle with pumps and the vicar
> Attempts to hang on to his accent.
>
> (SEAN O'BRIEN, 'After Laforgue')[5]

Note how these lines variously begin at all three possible positions in the triple pattern. Generally speaking, content words in triple metre are also more easily demoted to w stresses when they land

---

5 Sean O'Brien, *HMS Glasshouse* (Oxford: Oxford University Press, 1992).

on a w position ('It is Londesborough Street with the roof <u>gone</u>'). In duple metre, such a stress-position/lexical stress contradiction ('It's Borough Street with all the roofs <u>blown</u> off') would usually constitute a 'tension', but the momentum of triple metre makes the demotion smoother (as does the fact that the first w of the pair often has a little more pitch height as it negotiates between the s stress and the second w stress; for this reason tensions on the second w — 'It is Londesborough Street with the roof on <u>fire</u>' — are somewhat rarer, but smoothly accommodated nonetheless).

In the context of 'loose' metrical composition, the two metres can also be cheerfully alternated to effect changes of tempo, reminding us that the w position is a durational, flexible space which can be variously inhabited:

> They fought the dogs and killed the cats,
>   x   /   x / x   /   x /
> And bit the babies in the cradles,
> x   / x / x /   x / x
> And ate the cheeses out of the vats,
> x   /   x   / x / x   x /
> And licked the soup from the cooks' own ladles,
> x   /   x /   x   x /   x   / x
> Split open the kegs of salted sprats,
> x / x   x / x / x   /
> Made nests inside men's Sunday hats,
> x   /   x /   x   / x   /
> And even spoiled the women's chats,
> x   / x   /   x / x   /
> By drowning their speaking
> x   / x   x   / x

With shrieking and squeaking

x   / x x   / x

In fifty different sharps and flats.

x / x / x   /   x   /

(ROBERT BROWNING, 'The Pied Piper of Hamelin')[6]

---

6   James F. Loucks and Andrew M. Stauffer (eds), *Robert Browning's Poetry: Authoritative Texts, Criticism* (New York: W. W. Norton, 1979).

'RESTING STATE' PROSODY

When we scan lines, we generally look first at the tension between the metre and lexical stress. I will refer to this pattern of lexical stress as the lines' 'resting state' prosody or RSP. (I use the phrase to include such prosodic qualities as we may also want to take account of at the phrasemic and syntactic-phrasal level too.) By 'resting state', I mean such prosody as already inheres in the language (a) before any larger contextual sense has been derived and performed and (b) before any metrical frame has been diagnosed and projected into the verse.

Wherever the underlying metre is not immediately apparent (i.e. whenever the line is in either loose or light metre), the RSP of several lines will indicate or confirm the metrical template on which they converge. However tight or light, a line works to an identical under-lying metrical frame; therefore metre is always marked in exactly the same way. My rough procedure is as follows. The metre is 'decided upon', and then indicated by marking strong positions with a /, and marking the position or medial point of the weak placeholders with an x or -x-; the metre is then compared to the actual line's lexical stress; points of disagreement are registered; and then a sense-stress scansion is conducted. The result is a blueprint for performance which can and should be open to a variety of competent interpretations.

INTROJECTION, PROJECTION,
METRICALITY AND CONVERGENCE

Verse metricality is intrinsically unstable: I'll try to defend this assertion. (Readers may also read this – correctly – as yet another assault on our inherited New Critical values: what I call 'introjection' and 'projection' are, respectively, aspects of intentional and affective forces entirely necessary to the existence of poetry as aesthetic event.) The phenomenon of verse metricality arises through a variable combination of three things. These are **introjection**, the poet's engineered coincidence of speech-rhythm and metrical template; **projection**, the reader's determination to *hear* such a coincidence, whether it exists or not; and the **metricality** proposed by the resting state prosody of the line itself.

The scansion of a poem's RSP may reveal a metricality either stronger or weaker than that which the poet believes imprinted there, or the individual reader thinks they have heard. This metricality should not be confused with the poet's intentions; what poets intend is often not well communicated, and their metre is no different. Poets are fallible, and – as readers of their own lines – just as capable of erroneous projection as readers are, which affects the reliability of their calculations and claims. Similarly, readers are capable of remarkable acts of 'willed metricality', where subtle and unconscious shifts of emphasis can result in the perfect lining-up of speech rhythm and metre in a way that appears wholly deliberate on the poet's part, but is often nothing of the sort. (This is the bane of most prosodic theories; indeed theorists are perhaps the readers *least* exempt from this bad habit.) These three readings are broadly equivalent, if you like, to the intentional force, the affective force and the disinterested close reading of the text. The refusal to acknowledge or be aware of the extent of one's introjection and/ or projection has often led to the erroneous assumption that x or y passage is *intrinsically* metrical. However, an unread text can no more incarnate its own metricality than possess its own meaning. The RSP may *suggest* the presence of a metrical template, but only the reader confirms it.

Convergence represents the extent to which the introjection and projection of a metre successfully converge on the RSP of the line. A verse with high convergence will be found overwhelmingly and unequivocally metrical, and it may take only one or two lines to confirm this; verses — especially in light metres — with lower convergence will be unstable, and even after several lines will remain open to different metrical interpretations. (See the later analysis of Auden's 'Epitaph on a Tyrant'.) Strictly speaking, *no one line can confirm the presence of a metrical template*, only several lines which are felt to be organised by it. (However, some frames — common metre and i.p., for example — are so strong and culturally ingrained that the reader can often project the metre with near-certainty from a single instantiation.)

Sometimes introjection is very weak. The poet may deliberately be writing only loosely to their metrical template; alternatively, they may be in the grip of only a half-realised, partly unconscious or naive one. This is remarkably common. Not only doggerelists, but many decent contemporary poets untrained in metre will stumble into a loose common or ballad template, entirely unconscious of having done so; or they will write a few approximations of 4-strong, vaguely aware that they are 'having a bash' at metred lines — but with no ability to repeat the trick consistently, or accurately scan the lines they already have. (Significantly, iambic pentameter is never written 'naively'; I'll return to this later.) Often 'projection' is weak, and if the reader has no ear for metre, the poet's introjection must do the job alone — as it often does in metrically naive theatrical readings of Shakespeare, where the metre is still communicated to the listener, even if the actor neither feels it nor performs it.

OVERDETERMINATION

How little the morning needs us!

 x / x x / x / x

So is it with all our morrows;

 x / x x / x / x

If we count them, we will lose them —

 x x / x | / x / x

They our glories, we their sorrows.

 x x / x | / x / x

As unto the bow the cord is,

 x / x x / x / x

So unto the man is woman;

 x / x x / x / x

Though she bends him, she obeys him;

 x x / x | / x / x

Though she draws him, yet she follows.

 x x / x | / x / x

Exactly like all complex musical rhythms, any line can be (and generally is) broken down into simpler components of twos and threes, no matter how complex its prosody.[1] This might permit the emergence of a metre-type upon which other lines may converge, or allow a complex template to be designed from scratch. *All* metres are possible with sufficient introjection or projection: any mad variation you like, when accurately repeated, will create an

---

1 Unlikely as this sounds, this is an uncontroversial remark in music rhythm analysis.

expectation of its further recurrence; the accurate repetition of a caesura, too, can form part of such a template. As I mentioned in discussing the foot, metre-types are overwhelmingly duple or triple, with 'paeonic' / xxx types very occasionally cropping up in light 4 × 4 metres. In the above example by John Greenleaf Whittier (two stanzas from a much longer poem, 'The Ball of Clava') – we see the unusual trimeter verse-form

```
x  /  x  x  /  x  /  x
x  /  x  x  /  x  /  x
x x  /  x  |  /  x  /  x
x x  /  x  |  /  x  /  x
```

In this feminine-ending stanza, we might, if inclined, analyse the lines as follows: iamb/anapaest/amphibrach, x2; [anacrustic w] amphibrach / trochee / trochee, x2. (Note that a foot should not – if it is to have any integrity as a useful concept and analytical tool – cross a clear caesura any more blithely than it would a line-boundary. To analyse the second couplet as anapaest/iamb/amphibrach would be 'accurate', but pretty unsympathetic to what was going on.)

Overdetermination describes the *degree* of convergence which guarantees the identification of a metre-type, and occasionally its strength means that the metre is conjured far more powerfully that it would be in normal compositional or reading practice. This includes more strenuous forms of projection, some of which can loosen and even override such relatively locked aspects of prosody as lexical stress. The important distinction is that, while metrical template is only a lineated series of strong positions and weak placeholders, metre-*type* can be additionally overdetermined by a number of lines' sustained convergence on a specific pattern – and then seem to insist on a precisely ordered count of w- and s-syllables. If the syllabic count-pattern is consistently sustained, it may (as in the 10-position i.p. line) be thought of as forming part of the template itself. Looser or tighter verses, however, will simply take a looser or tighter approach to the *overdetermination* of metre-type without any change to the basic metrical pattern on which they are built, and these relatively loose or tight approaches can also be components of the cognitive template (best thought of, really, as 'the rhythmic expectations one has of the line').

For example: trochees are generally not sustained in duple metre, as more poets prefer to retain a syntactic latitude in their composition, and the freedom to begin the line with either a w or s stress. However, we know that trochaic verse can be sustained by strenuously *rejecting* that latitude, and overdetermining the metre of the line:

> By the shores of Gitche Gumee,
> By the shining Big-Sea-Water,
> Stood the wigwam of Nokomis,
> Daughter of the Moon, Nokomis.
> Dark behind it rose the forest,
> Rose the black and gloomy pine-trees.

> (HENRY WADSWORTH LONGFELLOW,
> 'The Song of Hiawatha')[2]

to quote a snatch of that estimable trochee-athon. And as some of you will have suspected, Whittier did not write anything called 'The Ball of Clava' (an infamous Dundee 'properism' heard among the aspirant classes, along with the sport of 'badminting'). I made up the garbage of the first verse to overdetermine the metre of the second, so you heard:

> As unto the bow the cord is,
> x / x x / x / x

2 Henry Wadsworth Longfellow, *Poems and Other Writings*, ed. J. D. McClatchy (New York: Library of America, 2000).

So unto the man is woman;

x /   x   x   /   x   /   x

Though she bends him, she obeys him;

x   x /   x | / x /   x

Though she draws him, yet she follows . . .[3]

x   x   /   x | /   x / x

However, these lines are from 'Hiawatha'. Here, because of the overdetermination of the trochaic pattern — which by this point in the poem has great momentum — you would have heard instead:

As unto the bow the cord is,

/   x   /   x   /   x /   x

So unto the man is woman;

/ x   /   x   / x   /   x

Though she bends him she obeys him;

/   x /   x   / x /   x

Though she draws him, yet she follows,

/   x   /   x   /   x / x

Useless each without the other!

/ x   /   x   /   x /   x

With the template firmly embedded in our ear, we hear these lines as trochaic; but if had they been the *opening* lines of the poem, the lexical scansion we would have instinctively made would have proposed a template nowhere *near* the trochaic regularity of 'Hiawatha', and might indeed have been something far closer to the 'Ball of Clava'. Metre-type, like almost everything else in life, is not intrinsic but determined by contextual forces.

3   It might have also been easily projected as two 3-stress lines (i.e. catalectic 4-strong) with triple variations, and two lines of an elaborately overdetermined 2-stress line consisting of two 'third paeons' [xx/x].

Precedents are crucial. A beginner's error is to start a metrical poem with a line or stanza in which there is some metrical ambiguity, or in which many variations occur: the template will then take far longer to be confirmed in the ear of the reader – and indeed they may never hear it at all; 'variations' are meaningless without a fixed template to vary *from*.

The only thing keeping these lines from 'Hiawatha' trochaic is the reader's projection. However, while there are a couple of tricks one can use to avoid trochaics getting repetitive – such as commencing lines with two monosyllabic function words, or using the imperative mood – there are too few to give the trochaic line the flexibility it would need to enter the mainstream of compositional practice. Though as soon as it did so, in its sophisticated use it would soon be indistinguishable from the so-called 'iambic' line, other than in its feminine endings: as I've observed, by 'iambic' we almost invariably mean simply 'duple'. (Trochees are a little unnatural to sustain, and this does seem to give them a rather 'otherworldly' or exotic feel; Longfellow's choice of trochaics here is, of course, really a kind of racist caricature, akin to a composer using a pentatonic melody played in parallel fourths to signify 'Chinese'. Shakespeare exploits this effectively, though, in his habit of setting the speech of supernatural beings in trochaic metres: 'Eye of newt, and toe of frog, / Wool of bat, and tongue of dog, / Adder's fork, and blind-worm's sting, / Lizard's leg, and howlet's wing, / For a charm of powerful trouble, / Like a hell-broth boil and bubble.'[4])

An overdetermined metrical rigidity and strength can be achieved not only through the determined repetition of fixed metrical patterns, but also by 'writing to' classical forms or their Anglo-Saxon

---

4 I can vouch for the inherently 'rising' feel of English, having almost driven myself crazy making and setting an English version of Striggio's libretto for Monteverdi's *L'Orfeo*. It meant flipping the polarity of the whole language: English rises, and mostly goes *duh DAH*. Italian falls, and mostly goes *DAH duh* – and therefore so does any music written for it; it felt like trying to squeeze a set of spanners into a velvet box made for a dinner-service.

equivalents; writing to song forms (song doubly fixes prosody by attaching an audible quantitative dimension to the vowel); isocolonic patterning (i.e. the repetition of syntactic structure, as seen in the 'Whittier' example earlier), and so on. However, this fixity often comes at an expressive price: it simply sounds unnatural, in no small part because it limits the use of the free and subjectively placed suprasegmentals that we associate with the more expressive and dramatic modes of performance.

Metrical variation in strenuously overdetermined metres is oxymoronic, and either extremely difficult or logically impossible to achieve; the line, by definition, requires a far higher degree of projection to be maintained, meaning that syllable count must be pretty rigid, as liberties are likely already being taken with lexical stress. Such lines are very brittle, and sustained more by readerly projection than by the lines' RSP; the reader will quickly lose the metrical frame if the line makes even a single radical deviation from the expected pattern. Even triple metres can suffer very little variation before they decay into mere natural stress-rhythm, and halfway-house, duple-triple approaches often create the perception of doggerel – at least in the hands of almost everyone but Louis MacNeice, whose metrical success remains something of a cosmic mystery:[5]

> In the top and the front of the bus, eager to meet his fate,
> He pressed with foot and mind to gather speed,

---

5 Once we have decided to identify such metrical eccentricity as a 'style', we will often let it pass. A style is generally regarded as deliberate matter, and not perceived as a form of incompetence; this is surely the correct diagnosis in MacNeice's case. However, this generosity usually depends on the author's name – with which comes all their previous poetic success – being firmly attached to the work; whether we would extend that generosity to an anonymised reading very much depends on the reliability of our taste and critical discrimination. I would dare not rely on mine, and for this reason I regard 'reputation' as a very useful thing – not, as some do, as the means by which otherwise unpublishable work is smuggled into print by a self-serving cabal.

Then, when the lights were changing, jumped and hurried,
Though dead on time, to the meeting place agreed,
But there was no one there. He chose to wait.
No one came. He need not perhaps have worried.

(LOUIS MACNEICE, 'Figure of Eight')[6]

If they can stay the right side of contrived artifice, overdetermined strategies can offer some interesting possibilities. They allow for far better analogues of quantitative classical forms than those which attempt to count vowel length (pointlessly: in English, length is certainly present as a feature, but it's rarely a salient one). 'Sapphics', for example, approximate three lines of /x/x/xx/x/x (two trochees, a dactyl, and two trochees) and one of /xx/x (a dactyl and a trochee). Swinburne makes a decent fist of it in 'Sappho' (in stark contrast to, say, Auden's or Bridges's quantitative experiments), and the template becomes audible after only a few stanzas:

. . . Saw the white, implacable Aphrodite,
Saw the hair unbound and the feet unsandalled
Shine as fire of sunset on western waters;
      Saw the reluctant
Feet, the straining plumes of the doves that drew her,
Looking always, looking with necks reverted,
Back to Lesbos, back to the hills whereunder
      Shone Mitylene.

(ALGERNON CHARLES SWINBURNE, 'Sappho')[7]

---

6 Louis MacNeice, *Collected Poems*, ed. Peter Macdonald (London: Faber & Faber, 2007).
7 Algernon Charles Swinburne, *Selected Poems*, ed. L. M. Findlay (New York: Routledge, 2002).

Though any arbitrarily constructed pattern will work just as well, and – as we've seen – may even include caesurae, which can be a metrical effect if (and *only* if) repeated regularly. Take /xx/ | x///xx (something like: dactyl, catalectic trochee, caesura, bacchius, dactyl, if you're the sort to care – though I might scan it as an 'overdetermined light metre' 4×4, i.e. a 4-strong line with variations and a mora taking the place of the caesura, for reasons later explained). These nonsense lines were written in ten seconds flat, so forgive me – but you'll get the idea:

> Give me that knife, you great mad idiot!
> Put it away, and kill all wrathfulness . . .
> Set it aside, or take yon blunderbuss
> down from the wall, and shoot that rattlesnake.

The 'success' of the molossus of 'great mad id-' / 'kill all wrath-' / 'take yon blun-', etc., might appear to suggest that *any* foot might be conceived of as a non-variant if it can be located in the template, albeit one initially formed by successive identical instances of 'anomalous' lines. This would be one way of 'proving' the possibility of the true English spondee, which many theorists feel cannot exist (on the principle that if two strong stresses occur together, one must weaken to preserve alternate stress): if a spondee merely realises part of an abstract metrical frame which contains successive strong-stress positions, then it 'exists'. To 'disprove' that, one would have to then argue the illegitimacy of the frame itself, and claim that *all* frames are, 'beneath it all', composed of only alternate w-s patterns. (I might not go quite so far, but would certainly argue that these overdetermined templates nonetheless *ride* on the tickertape of the endless w-s pattern. But this misses the point: a spondee is a *verbally realised* foot; if two strong positions occur successively as a part of an overdetermined abstract frame – designate that part of the template a 'spondee', by all means; just understand that this points to something which does not exist. But overdetermined templates can *encourage* the spondee, and spoken words can then realise it. Damn right.)

The closer this kind of patterning dovetails with the 4 × 4 form (as it often does), the more robust it becomes:

> High on the shore sat the **great god Pan,**
>> While turbidly flow'd the river;
> And hack'd and hew'd as a great god can
> With his hard bleak steel at the patient reed,
> Till there was not a sign of the leaf indeed
>> To prove it fresh from the river.
>
> He cut it short, did the **great god Pan**
>> (How tall it stood in the river!),
> Then drew the pith, like the heart of a man,
> Steadily from the outside ring,
> And notch'd the poor dry empty thing
>> In holes, as he sat by the river.

(ELIZABETH BARRETT BROWNING,
'A Musical Instrument')[8]

After several verses in which certain lines keep more or less doggedly to the same syllabic pattern, lines which in a single instantiation would sound like a metrical variation *now* sound as if they are realising part of the form. The first line scans as

```
    x    /    -x-    /    -x-    /    x    /
    High on the shore sat the great god Pan,
     /    x - x    /    x - x    /    \    /
```

8 Elizabeth Barrett Browning, *Selected Poems*, ed. Marjorie Stone and Beverly Taylor (Peterborough, ON: Broadview Editions, 2009).

— in my system.[9] However, suppose that this first epistrophic line had *not* been repeated in the prominent initial position, and that the whole poem *not* been written to a fully realised 4-strong template, but instead had read like this:

> **There**! The dark **shape** of my **reck**oning —
> **Near** the back **door** of his **car**avan,
> **Rais**ing his **left** hand and **beck**oning . . .
> High on the shore sat the great god Pan.

The line last would conceivably be scanned as trimeter, thus:

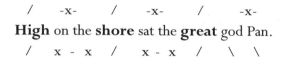

—A stretch, but the more such triple-rhymed stanzas had preceded the line, the greater the chance of a trimeter being overdetermined. And for my next trick, iambic pentameter:

> '*The* shore? What shore? This shore here? Oh shit!'
> He could be anywhere, this capric man . . .
> But this was no shore indeterminate:
>   / x / x / x / x /
> **High** on **the** shore **sat** the **great** god **Pan**.

In the final line, this requires the reader to read the 'the' in '*the* shore' as emphatic /ði/, of course, but it just about works. Contrived as it is, the principle is identical to the one we found at work ensuring 'Hiawatha' stayed trochaic.

---

9 One would likely perform a mora after 'god'; the overdetermined metre-type is triple, but in this foot, the expected consecutive w stresses are met with a single

Similarly, precisely timed overstressing of the sort we find in well-known stagings of Sitwell's *Facade* or Auden's 'Night Mail' can overdetermine a metre by taking lexical stress prisoner. In the latter case, the performance converges on the rhythm of Britten's score through adding the odd mora (a pause-length of about half a w-stressed syllable, here corresponding to a semiquaver rest in the score) between syllables and phonemes to add some quantitative fixing, as well as the use of strictly timed, w-substituting caesurae [-x-] between phrase boundaries.

> THIS [:] is the NIGHT[:]mail CROSSing the BOR[:]der,
> BRINGing [:] the CHEQUE [:] and the POST[:]al ORDer,
> LETTers for the RICH, [-x-] LETTers for the POOR, [-x-]
> The SHOP [:] at the CORNer and the GIRL [:] next [:] DOOR.

Any text, however, can be made to fit a metre if lexical stress is ignored:

> SIMilARly, PREEciseLEE timed OVerSTRESSing OF the SORT we FIND in WELL-known [switching to triples] STAGings of SITwell's FaCADE, -x- or AUDen's Night MAIL -x- can OVerdeTERmine a METre by TAKing lex-EE-cal stress PRISoner.

This is the kind of hellish mangling many song lyrics regularly undergo, through the strategies of vowel shortening, elongation, elision and division, and the splitting of diphthong.[10] However, songs

---

s stress, which is then demoted. This means it also requires some quantitative compensation, hence the mora. I have notated the one-size-fits-all AS pattern on top, not that of the overdetermined template. Arguably a fuller scansion of these metrical curiosities would include the AS pattern *and* the overdetermined template above the line.

10 This accounts for many a mondegreen, including my own mishearing of 'Islands in the Stream' by Dolly Parton and Kenny Rogers – lexical stress [/x x x /], but

have other merits, and we have rewarded them by naturalising their very strange procedures. In contrast, Sitwellian novelties tend to be resisted for the simple reason that their odd metre will quickly become the most memorable thing about them.

---

performed something like [/ x / x x] to fit the note-lengths and rhythm of the song –
as 'Ireland's Industry'. Which I did, bewildered, for years.

THE LINE AND MEMORY

Average poetic line length is determined in large part by human neurology. Firstly, syllable length and delivery-rate show a rough correspondence to our minimum auditory stimulus response time, which would make some basic evolutionary sense: presumably requests for lion-related assistance from the very fastest talkers went both uncomprehended and unheeded, while the drawlers and the mumblers were eaten before the words were out. Secondly, there's the matter of the 'specious present'. William James defined this notional period as a kind of ur-unit of time perception, being 'the short duration of which we are immediately and incessantly sensible',[1] i.e. the frequency of our conscious being. We now have a measurement for this duration, which it comes in at about 2.5 to 3 seconds. It would appear that this is the length of the 'auditory present', our hearing being the sense best equipped to follow and measure a time-event.[2] (Sight is half as quick in its reactions; smell is singularly poor

1 William James, *Principles of Psychology* (New York: Henry Holt, 1890), vol. 1, 631.
2 As mentioned earlier, Pöppel and Turner's paper 'The Neural Lyre' (1983) first proposed and elaborated this idea, but it also drew some very unfortunate reactionary and pro-New Formalist conclusions, using the three-second rule to declare the innate and superior fitness of certain line types over others. This, from a remarkable attack on Charles O. Hartmann's *Free Verse* (Princeton, NJ: Princeton University Press, 1980): 'His argument attempts to save free verse, and therefore defines verse in a hopelessly vague way; ours is content to abandon it as verse unless it consciously or unconsciously employs the human and universal grammar of metre. It may be an admirable kind of word play, and it might even be argued that it is a new art-form of our century. But it is not poetry . . .' Fast-forward ten years to New England symposia where young Republicans in bow ties give papers on Yvor Winters. Setting aside the stupid philistinism of Turner's declaration, while one is at liberty to say what one

in this regard – try counting fifteen minutes off with your nose. If it's thinking at all, and not screaming food, fear or filth, your nose is getting all dewy-eyed with the temporal cortex in its role as an access-point for long-term memory.)

We appear to divide time into psychological chunks based on the length of this three-second slot, and prepare our speech (as well as many other short-term actions, from handshakes to tennis serves) in roughly three-second units, with micro-pauses between them. As listeners, we attend to the speech of others in exactly the same way, dividing it up into manageable units of around three seconds. This three-second 'buffer' is then parcelled up and sent upstairs for processing, cyclically, over and over – forming a continuous three-second wavelength, a slow 'pulse' of attention, both to our own speech and that of others. If the information contained in this buffer sounds important, and needs to be consciously reviewed or memorised, it can be done so via the 'phonological loop'; this is a short-term memory slot about the length of the auditory present, which can be replayed for a short time. (If you snap your fingers in a silent room and listen to how long you can 'recall' the sound, how long the *very* sound itself seems to echo and persist in the mind's ear – that's about the number of times the loop can be replayed before the sound degrades into a memory; the exercise is a profoundly chastening and mortal one.) There is an important data-processing consideration attached. The loop is capable of holding around seven (plus or minus two) bits of information; this is why a seven-digit landline number is very much easier to recall on one hearing than a ten- or eleven-digit mobile number.[3]

---

thinks poetry is, one should never say what it is *not*: poetry is whatever we call poetry. Besides, as soon as you declare what poetry isn't, poets will just go and write that instead.

3 This insight originates with George A. Miller's influential paper 'The Magical Number Seven, Plus or Minus Two: Some Limits on Our Capacity for Processing Information', *Psychological Review* 63 (1956): 81–97. Atkinson and Shiffrin later

It should not surprise us to learn that most cultures have a default poetic line adapted to the length of the human auditory present, one which takes around three seconds or so to say aloud. (The kind of 'silent reading' we sometimes do when scanning a newspaper article or novel doesn't inwardly articulate the sounds of the words, and greatly increases our reading-speed. When reading poetry, however, this almost never happens; our 'lips move'. Or at least should.) Lines of a rough length of three seconds are more easily committed to memory, since they can be apprehended as an indivisible auditory unit. The data-limits of the phonological loop constrain us too, as do the number of syllables which can be slowly and deliberately spoken in this time: around ten, with the brain able to process around five or six pieces of content. Overload a line with content, and mind-leakage will occur. (I'm also struck by the coincidence of poetry's traditionally

proposed the dual-store memory model, where a 'buffer' can hold a short memory for a very limited time – R. C. Atkinson and R. M. Shiffrin, 'Human Memory: A Proposed System and Its Control Processes', in *The Psychology of Learning and Motivation*, vol. 2., ed. K. W. Spence and J. T. Spence (New York: Academic Press, 1968): 89–195. While this happens, it is bedding down its own semantic associations in the long-term memory – which, in contrast to the short-term memory, has a limitless capacity. Once there, it can be recalled by a contextual prompt. This memorising process is called 'consolidation', which is exactly what poetic lines attempt to achieve: if we fetishise their sheer beauty, truthfulness, originality and musicality, through rehearsal and re-rehearsal we will create the kind of meaningful associations by which they can enter the long-term archive. Here they can be strengthened by their periodic recall or 'recapitulation'. Baddeley and Hitch adapted the Atkinson–Shiffrin memory model to that of 'working memory'; this uses the short-term slave-systems of phonological loop and the visuospatial sketchpad, which are governed by a notional 'central executive', to hold different types of stimulus – A. D. Baddeley and G. Hitch, 'Working Memory', in *The Psychology of Learning and Motivation: Advances in Research and Theory*, vol. 8, ed. G. H. Bower (New York: Academic Press, 1974), 47–89. Later Baddeley added the 'episodic buffer', a vague holding-space for information from a number of sensory sources, but within which new kinds of cognitive representations might be created – which might point to the buffer also having a problem-solving role.

image-heavy tendencies and the 'visuospatial sketchpad', the visual equivalent of the phonological loop, and a major component of the mechanism of working memory.)

The poem, then, *is a succession of instances of the human present*. This line length of between 2 and 4 seconds roughly corresponds to a universal default, a line of around twelve (plus or minus five) syllables in non-tonal languages, and about half that number in tonal, where the metrical syllable is twice as long. The three-second line is a feature of classical Chinese and Japanese poetry, and of Latin, Greek, Hebrew, Slavic, German, Spanish and Gaelic verse; it corresponds to the French alexandrine, and in English to the 4-strong line. And it is the engine of the iambic pentameter, that bastard offspring of those princely three-seconders, the Italian hendecasyllable and the Anglo-Saxon alliterative line. (It's also the rough length of time it takes to read the schwa-infested tweet; there was nothing arbitrary in its 140 character limit 'feeling about right'. The average tweet-length is the same as the average sentence, of course: around 14 to 17 words and approximately a hundred characters, which a conversational reading speed will bring it at around the three-second mark. The recent doubling of the character limit stands a good chance of killing the platform.)

Any line of between roughly eight and twelve syllables is generally thought of as 'average length', i.e. neither long nor short. By the same rule, phonological memory decay dictates that there are about three seconds or so on either side of a word in which its sound can be prepared for or echoed, unless it has a salient position, like a rhyme-word: these are noisier – and so can be committed to memory, then recalled even several lines later. (The kind of analyses which point out buried lyric correspondences between non-salient or non-terminal words many lines apart are, alas, acts of either pure Kabbalism or wishful thinking.)

In any art form interested in being memorable, the ease with which it can be memorised is clearly going to be a major consideration; in an art form like poetry whose project is additionally *memorialising*, it's going to be a fundamental one. It should be no surprise that poetry's memorial project should naturally converge on those units of time that best reflect the way our brains encode memories. Those line-units are not discontinuous — one line runs into the next, as one moment bleeds into the next — but they do establish our deep poetic measure: the line is the carrier-wave of poetic sense, with three seconds its rough frequency.

LINE LENGTH

We instinctively categorise lines as 'short' or 'long' against this invisible, 8-to-12-syllable three-second-ish norm. 'Short' usually means anything around three s stresses or under; 'long', seven s stresses or over. A slightly longer line allows for more information, more description, more authorial opinion, but we tend to read it a little faster in an attempt to bring it down to something closer to the three-second wavelength, contracting the hiatus between lines considerably. The tactus of the poem – the pulse of its s stresses – speeds up; additionally, the content-word count is generally not as high, fitting the data constraint, and more s-stressed content is demoted to the functional and time-saving weak positions. This means that in the long-lined poem the semantic unit is dragged back towards the phrase, as in most conversation; in the short-lined poem, it is dragged towards the word. We gravitate towards the longer line when we write narratives, discursive arguments, polemic and so on, or when we mix authorial commentary with descriptive lines, or engage with the internal, abstract language of thought or feeling; these require a greater number of function words, as well as semi-functional and semi-phrasemic or stock-phrase language that often involves the demotion of content to function.

Conversely, we're often drawn to a shorter line when the poem is static, meditative and heavily imagistic, or when it declares an allegiance to song form. Here, the tactus of the poem slows down. We often find that a shorter line has more 'lyric' and imagistic content, more explicit use of musical effect, and tends towards the imagistic contemplation of the subject, rather than its argumentative discussion or narrative development. This results both in increased relative incidence of content words and (reversing the tendency we see in long lines) the promotion of function to content; this is also consonant with the idea that we will instinctively try to fill the five-bit quota in the line, if at all possible. There is a much longer hiatus after the short line, and (almost in imitation of song) a subtle elongation of the vowel, bringing the line back up to something closer to our three-second norm. This quantitative lengthening increases stress-prominence, which has the effect of making content even more salient. One thinks of the relief panels of Dickinson's poems:

> I started Early – Took my Dog –
> And visited the Sea –
> The Mermaids in the Basement
> Came out to look at me –
>
> And Frigates – in the Upper Floor
> Extended Hempen Hands –
> Presuming Me to be a Mouse –
> Aground – upon the Sands –
>
> (EMILY DICKINSON, 'I started Early –
> Took my Dog')[1]

– where the capitalised content gives the content words an even slower emphasis, and the dashes also serve (I think) to indicate brief caesurae or morae between grammatical phrases, and string the line out a little further. If we turn the ballad into 'fourteeners', they become noticeably cluttered:

> And frigates in the upper floor extended hempen hands,
> presuming me to be a mouse aground upon the sands.

1 Emily Dickinson, *The Collected Poems of Emily Dickinson* (Minneapolis: First Avenue Editions, 2016), 158.

The greater gaps between lines mean that advantage can be taken of the discontinuities proposed by them:

> My nipples tick
> like little bombs of blood.
>
> Someone is walking
> in the yard outside.
>
> I don't know why
> Our Lord was crucified.
>
> *A really good fuck*
> *makes me feel like custard*
>
> (SELIMA HILL, 'A Small Hotel')[2]

A very short line almost always reinforces the primacy of the individual 'image' or peristasis; there is a limit to how much one can elongate a vowel without singing it, and in passages of concrete description, nearly all but the most bardically inclined readers will instead opt for quantitative morae placed between the words themselves; this enhances both the sense of discrete detail and that detail's potential symbolicity. Take the 'Englished' haiku:

> Husking rice
> a child squints up
> to look at the moon
>
> (BASHO)[3]

2 Selima Hill, *Gloria: Selected Poems* (Newcastle upon Tyne: Bloodaxe, 2008).
3 My translation.

Here, the spoken delivery might well be something like:

> Husking [:] rice [————]
> a child [:] squints up [————]
> to look [:] at the moon [————]

One might even consider this elongated hiatus a *lineal* version of the weak placeholder: certainly, short-line poems are often remarkably content-heavy, as if grammatical function had been somehow been psychologically delegated to the weak interstitial duration of the hiatus itself. And one can also immediately see the difficulty – and indeed error – in trying to compose long-line poems full of content words, and short lines full of function words. However, when the poet *deliberately* uses the short line to promote function to content, the results can be dramatic:

> Through swing
>
> door after swing
> door I follow
>
> him until
> where he is to
>
> leave me as I leave
> well after midnight
>
> it is so quiet in
> the hospital
>
> (CIARAN CARSON, from *Until Before After*)[4]

---

4 Ciaran Carson, *Until Before After* (Winston-Salem, NC: Wake Forest University Press, 2010).

It would be very difficult to write a conversational, philosophical or narrative poem with a very short line: the long hiatus at the end of each line would be constantly undermined as the phrasal sense was obliged to ignore it, and the continual enjambment would soon become an irritation to the reader. (When there is a *persistent* disagreement between phrase and line – that is to say when the poem appears to enjamb excessively, and the line-break constantly drives against the grain of the syntax – it's usually a sign that the poem has just been written in the wrong line length. The good default is that line length is broadly reflective of phrasal rhythm, and phrasal rhythm varies with literary mode.) Conversely, long lines full of content can be as unmemorable and unwieldy as 13-digit telephone numbers. Better strategic accommodations are those such as C. K. Williams's signature long line: full of function words, but also with much of its content demoted through de-accent, as can be shown through a sense-stress scansion which reveals a high degree of 'phrasemicity', a horrible word we will soon be obliged to fling around with some abandon. (As will be later discussed, the brain treats the phraseme like a word, filed on the paradigmatic word-axis, and giving it one primary stress while partly or wholly demoting all others.)

The simplified scansion I've given to the following lines will, I hope, be intelligible enough for now. [/ ,] represents an s-stressed content word which receives a contextual de-accent, and [x'] a w-stressed function word with an emphatic accent:

'Water' was her answer and I fell instantly and I knew self-
/ x   x   x   / , x x   x / , /   x   x x   x   / , /
    destructively in love with her,
     x   /   x x x   /   x   x
had to have her, would, I knew, someday, I didn't care how,
x'   x x   x   x'   x   / , / ,   x x x x   / , x
    and soon, too, have her,
     x   x'   x' x   x

though I guessed already it would have to end badly though
   x   x   /   x / xx   x   x   x /, / x   x
not so disastrously as it did.
   x   x x /   x   xx x x'

(C. K. WILLIAMS, 'The Game')[5]

Despite their length, many of Williams's lines average only four or five genuinely strong stresses, once one takes account of de-accented content and accented function through a sense-stress scansion. (Note that in non-metrical verse, the operations 'promotion' and 'demotion' are not possible, but accent and de-accent accomplish much the same thing – i.e. they can reverse or part-reverse the roles of content and function.)

5   C. K. Williams, *The Vigil* (Newcastle upon Tyne: Bloodaxe, 1997).

LINE-BREAK AND ENJAMBMENT

Many aspects of lineation could just as easily have been discussed under 'meaning'. It can be quickly demonstrated that the lineation of a prose paragraph is capable of *enacting* much sense hitherto merely stated, making explicit sense of what was merely implied, or releasing and orchestrating sense which was either deeply buried or simply absent. This points to the line itself being a fundamental means of poetic sense-generation – a point perhaps more easily proven by reversing the operation and de-lineating a good poem to render it as prose. The first exercise artificially isolates smaller units of meaning within flowing speech; the focus those units provide and the syntactic fracture they create can release new or additional sense. The second exercise destroys such meaning as the line alone provides, and withdraws the poetic freedoms (contentual density and linguistic novelty, primarily) the slower and bounded space of the line-unit legitimates. I will discuss some of those effects here, though I'll try to keep the focus on the line as metrical rather than semantic tool.

The metrical unit of poetic composition is the line, a series of words with a typographically indicated pause at the end. This pause may be observed or overridden by following the syntactic cues in the poetic sentence itself. The line ending is the single most important metrical device in poetry, not least because it's the most obvious way in which poetry differentiates itself from prose, and advertises its desire to be treated as both excessively significant and excessively signifying language. While I'll continue to use it for convenience, we would ideally avoid the term 'line-break' in discussion of tight or loose metres; the poet should be trying to 'think in lines' – and, therefore, in terms of agreements and tensions produced by clause-coincident end-stopping and non-coincident enjambment, rather than 'breaks'. These variations are produced by holding a lineal template in the mind with which a phrase will agree or disagree, and into whose shape a phrase will frequently fall (i.e. lineal composition works in much the same way as other kinds of metred speech at the level of metrical rhythm or stanza). Workshop conversations about 'where to put in the line-breaks' tend to smack of the scissors and the pastry-cutter; these are perhaps necessary conversations, but it probably shouldn't be taught that working out 'where lines should break' is good compositional practice. The poet would be better guided towards a more organic method of lineal composition, and use 'line breaking' as a tool of correction. However, in unrhymed free verse and very light metres, the 'line-break' is definitely closer to a distinct technique, and is often more deliberately or consciously placed, since the metrical template itself has little or no power to direct or generate line endings. By contrast, in tight or loose metres the line-break is often the product of compositional exigencies other than line length, such as rhyme and metre. The effective defaults for breaking and enjambment are broadly the same regardless of metrical approach, however, except in the case of free verse, which is in some regards a special case, and will receive some brief separate discussion.

The line-break is a fairly straightforward business, and not, I feel, one that deserves lengthy treatment – although it has certainly received it elsewhere. When a line stops, speech is interrupted. If this coincides with a sentence- or clause-ending, we experience a pause. If the line stops mid-phrase, the sense impels us to minimise the interruption, and we elide the hiatus to create an enjambment. Generally speaking, consistently end-stopped lines, where sentence- or clause-ends coincide with line endings, are perceived as too predictably regular; consistently enjambed lines, where the sense and syntax flow over the line-break, are perceived as too gratuitously disruptive, and merely have the reader thinking 'So . . . *Why* did you bother to write it in lines at all, if these obvious breaks *never* coincide with the sense?' End-stopping is the natural default; enjambment is a natural tool of variation, and between them they achieve the ideal 'pink' balance of brown and white noise, predictability and surprise, syntagm and paradigm, rule and transgression that the brain most enjoys. One might also think of the end-stopped line as the brake, and the enjambed line as the accelerator, since they are crucial in controlling and varying the pace of a poem's delivery. Tactus slows towards the end of an intonational phrase, and phrase-coincident lines slow in the same way – but they will maintain a steadier pace if the syntax flows over the line.

Compare these two passages from MacNeice's 'Soap Suds'. The earlier part of the poem enforces its pauses:

And these were the joys of that house: a tower with a telescope;
Two great faded globes, one of the earth, one of the stars;
A stuffed black dog in the hall; a walled garden with bees;
A rabbit warren; a rockery; a vine under glass; the sea.

– in stark contrast to the closing lines, which propel the reader towards the end:

Then crack, a great gong booms from the dog-dark hall and the
      ball
Skims forward through the hoop and then through the next and
      then
Through hoops where no hoops were and each dissolves in turn
And the grass has grown head-high and an angry voice cries Play!
But the ball is lost and the mallet slipped long since from the
      hands
Under the running tap that are not the hands of a child. [1]

---

[1] Louis MacNeice, *Collected Poems*, ed. Peter Macdonald (London: Faber & Faber, 2007).

In their extreme enjambment and deliberate lack of punctuation, the final lines refuse to allow the reader a breath — and create a hyperventilating, terrified and headlong rush towards the poem's silently devastated conclusion.

A simple algorithm could probably be written for breaking any prose passage 'effectively' into poetic lines. Based on what one might intuit of current 'best practice' in the lyric poem, this would likely involve:

a) a balance of end-stopped and enjambed lines;
b) a tendency for thematically significant or 'interesting' material to be made salient by placing it as the final word (or 'teleuton');
c) the use of certain emotionally loaded words in terminal positions to create tension;
d) the occasionally gratuitously disruptive break to keep the reader on their toes, and 'misread' across-phrase breaks as on-phrase breaks (this often involves the brief misreading of the part of speech formed by the teleuton);
e) the use of deictically loaded words in a terminal position to create metatextual or metapoetic interest, by pointing to or 'playing on' their own terminality. (This is especially a feature of the more self-consciously placed teleutons of the free verse line.)

Here's a sonnet made from a random lump of Wikipedia:

Terang Boelan was a commercial success
in both the Indies and abroad, earning
200,000 Straits dollars in British Malaya.
This success revived the faltering domestic film industry
and inspired films aimed at Malay audiences
in Malaya, creating a formula

of songs, beautiful scenery and romance
that was followed for decades afterwards.
Modern critical reception of the film, which has been lost
since at least the 1970s, has generally been
positive. The Indonesian film historian
Misbach Yusa Biran described it as a turning
point in the history of Indonesian cinema for its
catalytic effect on the industry's growth.

Which we can analyse as:

Terang Boelan was a commercial success
    (enjambment on clause boundary)
in both the Indies and abroad, earning
    (enjambment across clause boundary)
200,000 Straits dollars in British Malaya.
    (end-stopped)
This success revived the faltering domestic film industry
    (end-stopped on clause)
and inspired films aimed at Malay audiences
    (apparent end-stopping on clause, revealed as enjambment)
in Malaya, creating a formula
    (enjambment on phrase boundary)
of songs, beautiful scenery and romance
    (enjambment on phrase boundary)
that was followed for decades afterwards.
    (end-stopped)
Modern critical reception of the film, which has been lost
    (apparent end-stopped on clause, revealed as enjambment)
since at least the 1970s, has generally been
    (enjambment across clause boundary)
positive. The Indonesian film historian
    (enjambment on phrase boundary)

Misbach Yusa Biran described it as a turning
    (apparent enjambment on phrase boundary, revealed as
       enjambment across it)
point in the history of Indonesian cinema for its
    (enjambment across clause boundary)
catalytic effect on the industry's growth.
    (end-stopped)

(I was far too heavy on the enjambment there, but I was having some fun with it.) Enjambment, as the above example shows, is capable of destabilising effect and can create brief 'misreadings'; these have the advantage of forcing the reader into quick reconsideration of the passage, so it can be correctly parsed. In language, give or take a few intermediate categories, the hierarchy of units in the syntagm is phone–phoneme–syllable–word–phrase–clause–sentence. Connected elements both within each level and between contiguous levels are bonded by a force of steadily diminishing strength. As one moves up from the smaller to higher units, the kind of cuts and divisions that line length produces are easier to make. However, within levels there can be great variety: within phrases, for example, the bond between determiners and following nouns is stronger than between adjectives and nouns, meaning enjambment on the former is more disruptive than the latter.

To summarise: a line is 'end-stopped' if it coincides with the end of a complete sentence or clause and is marked by some form of punctuation or implied punctuation, i.e. where punctuation would be present under normal grammatical rules. A line is enjambed if it breaks across a clause and the sense runs on until the next line. (This is an absurdly crude division; we should admit at least one intermediate category: lines which run on without punctuation but break on the clause boundary. I've always referred to these casually as 'half-stopped'. See the line 'This success revived the faltering domestic film industry' in the above example.) Back in the day, hyperbaton (which compensated for the difficulty of full rhyme and perfect metre) could more easily engineer a coincidence between phrase- and line-end; this was another frustration that the unofficial ban on poetic diction introduced to formal verse, making free verse an even more appealing alternative. The disruptive effect of line-breaks is a matter of degree, and linked to the hierarchical unit it cuts across.

Line-breaks which break sentences but observe clauses are least disruptive:

> What is this fear before the unctuous teller?
>
> (MICHAEL DONAGHY, 'Smith')[2]

Those which break clauses but fall on phrase boundaries are slightly more so:

> Why does it seem to take a forger's nerve
> To make my signature come naturally?
>
> (MICHAEL DONAGHY, 'Smith')

Those which do not observe phrase boundaries but divide them between qualifier and noun are yet more so:

> I drop my crumbs into the shallow
> Weed for the minnows and pinheads.
>
> (W. S. GRAHAM, 'Loch Thom')[3]

(Adjectives placed as teleutons not only challenge the prime position of the noun phrase – in English they also introduce a glitch, as many adjectives double as nouns and will be read as such in the first instance.

2 Michael Donaghy, *Collected Poems* (London: Picador, 2009).
3 W. S. Graham, *New Collected Poems* (London, Faber & Faber, 2004).

The reader usually has to reread to make sense of the line; this can be a fine tactic when used sparingly.)

Those on non-boundary function words are more disruptive still:

> [. . .] to touch him again in this life. I ran, and the
> bags banged me, wheeled and coursed [. . .]
>
> (SHARON OLDS, 'The Race')[4]

Those which divide lexemes themselves are most disruptive of all:

> Last night I
>   of your very hard and
> real I have put my fingers
>   on you and your fa
> ce if you were
>   here Russ Cheng
>
> (KESTON SUTHERLAND, 'Hot White Andy')[5]

And I'm sure I could hunt down something from a L=A=N=G=U=A=G=E poet which broke a phoneme into constituent phones. Putting the effect of tribal allegiances and 'school songs' in stylistic practice aside (New Formalists like end-stopping, L=A=N=G=U=A=G=E poets like breaking on particles, etc.), the various forms of enjambment generally tend to show up, as you'd expect, with a frequency inversely proportional to their disruptiveness. The cline of least-to-most disruptive line-breaks might go something like:

1) end-stopped on sentence;
2) end-stopped on clause;

---

4 Sharon Olds, *Selected Poems* (London: Jonathan Cape, 2005).
5 Keston Sutherland, *Poetical Works 1999–2015* (London: Enitharmon, 2015).

3) enjambment on clause boundary;

4) enjambment across clause boundary;

5) apparent end-stopping on clause, revealed as enjambment on phrase boundary;

6) apparent end-stopping on clause, revealed as enjambment against phrase boundary;

7) apparent enjambment on phrase boundary, revealed as enjambment across it;

8) enjambment on clitic, particle, etc.;

9) enjambment on compound word or phraseme;

10) enjambment on word, between lexeme and affix;

11) enjambment on word between phonemes;

12) enjambment within phoneme.

LINE BEGINNINGS

Lines follow the direction of time. All spatial and architectural analogies are suspect unless they are applied to purely typographical considerations. Some poets have – quite misguidedly, I feel – talked of the start of the line as being as important as the end, the opening word as important as the last, and have used this to justify the use of consistently disruptive line-breaks to facilitate the placing of 'interesting' words at the head of the line.

> In the taxi alone, home from the airport,
> I could not believe you were gone. My palm kept
> creeping over the smooth plastic
> to find your strong meaty little hand and
> squeeze it, find your narrow thigh in the
> noble ribbing of the corduroy,
> straight and regular as anything in nature, to
> find the slack cool cheek of a
> child in the heat of a summer morning—
>
> (SHARON OLDS, 'The Daughter Goes to Camp')[1]

---

1 Sharon Olds, *Selected Poems* (London: Jonathan Cape, 2005). Olds, like a number of poets of the first rank, succeeds despite and not through her technical experimentation. (I suspect her refusal to be bound by the conventions of the line ending is symptomatic of her rebellion against her own 'hellfire Calvinist' upbringing.) Though one might make an argument that perhaps in her case it *does* work: perhaps her viscerally moving poetry *needs* to looked as if it was torn out from the book, for all its meticulous construction.

If this approach was more than a novelty, poets would have been employing this 'ragged edge' technique for considerably longer than they have. Asking the first word to be as important as the last is asking time to run backwards: the hiatus means that the last word in the line reverberates briefly in its silence. Regardless of whether the word is 'elephant' or 'the', it will inevitably gain in semantic weight. But if it's 'the', and there is no good *reason* for the pause, the effect is one of a gratuitous disruption; compositionally, it seems a weak choice and a wasted opportunity. This technique most often gives these terminal function words an absurd and counterproductive salience, one its poets tend to deny; however, its *consistent* deployment can diminish the disruption, as the expectation of effective line endings are lowered. (Though *why* one would want to limit the power of the poem's most important formal feature is another question.)

Because of its temporal linearity, the start of the line is the ideal place for cramming in the extra weak syllables of the function words needed to propel the syntax forward at the start of a new phrase. They will read more quickly here that at any other position in the line, because the high-to-low model of the intonational phrase (with which line-template broadly tends to concur, and from which it is partly derived) also starts its syllable count fast, and slows towards the end. The effect is identical to the pickup bar in music, which shares the term 'anacrusis': the listener perceives the initial short notes as still belonging partly to the previous bar — or in poetry, the w stresses to either the hiatus or the ghost metron, if one occurs:

> They sang, but had nor human tunes nor words,
> Though all was done in common as before;
>
> <u>They had</u> changed their throats and had the throats of birds.

(W. B. YEATS, 'Cuchulain Comforted')[2]

---

2 W. B. Yeats, *The Collected Poems of W. B. Yeats* (Ware: Wordsworth Editions, 2000), 299.

Were one to sing the last line, 'changed' would be naturally placed on the downbeat, with 'they had' crushed into the end of the previous bar.

At an even more basic level – when the line begins, the reader's attention is as much taken up with its breaking the silence as with its sense, and this makes for a good opportunity to slip in all the messy and unmetrical stuff. Together with the function-first and masculine-ending tendencies of English syntax, it is the main justification for cutting into the metre-wallpaper before the weak stress, and gives the impression of a rising iambic default in duple metre.

Regular lines with odd-count stresses tend to invite more end-stopping; this is because the alternate stress rule places a natural counted pause – which I refer to as a 'ghost metron' – at the end of the line to even the numbers. Enjambment between odd-stress lines is a far more radical gesture than it is between even-stress lines, as it elides the ghost metron which elongates the hiatus. Counting errors often occur after enjambment in odd-stress metres, but especially in i.p. Syntax and clause-boundary are often influential factors; but often when i.p. lines enjamb, a dimetron is formed from the last iamb of one line and the first of the next; this produces a strongly even feel, especially when the phrased is closed by an initial caesura. As a result, the remaining four stresses of the second i.p. line are felt to *even out* the stress count – when it's the *odd*-stress line the reader feels they need to hear re-established. This means that under those conditions, lines of correct length often feel 'wrong':

> You were the one for skylights. I opposed
> Cutting into the seasoned tongue-and-groove
> Of pitch pine. I liked it low and closed,

> Its claustrophobic, nest-up-in-the-roof
> Effect. I liked the snuff-dry feeling,

(SEAMUS HEANEY, 'The Skylight')[3]

Here, the 'the roof / effect' is felt as even, and the 3-stress 'I liked the snuff-dry feeling' does the job of restoring the odd-count asymmetry of the i.p. It's still a miscount – and technically, I suppose, a goof; but Heaney's line shows how so-called error can work entirely to the poem's euphonious advantage. Only a fool would claim 'Its claustrophobic, nest-up-in-the-roof / Effect. I liked the dandruffed, snuff-dry feeling' was a better line on the grounds of its acatalexis; my rotten addition apart, it simply sounds too long. The 'mistake' is likely to have been wholly intentional, or at least a triumph of sound instinct over rule.

---

3 Seamus Heaney, *New Selected Poems 1988–2013* (London: Faber & Faber, 2014).

CLOSURE

I would ask that the reader indulge me a little here; the matter dealt with is not really a metrical one. It is, however, the direct product of a metrical phenomenon, that of the line, without which closure would not exist in the same form. Closure is a field of study in its own right, but I would be remiss if I did not make some brief account of it.[1]

With 'closure' I refer to the end-points of the larger structural elements of the poem, which, in their proximity to silence, inevitably produce expectations of significant information. In both symmetrical or regular forms and in free verse, the poet takes advantage of this pattern of anticipation, and often concentrates new or important semantic content at these points, preparing their shocks, surprises, revelations, punchlines and 'moving' details. 'Cadence' is a notoriously slippery term, and has gained an un-deserved credibility through its importance and clear definition in music theory. We would be better to confine its use to intonational phenomena, and replace it with the term 'closure', with which it seems to be more or less synonymous in this context. (I have for now ignored the grave limitations of the word itself and the various conceptual metaphors it brings with it; as Jennifer Baker points out, their domains and connotations have unnaturally narrowed our discussion of 'the end of the poem', a far richer and more varied field than mere 'closure' could ever accommodate.)

---

1 Most academics have been trained to reflexively yell Agamben! at this point, whether they have read him or not – see Giorgio Agamben, *The End of the Poem: Studies in Poetics* (Stanford, CA: Stanford University Press, 1999) – but the relevance of his work to the nuts and bolts of poetic closure has been overstated, and is not really relevant to our specific purposes here.

Closure remains — and *must* remain — an inexact science. It is as instance-specific as metonymy, and has a terrifying number of salient parameters, leaving the would-be taxonomist with an impossible and pointless task. These few remarks are offered in lieu of a more in-depth study.[2]

Poems are initially read as linear, temporal sequences. On re-reading, the reader's experience becomes more spatial: the domain is revisited as a semantic space in which connections between non-contiguous elements can be forged across greater textual distances and in any direction. Often the reader is prompted to do so by new, re-contextualising information, frequently made salient by its occurring at significant and rhythmic points in the poem's structure, especially before its patterned silences. This new information can do more than merely recontextualise: it can declare the poem as actually 'about' something else entirely — revealing, say, some new meaning hitherto latent in the title; it can have a catalytic effect, freezing the whole poem into shape, like a single ice crystal in a bottle of cold water, making suddenly manifest and tangible hidden structural properties of the whole domain. At this point — the discovery of connections, relations between lines, 'images' and themes — the reader additionally enters a spatial territory that is much more akin to the poet's own

2 Barbara Herrnstein Smith's study *Poetic Closure: A Study of How Poems End* (Chicago, IL, and London: University of Chicago Press, 1968) remains the single important monograph on the subject, but is now rather dated. Several points in this short section have their origin in insights borrowed from a St Andrews PhD candidate, Jennifer Baker, or emerged jointly from our conversation. Specifically, her work looks at varieties of terminal deictic and non-deictic shift (between them comprising a real-world and literary origo) and their centrality to the effect of closure, which forms a smaller part of what she calls Closural Poetics. All this occurs within in a dynamic frame where the poem is effectively 'spatialised' after its initial temporal reading; this spatialised and part-memorised reading is itself often further shifted, following the radical recontextualising effects of closure itself. (I.e. not only do we read the poem again and link memorised elements in a non-linear way, we often also go 'Oh — *that* was what it was about!' and then reinterpret the meaning of those elements.)

compositional experience, that of a network of linked elements; they have entered the realm of creative authorship. Closure, then, often provokes the very rereading needed to turn the poem from a series of elements experienced in linear time to a set of memorised, spatial elements which can also be connected in parallel. (Again, this process projects paradigmatic parallelism into syntagmatic series, and represents the 'neural network-ification' of the poem itself.)

The reading eye or ear begins in anticipation; as it moves through the poem, what has been anticipated is then read and processed; if it is memorable, it becomes memory, if it is not, the mere past. Anticipation starts to grow around line and stanza endings, with the principal weight of expectation bearing down on the last line or lines, to the extent that poem-endings constitute part of the cognitive template; they are a promise of significance – one which will be projected into those lines, regardless of whether the poet has created an effective ending or not. Try the simple experiment of showing readers half a poem, and telling them it is the *whole* poem: the meaning of medial lines transposed to a terminal position are wholly altered. Here in its entirety is Matthew Arnold's famous sonnet, 'Dover Beach':

> The sea is calm to-night.
> The tide is full, the moon lies fair
> Upon the straits;—on the French coast the light
> Gleams and is gone; the cliffs of England stand,
> Glimmering and vast, out in the tranquil bay.
> Come to the window, sweet is the night-air!
> Only, from the long line of spray
> Where the sea meets the moon-blanch'd land,
>
> Listen! you hear the grating roar
> Of pebbles which the waves draw back, and fling,
> At their return, up the high strand,
> Begin, and cease, and then again begin,

With tremulous cadence slow, and bring
The eternal note of sadness in.[3]

Ah . . . How that note of eternal sadness seems to infect every earlier line in Arnold's little poem. Don't you think? (Setting aside his rather wayward rhyme-scheme, of course.)

If the title is often neutrally 'what the poem is about', or at least subverts that convention to some degree – final closure is sometimes the 'key', the 'secret title' by which the full meaning of the poem will be unlocked, and often wholly recontextualised. As with titles, this expectation may be subverted: while the poem must play out against this expectation of final significance, it need not actually honour it.[4]

---

3   Matthew Arnold, *Dover Beach and Other Poems* (New York: Dover Publications, 1994).
4   One thing of which I am certain is that closure is *not* a patriarchal structure. Any writer who gets halfway down a page and decides that this is where the writing stops is in engaged in an act of self-conscious, knowing termination – and attempts *not* to inscribe this fact somewhere, in some way, in the final line are invariably far more strenuous than actually doing so. This is all closure is: the deliberate as opposed to the accidental cessation of poetic speech. We must distinguish this from less neutral definitions. One knows just what Lyn Hejinian means when, in supplying a bad example of a 'closed text', she arraigns 'the coercive, epiphanic mode in some contemporary lyric poetry [which] can serve as a negative model, with its smug pretension to universality and its tendency to cast the poet as guardian to Truth' – Lyn Hejinian, 'The Rejection of Closure', in *The Language of Inquiry* (Berkeley, CA: University of California Press, 2000), 41. And, more often than not, therein will we find the patriarchy deeply inscribed, in all its self-satisfaction, in all in the uninterrogated presumption of its own power and rectitude. However, I feel we must allow for the possibility that a handful of poets may *well* be the Guardians of the Truth, and that their articulation of the universal might actually be well served by just such rhetorical 'coercions'. That particular closural mode might serve fools badly, and indeed make them look more foolish than ever; but it sat pretty well with Emily Dickinson. More generally: 'closure' may appear to map easily to certain sociopolitical structures many of us detest, but this is mere correlation; to say it is *continuous* with those structures and that its use perpetuates them is a far harder thing to prove. By all means go nuts, but it sounds to me like another case of the 'fallacy of reciprocity'. Besides, any argument which ignores all *actual content* and focuses purely on the means

Endings may be roughly categorised as either more or less 'surprising'. Those that do not surprise usually honour the thematic propositions of the title, engage with the summed semantic content of the previous lines and do little to disturb the slowly building thematic domain; but these are relatively rare. Endings will often provide the reader with the now-expected 'unexpected' semantic surprise. They do so, *almost invariably*, through the drama of some form of deictic or metatextual shift. While deictic shift need not be an essential *aspect* of this new data or content, it is very often the means by which it is made salient. (Such shifts are themselves often flagged by being allied to other 'arresting' devices: syntactic, lineal and stanzaic effects, most of them 'slowing' in their effect, like shorter sentences, parataxis, unusual punctuation, end-stopping, odd line-lengths or monostichs; or anomalous metrical, lyric or rhyming strategies.) It will achieve this via the four familiar deictic routes: the temporal, the locational, the pronominal and the metatextual (i.e. various destabilisations of the mimetic 'reality' conceit).

All the examples below are from Michael Donaghy's *Collected Poems*.

a) *Changes of tense or dramatic jump in chronology*

> [. . .] instead of now, when I hear of your death,
> after your stroke at my age give a month or two,
> now, when you never made it to Mexico
> And Claire remarried and never had children
> And the clapboard safe house fell down at last
> And the blue pickup went for scrap years back.

('From The Safe House')

---

of its presentation tends to bear little scrutiny. Hejinian, for example, is notably weak on evidence, and the adduction of a terrible poem proves nothing other than that the poem was terrible. If you intend to prove that anti-closural practice is superior, you have to go after the canon, claim some evolutionary or cultural advancement (one sees none), or defend it as an adequate symbol for our unclosed times.

b) *Movements or jump-cuts to another location*

> Accept this small glass planet then, a shard
> Grown smooth inside an oyster's craw.
> Like us, it learns to opalesce
> In darkness, in cold depths, in timelessness.
>
> ('More Machines')

c) *Changes in address (which may affect either pronoun, voice, addressee, manner, or rhetorical pitch)*

> We long to lose ourselves amid the choir
> Of the salmon twilight and the mackerel sky,
> The very air we take into our lungs,
> And the rhododendron's cry.
> And when you lick the sweat along my thigh,
> Dearest, we renew the gift of tongues.
>
> ('Pentecost')

> The morning of the first snowfall, I was shaving,
> Staring into a mirror nailed to a tree,
> Intoning the Christian names of the Andrews Sisters.
> 'Maxine, Laverne, Patty.'
>
> ('Shibboleth')

d) *Destabilisation of the literal conceit*

This can be done through moving into the imaginary or figurative from the natural-mimetic, or vice versa; from moving from the concrete to the abstract; and (increasingly, these days) through metapoetic effect, either punning of the word or line to draw attention to its position or role within the poetic structure, or even 'breaking the fourth wall' by some form of self-reflexive movement, and declaring the poem to be a poem.

> I know. My world's encircled by this prop
> Though all my life I've tried to force it shut
>
> > ('Upon a Claude Glass';
> > the omitted final period was deliberate.)

e) *Changes within two or more deictic aspects simultaneously*

> [. . .] and when you spoke
> in no child's voice but our of radio silence,
> the hall clock ticking like a radar blip,
> a bottle breaking faintly streets away,
> you said, as I say now, *Don't be afraid*.
>
> > ('Haunts')

In the last example we see shifts of tense, location, address, and — in referring to the very poem we are reading with 'as I say now' — a metatextual, 'fourth-wall' shift too.

Often the ending will be anticipated or foreshadowed at a significant point (first line, line ending, stanza-ending, turn, etc.) to give it salience, either strongly (in which case it *specifies* the nature of the anticipation) or quietly (where the cue may be rediscovered or unearthed in the rereading the closure itself prompts).

However, even at the closural level of the line ending, we often see identical deictic shifts in miniature: the teleuton will metatextually pun, play or lean on its own terminal position. If we look at those lines from Heaney's 'The Skylight' again:

> You were the one for skylights. I opposed
> Cutting into the seasoned tongue-and-groove
> Of pitch pine. I liked it low and closed,
> Its claustrophobic, nest-up-in-the-roof
> Effect. I liked the snuff-dry feeling,

we see several examples of virtuosic, self-aware line endings: 'opposed' stands oppositionally before the break, with the next line beginning with the even more boldly oppositional trochee, 'cutting'; 'closed' is closurally end-stopped, and so on. Note too the extravagantly disruptive later lines 'But when the slates came off, extravagant / Sky entered and held surprise wide open.' Here the syntax is driven against the frame of the metre – and the sparks fly as the line executes a handbrake turn on the bend, to beautifully expressive effect. Such disruptive enjambments give the teleuton great prominence, and provide the opportunities for all sorts of quiet metatextual paronomasia, where the reader is asked to consider not just the word, but its position within the line. The artifice of closure potentiates a little moment of self-consciousness or awareness which the poet can exploit: when placed just before the gap, the word seems to wake up to its own word-ness.

Poetic closure varies not only in its logical form but also in its strength, and in the degree of its 'surprise'. This last quality, while far too subjective and vague for serious attention, usefully allows for some broad caricature. These types frequently occur at the other closural points of the poem (i.e. stanza endings and line endings) to lesser degrees.

1. 'The non sequitur'

This effect is often – or intends to be – shocking, disruptive, surreal, 'stream of consciousness', or part of a discontinuous strategy (assuming the whole poem does not pursue this strategy globally, in which case it comes as no surprise at all).

> To my right,
> In a field of sunlight between two pines,
> The droppings of last year's horses
> Blaze up into golden stones.

I lean back, as the evening darkens and comes on.
A chicken hawk floats over, looking for home.
I have wasted my life.

(JAMES WRIGHT, 'Lying in a Hammock at
William Duffy's Farm in Pine Island, Minnesota')[5]

2. 'The punchline'

'Joke'-type 'bisociative' endings – though the effect is often not
humorous. Nonetheless they will rely on the same technique of
engineering the collision of domains or contexts, where an expectation
will be both delivered and simultaneously confounded, often through
pun or paronomasia.

Was it the white pine face like a new moon?
The wet splutter and moan of the shakuhachi?
Was it the actor's dispersal in gesture and smoke?
What part of Noh did you not understand?

(MICHAEL DONAGHY, 'Hazards')[6]

You're like book ends, the pair of you, she'd say
Hog that grate, say nothing, sit, sleep, stare . . .
The 'scholar' me, you, worn out on poor pay,
only our silence made us seem a pair.

. . .

5   James Wright, *Above the River: The Complete Poems* (New York: Farrar, Straus &
Giroux, 1992). The non sequitur is often a bluff. This is a fine example of an ending
that – in its very unexpectedness – pretty much demands that we read the poem
again, in case we had missed some cue. And on doing so, we discover the shared
patheme, the ground of the tonal metaphor that seems to unconsciously prepare the
mind of the speaker for the final outburst: there is a movingly distinct note of *départ*
running through every image.
6   Michael Donaghy, *Collected Poems* (London: Pan Macmillan, 2014).

Back in our silences and sullen looks,
for all the Scotch we drink, what's still between 's
not the thirty or so years, but books, books, books.

(TONY HARRISON, 'Book Ends I')[7]

3. 'The clincher'

These usually both belong within and indicate argumentative or
narrato-argumentative forms, where closure delivers the sealing
remark – one which the reader need not see coming, though in
retrospect it often seems logically inevitable. (Weaker versions of
'clinchers' can often be seen in the infamous couplet of the English
sonnet; these can stray perilously close to mere summary, moralising
homily, or over-obvious sententiae.)

Mark well, dear boy, whilst these assemble not,
Green springs the tree, hemp grows, the wag is wild;
But when they meet, it makes the timber rot,
It frets the halter, and it chokes the child.
Then bless thee, and beware, and let us pray
We part not with thee at this meeting day.

(WALTER RALEIGH, 'To His Sonne')[8]

Then No-No lifts up Clumsy's trembly chin,
And leans to hiss with loud stage whisper in
The big pink ear of Clumsy, 'My dear friend,'
No-No enunciates. 'This is The End.'

(GJERTRUD SCHNACKENBERG, 'Two Tales of Clumsy')[9]

7 Tony Harrison, *Selected Poems* (London: Penguin, 1987).
8 Sir Walter Raleigh, 'To His Sonne', in Willard M. Wallace, *Sir Walter Raleigh*
(Princeton: Princeton University Press, 1959), 267.
9 Gjertrud Schnackenberg, *Supernatural Love: Poems 1976–2000* (Newcastle upon
Tyne: Bloodaxe, 2001).

4. 'The dying fall'

The standard closural device of the lyric narrative or meditation. The ending is not a 'surprise', and is continuous with the flow of the whole; it nonetheless contains enough unexpected information to create a 'poignancy', often through a peristasis that carries some element of deictic shift, or some original but non-disruptive abstract phrase-making. The effect is often tonal and emotional, i.e. works through the invocation of an often inarticulable patheme shared between the poem's elements.

> Until Laertes recognised his son and, weak at the knees,
> Dizzy, flung his arms around the neck of great Odysseus
> Who drew the old man fainting to his breast and held him there
> And cradled like driftwood the bones of his dwindling father.
>
> (MICHAEL LONGLEY, 'Laertes')[10]

> The clock-a-clay is creeping on the open bloom of May,
> The merry bee is trampling the pinky threads all day,
> And the chaffinch it is brooding on its grey mossy nest
> In the whitethorn bush where I will lean upon my lover's breast;
> I'll lean upon her breast and I'll whisper in her ear
> That I cannot get a wink o'sleep for thinking of my dear;
> I hunger at my meat and I daily fade away
> Like the hedge rose that is broken in the heat of the day.
>
> (JOHN CLARE, 'Summer')[11]

10   Michael Longley, *Collected Poems* (London: Jonathan Cape, 2006).
11   John Clare, *Selected Poems* (London: Penguin, 2000).

5. 'The anticlimax'

This ends the poem on a quieter note than mere tonal neutrality, defying the expectations of more conventional closural strategies that have perhaps been hitherto encouraged by the poem. It is often a kind of double-bluff, however, and just a 'clincher' in disguise. Take the unexpectedly low-key end to Hecht's 'A Hill', to my mind the epitome of 'quietly devastating':

> All this happened about ten years ago,
> And it hasn't troubled me since, but at last, today,
> I remembered that hill; it lies just to the left
> Of the road north of Poughkeepsie; and as a boy
> I stood before it for hours in wintertime.
>
> (ANTHONY HECHT, 'A Hill')[12]

6. 'The non-ending'

This might be identified as an 'anti-closural device', if one believes in such things: here, the poem appears to less 'end' than stop. Outside avant-garde practice, this kind of closure is rare; its closural quality depends largely upon its simply occupying a terminal position, and the reader's inevitable projection of closural importance (some post-modern and L=A=N=G=U=A=G=E poets such as Lyn Hejinian seem to explicitly request that their poems *not* be read closurally; whether they have the right to do so is questionable). Ironically, because the non-ending is highly destabilising in its refusal to honour traditional closural expectations, it's therefore a perfectly effective closural

---

12 Anthony Hecht, *Selected Poems*, ed. J. D. McClatchy (New York: Random House, 2011). This poem has haunted me for years, and I invite the reader to tilt the plane on Google Earth and follow the road Hecht describes in the poem; soon they will encounter this miserable, bare, mole-coloured little knoll, just as he paints it.

technique – so long as only a few closural refusniks exist and we don't all start doing it.[13] Michael Hofmann has, from the start of his career, used it to brilliant effect:

> The motor-mews has flat roofs like sandpaper or tarpaper.
> One is terraced, like three descending trays of gravel.
> Their skylights are angled towards the red East,
> some are truncated pyramids, others whole glazed shacks.
>
> (MICHAEL HOFMANN, 'From Kensal Rise to Heaven')[14]

> Someone brought me some cigarettes from America
> called Home Run, and they frighten me half to death
> in their innocuous vernal packaging, green and yellow.
>
> (MICHAEL HOFMANN, 'Snowdrops')[15]

13 For the record, I consider the 'anti-closural' an entirely false category. As much as some theorists desire it to exist, *will* it to exist – usually for perfectly admirable political or ideological reasons – it cannot. If you contrive such a thing, you are plainly engaged in consciously constructing closure of *some* kind, and are simultaneously calculating for its effect. In literature, things do not stop unselfconsciously unless the author is shot mid-sentence. Readers know this, and invariably project closural expectation wherever they see writing end. (I have also seen too many occasions where the critical diagnosis of 'refused closure' did not seem justified. Poems we do not understand tend to read as 'open'.)

14 Michael Hofmann, *Acrimony* (London: Faber & Faber, 1986). Excepting those youthful gunslingers who will learn soon enough, the poetry of our 'bravest critics' is invariably revealing – in exactly the same way. Most of it seems modest and conservative to a fault, as if they were trying to make their work as small and inoffensive as possible. They all write like baby hedgehogs. Hofmann is a notable exception, and seems somehow to have parlayed Ian Hamilton's 'English cringe' into something like a powerful, Lowellian indifference to the consequences of honest speech – including saying no more when one is done talking. I feel his endings are often far closer to the 'anti-phallogocentric' structures others identify elsewhere, and they seem have little interest in either convincing or impressing anyone via the usual Flash-Harry tricks, epiphanies, look-at-me zingers or wise conclusions.

15 Ibid.

I freely confess that I find this a rather silly little cline; nonetheless it may propose a more systematic one that others will have the time to pursue.

THE CAESURA

By 'caesura' I refer to the intralineal syntactic break. In some ways it would be better to *call* it that, or at least some less unwieldy alternative – but the caesura's currency is, alas, far too wide. Like most other prosodic terms it belongs to the language of classical quantitative prosody, which is where we might have left it.

General remarks on the caesura are perhaps of limited value, as its effectiveness will very much depend on the extent to which its deployment enhances the meaning and performance of the individual line. Each case will be different. While the caesura has metrical consequences, in English it is not (unlike its French counterpart) a metrical effect per se; the caesura only becomes one when its occurrence is regular (as that which divides the Anglo-Saxon hemistich). The caesura is the product and evidence of an expressive tension between the poet's speech and their metrical template; together with enjambment, it is often a sign of the kind of formal-syntactical disagreement that we read, quite correctly, as evidence of strength of feeling. The symmetry of the template provides a contrastive means to make salient the naturalism and authenticity of our speech; it does this by foregrounding the *asymmetric* nature of the often complex, hypotactic syntax (the language of argument, consideration, qualification, conditionality, parenthetical aside) that we need as proof of both the vulnerable humanity and intellectual sophistication of poetic thought. Not only will speech-clauses run expressively counter to the lineal template; the template may also insist on pauses and hesitations that the speech, if presented in an unlineated form, would simply not imply. Thus poetry's expressivity is *increased* via the friction, grinding, tension and fracture introduced through the disagreement between lineal and stanzaic form and speech. It may therefore be regarded as a higher-level metrical disagreement of the kind we see in lower-level metrical stress position/lexical stress tensions. (Indeed there's some mileage in considering enjambment and caesura forms of higher-level metrical tension.)

It's probably not worth giving a systematic account of the caesura, since it's an anti-systematic feature of the line whose purpose is to generally to help it sound more organic and improvisatory. Though it need not *interrupt* the metre the way prosodic variation does, it shapes metre to its will, inserting pause, silence, breath, cadence and inflection; it naturalises and softens metre's more mechanical effects to give the line a plausible, spoken-word verisimilitude. I feel it should emerge just as unselfconsciously in poetic composition; the caesura should be the mere product of the agitation between the isometric, recursive fixity of the template and the fluid rhythms of real speech, not a matter of conscious deliberation. (Unless it is a feature *of* the template.) Its successful effects are achieved by virtuosity alone; no one I know thinks of 'where to put in a caesura', the way they might sometimes do the line-break.

The caesura appears to 'insert' a pause or a silence within the line, but in reality merely *is* a pause that arises through a syntactic not a metrical exigency. It generally falls between clauses, and is almost always marked by punctuation or by some other typographical convention (such as the space employed by certain Beat and Black Mountain poets). My certainty here is controversial. Standard definitions also allow for caesurae to be merely inferred by the reader, and 'placed' at unmarked pauses on phrase-boundaries. However, such latitudes lead to immense confusion, as well as the subjective diagnosis of pauses the poet frequently did not intend. When poets want a pause, silence or a breath, they will generally indicate it. The caesura should only *rarely* be inferred or divined from the syntax where no typographical prompt is given – and even then, only as the stylistic elision of a punctuation mark. (Unless, of course, it forms a diagnosis of deliberate omission or incompetence.) But if a poet appears have run two clauses together, they probably didn't want you to pause for breath.

Like the line-break, the caesura can be classified as masculine or feminine if the last syllable before the indicated pause is strong or weak.[1] (Examples are from Richard Wilbur's 'The Mind Reader'.[2])

> Lobs up a blink of light. The sun-hat falls (masculine)
> x / | x /
>
> [. . .]
> There would be obfuscations, paths which turned (feminine)
> x / x | /   x   /

Much as we saw with the line ending and line-beginning, the caesura accommodates metrical variation more smoothly than would be possible without it:

> The mind is not a landscape, but if it were,
> /   x | x / x   /
>
> Yet seem, too, to be listening, lying in wait
> / x x | / x x   /

The notion that a pause may fill up the missing part of a metrical line belongs to discredited temporal theories of metre, but it is a mistake to dismiss this out of hand. It holds perfectly well that within

---

1 An old convention for describing 'strong' and 'weak' endings that I observe here with reluctance. I will, however, attempt to reclaim the words for neutral use, and remind readers that they originate not in a sexual power-metaphor but in a quirk of French, where words of feminine grammatical gender have the tendency to end in a more lightly stressed syllable, and words of a masculine in a more heavily stressed. Passing the buck, but take it up with them.

2 Richard Wilbur, *The Mind Reader: New Poems* (San Diego, CA: Harcourt Brace Jovanovich, 1976).

the metrical line-unit a pause can occupy the place of a weak syllable with little disruption. It's natural to have the caesura occasionally stand in for a w; a comma, say, is a *genuine* temporal gap, and can be easily read as a syllable-substitute, as it makes the reader physically perform the weak placeholder. This coincidence of omitted syllable and punctuation also lengthens and emphasises the caesura, and to a degree 'times' it:

> Downstairs it's New Year's Eve. Drink and shrieks.
>
> /　　x　　/　[x]　/　　x　　　/
>
> (MICHAEL DONAGHY, 'Black Ice and Rain')[3]

> [. . .] And realisation of it rages out
> In furnace-fear when we are caught without
> People or drink. Courage is no good:
>
> 　　x　　/　[x]　/　x　/　x　/
>
> It means not scaring others. Being brave
> Lets no one off the grave.
>
> (PHILIP LARKIN, 'Aubade')[4]

However, classifying these variations as hypercatalectic, acephalic and so on strikes me mere trainspotting, and gives the false impression that the caesura is as metrical as the hiatus and the ghost metron. It can, however, be *exploited* for metrical effect.

The variation of caesural placement is the sign of a supple and adaptive syntax, evidence that the template has not *dictated* the kind of sentences the poet writes, but instead — like enjambment — encouraged some productive resistance between syntax and lineal frame. As I've mentioned, the pattern of concurrence and disagreement between phrase length and line length is closely analogous to the lower-level

3　Michael Donaghy, *Collected Poems* (London: Pan Macmillan, 2014).
4　Philip Larkin, *Collected Poems*, ed. Anthony Thwaite (London: Faber & Faber, 2003).

relationship between lexical stress and metrical position; caesura is a kind of free variable operating between the two. It mitigates against any metrical extremes: too little syntactic resistance to the template can produce an uncomfortable isometrism that results in something we can experience as robotic speech.

In i.p. and longer lines, the caesura affords us a means of quietly entertaining the reader through variation. (In shorter lines – because the neat coincidence of line-break and phrase-length is far easier to casually engineer, something readers instinctively understand – its overuse is more conspicuous.) As usual, our default is variation within repetition. Lines which do nothing but vary and disagree – i.e. which constantly enjamb, constantly vary the placement of the caesura – become highly predictable. The virtuosic and sparing use of enjambment and caesura is a sign that the line has a robust purpose: the poet feels strongly enough about something to go against the grain of the metre. It is perceived by the reader unconsciously as another level of interest in the language, providing them with unexpected places to breathe and pause, lengthening and slowing the line as it reaches the phrase boundary; it is one of the quietest ways of 'ringing the changes'. The analogy doesn't survive close inspection, but the poet might think of it as strengthening the poem in the way that irregular verticals strengthen brickwork: a poem whose vertical mortar-joints are aligned is less strong that one which varies them.

We might make a rough classification with the terms masculine, feminine, medial, terminal and initial (though the last three are inevitably vague). If we also take account of line endings, we can quickly account for the poem's lineal variation. For now I've just marked the lines as end-stopped, half-stopped (i.e. enjambing at a clause boundary) or enjambed, though using my 'cline of disruption' will give more granularity to the description.

Go from me. Yet I feel that I shall stand
    [feminine initial, enjambed]
Henceforward in thy shadow. Nevermore
    [feminine terminal, enjambed]
Alone upon the threshold of my door
    [enjambed]
Of individual life, I shall command
    [masculine medial, enjambed]
The uses of my soul, nor lift my hand
    [masculine medial, enjambed]
Serenely in the sunshine as before,
    [end-stopped]
Without the sense of that which I forbore –
    [end-stopped]
Thy touch upon the palm. The widest land
    [masculine medial, enjambed]
Doom takes to part us, leaves thy heart in mine
    [feminine medial, half-stopped]
With pulses that beat double. What I do
    [feminine terminal, enjambed]
And what I dream include thee, as the wine
    [feminine terminal, enjambed]
Must taste of its own grapes. And when I sue
    [masculine medial, enjambed]
God for myself, He hears that name of thine,
    [masculine initial, end-stopped]
And sees within my eyes the tears of two.
    [end-stopped]

(ELIZABETH BARRETT BROWNING, 'VI',
Sonnets from the Portuguese)[5]

5 Elizabeth Barrett Browning, *Selected Poems*, ed. Marjorie Stone and Beverly Taylor (Peterborough, ON: Broadview Press, 2009).

(This is E.B.B. giving another masterclass in how one manages caesural and line-end variation within an unforgiving formal frame; poets will learn much from a careful study of her technique.) We might then abstract the following common-sense rules regarding caesurae in medium-length lines (i.e. of 8 to 12 syllables):

- a) medial caesurae are generally the least conspicuous and are felt as least disruptive, since they occur at the furthest distance from both the line beginning and line ending.
- b) caesurae nearer the end of the line are generally *more* disruptive, since the line-break will then occur soon after the start of the new phrase, whether it is enjambed or not.
- c) caesurae at the start of the line are generally the *most* disruptive, since we don't expect the line to be interrupted so early after its inauguration, especially if the previous line was end-stopped. (This is borne out by the classic miscounting error, where a stress is dropped in the line immediately following an enjambment, if that line contains an initial caesura.)

The relative frequency of the initial, medial and terminal caesurae roughly reflect these rules.

As discussed elsewhere, the use of metre and rhyme can mean fixing some elements of the line earlier in the compositional process than others, and the syntax then has to prepare for their effortless fall. Syntax is the capacious variable that restores the combinatorial possibilities that formally fixed elements can drastically reduce, especially in our post-poetic diction era, when hyperbaton is regarded as an embarrassing anachronism. (Rhymed poems often produce more varied caesurae than unrhymed poems – and *far* more than in free and irregular-lined verse, which often finds itself shaped to its clause-lengths, since the form offers no particular resistance to its doing so.) In formal verse, a fluid and adaptable syntax will often make use of caesurae to naturalise speech which otherwise might draw attention to itself.

PUNCTUATION

One is occasionally asked by students if there are 'good rules' for how to punctuate a poem. The answer has to be simply that there's no particular reason for poems to be punctuated any differently from prose beyond the freedom to experiment we sometimes allow poetry as 'radically original speech'. There is little to say about punctuation, other than it tends to receives the same excessive attention from the poet as does the individual word: a well- or badly placed comma will often make or ruin a line. Punctuation in poetry does a great deal more than making grammatical structure explicit. In compelling precisely timed rises, falls, breaths and pauses at the ends of phrases, punctuation marks not only foreground significant material and prepare the reader for the syntactical form of the next phrase, they also direct the cadences of human emotion.

Generally speaking, as long as the rule is consistent (i.e. the poet has not told the reader it's a football game, only to start playing cricket halfway through) the reader will accept *any* local convention, however non-standard. Otherwise a comma is still a comma, whether it appears in a sonnet or a match report. Nonetheless one occasionally hears a poet maintain that the poem should have special exemption, and insist that poems have no need of colons, or dashes,[1] or indeed any punctuation all; some others simply adopt this approach without defending it. Unless the poet can offer some explanation for this

---

[1] Douglas Dunn once told me that 'brackets have no place in a poem: if you're going to say it – say it'. I disagree, but I know what he meant. If poetry is a distinct mode of speech, perhaps it just doesn't *have* brackets, in the same way that reported speech doesn't have semi-colons – or at least looks absurd when it does. We don't use bracket parentheses when we sing songs either.

strategy (and there are some noble ways to defend it), we needn't be detained by this nonsense; apart from anything else, written English is already impoverished enough in this regard. (If it were left to me, I'd introduce *degrees* of italics.[2])

However consistent underpunctuation, in either its light or extreme forms, can be hugely effective. Especially (perhaps almost solely) in short-lined or odd-stress-count poems where the hiatus is longer, the space after the line can be used as a neutrally inflected punctuation-zone, and can easily serve as a multi-purpose punctuation mark. The neutrality of these blank pauses is their novelty: as I've said, we are used to being directed by the punctuation at the end of the phrase – and to remove it is to remove all the intonational ups and downs of final cadence we would otherwise encounter, as well as most of our emotional cues. The omission of all punctuation marks is the explicit *repudiation* of such cadences, and is always a 'statement' of some kind. (A general absence of caesurae, though, often indicates a repetitive and overly paratactic syntax.)

Usually unpunctuated poems 'unhumanise' their tone. By removing the intonational rises and falls of expressive cadence, the poet can enforce an even, flat, monotonous delivery. This delivery can be perfectly appropriate to – and indeed enhance the expression of – absolute emotional states: great ecstasy, all-consuming depression, pitiless judgement, blank disillusion, or unspeakable tragedy and horror:

> Like every living Jew I have
> in imagination seen
> the gas-chamber the mass-grave
> the unknown body which was mine

2 The banning of italics for contrastive emphasis in the house styles of certain academic presses on the grounds that *all* emphases in a well-written article should be easily derived from context is an almost illiterate practice.

and found in every German face
behind the mask the mark of Cain

(KAREN GERSHON, 'Race')[3]

The omission of the final full stop can be a powerful device, implying (for once) genuine non-closure. While it may read merely as a pretentious affectation in weak poems, it can also reinforce a sense of continuation or 'timeless suspension':

and went on running with that bindweed will of his
went on running along the hedge and into the earth again
trembling
as if in a broken jug for one backwards moment
water might keep its shape

(ALICE OSWALD, 'Body')[4]

---

3 Karen Gershon (ed.), *We Came as Children: A Collective Autobiography* (London: Papermac, 1989)
4 Alice Oswald, *Falling Awake* (London: Jonathan Cape, 2016).

A NOTE ON THE PROSE POEM

The prose poem presents a special case. It rejects one of the strongest core attributes of the conceptual domain of 'poem', which is that it be written in lines. The prose poem must compensate for its having relinquished all the conventional typographic advertisement of its poem-status or poetic nature, and find an alternative way to *sell* itself as a poem, so that it can then be read as one. For this reason, early prose poems – especially those of the British Decadents – often found themselves reaching for an *overly* poeticised diction, one into which their authors might not have been tempted had they been working in the more relaxed, self-assured, traditional environment of the lineated poem. (The earlier experiments of the French Symbolists seem far less self-conscious, partly because opening gestures have the confidence of genuine iconoclasm, and partly because French poetic prosody is a little closer to speech than English; the French prose poem 'connotes' the poetic by different means.) These days, poets are generally wiser to the pitfalls. But in its need to distinguish itself categorically from prose – having abandoned the simplest means by which it could have done so – the prose poem can still be an affected and self-conscious affair.

Prose poems which do not distinguish themselves in diction, scheme or intention from prose *are* prose in all but strenuous designation. They may be praised for vague qualities of 'sonorousness' and 'rhythm' in lieu of lyric and metre, but these are the qualities we already ascribe to prose when we're inclined to call it 'poetic'. Though it may be that 'designation' is all we need; perhaps all the prose poem requires is to be found in a book called *Poems*.

The alternative is a circular and pointless discussion about what constitutes 'poeticity'. This notion may be saved only by the kind of relativism a French casuist would dare attempt:

> Prose is only a moderate kind of poetry [. . .] [poetry is] the most passionate form of literature, the paroxysmal degree of style. Style is one. It comprises a finite number of figures, always the same. From prose to poetry and from one state of poetry to another, the difference is only in the audacity with which language employs the processes virtually inscribed within its structure.[1]

This is just about credible, although I have read much stylistically audacious prose, and possibly even more miserably craven and conservative poetry. Eliot came round to a similarly relativistic stance, though I prefer his initial judgement that 'verse and prose still conceal unexplored possibilities, but whatever one writes must be definitely and by inner necessity either one or the other'. I feel the problem lies simply in its *declared* hybridity, combined with the usual uninterrogated belief in the intrinsicality of certain qualities – like 'poeticity'. Call it 'unlineated poetry' and the problem virtually disappears:

> The questions I asked all the time, but never aloud: where
> is the soul? What does it most resemble? I had an image of
> something transparent, a fine yet indestructible tissue of
> buttermilk or chitin.[2]

> (JOHN BURNSIDE, 'Aphasia in Childhood')

1 Jean Cohen, *Structure du Langage Poétique* (Paris: Flammarion, 1966).
2 John Burnside, *Feast Days* (London: Secker & Warburg, 1992).

In the hands of a poet conscious of these dangers, the prose poem can be a brilliantly subversive form. The nagging worry is that because it is negatively defined – poetry-but-not-poetry, 'non-generic prose', etc. – there will *always* be the sense in which it is a transgressive and oxymoronic project; 'subversion' is rather tediously built into its contract. But the form can quickly become normalised by context, and by its own emerging tradition. And perhaps more 'poeticity' is conferred by context than we would like to admit. For example, we 'attend' to Lowell's brief prose memoir '91 Revere Street' very differently than we would otherwise, simply on account of its appearance halfway through *Life Studies*.

The 'stanza' of the prose poem is the paragraph, and in terms of their function the two are passably close. By and large the prose-poem paragraph will conform to the reader's expectations of normal stanzaic definition, and exhibit episodic closure: a series of paragraphs will create just the same expectation as would a series of long stanzas. However, the longer the poem goes on, the more it will seem to converge on longer, received prose forms, principally that of the short story; the reader's concomitant narrative projections will be frustrated, leading to eventual disappointment. The default high contentual density of poetry is not suited to extended prose forms, and poetic form is – in one straightforward sense – just a way of mitigating a mode of speech that would otherwise be found insufferably pretentious and costive.

However, some of the most effective prose poems are really indistinguishable from tiny short stories that don't hang around for long enough for us to worry over their fruitfully indeterminate genre (see, for example, Elizabeth Bishop's astonishing version of Max Jacob's 'Hell is Graduated'), or surreal microessays –

Napoleon's hat is an obvious choice I guess to list as a famous hat, but that's not the hat I have in mind. That was his hat for show. I am thinking of his private bathing cap, which in all

honesty wasn't much different than the one any jerk might
    buy at a
corner drugstore now, except for two minor eccentricities [. . .]

[. . .] The second eccentricity was that it was a tricorn
bathing cap. Scholars like to make a lot out of this, and it
    would
be easy to do. My theory is simple-minded to be sure: that
    beneath
his public head there was another head and it was a pyramid
    or something.

                        (JAMES TATE, 'The List of Famous Hats')[3]

– whose poetry lies in the spatial connections one can forge between its constituent elements after an initial linear reading. (In the above example, it also resides in the hilarious, insane bathos of its ending.) In this way, it is much like any other decent poem; perhaps we read *all* poems as prose first, *then* poetry, though that statement would probably sound better if I was waving a Gauloise. After its lineation, a poem's structural integrity and the 'spatial interdependence' of its parts are, I feel, the qualities by which we may most readily identify it *as* a poem. As we've seen, this is the model most often projected by the reader: an initial temporal reading in which the elements are absorbed in series, then more spatial rereading, where – having been memorised – the elements can be reconnected in parallel. If the model coincides satisfactorily with what they find there, the poem succeeds as a poem. At the end of the day, though, the poet cannot really complain if something they insist on calling 'prose poetry' is read in a way that is guided as much by the conventions of the former as the latter.

3 James Tate, *Selected Poems* (Middletown, CT: Wesleyan University Press, 1991).

THE ALTERNATE STRESS RULE

We'll now return to more technical matters. The alternate stress rule (ASR) arises from two phenomena. The first is isochrony, whose nature I will quickly recap. Through its manifestation in pulse, breath, brain-wave, ambulation, sleep-cycles and so on, isochrony is intrinsic to the condition of physical being. To a consciousness inclined to sense, project or measure them, isochrony can conjure weak interstitial spaces between its salient events. These can be perceived as 'ghost placeholders' which 'negatively' reinforce the even distribution of 'positive' icti. Governed by whatever resistance and tension there is in the system — whether it's a pair of lungs taking a few seconds to reinflate before the next exhalation, or the sun and moon slowly swinging into alignment between spring tides — these gaps effectively repel the events on either side to maintain their regular recurrence. The second phenomenon is the 'tick-tock' effect, the tendency to hear close, isochronically distributed sound events as differentiated in value, with the first beat stronger. This effect works hierarchically: we soon hear TICKtock ticktock, and then *TICK*tock **tick**tock **TICK**tock ticktock — with two, and then four, alternating, gradated strengths of strong 'tick'. Hierarchical alternation forms a literal 'measure', a way of experiencing parcels of time through applying an asymmetrical value to a symmetrical system.[1] And if measurement creates 'the passage of time', then its child is rhythm, the very patterns of recurrence themselves.

---

1 The reader may recall endnote 2 on Matte Blanco: without asymmetrical sequence there can be nothing but symmetry, and therefore nothing but 'timelessness'.

It seems probable that there will be material explanations for the existence of the ASR: our intrauterine experience of the heartbeat and our slightly lopsided bilateral body-symmetry may account for it. But since no other animals seem to respond to rhythmic series, other human-specific reasons for the ASR have been advanced: for example, rhythmic 'hypnosis' may have been important for social or team-building reasons, such as battle-trance and courtship ritual. AS seems to lie behind what biomusicology calls 'beat induction', the active perception of a pulse (this can then lead to 'entrainment', the collective synchronisation of humans to a perceived rhythm that allows them to dance, sway or foot-tap together; only humans dance²).

It has always struck me, though, that ASR must also be derived from the transient-silence-transient-silence pattern of isochrony itself. A ghost-event is *projected* into the interstitial gap, so a ghost off-beat is 'heard' in the space. We often count a slow beat not by going one . . . two . . . three . . . four, but by projecting an offbeat: one *and* two *and* three *and* four *and* . . . This strong-weak-strong-weak asymmetric series (as opposed to an ictus-nothing-ictus-nothing symmetric series) is an important cognitive shift. It can then be projected into higher groups of beats. In other words, the ASR may emerge directly from slower pulses via a kind of human reflex which simply 'abhors a vacuum', and will project an imaginary event to fill the miniature, abyssal horrors of the gaps. I suppose I'm claiming that AS really arises through an inbuilt condition of existential crisis, and that its roots may lie in a kind of ingrained 'fear of nothingness' more generally; other more existentially secure animals seem not to make this projection. It may also be a product of our exceptionally strong awareness of our own impending annihilation: this indeed causes us to 'structure time', as the anticipated death of the self creates a life that is a 'rhythmic unit', which can then subdivide into year, season, week, minute, 'the seven ages of man', and so on (whether

2 A lie. So, confusingly, do some breeds of parrot.

we intend to close our life-poem with a deictic shift to the heavenly sphere or not). A deep-seated, inner 'drive to measure' would be consistent with the rejection of 'meaningless' isochrony in favour of 'meaningful' rhythmic measurement, which would have to begin with the projection of AS. (It is possibly *the* most primal, meaning-creating supra-domain reframing of them all.) To say that it arises from isochrony *itself*, and not the projection of an alternate pattern into a series of events, is to say we that we are instinctively driven to reject the existence of empty, meaningless space, and will instead actively interpolate the role of function in its place. But perhaps the more interesting question is why we then project AS recursively, into self-similar, higher metrical units. [3]

3 Generative metrics is a form of prosodic analysis derived from the principles of generative grammar, and has AS at its heart. I think it's broadly unsuccessful, but in idle moments I have wondered, ignorantly, if the cart is before the horse – and whether generative grammar's rules, which recursively generate the structures of well-formed expressions, are *themselves* the product of recursion in AS.

ALTERNATE STRESS IN LANGUAGE

Isochrony arises in nature, whether in the form of successive sunrises, cave-drips or heartbeats. AS does not. It is an active mental projection, allowing us to perceive and measure the passing of time through the metrical divisions of binary groups.

AS is projected into the tactus of our speech when the isochronic distribution of strong stresses becomes exaggerated enough to be plainly heard. These occasions are 'emotional speech acts', which are both imitated and invoked under poetic conditions. Often we find the isochronic effect also overdetermined by metre. As well as binary units like iambs and trochees, our syllables can also be arranged in ternary units, such as triple metres – a happy possibility, helped by several factors: the longer length of s-stressed syllables, and their easy isochronic alternation with two weak syllables; and the grammatical alternation of strong-stress content and weak-stress function words (added to the fact that there are generally more of the latter in any typical speech act). [1]

As know from the tick-tock effect, AS is hierarchical, which is to say that once established, groups of strong-weak-strong-weak beats will form larger units where the s-w alternation *between* them is still maintained. Thus strong-weak-strong-weak is heard as STRONG-weak-strong-weak; STRONG-weak-strong-weak-STRONG-weak-strong-weak is soon heard as **STRONG**-weak-*strong*-weak-STRONG-

---

[1] Ternary patterning is possibly also present at a dimetronic level in the over-determinations of the literary line we call iambic pentameter. I'll describe this way of looking at i.p. as a ternary Apollonian sophistication, a kind of Ubermensch waltz, a little later. I think it's a minor feature of the line, but it may be weakly perceptible at times.

weak-strong-weak, and so on. Ternary groups are non-hierarchical, and such is the immense AS pull of the duple, they have a strong tendency to resolve themselves as binary at the next level up, if they possibly can. Musicians will know that a $3/4$ time signature strongly resolves into two-bar measures, and does not propose three-bar cycles; if one uses melody or repetition to overdetermine a $3 \times 3/4 = 9/4$ time signature, it will then strongly pull to a longer two-bar measure of $2 \times 9/4$; ditto $3 \times 9/4$, which will pull towards a long binary strophe. The AS binary is simply a cognitive frame we find impossible to kick, and arises instinctively as soon as there is no overdetermining frame to prevent it from doing so. A point to bear in mind is that the binary is countable at all these various levels *only* because it maintains the natural asymmetry it possesses at the smallest level – in our case, the syllabic – through every larger unit. Larger s-w binary strophes *not* built up from low-level metrical AS are certainly possible, but they are not particularly strongly felt.

We have a distinct preference for AS in our word-combinations, and the so-called 'rhythm rule' shows the ASR is observed wherever it can be. The stress in a word will often shift in order to avoid consecutive, non-alternating stresses: thus GlenCOE, but GLENcoe MASSacre; FIFteen WINdows, but the FIRST fifTEEN. AS enters non-phrasemic speech too: unSAFE, but UNsafe STRUCTure; at a university council meeting the other day I heard, in a single sentence, both inSANE iDEA, and INsane POLicy. Words are generally keen to shape themselves to alternating pattern; while the lexical prosody of many bisyllabic and polysyllabic words is relatively fixed, w stress monosyllabic function words and functional affixes are often cheerfully enlisted as free agents for 'promotion' when the metrical context requires them to step up – and s stress content words and lexemes will take a demoted back seat when asked to.

Polysyllabic words which contain consecutive weak stresses will often allow one of them to be promoted. Thus 'American' is generally spoken x/xx; but in an iambic frame – 'Americans are mostly English-speaking' – the third syllable is felt, marginally, as a secondary s stress, allowing us to scan it in its metrical context as x/x/. (Frames have to be held in the mind *before* the words are spoken to exert any influence over their prosody.) 'Words have one strong stress, and if you hear two, it's two words' is still a good general rule to hold by, though polysyllabic words do have *light* secondary s stresses. These are often heavily exaggerated under metrical circumstances when the ASR requires them to be; but this phenomenon has led some prosodists to reify secondary s stress, and talk as if its presence in real speech – as opposed to its performance within metrically overdetermined lines – is far greater than it really is, to the extent of marking secondary s stress in lexical stress analysis.

Some generative theorists hold that AS is so powerful, the spondee is impossible, since one stress will always incline to be the weaker. I doubt this is true. A more reliable rule is that whenever we encounter *three* consecutive s stresses bounded by w stresses, the middle one will weaken to maintain the alternate pattern; with three w stresses bounded by s stresses, the middle will strengthen. (I'll discuss this in detail later.) It would to more reasonable to say that two consecutive s stresses are *unstable*, and are more likely to adapt to their metrical, semantic or contextual circumstances through one of them weakening, or through the interpolation of a weak-substitute mora; but there is no logical reason why they should not also occasionally *defy* the ASR for much the same reasons.

As mentioned previously, monosyllabic content words tend to take a strong stress, monosyllabic function words, a weak. Often the w stress part of bisyllabic or polysyllabic words is a functional affix. Thus the underlying, alternating pattern of isochronic English is not just between weak and strong, *but between function and content* (i.e. between grammatical and lexical function, and so between the universal forces of the syntagmatic and paradigmatic). Strong stresses tend to foreground lexis, weak stresses tend to background grammar; *imposing* a regular strong-weak alternation will therefore reinforce this arrangement. In metrical English, more s stress is introjected than in normal conversational English, and this gives the strong psychological impression that poetic language is relatively content-heavy, 'dense with information' — one of several factors that account for its famed 'difficulty'. The corollaries of this deep relationship between w and s stress and the conceptual categories of function and content are highly complex, and crucial to any real understanding of poetic speech. For now, I would ask the reader to take it on trust that the connection between the two is virtually mechanistic: despite them having no immediately apparent connection, a change in state of one will immediately effect a change in the other.

THE AS MATRIX

Let's turn now to a more practical application of the ASR. What I'll call the 'alternate stress matrix' is derived from the principle that the ASR preserves some kind of s-w, high-low alternation at every hierarchical level of the metrical template; the mathematical consequence of this statement is that no two stresses can have exactly the same value. What is proposed below is a method of stanzaic analysis, but whether this should be incorporated even into an exhaustive scansion is doubtful. I think it may overcomplicate the exercise pointlessly (the notational complexities are mind-boggling) and we might do best to think of the AS matrix as not contributing to a scansion per se, but providing a separate means of analysing larger structural units and their relative key-falls and rises. However, certain saliences in the pattern may also be compositionally influential, and these might well be worth taking into account when we scan units greater than a line in length.[1]

The empty form of the line, couplet, or stanza seems to function as a coherent metrical-intonational unit if and *only* if the cognitive frame of the metrical template is anterior to the poem — that's to say if the speaker has the form already in their mind as a w-s, 'duh-*dah* duh-*dah*'

---

[1] The basic idea is not particularly original; discussion of the principle can be found in various generative theorists, as well as Cureton *et al*. I stumbled on the idea independently many years ago while I was involved in more youthful Kabbalistic researches: I was trying to discover whether there was an optimal place where 'key terms' in a poem might be buried or foregrounded for subliminal effect. As much as this sounds like a piece of neuro-linguistic programming nonsense, I still think there may be something in it, and will discuss the matter later.

pattern *before* the words have filled it in.[2] Above the w–s syllabic level, the AS matrix might seem a purely human projection, and not 'intrinsic' to poetic form, let alone language; its existence seems to depend upon our determination to impose it, and then perform it – which we naturally confuse with hearing it 'actually there'. However without the larger structures the AS matrix describes, poetic form itself would not exist; the matrix might be said to have as much 'real existence' as the weak-strong alternation of stress at syllabic level.

To put it another way: w–s syllabic AS is just as *much* of a projection as AS at any other level. Recursive patterns of AS at higher levels are telling us only about the reality of our own internal auditory and temporal structures, and lines and stanzas are themselves only external projections of this pattern. To repeat the war cry: there is no intrinsicality, and in ascribing qualities to forms, many AS fantasies forget this. This is different from saying the structures created by AS aren't real: things can be present and manifest without possessing any intrinsic qualities. (I always feel that 'reality' is a less troublesome idea than we make it, being merely the category of everything which 'obtains'.)

The character of AS at the level of syllable, metron and dimetron is predominantly a s–w stress pattern, reflective of the s–w stress patterns of speech. As the units double, however, it takes on a steadily increasing *intonational* character, reflective of the high-low speech pattern of the intonational phrase. By the time we get to line, distich and strophe, these distinctions are predominantly related to pitch, and

2 The line, stanza and poem itself – if conceived of by the poet as coincident with the distinct units of speech – tend to exhibit just the high-to-low, fast-to-slow syllabic pattern you would expect, with a particular drag being enacted in the final line, one often experienced as metrically 'heavy' even in free verse. This often semi-deliberate reversion to an evenly stressed (or even overtly metrical) line at the end of the poem can also act as a kind of retrospective assurance that what the reader had just experienced *was*, in fact, a piece of syntactically and emotionally coherent speech, lest they were still unconvinced.

better thought of as overall key-falls, not stress differences. This is a slippery idea intuitively understood, as can be heard if you get a group of schoolchildren to 'duh-dah' their way through an imaginary two-stanza 4-strong poem. The first stanza will sound something like this:

duh ***DAH*** duh DAH duh ***DAH*** duh dah
duh ***DAH*** duh DAH duh ***DAH*** duh dah
duh ***DAH*** duh DAH duh ***DAH*** duh dah
duh ***DAH*** duh DAH duh ***DAH*** duh dah

— with the lines themselves falling in pitch, while nonetheless maintaining their alternation: if 4 is high and 1 low, the relative pitch of each line would sound 4, 2, 3, 1. (Phonology has far better systems of notation for real speech, but perversely they're ill-suited to our crude purposes.) To see the effect this has on a real poem, let's look at Edna St Vincent Millay's 'First Fig'. This is a clear common-metre poem with a single variation (i.e. the lengthening of 'burns' in line 1 to accommodate a trochee; an easy enough trick in any dialect like Scots or American with a semi-consonantal 'r').

$$x \ / \ x \ / x \ / \ x \ /$$
My candle burns at both ends;
$$x \ / \ x \ / \ x \ / \ \ [x \ /]$$
It will not last the night;
$$x \ / \ x \ / \ x \ / \ \ x \ /$$
But ah, my foes, and oh, my friends —
$$x \ / \ x \ / \ x \ / \ \ [x \ /]$$
It gives a lovely light![3]

---

3   Edna St Vincent Millay, *Collected Poems*, ed. Norma Millay (New York: HarperPerennial, 2011).

If we remove the w stresses, we can hear the alternations at the level of metron:

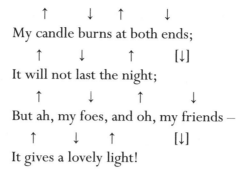

↑　　↓　↑　　↓
My candle burns at both ends;
　↑　　↓　　↑　　[↓]
It will not last the night;
　↑　　↓　　↑　　↓
But ah, my foes, and oh, my friends –
　↑　　↓　↑　　　[↓]
It gives a lovely light!

Now the dimetron:

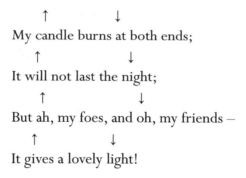

　↑　　　　↓
My candle burns at both ends;
　↑　　　　↓
It will not last the night;
　↑　　　　↓
But ah, my foes, and oh, my friends –
　↑　　　↓
It gives a lovely light!

Now the line (the arrow is now really indicating pitch contrasts between whole lines):

　↑
My candle burns at both ends;
　↓
It will not last the night;
　↑
But ah, my foes, and oh, my friends –
　↓
It gives a lovely light!

Then the distich:

↑
My candle burns at both ends;
It will not last the night;
↓
But ah, my foes, and oh, my friends —
It gives a lovely light!

. . . And, for the sake of argument, the tetrastich or strophe (which would obviously only be perceived if the poem was at least two verses long):

↑
'Heaven bless the babe!' they said.
'What queer books she must have read!'
(Love, by whom I was beguiled,
Grant I may not bear a child.)
↓
'Little does she guess to-day
What the world may be!' they say.
(Snow, drift deep and cover
Till the spring my murdered lover.)

(EDNA ST VINCENT MILLAY, 'Humoresque')[4]

Because the matrix is conceived of in the mind as a single intonational unit falling from high to low, the first accent of the stanza must be higher than others, and the last the lowest. Within this rule, though, AS must be maintained at all the other levels. As previously stated, the alternation at higher levels of line and above is perceived less as 'stress'

4 Edna St Vincent Millay, *Collected Poems*, ed. Norma Millay (New York: HarperPerennial, 2011).

than as a steady stepped *falling*, with the 'key' of the second unit of any pair lower than the first. This means that the number of height-gradations needed to express *all* the arrow-falls and rises accurately within any larger unit are exactly the number of s stresses. (e.g. in 'First Fig', 'will' in line 2 must be higher than 'night' in the same line to preserve the dimetronic AS – but lower than 'candle' in line 1 to preserve AS at the level of the line, and so on).

AS only works on binary pairs, and many forms do not exactly fit it. The point is controversial, especially when we get to forms which leave large parts of the matrix blank; but because the matrix *precedes* the poem, the values remain the same regardless of the poem-shape, and the poem is merely 'plugged in' to the matrix regardless, in the way than most easily and instinctively fits. For example – in 'First Fig' we include the ballad-metre ghost metrons of lines 2 and 4 in our calculations, as their stress value is 'felt', if not directly experienced; and so too the 'missing lines' of, say, the sestet of an Italian sonnet, where we would still bracket in the matrical values of the non-existent lines 7 and 8 of the distrophe, i.e. the two lines after the sestet. This proposes that asymmetric stanzas are unconsciously measured against a symmetric norm. (Of course this involves buying into the theory that the ASR operates at very high unit levels; but remember it's a phenomenon that consists – no more, no less – in the strength of its own *projection*. In other words if I hear it, I hear it. My suspicion is simply that others do too.)

In Millay's ballad, this leaves us with something like:

$$\uparrow 16 \quad \downarrow 8 \quad \uparrow 12 \quad \downarrow 4$$
$\uparrow$ My candle burns at both ends;
$$\uparrow 14 \quad \downarrow 6 \quad \uparrow 10 \quad \downarrow 2$$
$\downarrow$ It will not last the night;
$$\uparrow 15 \quad \downarrow 7 \quad \uparrow 11 \quad \downarrow 3$$
$\uparrow$ But ah, my foes, and oh, my friends –

↑13   ↓5   ↑9   ↓1
↓ It gives a lovely light!

If the effect is real, it immediately explains one of the key advantages of ballad metre: the 'lift' we get on the last word of the stanza, relative to that of the tetrameter quatrain:

16   8   12   4
Thine are these orbs of light and shade;
14   6   10   2
Thou madest Life in man and brute;
15   7   11   3
Thou madest Death; and lo, thy foot
13   5   9   1
Is on the skull which thou hast made.

(ALFRED LORD TENNYSON,
In Memoriam, Prologue)[5]

This 16-8-12-4 / 14-6-10-2 / 15-7-11-3 / 13-5-9-1 frame is common to all 4-strong forms, and allows us to analyse them intonationally: in Keats' 'La Belle Dame Sans Merci', the last line has a double ghost metron, and the last word of each stanza ends on a note we may describe as low and neutrally flat, a bleak effect frequently reinforced in the poem by a strong lexical stress in a weak position on the penultimate word (the effect is repeated often enough for it to become an overdetermining part of the metrical template) – as well as, of course, the line's sense:

5 Alfred Lord Tennyson, *In Memoriam*, ed. Eric Irving Gray (New York: W. W. Norton, 2004).

16   8   12   4

And this is why I sojourn here,

14   6   10 2

Alone and palely loitering,

15   7   11   3

Though the sedge is wither'd from the lake,

13   5 [9   1]

And no birds sing.

This effect will be heard over the longest units that can be felt as a single intonational phrase, but it is also a product of other over-determining factors, with versification and syntax prime among them. If lines are written in stanzas which coincide with syntactic closure, AS across longer units will be likely be performed more emphatically.

So we see a complex pattern proposed, where each successively larger binary unit will effectively contribute towards a greater perceived contrast between high- and low-numbered stresses. The upper limit to the influence of these larger units is simply whatever can be held in the reader's mind as a binary 'matrical expectation'; if the reader can *feel* the alternation of the strophic unit, they will likely hear and perform some degree of intonational differentiation between them. However the influence of each higher unit is successively weakened, and contributes less and less to the individual vowel stress (meaning that the true scale is likely to be logarithmic, not smoothly numeric). Beyond the level of two distrophes (i.e. sonnet length + 2 lines) I suspect its prosodic strength is minimal, and at this level we can declare the influence of AS more or less negligible.

THE LIMITATIONS OF THE AS MATRIX

In longer stretches of *non-stanzaic* 4-strong, i.p. or blank verse, AS matrix analysis is of very little use, as larger units are simply not projected. The opening lines of 'Frost at Midnight' will illustrate this. If we start to isolate the metronic, dimetronic, stichic, and distichic ASR, the scheme becomes simply nonsensical after the second level:

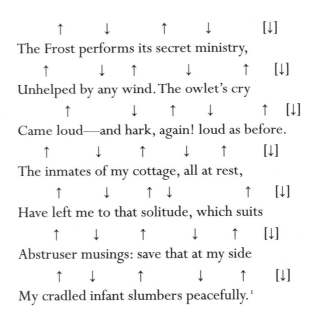

The Frost performs its secret ministry,

Unhelped by any wind. The owlet's cry

Came loud—and hark, again! loud as before.

The inmates of my cottage, all at rest,

Have left me to that solitude, which suits

Abstruser musings: save that at my side

My cradled infant slumbers peacefully.[1]

1 Samuel Taylor Coleridge, 'Frost at Midnight', *Coleridge's Poetry and Prose*, ed. Nicholas Halmi, Paul Magnuson, and Raimonda Modiano (New York: W. W. Norton, 2004), 120.

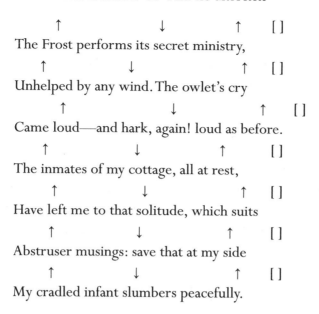

Already we can see that it's not worth proceeding. The problem is twofold: firstly, the line appears to be ternary at the level of dimetron (another way of saying that it's in i.p.); this means consecutive high accents on immediately successive final and initial stresses (↑ ↓↑/↑ ↓↑). There are more complex and interesting explanations for this phenomenon, discussed in due course. I.p. couplets under 'empty recitation' circumstances *sometimes* display a vestigial ↑ ↓↑/↓↑↓ alternation, to my ear, but are soon overtaken by more pressing local concerns. Secondly, AS is receiving little or no help from the versification or syntax itself. In seven lines we have three enjambments, meaning that the ghost metron, such as it is, is elided. (In the context of i.p., the phenomenon of the ghost metron is vexed. If the line is also considered as a dramatic 10-position unit, it is almost monadic: a hiatus is *only* a hiatus when a second line is implied in the metrical structure of the first. If the line is considered as a lyric, 2 × 4-strong unit, the hiatus is, potentially, 3 metrons long.) While we might claim that the lines exhibit paired or even strophic tendencies, they do not show themselves interested in any regular distichic patterning.

Even though there is a 'break' between the strongly stress-based AS at metronic and dimetronic levels and the strongly key-based AS at stichic and above, hierarchical levels in AS are generally formed from the bottom up: when the line-unit *itself* does not sustain it, it will have difficulty forming at stichic, distichic or strophic levels unless strongly reinforced by formal couplets or other regular stanzas.[2] It may be the case that the AS matrix can be sensibly applied only to poems that exhibit explicit binary patterning at both the syllabic and stichic levels.

2 Phrase rhythm analysis and Attridge's analysis of phrasal movement hold out more promise for these passages, but I would maintain that these analyses are often more phonologically than metrically descriptive, and that the word 'rhythm', as in 'his sentences have a lovely rhythm to them', is straightforwardly misapplied, unless that rhythm is consciously perceived or objectively measurable.

THE PROBLEM OF NOTATION

I have been rather breezy about all those numbers, and we should take a closer look at them. We've seen that within the matrix, self-similar patterns of alternation occur within any unit or sub-unit, and that the second of any unit-pair must always fall in relation to the first. Individual stresses can be given a numerical value, summing the weak and strong values of all the various levels to which they simultaneously belong, i.e. where they occur within the pattern of alternating metron, dimetron, stich, distich, strophe and distrophe (which I'd claim is their reasonable limit). Below is an analysis of the first stanza of Auden's 'The Fall of Rome',[1] but any 4-strong or common metre stanza would do (as we'll soon see, this is code for 'any metrical poem not in i.p.'). The smaller the unit, the stronger its influence; this is why most metrical scansions *only* take account of syllable stress, where the AS pattern exerts its greatest pull. This is the same as saying that the larger the unit, the less power it has; as we move through the higher units, their strength-conferring influence over the individual syllable is halved until it becomes negligible.

Before we try to find the most sensible way to notate this, I'll first make a note of the s-w patterns of paired units at every level in a four-line stanza (which for the sake of argument we'll consider as the first of a pair of stanzas, hence the 'strophic' row). In this pair of stanzas, we would have 32 s stresses, all of which would be differentiated in value. The forward arrow indicates that the given s or w value extends to the unit division or end of the unit.

1 W. H. Auden, *Collected Poems* (London: Faber & Faber, 2007).

(Note that 'metronic', 'stichic' etc. in the column below refer to contrasting *pairs* of those units. The procedure is cognate with the 'metrical grid' in the field of metrical phonology, a way of displaying hierarchic levels of syllabic salience.)

line 1

The piers are pummelled by the waves;

		1		2		3		4
syllabic	[w]	s	w	s	w	s	w	s
metronic		s	|	w	|	s	| w |
dimetronic		s	→ |			w	→ |
stichic		s		→				
distichic		s		→				
strophic		s		→				

line 2

In a lonely field the rain

		1	2		3		4
syllabic	[w]	s w	s	w	s	w	s
metronic		s |	w |		s |		w |
dimetronic		s	→ |	w →		|
stichic		w		→			
distichic		s		→			
strophic		s		→			

line 3

Lashes an abandoned train;

		1	2	3			4
syllabic	[w]	s	w s	w s	w		s
metronic		s |	w |	s |			w |
dimetronic		s →		| w →			|
stichic		s		→			
distichic		w		→			
strophic		s		→			

line 4

Outlaws fill the mountain caves.

		1	2		3		4
syllabic	[w]	s	w	s	w	s	w	s
metronic		s		w		s		w	
dimetronic		s	→			w	→		
stichic		w		→				
distichic		w		→				
strophic		s		→				

One can immediately see that the relative strength of a stress can be given by summing the number of strongs in each column. As I've said, the influence of the s on the individual s stress syllable will diminish as the units increase in size. All s stresses at the syllabic level are equal, so we can attach a base value of 1. Let's assume a two-stanza poem of 4-strong metre. Let's arbitrarily assume strength is halved as each level doubles in size, and that w-marked spaces counts as 0. So an s at the metronic level is 16; at the dimetronic, 8; at the stichic, 4; and so on. The first stress would then have an s-number of $1 + 16 + 8 + 4 + 2 + 1 = 32$. The third stress in line 3 would be $1 + 16 + 0 + 4 + 0 + 1 = 22$; the weakest stress in the stanza would be the fourth stress in the fourth line, with $1 + 0 + 0 + 0 + 0 + 1 = 2$. The lowest, 1-value stress in this two-stanza form would be the final stress in our *second* stanza, strophically marked 0. Each time a level is added – let's say we wished to project a distrophic frame of alternating eight-line stanzas – the values would double, with 32 as the metronic s, 16 as dimetronic s, etc. (Note that a four-stanza poem in tetrameter quatrains analysed in this way could arguable have 64 degrees of stress: this is borderline absurd, and is likely to have little relation to its actual spoken delivery. However, this kind of analysis is a highly useful tool in identifying extreme and median values, and any given poem's deviation from them.)

All this leaves us with a distrophic matrix of:

```
32   16   24    8
28   12   20    4
30   14   22    6
26   10   18    2

31   15   23    7
27   11   19    3
29   13   21    5
25    9   17    1
```

And if we plug in the first stanza, we get:

32   16   24   8

The piers are pummelled by the waves;

28 12 20   4

In a lonely field the rain

30   14 22   6

Lashes an abandoned train;

26   10   18   2

Outlaws fill the mountain caves.

Remember that while AS at unit levels *below* the stichic is strong-weak in character, for stichic and above it will pull towards high-low, with the quality of *pitch* being the dominant character of its 'strong stress'. These summed values convey nothing of that. We might try something like this:

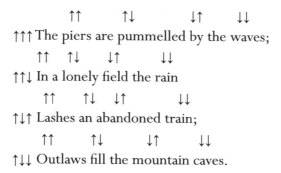

↑↑↑ The piers are pummelled by the waves;

↑↑↓ In a lonely field the rain

↑↓↑ Lashes an abandoned train;

↑↓↓ Outlaws fill the mountain caves.

— where the metronic and dimetronic strongs are placed above the line, and stichic and above alongside it; but this is hardly an improvement, and as a performance blueprint, worse than useless. The problem is relatively simple, though: since the AS matrix at the level below stichic does not change from one line to the next, all we are really seeking to represent is the relative height of an intonational contour — essentially, a melody transposed into different keys. While the representation below does not have the granularity of our numerical representation, it's more sympathetic to the general idea:

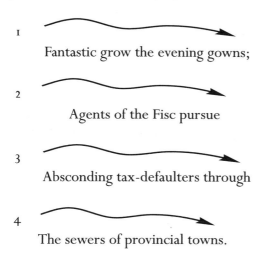

1

Fantastic grow the evening gowns;

2

Agents of the Fisc pursue

3

Absconding tax-defaulters through

4

The sewers of provincial towns.

And if we assume the schwas too short to carry perceptible information, the tonal information might even be caricatured as this kind of thing:

Alas both methods are impractical and do not even provide a way of supplying 'fake' precision, nor of dovetailing with a conventional metrical scansion. But if the numerical AS matrix is taken at face value with its serious limitations acknowledged, I believe it may be a useful tool for identifying hidden features of stress. So when we use the AS matrix in metrical analysis, I'll use the numerical system, identifying it with its appropriate matrical frame. For reference, these are:[2]

2 Note that despite the ghost metron being something of a fiction in i.p. – it is an indeterminate pause only counted under specific modal circumstances – it's a necessary one, if we are going to apply accurate AS numerical values in this way. I've included here the values for the AS matrix in i.p. at levels beyond the stichic, even though I think their existence is highly moot; I discuss a radical alternative in a future chapter. Much depends on the *stanza* form in which i.p. appears: while sonnets imply a clear hierarchical binary frame at the level of line, distich and tetrastich which will at least be felt as a pattern of alternating key-fall – generally speaking, lumps of blank verse will generate little sense of alternation above the stichic. Therefore one might say that larger AS matrices might conceivably be applied to sonnets, but not to blank verse. However, I will later argue that the more common reason for AS emerging at higher units in i.p. is down to i.p. entering a lyric mode in its stanzaic forms, one with a radically different metrical template.

line matrix in 4-strong: 4-2-3-1

line matrix in i.p.: 6-3-5-2-4-[1]

distichic matrix in 4-strong:

8	4	6	2
7	3	5	1

distichic matrix in i.p.:

12	6	10	4	8	[2]
11	5	9	3	7	[1]

strophic matrix in 4-strong:

16	8	12	4
14	6	10	2
15	7	11	3
13	5	9	1

strophic matrix in i.p.:

24	12	20	8	16	[4]
22	10	18	6	14	[2]
23	11	19	7	15	[3]
21	9	17	5	13	[1]

distrophic matrix in 4-strong:

32	16	24	8
28	12	20	4
30	14	22	6
26	10	18	2
31	15	23	7
27	11	19	3
29	14	21	5
25	9	17	1

distrophic matrix in i.p.:

$$
\begin{array}{ccccccc}
48 & 24 & 40 & 16 & 32 & [8] \\
44 & 20 & 36 & 12 & 28 & [4] \\
46 & 22 & 38 & 14 & 30 & [6] \\
42 & 18 & 34 & 10 & 26 & [2] \\
47 & 23 & 39 & 15 & 31 & [7] \\
43 & 19 & 35 & 11 & 27 & [3] \\
45 & 21 & 37 & 13 & 29 & [5] \\
41 & 17 & 33 & 9 & 25 & [1] \\
\end{array}
$$

I refer to the highest value in any given matrix as *zenith*, the lowest as *nadir*.

AS AND GHOSTS

Since the matrix is a cognitive template, a 'structured expectation', and is generally binary and inflexible – lines and forms are merely plugged in to whichever matrix can be most easily projected into them, regardless if all the positions are filled or not. Feet may be missing (as we saw with 'La Belle Dame Sans Merci'), whole *lines* may be missing – but both ghost feet and ghost lines are still accounted for, and also given a numerical value. The sense of this apparently odd move will be seen when we compare the matrix-patterns of 4-strong lines and i.p. The AS pattern in one line of 4-strong is 4-2-3-1; in one line of i.p. it is 6-3-5-2-4-[1].

```
   x   /   x / x  / x  /
By God, ye be a pretty pode
   4       2     3      1
```

(JOHN SKELTON, 'Mannerly Margery
Milk and Ale')

```
  x  / x  /   x    /   x / x  /  [x/]
My dearest dust, could not thy hasty day
  6      3        5      2    4    1
```

(CATHERINE DYER, 'Sonnet')

One can see immediately the stark difference between the two lines: the final s-syllable has an intonational *fall* in 4-strong and a *rise* in i.p., explaining the effects that tend to be strongly performed in group recitations, or group performances of the 'duh-DAH' pattern of the metres.[1]

If we plug in the distichic matrix:

```
x   /   x / x  / x  /
By God, ye be a pretty pode,
    8       4   6   2
```

```
x  / x   / x   /   x   /
And I love you an whole cart-load.
   7       3       5        1
```

```
x  / x   /   x   /   x / x  /  [x/]
My dearest dust, could not thy hasty day
  12      6         10     4   8  [2]
```

```
x  /   x  /  x / x   /   x   /  [x/]
Afford thy drowzy patience leave to stay
  11       5     9       3       7  [1]
```

— at the very least I suspect that even if the alternation at the level of metron or dimetron is not perceptible because of metrical variation or local sense-stress complications, perceived *pairs* of lines, distichs and strophes exhibit high and low alternations of overall key.

1 The situation is further muddied by the fact that end-stopped i.p. lines – of the sort that elegiac or 'deadly serious' verse often favours – aligns with the sort of intonational unit where the line falls in key from high to low anyway, and the last strong position coincides with the rise on the nuclear stress; the NS more usually appears in the *second* line of any 4-strong couplet. (The balladic form of the 4 × 4 neatly engineers a coincidence between nuclear stress and a high matrical value; see below). AS is just a little *too* conveniently easy to project into such lines, so they should not propose a rule; especially when we see blocks of i.p. are almost incapable of forming higher-level units of the sort that would make AS more explicit. (The theory of dramatic and lyric modes of i.p. offers a better explanation, I think, for our rising final s stress.)

NUCLEAR STRESS IN THE AS MATRIX

An exquisite – or at least exquisitely agonising – complication is that the most prominent stress in both music and in English speech tends to land on the rightmost (i.e. the last) s stress of a prosodic unit. (Poetry can be considered almost straightforwardly music *and* speech, which if anything reinforces the effect.) In 4-strong metre, the need to preserve this nuclear stress (NS) against the low matrical value of the final stress in the line often results in an additional intonational lift being added to the final stress of each distich (distichs more so than lines, especially in vaguely 4-strong form, as they carry the expectation of being sentence- and clause-coincident, where single lines can often be merely phrase-coincident).

This can be clearly heard in group recitations of 4-strong lines, which often default to: duh *dah* duh *dah* duh *dah* duh *dah* / duh *dah* duh *dah* duh *dah* duh *DAH*↑. This lift essentially *forms* part of the distichic 4-strong template: 8 4 6 2 / 7 3 5 1'. In i.p. no such compensation is felt as necessary, as the 6-3-5-2-4-[1] pattern means that there is already an audible built-in rise from the fourth to the fifth stress, making it ideal for normal clause-units of performed speech. Similarly, the distich pattern of common metre – 8 4 6 2 / 7 3 5 [1] sees a rise between the second and third stress of the second line, which will accommodate most final-position nuclear stresses neatly.

In group recitations of the full 4 × 4 strophe (with the 4-strong pattern 16 8 12 4 / 14 6 10 2 / 15 7 11 3 / 13 5 9 1) I've heard an odd phenomenon. Despite the fact that the ASR marks the last stress of each line as a fall, the voice occasionally performs a strange turn on lines 2 and 4, where the stresses are weakest. In line 2 it takes the form of a high pitch, which glides to a low and then immediately rises

METRE: THE RHYTHM OF THE POEM

to a medial level; in line 4, a high pitch which glides to low. I'm fairly
certain this is again an unthinking performance of the NS, which has
been built into the cognitive template. The high accent in line 2 is a
NS, and the fall and subsequent rise is an effort to compensate for
the extreme break with the matrical frame. What would stay merely
high as a single spoken phrase will drop again, in deference to its low
matrical position, then rise a little in a performed acknowledgement
of the fact that the form is not yet closed, the first distich is higher in
key than the second, and that we must retain the final 1-value drop for
the last position in line 4. Which is where we find it, dropping down
to a low after an initial NS 'high'. This instability means not only that
the NS is already incorporated into the matrical frame as an inton-
ational accent, but also that the mind *already* perceives it as an area of
metrical tension before any has been introduced by sense stress: in a
way, the final s of a 4-strong couplet occupies *both* a w- and an s-stress
position.

> And since to look at things in bloom
>   ᴜ
> Fifty springs are little room,
> About the woodlands I will go
>   ᴄ
> To see the cherry hung with snow.
>
>   (A. E. HOUSMAN, 'Loveliest of trees . . .')[1]

I don't doubt that such an inbuilt, self-questioning tension in
the 4-strong form must eventually draw out unconscious semantic
expectations on the poet's part. These manoeuvres are *not* performed
on the final stresses of lines 2 and 4 in common metre, where NS
and a high matrical position tend to coincide: the 4/3/4/3 s stress
balladic version of 4 × 4 largely avoids this instability, as the terminal

1   A. E. Housman, *A Shropshire Lad* (New York: Dover Publications, 1990).

stress-value on lines 2 and 4 (10 and 9) is both rising and high anyway. Indeed, one of the most salient and undervalued aspects of common metre is the engineered coincidence of NS and a high stress position (i.p. often benefits from a similar arrangement).

> A slumber did my spirit seal;
>
> 10   [2]
>
> I had no human fears:
>
> She seemed a thing that could not feel
>
> 9   [1]
>
> The touch of earthly years.
>
> (WILLIAM WORDSWORTH,
> 'A slumber did my spirit seal')[2]

In contrast to the ballad form, might the 4-strong form of 4×4 stanza be better suited to tense, questioning or argumentative subjects or approaches? Possibly, possibly not; but it doesn't strike me as entirely outlandish to suggest that anglophone poets may have been unconsciously influenced by the contour of the matrical form, and that it may have led them to a more 'rogatory' style (and by extension, strategy) than they might otherwise have lighted upon.

While the AS matrix may occasionally encourage the poet towards certain kinds of statement, the suggestion that AS might exert some deeper compositional influence is probably rather Kabbalistic and far-fetched. Nonetheless the more ingrained the template, the more likely it seems that its extreme values, at least, may be unconsciously put to compositional work. In the 6-3-5-2-4-[1] matrix of the i.p. line, the nadir falls on the fourth stress; my feeling is that, across the poetic corpus, a fair bit of intonational demotion, function-word promotion or de-accent falls on that stress, because it 'feels right'. Taking a larger matrix: 'To the Etruscan Poets' by Richard Wilbur is

---

2 William Wordsworth, *Selected Poems*, ed. Stephen Gill (London: Penguin, 2004).

a six-line pentameter stanza. We would treat the default matrix as a distrophic, even though the poem is 'curtal' relative to such a matrix. In its i.p. form, this matrix has 6 × 8 icti, i.e. 48 stress positions. They take these values:

48	24	40	16	32	8
44	20	36	12	28	4
46	22	38	14	30	6
42	18	34	10	26	2
47	23	39	15	31	7
43	19	35	11	27	3
45	21	37	13	29	5
41	17	33	9	25	1

Here are the numbers slotted into Wilbur's poem:

```
            48   24        40        16          32      [8]
Dream fluently, still brothers, who when young
   44              20       36       12       28         [4]
took with your mothers' milk the mother tongue,
      46          22      38      14          30         [6]
in which pure matrix, joining world and mind,
         42        18       34     10    26              [2]
you strove to leave some line of verse behind
         47    23     39     15        31                [7]
like a fresh track across a field of snow,
      43     19      35         11       27              [3]
not reckoning that all could melt and go.³
    [45   21    37     13    29    5]
    [41   17    33    9    25    1]
```

---

3   Richard Wilbur, *Collected Poems 1943–2004* (California: Harcourt, 2006).

(The reader will have to trust me over the positioning of some of these stresses for now: the second line, for example, is the initial variant of the 'displaced weak rule', later explained.) The first observation I'd make is that there's a lovely coincidence between NS and rising values on the fifth stress. Additionally, the content word 'fluently' occurs at the zenith, but with 'dream' forms a strong variation; we often see bold variation in initial positions (lines 2 and 5 have them, in this poem), but especially so in those matrical positions at which the poet senses more energy. Here, this matrical zenith probably aids the near-spondee 'dream flu[ently]'. 'verse' occurs at the nadir of the matrix (excepting, of course, the last two empty lines). The poem is about the evaporation of an entire poetry, an entire language; its position may, of course, be entirely coincidental, but to my ear exquisitely performs the diminishment of 'verse'. The de-accented 'mother' (closely repeated content words in speech are usually de-accented to functional anaphora) appears on the second-lowest value.[4]

If a sonnet is regarded as a kind of long-form common metre,[5] the low values will occur in the fourth stress positions in lines 8 and 12; I have a fair bit of evidence for deliberate 'burying' in just those positions. Shakespeare's Sonnet 86 ('Was it the proud full sail of his great verse') is a striking example, with the repeated word 'verse', the poem's agonised subject, falling on the nadir of the fourth stress position in the eighth line, and the fourth stress in the twelfth line coinciding deliciously with 'fear' in 'I was not sick of any fear from thence' – as the poet dismissively rejects the possibility that the rival's prowess might be causing his writer's block, almost reducing 'fear' to the status of grammatical anaphora; but a random sampling suggests

4 My later, controversial suggestion that i.p. in its lyric mode fits or at least can readily fit itself to a 2 × 4 pattern actually makes no difference whatsoever to the matrical extremes, once we do the arithmetic; the nadir and zenith occur at the same positions.

5 A 'curtal tetrastrophe': a term so ripe for Spoonerism it probably also establishes the sensible limits of my terminology.

that Sonnets 17, 25, 29, 60 and 65 may also have been influenced by their nadiral positions too, and that a more systematic study might be at least halfway worthwhile. Elsewhere the case is harder to prove, with the matrical nadir showing no more than a mild tendency to coincide with function words, which would be expected from the stichic matrix alone. But while all this might not amount to what we could call a governing influence, it may well fall into the category of 'underexploited effect'.

Over long AS units, far too many other semantic, syntactic and thematic factors come into play. Indeed, the AS matrix is continually trumped, overridden, undermined and elided by semantic considerations. Consider just some of the phonological phenomena a random passage might encounter: the 'paratone', an expansion and a final constraining of the pitch range at paragraph (or strophe) level, corresponding to the introduction of a new topic; the fact that asides and parentheticals are characterised by an initial constrained range and a low-rising intonational contour; the disruptions provided by question or exclamation marks . . . The list is very long. Such additional information will likely drown out the subtler effects of the AS matrix, if the performer is paying proper attention to the poem's larger phrasal structures and the intonational contours that go along with their performance. Even so, many speakers of poems will unconsciously make a kind of global 'metre-strong' reading to preserve a sense of the AS matrix regardless, leaving metrical poetry significantly unlike normal speech.

The relationship between the larger structures of AS and the natural intonational contours of the spoken phrase would *ideally* provide the exactly same kind of expressive tension and variation we find at the level of syllable, between lexical stress and metrical position. The truth, alas, is that the higher (i.e. larger) the unit structure, the more complicating phrasal-semantic factors there are – and such neat contrapuntal tensions and consonances are very quickly buried.

AS: KEY POINTS

In summary, here are a few of the key points relating to the AS matrix and the ASR generally, and some practical consequences AS has for the poem.

a) Odd-stress lines, such as i.p and the common metre 4+3 couplet, end on rises; because the pattern is curtailed, the falling position occurs in the hiatus. This means that those lines tend to accommodate NS comfortably.

b) The effect is scaled up: stanzas which curtail the pattern by omitting whole lines may end on lines of an overall higher or lower *key*, depending on their position.

c) Even-stressed lines will often demonstrate a natural, emphatic rising accent on the final s position in the second unit of any distich to counter the coincidence of falling matrical value and rising NS.

d) The zenith and nadir of each successive hierarchical unit will become cumulatively more salient, and at the higher, larger unit levels these nodes *may* have sufficient salience to exert some compositional influence as potentiated, expressive positions. Metrical variation is most likely to take place at the zenith and the higher nodes, probably on an unconscious 'the stronger the position, the more disruption it can take' principle, and the fact that there is more energy to be distributed at those points. And although I have no more than anecdotal evidence for this, the nadir and the other lowest nodes may tend to coincide with content words which are de-accented for argumentative, thematic or syntactic reasons. (Poets could certainly take more manipulative advantage of these 'secret' stations in the matrical frame.)

e) As is well known, enjambment between odd-stress lines is a far more radical gesture than even-stress lines, because it elides the ghost metron. However, as can be seen from the matrix, it also means three successive s stress rises: in i.p., 12 6 10 4 8 [2] / 11 5 9 3 7 [1] becomes 12 6 10 **4 8** / **11** 5 9 3 7 [1]; this may encourage stress-miscount under certain syntactic conditions, but also suggest a potentially expressive technique. (The rising effect is also present in enjambed trimeter: 8 **4 6** / **7** 3 5. It would be apparent, too, if we enjambed the second and third lines of common metre.)

f) The effect of AS at the metronic and dimetronic level is radically weakened by metrical variation at the level of syllable. Additionally, the looser the metre, the slighter its effects. However, at units of the syllabic, metronic and dimetronic, AS is primarily felt through stress-alternation. (The difference between a syllable which is strong only at syllable level, and one which is strong at syllable, metronic and dimetronic levels – i.e. in the stichic matrix of 4-strong, the last and first syllables respectively – is certainly pronounced enough to be exploited for expressive purposes.) At units of the stichic and above, AS is primarily experienced as intonational effect, of key-rise and key-fall. They may enjoy a fair degree of independence from one another; while loose, light and free metres may limit or elide the effects of AS *within* the line, lines syntactically experienced as binary groups may still vaguely be felt to alternate:

4 To what purpose, April, do you return again?
2 Beauty is not enough.
3 You can no longer quiet me with the redness
1 Of little leaves opening stickily.

(EDNA ST VINCENT MILLAY, 'Spring')[1]

1   Edna St Vincent Millay, *Collected Poems*, ed. Norma Millay (New York: HarperPerennial, 2011).

TIGHT, LOOSE AND LIGHT METRES

The relative regularity of a metre is decided on the strength of its convergence. Usually, the same frame will be introjected and projected into a line, then a number of successive lines will establish a convention of stricter or looser interpretation of that frame. The first lines in the poem are especially important in announcing this convention: most poets who work in form intuitively understand that too much wild variation in the initial lines will mean that the frame may never be clearly projected. The relative tightness or lightness of the metre, the bandwidth of what the reader perceives as 'tolerable' variation, *is an aspect of the metrical frame itself*, and is built into its pattern through the careful advertisement of certain expectations. It will then establish a local convention within which each individual poem is read.

These conventions might be roughly caricatured as 'tight syllabo-tonic metre', 'loose syllabotonic metre',[1] and 'light metre', the last being the least metrically insistent. These metres describe the relative influence of the binary frame, and the degree to which speech has become magnetised to that pattern.[2] Confusion has been introduced by prosodists who love to count, and will establish the 'existence'

---

1 Used here in preference to 'accentual-syllabic'.

2 Light metre is sometimes mistaken for 'accentual metre' but they are very different: the poet working in light metre is introjecting a strong stress / weak placeholder pattern as usual; they are not merely counting strong stresses. If the poet *is* merely counting the stresses, this is merely a form of free verse in which the lines happen to be roughly regular: the metre would be posterior to the composition, whereas for it to have any generative force it must always be anterior. This will receive separate discussion.

of regular metres in very loose or free verse through totting up the stresses. Counting is *not* projection, however; and *only* the projection of the whole metrical template echoes and is sympathetic to the poet's own procedure of introjection. For that reason I'd prefer to introduce the terms 'tight', 'loose' and 'light' metres for tight syllabotonic, loose syllabotonic and very light syllabotonic (occasionally mistaken for so-called 'accentual metre'). These are distinct but not cleanly categorical differentiations.

Strictly speaking, one can *never* say that any single line read in isolation is 'in iambic pentameter', or indeed anything else. The presence of the metre which the poet has introjected can only ever be determined by the convergence of several lines upon it. (We might even be inclined to get all Popperian about it, and claim that all such determinations must remain theoretically provisional; the possibility we are projecting the wrong frame is never entirely removed.) The weaker this convergence, the looser the metre; and the looser the metre, the longer a template's 'presence' will take to be confirmed.

With the very tightest kind of syllabotonic verse the frame is least inflexible, as its syllable count is relatively fixed and expectations of isochronic regularity are far higher. As a consequence, the perception of unmetricality has a low threshold. Loose and light metre follow the same rules, but more laxly. While it may be qualified by various syntactic and phonological expectations, the metrical frame has only two principal properties: (a) its binary nature and (b) the relative 'magnetic' strength of the template, which lends the perception of its tight, loose or light form, and determines latitudes over syllable count. 'Metricality' depends on whether the metrical template is adjudged by the reader to have survived its encounter with the speech act. This perception can be 'felt' and need not be conscious. I'll now look at tight, loose and light metres in turn.

Tight metres will tend to observe very strict stress-to-position coincidence (w stresses will coincide with w positions, and s with s), favour end-stopped lines, and have a more or less perfect, acatalectic syllable count. Strict syllabotonic verse is merely the most rigid verbal realisation of the strong position/weak placeholder template. We can be reasonably certain after a line of two of this kind of thing:

> Now, out of doubt, Antipholus is mad,
> Else would he never so demean himself.
> A ring he hath of mine worth forty ducats,
> And for the same he promis'd me a chain:
> Both one and other he denies me now.
> The reason that I gather he is mad,
> Besides this present instance of his rage,
> Is a mad tale he told to-day at dinner,
> Of his own doors being shut against his entrance.
> Belike his wife, acquainted with his fits,
> On purpose shut the doors against his way.
>
> (*The Comedy of Errors*)[3]

— that we are dealing with the tight metre form of i.p.

Loose metres are, generally speaking, the most sophisticated in their approach to metrical composition. They tend to feature more variation, more disagreement between realised stress and position, and more variation in syllable count — and therefore take a little longer to establish themselves; but once the underlying frame *and* the degree of metrical latitude have been made clear to the reader, loose metres can win the poet great expressive liberties. (Nonetheless a tight-metre poem which takes advantage of tensive possibilities can be equally expressive, and often has greater interpretative instability.) The extent to which these liberties can be taken without the perception of unmetricality is the test of a poet's skill; the prize is a

---

3 William Shakespeare, *The Comedy of Errors*, ed. Charles Whitworth (Oxford: Oxford University Press, 2002).

considerable increase in the expressive potential of the line, through the exploitation of the tensions between speech stress and metrical pattern. Loose metre is a disease of degree, and its designation more subjective; tight and light metres are more easily defined and identified, representing, if you like, 'extremes of practice'. But this should direct us to a simpler truth: in practice, 'loose metre' encompasses *all metrical procedure*, and 'tight' and 'light' metres, while broadly distinct, are really the result of overdeterminations and underdeterminations of the ruling 'loose' frame (often caused by the pulls of metre and song respectively). This means that loose metre demands more sophistication from the reader as well as the poet, since its projection and introjection require a reciprocal sensitivity. Here's a passage from Elizabeth Barrett Browning's *Sonnets from the Portuguese*, where we can hear the tight metre slacken off considerably through the use of metrical (and caesural) variation:

> Let the world's sharpness, like a clasping knife,
> Shut in upon itself and do no harm
> In this close hand of Love, now soft and warm,
> And let us hear no sound of human strife
> After the click of the shutting. Life to life—
> I lean upon thee, Dear, without alarm, [. . .][4]

And here are a few lines from Richard Wilbur's 'The Mind-Reader':

> Imagine a railway platform –
> The long cars come to a cloudy halt beside it,
> And the fogged windows offering a view
> Neither to those within nor those without;
> Now, in the crowd – forgive my predilection –

4 Elizabeth Barrett Browning, *Selected Poems*, ed. Marjorie Stone and Beverly Taylor (Peterborough, ON: Broadview Press, 2009).

Is a young woman standing amidst her luggage,
Expecting to be met by you, a stranger.
See how she turns her head, the eyes engaging
And disengaging, pausing and shying away.[5]

Both passages take considerable liberties with the frame, and yet strongly preserve its character. (However – and I will deliberately avoid expanding on this subject for now – loose i.p. is a special case. For reasons which reflect a deep cultural shift in the use of poetry itself, i.p. also contains within it a second template, that of a *10-position line*. I'll cover this in the chapter 'Two Kinds of Line'.)

Loose metres can take additional liberties with line length. In its variable 3- or 4-strong lines, the following passage displays a relationship to the 4-strong template one quickly and instinctively identifies:

```
      x  /   x   /  x /   [x /]
   That day will still exist
   x   / x / x   /      x    /
   Long after I have joined you where
   x    / x/   x  / x /
   Rings radiate the dusty air
   x   /   x  /   x   /   x      /
   And bangles bind each powdered wrist.
   x   /      x  / x /    [x /]
   Here comes that day again.
     x   / x / x   /    x   /
   What shall I do? Instruct me, dear,
   x  / x  /   x   / x /
   Longanimous encourager,
```

5 Richard Wilbur, *The Mind Reader: New Poems* (Palo Alto, CA: Harcourt, 1976).

```
x   /  x  / x  / x  /
Sweet soul in the athletic rain
x    /   x   /   x   /   x   [/]
And wife now to the weather.
```

(DOUGLAS DUNN, 'Anniversaries')[6]

Light metres are by definition either difficult or straightforwardly impossible to confirm, mainly on account of the freedoms taken with how the w placeholders are populated. It is an incorrect procedure to 'nail' light lines to a metre; we can do no more than identify a shifting relationship towards it. What would have been called 'variation' under tight- or loose-metre rules — i.e. the deliberate creation of expressive tension — is here mere 'liberty'; the rules of play are different. Variations in light metres do not create tensions, and cannot be characterised as 'disagreements'. In the following example, a free and rough 'groove' playing on something like common or ballad metre is audible below the stresses (the positioning of the frame is here necessarily rough and subjective):

```
x    / x /  x  / x /
On my decline, a millipede
 /     x / x   /    [x/]
Helped me to keep count;
x / x   /   x /    x  /
For every time I slipped a foot
 /  x  /    x / x    [/]
Farther down the mountain
```

---

6 Douglas Dunn, *Elegies* (London: Faber & Faber, 1985).

```
    x    /   x / x  /   x   /
She'd leave a tiny, cast-off limb
  x   /   x  /   x   /    [x /]
Of crimson on my cheek
  x  /  x  /    [x / x /]
As if to say —
    x     /    -x-    /    -x-     [/ x /]
You're hurting us both, Mick . . .
[. . .]
[. . .]
    x   / x     /  x / x    /
This thousandth morning after, though
    x    / -x-     /   [x / x/]
(Or thousand-and-first)
  x /   x  /  x  / x    /
I miss her, and a bedside mirror
    /    -x-   /      [x / x/ ]
Bellows the worst —

  x /   x   / x   /    x    /
A big, new, bilberry birthmark, stamped
    x   /  x / x  /   [x /]
From ear to livid ear,
    x    / -x-/  -x-  /         [x/]
Her whole body of blood's
  x  /  x   /    [x / x /]
Untimely smear.
```

(MICK IMLAH, 'Birthmark')[7]

The strength of very loose and light metres is also their weakness: their scansion can never be agreed, as great interpretative latitude is

---

7 Mick Imlah, *Selected Poems*, ed. Mark Ford (London: Faber & Faber, 2010).

granted the reader as soon as syllable count is abandoned; this gives them much more freedom to position the weak placeholders and place the stresses. (I have nonetheless heard poets literally *scream* that their 'accentual' lines are scanned *this* way and this way alone, wholly oblivious to the subjective projections of their own performance.) In their lack of definitive s syllable-to-s position alignment, there can be little metrical 'variation' in the sense we normally understand it. As will become clear, light metres are only really a 'thing' in 4-strong-derived forms such as the song-strong 'Dolnik', and what I call the 'two-step' metre (a very loose short line which usually features two items of content, and any number of functional schwas – essentially a cut-in-half Dolnik with an even freer template than Dolnik allows, currently a common form in English verse, if a very underidentified one). The template of i.p. is ultimately *too* inflexibly syllabotonic to accommodate these variations and cannot really sustain anything like a light metre while retaining its character.

FREE VERSE AND FREE METRE

One of the more misleading bromides one still hears is that 'it is just as hard to write good free verse as good formal verse'. Since the only sensible purpose of formal rule is to prevent the poet from writing the dull or stupid thing they'd intended to write and force them to write something surprising or intelligent instead – this statement cannot be true.[1] As terrible a soundbite as it makes, what would be truer to say is that 'free verse which compensates for the lack of resistance inherent in its formal rules through the introduction of *other* kinds of procedural resistance . . . is as hard to write as formal verse'. (Also true is 'bad free verse is just as easy to write as bad formal verse'.) If this resistance is not in place, in whatever form – the poet is *indeed* making it easier for themselves. If the goal of both formal and free verse is natural, original, memorable and felicitous expression, then the method with the most built-in resistance is going to be straightforwardly 'harder' to write. With the best will in the world, poets cannot always rely in their own good taste, vigilance and quality control as sources of formal resistance. A few, however, clearly can; though those poets – James Wright and Sylvia Plath come immediately to mind – were often meticulous in their early formal training.

In order to make the 'free' game worth playing, most decent poets will replace a formal rule for a compositional one. But this is a risk: if that rule provides too little resistance, they might put the ease and fluency with which they write down to nothing their own uncommon skill and artistic vision. Indeed that may be the case; but formal

---

1   As for form's alleged 'constraints': 'Form is a straitjacket the way a straitjacket was a straitjacket for Houdini' – Paul Muldoon.

resistance — in the shape, say, of metrical pattern, rhyme or form — performs the useful service of reminding most of us we are not geniuses. Poets who believe themselves to be so tend to burden their poetic practice with very little formal inconvenience of the kind that would challenge this conceit of themselves. (See, for example, the late work of Ezra Pound or Ted Hughes. I once heard of a notoriously prolific poet who was asked the secret of his remarkable productivity: he answered, unsmilingly, 'I have a very fertile imagination.' There are also a number of fluent versifiers who imagine themselves great masters of the poetic art on account of their mere facility; but there, the problem is usually the absence of the various kinds of *non*-formal resistance that make a good poem, mainly a commitment to original phrasemaking and truth-telling, and to the sophisticated, parallel integration of the poem's elements.) Yes, 'no verse is free for the man who wants to do a good job', but good jobs are guaranteed by checks, procedures and gold standards which make the bad ones easy to spot.

Outside of its historically specific sense of Laforgueian *vers libre*, 'free verse' is a meaningless term, and 'freedom' is as much a disease of degree as 'formality'. 'Free' latitudes may be taken with metre, line, stanza, rhyme-scheme and so on; the absurdity of the phrase is clear when one posits a verse free from *all* those 'strictures'. What's required is neutral description, and a first step towards this would be abandoning the word 'free' altogether: the word 'freedom' has positive associations that bad poems do not deserve, and confers on these poems a kind of fuzzy, undeserved merit. Nor is 'free' metre in any way analogous to loose or light metre, since its composition is often *more* complex than tight formal metre. For now, let's take free verse as meaning 'unrhymed verse which demonstrates no adherence to a metrical pattern'; but since we're focused solely on metre here, there's no reason not to talk of a poem as written in 'free metre'.[2]

---

2   It is absurd to subject to a metrical scansion free verse which has not been deliberately composed to a metrical frame. This is a bit like scoring a boxer on the

There is a great deal to say on the subject of free verse, but most of it is beyond the scope of this book. However, the purely *prosodic* implications of free verse are not complex, and nor are its rules substantially different from those we apply to light-metre verse.

The most significant feature of free verse 'prosody' – the inverted commas are not placed sarcastically but to acknowledge the limited usefulness of the word here – is line-end and phrase boundary co-incidence or non-coincidence. Enjambment is a far more significant gesture in free verse than in formal verse, for one simple reason: the reader intuitively *knows* that the poet, in the absence of any visible or audible formal scheme of regular lines that might drive against the naturally loose rhythm of her phrases, could easily have broken the line at its most natural point, the phrase boundary – and has *deliberately chosen not to*. There is no frame to blame, as it were. (The deliberate-ness of the gesture also exaggerates any metatextual 'play' on the teleuton.) This feature can be analysed with the same cline we used when discussing line endings, on a scale of least-to-most disruptive.

Claims for the *metrical* versatility of this crucial feature have been badly overstated (Charles O. Hartmann's otherwise highly useful book *Free Verse* exaggerates its versatility to the point of ludicrousness), though perhaps understandably so, since in free verse it represents the primary and often sole locus of expressive tension between frame and speech. However, because of the line-break's expressly wilful positioning, it encourages the reading of the last lexical stress in the line *as the nuclear stress,* whether it is or is not – and for this reason we often see an exquisite lingering over the teleuton that is quite impossible to replicate in formal verse. When combined with free verse's other secret

---

aesthetic quality of his footwork. Beyond average phrase and sentence length, etc., the only rules in force under such circumstances are the same as those in play with *any* random chunk of language which has been lineated: (a) the three-second rule (b) isochrony, tightened under the three-second rule (c) and any unconsciously projected metrical frame.

weapon – the flexibility of the hiatus, which permits the introduction of variable silences against the median length of the poem's lines (as well as, no doubt, the three-second frame) – this terminal 'lingering' can become a procedurally distinct and subtle tool of emphasis:

> And everything is gone, the body is gone
> completely under, gone, entirely gone.
> The upper darkness is heavy as the lower,
> between them the little ship [   ]
> is gone [   ]
> she is gone. [   ]

(D. H. LAWRENCE, 'The Ship of Death')[3]

Many examples of free verse seem in the grip of unconsciously introjected templates, principally the ur-form of the 4-strong line; at the very least the three-second rule certainly seems to influence the median line length itself:

```
       /    /          /   /           /        /
6 The broken pillar of the wing jags from the clotted shoulder,
       /   /         /            /
4 The wing trails like a banner in defeat,
       /      /        /   /        /            /
6 No more to use the sky forever but live with famine
       /     /    /    /         /
5 And pain a few days: cat nor coyote
       /           /       /         /               /
6 Will shorten the week of waiting for death, there is game
       /
   without talons.
```

3 D. H. Lawrence, *The Complete Poems of D. H. Lawrence* (Ware: Wordsworth Editions, 2002).

       /   /   /

3 He stands under the oak-bush and waits

      /   /   /   /   /   /

6 The lame feet of salvation; at night he remembers freedom

      /   /   /   /

4 And flies in a dream, the dawns ruin it.

(ROBINSON JEFFERS, 'Hurt Hawks')[4]

Were we to examine the whole of 'Hurt Hawks', we'd see that the strong stresses work out at a rough mean of five per line, suggesting a strong 'auditory present' influence (the alternating line lengths might also put one in mind of common metre).

There is absolutely no point in making even a lexical stress analysis of a long free metre line, as speed increases schwa-count considerably, and under such circumstances sense is parsed more at the level of phrase-unit, while individual words demote much of their content to w-stressed function. Far better to immediately make a sense-stress analysis (we haven't yet looked at this procedure in any detail, but for now it will suffice to know that ['] or [,] after an x or / represents an intonational accent or de-accent derived from *semantic context*, and can be counted as prosodically equivalent to a strong or weak stress respectively, regardless of the mark it follows):

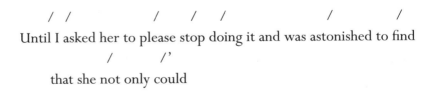

     / /   /   /   /   /   /

Until I asked her to please stop doing it and was astonished to find

          /   /'

      that she not only could

4 Robinson Jeffers, *The Selected Poetry of Robinson Jeffers*, ed. Tim Hunt (Stanford, CA: Stanford University Press, 2001).

       /   /   /'   /, /,

but from the moment I asked her in fact would stop doing it,

        /   /   /

   my mother, all through my childhood,

  /   /   /

when I was saying something to her, something important, would

     /   /   x'   /'

   move her lips as I was speaking

       /   /   /   /   /   x'

so that she seemed to be saying under her breath the very words I

   /,   x'   /

   was saying as I was saying them.

x'   /'   /,   /' /,   /'

Or, even more disconcertingly – wildly so now that my puberty

      /,   /'

   had erupted – *before* I said them.

  /   /   / /   /

When I was smaller, I must just have assumed that she was

    /   / /'

   omniscient. Why not?

    /   /   /   /   /   /

She knew everything else – when I was tired, or lying; she'd know

    /   x'

   I was ill before I did.

    /   /   /   x'   /

I may even have thought – how could it not have come into my

    /'   /'

   mind? – that she *caused* what I said.

                 (C. K. WILLIAMS, 'My Mother's Lips')[5]

5   C. K. Williams, *Collected Poems* (New York: Farrar, Straus & Giroux, 2006).

(Note how the long, function-heavy line accounts for the *ease* with
which semantically determined accent and de-accent can be applied:
for example in line 2 '. . . would stop doing it', we can unthinkingly
promote 'would' to emphatic content, and drop 'stop doing it' to
de-accented anaphora.) We immediately note several features: the
surprisingly regular number of marked stresses per line (between 7 and
9 here, although one could very easily give just as plausible scansions
which varied them a great deal more); the near-organisational force
of the terminal NS; and the tendency for high accent to demand an
immediate fall on an adjacent stress (more, perhaps, through the need
to achieve its own contrastive salience than any application of the
ASR, which is just how it would feature in conversational speech).[6]

6   One immediately suspects the presence of an unconscious 2 × 4 template. Is
the long line frequently just an 'accentual fourteener', or a 2 × 4 line? Try reading
Williams's poem against a triple-metre fourteen / 8-strong template; the results,
while far from conclusive, show far more convergence than you might expect, e.g.:
When I was smaller, I must just have assumed that she was omniscient. Why [xx] not?

POLYSEMIC VERSE AND STRESS

One major complication thrown up by postmodern, avant-garde, 'linguistically innovative' or 'other' (their word, not mine) poetries[1] lies in their relationship to stress. The problem is simply stated. Any verse in which automatic sense-interpretation is either impossible, highly unstable, or suspended until such point as its secondary exegetic text is generated cannot receive any sense-stress emphasis beyond that proposed by its resting state prosody or lexical scansion. Anything further will be to some degree arbitrary, which is to say there will be too little convergence, since the text cannot confirm the accuracy of any one scansion. Often readers will initially read such poems in a tone deliberately devoid of intonational contour, since even a rough sense-interpretation and sense-performance cannot be made on a cursory reading.

However, when this sort of poem is performed by its author, a clear sense stressing is almost *always* made – one which points, obviously, to their superior understanding of the semantic intentions of their own text. In this way, both postmodern verse and performance verse are closely connected, and I do wonder if the allegiance forged between these two apparently very different camps during the British Poetry Revival was less to do with shared countercultural concerns than

---

[1] Everyone should be allowed to call themselves whatever they want, but their banners should not imply that other more traditional poetries are *intrinsically* inferior; 'linguistically innovative poetry' comes dashed close to implying its own superiority. My current favourite piece of I'll-stay-up-as-late-as-I-want *soi-disanterie* is 'non-conformist verse', a phrase so exquisitely loaded I don't know where to begin. One clarifying solution might be to hold a conference of Conformist and Linguistically Conservative Verse, and then see who showed up.

their common late-Romantic, expressionist tendencies, where text and authorial performance were more closely intertwined. Below are the opening stanzas of a poem by Tom Raworth: I have scanned it according to the author's own performance, but defy any reader to derive enough *clearly* decided sense to make either a similar or as confident a scansion:

>
> though it might have been chronic
>   x   x /' x   x   / x,
> around his neck and shoulders
> x /   x / x   / x'
> filled with thick high weeds
>   /   x /' x   /
> the road was lined with stone
>   x /   x /   x   /'
>
> almost entranced she started
> / x x /'   x / x
> ordering quantities of everything
> /   x x   / x x x /' x x
> down the windows of your station
>   /   x / x   x   x   / x
> combed and perfectly normal
>   /   x   / x x / x'
>
> bees through blood and perhaps
>   /   /   / x   x /
> night air while we rode back
>   / /' x   x /   /'
> followed him to the front porch
>   / x   x x x /   /'
> and the chimney bricks were fallen
> x   x /' x   /,   x /, x

she hasn't heard from him since [. . .]

   x /'x /   x   x   /

(TOM RAWORTH, 'All Fours')[2]

Raworth's subtly inflected and enjoyable performance reveals much hitherto buried or obscure sense, and has the immediate effect of narrowing the polysemy encouraged by his lightly disjunctive method, strongly mitigating the effect of the text's syntactic and narrative discontinuities – and reducing the 'difficulty' of the poem overall. There seems no doubt that the poet 'understands' his poem perfectly well, and – for all its instability and complexity – reads it with the clear, intonationally contoured semantic intent of someone relating an anecdote. This example also points up the *total* inadequacy of a rule-derived prosodic scansion, whether traditional or generative, to arrive at a useful picture of a strongly polysemic poem's stress pattern or inherent tensions. Polysemy is directly related to the instability of stress; this means that, unless prosody is of no concern to the poet, its author-performance may actually be *necessary* to and continuous with the realisation of the poem; without such a performance, we risk being left with a poem whose sense is so unstable that too many mutually exclusive interpretations can be generated than would be either purposeful or 'fun'. Essentially what the above scansion accomplishes is a kind of ham-fisted but not inaccurate pragmatic analysis which takes some account of phonological feature (i.e. the means by which intention and interpretation are conducted); the runs of high accent and s stress, low accent and w stress, are really tonal suprasegmentals – whose purpose is to constrain the sense *to that which the author intends*, and thus reduce polysemy to a manageable degree. In the context of poetic prosody, these effects cannot be adequately represented on the page; although I suppose this could be accomplished by revisiting something like sprung rhythm, or at least some system of

---

2 Tom Raworth, *Collected Poems* (Manchester: Carcanet, 2003).

'pragmatic overstressing', an option one half-wishes the avant-garde would consider. At the moment they seem to be either ignorant of or in total denial over the semantic gulf that exists between the textual presentation and the performance of their own poems. One feels sometimes that the book is a bit like a Xenakis score — that is, a mere blueprint that can be enjoyed by a handful of cognoscenti; whereas the music itself is accessible to many, and only requires a committed performance. However, unless a broad sense can be derived from the text, no such broad sense can be performed; only such semantic and pragmatic information as inheres in the 'resting state' rise and dip of syntactic contour will be derived from the poem. The reader has no alternative but to fall back on a performed reading based on lexical stress and 'default' nuclear stress alone — which will have the effect of *further* weakening the phrasal structure. [For some mildly unprofessional remarks on avant-garde practice, see endnote 18.]

STRONG STRESS METRE: ANGLO-SAXON VERSE, 'ACCENTUAL METRE' AND RAP

There is no longer such a thing as purely 'strong stress' or accentual metre as a compositional procedure in written English poetry. It had its heyday with Anglo-Saxon verse, which overdetermined the metre in a number of ways: principally, a strongly rhythmic and incantatory performance-style (or so we think), combined with two strong technical features: a regular caesura between two 2-stress hemistichs, guarding against mid-line slippage; and the alliteration of two or three of the four s stresses in the line, which gives them considerable salience. Between them, a deep familiarity with these features would have supplied a cognitive template strong enough to attract language towards its form, and make such poetry easily composed. Beyond Anglo-Saxon pastiche verse, no such template exists for the contemporary accentual versifier, with the highly important exception of rap, which I'll discuss shortly.[1]

In contemporary poetry, pure accentual verse (just like syllabics, with the exception of 10-position i.p., discussed elsewhere) is only

---

[1] The notorious 'sprung rhythm' of Gerard Manley Hopkins was partly derived from a misreading of light metre folksongs – though 'light metre folksongs' is really oxymoronic, as the fixed structure of song itself provides a overdetermining isochrony, and therefore more latitude to cram weak syllables into metronomically spaced weak placeholders. In the absence of music to overdetermine the distance between the position of s syllables, Hopkins attempted to do so using printed accents. As fine as some of these poems are, they are broadly unscannable as Hopkins intended them, and sprung rhythm – like Robert Bridges's quantitative experiments and William Carlos Williams's 'variable foot' – should be filed decisively under 'lousy ideas by good poets'.

employed as a way of organising the free verse or unmetred line through retrospective *count*. For compositional purposes, it has no generative force. The employment of mere stress-count points to the absence of an even-timed placeholding in the underlying metre, and results in a line whose only regularity is derived from such vague isochronic effect as already inheres in the language. If successive lines are *not* heard to converge on something approximating an even stress-distribution (i.e. if the metrical template can't be projected), the result is soon perceived as free verse, unmetrical verse, or 'doggerel'. Without perceptible, even-timed placeholding, the reader has far too much latitude in placing the s stresses wherever lexical stress guides them, or interpreted sense inclines them.

Therefore if an underlying metre *can* be more or less definitively established, the poem has been written in 'light metre', and with a template in mind. In purely accentual metres, there *is* no w-s metrical template to guide their position, and in English, scansions can never be even vaguely agreed. Here is a passage from a poem written in a rough 4-strong line, with two alternative and entirely plausible scansions — the line above marking (for the sake of argument) a low-key conversational minimal stress approach, the lower, a more rhetorical, dramatic maximal:

```
             /           /
While I was shawling the strawberries
   / /       /          /


      /          /          /
with fine green netting, you told me
   /    /   /      /  /


        /          /         /
about the cow that swam to the island
   /       /        /          /
```

```
   /             /              /
to stand there mooing until the seals
    /      /     /       /       /

         /        /           /
came in close to add their own belling,
   /        /      /       /      /

          /               /     /
with the seagulls circling above, kao-
   /        /       /        /     /

  /                         /       /
kaoing – and after you'd stared enough
   /          /           /       /

       /          /                  /
you ran to the farmer, who didn't believe
     /         /            /        /

          /            /
until he saw for himself, then asked
     /      /         /         /

           /          /            /
if you'd row him out there, to ferry
   /       /   /    /    /        /

the creature home . . .
```

(MATTHEW SWEENEY, 'In the Garden')[2]

Purely strong-stress templates as theoretically described are a myth, as far as compositional method is concerned. The proof is anecdotal, but, I think, compelling: how can one compose *within* a line

---

2 Matthew Sweeney, *Poetry London* 62 (2009).

one cannot feel, and which has no abstract correlate? Anyone over the age of seven with half an ear can be taught to speak i.p. in ten minutes, and have the rhythm of their spoken sense-making fall into rough step with the template – but I've yet to hear anyone speak in purely accentual metre.[3] (With, as I'll discuss, the single exception of extemporised rap.)

3 One might think this was also true of syllabics, there being no template in English to distribute all syllables evenly except by impersonating a Dalek. The English ear doesn't count syllables, but s-stressed vowels. However, the very peculiar business of the 10-position loose i.p. line, discussed elsewhere, challenges this. Accentual verse is in a lousier position, since no one can even agree the *number* of s stresses; unlike syllabicity, s stress is not necessarily intrinsic. Nonetheless, *any* arbitrary or random scheme can be prove productive for the poet; stress-count and syllabics are both excellent ways of dragging strange things from the mind. They are not metrical strategies, however, which makes syllabic verse's addiction to weakly disruptive line endings all the more confusing: there is no unusual resistance inherent in, say, a 13+11+6+3-syllable template that justifies lines ending randomly and raggedly in meaningless enjambment and dangling function words. Look, for example, at this stanza from Marianne Moore's 'Virginia Britannia':

> Powhatan as unflattering
> as grateful. Rare Indian, crowned by
> Christopher Newport! The Old Dominion has
> all-green box-sculptured grounds.
> An almost English green surrounds
> them. Care has formed among un-English insect sounds,
> the white wall-rose. As
> thick as Daniel Boone's grape-vine, the stem has wide-spaced great
> blunt alternating ostrich-skin warts that were thorns.
> Care has formed walls of yew
> since Indians knew
> the Fort Old Field and narrow tongue of land that Jamestown was.

> Marianne Moore, *Complete Poems* (London: Penguin, 1994)

The poem remains a good one, and the template clearly helped the composer write it; however – for this reader at least – it succeeds *despite* and not because of its syllabically regular, pastry-cutter-from-hell stanza. ('But I was making the rhymes' is of course no defence.)

Poetry, I believe, is stronger when it arises from speech. All the composer of 'accentual verse' does is count *x* number of strong stresses, chop the line, rewrite it if it chops in a bad place, and then start another one; or they chop the line, count the s stresses, find they are one or two over or under, and rewrite. This is by no means a bad way of imposing a very rough groove – but it is simply not the same as metrical composition, where the template is anterior to the poetic line. Accentual metres cannot fish in the unconscious of the poet for material, as they have no net: with no empty and fixed, evenly spaced pattern, they have no way of magnetising speech to their template. (Reciprocally, the reader can no longer rely on the stress-salience that metre creates as a *semantic* foothold.) If the s stresses are not held apart by even-length placeholders in the cognitive template, there is no overdetermined isochrony to fall in step with, and nothing to sing along to.

Events which are rhythmic are held at a distance from one another by real, not magical forces; and while the brain is good at imposing a series of even temporal units when there is little noise for the louder transients to compete against, it is not a metronome. The confusion introduced to a line by an additional eight, twelve or fifteen contracting, expanding and jostling schwas will soon result in its non-metricality. *Pure* accentual metre in written verse is a method of counting, not of organising stress.

The sole contemporary exception to this is hip-hop, rap and some related kinds of performance poetry, which achieve accentual regularity through similar techniques to Anglo-Saxon verse: quantitative fixing through metronomic performance, and (instead of alliteration) forceful end-rhyme and internal rhyme, often achieved through assonantal exaggeration, dialectal pronunciation and a flexible approach to lexical stress and end-word pronunciation. They make radically *song-strong* interpretations of the metrical template. This is just about the only form of poetry which can be successfully analysed in terms of temporal metrics, since it is almost invariably performed with either a metronomic beat-pattern or, if unaccompanied, to an overdetermined metronomic pulse. It has, in effect, an *absolute* accentual isochronicity, whereas in other poetries – even those written in tight metres – isochrony is always a mere tendency. It has a further subtlety in that, depending on the individual style of the performer or the sub-genre of rap they work within, the entire phrase-unit can be shifted behind or ahead of the beat; this gives the impression of an improvised and conversational delivery that just happens to miraculously coincide with the underlying rhythm. (Behind-the-beat delivery may also be an advantage in 'freestyle' improvised flytings, as it wins an extra fraction of a second to think in.)

Written out, this excerpt from Kanye West's scabrous 'Gold digger' barely looks like it will scan at all:

> Eighteen years, eighteen years
> She got one of your kids got you for eighteen years
> I know somebody paying child support for one of his kids
> His baby momma car and crib is bigger than his
> You'll see him on TV any given Sunday
> Win the Superbowl and drive off in a Hyundai
> She was s'pose to buy ya shorty Tyco with ya money
> She went to the doctor got lipo with ya money
> She walking around looking like Michael with ya money
> Shoulda got that insured, Geico fo' your money[4]

4 This motor-vehicle-obsessed verse goes something like: 'eighteen years, eighteen years / if she has your baby, she owns you for eighteen years / I know somebody who is paying child support for one of his kids / the mother of his child has a car and house that are bigger than his / you'll see him playing professional football on TV on Sundays [*Any Given Sunday* is an Oliver Stone movie about American Football] / [if he] wins the Superbowl, he'll drive off in a cheap little Hyundai car / She was supposed to buy your child toy cars with your money / [but] she went to the doctor and got liposuction with your money / [now] she's walking around looking like Michael Jackson with your money / you should have taken precautions, and got some

– though this is far from the most extreme example I could have chosen from the genre. However, the lines are roped together with brutally effective, forced rhymes, overdetermined via some of the strategies mentioned above (years/kids/his [pronounced 'keeds', 'heez']; Sunday/Hyundai ['Hunday']; and Tyco/lipo/Michael/Geico ['Tie-ko', 'Lie-po', 'My-ko', 'Guy-ko']); then a firm and metronomic template is introjected, nailing the position of the four principal stresses on the first beat of the bar, permitting a very high level of free play with the weak placeholders. In rap, these can be populated with a high number of w-syllables, many of which are forcefully demoted content words – or they can be left empty. These syllables are always musically timed, and can appear not just in duple and triplet groups of quavers and semiquavers but more complex arrangements of tied notes, triplets and dotted notes, or even compound, fractional or additive groups reinforced by sub-stresses (see, for example, the work of Aesop Rock, Angel Haze or Jay Electronica); the performer is always safe in the knowledge that a beat, real or imaginary, is counting out the bars in a way that guarantees the even distribution of the major s stresses. The anacrustic syllables fall into the last bar of the line, in this case giving something like (ignoring a handful of 'pushed beats'):

---

insurance [such as the automobile insurance that Geico provide] with your money.' In the form of a prenuptial agreement, it then transpires. I accept that my rendering may have lost a little of the force of the original.

[EIGHTeen]	[YEARS]	[EIGHTeen]	[YEARS she got]
[ONE of your]	[KIDS got you for]	[EIGHTeen]	[YEARS I know]
[SOMEbody paying]	[CHILD support for]	[ONE of his]	[KIDS His]
[BAby momma]	[CAR and crib is]	[BIGGer than]	[HIS You'll]
[SEE him on]	[Tv]	[ANy given]	[SUNday]
[WIN the Super]	[BOWL and drive]	[OFF in a]	[HYUNdai She was]
[S'PPOSE to buy ya]	[SHORTy]	[TYCo with ya]	[MONey She]
[WENT to the]	[DOCtor got]	[LIpo with ya]	[MONey She]
[WALKing around]	[LOOKing like]	[MICHael with ya]	[MONey Shoulda]
[GOT that ins-]	[URED,]	[GEICo fo' your]	[MONey]

This, one feels, punching the air, is exactly what accentual metre should sound like: poetry dragged back into a musical, rawly temporal rhythmic frame, not noodling around with stresses one can barely hear. (Or at least one does before one starts fretting over its sexual politics, for all it may not be my culture to fret over.) Effectively, rap *is* the argument against the speciousness of current so-called 'accentual' approaches to the verse line, which are really just musclebound syllabics. I can see no other way to achieve a strong-stress metre, other than by similar means of overdetermination. There is, of course, no good reason why 'page poets' could not return to the Anglo-Saxon model[5] – but its rough, war-drum, incantatory music is just not what we do round here these days. Rap, though, provides a song-strong performance model that may have a great deal to teach 'page poets' about re-engaging a general readership.

5 Insofar as we can intuit it. As Attridge wisely points out: 'comparing rap lyrics on the page with actual performances leads to the realisation that Old English verse, for which we only have the words on the page, may never yield up its secrets.' – Derek Attridge, *Poetic Rhythm: An Introduction* (Cambridge: Cambridge University Press, 1995), 94.

PHRASEMIC ANALYSIS

A phraseme is an idiomatic expression or 'set phrase', where at least one word or element is chosen not by the speaker but by conventional usage. They can take the form of idioms and clichés ('a storm in a teacup'; 'it made my blood boil', 'hit the road', 'king of all he surveys'), collocations ('boxing match', 'strong coffee', 'balance sheet', 'dinner date'), pragmatic phrases or pragmatemes ('serving suggestion only', 'best before', 'beware of the dog') and all the varieties that 'received' language can take, from song- and movie-titles to proverbs and quotations.

'Collocation' is the conventional or habitual placing of one specific word with one or more other specific words, one of which is chosen freely and one not. It is a fixed series of words that occur together more often than chance would dictate. Often the convention is to place the 'base' – the 'freely chosen' word – in small caps to distinguish it from the 'collocate' dragged along for the ride: 'legal ADVICE'; 'dinner DATE'. However, either base or collocate can take the major stress, as can be seen from the last two examples, where the stresses are on 'advice' and 'dinner' respectively. We can usually tell when we're really thinking of these as compound words, because the stress will come as far forward as it can; thus 'dinner date' is a compound but 'legal advice' is still being stressed as a qualified noun (unlike the more compound-like 'legal firm').

The closer to a 'set phrase' a phraseme becomes, the more it becomes lexicalised – which is to say stored in the brain as a word, not processed as a phrase along the rule of the syntagm. If it is stored as a word, it can then be accessed along the vertical 'axis of equivalence' and compared with other words; it will have an articulable paraphrase, a 'definition', as well as synonyms or near-synonyms. (In conversation, someone might make quick, context-appropriate choices between various part-synonyms like 'conceived', 'fell pregnant', 'in the family way', 'with child', 'bun in the oven', 'up the stick' and so on, without much thought as to whether they are using a word, idiom, euphemism, dysphemism, cliché or collocation.)

Just as words are memorised along with their prosodies – we learn to say POMegranate, toMAto and TANgerINE – so lexicalised phrasemes have their stresses relatively fixed. It is rare that we have to shake the phraseme from its slumber, process it consciously along the line of the sentence (which is to say drag it from paradigm to syntagm) and give the stock phrase any more than its 'stock emphasis'. Unusual circumstances would be required to justify saying 'It's on the balance *sheet*' (as opposed to the balance report, which you picked up first) or 'they're planning to *start* a family' (to correct your mishearing 'dart a family', or something).

When a collocative phrase becomes phrasemic, its lexicalisation or semi-lexicalisation will means its prosody will not be just fixed but also likely simplified, as it is essentially being processed as something close to a polysyllabic word; as with polysyllables, this tends to mean that in longer phrasemes the principal stress will fall on the last strong syllable that it can.[1] The number of near-w syllables will increase compared with a semantically equivalent but non-phrasemic phrase. In other words, phrasemes are often stressed just like words, with one principal stress.

---

[1] Mark Liberman's word rule applies here, which basically states that the stress will come on the last 'branching' (i.e. followed by a w) strong stress in the word. Thus 'ad*mini*strate', but 'adminis*tra*tion'. Again, note how in a phrasemic context the principal stress will shift to the first position when we perceive it as a compound: compare the mere collocation 'current adminis*tra*tion' versus the compound '*Obama* administration'. – Mark Liberman and Alan Prince, 'On Stress and Linguistic Rhythm', *Linguistic Inquiry* 8 (1977): 249–336.

Although useful lexicographic and morphological distinctions have been made, 'phrasemicity' is a disease of degree, and often difficult to identify. What we might call the 'phrasemic treadmill' starts to drag just about *everything* we say more than three or four times towards somnambulant stock-phrase weakness. The more brain-dead the conversation, the more it consists of the zombified sewing-together of stock phrases, the less stress we will hear – and the more the function of that speech will be purely phatic, i.e. two mammals doing little more than enjoying their empty mutual twitter. The phraseme might be said to run from easily identified idioms and clichés right through to the 'tired phrase'. What it *cannot* be is dismissed as a prosodic phenomenon. As Ray Jackendoff remarks, 'There are too many fixed phrases [. . .] to be "on the margin" of language'; [2] and if the phraseme is a crucial aspect of language, its distinct prosodies should be accounted for in any sensitive poetic scansion.

The more one can assume our words already 'known', the less emphasis they tend to require. We alert our interlocutor to the presence of a phraseme (and anticipate their familiarity with it) by using only one primary stress, and heavily de-accenting any other s stress in the phrase; this in turn saves them energy and processing power, and rather than 'try to understand' the phrase, they will instead hear something relatively lexemic – and incorporate this into their parsing of the larger phrase in which the phraseme occurs, much as they would any other word. This works much in the same way as de-accented content; the speaker will de-emphasise material because they assume it to be well known, either through domain-rule tagged 'already understood information', or because it has already been stated; in the latter case, the repeated words perform a merely anaphoric function, and are treated *as* function, much as they would be if they were replaced by 'it', 'that' or 'do' (For example the word 'function' in that last sentence

2 Ray Jackendoff, *The Architecture of the Language Faculty* (Boston, MA: MIT Press, 1997), 177.

is de-accented, and performed as would be the word 'such', i.e. as a word which merely grunts towards the earlier antecedent.) I believe one should also take prosodic account of this phenomenon, and there is an example of a de-accented anaphora in the Paul Muldoon poem I've scanned at the end of this chapter. Within the phraseme, the de-accented material also acts as a 'psychological anaphora', and performs the listener's assumed familiarity with the phrase.

The phraseme's one salient stress is enough to provide an auditory 'mug handle' by which the whole lexemic phrase can be picked up; the other stresses don't need to flag their existence. Take two content-equivalent statements:

Well – that's the sixty-four thousand dollar question.
/   /   x /, x /,   /, x   /, x /' x

then

Well – that's the fifty-three million pound answer.
/   /   x / x / / x / /   x

The first is a phraseme derived from an American game show from the 1950s, and has become lexicalised; the s-stressed syllables have been intonationally demoted to functional roles, reinforcing the dominance of a single (in this case nuclear) stress; it is, essentially, just a single-entry word which has come to mean 'the crucial, difficult question', 'the big question', 'the mystery', or 'what we need to find out', etc., depending on context. 'Question' has been freely chosen; the other words are just being dragged along for the ride. The second statement is an unfamiliar phrase, and so must be processed along the syntagm, and its words will default to a normal, content-strong/function-weak prosody. However, phrasemes, when identified, should be treated as words; were we to encounter 'the sixty-four thousand dollar question' in a poem we would write its lexical stress *against* the metre as x x x x x x x x / x and derive the prosody accordingly. (If de-accented s stresses are *built in* to the phrase, it's easier to treat them as weak in their lexical prosody.) Perverse as this may seem, this will then give an accurate account of the tensive relationship between the phraseme and the metre.

One serious failing of existing methods of scansion is that none, as far as I can tell, take any account whatsoever of phrasemic or collocative material. Given that so much original poetic effect depends on the clever use and the subversion of 'the already known', this strikes me as a bizarre omission from a scansion with any claim to sensitivity. In a metrical context, phrasemic analysis would not only have to identify the phrasemic material and mark its simplified lexical prosody, it would also have to decide, during the process of the sense-stress analysis, whether it had been regrammaticalised by its new poetic context — in which case we would be obliged to mark the *restoration* of the lost stresses.[3]

The subversion of the phraseme is hardly straightforward, but nor would we want it to be. To return to the Paul Muldoon poem 'Mules', mentioned in Part II (I'll adopt the convention of underlining any phrasemic material):

> We had loosed them into one field.
> I watched Sam Parsons and my quick father
> Tense for the punch <u>below their belts</u>,
> For what was <u>neither one thing or the other</u>.[4]

---

3 All this is another argument for the reader's flawless first-language fluency. Even a slight insensitivity to idiomatic nuance has serious consequences in terms of metrical projection. As soon as the reader hears a phrase they've heard before — even if neither they nor a linguistician would *identify* it as a phraseme — they will unconsciously understress it. But poetry's naturally high s-stress count means all such material is prosodically destabilised and has the potential to be reinvigorated, and consciously forced along the syntagm. Whether it is or is not is entirely dependent upon the sensitivity and sophistication of the reading.

4 Paul Muldoon, *Poems 1968–1998* (London: Faber & Faber, 2001).

You'll recall that I claimed that, guided by the rules of the thematic domain, the phraseme has been reinterpreted, and phrasemic lexicality has been weakened as it becomes *both* cliché and a mere series of words to be processed as a regular phrase. In English, 'below the belt' – meaning 'underhand, illegal' – has become heavily lexicalised, and is stored in that part of the brain that deals with word and 'memorised item', and is capable of paradigmatic substitution. Its status as collocation is often indicated by the presence of a strong primary stress: 'that was a bit below the BELT'. (Whereas in the exchange: 'Where do you want this boxing trophy placed in the display cabinet?' 'Below the belt, please', the second syllable of the word 'below' will take a stronger stress than it would in the phraseme, since it imparts important information. Similarly, 'he bought the farm', meaning 'he died', will often de-accent the s stress on 'bought' and leave the primary lexical stress on 'farm' more exposed, whereas a property developer who 'bought the farm and the surrounding land' will obviously require a full s stress on 'bought', as the phrase is non-phrasemic.) In 'Mules' we are aware of the phrase *both* given a new sense *and* returned to its origin: the literally and physically sickening conception of the sterile mule as a kind of crime against nature, and (in the connecting domain of 'genital activity') its origin in the 'low blow' of boxing, where a punch to the lower abdomen or testicles is reasonably considered bad form. [5]

5 These metonyms are often just the means by which the phraseme itself comes into being; once accepted into general vocabulary, a phrase like 'kicked the bucket' is used in a more or less wholly lexicalised way, with none of the original sense of 'kick the bucket away from under a hanged man's feet' – and likely with no *knowledge* of this origin, any more than one might be aware of the tropic genealogy of any other word. Indeed, these 'origin stories' are now *mere* etymologies; and if a poem reawakens our awareness of them, we see a version of 'etymological pun'. Note that – as convenient as it would be to claim that 'kicked' is radically de-accented as a result of the lexicalised phraseme – it is reduced only to something like the secondary stress of a polysyllabic word, and will therefore be processed by the brain as isolable content to *some* degree, albeit a reduced one; i.e. the metaphor is not wholly disembodied;

The consequences of such recontextualising will force the brain to process the dead trope along the syntagm, and the function word 'below' will – if sensitively performed – likely be restored some of the stronger stress it enjoys in a non-lexicalised phrase such as 'your hat's below the chair'. I say *some* of the stronger stress; to perform it *all* would also fail to acknowledge the phraseme, and would be missing the two-edged point. A 'reawakened phraseme' receives its 'ideal' performance, I would suggest, when the non-principal stresses in the phraseme are regarded as tensive promotable ws, and the principal stress of the phraseme as a marginally *demotable* s, in the form of a tensive intonational de-accent. (To my ear the overwhelmingly strong principal stress of the phraseme often needs pulling back when the same words are used syntagmatically: 'like the back of my hand' in 'I know this town like the back of my hand' is something like xx/,xx/'; whereas in Q: 'Do you recognise this picture?' A: 'It looks like the back of my hand', the phrase is simply xx/xx/.) This keeps both readings alive, and leaves the whole phrase broadly tensive, which would make sense if we regard it as essentially *both* syntagmatic and paradigmatic. Its paradigmatic aspect means it comes with a fixed prosody that functions like a little metrical template, *against* which any new syntagmatic sense will stress.

In a poetic scansion that isn't going to end in tearing one's hair out, we should simply treat the phraseme 'as any other word', and take its w-s pattern as *fixed*, not as tensive *against* any 'normal' syntagmatic reading. That's to say the lexical stress of 'like the back of my hand' would be notated not as xx/,xx/', but as the binary template xxxxx/. Any 'subversions' of the phrase such as those above would emerge when accounting for sense stress.

---

the brain will presumably still enact a light kick, and all is not bucket. In a metrical context the phrase would be scanned like any other polysyllabic word. This means that there are metrical situations where 'kicked' could be effortlessly demoted, such as triple metre: 'so *Dave* hit the *gin* when his *cat* kicked the *buck*et' is no more a stretch than 'so *Dave* hit the *gin* when his *cat* disap*peared*'.

This is a deliberate simplification which underplays secondary
s stresses in the phraseme, which are arguably fixed. Its effect is
to favour a speech-strong scansion and to emphasise and increase
metrical tensions. The reader will note that I use the same barbaric
convention with polysyllabic words too, and scan polysyllabic
words with a single principal stress. My argument is simply that
they are more likely to be performed as such in the flow of speech;
what sounds like a fixed secondary stress in isolated performance
– SECon_dary, say – has the habit of disappearing in conversational
flow (the same applies to phraseme, only slightly less so). The
result is again a deliberate speech-strong bias on my part, with the
corresponding increase in the identification of tensive effect and
'consequently' interpretative latitude. In polysyllabic words, the
ASR will leave some secondary stresses (but now marked as w)
more easily promotable than others – SECon_dary being a case in
point; but to treat secondary stress as a form of *fixed* median stress
introduces hideous notational complexities (one requires a third
type of prosodic symbol below the line), favours the kind of stagey
metre-strong readings that I am keen to avoid, and overstates an
effect whose prosodic merit *is* its instability. The convention one
occasionally encounters of scanning secondary lexical stress as
simply *strong*, on the other hand, leads swiftly to metre-strong
scansions of the most unnatural kind.

Stronger promotions will be seen on newly de-collocated content
words. Let's explore some potential complexities:

So who were we to want to hang back there
In spite of all?
In spite of all, we sailed
Beyond ourselves and over and above

> The rafters aching in our shoulderblades,
> <u>The give and take</u> of branches in our arms.

(SEAMUS HEANEY, 'The Swing')[6]

The first phrase 'in spite of all', through its repetition and duple-metre emphasis, has us correctly wondering if there may be more mileage in it than first appears. It means 'paying no heed to any of it'; but here it is mildly subverted by the omission of the 'it' usually heard in 'in spite of it all', or a grammatical continuation, like 'in spite of all she'd done for them'. This salience gives 'all' in the first phrase the more concrete, anaphoric sense of 'all of that stuff I just mentioned in the previous stanza', but in the subsequent repetition it seems to indicate something more like 'everything'. This is because its repetition restores something of the phraseme to the phrase; for that reason I might be inclined to stress the first phrase x/x/ and, relative to it, the second x /, x /' – the de-accent on the content-word 'spite' denoting both its anaphoric, 'known' quality, and the phrase's now being delivered as a phraseme. (Remember that if we considered this as phraseme *alone*, we would write its lexical stress as xxx/.) In a sense-stress analysis I'd add, too, a contrastive NS accent on the last syllable: the word 'all' carries a great deal more semantic freight than the word 'belt' did in 'Mules'.

The phraseme 'over and above' is often used as a kind of compound preposition meaning 'emphatically beyond', a phrase of pure function, receiving little or light stress (as in 'we must consider the cost of crowd policing <u>over and above</u> normal duties'). Here it is re-presented as entirely literalised and metred, and rises from xxxxx to something like /xxx/ (aided, I suspect, in many readers' minds by the echo of Heaney's own Ulster pronunciation, 'abōve'). Finally, 'give and take' usually just means 'compromise', but again the thematic domain of 'swing-stuff' almost literalises the phrase, and it will rise

---

6 Seamus Heaney, *New Selected Poems 1988–2013* (London: Faber & Faber, 2014).

from its more usual xx/ ('this won't work without a little <u>give and</u> <u>TAKE</u>') to /x/ (or contrastively, x'x/) as the words are driven down the syntagm, and rediscover themselves as content again.

I say *almost* literalises the phrase . . . The point will be understood better after the chapter on scansion, but one might prefer to add a further nuance to 'give and take' and scan it as \x/ to indicate that 'give' is here *tensive* – which is to say unstable, with its stress-performance more open to interpretation: this is because it both *is* *and is not* part of the phraseme. (One might argue that the first stress of 'over' in 'over and above' might be marked the same way for the same reasons, but I hear that phrase as more robustly literal.) Usually tensive marks require the projection of a metrical frame; however the phraseme provides one in miniature, and while it can be subverted by the syntagmatic use of the phrase (i.e. by ignoring the phraseme), it can never be wholly erased. This extra level of lexical/sense-stress interaction would add a pointless and unwieldy notational complexity, though, so sensible ways will be found of simplifying it.

The reinvigoration of these phrases is achieved not only by the thematic domain but also by the high s stress expectations of the poetic line (and if the poem is metrical) by metre itself; this allows s stresses which may have been lost in the phraseme to be more easily revived. This restoration of content is not unusual, and shows again that *metre increases referentiality*. This is one reason poems seem more vividly 'about' the world: their 'contentuality' has been over-determined. When metre restores stress to 'known' dead phrases, the brain reacts with a little shock and delight at the paradox of simultaneous recognition and novelty. Often we will find the phraseme re-grammaticalised by semantic context, and thus capable of receiving a variety of alternative stress-performances according to the new interpreted sense. Sometimes it's the case that the most sympathetic readings simply honour the phraseme:

> <u>I remember it like it was last night,</u>
> Chicago, the back room of Flanagan's
> malignant with accordions and cigarettes . . .[7]
>
> (MICHAEL DONAGHY, 'The Classics')

'I remember it like it was last night' is a near-cliché, semi-lexicalised, and filed on the paradigmatic axis somewhere under 'indelible memory stuff'. As a result the lines' natural lexical stressing of x x/x x x x / / might be delivered more as x x /, x x x x x /, /' – where we lexicalised the whole phrase, with only the *one* intonationally distinguished accent, on 'night'. Some might resist this, 'since it's a poem', and we rarely associate such long runs of near-schwa with poetry; the phrase is weak enough, even as a non-phraseme. However, the sophistication of this rigorously underplayed, speech-strong approach to the performance of the phraseme becomes clearer when – after an anecdote about an Irish accordionist who falls asleep while still playing, and has to be woken up, mid-tune – we reach the final lines:

> What does it matter now? It's ancient history.
> Who can name them? Where lie their bones and armour?

Donaghy's point being that it is from such local, small materials that our unforgettable stories and heroes arise; that Homer 'made the Iliad out of such a local row'.[8] The throwaway-yet-ominous cliché 'I remember it like it was last night' (the speaker later admits he may have just 'heard it told so well / I've staged the whole drunk memory') *must* be 'thrown away' in its phrasemic form for the poem to really work; this way, it can manage the symbolic contrast between the first

---

7 Michael Donaghy, *Collected Poems* (London: Pan Macmillan, 2014).

8 Patrick Kavanagh, 'Epic', *Collected Poems* (London: Allen Lane, 2004); the line one senses may have 'invented Seamus Heaney'.

line's anecdotal chattiness and the final lines' beautiful 'classicising' of the anecdote. (We might scan 'Who can name them? Where lie their bones and armour?' /x /x' | x'/ x / x /x – leaving us with something that feels like *seven* strong stresses.) I would argue that a performative default which *always* attempted to restore content to the phraseme will end by half-destroying the poem. And yet one still occasionally hears the silly assertion that the poem is a place in which 'each word should receive its due weight'. This is only true if we arrive at a more sophisticated understanding of what a 'word' really is.

TOWARDS A DEFINITION
OF POETIC FUNCTION

The following paragraphs can be gaily skipped, as I have not yet managed to formulate this idea in a particularly coherent way, let alone an elegant one. But let me attempt a more careful description of what has happened in the preceding example. What follows is a little more speculative than other aspects of my argument, but I'll lay out the case as carefully as I can.

Through a process of reinterpreting the words along the syntagm, guided additionally by the rules of the thematic domain and reinforced by reader-projected metre, phrasemic lexicality has been weakened. These phrasemes are now *also* mere series of words, which then also have to be processed along the syntagm – as would be the words of any new sentence. However, the weakening of the lexical phraseme has been accomplished by a syntagmatic function *itself* strengthened by a parallel, i.e. paradigmatic effect: rhythm. Metre has therefore increased referentiality and the overall degree of lexicality by restoring discrete content to the component words of the phraseme.

Syntax is, of course, a form of syntagmatic function, but so are the arbitrary rules of the thematic domain. On current evidence the picture seems rather more complex than 'the projection of the principle of equivalence from the axis of selection into the axis of combination'; as I have mentioned repeatedly, I have long suspected the truth is that the poetic function collapses the axes of *both* selection and combination. It is less the operation of one axis being projected into another than an initial destabilising move, one that has serious and complex consequences for both axes. Metre and lineation, while projecting a function of similarity along the syntagm, also enforce the relatively slow delivery of the poetic line. This then forces the reader to *heed* every single stressed content-word; this simultaneously strengthens the syntagm's referentiality and weakens all lexicalised phrasemic content, from the hoariest of clichés to the lightest of collocations; and this in turn shifts our semantic parsing a little away from the phrase-unit and tilts it towards the word-unit, introducing a far higher degree of lexicality than we see in normal speech or prose. In restoring each word to its native part of speech, we then see a *strengthening* of the syntagmatic rule of both sentence-syntax and thematic domain – which we then require to process the new or rediscovered sense.

Then again – 'Speaking of contraries, see how the brook / In that white wave runs counter to itself.' The complexity of their interrelation is brain-melting. The true picture is a whorl: the poetic function, in addition to increasing referentiality in the line, is also doing precisely the opposite. As we move from disagreements between lexical stress and metre toward scansions which incorporate the context-specific accents and de-accents of performed sense, we hit a contradiction. Patterns of emphasis and de-emphasis communicate our under-standing of a line. This semantic stress is context-dependent, and cannot be derived from the rules governing patterns of agreement and tension between metre and 'resting state' prosody of the sort that form most scansions; but even more problematically, sense stress in a *poetic* context can't even be firmly or consensually decided, as poetic sense is only partly paraphrasable.

'Paraphrasability' decreases as the poetic function increases, regardless of its drive toward increased lexicality. Paraphrasability works through a process of 'synonymisation', i.e. 'finding words for other words', and takes place along the axis of selection. This axis – i.e. the list of corresponding items with which a term might be meaningfully exchanged – has, however, been fatally weakened by the presence of a global shift from denotation towards connotation, resulting in unique and *unparaphrasable* terms composed of new and larger word-combinations. These new 'super-words' are bound together by trope, phonestheme and metre (and sometimes diachronic or synchronic effects like etymological pun and intertextuality) effectively to create new, semi-lexicalised instantiations at the level of phrase.

These new 'self-employed' phrasemes are strengthened in both their fixed prosody and *subjective* monosemy by rereading; I suspect what most drives the phrase toward the condition of a near-proverbial phraseme is its sheer poetic memorability. The paradigmatic rule, which provides the parallel effects of metre, connotation and lyric correspondence which blur the discrete, sequential components of the syntagm, is now essentially 'overbonding' words far above and beyond the strength of their mere syntactic connection, to leave 'meaning' running on parallel as well as serial circuitry. Non-paraphrasable sense simply means we see a weakened consensus regarding what a poetic line *means*; as a result the line is open to a variety of legitimate interpretations. A further corollary is that there will now be a variety of ways in which that sense can be performed.

Poetry can be defined as that mode of speech which *fuses* syntagmatic and paradigmatic function. (I sense it works as something like a cross-hemispheric corrective to left-brain distortions of language.) We seem to possess a deep and unconscious understanding that syntagm and paradigm are all there is; poetry seems an attempt to unify them, through a clever involution of the sign-system (one by-product of which is the symbolic function, earlier discussed). Its occasional success probably accounts for poetry's reputation as a transcendent, spiritual or transgressive pursuit.

TWO KINDS OF LINE:
4-STRONG AND IAMBIC PENTAMETER

There are only two kinds of metrical line in English. In their stylistic tendencies they reveal their contrasting origins: the high and low, the 'folk' and the literate, the oral and the written, the Dionysian and the Apollonian, the anonymous and the authored. One is duple in essence or 'spirit'; the other can almost be defined as a deliberate complication of everything that the 4 strong-stress, duple line proposes. In their 'deep template' ur-forms, I'll refer to them as 4-strong, and (with some reluctance) as i.p., in the hope that we may eventually forget that it stands for iambic pentameter — a name which barely tells half its story.

The 4-strong line

For a long time in English poetry, there was little but the 4-strong form, which was pressured naturally into being from isochronic, alternate stress and 'auditory present' constraints, as well as breath capacity (the 'sung strophe' of two 4-strong lines is close to an optimum lungful). The line itself and its 4×4 stanza-form are remarkably robust, and seem able not only to bend syllables to their will, but also to shape a considerable amount of silence into accurately timed ghost metrons. (Trimeter lines are invariably heard as catalectic 4-strong with a ghost metron, but far more radical variations are possible too.) This allows it to take many shapes: the Anglo-Saxon 4-strong alliterative/caesural line; the duple and triple variations of common or ballad metre (where the second line has a ghost for breathing in song); the duple and triple variations of tetrameter or trimeter; the 'standard Habbie' or Burns stanza;[1] the limerick;[2] the light metre 4×4 form that Attridge and others refer to as 'Dolnik' verse;[3] the 'double dactyl';[4] the hemistichic

[1] Three lines of tetrameter, one of dimeter, one of tetrameter, and one of dimeter, rhymed AAABAB; the dimeter lines have two perceptible ghost metrons. (This is straightforwardly verified in almost all musical settings of Burns's stanzas, where a minim rest is placed after the short lines to pad out the bar.)

[2] Two lines of triple trimeter, two hemistichic lines of triple dimeter, one line of triple trimeter, rhymed AABBA.

[3] The Dolnik is a 4×4 Russian metrical form which (it is often claimed) is written to a template that is somewhere between a syllabotonic and an accentual one; its template *includes* the potential to take great latitude with the w stresses populating the weak placeholder positions. In the Dolnik, and in the Western versions of the form variously diagnosed, unmetricality is avoided by keeping the ictic s-syllables *more or less* evenly spaced. Whether it substantially differs in template or character from what we might otherwise call light 4×4 is a matter of debate (in my head, if no other), although its cognitive template seems to have subsumed some of the quantitative regularly and w placeholder flexibility of the song form. Song-strong 4×4 might be an alternative description.

[4] A metrically overdetermined hemistichic comic form, with rules too bananas to explain here. Oh all right:

> /xx/xx (nonsense word, x2)
> /xx/xx (proper name)
> /xx/xx
> /xx/ (rhyme)
>
> /xx/xx
> /xx/xx (six-syllable word)
> /xx/xx
> /xx/ (rhyme)

The second stanza is shaped by my favourite rule in all formal poetry: it must contain one six-syllable word, which can occupy any of the first three lines – but once the word is used, it must *never be spoken again in one's lifetime*. Thus:

> Syltetøj-syltetøj
> J. O. H. Jesperson
> scanned English better than
> Englishmen could;

dimeter line, including the popular contemporary form of the 'accentual' two-step (see for example Heaney's 'Mossbawn: Two Poems in Dedication. I: *Sunlight*'); the caesural hexameter (discussed below); the 'long-common' line of the fourteener.[5] Except for the Anglo-Saxon line, rarely used for anything but literary pastiche, these forms all survive. All, I would maintain, are no more than variations on the same ur-form, the same deep 4-strong template, a series of stresses separated by weak placeholders:

$$-x- \ / \ -x- \ / \ -x- \ / \ -x- \ /$$

While Marina Tarlinskaja[6] and Derek Attridge have both defined it very cleanly, I would still gently question the burning need for the near-strong-stress 'Dolnik' category as a distinct template, and will invite their disagreement by stating that it can still be defined adequately by 'light metre or song-strong 4 × 4'. However, *whatever* we call it, it plainly exists, and in honouring and accounting adequately for its own long tradition across many languages (as one would expect from a form which arises so naturally from the human body), one must take on board that the analytical language we use to describe the light metre form of 4 × 4 remains conceptually distinct from that of i.p. and all other templates influenced by classical metres. The language of

---

> I'd like to think that his
> phonosemantic'lly
> predisposed ears were what
> made him so good.

5 Monometer is a novelty. English duple hexameter which avoids the medial caesura is impractical for a number of reasons, and on those rare occasions where it has been used successfully – by Ciaran Carson, for example – its inbuilt awkwardness has been heavily mitigated by the poet's native virtuosity, and self-conscious nods to the French Alexandrine. Carson himself further cites the influence of the strophes of *Sean-nós* ('old style') traditional Irish singing.

6 Maria Tarlinskaja, 'General and Particular Aspects of Meter: Literatures, Epochs, Poets', in *Phonetics and Phonology*, vol. 1: *Rhythm and Meter*, ed. Paul Kiparsky and Gilbert Youmans (San Diego, CA: Academic Press, 1989), 121–52.

feet, inversion and so on is not merely inappropriate to this form, but irrelevant to it. Its apparent bombproof flexibility strikes me as the inevitable product of timed syllables and elongated vowels, i.e. from its being – cognitively, at least – a sung form. I would concede that this possibly makes light metre 'Dolnik' a distinct subset of the 4×4: its song-template means that the weak placeholders of 4×4 carry an element of overdetermined timing. (In song, only the transient of the stressed vowel is strong; its elongation pushes into weak space, which can lengthen and contract to perfectly accommodate whatever number of weak syllables occupy it, from none to three or four). If we think of a form 'as song' it becomes far more flexible in terms of weak placeholder variation than purely metrical templates.[7]

To develop this point a little further: it's telling that the examples adduced as evidence of the existence of a quasi-accentual template at work behind the 4×4 are often lyrics, and that, when sung, their metronomy – despite their apparently chaotic relation to w-syllable count – is neatly overdetermined by the quantitative nature of song-performance. When the line itself is spoken, it is not only 'unaccompanied' but also *de-quantified*, and in the absence of timed vowel lengths, has to generate its own isochrony. Isochrony, being partly a psychological projection, is elastic – but not infinitely so. In the absence of overdetermining factors (like alliterative salience and hemistichal pause in the Anglo-Saxon line), freedoms are curtailed. The tactus-projecting part of the brain is always working to a template that includes both evenly spaced transient events *and* alternating durational placeholders, and this is our *only* template of metre. Unlike dramatic i.p., there is no 'syllabotonic template', just one 4-strong pattern of which

---

7 I would argue that rhythmically patterned 'song' is the third master template alongside 'metre' and 'speech'; poems are open to *three* forms of reading bias: 'metre-strong' for readings, 'speech-strong' for naturalistic, and 'song-strong' for quantitative. Since 'song-strong' only applies to the 4-strong line, there may be a case for claiming that while i.p. is capable of tight, loose and light interpretations, their analogous forms in 4-strong are really metre-, speech- and song-strong templates.

different interpretations are made, 'Dolnik' or light metre 4×4 being merely one of them. However, one might reasonably argue that Dolnik or light 4×4 is *defined* by the echo of song-like timing, and therefore – while the fixed pitch-series of song is lost – the overdetermined timing of s-position stress (or the compensatory elongation of weak space, which amounts to much the same thing) *persists as a component of the template itself*, rendering it to some extent distinct. (To feel what this sounds like, try reciting a poem that you already know far better as a song. In my case it might be something like Dick Gaughan's version of Burns's 'Westlin' Winds', otherwise known as 'Song Composed in August'. It's almost impossible to recite *without* some imitation of the timed rhythm of its sung form, and one pauses continually, albeit in a semi-naturalised way, for 'the speech to catch up with the beat'; thus the cognitive template in such a spoken performance is really quantitative.) On the other hand, I would rather just claim that both light 4×4 and the sung 4×4 are often composed and performed to the same ur-template – one ur-enough to invoke a time when poetry and song were barely distinguishable arts. This template, for atavistic reasons, seems to have retained an element of what we hear as either quantitative regularity or of metronomy, of either regularly measured weak space or timed s stress counted in elongated vowels, depending on whether we choose to make a poem or a song out of it.

If we stand back, we see a nicely balanced picture: loose and light metres establish conventions of interpreting the weak space freely, but often maintain isochrony through some degree of quantitative performance; tight metres maintain isochrony by overdetermining it rigidly through syllable count, a quantitative 'fix' that means a freer approach to actual *performance* becomes possible. Our two types of line demonstrate opposing tendencies: 4-strong pulls towards the loose and light; i.p. towards the tight. (While, broadly speaking, tight and light metres are points at either end of a continuum, and distinctions of degree, i.p. and light 4×4, on the other hand, may be reasonably thought of as forming very distinct cognitive templates.)

The 4-strong line works at three unit levels, all of which seem to exert an equally deep and primitive hold on the mind: the mono-stichic form of the 4-strong line; the distichic 'sung lungful' that partly influences the strophe of the ballad or common metre line (and arguably all light 4 × 4 forms); and the many forms of the 4 × 4 stanza. All proceed naturally and inevitably from hierarchical units of AS. [x/] is soon [x/x/] , then [x/x/x/], then [x/x/x/] [x/x/x/], then [x/x/x/] [x/x/x/] [x/x/x/] [x/x/x/]. The forms are so robust, so deeply embedded in the communal ear, that they can survive a truly remarkable degree of variation in their realised form. In its light and song-strong forms, variation in the w-placeholders can be almost chaotic, and certainly flip cheerfully between duple and triple metres (paeonic triple-weaks also appear, depending on how the line is performed – as well as mora substitutes for no syllable at all); ghost metrons can be substituted for unspoken strongs, with the 4-strong line happily reverting to a 3 + ghost or 2 + double ghost line. Here's what I'd think of a typical example of song-strong 4 × 4 in recent English verse:

<pre>
    /   x   /   -x-   /   x   [/]
Who's that knocking on the window,
    /   x   /   -x-   /   [x /]
Who's that standing at the door,
   / x   /   x   / x   [/]
What are all those presents
    /   -x-   /   x   /   [x /]
Laying on the kitchen floor?

    / -x-   / x   /   x   [/]
Who is the smiling stranger
   x   / x   / x   /   [x /]
With hair as white as gin,
    / -x-   /   -x -   /   x   [/]
What is he doing with the children
</pre>

x　　　 / 　-x-　 / 　x 　/ 　 [x /]
And who could have let him in?

(CHARLES CAUSLEY, 'Innocent's Song')[8]

(In 'Who is the smiling stranger', 'who' might well be elongated to 'whooo', because a paeonic feel – /xxx /xxx etc. – has by then been well enough established to overdetermine the metre, and the vowel must take up the space of a missing weak – at least in a song-like performance.) Here, the triple weak substitutions can easily flip to weak-strong-weak (according to the 3-stress rule, later explained):

/ 　x 　/ 　x　 / 　x　 / 　x
Who's that knocking on the window,
/ 　x 　/ 　x　 / 　x　 /
Who's that standing at the door,

– and indeed you may have immediately defaulted to *this* reading, as I did to mine; but light 4 × 4 will often offer the scope for radically different performances, all of which can maintain the metronomic distribution of the 4 s stresses. Some readers will even make a 'double-time' performance with little effort, 'grunting in' morae between strongs:

/ : /: / 　x　 /　　 x
Who's that knocking on the
/ : / 　 [x / x /]
window,

Though one could conceive of any number of extreme yet still-just-about-viable 4 × 4 variants:

x ⁷ x 　/ 　x 　/ 　 [x /]
The King of France is bald

8　Charles Causley, *Collected Poems* (London: Picador, 2000).

x / x /   [x / x/]
Or so it's said;
    -x-   /   -x- /   -x-   / -x-   /
Though I'd rather we talked about absolutely anything else
x /   [x / x / x /]
Instead.

(See, too, the 'Clerihew', whose humour depends upon stretching the 4×4 to breaking point.) Note that we tend to take a freer approach to the omission of s stress count in the alternate lines 2 and 4 in the 4×4 template, hinting strongly that the bulk of the responsibility for maintaining even timing through 'silent counting' falls at the end of a *distichic*, 8-strong frame. However, we might be better to intuit from this a more general rule that more omission and variation is permitted in weaker AS lines than stronger (i.e. the *second* unit of any binary pair) across the whole form – because as soon as *anything* takes a relatively weak position, in a cognitive sense *it also takes up some degree of placeholding function*. If this is true, it would represent a very deep and almost wholly unconscious aspect of the template. The ballad form is, of course, the most obvious example of this kind of variation, and its short second and fourth lines may be justified by more than just human lung capacity. If we look at the 4-strong strophic matrix (marking the dominant couplet +, and the hierarchy of the lines A, B, C and D)

+A 16 8 12 4
 C 14 6 10 2
- B 15 7 11 3
 D 13 5 9 1

I have a strong feeling that the second couplet can generally stand (and will have been historically subjected to) more variation than the first –

```
 x   /   x   /   x   /
```
The grand old Duke of York
```
 x  /  x   /  x    /      [x /]
```
He had ten thousand men
```
 x   /      x  /  -x-  /   -x-   /
```
He marched them up to the top of the hill
```
-x-  /        x   /   x  /    [x /]
```
And he marched them down again

— as do lines C and D relative to lines A and B here. (In most musical performances of ballad form, the first two lines are often melodically either identical or very similar, and the third line will often introduce a radical variation or an entirely new melodic line, with the fourth line resolving its tension; I hear this model frequently echoed in our default patterns of metrical variation.) S-stress omissions affect only overall line length, but only the second lines of distichs will generally accommodate the loss of more than one stress (trimeter substitutions for any 4-strong line are common enough, though far more so in the alternate lines — and it's very rare to see them in the strong first or third lines and not in the weaker second and fourth too).

Thus (tidying Dickinson's verse a little for the sake of clarity):

A The brain is deeper than the sea,
       16   8   12   4

C For hold them, blue to blue,
      14   6   10   [2]

B The one the other will absorb
      15   7   11   3

D As sponges buckets do.
      13   5   9   [1]

Let's make some radical variation in the weaker alternate lines:

A The brain is deeper than the sea,
      16   8   12   4

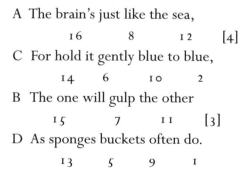

C For hold them up —

14   6   [10]   [2]

B The one the other will absorb

15   7   11   3

D As sponges buckets do, or cups.

13   5   9   1

This is just about tolerable. However, if we do the same in the strong A and B lines:

A The brain is like the sea,

16   8   12   [4]

C For hold them, blue to blue,

14   6   10   [2]

B Both will gulp

15   7   [11]   [3]

D As sponges buckets do.

13   5   9   [1]

In the context of the ballad-form, that variation on the first line will seem grimly amateurish, and the third a disaster. Trimeter quatrains are, of course, perfectly good 4 × 4 forms, but if we flip the 4 / 3 / 4 / 3 of common metre:

A The brain's just like the sea,

16   8   12   [4]

C For hold it gently blue to blue,

14   6   10   2

B The one will gulp the other

15   7   11   [3]

D As sponges buckets often do.

13   5   9   1

it 'sounds all wrong'.

Turning to w stress additions and omissions:

A The brain is deeper than the sea,
    16   8   · 12   4

C For hold blue to blue,
    14   6   10   [2]

B The one the other will absorb
    15   7   11   3

D As sponges some buckets will do.
    13   5   9   [1]

The w stress omission in line C between 'hold' and 'blue' can be accommodated with a mora (and even more easily with a comma); the move into triple metre in the final line is also a breeze, as its 'timed' nature allows 4×4 very free play between duple and triple. However, if we attempt the same trick on the strong A and B lines:

A The brain is deep. Take the sea:
    16   8   12   4

C Now hold them, blue to blue,
    14   6   10   [2]

B The bigger the smaller one will absorb
    15   7   11 3

D As sponges buckets do.
    13   5   9   [1]

The first line is now plain awkward; the third is, to my mind, slightly less acceptable than the corresponding variation just seen in line D, though the effect is mitigated by the second couplet being weak relative to the first and therefore able to access some 'placeholder-style' freedoms, as well as the third-line variations of sung tradition.

As for the smooth accommodation of variations *within* the 4-strong line: for now it can be simply stated that medial variations are more difficult to perform than initial or terminal, and that weaker dimetronic positions – i.e. the second half of the 4-strong line – appear to accommodate variation more easily than the strong first.

Time and space prevent me from making a deeper study of this 'scalable weak' phenomenon, but I strongly suspect it obtains at higher AS levels too. Taking the strongly distrophic 'King Henry' (Child ballad 32), we see strong triple variations in the seventh and eighth lines in almost every double stanza, e.g.:

> More meat, more meat, you King Henry, / more meat you
>   give to me!
> Oh you must kill your good greyhounds, / and bring some
>   meat to me!
> And he has slain his good greyhounds, / it made his heart full
>   sore
> *For she's eaten them up, both skin and bone, / left nothing but hide*
>   *and hair!*

To return to the robustness of the 4×4 form: one might even think of situations where both (hemistichic) dimeter and tetrameter templates can be projected into the same line:

/   x x / x   x

Storm'd at with shot and shell,

/ x x / x   x

Boldly they rode and well,

/ x x / x x

Into the jaws of Death,

/ x x /   x x

Into the mouth of Hell

/   x x / x

Rode the six hundred.

Or

<pre>
        /   x x   / x   /   [x /]
        Storm'd at with shot and shell,
          / x x /   x   /   [x /]
        Boldly they rode and well,
        / x x /   x   /   [x /]
        Into the jaws of Death,
        / x x   /   x /   [x /]
        Into the mouth of Hell
          /   x x /   x   [x / x /]
        Rode the six hundred.
</pre>

A song-template where the morae are performed as vowel-elongations might even produce the fully realised 4-strong line:

<pre>
        / x   / x   / x   /
        Sto[:]rm'd at with shot and shell,
          / x / x / x   /
        Bo[:]ldly they rode and well,
        / x /   x /   x   /
        In[:]to the jaws of Death,
        / x /   x /   x /
        In[:]to the mouth of Hell
          /   x / x /   x /
        Rode the six [:] hund[:]red.
</pre>

As an example of the tenacity, adaptability and pervasiveness of the 4-strong template, look at the so-called 'English hexameter' (a hexameter with a triple-metre feel) favoured by Arthur Hugh Clough. Despite its *apparent* similarity to i.p. – the final ghost metron being merely infilled with content – in reality, it behaves very differently. It is often far closer to a 3-stress line with a silent beat at a medial caesura and a ghost metron in the hiatus — which is to say it behaves much like two 4-strong lines, and is really metrically cognate with the fourteener. In the following passage, ask yourself if it's more natural to pause after the third line than to enjamb it; given the line is even-numbered in its stresses, we would expect no pause — and yet a silent 'seventh' beat is, to me at least, palpably felt. If this is so, a medial beat after the first three stresses is also necessary — but easy to place, as we often find phrase-boundary coincidence:

Rome disappoints me still; [/] but I shrink and adapt myself to it. [/]
Somehow a tyrannous sense [/] of a superincumbent oppression [/]
Still, wherever I go, [/] accompanies ever, and makes me [/]
Feel like a tree (shall I say?) [/] buried under a ruin of brickwork. [/]

(ARTHUR HUGH CLOUGH, 'Amour d'voyage')[9]

(The demotion of 'buried' to xx would be very difficult without the medial ghost, which allows it to be performed anacrustically.)

Often the caesura aids this division:

Sea-fogs pitched their tents,   and mists from the mighty Atlantic
Looked on the happy valley,   but ne'er from their station descended.
There, in the midst of its farms,   reposed the Acadian village.
Strongly built were the houses,   with frames of oak and of chestnut,

(HENRY WADSWORTH LONGFELLOW, 'Evangeline')[10]

Though often it's present only through phrase boundary, here in the same poem:

9 Arthur Hugh Clough, *Arthur Hugh Clough*, ed. John Beer (London: Orion Books, 1998).
10 Henry Wadsworth Longfellow, *Evangeline and Other Poems* (New York: Dover Publications, 1995).

And of the white Létiche,	the ghost of a child who unchristened
Died, and was doomed to haunt	unseen the chambers of children;
And how on Christmas eve	the oxen talked in the stable,
And how the fever was cured	by a spider shut up in a nutshell,
And of the marvellous powers	of four-leaved clover and horseshoes . . .

— and after a while starts to sounds like an elongated Anglo-Saxon metre. Either way, a 'strong mora' will often instinctively be performed mid-line to preserve the 3-stress hemistich, and hint at the underlying 4-strong template.

Iambic pentameter

'Iambic pentameter' remains a very poor term for the 5-metron duple/10-position line, but it has the merit of being widely known and understood (or at least tolerably misunderstood) so I'll persist with it here, and continue to use 'i.p.' as a shorthand. Deeper differences exist between the tight, loose and light metres in i.p. than do between these metres in 4-strong; in i.p. they really constitute alternative templates. They remain, nonetheless, points on a scale, and there exist confusingly intermediate forms. Tight i.p. is a syllabotonic metre which permits relatively little variation in syllable count, though in its more sophisticated dramatic forms it is influenced by the fixed 10-position syllabic template; loose i.p. is a hybrid template which contains both an AS syllabotonic and the 10-position template, and also sanctions a fair degree of variation within the w-placeholders; light i.p. is a kind of 5-strong, which shows immense variation in the w-positions — but since it does not propose the hierarchical AS structures of its 4-strong cousin, can rapidly degrade into vaguely accentual speech rhythm, and is often recognised as i.p. only in the mind of the composing poet, i.e. it is not easily perceptible as such. There are also two distinct modes of i.p. performance, the lyric and the dramatic; these modes radically influence the metrical template itself.

I.p. is sophisticated, unstable, tensive and endlessly expressive *because* it can host a number of different templates; it can also switch between them (and indeed superimpose several of them) with ease. The picture I will describe does not show the clean division of metre-types some might prefer; however, the beautiful complexity of the templates that emerge reveals a neutral form that, while it has no intrinsic rhythmic character, is capable of hosting a myriad of different rhythms through introjection and projection.

To jauntily summarise a complicated tale: for a long time, variants of the AS, 4-strong oral line, the line of singing and of public recitation, ruled the roost. Then Chaucer returned from Italy with something new: a 5-metron, syllabically fixed line derived from Petrarch's hen-decasyllable. This was and remains largely unsingable,[11] but it was a line perfectly suited to 'art poetry' written by individual poets, often consciously striving for literary originality; this was poetry composed for the consumption of an educated, literate readership (as distinct from that inclusive 4-strong cohort which contained both audience *and* performer, and who often used poetry for the more primitive purposes of mnemonic and mere entertainment; common metre was also 'held in common'). I.p. is a longer line capable of a flexible caesura, and ideally built to accommodate the longer, hypotactic phrasal structures of personal expression, whether in argumentative or dramatic forms; by contrast, 4-strong is ideal for serial, paratactic

---

11 When attempted *consciously*; however I believe an 8-strong line lurks within it, and is revealed in lyric (or indeed elegiac) delivery, but we'll get to that in due course. For some reason composers remain immune to this easy solution, and will usually set i.p. by more roundabout or perverse means. Among the more impressive recent attempts are those by Rufus Wainwright: *All Days Are Nights: Songs for Lulu* (2010) has several enjoyable settings of Shakespeare's *Sonnets*. However, here the metrical problem is less resolved than simply magicked away by some unabashed quantitative mangling, with the i.p length either wrestled down to a good old 4-strong template with the kind of reckless freedom only singers enjoy, or overdetermined by a wholly alien frame (a ternary one, in the case of Sonnet 43).

narrative, and for songs and anonymous ballads. The popularity of i.p. was culturally symptomatic of a move from oral, sung, anonymous and communally held verse of an illiterate community to the written, spoken, authored expression of a literate elite. (Since both lines nonetheless tend to converge on the three-second wavelength, i.p.'s higher syllable count implies a slightly more rapid delivery, suited more to speech than to song or 'intoned' recitation.) It has, however, never bedded down in the popular consciousness, and is never written 'naively'. Only poets work in it, and that may indeed be the point: i.p. is not only i.p. – it is, emphatically and definitively, *not* 4-strong. (You will never find that any 'uncouth rhymes' in the obituary column of a local newspaper written in i.p.) The dramatic i.p. line has a speech-strong prosody where 4-strong tends to have a metre-strong, or song-strong.

Before we attempt an accurate description of the i.p. template, let's look briefly at some 'different ways of hearing it'. One can encounter a number of alternative descriptions of its distinct rhythmic character, and all can seem plausible, if perhaps not equally obvious. The most widely used is the 5-metron, strictly w-s alternating *duhDAH-duhDAH-duhDAH-duhDAH-duhDAH* template; and because the number of s stresses is odd, we tend to insert a ghost metron between lines in order to maintain AS. (The falling AS matrical pattern 6-3-5-2-4-[1] means that the final realised s stress sits at 4, and is relatively high in pitch, handily and seamlessly coinciding with the usual position of the nuclear stress in a typical phrase; this is one reason it's marvellously suited to dramatic verse.)

duhDAH-duhDAH-duhDAH-duhDAH-duhDAH might be how we teach those encountering it for the first time, but any poet who has worked extensively in the line will tell you there's a great deal more going on. For example: the i.p. line can also be heard as a triple dimetronic, with its end catalectically shorn, like the ballad line with its silent final beat. However, the fact that it can often be felt as heavily in three as five –

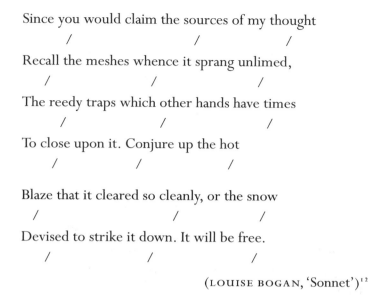

Since you would claim the sources of my thought
    /   /   /
Recall the meshes whence it sprang unlimed,
    /   /   /
The reedy traps which other hands have times
    /   /   /
To close upon it. Conjure up the hot
    /   /   /

Blaze that it cleared so cleanly, or the snow
  /   /   /
Devised to strike it down. It will be free.
  /   /   /

(LOUISE BOGAN, 'Sonnet')[12]

— is really just a product of alternate stress within the 5-metron sequence. Although one might say i.p. has a ghost metron in the sixth position (this is highly moot, for reasons we will explore), to describe the line as a 'permanently catalectic hexameter' is definitely missing the point. One might sensibly choose to sing this dimetronic line as a slow 3/4; another obvious solution for composers attempting to set i.p. would be to treat it as kind of a very slow waltz-time ballad, each syllable a semiquaver in length, with a quaver rest at the end of the bar — or as 12/8, in a similar fashion.[13]

Possibly one might also try singing it as a trimeter *ballad*, i.e. a double trimeter line with a silent foot and a silent dimetron, bring it up to a slow 4:

12 Louise Bogan, *Body of This Death* (New York: R. M. McBride, 1923).
13 This is roughly the idea proposed in Nicholson Baker's highly amusing *The Anthologist* (New York: Simon & Schuster, 2009), though the theory is not as original as the author hoped.

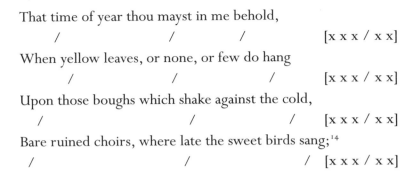

That time of year thou mayst in me behold,
/   /   /   [x x x / x x]

When yellow leaves, or none, or few do hang
/   /   /   [x x x / x x]

Upon those boughs which shake against the cold,
/   /   /   [x x x / x x]

Bare ruined choirs, where late the sweet birds sang;[14]
/   /   /   [x x x / x x]

Where here the base foot (x/xx) is the second paeon, which is prob-
ably never a good thing. Note that the long hiatus is by no means
wholly unnatural in the context of a 'stately delivery'; an alternative
explanation for this will follow soon.

But the truth is that lines can suffer all sorts of metrical reframings,
and the waltz-time and 'trimeter ballad' templates are really pure
projection: there is little introjection, and poets do not generally
compose i.p. to this template or anything like it. Besides, as soon as
we see a more varied or sophisticated use of the caesura, the triple
effect is quickly lost. (Projecting it into, say, any of Barrett Browning's
Sonnets from the Portuguese would prove very difficult.)

The 'triple dimetronic' approach seems hard to sustain in all but
the tightest metres, and while it might sometimes sound close to a
prosodic reality, it is probably never a compositional one.[15]

---

14 Katherine Duncan Jones (ed.), *Shakespeare's Sonnets* (London: Arden Shakespeare,
1997), 257.

15 There is perhaps more mileage in considering i.p. as *both* as a 5-strong metronic
and 3-strong dimetronic in a duck-rabbit way; but for the 3-strong dimetronic line
to have some compositional value it would have to prove itself capable of variation.
A dimetronic analysis might explain such head-scratching phenomena as the relatively
common xx//-for-x/x/ variation (often seen in 4-strong metres too), something
which cannot be satisfactorily explained in terms of metronic variation, and which
will be discussed shortly; but perhaps if, at some level, we hear x/x/ as a *unit*, we
might also hear xx// or //xx as a permissible variation. The proposition would,
however, be falsified if we heard xx// for x/x/ as a legitimate variation *across*

In loose i.p., this dimetronic effect disappears entirely:

> I prithee, let me bring thee where crabs grow;
> And I with my long nails will dig thee pignuts;
> Show thee a jay's nest and instruct thee how
> To snare the nimble marmoset; I'll bring thee
> To clustering filberts and sometimes I'll get thee
> Young scamels from the rock. Wilt thou go with me?[16]

— not least because when i.p. moves into its loose dramatic mode, another frame dominates, that of the 10-position line.[17]

Generally speaking, we are correct to assume that anglophone poets compose to short, fixed-length templates of weak placeholders and strong events. However, at its most virtuosic and in its most expressive loose form, i.p. challenges and modifies this model of cognitive introjection. It is clear that many poets hear the dramatic i.p. line simultaneously as *both* 5-metron and 10-position. 'Simultaneously' is a crucial condition: the 10-position template does not *replace* the alternating pattern of w-s stress, but imposes a kind of decimal mitigation, which evens out the differences between

---

dimetronic boundaries. However, this variant is just as smooth or disruptive whether it crosses boundaries or not; the dimetronic boundary is likely just as illusory as the foot-boundary. xx//, incidentally, has been advanced by Robert Wallace (1997) as a legitimate foot called a 'double-iamb', which would get us round having to use the pyrrhic foot at all. There isn't space to explain the many ways in which this is wrong-headed, so for now I'll confine myself to observing again that 'feet are not a thing'.
16 Richard Proudfoot, Ann Thompson and David Scott Kastan (eds), *The Arden Shakespeare: Complete Works* (London: Arden Shakespeare, 2001), 1084.
17 Describing the frame in these terms is something I have resisted for years; but it now seems to me the only way to explain certain effects I was accounting for by increasingly perverse means. I have Derek Attridge to thank for the change of heart, especially a few remarks made in personal correspondence. What follows does not wholly align with Attridge's position, however, and should certainly not be confused with it.

the placeholders and event-markers in the line so that *all* can be consciously perceptible. (I strongly suspect the 10-position line may be close to the limit of how many undifferentiated syllable-slots on can synchronously hold in one's head *as* a template, much as it is hard for the eye (or at least the 'visuospatial sketchpad') to immediately perceive more than eight or nine balls on a pool table in a single glance.) This creates a finite event-series perceptible not only as a single but also as *monadic* — rather than propositional of further lines, in the way the AS momentum of the 4-strong line invariably is; by contrast, we are rarely surprised when the i.p. stops. *4-strong is a rhythm; i.p. is a Gestalt.* For this reason the ghost metron, when the line is dominated by the 10-position template, cannot really be said to be 'counted' at all; it is an indeterminate pause, and is elided, counted or stretched entirely according to local exigencies. (I feel its indeterminacy is also produced through the line being awkwardly pulled between a 5-metron, 10-position measure and an 8-strong one of 5 s stresses and a 3-metron hiatus, on which I'll have more to say in due course.)

A second component of the dramatic i.p. template is that it is negatively defined. It is self-consciously *not* 4-strong, i.e. it exists in careful contradistinction to the 4-strong line and will actively resist any confusion with it. In its dramatic mode it is actively '*anti-song*', a speech-strong line to be spoken, as distinct from a metre-strong line to be sung. Indeed, I would be inclined to go further: when i.p. approaches the essence of its 'loose' form, with the addition of the 10-position template to the 5-metron one (i.e. *dit-dit-dit-dit-dit-dit-dit-dit-dit-dit* + duhDAH-duhDAH-duhDAH-duhDAH-duhDAH), things change more critically. In terms of how the brain treats the two kinds of line-template, I suspect the difference is close to that between our two means of data-delivery, the analogue and the digital. I will spare the reader any extended analogy, except to observe that it is my impression that the 4×4 sung form has a tendency to convey its emotion directly, through the medium of elongated vowel (and all the gradations and variety of feeling that vowel can physically convey); whereas dramatic i.p. tends to operate more indirectly, with language which is first understood and then *interpreted* as tokens of the feeling it represents. I will not overstate this effect, nor suggest that it is anything more pronounced *than* a tendency, but I detect a distinct difference of mode as well as of form. The smoothly gradated highs and lows of stress-strength and -weakness in 4-strong follow those of the sine wave; the on-off, datum/null pattern of the 10-position line is closer to that of a square-wave, binary system. Finally, the first is in more danger of being corrupted by the noise of its transmissionary medium, and by the highly performance-dependent nature of its own signal, whereas the second, being as much written as spoken — almost experienced from a graphocentric perspective, as speech which is 'written into the air' — is broadly incorruptible and noise-resistant.[18]

Note that, as the more deeply planted and robust template, 4-strong can cheerfully alternate between duple- and triple-metre forms, both *between* lines, and *within* lines. In terms of syllable count, content and syntax, the 4-strong triple-metre line is broadly equivalent to i.p., and in composition tends to raise closely comparable issues — note, for example, the smoothness with which a poet like Sean O'Brien shifts between them (I have underlined the duple metre in the following passage):

Home to dead docks and the vandalised showhouse.
Home for Mischief Night and Hallowe'en, their little tales,

---

18   I'm sure it's just an odd and pleasing coincidence, since the phenomenon is not interlingual, but 4-strong is very much the atavistic line of the four limbs, of dance, of physical performance, of the body of the human animal, whereas i.p. is indeed digital, and counted on the eight fingers and two opposable thumbs that got us into this fine mess in the first place.

When the benches (the sodden repose of old bastards in dog-
    smelling overcoats)
Vanish, when council employees dragged from the pub
Will be dragging the lake in the park,
Watching their footprints fill up
<u>And hating those whose bastard lives</u>
<u>Are bastard lived indoors.</u>

(SEAN O'BRIEN, 'After Laforgue')[19]

However, while i.p. occasionally suggests triple metre, it very rarely sustains it, most probably as it makes the line too long and unwieldy, e.g.

. . . to clustering filberts and maybe I'll get thee young scamels from under the rock; wilt thou go with me sometime tonight?

seems to push it into Gilbert and Sullivan patter-song territory, and the world of metrical novelty. The line's strict syllabotonic nature seems to be part of its template.

To repeat an earlier caution: no single instantiation points to the presence of a metre. To address one form of 'rookie error', the kind of i.p. we might identify in the comic song –

<blockquote>
There's a fascination frantic
In a ruin that's romantic;
-x-   /   x / x / x   / x   /
Do you think you are sufficiently decayed?
</blockquote>

(GILBERT AND SULLIVAN, The Mikado)[20]

---

19 Sean O'Brien, HMS Glasshouse (Oxford: Oxford University Press, 1992).
20 Ian Bradley (ed.), The Complete Annotated Gilbert and Sullivan (Oxford: Oxford University Press, 2001), 646.

— is a bad misdiagnosis, in this case due to an inaccurately projected frame encouraged by some highly misleading lineation. The form here is our bomb-proof 4 × 4 —

<pre>
        -x-   / x / x   / x   [/ x]
   There's a fascination frantic | In a
   / x   /   x / x   [/   x]
   ruin that's romantic; | Do you
      /   x- /   x / x   /
   think you are sufficiently
   x /   [x / x / x /]
   decayed?
</pre>

— as can be heard clearly from its musical setting. Thus the last line is really the last *two* lines of the 4 × 4 template. However, I am convinced that in certain circumstances the 4-strong line *can* imprint itself into i.p. in much the way W. S. Gilbert succeeds in doing in the above example.[21]

Before we turn to look at the two modes of i.p., I'd like to clarify a point. I mentioned earlier that there exists some disagreement as to whether we should call neutrally performed syllables 'weak stresses' or 'unstressed syllables', given that the terms have very different implications. I prefer to call them 'weak stresses'. This decision has some serious corollaries (which will ultimately illuminate key differences between tight, loose and light pentameter). Firstly, under the superimposition of the 10-position template, 'weak stresses' are more easily raised then evened out. By contrast, 'unstressed syllables' would have to gain the quality *of* stress before they could operate within a 10-position template, and this seems incorrect.

---

21   The definitive critique of patter-song remains Peter Griffin's infamous performance of 'The Major-General's Song' in the US TV comedy *Family Guy*.

Secondly, there is an honourable semantic objection to 'weak stresses', which I nonetheless reject: while 'unstressed syllable' implies (correctly) that a series will be heard as an undifferentiated stream, 'weak *stress*' might seem to propose that there might exist, contra-distinctively, some even weaker *non*-stress, producing between w and non-stress not a neutral isochronic stream — but *a weak syllabic rhythm* (against which the superimposition of a further alternating *strong* syllabic pattern would produce the metrical template). However, for this to *be* a rhythm, it would have to be intuitively countable, i.e. demonstrate some perceptible alternation, constituted by the contrastively weaker space between each weak syllable. However, this null interstitial simply passes too quickly to be felt, and, such as it exists at all, falls well below the limen of conscious processing. So I say 'weak stress' in contrast to 'strong stress' in the context of an alternating rhythmic flow, but *not* to additionally propose an under-lying weak-stress rhythm. Once again: (a) the flow of isochronic pulse *is not rhythm*, and therefore not countable, even when repeated in evenly divided units; (b) isochronic pulse is reflected in the flow of syllables; (c) stress is merely a neutral property of all syllables. Even while we may indeed consider the cognitive template of the i.p. line a 10-position one, and compose within that metrical 'conceit' — this does *not* imply that there exists a countable, weaker 10-stress rhythm on which an alternate 5-strong stress pattern flows; the ten positions are not counted out, but merely an auditory-present-sized, snipped and trimmed section of our endless isochronic flow, which we can learn to apprehend *as* an indivisible chunk. Our 5-metron AS then rides upon it, as a ripple on a small pond.

THE DRAMATIC AND LYRIC MODES OF I.P.

I have, to this point, been discussing i.p. in its dramatic mode — one which most poets and readers will inhabit by default; the qualification 'dramatic' may even seem redundant. What follows is an attempt to show that the 5-metron i.p. line is capable of sustaining *two* different metrical templates, which are themselves aspects of two modes of performance, namely the dramatic and the lyric. (For any lay readers still with me: I should make it clear that my remarks on the alternative template of lyric i.p. are resolutely non-mainstream.)

Dramatic i.p. and the 10-position line

Dramatic loose i.p. is the 'virtuosic' poetic line par excellence (its template is still best intuited in the late work of Shakespeare, and perhaps most effectively contrasted with the tight i.p. of his earliest work). Its sophistications arise from the simultaneous management of two superimposed templates, the 10-position and the 5-metron, which between them allow for far greater prosodic complexity than other single templates. While this is partly predicated on their being realised by a sophisticated reader, the 10-position template is primarily *introjected*, which is to say it is a conscious compositional technique that produces different kinds of statement than would AS alone; it is therefore a line whose effects need not *depend* on 10-position projection in order to be felt (indeed, excessive projection would be counterproductive). The poet in English who employs the 10-position template must deal with an underlying and non-negotiable AS. The 10-position, semi-syllabic 'feel' is maintained through the partial conversion of weaker to stronger stresses and stronger to weaker, i.e. of duration-positions to event-positions, and (to a lesser degree) event-positions to duration-positions. While weak durational positions rise *towards* the status of timed syllabic event, it remains an inferior one, one which still easily allows for perceptible AS when the syllable is realised. Despite its name, the 10-position line need not wholly overdetermine the syllable count, and a modest degree of variation in the number of w stresses found in the weak placeholders is common. Mostly, however, its variations come from the fact that its frame makes the demotion of every strong syllable and the promotion of every weak syllable far easier than would a purely AS template; 10-position actively *proposes* expressive variation in the line.

It is my impression that since the 10-position line affords the poet the latitude to strengthen w *or* weaken s, their dramatic and self-dramatising tendencies are easily indulged: the weak invariably rises more than the strong falls, which is to say there is a *net increase* of event-presence and stress-strength overall, and a concomitant increase in content, vowel length, line length, pitch, declamatory tone and overall drama. An active poet–reader collusion will therefore help sustain it, though *what* is projected by the sympathetic reader is less a template and more a mode of performance. (In theory, the line could just as easily accommodate *understatement*, through the consistent demotion of content to function – but such an inclination tends not to be very common within the poetic community.)

The loose i.p. line is delicately balanced. While 10-position actively requires a process of compositional introjection, the frequent presence of an inflexibly projected, 5-metron AS template (e.g. its delivery by a tone-deaf actor) means the 10-position effect – if not actively embedded in the language itself – can be lost, and the line can flip to tight, rum-te-tum syllabotonic i.p., incapable of supporting the kind of variation the sophisticated 10-position line proposes: think of the surely superior 'WAS it the PROUD FULL SAIL of HIS GREAT VERSE' versus the lame 'Was IT the PROUD full SAIL of

HIS great VERSE'. The 10-position line demands either a readership sophisticated enough to allow for this new freedom in the 5-metron line or, failing that, one so ignorant of the 5-metron line that they simply treat it as chopped speech (rather ironically, this will often do far less damage to the line than projecting AS too boldly, though with *enough* projected ignorance, loose i.p. can quickly degrade to light i.p. speech-rhythm). But the point is worth repeating: the introjection of the 10-position line in effect *potentiates* the possible promotion and demotion of every syllable, thus greatly increasing poetry's metrical instability – and so its expressive potential and capacity for individual interpretation.

But let's not overstate the case. While finding in

> Oh it was strong and bold and terse,
> The proud full sail of his great verse

the variation

> Oh it was strong and bold and terse,
> the PROUD FULL SAIL of HIS GREAT VERSE

– is by no means impossible, sustaining such tension over a rigid AS frame like loose 4-strong is far more difficult than it would be in blank verse or rhymed, 10-position i.p. couplets. (The variation above is only possible through a 'speech-strong' reading, one which favours sense stress over metrical stress, and this will be explained in detail later. Such speech-strong interpretations are far easier to make when aided by the 10-position frame.)

Let's look at a passage of loose i.p.:

```
-x-    /    x    /    -x-  / x   /  x    /
   Tamed by Miltown, we lie on Mother's bed;
    1      2  3 4     5 6 7    8  9    10

   x / x   /  x   /   x    /  x  /
   the rising sun in war paint dyes us red;
    1 2 3   4 5    6   7     8  9 10

   x    /   x /   x  / x  /  x      /
   in broad daylight her gilded bed-posts shine,
    1    2    3 4    5  6 7  8   9    10

   x /  x    /  x   / x / x /
   abandoned, almost Dionysian.
    1 2  3    4  5    67 8 910

   x  /   x  / x    /   x   /  -x-      /
   At last the trees are green on Marlborough Street,
    1 2    3  4 5     6   7    8    9       10

-x-    /    -x-  /   x   / x / x /
   blossoms on our magnolia ignite
    1     2    3   4    5   6789 10

   x  /  x   /   x   /  x   /  x     /
   the morning with their murderous five days' white.
    1  2 3    4    5    6   7   8    9     10
```

(ROBERT LOWELL, 'Man and Wife')[1]

If, as I suspect, Lowell was also 'feeling' the line in ten positions, what has changed by his superimposition of this decimal template over the familiar AS pattern? The difference is inevitably subtle, but I think it is present. Yes, we still see a tight coincidence of s-event to even number, maintaining the AS; and with the obvious exception

---

[1] Robert Lowell, *Life Studies* (London: Faber & Faber, 1959).

of 'Dionysian', we see a strong nuclear stress to high s-position correspondence within the AS template (the syllable at position 10 coincides with a 4 on the AS matrix for i.p.). However, I would claim that with a 10-position 'awareness', the AS is somewhat less insistent, and that the independent integrity of the individual line — and that of the statement it makes it — has strengthened considerably as a result of the stronger bound limits of the 10-position template; Lowell's phrasemaking seems more boldly monolineal than ever (it's significant that elsewhere Lowell's inclination is often not to vary merely through caesura, but by actually breaking the i.p. line into two lines). As to the increased level of content realised by s-potentiated w stresses, and the richer variety of interpretations this might subsequently introduce . . . While *I* may perceive that this has indeed occurred, I admit it is largely subjective. It is vitally important to bear in mind that *articulating* the effect of the 10-position template on a line is going to be roughly as hard as trying to nail down the 'definition' of a single phonestheme. It is less a slippery concept than a concept defined by its own slipperiness — in this case because all 10-position composition *does* is potentiate more interpretative variation, or a kind of 'prosodic connotation', partly through its cognitive fudging of s and w, content and function, and the operation of paradigm and syntagm. If we again take the line

x   / x /   x / x / x   /
in broad daylight her gilded bed-posts shine,
1   2   3 4   5 6 7 8 9   10

Under a 'normal', tight i.p. scansion, we do little more than line up metrical pattern and speech and see where they agree or disagree. However, with the introduction of the 10-position frame, we are negotiating between in **broad** day**light** her **gild**ed **bed**-posts **shine**,

and the neutral, digital, metronomic 'Dalek' stress of

in — broad — day — light — her — gild — ed — bed — posts — shine

Obviously variations like '*day*light' will be eased and aided by the blanket, near-syllabic neutrality of 10-position, but the content-syllables 'light' and 'posts' could easily find themselves performed with extra vowel-quality, enough to push 'daylight' and 'bedposts' further towards spondee; furthermore, 'in' might find itself quietly promoted to a slightly more emphatic role, emphasising the contrast with the night the couple have just seen out, and during which the golden bed was dim. The overall effect will be to *increase the perception of content,* and so of significant information.

Let's now look at a very different example with only two content words:

x / x   /   x   /x / x/

abandoned, almost Dionysian.

1 2 3   4   5   67 8 9 10

The i.p. frame will attempt to draw five syllables from 'Dionysian' here anyway (elsewhere the word could easily be shrunk to a three syllables by making it three monophthongs, as in the i.p. line 'their crazed Dionysian revelries', where we would say 'Die-nize-yin', and stress the word x/x); but 10-position asks for the syllabic segmentation of the word into Di-o-ny-si-an more strongly than does the mere AS i.p. frame, giving the word great length and prominence. It is also an effect of 10-position to make polysyllabic classical lexis sing rather better in English, by introducing a very light version of its own quantitative scansion (see 'magnolia' earlier). For this reason a poet using 10-position loose i.p. is also, I'd propose, far less bound by the old 'Anglo-Saxon default' in their choice of lexis. Polysyllabism is accommodated in i.p. by more than just having a longer line to work with: 10-position *makes polysyllabism lyric*. Because of the slightly evened-out spacing of all syllables, schwa has more time to take on a little of the colour of its vowel. All this has consequences for the not only the lexis poets are inclined to employ in i.p but also for readers: it will require a more sophisticated and educated audience to understand it.

Readers are well within their rights to choose *not* to enact these potentiated variations, however, and one should not lose track of the fact that they are merely that: potentiated. Let's look at another example:

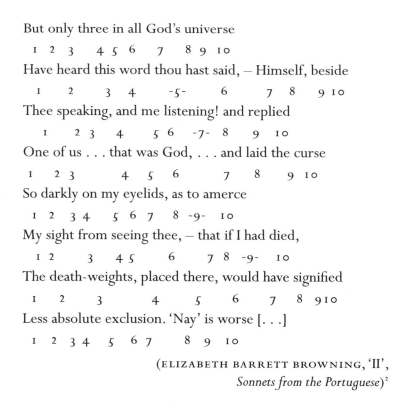

But only three in all God's universe
  1 2 3   4 5 6   7   8 9 10
Have heard this word thou hast said, – Himself, beside
  1   2   3 4   -5-   6   7 8   9 10
Thee speaking, and me listening! and replied
   1   2 3 4   5 6 -7- 8   9 10
One of us . . . that was God, . . . and laid the curse
1   2 3   4 5 6   7   8   9 10
So darkly on my eyelids, as to amerce
  1 2 3 4   5 6 7 8 -9- 10
My sight from seeing thee, – that if I had died,
  1 2   3   4 5   6   7 8 -9- 10
The death-weights, placed there, would have signified
  1   2   3   4   5   6   7   8 9 10
Less absolute exclusion. 'Nay' is worse [. . .]
  1 2 3 4 5 6 7   8 9 10

(ELIZABETH BARRETT BROWNING, 'II',
Sonnets from the Portuguese)[2]

2 Elizabeth Barrett Browning, *Sonnets from the Portuguese and Other Poems* (New York: Dover Publications, 1992).

Do the odd-numbered syllables gain any strength through the poet's introjection of the 10-position template? My own feeling is that they do – sometimes smoothing out what would usually be felt as tension, i.e. as promotion or demotion, to a more direct stress ('But only three in all God's universe'); sometimes lyrically drawing out the length of polysyllabic words (in 'Less absolute exclusion' we might hear the second word as a *little* closer to ab-so-loot than we would in other AS or conversational frames, where the last two syllables are mere schwa; ditto 'ehx-cloo-zhuhn'); sometimes raising phrases more easily to spondee ('placed there'); sometimes raising a run of functional schwa to something far more emphatic and evenly stressed ('that if I had died'); sometimes introducing a delicious instability to the phrase ('One of us . . . that was God . . .), and so on; though I freely admit the existence of these effects also depends, at least in part, on my own projection. Nonetheless I believe that the 10-position frame must also have aided the composition of these lines, and the richly tensive possibilities they propose, possibilities that I am then able to explore as a reader.

Some corollaries of the 10-position line

To summarise the differences between tight, light and loose i.p.: tight i.p is not functionally 10-position; it is introjected and projected as a syllabically overdetermined 5-metron AS line and so has a very high degree of convergence. Light i.p. is not 10-position either, as it returns the weak odd-numbered stresses to durational placeholders, where weak syllables might be more freely placed or removed (although because i.p. has no 'Dolnik' form it can swiftly degrade into McGonagallesque unmetricality). 10-position i.p. *is* the definition of sophisticated loose i.p.; but it will remain poorly understood until it is accepted that its essence is its very instability, since tension is written deep into its template – consisting as it does of the superimposition of *two* metrical templates. 'Loose i.p.' *contains both syllabotonic and syllabic schemes.*

Let's work out the consequences of this assertion a little more carefully, because they are thoroughly strange. If we assume that the 10-position introjection is at least a compositional reality, then there are several interesting corollaries. In order to make it a 10-position line countable, we need two things: a boldly circumscribed unit that can be apprehended *as* such, and a flattening out of w-s alternation. This leads to a less pronounced distinction between function and content, the latter promoted and the former (slightly) demoted. To some extent their cognitive roles move far closer to being, if not interchangeable, in flux. It will generally require more cognitive processing than the 4-strong line, because of the relative salience of each syllable. The line is therefore information-heavy, and so better designed for art-speech, not folk-song.

Furthermore, if the Gestalt of the line is strongly reinforced so that the template can be apprehended as a whole (this overdetermination is necessary simply because it's an alien concept, being a syllabic template in a stress-timed language), it becomes *monadic*, and – unlike 4-strong – does not imply hierarchical structure (though sometimes we can some see explicit *stanzaic* overdetermination). This makes it more attractive to and accommodating of independent statement and perception. It may also point to 10-position i.p. being essentially *monostichic*, where the hiatus is more a terminal or at least indeterminate space than the interstitial gap it is after, say, the second line in common metre; this would explain enjambment in i.p. being far more confusing than its merely odd-numbered strong-stress nature would imply (something we can see from the number of miscounts that occur in run-on lines).

However, if the i.p. line *does* include the ghost metron in its template – I would say the tight i.p. template probably does – it follows that it can only exist if a second line is anticipated. This means that, while AS never really 'gets going' in i.p., there may be some grounds for at least considering *tight* i.p. a fundamentally distichic form, with the heroic and closed couplets its most natural variations.³ (By contrast, in loose i.p. AS will function less strongly at the sublineal level, since the 10-position template make w-s difference less pronounced, and also at the lineal level, since the line itself tends towards the monadic. Higher-level AS is felt only when the line can be heard as a rising and falling unit, and this effect is generally the preserve of stanzaic tight

---

3 An alternative explanation for this is tabled next, and I apologise for the endless drum-roll. Note that if it were the case that tight i.p. was distichic, we'd have a 12-metron form, with the first and thirteenth places occupying the first stress of each successive couplet – a thought to excite Fibonacci bores everywhere. We might then consider the eighth-placed stresses the 'dominant', the golden ratio tension within the couplet's chromatic 'scale', and look for some unconscious positioning of significant content:

> 'Tis hard to say, if greater Want of Skill [x/]
> Appear in **Writing** or in Judging ill, [x/]
> But, of the two, less dang'rous is th' Offence, [x/]
> To tire our **Patience**, than mis-lead our Sense:
> Some few in that, but Numbers err in this, [x/]
> Ten Censure **wrong** for one who Writes amiss; [x/]
> A Fool might once himself alone expose, [x/]
> Now One in **Verse** makes many more in Prose. [x/]
> – Alexander Pope, 'An Essay on Criticism'

I leave the reader to decide if this is a brilliant new insight or a lunatic distraction, though I'd say the smart money is definitely on the latter.

If the reader additionally projects a strong 10-position feel into *tight* i.p, it will likely lead to a firm, evening ghost-metron at the hiatus, leaving a twelve-syllable count, easily felt in groups of 4; that's to say it may potentiate the kind of a triple dimetronic count earlier discussed, with supratonic stresses on positions 2, 6 and 10. These maddening complications really just reflect a simple underlying truth: roughly fixed syllabic lines are capable of playing host to a number of projected metrical templates *simultaneously*, with each new template and combination of templates providing its own unique complexities. This situation will be horribly familiar to anyone who has spent any time investigating the number of harmonic systems that can be hosted by the 12-note chromatic scale – a vortex which has cost many musicians their entire lives.

i.p. (Even then, its limits are probably reached quite swiftly, and I doubt they can extend beyond sonnet length.)

As I've mentioned, dramatic i.p. defines itself in opposition to 4-strong, and the 10-position template emphasises that while 4-strong has the heart of a tonic/accentual line, i.p. is contrastively at least part-syllabic. *To a degree*, 4-strong introjects an accentual template, and 10-position i.p. a syllabic one. The reality of loose i.p. is that it tends to seek a middle ground, and is *both* an AS template and a 10-position one. Any syllable in loose i.p. is, by birthright, a mixture of timed placeholder and durational event. This surely has the capacity to lend the loose i.p. line some additional dynamism, as well as dragging the line decisively towards, if not a quantitative prosody, then at least a rather French one (as it likely fell on the ears of an educated Elizabethan audience). It is additionally capable of 'lyricising' the polysyllable, for the reasons explained earlier, and thus making a classical lexis 'sing' in English.

Here I've really been referring to the kinds of lines that 10-position thinking is likely to *produce*. However, in order to be *perceived* as 10-position, our functional w stresses must all receive a degree of 'promotion'; but 'promotion and demotion' are the wrong way of thinking about it. The additional *projection* of a 10-position cognitive template would produce a degree of convergence which would effectively insist on a subtle revision of the function of parts of speech. Ten positions of relative equality means the elongation of schwa, and the concomitant stressing of function. Making grammatical function an aspect of the sentence that now must be consciously processed will increase both its versatility and its difficulty: 'Who is it that says most, which can say more, / Than this rich praise, that you alone are you, / In whose confine immuréd is the store / Which should example where your equal grew?'[4] — and one can immediately see the appeal

4   Katherine Duncan Jones (ed.), *Shakespeare's Sonnets* (London: Arden Shakespeare, 2010), Sonnet 84, 279.

of 10-position to Shakespeare, the most grammatically experimental of poets.

However, s stress suffers a metronomic pull down towards the quiet zone of timed placeholding function too, so there may be a slight overall increase in 10-position line length, and the perception of the s/w/s/w/ weave being more of a gentle kink than an emphatic wave. While in *theory* it might all balance out, because of the social and cultural purpose to which poetry is put (and, let's be frank, the hysterical temperament of poets generally), we tend to see instead that 10-position is exploited as means by which the event- and pitch-floor can be *raised overall*. A frame perceived as a monadic Gestalt is far more easily raised up as a single unit than would be an AS frame whose purpose is to *preserve* the strong pitch-alternation between content and function, weak and strong.

In 10-position, pitch variation between content and function words is flattened out in neutral readings; this means that the pitch-contours, emphases and de-emphases of sense stress, those which occur as a result of semantic, phrasal, syntactic or dramatic exigency, will stand more saliently against it. This makes loose i.p. ideal for dramatic performance and for personal interpretation; the attenuation of AS means that there is little pitch variation *inherent* in the line's rhythm, meaning that its performed *sense* can be accommodated readily without perceived damage to the integrity of the line.

Finally, the partial erosion of event/placeholding roles further aids the collapse of the content-ruled axis of paradigmatic selection into the function-ruled axis of syntagmatic combination. Or to put it more simply: dramatic loose i.p. can hold more content that English sentences of the same length can usually sustain.

Lyric i.p. and the 8-strong measure

There is a significant complication to this picture. It depends upon our accepting that there are two distinct modalities, two larger cognitive templates in play, which the co-composing poet and reader may switch between (they need not coincide, but, as ever, a convergence of introjection and projection is our ideal): namely *those of lyric and dramatic speech*. This theory is plausible only if we can subscribe fairly wholeheartedly to my creed of non-intrinsicality: here, this means that i.p. as a 5-metron duple line generates no secondary template but its own, and is merely a neutral construct onto which other templates can be culturally projected.

Whatever its muddy origins and confused entry into the language, it would be no surprise to anyone if i.p had occasionally accommodated itself to the most pervasive metrical template of poetic speech, the 4-strong line. I feel increasingly that the 5-strong duple line is a neutral frame which has interacted with two performance traditions, the lyric and the dramatic, and has become a line capable of *both* 'analogue' and 'digital' interpretations; while these interpretations lie at opposite ends of the metre-strong/speech-strong performance spectrum, they might nonetheless freely interact in a way perceptible to, or at least registered by, an attuned listenership.[5] Not only that, but

5 This theory coincides with my own experience as an improvising musician. There, I hear two metrical approaches to the improvised melodic line, which I mentally characterise as 'isometric' and 'chrysometric'. The first divides or multiplies the bar evenly and mathematically; most characteristically it would be something like the machine-gun 'digital' delivery of semiquavers over bebop changes, Charlie Parker-style. The second is ruled by the far more organic, asymmetric phrasal patterns of spoken conversational language, ruled (through a kind of projection of harmonic-series asymmetry into rhythm itself; pitch is a human projection, and just our way of hearing very fast rhythmic cycles) by golden section and Fibonacci ratios (hence 'chryso-', gold). Musically this might correspond to the speech-like phrasing of those musicians conventionally thought of as 'lyric' – Bill Evans, Miles Davis or John Abercrombie. (One common technique that jazz musicians use for learning conversational phrasing is to play along as one reads out a piece of prose fiction, following the shape and pitch-contour of the sentences in their larger narrative context.) The 4-strong interpretation of the i.p. line *may* be considered a kind of 'chrysometric', radically asymmetric 'Fibonacci ballad'. This means the lyric i.p. line divides an 'octaval' 4 × 2, 8-strong template at the golden section (s stress position 5),

the notorious instability of the i.p. hiatus might be partly explained by i.p.'s swithering *between* the two modes. (The old argument one occasionally still hears about the i.p. line 'really only having four stresses' – owing to some mysterious and inherent inability of the self-contained English phrase to sustain any more – is unrelated to what follows, and not worth our serious attention.) My admittedly controversial proposal is this: under lyric, end-stopped, stanzaic conditions, we sometimes see the spoken performance of i.p. *tend* towards an 'analogue', 8-metron, 'chrysometric', tonal, double-supratonic, generative line, one composed of five strong stresses and a hiatus roughly counted as three metrons. Sing or 'intone' a line of i.p. in this way, and you will soon hear it as two four-strong lines.

In dramatic blank verse, it tends towards a more 'digital', 10-position, isometric, syllabic, 5-strong, monadic line, composed of five duple-metre metrons and (as it is monadic) an uncountable, short hiatus of wilfully indeterminate length. (Anyone who ignores the word 'tends' will find this theory very easy to refute; my focus is on the performance of the line as it might be affected by the introjection and/or the projection of two different templates, which are themselves the formal aspects of two different performance modalities. It's the existence of those English ethnolinguistic metrical frames I'm trying to show, not any 'inherent characteristics' of the 5-metron line, which – to repeat – is a neutral and empty construct.) The performance and perhaps composition of i.p. negotiates between these two extremes. Actors' performances of poetic or lyric i.p. are rarely to be trusted, as they are *almost* invariably speech-strong, a mode only really appropriate to i.p. in blank verse, which, of course,

---

leaving a 3-foot interstice which works in an interlineal placeholding function. (One might easily see an analogue of the V-I perfect cadence being enacted between lines – the intonational jump between stresses 4 and (nuclear stress) 5 may even *perform* something close to it – from which one might derive the correspondence: strong = perfect, bright, sharp; weak = plagal, dark, flat.)

they tend to speak supremely well. (Here is not the place to whine at length about all the great lyric poetry ruined by an actor's desire to 'put something of themselves into it'.) For the 4-strong effect within i.p. to be heard, one requires a measured and unexcitable performance, metre-strong and consistent with the conventions of lyric delivery, i.e. with a slower speech tempo and the downplaying of 'interpretative emphasis'.

The argument for its existence runs as follows. To start with my conclusion: in addition to the neutral 5-metron and the dramatic 10-position templates, the i.p. line *can also be an expression of two measures of 4-strong.* (These metrical, dramatic and lyric modalities are i.p analogues of the metre-, speech- and song-strong interpretations of the 4-strong line, i.e. they provide a similar expressive latitude by different means.) I arrived at this while asking two questions. Firstly, why does the way we *claim* that we time the hiatus often differ so much from actual performance? And secondly, how would one go about setting i.p. for the singing voice? I was listening on YouTube to the Scottish actor David Tennant give what I would call a very natural, unaffected and lyric performance of Sonnet 18: he pauses longer than other actors at the interlineal hiatus. Actors are very good at blank verse, but are mostly lousy performers of the lyric mode, where they tend to rush, shortening the vowel, kinking the line with expressive accent and generally diminishing the musical experience – i.e., they read it as they would dramatic blank verse. In these circumstances, obvious, line ending-coincident syntactic breaks will receive a longer pause, but the i.p. line *itself* seems neither to imply nor compel any. Tennant paused at the end of each line in a way that seemed perfectly natural and, more importantly, timed and rhythmic; but for far longer that one would expect from a line which was merely making up its length to an even 6-strong stress positions by the addition of a single ghost metron. Suddenly I heard that all he would have to do would be to sing his syllables for Sonnet 18 to fit a four-bar measure almost perfectly. And indeed he basically *was*: Tennant was, in effect, giving a timed lyric performance of a line most would treat or read dramatically; and in doing so, fitting it almost perfectly, instinctively and effortlessly to a 4-strong template: the final stress was treated as the first stress of a new line of 4-strong, with the remaining strongs counted in silence. The availability of this alternative cognitive template suddenly made sense of much that had troubled me over these inconsistencies in our analysis.

While it is sensible to argue that the dramatic i.p. line is a kind of freelance monostich, incapable of proposing the larger stanzaic structures easily conjured from the alternate-stress-ruled 4-strong – i.p. *feels* bounded, odd, independent – when the line inclines to the *lyric* form, we find them in just such stanzaic structures all the time. Within those non-blank verse structures, we assume, I think, that we are placing something like a ghost metron to even it up, i.e.

> So now I have confessed that he is thine, [x/]
> And I my self am mortgaged to thy will, [x/]
> Myself I'll forfeit, so that other mine [x/]
> Thou wilt restore to be my comfort still: [x/]

This argument holds reasonably well for modally *neutral* performances; indeed there, the hiatus need not be thought of as more than an optional – *uh* – between lines, one easily skipped by enjambment. And whenever the line leans more emphatically towards a *dramatic* delivery, the length of the hiatus varies greatly depending on the sense, and is very often cheerfully elided by enjambment produced by the dramatic necessity of the speech; compared with the 4-strong line and its 'stanzaic consequence', the 4×4 form, we think of i.p. as less lyric, and more conversational; less sung and 'felt', and more spoken or 'acted'; less vowel- and weak-space elongated (it has no 'Dolnik' form), and more schwa-populated; less metre-strong, and more speech-strong in its prosody, with the speech tempo generally a fair bit faster. However, this only really applies to i.p. in its blank verse forms, and the loose versions of its metre. In the case of poems composed of *obviously* lyric, frequently end-stopped i.p. lines, such as we often encounter in more formal sonnets, the one-metron hiatus is clearly insufficient, and, I would argue, not reflected in sensitive performance; in its lyric incarnations, the single-stress hiatus can create an unnaturally rushed effect. But when I yell at a student, as I often do, to 'read it slowly', in a manner sympathetic to its author's lyric intentions – another template will emerge: there's really not that much difference, to my ear, between the effective performance of strongly *lyric* i.p. and 4-stress.

I think the failure to diagnose this lies in the refusal to acknowledge that there *are* two distinct and alternative templates, each appropriate to our two modalities, our 'genres' of i.p. On more than one occasion I have found myself in arguments with actors who insist that the *Sonnets* are a long dramatic poem, and should be read accordingly; it seems to me self-evidently the case that they are nothing of the kind. The 'indeterminate ghost metron' (it's significant that this is rather oxymoronic) between lines:

> So now I have confessed that he is thine – x DAH
> And I my self am mortgaged to thy will – x DAH

is felt (i.e. sort-of-counted) in *half time* in lyric i.p. and takes up something slower to the space of *three* metrons, i.e. [– DAH –] is more [– uh – DAH – uh –]. If we insert the weak placeholders:

> So long as men can breathe and eyes can see [x /x S x /]

Nor is this 3-metron hiatus perceived as particularly overlong, as the speech tempo of the lyric mode is far slower than the dramatic.

I believe this long interlineal gap is merely the product of a wholly instinctive mapping of i.p. to 4-strong. Consider the possibility that i.p. might be felt as a 4-stress couplet *with only the first stress of the second line realised*:

```
    x  /   x   /   x    /    x   /
    So long as men can breathe and eyes
      x   /   [ x /   x /   x /]
    can see
    x /   x    / x    / x    /
    So long lives this, and this gives life
      x   /   [ x /   x /   x /]
    to thee
```

And lyric i.p. become as form of curtal ballad. I am aware that *always* counting 2, 3, 4 after every line of end-stopped lyric pentameter may feel strenuous, and I would suggest that the 3-metron hiatus is more 'a potential space that can be comfortably expanded into' than always realised; generally speaking, it is *gestured* toward by a much-longer-than-usual hiatus, and need not always be fully timed. This may be because lines often move freely between dramatic and lyric modalities, and the hiatus is therefore open to either a 1-metron or a 3-metron half-time interpretation, but is most characteristically a tensive space somewhere between *both*, from which *either* can also be realised — one we perhaps think of as especially characteristic of the i.p. line. Certainly, a 1-metron gap feels much too short in lyric i.p.; but increasingly I hear most i.p. verse gain one of its characteristic tensions as it is pushed and pulled between the modal templates of the lyric 2 × 4-strong measure and that of the dramatic, 10-position line. Whether a line is read one way or another will often be directed by content, i.e. various semantic and syntactic cues — but also by lyric properties, word choice, function-to-content ratio and so on. When an i.p. line is read in the slow, end-stopped lyric mode, the elongation of the line makes the 2 × 4 template easily available as a metrical alternative. It is not intrinsic to the form, but potentiated when i.p.

lines imply a lyric performance. Much of the hiatus's indeterminacy, therefore, rests on our being unsure if the hiatus is 1- or 3-metron, i.e. to be counted in single or half time, as we first need to be sure of a line's dramatic or lyric modality, which affects tempo. (Another factor steering some readers towards a half-time, 3-metron hiatus may be the ternary dimetronic reading of i.p. that tends to emerge under tight-metre, endstopped conditions; here, the felt 3-strong of And SUMMer's lease has ALL too short a DATE [xxx] can easily rebalance itself as a half-time 4-strong, i.e. And SUMMer's lease has ALL too short a DATE [x/x S x/].) Is there any validity in claiming the existence of a template few poets or actors *explicitly* perform, and which could perhaps be as well explained away by the mere expressive elongation of what we all 'just feel' to be an indeterminate hiatus? I believe so; not least because it explains the indeterminacy of the hiatus itself without resorting to mysterious claims of intrinsic properties, and the cognitive presence of 8-strong would explain the larger symmetrical stanzaic structures into which our allegedly monadic i.p. readily forms itself under lyric circumstances.

(Again, one could easily cite the performances of the poets themselves, but as the most self-conscious performers on God's earth, they are rarely reliable guides. Although Frost delivered the shorter, more lyric i.p. of 'Design' more slowly than he batters through 'Birches', he was a notorious rusher; to my ear 'Design' works far better read in something close to the lyric i.p., 2 × 4 template. On the other hand, Yeats was once asked why he paused so heavily at the end of every line; he replied, 'So they can hear the work I've put in.')

Some corollaries of the 8-strong template in i.p.

If we plug some i.p. into the numerical values of the 4-strong distrophic matrix, we see the following:

    32   16   24   8

Shall I compare thee to a summ-

    28   12   20   4

er's day?   [x/   x/   x/]

     30   14   22   6

Thou art more lovely and more temp

  26   10   18   2

erate.   [x/   x/   x/]

      31   15   23   7

Rough winds do shake the darling buds

   27   11   19   3

of May,   [x/   x/   x/]

   29   14   21   5

And summer's lease hath all too short

  25   9   17   1

a date.   [x/   x/   x/]

Factoring in the above will help explain a few phenomena, and propose a few interesting corollaries:

1. This is why lyric i.p. feels not just monadic but *bounded*: blocked out by a conspicuous silence at its end, and carrying both an initial high stress *and* a terminal one – and yet rhythmically balanced. What we have in lyric i.p. is a *double supratonic line*, derived from the high initial stress on each first stress of the 2 × 4 form. We now see the additional pressure on the final word of lyric i.p. to carry some significant semantic weight, given the greater size of the space it must resonate into – and its being thrust into a semi-symbolic role, almost through its Janus-facing position alone. (One feels one could *almost* reconstruct the sense of the whole poem from *day? / temperate: / May, / date: / shines, / dimmed, / declines, / untrimmed: / fade, / ow'st, / shade, / grow'st, / see / thee.*) Approximate rhythm between supratonic stresses is maintained by

the three silence metrons performing the 'placeholder role' of the
s stresses in the middle of the line:

> So *long* as <u>men</u> can <u>breathe</u> and <u>eyes</u> can *see*   [x/ x/   x/]
> So *long* lives <u>this</u>, and <u>this</u> gives <u>life</u> to *thee*   [x/ x/   x/]

Silent counts contract, and this 3-metron space is often performed
a little shorter, though nothing like a 1-metron count.

2. This is why the last stress of lyric (not dramatic) i.p. feels unusually
strong and high. I had ascribed this principally to the effect of
default nuclear stress in the normal English prosodic phrase with
which i.p. regularly coincides, but in this analysis, it's part of
the template: the high value of the fifth stress is merely the high
position of an *initial* stress in 4-strong.

3. This makes i.p. potentially subservient to *three* templates: to a
10-position line in its dramatic form, a double supratonic line in its
lyric 2 × 4 form, and a neutral 5-metron AS line which negotiates
between the two.

4. This would mean that larger AS structures *are* in fact implied by
i.p., because the single line is, in a sense, already a couplet. The i.p.
couplet is then merely another expression of 4 × 4, which would
explain the feeling that the heroic couplet is its natural lyric form.
The common-sense assumption that i.p. has no momentum because
its five strong stresses do not imply larger stanzaic structures has
never been very well borne out; we feel it *does*, and can point to
any number of examples of stanzaic, lyric i.p. where it appears to
do just that, and which we can now explain.[6]

---

6 The terminal caesura after s stress position 4 might *theoretically* be less disruptive in
a line of lyric than 10-position dramatic i.p., since it would mark the end of a four-bar
measure. The question remains as to what extent a poet writing i.p. in the lyric mode
will be affected by the underlying 2 × 4 line; my sense (reviewing my own work in this

5. Wherever we detect an 8-strong template, we may then decide to also make some account of the ASR at the higher unit levels, including alternating key-fall patterns and larger matrical structures. I.p. can be plugged into the 4-strong AS numerical matrices, so larger forms can be analysed with none of the hesitation one would have over the 6-value (5, plus the ghost strong) line matrix earlier discussed. An i.p. quatrain would map to an eight-line distrophic 4×4 matrix; here, the zenith is first stress of first line, the nadir is fourth stress of fourth line, as in this short poem by Frost:

```
   32        16    24    8      28     [12 20 4]
Here come real stars to fill the upper skies,
   30     14       22   6     26       [10 18 2]
And here on earth come emulating flies,
   31        15  23    7    27         [11 19 3]
That though they never equal stars in size,
   29      13   21    5     25         [9 17 1]
(And they were never really stars at heart)
Achieve at times a very star-like start
Only, of course, they can't sustain the part.⁷
```

And lo, what do we find at the nadir but . . . The false stars of the fireflies. It's hard to believe that Frost, in making this beautiful effect, didn't instinctively sense that the de-accented, anaphoric repeat-word 'stars' and the 'distrophic nadir' should be coincident. (Note that in lyric i.p., while the highest value falls on the initial position, the lowest in the 4-strong distrophic matrix is always the penultimate stress of the first strophe, if the second is not complete.

context) is that I am definitely inclined to less caesural variation, but beyond that I see no pattern. However, since 4-strong is a continuous line, it implies no hiatus – and therefore no caesura here.

7 Robert Frost, *The Poetry of Robert Frost: The Collected Poems, Complete and Unabridged*, ed. Edward Connery Lathem (New York: Henry Holt, 2002).

THE DRAMATIC AND LYRIC MODES OF I.P.

This is different from the position of the nadir in the strophic matrix of i.p.; the difference is in the numerical values, indicating a psychologically lower position for the nadir relative to the zenith in the 4-strong distrophic matrix – $5/32$ as opposed to $5/24$ – and likely reflected in a more exaggeratedly performed drop in pitch.) Though I suspect the lyric i.p. nadir can be used for more than the smooth accommodation of strong-position function, the demotion of content to function (and, as above, the burying of a repeated word to reinforce its anaphoric role), and may be deployed as a general tool of bold de-accent: in line 8 of 'To His Sonne', with the slyest fake insouciance, Raleigh drops in the following:

The wag, my pretty knave, *betokeneth* thee.

. . . And to my ear – by mere dint of its matrical positon – Raleigh suggests we might drop our voices down a fifth or so, Edmund Blackadder-style. (Note that the weakness of this position also makes it especially accommodating of schwa, and so polysyllabism.)

6. The numerical values leave a line with a greater overall *height* than two lines of 4-strong, as the lower-value final three syllables of the second 4-strong line are missing. This may psychologically confer a greater overall sense of emotional urgency on the i.p. line when read within this template. Similarly, alternating key-falls between lines will be pitched at a far higher level, leaving lyric i.p at a higher overall pitch that an equivalent passage of 4×4. This leaves it, naturally, a better form for 'heightened' language than 4×4 since the pitch floor itself is naturally raised by the effects of AS.

7. This has major implications for the content–function ratio, with an area of silent 'weak function' being delegated to the 3-metron space after each line. This leaves a speech-to-silence Fibonacci ratio of $5:8$, which may have some content-to-function echoes.

Speculatively (a word which should always follow 'Fibonacci'): might the line and its long after-breath affect or effect larger structures? Might the roughly 8:5 exposition-to-development ratio of the sonnet correspond to a merely scaled-up version of 5:3 content–function line? In a sense, this would imply a scalable, 'chrysometric' version of AS.

8. The variable length of 3-metron hiatus is a further sophistication offered by the form. Its full value may or may not be realised, but its occasional contraction in enjambment (which occurs with considerably less frequency in its lyric forms than its dramatic) is a far more radical gesture than one would find in, say,

> And down by the brimming river
> I heard a lover sing
> Under an arch of the railway:
> 'Love has no ending.'

This leads to the increased sense of dramatic momentum wherever the hiatus is elided or shortened in lyric i.p.:

> Was it his spirit, by spirits taught to write
> Above a mortal pitch, that struck me dead?

since it not only elides a longer gap but also effectively brings two supratonic stresses ('write/above') together. The effect is far stronger than such an enjambment would achieve within our bundles of blank verse.

Conclusion

Poets who wish to write metrically have either a 4-strong analogue line or a 5-metron, 10-position digital line to work with, and that's pretty much the whole show. The looser, popular 4 × 4 template tends to populate or depopulate the weak placeholder freely, and can easily shift between duple and triple metres. The upmarket i.p. line tends to overdetermine its timing more rigidly through a largely fixed syllable-count, but often takes advantage of an additional 10-position template to upgrade the weak placeholder to event-position, with predictable consequences for the syllables it then hosts. The 10-position line is a superimposition upon and not a replacement for the AS frame: its effects therefore should not be overstated. They are crucially dependent on introjection and projection, since the 10-position line would not, of course, be detected in any purely resting state prosody; it is a product of collective cultural will. This line is further complicated by folk-echoes of 4-strong itself under lyric circumstances.

Both kinds of line maintain isochrony through a degree of quantitative fixing: 4-strong through metronomic (and sometime sung, or near-sung) performance, i.p. through syllable count: one partly counts through tone, the other partly counts through syllable. The constraints inherent in both are, in practice, balanced by 4-strong's freer w-syllable count, and i.p.'s greater expressive latitude.

SCANSION: NOTATIONAL SYSTEMS
IN THE FOUR METRE-TYPES

Different metres require different kinds of scansion. There are four broad types of metrical composition: **tight, loose, light,** and **free**.

Tight metres disallow all but the smoothest and least radical variations, and can be described by four lexical scansion symbols:

/ — strong syllable on strong position

x — weak syllable on weak position

\ — strong syllable on weak position; potentiated demotion

X — weak syllable on strong position; potentiated promotion

The loose-metre template differs from tight metre in that it allows some freedom with syllable count in the form of w additions and omissions, and can sustain a greater number of tensions. Convergence is diminished, which is to say that the confirmation of metrical template is more difficult. I prefer to employ -x- in the top line where the weak placeholder occurs over two or more syllables, as its durational status is more evident; I save x for single-w, accurately coincident positions. (The objection here is that in using -x- you've gone beyond the mere projection of the frame, and have started to scan the line; to which I'd have to answer than the projection of the frame *is* scanning the line: the process is subjective from the start.) Otherwise the loose-metre notational system is identical to the tight, with the addition of:

    x-x   – double weak (either syllable of which might be subject
          to the usual promotions, though *not* both)

    [x]   – omitted weak

    :   – mora (a very short pause used as device of quantitative
          compensation).

These three additions are, however, syllable count and quantising
marks; the basic four symbols remain the same. After a sense stress
scansion, we will also encounter

    /'   – accented s (the 'high' syllable)

    /,   – de-accented s

    x'   – accented w

    x,   – de-accented w (the 'buried' syllable)

as well as some compound signs; in these, accent or de-accent is the
more salient quality, and trumps w or s stress-qualities; it essentially
'calls' a tension and determines its final performed strength:

    X,   – promoted w with de-accent

    X'   – promoted w with accent

    \,   – demoted s with de-accent

    \'   – demoted s with accent

giving us twelve possibilities in total.

    Thus, for example, [X] indicates a tension, in this case a promoted w;
but [X,] indicates a tension that a sense-stress analysis has subsequently
de-accented. Two kind of information are now presented. One
is simply binary, and shows either agreement or tension between
position and lexical stress. Tensions indicate that the w or s syllable
will *likely* be promoted or demoted in performance – rarely to full s or
w stresses, but some lighter approximation of them. However, with a
sense-stress scansion, we add a more subjective, performative dimen-
sion – and sometimes an accent or de-accent will contradict a tension.
This will effectively return the syllable from its potentially lowered

position to its previous prominence, or vice-versa; but interestingly 'problematised', and deriving its complex character from *both* stress-position and pitch.

It would be performatively difficult to request an accent on a demoted s syllable that returned it to a position *equally* salient as an accent on a simple s syllable; the w position of an s syllable that is clearly accented (or, conversely, the s position of a w syllable that is de-accented) provides one of the most subtle and nuanced of available tensions: in the case of our s syllable, one which has been stress-demoted but accent-promoted. 'Confusion' results only when we refuse to treat it as an intrinsically unstable and tensive phenomenon. To demonstrate this complexity, let's look at the following example:

$$\text{x} \quad / \quad \text{x} \quad / \quad \text{x} \ / \ \text{x} \quad / \quad \text{x} \quad /$$
Rough winds do shake the darling buds of May
$$\text{x} \quad / \quad \text{x} \quad / \quad \text{x} \ / \ \text{x} \quad / \quad \text{x} \quad /$$

Giving:

Rough winds do shake the darling buds of May
$$\backslash \qquad / \quad \text{x} \ / \quad \text{x} \ / \ \text{x} \quad / \quad \text{x} \quad /$$

Marking a tension at the first syllable. *A tension marks a place of metrical controversy*, and 'rough' may or may not be demoted; the voice will often perform a syllable neither exactly w *nor* s.

However, in the next step in our scansion, that of sense stress analysis, I feel we might have:

Rough winds do shake the darling buds of May
$$\backslash' \qquad /' \quad \text{x} \ /, \quad \text{x}, /, \text{x}, \quad /, \quad \text{x} \quad /$$

Here 'rough' is *sustained* against its weak position for syntactic (monosyllabic qualifier + monosyllabic noun often results in near-spondee, especially in the initial position) and emphatic sense-stress reasons (the sense demands that the subject is *not* 'winds' plus a casually descriptive qualifier, but '*rough* winds' as a metonym for 'bad stuff'). Note that one cannot arrive at the judgement of 'sustained against weak position' (i.e. a 'refused demotion') from a lexical scansion alone, which merely *indicates* tensions; it does not resolve them. Only a sense interpretation does. Nor is accent or de-accent always handily provided to resolve them either, of course. (And nor do they then *necessarily* resolve them; in some ways pitch accent and stress pattern can be coexistent frames, even though apparently contradictory values attach themselves to the same stress.) As I've mentioned, many tensions are left hanging in performance – equivocally and rather deliciously at a *medial* stress position, making a great variety of stress-contours – i.e. alternative interpretations – available to the line. An accent on the demoted s of 'rough' returns the stress to something close to its original s *salience*, but via a pitch, not a stress compensation.

My reasons for scanning 'the darling buds' as [x, /, x, /,] I'll discuss in due course. Note one miserable complication: polysyllabic words which take an accent tend to take it only on the s-syllable, and keep their weak stresses in a largely unchanged position to maintain contrast; however *all* syllables in the word will usually suffer the same *de-accent*, as pitch here is suprasegmental. The performative reality is that an entire phrase will often take the same low accent too; but for sanity and simplicity's sake I mark only *strongly* phrasemic material in this way, i.e. such material in the line that is strongly lexically bound, and therefore likely to be de-accented all of a piece. (Although suprasegmental de-accent is often strongly indicated by a consecutive run of low [x]s and [x,]s and [/,]s. I had considered merely underlining the words through which the suprasegmental accent runs, but owing to the messiness of a balancing system of overlining for *accent* – accent most often occurring singly – I abandoned it. Phonology has its own precise systems for these things; the merit of our system *is* its approximate nature.) Note that my rough numerical system of intonational analysis described below preserves the same s-w difference between the two syllables of 'darling' as one would find in its un-de-accented state, while nonetheless marking the word's overall intonational 'demotion'; the information is not summed.

While I'll describe this in more detail, the scansion procedure with tight and loose metres is roughly as follows:

1. Make a lexical scansion by projecting the template above the line, and marking the 'resting state' lexical prosody below it (this would include the analysis of any lexicalised phrasemic material):

x / x /   x / x /   x   /

Shall I compare thee to a summer's day?

x x x   /   x xx /   x   /

2. Consolidate the information in a single notational system (after a little practice one can do this immediately, making it step 1):

Shall I compare thee to a summer's day?

x X x   /   x X x /   x   /

3. Make a sense-stress analysis, factoring in the phonological rules of syntax and phrase, and marking such accent and de-accent as appropriate:[1]

Shall I compare thee to a summer's day?

x X, x   /,   x X, x /   x   /'

---

[1] The fact that these analyses are highly subjective and must be justified by articulated explanation is precisely *why* we should make them; they are concerned with the intelligent interpretation and performance of the line. Without them the whole process of lexical scansion can be automated, and some basic computer programs have been written to accomplish just this. (They do not, of course, conduct phrasemic analysis, which would be a sophistication only the military could fund.) The results are broadly accurate and even more broadly without any value.

4. Derive an intonational contour.

This last move is, I fear, my own 'sophistication'; it is really a simplification, but one I believe worthwhile. Suppose that we now assume strong stresses have, as a component of their stress-quality, a normative pitch accent value of 2, and weak stresses one of 0. Our demoted s or promoted w tensions will generally lie somewhere in between, being 'pitch-adjusted' through the pitch-component of their stress position, so can both receive a value of one (although as merely *potentiated* changes they are unstable, i.e. 'tensive' – and will be marked as such, with an asterisk). Accent and de-accent add and subtract one respectively. This leaves us with:

$$/ \ = \ 2$$
$$x \ = \ 0$$
$$, \ = \ -1$$
$$' \ = \ +1$$
$$\backslash \ = \ 1$$
$$X \ = \ 1$$

Working our way through the twelve permutations produces:

$$/' \ = \ 3$$
$$/ \ = \ 2$$
$$\backslash' \ = \ *2$$
$$X' \ = \ *2$$
$$x' \ = \ 1$$
$$/, \ = \ 1$$
$$X \ = \ *1$$
$$\backslash \ = \ *1$$
$$\backslash, \ = \ *0$$
$$X, \ = \ *0$$
$$x \ = \ 0$$
$$x, \ = \ -1$$

This gives five pitch gradations derived from our final scansion, with the unresolved tensions marked with an asterisk to indicate that the value is unstable, and that the stress can weaken or strengthen a little where the line needs to preserve ASR. (For instance a double tension [X \] will not be felt as a '1 1' spondee, since AS will usually imprint itself; the tension, marked '*1 *1' allows it the instability and therefore the latitude to do so.) The bell-curve distribution of the five values is important, as extremes should be rarer than median stresses. This run of numbers makes explicit two obvious phonological phenomena: where we see a large numerical difference, we will likely perform a sharp rise or fall in pitch; and where we see a run of the same or similar low or high numerical values, we will see the strong potentiation and very likely appearance of suprasegmental effect in the form of sustained and even pitch (note that this is more often *neutrally* even than either high or low).

Thus:

$$\text{o} \quad \text{o*o} \quad 1 \qquad \text{o} \quad \text{o*o} \quad 2 \qquad \text{o} \qquad 3$$
Shall I compare thee to a summer's day?
$$\text{x} \quad \text{X,x} \quad /, \qquad \text{x} \quad \text{X,x} \quad / \qquad \text{x} \qquad /'$$

and

$$2* \qquad 3 \qquad \text{o} \quad 1 \qquad -1 \quad 1 \quad -1 \quad 1 \quad \text{o} \quad 2$$
Rough winds do shake the darling buds of May
$$\backslash' \qquad /' \qquad \text{x} \quad /, \qquad \text{x,} /, \text{x,} \quad /, \qquad \text{x} \qquad /$$

This forms our final scansion and accounts for both stress-value and pitch contour. Although this has little granularity, it still allows us to see the rough intonational contour of the line, and is useful as a 'performance tablature'.

The danger of this system is that the numerical line provides only the very limited information of a rough performance note — ideally we would convert it to a single rising and falling line – and the lower line too *much* information, which (in, for example, resolving tensions as a single sign rather than allowing them to *stand* as tensions) loses the sense of a scansion as a wholly subjective interpretation. Moreover, it fails to register the suprasegmental *flow* of accent and de-accent, and notes them as syllabic-specific marks. (As I mentioned, I considered consolidating runs of suprasegmental accent thus:

Rough winds do shake the darling buds of May
\   /   x /,   x   /   x   /   x   /

but I'm wary of introducing further notational marks, and these don't aid the rapid calculation of numerical values; consecutive runs of accents can be easily seen. It may nonetheless be a system worth developing in the future, as it enjoys the advantage of showing that while syllable segments, sense flows.)

At this point one might recall T. F. Brogan's warning with a shiver, but to repeat: the alternative is a scansion that *entirely ignores the sense of the poem*, which might as well be a lineated plumbing manual. And where sense is concerned, as we will see, there is no alternative but discussion, flexible strategies of analysis, and a little subjective description. It's no bad thing to be reminded that we are not dealing with a branch of the sciences; nor should we aspire to be.

I will mention, however, a hugely simplified notation I use for making rapid notes on other metrical poems, including my own, so I can recall what sense I originally made of them when I return to them later. This is especially useful if I'm required to read them in public. The dots over the vowel never occur in isolation (i.e. they indicate a suprasegmental phenomenon), and represent runs of roughly even, mid-strength consecutive stresses, usually produced by normal w promotion or s demotion (especially frequent in the 10-position loose i.p. line, where any 'felt' alterneity will depend on the ASR alone); the accent and de-accent marks are derived from sense stress analysis. The stress-position agreement is unmarked, which is to say the metricality of the line is taken as given (i.e. I *know* this is in i.p.).

I found a dimpled spider, fat and white,

On a white heal-all, holding up a moth

Like a white piece of rigid satin cloth —

Assorted characters of death and blight

Mixed ready to begin the morning right,
Like the ingredients of a witches' broth —

A snow-drop spider, a flower like a froth,

And dead wings carried like a paper kite.

What had that flower to do with being white,

The wayside blue and innocent heal-all?

What brought the kindred spider to that height,

Then steered the white moth thither in the night?

What but design of darkness to appal?—

If design govern in a thing so small.

(ROBERT FROST, 'Design')[2]

---

2 Robert Frost, *The Collected Poems* (London: Vintage Classics, 2013).

(The words 'white' and 'design' are repeated, and their second appearances treated as anaphors; the other marks are, I hope, self-explanatory in the context of the poem.)

Light metre in its purest form would theoretically allow all weak placeholders to be populated with any number of w-syllables, including zero; however, this would constitute a definition of accentual verse, and in reality we must establish a 'viable threshold' *before* that point is reached (the deep problems with 'pure' tonal/accentual and strong-stress metres in English have been separately discussed). The closest we get to accentual verse in English are the very freest song-strong Dolnik interpretations of 4-strong; light metre cannot happily exist as a form of i.p. Some might feel that 'Dolnik' is really a *synonym* for light metre in English, but this would omit such common 4-strong-derived forms as the light 'two-step', a kind of slow, roughly measured, content-heavy, half-time, 2-strong line very common in contemporary poetry.

Its notation is simplified, as tensions are impossible without a clear correspondence between stress position and stress; as the number of syllables in the line becomes more and more variable, such a position-based correspondence becomes impossible to maintain in the ear, with extra or omitted syllables heard *not* as variations in fixed syllable count, but as part of an inbuilt latitude in the template itself. This means that we cannot derive the numbers of our intonational contour; but this is just as is should be, since the fluidity of the line also affords considerably more latitude in its sense-stress interpretation. All we require here are the following:

-x- — w position or placeholder
/ — s position
/ — s syllable on s position
x — w syllable on w placeholder

/' or x' – accent
/, or x, – de-accent

and (if we're inclined):

x-x or x-x-x – double or triple weak
[x] – omitted weak

Free metre has no metrical template, and can be described by a single scansion line:

/ – s syllable
x – w syllable
/' or x' – s or w accent
/, or x, – s or w de-accent

However, anyone proposing a more sophisticated method of scanning free metre would have to make especial account of variations in the teleuton, free verse's unique prosodic quality. (A start might be to attach numerical values to the line-break cline to indicate relative degrees of smoothness or disruption.)

TWO CRITICISMS

Word boundaries

It is unlikely that word boundaries represent a prosodic aspect important enough to be worth bothering to account for in poetry. The first point to make is that two monosyllables have more fluidity in terms of how their stress can be interpreted than the more fixed prosody of a bisyllabic word, and this is an important consideration when establishing sense-stress latitudes; the second is that there is a good chance that the poet will have given this matter no thought whatsoever in the course of an entire lifetime. This means that such effects as are produced by the coincidence or non-coincidence of word-boundary and metrical pattern are wholly unconscious.

So to what extent Paul Kiparsky's so-called 'bracketing mis-matches',[1] (when the [w-s] [w-s] [w-s] [w-s] [w-s] foot-pattern he believed to be both present and indicative of higher structures is crossed by a word) makes any difference to our perception of the line really depends on the structural integrity we are prepared to grant the iamb. I would give it very little. As I've mentioned, the iambic rising 'flavour' of lines is as much a response to normative English sentence structure, its frequent need to start with a function word (as well as the relative paucity of feminine words with which to end the phrase); there are few other justifications for the habit of cutting into the metrical wallpaper at that point. To claim that (picking two lines from Wilbur's 'The Mind Reader' at random)

1   Paul Kiparsky, 'The Rhythmic Structure of English Verse', *Linguistic Inquiry* 8 (1977): 189–247.

My hand on theirs and go into my frenzy
[w s] [w   s] [w   s][w s] [w s]

can meaningfully be considered as less complex or more regular than, say

I scribble when I must. Your paramour . . .²
[w   s] [w   s] [w s]   [w   s][w s]

— simply because in the second line the strong-onset words 'scribble' and 'paramour' run across the w-s bracketed pairings seems absurd, taking into account (a) the issue of the perception of word-boundary itself, which is often just a psychological phenomenon; (b) the prosodic complications we find at the level of local instantiation — clitic, affix, polysyllabism, phrasemic strength, nuclear stress and forty other factors; and, most compellingly, (c) the fact that there are more trochaic than iambic bisyllabic nouns and adjectives in the language anyway (verbs are more often iambic). This means the negative status of 'mismatch' is risked almost every time we use a bisyllabic content word that is not a verb, which at the very least points to 'mismatch' being the wrong word for the job, or 'matching' itself being a waste of time. (That said — Kiparsky's use of the term is rigorously, if confusingly, neutral; I'm only complaining about the application of this theory to the poetic line.) 'Boundary violation' is not a form of perceptible 'enjambment', because there's nothing to violate. Unlike the phrase and the line ending, the word does not 'run on' across foot boundaries, because there *are* no foot boundaries, and in any case word boundaries themselves are often phonologically elided.

On the contrary, it might be said that a far more pleasing effect is realised when a strong onset coincides with a strong position. Nine-

2   Richard Wilbur, *The Mind Reader: New Poems* (San Diego, CA: Harcourt Brace Jovanovich, 1976).

month-old infants listen longer to bisyllabic words with a s-w pattern than to those with an iambic pattern,[3] and generally prefer words with strong-syllable onsets. In the flow of speech, they can also detect strong-onset words far more clearly than weak-onset, whether single-syllable or polysyllabic, and – contrary to the 'bracketing' principle – may establish word-boundary by isolating trochaic pattern in speech. (This is consistent with the tendency in nearly all higher-level intonational phrases to go s-w, or at least high-low, and is the basis of the ASR matrix.) Whether this leads to an increased salience of strong-onset words in adult conversation is not settled, but even a vestigial effect would likely be intensified by strong-position coincidence in metred verse. My sense is that there may be not only a tendency in poetry to favour strong-onset words in strong positions in metrical verse – but strong-onset words generally. Note too that, while strong-onset words can be used in radical metrical variations on weak positions, e.g. 'Rough winds do shake **harshly** the buds of May' or 'Rough winds **batter** the darling buds of May', weak-onset bisyllabic words on strong positions are almost never used in metrical variation, and are uncomfortable, e.g. 'Rough winds do shake the **maroon** buds of May'. I'm not convinced this is too mysterious: both require us to accommodate two metrical variations, one gentle and one more radical: the double w (*harshly the* and *the ma*roon) is a variation of the 'weak position rule', while the s-syllable on the w-position (*harshly the* and *the ma*roon) invokes the far bolder 'displaced weak rule', where we often make a mora compensation – 'Rough winds do shake [:] **harshly** the buds of May' or 'Rough winds [:] **batter** the darling buds of May'. But my sense is that such double variations

3   Martin H. Kelly and Susanne Martin, 'Domain-General Abilities Applied to Domain-Specific Tasks : Sensitivity to Probabilities in Perception, Cognition, and Language', *Lingua* 92 (1994): 105–40; Peter W. Jusczyk, Anne Cutler and Nancy J. Redanz, 'Infants' Preference for the Predominant Stress Patterns of English Words', *Child Development* 64 (1993): 675–87.

generally present in the order 'more radical → less radical', if the AS is to be re-established after the first glitch. Weak-onset bisyllables on s positions enact a 'minor variation followed by major variation', and feel like the template is being abandoned; the mora must be placed *after* the word, where its compensation only seems to make things worse: 'Rough winds do shake the **maroon** [:] buds of May'. For that reason they tend to scream 'unmetrical'.

Heavy use of strong-onset bisyllabic or polysyllabic words in s-positions probably contributes some minimal trochaic feel to the line, however, as weak onset words in w-positions will an iambic feel. But both these approaches, if applied consistently, would form a conscious or semi-conscious overdetermination of the metre; in other words, stress/word-boundary coincidence may influence where we take the start of the metron *from*. However, I find the difference vestigial, and for our purposes negligible. Perhaps we can try to argue that strong-onset content words in strong positions have unusually high salience, and may therefore be more theme-directive; but that would imply that weak-onset words can *never* enjoy such salience (a tiger will always leap out more than an impala, and a banjo sound more loudly more than a guitar). Even if there's a grain of truth here, it remains a grain, and the argument swiftly becomes silly. (So-called 'labelling mismatches', the disagreement of metrical and lexical stress, are the more serious phenomenon, simply because they are audible; however, these are largely identical to the tensions described in non-generative forms of prosodic analysis.)

Stress-tree analysis

The kind of stress-tree analysis derived from generative linguistics and favoured by Kiparsky and subsequent theorists is not, I feel, particularly helpful in analysing verse prosody. Where it seems far more successful is in the analysis of the resting state prosody (RSP) of short text samples — whether in verse or not. In making these analyses, the prosodist must take care *not* to colour the analysis with sense stress, and indeed make sure they subscribe rigorously to the more successful of the metrical-phonological rules (such as Liberman's rule for multiple-stress words, the normative operation of nuclear stress within spoken phrases, and so on) that govern the rhythms of well-formed speech and most written language.

However, despite its often rhythmic character, poetry provides *singularly* inappropriate samples for such analysis. Poetry is in some ways predicated on the immediate dismantling and subversion of its RSP, which falls to the exigencies and emergencies of metrical and emotional pressure almost immediately. It seems far more sensible to make a rough-and-ready lexical stress analysis, and then skip immediately to a sense-stress analysis. This, inevitably, provides only 'a blueprint for performance' — but to dismiss this as a piffling matter that can somehow be accounted for further down the analytic line is a grievous error. A poem fundamentally *is* a blueprint for its own performance. A scansion incorporating sense stress will give far more insight into what a poet 'meant', and to where they hear their pragmatic emphases and de-emphases, than any forensic description of the kind of higher-level tensions between syntax and rhythm that stress-tree analysis reveals or alleges; by the time we get to those tensions, they have already been undermined and rewritten by far more urgent linguistic, rhetorical and pragmatic concerns.

A stress-tree analysis of a difficult Shakespeare sonnet, say, would founder almost immediately on encountering Shakespeare's habit of turning language from solid to liquid through sheer emotional heat, echolalic patterning, an almost demented thematic reflexivity, and the consequent overdetermination of thematic domain. This means he will often detach words from their native part of speech and primary denotation, and allow them to orient themselves freely according to the magnetic force-field of the poem — one he has established through a mixture of lyric signature and domain-rule metonymy. (Stress-tree your way out of 'Even so, being full of your ne'er-cloying sweetness, /

To bitter sauces did I frame my feeding, / And, sick of welfare, found a kind of meetness / To be diseased, ere that there was true needing' or 'Mine eye hath played the painter and hath stell'd / Thy beauty's form in table of my heart; / My body is the frame wherein 'tis held, / And perspective it is best painter's art',[4] if you dare.) A word in a Shakespeare verse can make its contribution as much through a kind of 'semic ambience' as through any paraphrasable sense; and the skills of the generative metricists are, I am afraid, largely redundant in pursuing the considerable effects this has on the prosody of the line. What a more immediately subjective scansion can tell us, however, is how tensions between rhythm and phrase both dramatise his sense and provide room for a variety of sense-interpretations, which can be pursued or confirmed through the purely descriptive process of sense-stress analysis. Poems, in their semantic instability, their deconstruction and reconstruction of phrasemic material, their blurring of function and content, their metricality and deliberate overstressing, are 'all over the place'. A detailed tree structure hoping to unearth stress-contrast at higher phrasal levels is doomed to failure, because the connotative, unstable nature of poetic lexicality means that such structures are undermined from the bottom up.

Additionally, it is alarmingly unsympathetic to the way this poetic material has come into being. Such metrical-phrasal tensions as exist have arisen as artefacts of driving the urgent semantic and syntactic concerns of the poet against the resistance of the metrical template, not vice versa. To prioritise the metrical and prosodic in the hope that these will shed light on the semantic is the wrong way round, and places a primary emphasis on matters which, while important, are simply not as central to the art as they claim to be. Furthermore, it is also a too-easily self-justifying and circular exercise: when dealing with an unstable and polysemic text, *any* single reading is easily

---

4 Sonnets 118 and 24, *Shakespeare's Sonnets*, ed. Katherine Duncan Jones (London: Arden Shakespeare, 2010), 347, 159.

confirmed. One can easily find oneself in the position of someone standing in a garden in the middle of the night, reading a sundial with a torch, and proclaiming that they guessed the time exactly right.

No word steps into the same sense twice. (Unless it appears in a phraseme, of course, but even these are slaves to context.) Stress and sense are irrevocably connected. Stress is many things, but it is primarily a performative aspect of the properties of function and content, and these are properties which are psychologically conferred – and can therefore be switched. We've mentioned several times the way the second of two repeated content words in a sentence is often demoted to a weakly stressed anaphoric role: stress-tree analysis generally takes insufficient account of even this basic phonological phenomenon, never mind the more complex destabilisations of poetry. To claim that higher level w/s distinctions can be neutrally derived from lexical stress and a handful of rules ignores not only the fact that the individual signs are themselves unstable but also the fact that 'phrasal context' involves a higher-level, domain-ruled semanticisation – and hence a top-down supervenience on the syllabic stress of words which are *themselves* already problematised in their relationship to their own prosody. At the end of the day, generative metrics seems – like so much else – firmly predicated on crediting words with intrinsic value; but poetry demonstrates that this is something they possess even less than paper money or the art object. They are merely interpretable acts, and do not 'possess' meaning but indicate points of its contextual constraint. Poetry challenges and rewrites the generic context that confers sense on words, and can alter their local use beyond recognition.

PROJECTION ERRORS

Against 'inversion'

While they remain supremely insightful, I don't quite subscribe to what Attridge calls 'deviation rules', or more specifically the table of the order of their complexity.[1] These clines are problematic as there are too many variables, and single instantiations of so-called 'complexity' are mitigated or *further* complicated by metrical context. I prefer simply to declare the template tight, loose, light or free depending on the *median* level of variation, as demonstrated by whatever the reader thinks of as typical lines from a representative passage. One complication is that whatever might look fixed at the level of metrical scansion remains provisional until *some* contextual and syntactic account has been made of the material; this can often shift the projected template, and reverse the 'complexity'.

Serious differences in scansion arise depending on whether we hear a poet working to a tight or loose metrical frame. Additionally, different poets also hear the rules differently; part of a 'style' is hearing deviations which one poet may regard as radical as relatively non-disruptive – and vice versa. For example, we know that two ws can often occupy a weak position (Attridge's 'double offbeat rule' – that 'two unstressed syllables may realise an offbeat'). This is not generally

---

1 '1. Base rules 2. Double offbeat option of second base rule 3. Promotion 4. Demotion (mid-line) 5. Demotion (initial) 6. Implied offbeat and double offbeat 7. Promotion, implied offbeat, and double offbeat 8. Demotion, double offbeat, and implied offbeat 9. Two double offbeats and two implied offbeats.' – Derek Attridge, *The Rhythms of English Poetry* (New York: Routledge, 2014).

regarded as a radical or complex deviation; however, because Robert Frost only very occasionally employs it in a medial position, one can infer he treats it like one, and, to a careful reader of Frost, it also feels like one. Frost prefers his variation within an acatalectic frame, with one exception: w additions after the first stress. Confusingly, this variation is often called 'initial inversion', implying that the initial x/ iamb has been flipped to produce a trochee, leaving two successive ws. For example, in Frost's 'After Apple-Picking'[2] we see the following (I have notated only the deviations on the bottom line):

x /   x   /   x   /   x   /   x /

Cherish in hand, lift down, and not let fall.

/ x   x   /

According to this metre-strong description, the successive ws in 'Cherish in hand' are produced by 'inversion'. But compare them to the two ws which appear – in a rare deviation for Frost – in the middle of this line:

x   / x /   -x-   / x   /x   /

Magnified apples appear and disappear,

/   x x   /

According to the scansion, two ws occupy the position of the weak placeholder; therefore one is the result of a w addition. However, you will note that, like 'Cherish in hand . . .', this line also has two ws produced by 'initial inversion' too:

x   / x /   -x-   / x   /x   /

Magnified apples appear and disappear,

/   x x /

---

2   Robert Frost, *The Collected Poems* (London: Vintage Classics, 2013).

This leaves two /xx/ patterns in the line – apparently produced by different means. The problem is that the effect on the reader is identical: all *they* know is that Frost has briefly held out the promise of a triple metre. ('Magnified apples appear and then disappear' – /xx/xx/xx/xx – would sustain it.) While one is allegedly 'an inversion' and the other 'an addition', there is no palpable difference between either variation – meaning that our metrical accountancy is simply not aligning with perceived reality. I would, therefore, *not* say either of the above lines had suffered an inversion at all, but call them acephalic, i.e. lines where the initial w is dropped. This is because in a *speech*-strong reading – of the kind, for the record, Frost explicitly demanded – there *can be no inversion*; and this has serious implications in terms of where we position the metrical template. The w at the end of 'magnified' is a simple w addition, like the extra w in 'apples appear', and is registered as such. ('Magic apples appear and disappear' is also acephalic; it does not contain the extra w in 'magnified', the product of the so-called 'inversion' – but all is still well.) The difference between 'Cherish in hand, lift down . . .' and 'Cherish lots, lift down . . .' is merely a w addition. We should allow our analysis to accord with experience, or it will be of little value:

-x- / -x- / x / x / x /
Cherish in hand, lift down, and not let fall.
/ x x / \ / x / \ /

-x- / -x- / -x- / x / x /
Magnified apples appear and disappear,[3]
/ xx / x x / x / x X

---

[3] The lexical stress of 'disappear' here is emphatically /xx, to my ear – setting aside the ametrical run of three ws that xx/ (i.e. *and disappear*) would give us, its use here is contrastive to 'appear' – and when we make contrasts, the changing component (here *dis*-) is emphasised. In a fuller scansion, it would also receive an intonational accent.

The point is that 'inversion' implies a tension where none has been felt. (Unlike 'lift down', where the disagreement is palpable.) Frost merely has a preference for variation in the initial position, where it is most smoothly accommodated. I'd dispute that 'inversion' is *ever* an adequate description of the experience in the ear and mind of the reader. For all it looks that way in certain notated scansions – nothing is perceptibly 'inverted' by the 'inverted foot', any more than long mirror-image melodies are ever perceived as palindromic. This mistake arises through the reification of notational features (which involves unthinkingly converting temporal information to a spatial mark); it also has the fatal appeal of being more easily and less fussily notated than what's *actually* happening. Wherever we encounter lexical stresses 'out of place' we should first see if an alternative projection will accommodate them, and not assume that the apparent disagreement has produced a tension. We do this by remembering that an -x- or x in the metre represents a duration, not a position; and then moving, expanding or contracting the metrical frame written above the line. Failure to do so will swiftly lead to some serious misdiagnoses. (The fundamental issue at the root of all this is that, while a 'weak-stress position' looks conveniently fluid, a weak durational placeholder is far less so, and is largely non-negotiable.)

As we'll see, there always exists the possibility of a metre-strong performance, and this remains the quixotic preference of some readers, actors and poets. Here, the frame is projected differently, and tensions *will* be felt – often at the cost of natural speech. But even here, the word 'inversion' does not describe these tensions adequately.

The mora

For our purposes, the mora is a piece of quantitative fixing which takes the place of a weak stress in the form of a pause (nominally around the length of half a weak stress) between consecutive strong syllables. It arises in radical variations, when a w-syllable lands on a strong position but cannot be promoted. 'Cannot' is advised. Misunderstanding this point has led to serious errors of scansion. Let's look at that old prosodic chestnut, Marvell's 'Annihilating all that's made / To a green Thought in a green Shade.'

The template is a 4-strong duple line, or iambic tetrameter. The second line is often analysed thus:

$$x/ \quad x \quad / \quad x/ \quad x \quad /$$
To a green Thought in a green Shade
$$x\,x \quad / \quad / \quad x\,x \quad / \quad /$$

i.e.

To a green Thought in a green Shade
$$x\,X \quad \backslash \quad / \quad x\,X \quad \backslash \quad /$$

This scansion treats *every* metron as if it had undergone some variation. It potentiates the promotion of both 'a's and the demotion of both 'green's to something like a medial stress; it would mean that in 'in a green Shade' both syllables of 'a green' are potentiated as unstable; then, finding themselves the middle of three reasonably strong stresses (two tensive, one strong), both 'green's would be find themselves lightly demoted to maintain the ASR. There is, of course, no way this can ever be realised. In this strenuously metre-strong reading, the emphatic 'ā', which *could* take a stronger stress, can't be justified by semantic context; it is clearly the poet's intention that it remain weak, and that we should hear a radical variation. Since the dimetron xx// for x/x/ is by no means rare, this has led some theorists to rule that it represents a legitimate and metrical substitution or inversion.

The reality is more complex. The problem lies with the projection of the template itself – and the subsequently erroneous positioning of the w placeholders above the line. 'To a' is *not* a pyrrhic substitution for the first and third feet. Almost-imperceptible but performed morae (they can be thought of as a generally silent weak *uh* sound, attached to the end of the first strong stress in each pair, or an elongation or diph-thongisation of the first vowel) provides quantitative fixing by acting as a ghost weak, maintaining the ASR. The line is not acatalectic, but is radical because the poet has switched to a much looser metrical frame:

-x-   / -x- /   -x-   / -x- /
To a green Thought in a green Shade
x x   / : /   x x   / : /

'To' is anacrustic; 'in' is an additional syllable; and a realised w syllable has been omitted between 'green Thought' and 'green Shade', where it has been replaced with a very brief pause. I call this addition + omission process a 'displaced weak', since the mora is often – but not always – accompanied by the ghost-w it replaces, which shows up in the immediate vicinity to form a double w. Both the mora and the extra w are part of the same quantitative fix; the mora fills in for the empty weak placeholder, while the extra w makes up for any lost length. There are occasions when the 'displaced weak' is employed and the extra w does *not* appear, but life is usually simpler when it does. Try losing the double ws and making the line 'A green[:] Thought of green [:] Shade' work as tetrameter; the mora is working overtime very uncomfortably (unless you were to actually *voice* it as a w 'uh', your instinct will be to elongate the 'ee' in 'green' into upper-class diction).

The mora is really an exercise in spondee-avoidance when the metrical pattern is / -x- / but the weak placeholder realises no syllable. The mora can take the form of a tiny gap between a conson-antally closed coda and the next word's strong onset, but can also take advantage of a variety of phonological or morphological circum-stances: by 'leaning' on the first stress's vowel to elongate it ('cheap shot' performed to a /-x-/ template will tend to 'cheeeap [-uh] shot');

by taking any possible advantage of the potential to diphthongise the vowel ('bare bones' will tend to 'bay-ahr bones'); by placing micropauses between word and affix ('Dave's shed' will tend to 'Dave-iz shed'); elongating the second stress if it is easier to do so that the first ('big coin' tends to 'big coy-een'; or drawing a little more length from *both* stresses ('pooor moouth'). In other words, 'mora' is just a cover for any old strategy where the length of the line can be increased (ideally by a discrete w-impersonating segment but often just by opportunistic stretching) to cover the missing syllable. Note that these effects are fleeting, vestigial, and perhaps more psychologically present than performed — but they are necessary to retain the integrity of the template in performance. Take the third line in this passage:

> Whether or not I put my mind to it,
> The world usurps me ceaselessly; my sixth
> And never-resting sense is a cheap room
> Black with the anger of insomnia,

(RICHARD WILBUR, 'The Mind Reader')[4]

There is enough information in these lines to project a loose i.p. Just like the Marvell line, the xx// pattern of 'is a cheap room' is the result of a displaced weak, not an inversion or substitution, and in a speech-strong reading (I confess I have a tendency to favour them, although they are not always sympathetic to the line or the poet's projection) is corrected by a mora:

> x   / x / x   /   -x- / x /
> And never-resting sense is a cheap room
> x   / x / x   / x x / : /

4 Richard Wilbur, *The Mind Reader: New Poems* (Palo Alto, CA: Harcourt Brace Jovanovich, 1976).

One can hear that 'And never-resting sense is a crappy room' scans much the same way. (A metre-strong reading of the original line would either attempt to promote the w 'a' to an emphatic article, or argue for a non-existent 'inversion'.) However, there is a significant complication.

A slightly different line with a more easily 'promotable' weak syllable might have encouraged the template to be projected in a crucially different, *metre*-strong way (as would the original line having occurred within an identifiably tight-metre context):

x   / x / x   /   x / x   /

And never-resting sense is this cheap room

x   / x / x   /   x X   \   /

'This' is also a function word, but unlike 'a', it is capable of contextual promotion, meaning that it is far less likely to be heard as the radical 'displaced weak'. This means the line will be heard as acatalectic – and that we can line up the template directly over the syllables, leaving us with potentiated promotion on 'this', and a demotion on 'cheap', and an easily preserved AS in 'is this cheap room', with no quantitative easing required. (The numerical contour values are 0 1* 1* 2; remember, the asterisk indicates tensive instability, meaning that although both 'this' and 'cheap' are 1s, a tensive stress can either weaken or strengthen a little wherever it needs to preserve AS.)

In conclusion: half our 'tensions' are really misdiagnosed. Speech-strong scansions, especially, will reveal them as really either variations produced by initial acephalsis or anacrusis, or an internal displaced weak. The moral here is that we *cannot* project the metre correctly until some executive decision has been made over the poem's tighter or looser metrical frame – and that 'best practice' is probably to conduct lexical stress analysis and the projection of the template more or less simultaneously, so we can correct as we go.

– 605 –

THE RULES OF METRICAL VARIATION

These are produced through parsing the possible misalignments between the two binary systems of metrical and lexical stress, their limit being 'perceived unmetricality'.

1. The weak placeholder rule
2. The strong position rule
3. Tension rules:
   a) the initial rule
   b) the 3-stress rule
   c) the double tension rule
   d) the displaced weak rule

(Where uncredited, the example will have been drawn from Derek Mahon's 'Beyond Howth Head', a spectacularly virtuosic example of duple 4-strong loose metre.[1] Mahon's prosodic sophistication has been an insufficiently praised aspect of his work, but he has himself to blame; the extent to which his prosodic effects smoothly facilitate his sense have rendered it largely invisible, but poets, at least, have no excuse for not learning from him.)

It is important to point out that more than one legitimate scansion may exist even before we get to making a sense-stress analysis. Again, this depends on whether the reader chooses *a metre-strong or speech-strong performance*, which affects how the metrical template is projected. The main area of disagreement will then lie between double tensions and displaced weak stresses. These have a tendency to

---

1   Derek Mahon, *Collected Poems* (Oldcastle: Gallery Books, 1999).

go duck-rabbit on performers of the verse line, but the explanation is relatively straightforward, and essentially they offer two ways of rejecting the spondee, which the anglophone ear tends to regard as 'wrong'. AS is maintained through *either* a qualitative or quantitative solution: through taking advantage of the stress-instability of the tension itself, or though the introduction of a mora between the s-syllables.

The weak placeholder rule

W stresses can be omitted or multiplied in weak positions. Their metricality depends on the relative looseness of the template. Double ws and omissions are the most common variations:

```
-x-    /      x  / x /  x    /
of the drowned, and I put out the light
x    x   /
```

```
    x  / x  /  -x-  / x /
gruff Jeremiads to redirect
         /x   x  /
```

```
x / x   /   -x-   / x   /
Atlantic, hammering in its haste
x / x   /    x x  X x   /
```

Omissions are generally absorbed either by caesurae (a straight lexical scansion would mark the caesura with a [|], though the actual scansion will often see us employing the mora here):

```
x   / x / -x- /   x   /
or l'outre-tombe; make no noise
x   / x /   :  /    \  /
```

– or the smaller gaps between phrase boundary (where both omission and addition can be better accommodated). See, for example, the following passage of loose i.p.:

> You did say, need me less | **and I'll** want you more.
> I'm still shellshocked at needing anyone,
> used to being used **to it** | on my own.
>
> (MARILYN HACKER, 'You did say . . .')[2]

– or by the hiatus, especially where we see feminine endings in even-stress metres, where the hiatus is minimal. These are often followed by an acephalic line:

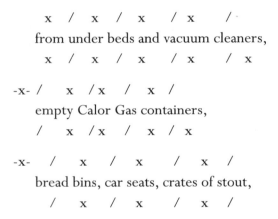

('bread bins' and 'car seats' are phrasemic.) Odd-stress metres like i.p. can absorb acephalic 'trochaic' openings after a masculine enjamb-ment easily, because the missing initial w coincides with the ghost metron, and the resulting spondee is easily avoided with a firm mora in the gap:

2 Marilyn Hacker, *Love, Death, and the Changing of the Seasons* (New York: W. W. Norton, 1986).

-x- /   x   / -x-   /   x / x /   [x /]
     Powre new seas in mine eyes, that so I might
-x-   /   x /   -x-   / x   / x / [x /]
     Drowne my world with my weeping earnestly

(JOHN DONNE, 'Holy Sonnet V')[3]

However, omitted ws *without* space for such compensation often fall to the quantitative fix of the displaced weak rule, and will see both the emergence of the w elsewhere as part of a w pair, and the introduction of a mora between the s stresses, avoiding the 'crime against nature' of the spondee.

The strong position rule

S positions *must* be occupied by either an s or a promotable w-syllable, otherwise the line is unmetrical. (One can have an empty space, but not a non-event.) S stresses which are additional to the template and *cannot* be demoted by tensions are by definition supernumerary, and therefore also unmetrical. Here's an example of a 'missing event':

      -x-   /   x   / x /   x   /?
        Meanwhile, for a word's sake,
        /   x X x /   \   ?

(The line could, incidentally, be corrected with a mora between the last two syllables, but it's an extreme solution. The poet's 'error' is a metatextual trick, and wholly intentional: see below.)

The next line in Mahon's poem contains an unmetrical s-stress *addition*:

---

3   John Donne, *Selected Poems* (London: Penguin, 2006).

Meanwhile, for a word's sake,

  -x-   /   x / x /   x /

the plastic bombs go off around Belfast;

[x /] x   /   x / x /   x /

— where the s stress on 'plastic' cannot possibly be absorbed by the w placeholder, giving us a pentameter line unmetrically crammed into a tetrameter frame — though, as can be seen from the short and self-descriptive previous line, the effect here is quite deliberately metatextual. Still more impressively, the poet has even shunted the missing rhyme into the line, in the 'correct' position: 'plast-' rhymes with 'Belfast' (whose position enforces its local, near-spondaic pro-nunciation); we see that the couplet is just a clever relineation of 'Meanwhile, for a word's sake, the plast- / ic bombs go off around Belfast'. Which realisation might, incidentally, lead us to reposition the template over the first line with the first weak over 'Mean-' and then apply the 'initial rule' (see below).

Tension rules

Potentiated tensive stresses are unstable, and have the latitude to maintain AS. A w stress on a strong position potentiates a promotion; an s stress on a weak position potentiates a demotion. The result is either a **single tension**, which results in the application of the 3-stress rule in any but the initial position, or a **double tension**, which can alternatively be interpreted as a displaced weak with a compensating mora (usually if the template is projected speech-strong rather than metre-strong — see below). They can also occasionally denote sense-stress accents, i.e. a demoted s can reinforce a de-accent, and a promoted w an accent.

Weak promotion:

```
x   /  x  /  x  /  x   /
and so by this declension fall
x    X  x   X  x  /  x   /
```

Strong demotion:

```
x    /    x   /  x   /  x  /
dark waves where bell-buoys dimly toss
\    /    x   /  x   /  x  /
```

Though double tensions such as:

```
x  /    x   /   x  /   x   /
installed his word-God on the throne
x  /    x   /   \  X   x   /
```

can also, theoretically at least, receive an alternate scansion and be read as a displaced weak:

```
x  /    x   / -x- /   -x-     /
installed his word-God on the throne
x  /    x   / :  /  x    x    /
```

However, even though *nominally* 'speech-strong', this is clearly far more difficult to perform naturally, and a compromise would be sought by most readers. See below for further explanation.

a) *The 3-stress rule*

This is one of the four possible outcomes of the tension rule. In duple metres, any run of three identical stresses, whether w or s, will see the centre stress respectively promoted or demoted to maintain AS if the first and third stresses are position-coincident.

Weak:

<pre>
    x   / x   /   x   /   x   /
The writing on the wall, we know,
    x   / x X   x   /   x   /
</pre>

Strong:

<pre>
    x /   x   / x / x /
the first flies cry to be let out,
    x /   \   / x / x /
</pre>

b) *The initial rule*

Tensions in the first weak position can create a near-spondee.

<pre>
    x   / x   / x / x /
'Stop here and see the sun go down.'
    \   / x   / x / x /
</pre>

('Here' is emphatic and should be labelled as content; 'go down' is phrasemic, and iambic.) This is controversial. The logic is simply that unless some artful enjambment has suggested otherwise, an initial strong will always be assumed to be indicative of an acephalic line, and s-positioned; it can then only be demoted through a metre-strong reading, as above, which wilfully aligns the first weak above the first syllable. This most often occurs where the reader knows the line already, and where the template is already being strongly projected.

However, in speech-strong readings, by the time the second s stress comes in, it is in effect too late to properly demote the first.

AS cannot operate effectively, since it ideally requires a run of three alternating or equal stresses ('and see — look there! — the sun go down' is a breeze); so either it will produce something like a genuine performed spondee:

<pre>
x   /   x   /   x /   x /
'Stop here and see the sun go down.'
/   /   x   /   x /   x /
</pre>

Or even a bizarre mora compensation for a displaced weak:

<pre>
x   /   x   /   x /   x /
'Stop here and see the sun go down.'
\   / : x   /   x /   x /
</pre>

— 'bizarre', as it does not split the 'spondee' as usual to fill the weak placeholder, but instead takes up the space of the missing displaced weak itself. (If 'stop here' occurred in any other position, it would fall to the 3-stress rule; there seems to be some unconscious acknowledgment of its unique situation buried in this odd move. Smoother alternatives are 'Stop here, and see the sun go down', where the caesura takes up the slack, or maybe 'Stop here and then see the sun go down'; but, of course, the line is virtuosic precisely *because* it does neither, and 'stops' its metre to echo its sense.)

Either way, variations in initial positions are highly anomalous, and unusual rules apply, depending on the projected frame.

Although triple tensions are generally unmetrical, we may occasionally accept them in the initial position. See the following lines from Richard Wilbur (later I explain my contextual reasons for marking 'down' and 'that' as strong):

[. . .] The sun-hat falls,
With what free flirts and stoops you can imagine,
x   /   x / x   / x/ x /
Down through that reeling vista or another,
/   x   / / x   / x x x / x

which consolidates as:

Down through that reeling vista or another,
\   X   \ / x   / x X x / x

— proposing that there may even be initial positions where we
encounter something like a genuine English molossus. See also the
first line of Frost's 'Fireflies in the Garden', which suggests the high
matrical position of the first stress may aid the spondee considerably:

6   3   5   2   4   1
Here come real stars to fill the upper skies,

c) *The double tension rule*

Successive tensions still allow AS to be maintained, though less
smoothly than runs of three same-stress syllables produced by single
tensions. They are subject to different interpretations, depending in
whether the projection is metre- or speech-strong.

In the following example

x   /   x   /   x /   x   /
each one, his poor loaf on the sea,
x   /   x   /   \ X   x /

the variation can be speech-strong too, and treated as a displaced
weak (see below):

x   /   x   / -x-/   -x-   /

each one, his poor loaf on the sea,

x   /   x   /: / x   x   /

Reading the line as a double tension depends upon the extent to which the reader wishes to overdetermine the rhythm via a metre-strong performance. There is arguably enough syntactic play with 'on' to allow it a promotion; in which case the latitude the tensions allow mean AS can be performed by demoting 'loaf', being the centre of the run of three moderate stresses (demoted, promoted, weak) 'poor loaf on'. The speech-strong reading here is a bit of a stretch, though could be accomplished by more clearly diphthongising the vowel of 'poor'. The rule is that more naturalistic speech-strong readings will resolve potential double tensions through interpreting them as displaced weaks, and more overdetermined metre-strong readings will preserve the double tension. Neither is 'correct'.

For all but the lightest metres, triple tensions are unmetrical:

x / x   / x / x   / x   /

they flee from me, Dave and Bob: yip, they do.

x / x   / \ X \ / x   /

However, they can very occasionally be mitigated by the 'initial rule', which legitimises the spondee; see above.

d) *The displaced weak rule*

Spondees produced by apparently successive tensions (i.e. 'inversion', where x/ or /x becomes /x or x/ respectively, producing sequences of x//xx/, x/xx// and so on) are rather often felt to be separated by a w-position-coincident pause or 'mora'. (This mora falls between the s syllables of the spondee regardless of how it was created, i.e. it may fall before or after 'the problem word'.) This very often receives further quantitative compensation in the form of a realised additional w in an adjacent w position. (Therefore because of this vestigial separation they are not technically spondees, which neatly solves the old conundrum of whether equally weighted, successive s stresses are possible in English at all; the answer is precisely 'sort of'.) They are not tensive substitutions, but a form of radical AS compensation.

The error has been perpetuated by the mistaken insistence that there is only one way the metrical template can be aligned. They may *also* be read as double tensions, discussed below — but the two approaches form radically different metrical solutions. Displaced weaks are the result of a naturalised or dramatic speech-strong solution; double tensions are more boldly 'artificed', lyric-oriented, metre-strong solutions. Once again: neither is correct, but usually just indicate different performance preferences. A genuinely sensitive scansion, however, should be able to flip between them and choose between the most effective result, based on semantic context and what one identifies as the poet's introjected intentions; especially in i.p. one may move between lyric and dramatic modes, and as we've seen this may also involve a dramatic shift of template.

Understandably, the clean symbols of w/s stress-only notation have been resistant to the messiness of the metrical reality. To give a few examples:

(a) metre-strong:

```
x  /    x /   x    /  x   /
among the rocks and the strict bones
x  /    x /   x    X  \   /
```

speech-strong:

```
x  /    x /      -x-    / -x-/
among the rocks and the strict bones
x  /    x /   x    x  / : /
```

(b) metre-strong:

```
x    /  x   /  x  / x    /
from the world-circles lovers make
x    X \    /  x / x    /
```

speech-strong:

```
-x-     /  -x-/  x  / x    /
from the world-circles lovers make
x    x  / : /  x  / x    /
```

(c) metre-strong:

```
x   /   x  /  x  / x  /
and old men at the water's edge
x   /   \ X  x  / x   /
```

speech-strong:

```
x   / -x- /  -x-    / x   /
and old men at the water's edge
x   / : /  x   x  / x   /
```

To my mind in the above examples (a) and (b) are best read speech-strong; (c) is best read metre-strong, though it could be effectively read in both ways. However, triple ws in a single placeholder introduce an alternative:

```
-x-  / -x- /   -x-     / x  /
love-play of the ironic conscience
/ : / x   xx / x  /    x
```

(In years gone by, an introjected speech-strong reading would have been ensured by writing it as 'love-play of th'ironic conscience'.) This will likely succumb to the 3-stress rule and be read as the metre-strong:

```
x    / x  / x / x  /
love-play of the ironic conscience
\     / x  X x / x  /    x
```

– depending on whether the reader's preference is for the more natural, speech-strong, 'resting state'-dominated reading in the first example (my own, I should admit, even if it's the more radical), or the more overdetermined metre-strong tensive reading of the second (where most readers will perform the emphatic '*thee*' for 'the' to aid its naturalism).

In the case of /xx/ at the beginning of the line (so-called 'initial inversion'), the metre is marked from and aligned with the first s stress in a speech-strong scansion. Obviously, no mora can be produced by the usual means, as the initial stress is isolated (unless one is inclined to mark it as a gulped pause at the start of the line – this is generally what I tend to do, though I'm aware I may be alone here), and the effect is smoother than a displaced weak in mid-line:

speech-strong:

```
-x-  /      -x-  / x /   x /
come and inspire us once again!
[:]  /   x  x  / x /   x /
```

metre-strong:

```
x   / x  / x /   x /
come and inspire us once again!
\    X x  / x /   x /
```

The metre-strong approach is unpleasant, and few would choose it. This is best considered an acephalic line where the omitted initial w has been displaced. As here, it will often appear after the first stress as an additional compensatory syllable, and it performs the service of restoring the rising rhythm of the metre, lest it be felt as trochaic (as might 'come inspire us once again!'). Although the missing initial w is easily absorbed by the hiatus (as in 'trochaic' lines), initial displaced ws are often also mitigated by feminine endings in the previous line, and are especially common after enjambment:

<pre>
        x / x / x   /   x   /
        eviscerations of the troubled
        x / x X x   X   x   /   x

-x-   / -x-   / x /   x   /
        waters between us and North Wales
        / x   x   / x X   \   /
</pre>

INTERPRETATIVE SCANSION: A METHOD[1]

What follows over the next few pages is intended to more fully illustrate the scansion procedure I have been sketching out. Given its relative complexity, I hope the reader will forgive some repetition. To be clear on the nature of the exercise: we are *not* attempting to work out 'how to stress lines of poetry'. This is a false question and as such can have no answer: any intelligent reader knows *exactly* how to do this already. They read aloud, or to themselves, with some awareness of the underlying metre, and with some understanding of the line — and allow the agreement and tension between the two to direct their performance. What we are instead attempting here is a

---

[1]   For a long time I called my own approach 'performative scansion'. I intended something a little less narrow by the word 'performative' than its conventional Austinian sense of 'pertaining to an utterance that effects an action through its own performance', but it amounts to much the same thing. There is a self-conscious and self-reflexive aspect to the poetic speech act which makes the entire enterprise an illocutionary one: it *always* has design, *always* has intent, and is *always* seeking to 'enact its sense' in some way. It achieves this through a formal overdetermination, of which its prosody is perhaps the most important aspect.

The phrase 'performative scansion' is originally John Hollander's, I believe; his main issue was less with subjectively prescriptive accounts of the poem per se, but their confusion with what their authors felt were objectively *descriptive* ones. The New Critical rejection of such performative approaches (see Wimsatt and Beardsley, etc.) is based on a superstitious fear of subjectivity. However, as the reader will now be aware, I believe that in the absence of intrinsicality nothing can said to be 'correct', and that highly subjective interpretation is built deeply into the most fundamental parts of the process; pretending it isn't merely upholds Hollander's original complaint. But there is nothing wrong with any subjective interpretation if you give your reasons for making it; thereafter it can be judged on its common sense and wisdom.

reasonably detailed description of the phenomenon of poetic rhythm. *How* detailed a prosodic description one might want to make is a matter of choice; there is no 'threshold of common sense' at which one should stop, beyond which one is detailing effects too small or too subjectively experienced to be verified. Who's to say? But there is a threshold beyond which one is becoming impractically remote from the aims of the exercise. We might have chosen to simplify this procedure greatly – or expand it more deeply into the field of pragmatics and phrasal analysis. For me this method represents as much information as I can sensibly extract before the exercise becomes either self-verifying or too distant from the field of poetics.

The purpose of performing such a scansion is *not*, however, to describe a poem's pattern of stress, and any scansion which stops there has lost track of its own project. The aim of a scansion is *to better understand the poem*, and to ally that understanding to a blueprint for its performance. Hence 'interpretative scansion'. As an interrogative exercise, it will generate little insight if conducted speedily; and if it's automated, it will be worse than useless.

The method I employ runs as follows:

1) We establish the metrical template. Essentially we 'project' the metre, based on what we can subjectively infer through a simple reading of the lines. We then notate the w-s pattern of the metre above the line, placing / and x as close to the vowel (or -x- at the mid-point of the w space) as we can. In metrical poems where liberties are taken with line length, the missing or ghost metrons can also be notated in square brackets.

We can hear that – despite its clear variations – the following passage converges quickly on an i.p. template:

```
x   /  x  /  x  /x  /  x    /
What does it think it's doing running west
  x  /   x / x  /   x   /    x   /
When all the other country brooks flow east
  x   /    x / x   /   x   /  x   /
To reach the ocean? It must be the brook
  x    /  x /  x  /  x  /  x /
Can trust itself to go by contraries
```

(ROBERT FROST, 'West-Running Brook')[2]

2) We then write the lexical stress below the line – rigidly, taking care not to inadvertently impose stresses derived through sense stress. This is a relatively simple matter: broadly speaking, words have a well-defined and agreed RSP, which can be taken from any good dictionary. While a word like 'the' 'but' or 'there' might appear to take a neutral stress, in its non-emphatic use within the flow of speech it takes very little stress, and its vowel heads towards schwa; emphatic function should, by contrast, be thought of as content.[3] Monosyllabic function words and grammatical affixes almost always take a weak stress, as their job is not to be consciously thought about, but to indicate a relation between contentual elements, or qualify them by inflection. After we have

---

2 Robert Frost, *The Poetry of Robert Frost : The Collected Poems, Complete and Unabridged*, ed. Edward Connery Lathem (New York: Henry Holt, 2002).

3 Their emphatic employment means they *were* 'thought about', and by definition are content words. In 'Dearest, note how these two are alike: / This harpsichord pavane by Purcell / And the racer's twelve-speed bike' ('Machines', Michael Donaghy) the word 'these' is emphatic and receives a strong stress; it should be scanned as if it were content. (Failing to note this would likely lead the reader to project a 4-strong triple-metre template into the first line, rather than scan it – correctly – as i.p.) The more expert versifiers will often have such emphasis coincide with s stress position (as above), so the promotion – should the word still be regarded as w function – will reinforce the emphasis.

worked through our list of prepositions, pronouns, quantifiers, conjunctions, determiners and particles, a word's 'functionality' – in metrical terms at least – becomes a slightly more complex matter. Auxiliary and modal auxiliary verbs (be/have/do, when not main verbs; can/may/will/shall/must) most often take a weak stress, but can often be easily and comfortably promoted in specific sense-contexts. (In 'Shall I compare thee to a summer's day?' 'shall' is easily – and often is – promoted, albeit only by completely misconstruing the sense.) For now they should be marked weak. Disyllabic and polysyllabic function words should of course be marked according to their lexical stress pattern ('about' is x/, not xx).

While we're doing this, we also mark the single-syllable content-words – nouns, verbs, adjectives, adverbs, proper nouns – with a strong stress, or with their lexical stress pattern, if disyllabic or polysyllabic. This leaves us with a *broadly* accurate pattern of their RSP outside the influence of a metrical or semantic frame.

```
      x  /  x  /  x   /x   /  x    /
   What does it think it's doing running west
      x   x x  /  x   /x   /  x    /

      x  /  x / x  /   x  /   x  /
   When all the other country brooks flow east
      x  /  x / x  /   x  /   /  /

    x /    x / x  /  x  /  x  /
   To reach the ocean? It must be the brook
    x /    x / x  x  x   /  x   /

     x   /  x /  x  /  x /  x /
   Can trust itself to go by contraries
     x   /  x /  x  /  x /  x x
```

One very simple way to check the analysis is to read the lines aloud as if they were perfectly metrical, overemphasising the weak/strong alternation of the template, and make a note of which words sound strange. This will indicate where the tensions lie:

```
x  /   x   /   -x-  / x /   x /
The long cars come to a cloudy halt beside it,
x    / x     / x   / x /  x  /
And the fogged windows offering a view
x  /  x  /   x /  x   /   x  /
Neither to those within nor those without;
x  /   x  /    x  /   x  / x /
Now, in the crowd – forgive my predilection –
x / x    / x  /   -x-  /   x  /
Is a young woman standing amidst her luggage,
x  / x   / x    x  / x  /
Expecting to be met by you, a stranger.
```

(RICHARD WILBUR, 'The Mind Reader')[4]

(Note: as we have seen in our discussion of the mora, there are also good arguments for making a lexical stress *first*, since there are many occasions when we will simply line up the template inaccurately or unsympathetically. The reality is that steps (1) and (2) ought to be conducted more or less simultaneously, so that corrections can be made on the hoof; they really constitute two parts of the single exercise of projection. The main thing to be aware of is that metre-strong and speech-strong performance styles will project the template differently, and that a degree of subjectivity is present in our scansion right from the start.)

4 Richard Wilbur, *The Mind Reader: New Poems* (Palo Alto, CA: Harcourt Brace Jovanovich, 1976).

3) We isolate any other phrasemic material that we feel to be lexically bound (I underline this material) and then adapt our lexical stress accordingly. This displays an open bias towards speech-strong interpretation (as I feel we usually should) and is a matter of judgement, since it introduces another subjective element into the process.[5] However, as we've seen, stress operates differently in collocations than it does in content-equivalent but non-phrasemic material. In the Frost passage two lines are affected. The phrasemic 'what do you think you're doing' has two s stresses if it's a reproaching question, one if it's a straight reprimand; here, I hear the former:

```
-x-        /      -x- /   x   /x   /   x    /
What does it think it's doing running west
         /   x   x   x   x   /x   /   x    /
```

4) In the fourth line the reflexive verb 'trust itself' is effectively phrasemic and scanned /xx. Now we have a metrical template and lexical stress. We now consolidate the two notations to mark double weaks, omissions and tensions, i.e. the out-of-position stresses that may be promoted or demoted. (Remember stress position tensions *potentiate* demotion or promotion, and are unstable; they cannot insist on them.)

5 This gives us two subjective variables already – and in that part of the process many theorists would prefer to think of as more or less automated. I confess this pleases me, as prosody is no place for the algorithm. Failing to account for differences between metre-strong and speech-strong performance, and of multi-word, lexically bound material are two good reasons scanning programs are currently pretty useless.

What does it think it's doing running west
/ x x   X x   /x   / x   /
When all the other country brooks flow east
x /   x / x /   x   /   \   /

To reach the ocean? It must be the brook
x /   x / x X x   / x   /
Can trust itself to go by contraries
x   / x X x / x /   x X

5) We then make a sense-stress analysis, accenting or de-accenting material according to our performance of its understood sense. This is entirely coterminous with an act of critical interpretation, and I believe a verbally articulated explanation must be made to justify such an interpretation, at the very least so other readers can disagree. To recap: while values of weakness and strength of stress are based on normative admixture of volume, pitch and length, sense stress adds a strongly intonational dimension, one difficult to represent notationally. It is what we add as *performers* of a line, as soon as we have semantic and emotional context. For our purposes, the primary functions of sense stress are (a) to contrastively foreground that which is new and important in terms of content; (b) to background and 'functionalise' information that the speaker assumes is already known, or wishes to remain low-key, or to provide the new material with contrastive salience; and (c) to add emotional information. Both (a) and (b) tend to be represented by pitch-change; (c) is communicated through a variable admixture of pitch, vowel length, loudness and timbre that it would be ludicrous to even try to represent with our (phonologically) simplified scheme, but an analysis of 'emotional sense', where it shades into the semantic, will often yield pitch accents too. The stress-alternation of our speech is really part of

a double sign, its two parts deeply and synaesthetically wedded: weak stress indicates function; strong stress indicates content. When stresses or accents are given to function words, and when weak stresses or de-accents are given to content words, they also shift in our perception from performing syntagmatic, functional roles to having paradigmatic, information-carrying roles, and vice versa. This is *especially* the case with accented and de-accented syllables. A de-accented content word which the speaker wishes to background because its information is already known to the listener performs *something* of the cognitive function of a grammatical anaphora, *whether the word is a repetition of an earlier word or not*; an accented function word, on the other hand, will carry some paraphrasable lexical content (that is to say it has synonyms on the paradigmatic axis).

We might perform our sense-stress scansion thus:

What does it think it's doing running west
  /   x x X x   /'x / x   /
When all the other country brooks flow east
  x /   x /' x /, x, /, \ /'

'Doing', I think, occurs in a phrase which parodies a kind of admonition, so takes a rise; 'other' is contrastive; 'country brooks' falls as both an 'already understood subject' and to facilitate the salience of 'other' (the de-accent is, as is often the case, suprasegmental and extends over all three syllables); 'east' is contrastive, and forms the high nuclear stress of the question; to place an additional accent on the neutral s stress of 'ocean' would be to misinterpret Frost's intentions, and diminish the contrastive effect of 'east'. (There is a good argument for de-accenting 'the ocean' or even 'to reach the ocean' as that part of the question that is 'common knowledge'; but while speech-strong *bias* is desirable, this would probably suggest its triumph. For poetry to sound like poetry, metre and speech have to be held in tension. Only actors are inclined to let speech wholly dominate.)

To reach the ocean? It must be the brook
x /   x / x   X   x' /, x   /

I hear 'must' as emphatic, and as often happens, contrast is preserved by de-accenting the next word, 'be'. The intonational contour values of 'it must be' will be [1* 1 1], though note that these 1-values have been arrived at via three different routes. Some metre-strong readers who arrived at the same conclusions would nonetheless then allow 'must' to fall gently to a version of the 3-stress rule, and maintain a vestigial sense of AS. I prefer the speech-strong wrestle, and in my quick-and-dirty performance-note system mentioned earlier, such runs of equal value would be marked with dots above the vowels.

Can trust itself to go by contraries
x   / x X x / x /'   x X

'Contraries' seems a straightforward nuclear stress.

6) Finally, we derive an intonational contour as a 'performance note'; this collapses information derived from all our previous analysis. Tensive *-marked stresses are unstable. Nuclear stress will generally be indicated by the highest number, or by the final stress by default, if it occupies a highest-equal position.

2   o   o   1* o   3 o 2   o   2
What does it think it's doing running west
/   x   x   X x   /'x / x   /

o 2   o 3 o I   −I   I   I* 3
When all the other country brooks flow east
x /   x /' x   /, x,   /,   \   /'

o 2   o 2 o I* I   I   o   2
To reach the ocean? It must be the brook
x /   x / x   X x' /,   x   /

o   2 o *I o 2 o 3   o *I
Can trust itself to go by contraries
x   / x X   x / x /' x X

Contours can be instructively compared by plugging the values into a 'contour grid', which I'll discuss under loose metre scansion.

7) If we are scanning the entire poem, we may take account of ASR at the higher hierarchical levels, if they exist, indicating alternating key-fall patterns at the start of each line. We then might notate the salient zenith and nadir matrical values of the various units (e.g. the nadirs of fourth stress of the eighth line of a sonnet, or the penultimate s stress of an i.p. couplet, etc.) and then look at the values they were represented by in the intonational contour grid.[6]

---

6 My own scansion does not take in nor try to find any replacement for Attridge's STATEMENT-EXTENSION-ANTICIPATION-ARRIVAL phrasal analysis; while attractive and elegant in its simplicity (especially when applied to free verse – an area crying out for some methodical prosodic 'coverage'), I worry that it might be too blunt an instrument. As I've mentioned, I'm also unsure of its strictly metre- and poem-specific credentials, and feel that the whole area might be better tackled as part of a contemporary rhetoric.

SCANNING TIGHT METRES

A sympathetic and sensitive scansion of tight metre should usually steer a path between metre-strong and speech-strong readings; tight metre makes far less use of the compensatory mora, and will therefore see far more disagreements marked instead as tensions. Tight metre does not show the w-placeholder variation we see in loose metre, but it finds its interpretative latitude through its tensive instability. In i.p. it can still be 10-position, but by definition is more metre-strong than would be loose metre; so it is usually enough to think of tight i.p. as simply 5-metron. However, where we find lines with a lot of tensive disagreement, we can usually take it as a sign that the poet has started to be influenced by the 10-position template too. (In the example below, we see Shakespeare already feeling the pull of 10-position, at a time when most of his contemporaries were writing a far more rum-te-tum version of tight metre.) As with the scansion of loose metre, the true purpose of the exercise is really just to work out what the lines *mean*, as will be apparent form what follows.

I'll analyse a few lines of Sonnet 18 here, following the procedure just described. The first line is deliciously unstable:

Line 1

x / x /   x / x /   x   /

Shall I compare thee to a <u>summer's day</u>?

x x x /   x x x x   x   /

consolidates as:

Shall I compare thee to a summer's day?
x X x   /   x X x X   x   /

A first reading might stress *shall*, since the context of the question is still unknown. But it quickly becomes clear that it was always the poet's *intention* to compare his beloved to a summer's day, and to pose the question as '*shall* I . . . ?' is a very silly misreading (although one often hears it). The sense is combative. 'OK, my dear — you dare me to compare you to some *summum bonum*, and find you in some way inferior? Let's pick something we can all agree on here. How about "a summer's day"? Fine. Game on.' I read 'summer's day' as phrasemic, especially here, where he's slinging it in very much as 'a thing you already know', and one can make a near-weak of the first vowel. 'Day' rises because of the question mark and the NS rule. (Note, however, that in performance the stress will either be high-falling or high-rising according to phatic inclination. High-falling, if you're looking to communicate a little swaggering, do-you-dare-me-to insouciance; high-rising if not.)

Furthermore the tensive promotion on 'I' is quite plausible; to resist it perhaps overnaturalises the reading at the expense of metrical robustness. The speaker might be inclined to compromise. Me, I'm a sucker for naturalism and a conversational tone — and if the poem isn't tending towards song, I like the metre to emerge from the sentence over the course of several metre-convergent lines, rather than leave the listener with too much sense of it being 'imposed' through an excessively metre-strong performance. So while 'I' is tensive, and marked with 1* —

o 1*o   2   o 1*o 1*   o   3
Shall I compare thee to a summer's day?
x X x   /   x X x X   x   /'

– I use its instability to keep it weaker and only promoted just enough to hint at the AS, where you may not. Similarly the run of weaks on 'thee to a summer's' I find attractive, so will generally resist much promotion of 'to'. Once again, note that the decision whether or not to realise a tension as a promotion or demotion is often one of simple metre- or speech strong preference, hence our 'unstable' asterisk. In speech-strong readings, an asterisk over a promoted weak might fall back towards to its original value; an asterisk over a demoted strong might rise.

Line 2

<pre>
    x /   x   / x /   x   / x /
Thou art more lovely and more temperate:
    x x   /   / x x   /   / x x
</pre>

<pre>
Thou art more lovely and more temperate:
    x X   \   / x X   \   / x X
</pre>

There are a number of legitimate sense-stress readings here. The first is stressing *thou* in contrast to 'summer's day'; however, I'm tempted to propose that 'thou' is largely understood by virtue of the quiet deictic cue of 'thee' in the first line, and that its stressing is somewhat redundant; a more dramatic or plain hammy approach would stress it, however. (This emphasis would occur with no help from our initial metrical scansion at all.) A second reading might give 'Thou art *more* lovely and *more* temperate': however, this deviation is hardly potentiated in the metrical tensions, where the adjective 'more' is demoted – so I would personally regard it as *just* too much of a readerly, speech-strong imposition, as reasonable an interpretation of the sense as it is. 'Thou art more lovely *and* more temperate' takes advantage of the weak 'and' being promoted by its position, and the fact that the sense matches the prosodic effect should tell us this was likely the author's intention: in fact I'd happily accent it in the sense stress too, and make it our high, emphatic NS. This is a classic case of a function word taking an accent because it plays a significant part in the informational structure of the line: the evidence is beginning to stack up against the poor 'summer's day', and that '*and*' has some serious content; it is saying something far more important than those 'mores' – the poem is *about* the inadequacy of comparisons, not the quantitative detail of those comparisons – and its strength should reflect this.[1] The copular 'art' takes a stress, but copulars can often duck down to something approaching w auxiliary stress in conversation. I feel we can let it take a w here, and have marked it so.

o 1*   1*   2   o 2*   1*   2   o   1*
Thou art more lovely and more temperate:
x X   \   /   xX'   \   /   x   X

This leaves a very tensive line with *five* asterisked disagreements – which explains why no two people read it the same way. However, I'll make an even more radical suggestion. The height of 'and' will be more salient if the stresses on 'lovely' and 'temperate' are dropped low to tonal de-emphasis, the semantic implication being that since these two things are already *such* well-known qualities of the summer's day, they really don't need foregrounding. (This means I revise my weakening of the copular 'art', and mark it s; a plain w here would give us a run of weak or de-emphasised syllables, and the line would only work with a very mumbled delivery.) Remembering that, unlike accents, de-accents are suprasegmental and work across all syllables of a polysyllabic word. This means we go from

---

[1] I am open to more elegant ways to notate all this, but do think that, for example, the way we say 'and' in this line *is* a result of its expressing the qualities of weak lexical stress/strong position/semantic accent/tension; and that any system which merely sums these qualities in one symbol has little value as accurate description.

o 1*   1*   2   o 2*   1*   2   o 1*
Thou art more lovely and more temperate:
x X   \   /   x X'   \   /   x X

to

o 2   1*   1   −1 2*   1*   1   −1 o*
Thou art more lovely and more temperate:
x /   \   /, x,X'   \   /,   x,X,

Line 3

x   /   x   /   x / x   /   x   /
Rough winds do shake the darling buds of May,
/   /   x   /   x / x   /   x   /

gives

Rough winds do shake the darling buds of May,
\   /   x   /   x / x   /   x   /

This is a good opportunity to discuss content monosyllables in a phrasal context, and this is an absolute corker. 'Rough winds' is a noun phrase. In a generative scansion, we would apply two rules: the NS rule – i.e. anything we can parse as a phrase takes its stress as far towards the end as possible; and the fact that we're not allowed spondees, as the ASR must always be applied. So 'winds' receives the stronger stress and 'rough' is demoted. However, there is a cognitive perception in English that those bold, contentual, mono-syllabic qualifiers placed next to nouns are making something halfway to a compound, where the stress always falls on the *first* syllable (e.g. 'SWIMming pool'; 'LOAN shark') – and so, depending on its phrasemic or collocative force, most speakers reach a kind of compromise, and give them something approaching equal emphasis, with perhaps a hint of a stronger stress on the noun. (This is further compounded by *really* well-known lines, which rise to the phrasemic status of the proverbialism.) But 'spondee' is too strong a word for it, and 'iamb' is too weak. 'Rough' really occupies a *kind* of genuine secondary stress; [\ /] tends to be the approximate resting-state prosody of those consecutive-monosyllable noun phrases in English that fall short of a full compound. And in this poem, of course, looking at the word in isolation, we see the demotion to a weaker stress is also potentiated by its metrical position. However, it depends on whether you buy my 'initial rule', which claims that tensions in the first weak position create near-spondees.

But stay your little blue scansion-pencil; we have been overtaken by events. Things are here further complicated by sense. 'Winds', I feel, requires an exceptional emphasis, because the poet's intention is this: 'Right — *here's* the evidence of your being more lovely and temperate. You know those darling buds of May? The picture just isn't as perfect as it seems. *Bad* stuff happens to them.' The bad vs good, 'winds' vs 'buds', means we see a contrastive accent on 'winds', and it's suprasegmental — 'rough', to which it is bound, will take one too:

> Rough winds do shake the darling buds of May,
> \\'   /'   x   /   x / x   /   x   /

I'd argue for a low accent at 'shake' (the low anaphoric 'sign of assumed understanding' indicating something along the lines of 'what *else* would those winds do to those darling buds?'); others might feel the effect too subtle and optional to mark. I'll also de-accent 'darling buds of May', as I hear Shakespeare's voice as almost sarcastically dismissive here, and the de-accent helps promote 'winds' to its position of NS (where 'May' would normally rise by default):

2*   3   o   I   o I −I   I   −I   I

Rough winds do shake the darling buds of May

\\'   /'   x /,   x /, x,   /, x, /,

– but the main reason I de-accent 'darling buds of May' is that it is simply a metonymic substitute for 'summer', and to some extent can perform a similarly anaphoric function as the repetition of the word 'summer' itself, which would automatically take a functional de-accent. There are cultural considerations here too. The sheer *fame* of the phrase 'the darling buds of May' (Shakespeare; H. E. Bates; the eponymous TV series) has arguably led to the formation of a phraseme, and certain readers will adopt a phrasemic stress in many performances (especially actors who might want to reveal their sophistication and overfamiliarity with the phrase by throwing it away), another reason for 'buds' receiving a de-accent, since the lexical stress of the phraseme is [x x x x /].

Line 4

x   /   x   /   x   /   x   /   x /

And summer's lease hath all too short a date:

x   /   x   /   x   /   /   /   x /

As a spoken phrase, 'All too short' takes a demotion to its central stress on the ASR alone, and this is reinforced here by metrical position. There's an argument, however, that it's more natural to read it as a phraseme, and that phrasemic prosody should dominate, which I tend to hear as an anapaestic [xx/]. This would leave

x   /   x   /   x   /   x   /   x /

And summer's lease hath <u>all too short</u> a date:

x   /   x   /   x   x   x   /   x /

So:

> And summer's lease hath all too short a date:
> x   /   x   /   x X x   /   x /

Turning to the sense stress, 'summer' takes a high accent, if we read the sense as 'this happens in May . . . and advancing on that, *summer's lease . . .*'. However, we should remember two things: firstly, Shakespeare is very much focused on the subject of the summer's day, and 'darling buds of May' was merely a metonym for it; secondly, the Elizabethans were very fuzzy about when spring ended and summer began. All of which leads me to conclude that 'summer' is not contrastive, and we can treat it as an anaphor with the antecedent 'summer's day' and just de-accent it, just as we would if it read 'its'. 'Short', to my mind, must take high rise, not least to avoid any sense that the NS is on 'date', where it would naturally land. 'Date' can't be allowed to declare itself as the significant new material of the sentence; it's the *shortness* of the time-span that's Shakespeare's contrastive point – short, unlike your *eternal* beauty – and when we subvert the position of the NS in this way, we usually scream it. (Unlike de-accents, accents only generally apply to one or occasionally two syllables in a phraseme, with the rest are kept low in functional contrast. Note that if 'short' were to be de-accented, *every* syllable in 'all too short' would fall as a lexemic unit.)

>   o   I   o   2   o I*   o   3   o 2
> And summer's lease hath all too short a date:
> x   /,   x   /   x X x   /' x /

Now the effects of ASR at the larger hierarchical levels can be marked. As previously stated the alternation is perceived not as 'stress' but a steady, stepped and alternated falling, with the key of the intonational contour of each second unit of a hierarchical pair lower than the first.

A numeral at the start of each line can indicate relative key height. Unless we apply an AS template, the alternating heights of stresses *within* the line should not be marked, as the only salient effect is of a stepped pitch-fall of the entire line contour: and as will now be obvious, there is far too much going on in the way of tensive, phrasemic and sense-stress variety to attempt to maintain a purely AS contour at a metronic or dimetronic level. (Just about the only time these lower-level ASR effects are heard is in tight metre 4×4 forms because of the extent to which they overdetermine the metre; but most sophisticated, dramatic and hypotactic verse will simply play havoc with them.)

The range of values available depends on the number of levels we deem perceptible. In the case of the sonnet, I don't think they extend much beyond the octave, but let's pretend that the sestet also bumps us up to a larger unit of 2×8 lines that can encompass the sonnet itself (with a ghost-couplet, remembering that the ASR can only work over equal-sized units). That would make paired units of lines + distichs + strophes + distrophes, i.e. four unit-distinctions. The need for every unit to fall relative to the previous unit means that there are as many gradations as lines.

The whole poem would then be marked as shown (the arrows are for visualisation purposes only):

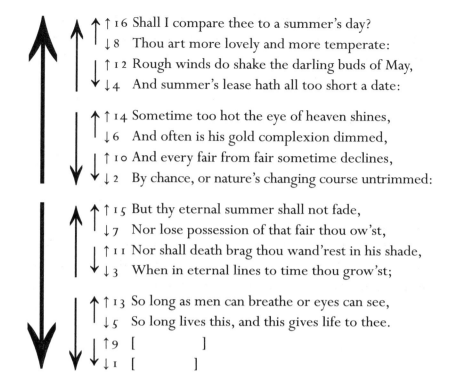

↑ 16 Shall I compare thee to a summer's day?
↓ 8 Thou art more lovely and more temperate:
↑ 12 Rough winds do shake the darling buds of May,
↓ 4 And summer's lease hath all too short a date:

↑ 14 Sometime too hot the eye of heaven shines,
↓ 6 And often is his gold complexion dimmed,
↑ 10 And every fair from fair sometime declines,
↓ 2 By chance, or nature's changing course untrimmed:

↑ 15 But thy eternal summer shall not fade,
↓ 7 Nor lose possession of that fair thou ow'st,
↑ 11 Nor shall death brag thou wand'rest in his shade,
↓ 3 When in eternal lines to time thou grow'st;

↑ 13 So long as men can breathe or eyes can see,
↓ 5 So long lives this, and this gives life to thee.
↑ 9 [   ]
↓ 1 [   ]

The more 'up' arrows, the higher the key of the line. The method of calculation has been explained at length already; essentially, to a base-level of one, the strong line adds 8, the strong distich 4, the strong strophe 2 and the strong distrophe 1. Therefore:

↑↑↑↑ 16 Shall I compare thee to a summer's day?
↑↑↑↓ 8   Thou art more lovely and more temperate:
↑↑↓↑ 12 Rough winds do shake the darling buds of May,
↑↑↓↓ 4   And summer's lease hath all too short a date

Leaving our final scansion as:

```
        o  1*o   2     o  1*o 1*   o     3
   16  Shall I compare thee to a summer's day?
        x  X x   /     x  X x X    x    /'


        o  2   1*  1 −1 2*   1*  1 −1 o*
    8  Thou art more lovely and more temperate:
        x  /   \   /, x,X'   \   /,  x,X,


        2*    3    o   1    o  1 −1  1  −1   1
   12  Rough winds do shake the darling buds of May,
        \'   /'    x   /,   x  /,x,  /,  x,  /,


        o   1   o   2    o  1*  o   3   o 2
    4  And summer's lease hath all too short a date:
        x   /,  x   /    x  X x   /' x /
```

Finally, we might make a contour grid, which will help to diagnose hitherto unconsciously experienced tendencies within and across the 10-position frame, such as musical contour, the concentration of the high stress at a particular stress position, anomalous lines, and so on:

key	w	1w	2s	3w	4s	5w	6s	7w	8s	9w	10s	w
16		o	1*	o	2	o	1*	o	1*	o	3	
8		o	2	1*	1	−1	2*	1*	1	−1	o*	
12		2*	3	o	1	o	1	−1	1	−1	1	
4		o	1	o	2	o	1*	o	3	o	2	

In the short sample above we can quickly identify a predictable height in the final s stress position, barring line 2, which boldly refuses it. The second strong position also shows high tendencies, and three of the four sixth-position strongs are tensive; were such a pattern to be sustained, it would revealing. There remains the question of whether too much subjectivity has already crept into the process; nonetheless a full scansion of the whole poem might even confirm some of these observations as *stylistic* tendencies, and by summing the columns and dividing by the number of lines, one might arrive at a mean contour — wherein may well be inscribed something of the poet's own typical song.

We might take one further step and compare the grid to the matrical AS values, but even from this short sample we can see there is a brilliant deviation at the zenith: sense stress has demoted the word 'I' in the first line, and this disavowal of the high opening s syllable gives the reader the sense of having arrived smack in the *middle* of an argument, not at the start of its laboured outlining. Not only that, but in this short sample, the nadir of the distrophic matrix – 'short' – is, of all things, a high 3. Compare with any old rotten sonnet by a contemporary like Barnaby Barnes to see the trends that Shakespeare was so freely bucking (in the example below, the zenith is the first syllable of 'glorious', and the distrophic nadir is 'so' in 'not be so remisse'):

O Glorious Patrone of eternall blisse!
Victorious Conqueror of Hell and Death!
Oh that I had whole westerne windes of breath!
My voice and tongue should not be so remisse [. . .]

SCANNING LOOSE METRES

Loose metres are usually diagnosed when projecting tight metre results in too many tensions; this is usually a good sign that a loose frame has been introjected and should be sympathetically projected. Nonetheless, we always have the *choice* between making metre-strong and speech-strong interpretations; but loose metre actively favours and 'asks for' a speech-strong approach with mora compensation. Let's look at the opening passage from Richard Wilbur's dramatic monologue 'The Mind Reader',[1] a poem into which we can confidently project a loose i.p., and apply broadly the same method we did to Sonnet 18, with minor variations. (It is simpler than some examples I might have chosen, as Wilbur has little fondness for the use or subversion of the phraseme; note, also, this poem is clearly written in the dramatic mode of i.p., and is resolutely *10-position*, with little hint of 8-strong anywhere in its template.) Each line emerges with a largely unique contour. First, a metrical scansion:

```
x      /   x   / x / -x-  /   -x-  /
Some things are truly lost. Think of a sun-hat
/      /   x   / x /  :  /   x-x  /   x
```

Devilment, I admit. Many would, I suspect, place x / over 'Think of', and call it a tension. I take a speech-strong approach, and read it as a displaced w with the mora on the caesura.

---

1   Richard Wilbur, *The Mind Reader: New Poems* (Palo Alto, CA: Harcourt Brace Jovanovich, 1976).

```
-x-   /    -x-    /  x  /  x / x /
```
Laid for the moment on a parapet
```
  /   x - x   /  x  x  x  / x x
```

The acephalsis is helped by the feminine ending of the previous line. Loose metre templates, as we've seen, will often project acephalsis where tight would produce a tension on the weak first position.

```
   x    /  x    /  x  /   x  /  x   /
```
While three young women – one, perhaps, in mourning –
```
   x   /  /   /  x  /   x  /  x  /   x
```

```
-x-  /    -x-   /  -x-  /  x  /   x    /
```
Talk in the crenellate shade. A slight wind plucks
```
 /  x - x   /  x - x   /  x  /   /   /
```

```
  x   /  x / x  /   -x-  /  x   /
```
And budges it; it scuffs to the edge and cartwheels
```
  x   /  x x x  /  x - x /  x  /  x
```

```
-x-/ -x-  /x  /  x  /   x  /
```
Into a giant view of some description:
```
 / x-x /x  /  x  x   x  /  x
```

```
-x-  /    -x-  /  x  /  x /   x   /
```
Haggard escarpments, if you like, plunge down
```
 /  x - x  /  x   x  x  /   /   /
```

'If you like' is a phraseme of the 'empty phatic filler' variety, and to my ear can take three weak stresses. This would overrule the strong 'like', creating a tension, and in turn propose the $xx/:/$ variant of the displaced w rule in 'you like, plunge down':

```
-x-  /   -x-  /  x  /   -x-   /  -x- /
```
Haggard escarpments, if you like, plunge down
```
 /  x - x  /  x   x  x - x  /  :  /
```

— though this would represent more speech-strong bias than I can reasonably summon. Most readers will position the template as I first notated it: acephalic, but otherwise coinciding with the syllables.

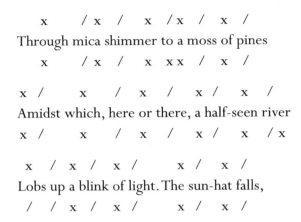

```
          x     / x  /  x  / x  /  x  /
     Through mica shimmer to a moss of pines
          x     / x  /  x  x x  /  x  /

     x  /    x    /  x   /  x  /   x   /
     Amidst which, here or there, a half-seen river
     x  /    x    /  x   /  x  /   x   / x

       x  / x / x  /       x  /  x  /
     Lobs up a blink of light. The sun-hat falls,
       /  /  x  / x  /      x  /  x  /
```

'Lob up' is a phrasal verb, albeit an unusual one; 'up' aligns well enough with the first s position, so I don't hear the line as acephalic.

```
          x    /  x  / x    /     x  / x  /
     With what free flirts and stoops you can imagine,
          x    /  / / x    /     x  x x / x
```

'You can imagine' is roughly phrasemic, reducing 'can' to a w. The next line is unstable:

```
     -x-    /        -x-   / x   / x / x /
     Down through that reeling vista or another,
            /      x -  x  / x   / x x x / x
```

'Down' I hear strong, as part of the interrupted phrasal verb 'fall down'. (Although if we read 'that' as firmly contrastive to 'another', it's emphatic, and therefore rises to s-stressed content; the line might then be scanned as acatalectic:

```
x         /       x  / x    / x / x /
```
Down through that reeling vista or another,
```
    /         x       /  / x    / x x  x / x
```

— though this would provide three successive tensions on 'down through that'. These are generally unmetrical but are very occasionally justified through a variant of the 'initial rule'.)

```
    x    /    x / x /   -x-    / x    /
```
Unseen by any, even by you or me.
```
    x    /    x / x / x - x   / x     /
```

Then we consolidate the information:

Some things are truly lost. Think of a sun-hat
```
   \      /    x    / x / : /   x-x /   x
```
Laid for the moment on a parapet
```
   /    x - x  / x   X x / x X
```
While three young women – one, perhaps, in mourning –
```
   x    /  \    / x   /   x / x   / x
```
Talk in the crenellate shade. A slight wind plucks
```
   /  x - x  / x-x   /   x /    \    /
```
And budges it; it scuffs to the edge and cartwheels
```
   x    /  x X x /   x-x /   x   /    x
```
Into a giant view of some description:
```
   / x-x / x   /   x  X    x / x
```
Haggard escarpments, if you like, plunge down
```
    / x - x /   x   X x /   \    /
```
Through mica shimmer to a moss of pines
```
     x    / x /   x  X x / x /
```
Amidst which, here or there, a half-seen river
```
   x /     x    / x   / x / x / x
```

Lobs up a blink of light. The sun-hat falls,
\ / x / x /   x / x /

With what free flirts and stoops you can imagine,
x / \ / x   /   x X x / x

Down through that reeling vista or another,
/   x - x / x   / x X x / x

Unseen by any, even by you or me.
x / x / x / x - x / x   /

Then we make a sense-stress analysis:

2*   2   o   3 o 1   3   o-o 2   o
Some things are truly lost. Think of a sun-hat
\'   /   x   /'x /, : /'   x-x /   x

The sense is 'some things are truly lost' (as opposed to most lost things, which we hear the speaker describe elsewhere as broadly findable). 'Lost' should take an anaphoric de-accent as 'the understood subject'. This is a fine rhetorical trick: the subject has not even been introduced yet, but the poem concerns itself with the nature of 'lostness', and the de-accent gives us the impression – absolutely correctly – of someone starting in medias res. ('Things' might too, but I prefer the even stresses on the first two syllables.) 'Think' is a bold imperative, and more important than 'sun-hat', the first of only a number of exempla; therefore 'think' receives an accent as the NS.

2   o - o   2   o   1* o 2 o 1*
Laid for the moment on a parapet
/   x - x   /   x X x / x X

This is straightforward – it's a long aside, really, and so the pitch range is tonally constrained.

```
   o     2  1*   2  o   2    o 2   o   2   o
While three young women – one, perhaps, in mourning –
   x    /   \    /  x   /    x /   x   /   x
```

Again, a flatly delivered line.

```
   2   o  -  o   2  o-o    3    o  2    1*    2
Talk in the crenellate shade. A slight wind plucks
  /    x-x    /  x-x    /'   x  /    \     /
```

Ditto, with a nuclear stress on 'shade', which we can accent to com-
municate a sense of intrigue. (Note how the brief dip into triple metre
enhances the 'talkiness' of the line.)

```
   o     2  o 1*o   2   o - o2    o    2      o
And budges it; it scuffs to the edge and cartwheels
   x    /  x X x   /   x - x /        /      x
```

```
  2  o-o 2o    2    o  o*   ⁻1  1  ⁻1
Into a giant view of some description:
  /  x-x /x    /    x  X,   x,  /, x,
```

I'd keep this monotone, although words like 'giant view' might cue
us up for a bit of drama; however 'of some description' reveal the
speaker as also dismissively throwing the example away as almost tire-
some, hence my de-accenting the phrase.

```
   2   o - o 3    o   1* o 2    1*    2
Haggard escarpments, if you like, plunge down
  /   x - x /'   x    X x /    \     /
```

I hear an 'oh all right then, if you insist' here, with a rise on
'escarpments'.

o   2 o   2   o 1*o   2   o   2

Through mica shimmer to a moss of pines

x   / x   /   x   X x   /   x   /

Here, the tensive 'to' should do a little to maintain AS, but otherwise remains below the radar.

o   2   1   2   o   2   o 2   o   2 o

Amidst which, here or there, a half-seen river

x   /   x'   /   x   /   x   /   x   / x

The emphatic and rhetorical use of 'which' will probably see it accented despite it being an anaphor. (Note the unusual *lack* of variation here: to see a run of neat os and 2s in the contour grid would indicate a very weak poem indeed.)

1*   2 o   2   o 3   o 2   o   2

Lobs up a blink of light. The sun-hat falls,

\   / x   /   x   /'   x   /   x   /

A forceful NS on 'light', I think.

o   2   1* 2   o   2   o 1* o 2 o

With what free flirts and stoops you can imagine,

x   /   \   /   x   /   x   X x / x

2   o -   o   2 o   2 o 1* o 2   o

Down through that reeling vista or another,

/   x -   x   / x   / x X x /   x

Letting the metre do the work in these last two lines . . .

o   2   o 3 o 2 o   o 2 o   3
Unseen by any, even by you or me.
x   /   x /'x / x - x / x   /'

A strong NS accent on 'any', after an intonationally flat couple of lines, and a sly rise on 'me' as the speaker introduces the subject of both himself and his peculiar expertise.

Marking the acephalic lines, this leaves us with:

2*   2   o   3 o I   3   o - o 2   o
Some things are truly lost. Think of a sun-hat
\'   /   x   /'x /, : /' x-x / x

x   2 o - o 2 o   I *o 2 o I*
Laid for the moment on a parapet
/ x - x / x X x / x X

o   2 I*   2 o   2   o 2 o   2 o
While three young women – one, perhaps, in mourning –
x   / \   / x /   x / x / x

x   2 o - o 2 o-o   3   o 2   I*   2
Talk in the crenellate shade. A slight wind plucks
/ x - x / x-x   /' x /   \   /

o   2 o I*o 2   o - o 2   o   2   o
And budges it; it scuffs to the edge and cartwheels
x   / x X x / x - x / x   /   x

x 2 o-o 2o   2 o o*   −I I −I
Into a giant view of some description:
/ x-x /x   / x X,   x, /, x,

x   2 o - o 3   o   I* o 2   I*   2
Haggard escarpments, if you like, plunge down
/ x - x /' x X x / \ . /

```
     o       2 o   2    o 1*o   2    o   2
Through mica shimmer to a moss of pines
     x     / x   /    x  Xx   /   x    /
```

```
   o  2      1     2  o   2   o 2   o    2 o
Amidst which, here or there, a half-seen river
   x  /     x'    /  x   /   x /   x    / x
```

```
 1*   2  o   2   o  3      o  2   o  2
Lobs up a blink of light. The sun-hat falls,
 \   /  x  /   x /'     x  /   x  /
```

```
   o     2  1* 2  o     2     o 1*o  2 o
With what free flirts and stoops you can imagine,
   x    /  \  /  x     /    x  X x  / x
```

```
x    2      o  -  o   2 o    2  o 1*o 2  o
Down through that reeling vista or another,
  /       x  -  x   / x    /  xX x  /  x
```

```
   o   2    o 3 o 2 o  -  o  2 o    3
Unseen by any, even by you or me.
   x   /    x /'x / x  -  x  /  x    /'
```

In a long poem like this without closed couplets or regular, even stanzas which show some clear stanzaic definition in their syntax, the ASR cannot operate at higher unit levels than the line, though it may be perceptible within clearly defined, longer sentence- and paragraph-units.

The contour grid

Plugging all values into a 10-position row allows us as before to compare echoed contours, detect overregularity, analyse the frequency of variation according to position, and so on. It can hardly be considered a 'statistical' tool, given the subjectivity of sense-stress analysis and its

effect of 'nailing' even unstable tensions to a value – but it will illus-
trate statistical and stylistic tendencies. Wilbur's lines display lots of
variety in the sixth and eighth s positions. The high nuclear stress of the
3s is very (and pleasingly) varied; it should be no surprise to find no 3s
in the first position, where the NS would be least expected. Only the
fourth and tenth w positions show any demoted syllables; the second
s position is rigidly consistent and the other positions are remarkably
regular. Weak placeholder variation is far more radical in the third
and ninth positions than the medial positions. It also demonstrates the
frequency of feminine endings + s stress line-beginnings, especially
where the line is enjambed; the fact that feminine endings smoothly
mitigate acephalic lines reinforces my claim that /xx/ arrangements
in the initial position are *not* the result of 'first foot inversion' but
merely a variation of the 'displaced weak rule', where the initial w has
been omitted, and the slack taken up by the extra w-syllable – which
also serves to re-establish immediately the rising iambic feel of the
metre. The grid overleaf has a column for key-fall alternation, and
if the lines had been stanzaic this would have been simple to fill in.
Nonetheless, the passage forms a very tightly structured paragraph-
unit, and to my ear AS key-fall is fairly easily projected *once the passage
is known*. The first accommodating binary unit is distrophic, so I've
marked in these values here.

key	1w	2s	3w	4s	5w	6s	7w	8s	9w	10s	w
16	2*	2	o	<u>3</u>	o	1	:	<u>3</u>	oo	2	o
8		2	oo	2	o	1*	o	2	o	1*	
15	o	2	1*	2	o	2	o	2	o	2	o
7		2	oo	2	oo	<u>3</u>	o	2	1*	2	
14	o	2	o	1*	o	2	oo	2	o	2	o
6		2	oo	2	o	2	o	o*	<u>−1</u>	1	<u>−1</u>
13		2	oo	<u>3</u>	o	1*	o	2	1*	2	
5	o	2	o	2	o	1*	o	2	o	2	
12	o	2	1	2	o	2	o	2	o	2	o
4	1*	2	o	2	o	<u>3</u>	o	2	o	2	
11	o	2	1*	2	o	2	o	1*	o	2	o
3		2	oo	2	o	2	o	1*	o	2	o
10	o	2	o	<u>3</u>	o	2	oo	2	o	<u>3</u>	

SCANNING LIGHT METRES

To give a rather extreme example of the sort of confusion that can arise when dealing with light metres: one theorist claims that the first two lines of Auden's 'Epitaph on a Tyrant' are 'in' tetrameter:

> Perfection, of a kind, was what he was after,
> And the poetry he invented was easy to understand;[1]

I'm pretty certain they're not. But the point is . . . *nor* am I certain they are in pentameter, or indeed anything else. However, my reasons for thinking that the poet *may* have had a pentametrical frame in mind lie in the last lines, when a metrical template is most plausibly established through two convergent lines (remember light metre scansions should *only* have -x- placeholders marked):

```
    -x-   /   -x-      /  -x-  /  -x-   /    -x-  /
When he laughed, respectable senators burst with laughter,
   x    x /      x  / x  x / x x   /    x  /   x
```

```
     -x-    /  -x- / -x- /  -x- /      -x-  /
And when he cried the little children died in the streets.
 x      x  x  /   x / x / x  / x  / x   x   /
```

1   W. H. Auden, *Collected Poems* (London: Faber & Faber, 2007).

My 'i.p. suspicions' are aroused as much by an underlying light-metre 3-strong scansion as a 5-strong scansion:

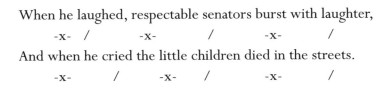

This retrospectively confirms my suspicion that lines 1–2 may also be written *to* (the prepositional distinction is crucial here) a 3-stress dimetronic or pentametrical frame. (I suspect '3-stress dimetronic' may *occasionally* be the light-metre equivalent, if one exists, of i.p. I.p. is for most poets a 10-position template, meaning that it rarely if ever moves from loose to light, and if it does may no longer *be* i.p. in any sense; unlike 4-strong, i.p. is almost never introjected unconsciously – but with Auden, all bets are off.)

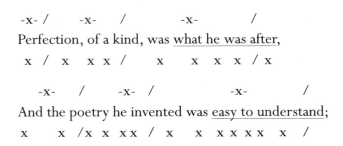

'What he was after' is borderline phrasemic, and tends to scan x x x / x; 'easy to understand' is semi-phrasemic, I feel – and can take a w on 'easy' and save its big stress for '-stand'. ('Understand' can scan as anapaest or amphimacer, but I feel the phraseme should always win, if it's not being regrammaticised through innovative re-presentation.) However, if we engage our projective capabilities, it hardly takes a great effort of will to turn the lines into tetrameter either:

```
-x- /      -x-  /      -x- /     -x- /
```
Perfection, of a kind, was <u>what he was after,</u>
```
x / x  x x /    x   / x  x / x
```

```
        -x- / -x-    /  -x-  /  -x-      /
```
And the poetry he invented was <u>easy to understand</u>;
```
x     x / x  xx / x   x / x  xx  x  /
```

Though there seems to me no compelling reason for doing so, especially on a second pass, when the bolder 3/5-stress of the last lines are now there for retrospective projecting.

If we try to read the middle lines as tetrameter:

```
   -x- /    -x-    /  -x-      / -x-     /
```
He knew <u>human folly</u> <u>like the back of his hand,</u>
```
 x  /   \ x / x x    x X  x  x /
```

```
      -x-  / -x-/      -x-  /   -x-     /
```
And was greatly interested in armies and fleets;
```
x     x   / x/ x    x x /   x x      /
```

'human folly' is a very borderline phrasemic collocation, and spoken as x x/x, so 'human' is an easy demotion. The weaks are just regular enough to imply a strong triple metre, which helps the demotion too. However, 'like the back of his hand' is definitely phrasemic, and often spoken x x x x x /; I would quite like to mark 'back' as an X, a promoted w but in light metre this seems a bit of a cheek really. The line 'And was greatly interested in armies and fleets' can be scanned as a loose tetrameter with reasonable ease, but this is perhaps the *only* line.

So if we can buy the notion that dimetronic 3-strong is a light-metre version of pentameter, one can again hear i.p. as Auden's introjected frame. At least, that's the way I prefer to hear it:

    /   /   /

Perfection, of a kind, was what he was after,

      /   /   /

And the poetry he invented was easy to understand;

    /   /   /

He knew human folly like the back of his hand,

    /   [/]   /   /

And was greatly interested in armies and fleets;

    /   /   /

When he laughed, respectable senators burst with laughter,

     /   /   /

And when he cried the little children died in the streets.

But line four doesn't fit, and this scansion is monumentally sub-jective. While such poems present interesting problems, they are *not* ultimately capable of proposing anything like a broadly agreed scansion – and should therefore be designated as metrically unstable, which is a perfectly admissible diagnosis. Light metre is often at the edge of free metre, and it's a waste of time our trying to project any template at all. In any sympathetic reading, *the act of projection* must *be commensurate to the act of introjection*, and if it greatly exceeds it – as I think does the above exercise – we move rather seamlessly from a metrical definition of projection to a neurotic one. The simple point should be made that, if it's *this* hard to project a template, the chances are that a template has not been introjected to any significant degree; Auden simply wasn't overthinking this one.

Far easier are those light metres which tend towards loose. I'll make a full scansion of a few lines of Paul Muldoon's 'Immram', in which I think a 4-strong line can be strongly projected, even though I suspect its introjection by the poet was an intuitive (though not unconscious) affair. While the sense stress scansion is as subjective as ever, I hear only the last line in this passage as metrically unstable, a significant part of its closural effect (especially the exquisite metapoetic strain on 'new strain'). Note that weak placeholders can be populated with not only multiple syllables in light metre, but also both ws *and* demoted s stresses. 'Out of the blue' and arguably 'little weight' are phrasemic. I have interpreted the second 'ass-hole' as anaphoric, and it should therefore be de-accented (a sentence I feel I have waited my whole life to type). I'll leave the reader to work out why I accented the other lines in the way that I did, and then – as they should, as a point of principle – disagree. Light verse *may* be scanned, provided one never tries to win any consensus and one realises that as soon as tension has been identified one has really switched to the projection of a loose template. Its definition *lies* in its permitting many interpretative possibilities.

```
       -x-  /   -x-      /   -x-  /   -x- /
    I was fairly and squarely behind the eight
    x   x  /’ x x     /’   x  x /    x /
    o - o   3  o-o      3   o - o  2    o 2


      -x-  /    -x-  / -x-  /  -x-  /
    That morning in Foster's pool-hall
     x   /  x   x  / x   /   x
      o   2  o - o   2  o    2    o


       -x-  /     -x-  /    -x-   /   -x-  /
    When it came to me out of the blue
      x  x /’    x  x, X  x    x  /’
      o - o  3     o  -1 1*  o - o  3


      -x-  /   -x- /    -x-        /  -x- /
    In the shape of a sixteen-ounce billiard cue
    x    x  /  x x /  x   x       /’ x    X
    o  - o   2   o-o 2  o    o       3  o   1*
```

```
    -x- /      -x-    /      -x-       /    -x-  /
```
That lent what he said some <u>little weight.</u>
```
    x  /      x   x  /  x    X  x   /
    o   2     o - o   2    o    1*- o    2
```

```
    -x- /  x /   -x- /   -x-    /
```
'Your old man was an ass-hole.
```
    x   /  :  \    X x  /'   x
    o   2     1* - 1*o  3     o
```

```
 -x-      /  -x-      /   -x- /  -x- /
```
That makes an <u>ass-hole</u> out of you.'
```
    X'  \    x  X,  x,  X   x   /'
    2*  1* - o  1*   −1  1*  o    3
```

```
    -x-  /    -x-    /     -x-  /   -x- /
```
My grand-father hailed from New York State.
```
    x   /   x  x   /    x   /  \    /'
    o    2   o - o   2      o    2  1*   *3
```

```
    -x-  /     -x-     /  -x-   /
```
My grand-mother was part Cree.
```
    x   /    x,  x,  X   \      /
    o    2    - 1 - - 1  1*  1*     2
```

```
    -x-   /   -x-     / -x- /   -x-    /
```
This must be some new strain in my pedigree.[2]
```
    x   X   x  x    / :  /  x   x  /' x  x
    o    1*  o - o     2     2  o - o  3  o - o
```

From the contour grid we can see that weak space is heavily (and sometimes adventurously) populated, tensions are concentrated mid-line, and there is a higher-than-usual degree of high accent:

2 Paul Muldoon, *Poems 1968–1998* (London: Faber & Faber, 2011).

1w	2s	3w	4s	5w	6s	7w	8s	
oo	3	oo	3	oo	2	o	2	
o	2	oo	2	o	2	o		
oo	3	o-1	1*	oo	3			
oo	2	oo	2	oo	3	o	1*	
o	2	oo	2	o	1*	o	2	
o	2	:	1*	oo	3	o		
	2*	1* o	1	—1	1*	o	3	
o	2	oo	2	o	2	1*	3	
o	2	—1—1	1*	1*	2			
o	1*	oo	2	:	2	oo	3	oo

A NOTE ON METRICAL COMPOSITION

I think there is almost nothing at all to say about the actual practice of metrical composition. You just do it, get better by doing it more, and find a way to practise it that suits your temperament. There are various ways of achieving the aim of making the forms useful, natural and invisible. I teach students how to write in i.p. by taking them down to the pub and insisting that no words may be spoken that are not in fluent pentameter. Two or three drinks in and they're all talking like Hamlet, having spared themselves writing a thousand lines of lousy blank verse (and discovering the usefulness of metrical elision and syntactic inversion in the process).

This section of the book may or not be useful in helping to explain the business of metrical composition; but as a dynamic and creative act, it's very simple. In a way, 'what really happens' is the reverse of everything I've described: language is introjected into the *frame*. A pattern is memorised and speech is magnetised to it; a metrical template draws words from the mind and pulls language into its close or rough shape. In the hands of a fluent practitioner, the resulting pattern of disagreement or agreement between words and frame both conveys and dramatises semantic intent. Infants can communicate with us and with each other without any lexis, through imitating the stress-alternation of content and function and the intonational contours of phrase-structure. Similarly, a poet can recite you a whole sonnet[1] – complete with a sophisticated argument, a devastating turn

---

1 The sonnet follows the emotional shape of the tonic/plagal cadence/perfect cadence of the twelve-bar blues form far more often than it does anything more dialectical or syllogistic. Indeed, the emotional contour and argumentative shape of

and a weighty, mind-blowing couplet — with nothing but a pattern of 'duh-*dahs*' and a scattering of accents, de-accents and supra-segmentals.

Such templates draw real words — like those of our prelinguistic chatterers — to the very tips of our tongues again. This method of metrical composition *replicates* that first joy in learning to speak, the sense of words being somehow sprung free from the mind by form and rhythm and structure alone. Metre is anterior to speech, and both generative and predictive of it. The words we could not yet speak were drawn out of us by phonological and prosodic structure; the words we dare not speak are tricked out of us in much the same way.

We are lent the courage to say what we dare not by rhythm. Poetry is just urgent human talk; that sheer urgency alone will naturally create both music and rhythm is an exquisite tribute to the symmetry of the physical laws that govern us. Poetry's urgent engine is rhythm, in the sense of both what draws it forth and what drives it forward: it gives us the courage of our convictions, and conveys the convictions of our courage; it injects its own excitement, its agitation, its dance,

---

the twelve-bar blues map to the sonnet closely enough to propose that some part of the brain regards them as deeply cognate, if not identical, forms. For those of us stuck with the sonnet habit, I suspect the aim is identical to a musician who plays the blues: to render the form invisible, as a kind of compositional motor skill. It's possible – as Shakespeare did with the sonnet, Dickinson with the ballad, Burns with the Standard Habbie, Bach with the fugue, and Charlie Parker with what jazz musicians call 'rhythm' changes (a particular set of chord changes based on the Gershwin tune 'I Got Rhythm') – to know a form so well, it's rendered a mere shaped space for thinking in, and for directing emotion. Its shape lays out a rough emotional and argumentative terrain across which a 'spoken plea' can be conducted, leaving the brain free to concentrate on original content alone. This sounds paradoxical if we also accept the sensible dictum of 'no art without the resistance of the form', but it's a balance: aspects of the form may still nag and snag productively, while others are unconsciously absorbed. Besides, ambitious artists can always find a way to make it harder for themselves.

into the minds of our readers. More than any other aspect of poetic composition, rhythm reminds us that the way up and the way down are indeed one and the same.

CONCLUSION

Speaking of contraries, see how the brook
In that white wave runs counter to itself.
It is from that in water we were from
Long, long before we were from any creature.
Here we, in our impatience of the steps,
Get back to the beginning of beginnings,
The stream of everything that runs away . . .

(ROBERT FROST, 'West-Running Brook')[1]

Everything in this universe is driven apart by increasing entropy; yet everywhere matter seems to resist, reflecting the weird state of order still inscribed in it by the primal singularity, our unbroken cosmic egg, and falling into wave, sphere, orbit, season and pulse. We reflect it too, as members of the set of natural objects; and so in turn does our complex system of language, which is just as deeply wrought with those symmetric whorls and rhythms and patterns as we are. Poetry discloses all this; and in making explicit, audible use of the patterns which shape our speech, poetry also sings of the underlying unity – the same song that sings under everything, the concentric circles that miraculously appear in your coffee mug when you tap the desk. Nonetheless it's a little sad to find yourself born into a universe founded on the principle of *nostalgia*. But it's a good one, perhaps, for poets, who start elegising things before they have even begun.

---

1   Robert Frost, *The Poetry of Robert Frost: The Collected Poems, Complete and Unabridged*, ed. Edward Connery Lathem (New York: Henry Holt, 2002).

ENDNOTES

---

1. A rule of five

This is not a book which discusses 'form' in anything other than a strictly metrical sense, but — at the risk of appearing even more of a crank — I have found the following little table useful in maintaining distinctions of formal procedure and structure. (It's derived, in part, from Vedantic *nyaya* traditions.) 'Structure' is generally far simpler in poetry than in other literary forms; our sophistications lie elsewhere. While the list below presents idealised categories, real-world poems often switch between these strategies freely, or nest one within another. The categories themselves can be interpreted in a great number of ways: they can be read as analogous to the operations of physical law, or those of the conscious and unconscious mind; or as descriptive of various logical, philosophical and literary procedures. The scale itself might be interpreted as (a) the progressive corruption of atemporal unity by temporal sequence; (b) the progression of an absolute singularity towards absolute dispersal, driven by entropy; (c) the non-sequential, symmetric unconscious moving towards sequential, asymmetric consciousness; (d) a progression from absolute innocence to an absolute skepsis, an absolute interconnectedness to absolute disconnectedness, or an absolute stasis to an absolute Heraclitean flux. There is a very odd (and likely coincidental) scalar correspondence to the perception of sound-events, which I will also include below; since hearing is the sense which measures time most accurately, it seems a relevant inclusion.

1. No A, no B: *unity*. There are no separable elements to be compared. Perceived simultaneity of auditory events (below 0.003 seconds apart). Continuous mode. No paradigm or syntagm. No temporal or causal sequence. *Via positiva*. Positively defined strategies. Pure 'image' poems; free-standing and deliberately inconclusive meditations; 'epiphanic' forms, such as haiku.

2. A is B: *symmetry*. Elements compared for similarity only. Perceived separation but not sequence of auditory events (above 0.003 seconds apart). Litanic mode. Strongly paradigmatic. Sequence without temporal or causal relation. List-poems; prayers; curses; incantation; dithyramb; blazon, etc.

3. A both is and is not B: *correspondence*. Elements compared for similarity and dissimilarity. Perceived sequence of auditory events (above 0.03 seconds apart). Argumentative mode. Paradigmatic and syntagmatic. Causal relation and sequence. Argument; conceit; syllogism; intertextuality; dialectic; eclogue, etc.

4. A is not B: *asymmetry*. Elements compared for dissimilarity only. Auditory response time to sound-events (i.e. time in which non-passive, asymmetrical reaction can be made): 0.3 seconds. Narrative mode. Strongly syntagmatic. Temporal and causal sequence. Narrative forms; dramatic monologue; epic; anecdote.

5. A neither is nor is not B: *disunity*. Elements are not compared. Limit of perceptible rhythm: i.e. sound events repeated 2–3 seconds apart. Discontinuous mode. Neither paradigmatic nor syntagmatic. Indifference to temporal or causal sequence. *Via negativa*. Negatively defined strategies. Surrealism; collage; *cento*; cut-up; postmodern or experimental discontinuous practices.

2. Symmetry and generalisation in the unconscious

Ignacio Matte Blanco proposed that the unconscious was structured by two principles. Firstly, the principle of generalisation, which states that 'Unconscious logic does not take account of individuals as such; it deals with them only as members of classes, and of classes of classes'; and secondly, the principle of symmetry: 'the Unconscious can treat the converse of any relation as identical to it; that is, it deals with relationships as symmetrical'.[1] Unlike the workings of the conscious ego, the unconscious deals with neither instance (it only understands sets) nor asymmetrical relation. If a relation exists, its direction is reversible and its agents interchangeable. If differences between things cannot be acknowledged, there can be neither chronology nor causality, since sequence requires differentiation. In the unconscious, what X did to Y, Y did to X; if I hate you, someone or something also hates me; the cat knocked over the vase both before *and* after it smashed; what happened yesterday is also happening today, and will happen tomorrow. The whole business will be fully addressed in the second part of the book, but I must make this point here: I feel the principle of generalisation erodes the paradigmatic 'axis of selection', which depends on family resemblances between stored items or 'individuals', while the principle of symmetry erodes the syntagmatic 'axis of combination', which depends upon rule-based category and sequence. Now: if the unconscious functions as a serious influence in the composition of poetry, Matte Blanco may have partly explained the psychological origins of Roman Jakobson's holy formula, 'the poetic function projects the principle of equivalence from the axis of selection into the axis of combination'. My position, which I will explain in due course, is that the principle of rule is *also* projected from the axis of combination into the axis of selection: the poetic

1 Matte Blanco, *The Unconscious as Infinite Sets: An Essay in Bi-Logic* (London: Karnac, 1998).

function is really a partial collapse and conflation of both axes. While it is probably unfalsifiable, Matte Blanco's hypothesis would explain this perfectly. This kind of thinking has, however, fallen out of fashion, and recent neuroscience seems to contradict both the clear-cut distinction between conscious and unconscious (consciousness seems more a matter of specific focus, and of our awareness *of* our awareness), and the idea of a childhood as an atemporal and indivisible Eden. But the fact that we continue to hark *back* to it as such – that we often see 'child-like presence' as an artistic or meditational corrective to the jagged discontinuities of the conceptualising machine – strikes me as almost as important.

3. Noise and meaning

White noise and brown noise can also be thought of as, respectively, the universe's paradigmatic and syntagmatic forces in their virgin state, i.e. when one is entirely unmitigated by the operation of the other. In the first case, all terms are interchangeable, and meaninglessly correspond; in the second, all terms are arranged by inflexible rule, and meaninglessly relate. 'Meaning', or 'meaningful arrangement', can be considered a human-projected consequence of the interrelation of both axes; or, better, a bootstrapping effect where a natural organism whose brain is *constructed* by the interrelation of both axes projects itself into a natural habitat which has evolved from the same principle: 'meaning' is a closed-system feedback process. When this stable, complex 'pink' system (i.e. 'us') projects itself into 'pink' features of nature, 'meaning' is equivalent to 'intentionality'.

'White' = lexis, 'brown' = grammar is another fun line to pursue, and might lead us to find poetry 'a browner shade of pink' than regular speech, given its fondness for rule-based structures which correlate its parts (among which I would also include the subservience of its elements to the overdetermined rules of the 'thematic domain', explored else-where). This appears to be an *opposing* tendency to that identified by

Jakobson, in that it is a strengthening of the axis of combination, but it might merely be a natural way of compensating for the projection of parallel arrangement across the syntagm. In other words, the rules of *the entire domain* are overdetermined in an attempt to limit the homogenising effect of the paradigmatic.

Incidentally, there are many 'colours' of noise described in acoustics and signal processing; my favourite is that unofficial racket known as 'green noise', which roughly corresponds to the sound of the world when you open the window: a low-level pink noise with an emphasis around 500Hz (just below C above middle C; the earth blows a little flat).

4. Computers as composers

As a result of the telescoping of the serial process of composition in computer-based music, all the analogue noise and error of us that we call 'humanity' has been moved to a different part of the compositional chain, and shifted from its traditionally frontloaded position (i.e. the recording of live performance); the fact that noise, delay, rubato, mistiming, timbral variation, error, slippage and goof are now *deliberately* inserted as part of a compositional procedure – and not left to performative expression and incompetence – appears to have affected the 'humanity' not a jot. Paradoxically, the necessity of 'programming in' the humanity has led to a bizarre expertise in the expressive *exaggeration* of human error, a music often full of glitch and crackle, staggered and staggering beats, over-hit snares and under-hit hi-hats. Computer-based music is already in its Romantic phase. By contrast, very few poets would dare to write 'badly', lest the gesture be misread as simple ineptitude. This 'constraint of demonstrable competence' is something one finds only in overdemocratised art forms: in poetry's case, the bar has been set very low by its *admitting* poets who could not write, poets from whom the rest would like to clearly distinguish themselves. The exceptions are pastiche or satire (see, for example, Peter Reading's *Stet*), or the poetry of those too smart, literate and self-confident to care (see Louis MacNeice).

Generative music programming – essentially the art of judiciously modulating 'white' aleatoric data with some 'brown' grammatical rules to produce something 'pink' – is fairly close to providing some very listenable music, and reminds us that Bach's genius was computational as well as inspirational. Poetry is a vastly more complex business, because its listable parameters are far more numerous, and its signs too quickly destabilised; but *not* – who would seriously claim this – because it captures any more of the human spirit than does music. Current efforts at generative poetry are still aspiring to the merely daft, alas, and most depend upon stochastic algorithms to produce surreal effects of 'the fatuous banana spliced my unwarranted windmill' variety, which appear 'poetic' only because nonsensical linguistic input overstimulates our connecting faculties – a feeling we reasonably might *associate* with poetry, but would be wise not to confuse with it. Poets, needless to say, have had nothing to do with their programming. An algorithm for poetry would be incredibly complex, but not infinitely so; and its detachment from such catastrophically overvalued and sentimental constructs as 'the individual voice' (the one all young writers are presently required to 'find') could be just the thing to see the cultural return of *anon.*, or even propel us into a new era of Classicism, should we desire or require such things. However, a fact too rarely pointed out is that a computer is going to have to be able to knock out a decent after-dinner speech, a piece of good journalism and a cracking short story before it gets anywhere *near* a great poem, which will be the very last thing it produces.

5. 'Allo allophones

Foreign allophones are the source of much mildly racist humour, but also the hinge on which many fatal shibboleths have turned. In the South-East Asian theatre in World War II, anyone approaching a US army checkpoint would be asked to say 'lollapalooza', which the Japanese l/r allophone makes very difficult to accommodate: anything close to 'rorraparooza' would be met with a burst of gunfire. Allophonic and 'missing phone' shibboleths have decided the fates of stuttering innocents throughout human history, from the Ephraimites who couldn't say the word for 'flood stream' (the original 'shibboleth', though it's sometimes translated as 'ear of corn') to the Dominican Haitians who couldn't say 'parsley' (the *perejil* of Rafael Trujillo's horrible 'Parsley Massacre'), right up to both Catholic and Protestant Northern Irish: one way or the other, your gunpoint recitation of the alphabet would stop at the eighth letter, since either *haitch* or *aitch* would declare your schooling, and therefore your sectarian allegiance.

To return to mild racism: I once heard of a jazz promoter who put together a tour of Japan featuring three guitarists chosen for no other reason than requiring that Japanese MCs announce 'Larry Coryell, Emily Remler and Bireli Lagrene'. A friend recounts an uncomfortable encounter with the p/f allophone in Filipino English: passing a garden party thrown by Imelda Marcos, she was treated to the hostess's rendition of the well-known Barbra Streisand number, 'Peelings'. But the problem is that smug Anglophones forget it cuts both ways. English 't', for example, is an allophone of *six* different sounds, separately differentiated in other languages. English allophones produce much Turkish and Mandarin hilarity, I gather, particularly in our (purely psychological) conflation of aspirated and unaspirated consonants. Even though we *use* both sounds, we have tuned out their differences so effectively we're quite unaware of them. Try saying 'nitrate' and 'night rate': you have to hold a candle-flame to your lips to make yourself aware of the clear difference in the articulation of the central /t/.

6. Present and absent zebras

If we set aside the arguments for its part-iconicity – the word 'zebra' is an arbitrary sign for both our real and conceptual zebra. However, let me offend the intelligence of every semiotician in the room and suggest that the word *functions* indexically when the zebra is visible or present to us, and symbolically when it isn't, designating the first and invoking the second. The ontological change in status of the referent from present to absent is hardly, I'd propose, a small matter; it entails a change in the function of the name from intra-domain to inter-domain – in this case, from one that works within the domain of a real and present world, to one that works *between* that real world (if we assume speech itself has a real-world presence) and its memorised simulacrum. I appreciate that this is an argument for the word 'table' in 'put it on that table' not having exactly the same referent as 'take it through to the table in the next room' – but I suspect that, given the opportunity, present-table trumps concept-table in a way that goes well beyond mere deictic convention, and that we simply neither think of nor use the words in *quite* the same way. (It also proposes that conceptualisation is very much a disease of degree. The table in the other room must be 'imagined', since it's not visible; though not to the extent that we have to 'imagine' a table that hasn't even been manufactured or purchased yet, but which we might still discuss as existing.) Nothing will settle this but an MRI scan, of course.

Our ability to hold the known world in our heads when it isn't physically present is unbelievably cool, but the facility came at a price: the consequent superimposition of 'the known' over the real world deepens the sense of all-pervasive dream, and diminishes our sense of our own real presence within that world. (Hence the parlous state of 'the' environment; the definite article stands before a pernicious misconception regarding our relationship to it.) It is precisely this superimposition that poetry alerts us to, undermines, punctures, and 'gets between'. Language is the main way in which we express, codify and consolidate what we hold to be the case; the poetic function is language's

ENDNOTES

built-in epistemological tool for challenging the truth of our casual certainties and broad assumptions wherever we sense them to be incorrect. *Were* language able to function only indexically, there would be no need for such a function; its symbolicity, however, demands it.

7. Overtones

In audio signal processing there is a procedure called 'additive synthesis'. It has its origins in the nineteenth-century French physicist Joseph Fourier's work on the heat equation. The Fourier series he subsequently developed decomposes the periodic functions of complex waveforms into an infinite series of simple sines and cosines. This led — much later — to the discovery that *any* sound, no matter how complex, could be replicated merely by stacking up sine waves (think of the pure tone you get from a pipe organ) at different powers, at frequencies corresponding to the partials of the harmonic overtone series measured from a fundamental or root tone. Nowadays it's possible to resynthesise even a complex musical sound — a violin note, a human voice, or a whole piece of music — and convert it to an additive series of sine waves. Computers allow us to visualise the whole thing spectrally, and 'see' how the sound is composed — as well as cut into it at any point, and change its inner composition as drastically as we like. The business of semantic connotation is central to how poetry works. In poetry, one is very conscious of not just the 'meanings of words', but also their 'overtones' — those secondary associations in the more peripheral regions of a word's conceptual domain, which are constrained, shaped and boosted by the context of the poetic line and the thematic domain as a whole. Even though I know the exercise is quite impossible, it strikes me that if you could 'resynthesise' a word's site-specific contextual meaning, you could visualise it as a unique semantic spectrograph, where connotative overtones would be expressed at various strengths over the harmonic fundamental of its denotative sense. Thus in a poem — to use my favourite

— 673 —

go-to noun – 'moon' might denote the heavenly satellite, but also carry aspects of whiteness, roundness, light-carrying, tide-pulling, coldness, remoteness, barrenness – at various amplified or diminished levels, depending on its various semantic, phrasal, lyric, syntactic and thematic circumstances. (The word's changing sense over time – which occurs through its subjective rereading and subsequent recontextualisation – maps beautifully to the more complex procedure of *inharmonic* additive synthesis, an analogy the reader will be relieved to know I do not intend to explore here.)

8. In defence of Lakoff

Patrick Errington, a St Andrews PhD candidate with whom I have argued long and hard over the chapter on 'The Conceptual Domain', feels the critical consensus is swinging back towards Lakoff, and writes to me (I have omitted most of his copious references; my italics):

> Numerous brain-imaging studies of linguistic and conceptual processing strongly suggest that word- and sentence-understanding recruits sensorimotor brain areas, particularly the motor and pre-motor cortices in action-verb processing, which, to my mind, throws something of a wrench in this reading of Pinker's theory. A general hypothesis, deeply tied to studies of what has been dubbed the 'mirror system', suggests that comprehension involves neural simulation of events and states that the words provoke (and not just as a side-effect), as well as simulation of *the action of producing the words themselves* in both speaking and writing. A recent survey of such studies by Giovanni Buccino et al. leads them to suggest that noun, adjective, and adverb comprehension recruits motor/pre-motor simulation as well, potentially due to interactive 'affordances' encoded by the hypothesised 'canonical neurons'

as well as emotional reflexes, which implies that meaning is based in collections of real-world experiences. Additionally, other research has shown fairly consistently that action words in metaphors (e.g. 'he grasped the situation') *do* recruit sensorimotor simulation in the processing of their meaning, though generally seem to show a diminishing level of activation inversely correlated to the subject's familiarity with the metaphor. This doesn't undermine Lakoff and Johnson's theory, but supports one based on a variation of Rachel Giora's 'Graded Salience Hypothesis', wherein I would suggest that novel metaphors (as all metaphors are, at one point, even our commonplace 'conceptual metaphors') recruit a wider or deeper spectrum of the sensorimotor systems to process it — though, over time, and with increased familiarity, the extent of the activation is diminished (there is research that may show a shift in activation from mostly right hemisphere to mostly left), with novel metaphors recruiting and eliciting greater emotional responses. Importantly, novel variations of familiar conceptual metaphors can still be understood *as* metaphors, as Lakoff and Johnson suggest ('the water went from hot to cold' can still be understood when it's changed to 'the water meandered from hot to cold'), which strongly suggests that those metaphors are not completely dead, and can thus be re-anchored in the wider-spectrum sensorimotor system by novel variations.

This 'embodied' approach seems to me a welcome middle way between the two positions, and is also consonant with what one might expect from good common sense. Lakoff has nonetheless exaggerated the power of conceptual metaphor, whose effects inevitably depend not on their verbal formulae but the actual deep referents themselves — which rise, sink, alter in metonymic emphasis or disappear, while the metaphor itself often retains the identical form of words.

9. Linguistic relativism

The idea that metaphors have the 'power' to reframe or shape thought is closely related to the linguistic relativism (or determinism, in its 'strong' form) of the Sapir-Whorf hypothesis. Only the weak version of the theory – the proposition that language influences, rather than determines, the thinking we do – has much credibility these days. As Lakoff has pointed out from the start, most of our basic metaphors are 'embodied', i.e. they emerge directly from our corporeal status, our physical orientation and topology, our spatiotemporal dimension, our proprioception, and so on; and therefore it might seem reasonable to assert that they do indeed 'shape our thought' to some degree. However, 'embodiedness' is not an arbitrary cultural convention, and I find it hard not to see these ur-metaphors as 'merely the shape our thought takes'. (I suppose one may consider our human embodiedness a 'culturally relative state', but this Olympian perspective is not one we have the luxury of indulging for long.) Even our original, newly coined metaphors are merely those which we are *capable* of thinking, and we are no more able to conceive of tropes outside that set than we are to imagine colours we cannot see. What looks like a *symbiosis* between a formal expressible idea and the dynamic thought that takes place within it may just be their consubstantiality. (Interestingly, this is a perceptual error that likely originates in the false propositional metaphor indicated by the words 'within it' – the result, if you like, of the ill-advised extrapolation of an otherwise perfectly useful embodied-type metaphor, adequate to some descriptions of reality but not others.)

Elsewhere, local, culturally fixed and unconsciously deployed conceptual metaphors can be explained in much the same way as anomalous linguistic systems of colour, number or tense: not as evidence of a fundamental difference of neural wiring, but mere reactions to cultural or environmental necessity, topographic circumstance, and so on. Doubtless these are self-reinforcing; doubtless they are censorious of certain kinds of thought – but I am sceptical as to whether they 'place limits on them'.

Whenever a genuine exigency presents itself – whether it's perceptual, sequential, economic, existential, sexual, or whatever – and *requires* us to think beyond those local conceptual metaphors, we tend to have little trouble in doing so. Our concept-blindness is then revealed as less a conditioning of our thought than merely a sensible and economical adaptation to a fairly stable set of cultural constraints. However, I would concede that – based on what I understand of the current evidence – the constant reinforcement of specific neural pathways can lead to their over-wiring, and possibly even the abnormal growth or contraction of parts of the brain's architecture; certainly there is now proof that neurogenesis occurs in the hippocampus of human adults, and appears to be shaped by personal experience and the patterns of behaviour that result from it, meaning that the brain is consequently 'individualised'. One would not be surprised to find that the patterns of an idiomatically distinct culture might have the same effect; the idea that a repeated thought should exert some downward causality and restructure its own material basis in a way that would then affect the kind of thought it subsequently produced – isn't an outrageous one. No thoughts are, after all, 'unembodied'; but this is a dynamic, not a 'deterministic' model. My gripe is with those who seem to insist that language influences or limits the mind through some magical supervenience. Language *is* merely an aspect of mind.

10. Figures of speech

Below is a reasonably comprehensive list of those rhetorical devices which still crop up in contemporary poetic composition. They have all occurred regularly in the poetry of the last 100 years, although most often go unidentified. However, as much as a few older scholars still like to present rhetoric as a subject which enjoys an unusual rigour, it is really a rag-bag of poorly defined, barely agreed, contradictory and often overlapping concepts. Moreover, the set of concepts that *should* be comprehensively reflected by these terms is covered patchily at best.

I would avoid – like the plague – making any proscriptive or prescriptive use of them: this is a recreational bug-hunt, not a proper discipline. (It *used* to be, but we should now take it about as seriously as alchemy, i.e. as a historically interesting precursor to more sensibly disciplined approaches.) Their arrangement here is, inevitably, a little arbitrary, and some terms could arguably have been as sensibly placed under different headings. I've made three divisions: first, rhetorical figures proper: these are performative devices concerned with *ways* of saying, of making convincing and manipulatively effective speech; secondly, those figures that describe deviations from and unusual ways of manipulating 'normal' syntax; and thirdly those figures that operate at the level of the single word. (These are useful in discussing older poetic dictions.) My rule of five – here used to distinguish figures of *addition*, *repetition*, *arrangement*, *substitution* and *omission* – is elsewhere often a rule of four, with addition and repetition conflated. The distinction seemed to me just about worth making, however. (The popular 'trope and scheme' distinction is terminally flawed.)

Either way, their names are still darned pretty, and occasionally they are clearly useful in the identification and description of an effect. I still use them frequently, but I appreciate that mine might be the last generation to do so; if that's the case, no tears should be shed, but something should be found to replace them. They are still a good, handy way of caricaturing a style: most poets can be identified by their excessive fondness for half-a-dozen of these figures, and noting examples of their effective use can be a highly useful exercise for the apprentice poet.

1. Rhetorical

i. Addition

exemplum: citing an illustrative example
metanoia: the correction of a statement immediately previous
apophasis: inclusion by affecting to omit
enumeratio: detailing parts, causes, effects, or consequences to make a point more forcibly

metabasis: a brief summary of what has been said and what will follow

asterismos: adding a word to emphasise the next statement

ii. Repetition

repetitio: irregular repetition of words or phrases

amplification: repetition of a word or expression, adding more detail

accumulatio: repetition in other words

antanaclasis repetition of a word used in a different sense

antithesis: repetition by the denial of the contrary

sententia: concluding or summarising foregoing passage in a pithy statement of general wisdom

iii. Arrangement

auxesis: material presented in ascending importance: can take the form of climax or bathos

iv. Substitution

periphrasis: more words for less

euphemism: pleasant words for unpleasant

dysphemism: unpleasant words for pleasant (or neutral words)

irony: any speech where the literal meaning of the words and their actual intention is opposed

hyperbole: overstatement for effect

meiosis: understatement for effect

litotes: a form of understatement, denying the opposite or contrary of the word which otherwise would be used

v. Omission

(figures of contraction, or ellipsis at the level of clause)

enthymeme: the omission of a clause which is logically implied

anapodoton: the omission of a clause which is not logically implied, but can be inferred by context

aporia: the profession of a doubt over what to say or choose

erotesis: a rhetorical question

aposiopesis: a breaking off, as if one were unable to continue

anacoluthon: the act of breaking off and finishing a sentence with a
different grammatical structure from that with which it began

praecisio: the omission of the whole: the conspicuous silence

2. Syntactic

i. Addition

pleonasm: addition of superfluous words

polysyndeton: addition of conjunctions between clauses

ii. Repetition

anaphora: repetitions of beginnings

epistrophe: repetitions of ends

epanalepsis: repetition of the beginning at the end

inclusio: epanalepsis at the level of passage

epanados: repetition in reverse order

chiasmus: epanados at the level of passage

anadiplosis: repetition of the end at the next beginning

gradatio: successive, linked anadiplosis

conduplicatio: similar to anadiplosis but it repeats a key word (not
just the last word) from a preceding phrase or sentence, at the
beginning of the next.

epizeuxis: immediate repetition or duplication

diacope: repetition, with a word or two between; a kind of
syntactic tmesis

isocolon, parallelism: duplication or successive similarity of
syntactic forms

paregmenon: the use of several words of a common root together

polyptoton: a paregmenon where the repeated word has a different
grammatical function

iii. Arrangement

hyperbaton: displacement of a single element; uncommon
syntactical usage

anastrophe: a hyperbaton in which noun and adjective, or two other elements are reversed

hypallage: an anastrophe which changes the sense

hysteron proteron: an anastrophe in which temporal order is reversed

metastasis: an unexpected change of tense

parenthesis: a word, phrase, or whole sentence inserted as an aside in the middle of another sentence

hypotaxis: using a series of subordinate clauses or phrases (the opposite of parataxis)

parataxis: the use of successive independent clauses, with or without conjunctions

iv. Substitution

metonymy: the substitution of a word for a related or aspectual term (such as cause for effect or effect for cause)

synecdoche: locally, the specific metonymy of part-for-whole

metalepsis: a double metonymy, a metonymy substituted for a metonymy

anthimeria: deliberately 'wrong' substitution for one part of speech for another

hendiadys: the use of 'and' to split a single qualified noun into two parts

antiptosis: using a prepositional phrase for an adjective

catachresis (often in the form of transferred epithet): an apparently 'inappropriate' substitution, usually for figurative purposes

enallage: an effective grammatical mistake

paronomasia: a pun, or play on words; a word used in a way that draws out its ambiguous meaning. It is behind some highly suspect 'suggestion' techniques in the quack science of Neuro-Linguistic Programming: here the 'top' meaning of a word used in a local sense veils a second meaning in a generic sense, or vice versa. (Poetry employs it in much the same way.)

v. Omission

ellipsis: omission generally

asyndeton: the omission of conjunctions

scesis onomaton: the omission of the main verb

zeugma: yoking two words to a single word which has a different meaning for both

3. Lexical

i. Addition

epenthesis: addition of letters to the middle

prosthesis: addition of letters to the beginning

proparalepsis: addition of letters to the end

ii. Repetition

alliteration: repetition of initial sounds

rhyme: repetition of terminal sounds

assonance: repetition of vowel sounds

consonance: repetition of consonantal sounds

palindrome: repetition of the same letters in reversed order

iii. Arrangement

tmesis: the splitting of one word into two, often separating it by another

spoonerism: the humorous switching of initial sounds between proximate words. (The Reverend Spooner's condition affected his perception of sequence, not words themselves. Once, at dinner, his hostess accidentally knocked over the salt-cellar: Spooner then helpfully tipped his claret into the salt-pile to soak it up. To save his embarrassment, his hostess then grabbed the bottle and threw it over her left shoulder, braining a housemaid. I invented that last bit.)

iv. Substitution

antisthecon: substitution of letters

metaplasmus: misspelling for effect

v. Omission

aphaeresis: omission of letters at the beginning of a word

syncope: omission of letters in the middle of a word

apocope: omission of letters at the end of a word

synaloepha: omission of a vowel when contracting two words
   to one

11. What's not in a name

While my acquaintance with the philosophy of language is that of a complete amateur, I've read just enough in Kripke and Frege not to be too breezy in my asseverations regarding 'names'. But there's a little infinite regress here: if 'Don Paterson' means 'he-who-goes-by-the-name-of-Don Paterson', then what does the proper name in 'he-who-goes-by-the-name-of-Don Paterson' mean? 'He-who-goes-by-the-name-of-"he-who-goes-by-the-name-of-Don Paterson"'? You see the problem. However, I think this nonsense also directs us towards the truth of the matter, which is a version of the 'use-mention' distinction. The name 'Don Paterson', when *interrogated*, can be seen to be commonly employed as a metonym for 'he-who-goes-by-the-name-of-Don Paterson'; however when the name occurs casually within in *that* sentence, it is being employed as an arbitrary name proper – that is, a pure 'asymbol' whose connection is forged by convention alone, the Millian idea of a 'name' as a pure denotation. Peirce thought their changing semiotic status was tied to one's degree of acquaintance:

> A proper name, when one meets with it for the first time, is existentially connected with some percept or other equivalent individual knowledge of the individual it names. It is then, and then only, a genuine Index. The next time one meets with it, one regards it as an Icon of that Index. The habitual acquaintance with it having been acquired, it becomes a

Symbol whose Interpretant represents it as an Icon of an Index of the Individual named.[1]

This passage still seems staggeringly insightful. However, while it seems to me that names are invisibly symbolic in their unconscious conversational *use*, they *still* appear indexical when consciously analysed in isolation, as one reacquaints oneself with the surprise of meeting them the first time: they are de-iconised. Again, one to be settled by the MRI scan, I suppose; but I'd point out that if you had substituted your *own* name in this self-conscious footnote, you would be just as struck by its strange, queasy index as I currently am by mine – enough to scream inwardly 'but that's not my *name!*' and try to either separate it from yourself, or attempt to flip it quickly into blissfully unthinking symbolicity, so as not to disown it completely. This seems to point to not just a trivial trick of the mind, but evidence of a fundamental change in its function under these conditions. (It also points to something else: the status of the name as both semiotic symbol *and* index means they are *doubly* arbitrary, suggesting that 'names' might be the wave-particle duality of language; although, as far as proper names go, I am not convinced that we can ever have much perspective on a linguistic phenomenon in which we are all so existentially invested. A conscious banana would probably be appalled to know what name it went by, and then spin off into something identically bewildered.)

I mention all this for one simple reason: I believe – in its fetishised attention to sound-detail, in its careful originality, in its deliberately slowed delivery – that poetry insists on our consciousness of words as strange indices, not mere symbolic tags in a sign-system. It 'novelises' language, and in doing so conducts a global shift towards the indexical function: this creates the paradox of moving language one step closer to the reality it seeks to represent, while reawakening us to the very strangeness of the signs by which it does so.

[1] C. S. Peirce, *The Collected Papers of Charles Sanders Peirce*, vol. 2, ed. C. Hartshorne and P. Weiss (Cambridge, MA: Harvard University Press, 1958).

12. Tonality, atonality and expressive range

At the end of Frost's poem – just when you feel things couldn't get any more depressing – the poem's apparently throwaway last line, 'If design govern in a thing so small', makes a deictic shift into a domain far more appalling than that of our merely evil demiurge. Frost's sudden reframing of his material is so radical, I can hardly read the line without feeling my stomach lurch: the poem, I think, is saying . . . 'Maybe God doesn't sweat the small stuff.' At least with the big stuff, we have the sense of *someone* taking an interest, even if it was a bitter or malevolent one – but one who nonetheless creates the horses, the forests, the sunsets, our children. Maybe what we're seeing in this Boschian Lilliput we find in the undergrowth is simply the nature of physical law. Unfortunately, it turns out that the physical law on which this universe is founded is a rebarbative, amoral, murderous enormity. One ends the sonnet nostalgic for the demon-designer of line 13; anything, rather than be left alone in a godless universe founded on such horrific principles.

Note that this line symbolises practically the whole rhetorical range of the traditional aesthetic, and the astonishingly complex and subtle effects it can produce. No experimental poem would ever 'throw away' its biggest line – nor arguably ever *could*, since this kind of nuanced understatement is possible only in the context of a poem which signs its allegiance to and is read within the traditions of consistent argumentative structure and rhetoric. I know that sounds like tedious finger-wagging, but I really do intend it as a neutral point: experimental poetry is not generally concerned with the kind of argument that could make use of such an effect in the first place. Either way, its saliences are rarely achieved by meiosis, something that may account for its attenuated expressive range.

This is a perennial limitation of the discontinuous approach in all the arts; an intrinsic lack of resolution is often culturally interpreted as a sign of tension, a tension which tends to then infect the whole domain. I recall a conversation with the late Michael Donaghy about the film

Amadeus (initiated by the fact that Donaghy was a hilarious double for its lead, Tom Hulce). In the film, Mozart's own music served as the sound-track to his life, in all its love and loss, its triumph and disaster. Imagine, Donaghy proposed, that the same trick had been attempted in a biopic about Schoenberg: you'd spend the entire ninety minutes – whether our hero was on the tennis court, sharing a candlelit dinner with a lover, hailing a cab, giving a lecture or wheezing on his death-bed – worried that the lunatic from *Friday the 13th* was about to jump out from the bushes or the cupboard with a machete. The emotional palette of non-tonal music is, for nearly all listeners, constrained and tense. The ear helplessly resolves everything into tonic-dominant patterns of tension and resolution, and while symbolic or ghostly substitutions for tonic resolution are possible – Alban Berg is the go-to name to drop here – we mostly perceive serial or atonal music as an extended and unresolved dominant sequence. (*Moses und Aron* put me in the same state of psychosis as would a month in the trenches.) The effect can be suspended and diminished through exposure, familiarity, and the slow letting-go of the deeply inculcated expectations of functional harmony, but it is *not* replaced by some atonal analogue of the tonal language of feeling.

Too much can be – and perhaps is – made of the tale of George Rochberg's conversion to tonality in the sixties. Rochberg was a very decent composer, but no one is pretending he was Webern. Nonetheless, the story is a poignant and instructive one. After the death of his son, Rochberg found that the icy angles, symmetries and dissonances of his serial technique simply could not express his grief: he needed a tonic as well as a dominant to compose music adequate to his tragedy. For the same reason, I would gently propose that a neo-modern experimentalist writing a 'heartfelt' poem for the funeral of a beloved friend or family member might find, say, the technique of switching out every noun for the next one in the dictionary inadequate to their purpose. The constriction of emotional range that discontinuous technique usually implies is another reason poets might be better to think of it as an occasionally useful mode, not a revolutionary solution.

13. Chicken and egg

So much depends, as they say, on what you think about things, and what you believe about reality. As for us poets: William Carlos Williams's absurd insistence on the integrity of the object and the intrinsicality of its own meaning was nonetheless driven by a laudable distaste for the way writers had rendered chicken, wheelbarrow and everything else unthinkingly subservient to hierarchical, classical, Eurocentric, colonial and patriarchal frames – a situation that, if anything, was made worse than ever by the palaeo-modernists WCW despised. However, his position remains that of a typical neo-modern absolutist: his distaste for all literary comparison (metaphor does indeed narrow our view of a thing, but it simultaneously makes it part of a new compound sign), and his embarrassing *Schwärmerei* towards Gertrude Stein, who, he famously claimed, 'has gone systematically to work smashing every connotation that words have ever had, in order to get them back clean'[1] reveals someone as clueless about the business of naming as he was about prosody. Mercifully we do not judge poets on the quality of their ideas. (As much for my own sake – I pray we do not.) By contrast, the arch-relativist Eliot's formula would run something like this: humans produce language and culture, and only culture produces reality; reality is therefore an adaptable construct in which the 'word' is *so* inevitably, so wholly continuous with the thing it denotes, combinations of words can create and destroy reality in a stroke. (Occasionally this omnipresent and invisible rule will burst into popular consciousness – see the furore around the revision of Pluto's status from major planet to dwarf, for example; its demotion was treated by some as a 'real thing', though we can be certain that Pluto itself was broadly indifferent to the matter. The beautiful, lonely little globe certainly looked that way on our recent flyby.) I would prefer to say that the word and/or the concept it denotes circumscribe a phenomenon; without this circumscription it is literally

1 William Carlos Williams, *Selected Essays* (New York: New Directions, 1954), 63.

unthinkable, and *with* it – however absurd or fantastical the thing may be – the thing exists by *virtue* of its mere adduction, its very 'thinkability'. My own position is therefore that if there is no intrinsicality, and if 'definition' is a human act of semantic circumscription, it follows that the ability to be 'thought of' is the only sensible qualification for 'a thing's' existence. (One thing remains arguably intrinsic: that of *intent*, i.e. that motive, emotion or desire which drives or informs our actions. But there, alas, I am not sure we are any further forward than Berkeley: '. . . *we cannot know the existence of other spirits otherwise than by their operations'*.²) As I trust may be apparent from these remarks, I line up behind Quine's anti-essentialism, and the assertion that all properties are 'accidental'. 'Things' may be partly composed of what I refer to as 'core connotations', but those are a mere matter of cognitive designation and cultural consensus. There are no primary qualities. An egg is not really an egg, but a set of expectations and assumptions about an egg. Of course the egg has 'chemical properties' and through these might initiate a 'process' – but 'process' is not 'motive' (the 'intentional stance' is a grand heuristic and predictive tool, but nothing else), and by 'properties' we do not mean anything like the 'properties' we intend when we ascribe meaning, role, function, and so on. (For a start, one can guarantee that the hen has a very different take on the thing – one that even humans might not dismiss as irrelevant.) Poets are mostly reality-sceptic, and expert in both pointing out these merely consensual frames, and positing the alternative lives of 'things'. 'What do you know / Of the revolutionary theories advanced / By turnips, or the sex-life of cutlery?'³

2   George Berkeley, *The Works of George Berkeley* (London: Macmillan, 1871), vol. 1, 231.

3   Derek Mahon, 'The Mute Phenomena (after Gérard de Nerval)', *Raw Materials* (Loughcrew: Gallery Press, 2011).

14. A brief defence of jargon

It's impossible to have a wholly nonsensical abstraction, as they always hold out the possibility of their own hypostatisation. This is why they can be so freely combined; randomly thrown-together terms like 'polysemic intransigence' or 'vectorised incoherence' meet with no real objection from the mind, and sound like (and indeed are) plausible or potential states or conditions. This is the idea behind the Sokal hoax and the 'Postmodern Essay Generator', but also the stylistic *raison d'être* behind this notorious, prize-winning corker from Judith Butler:

> The move from a structuralist account in which capital is understood to structure social relations in relatively homologous ways to a view of hegemony in which power relations are subject to repetition, convergence, and rearticulation brought the question of temporality into the thinking of structure, and marked a shift from a form of Althusserian theory that takes structural totalities as theoretical objects to one in which the insights into the contingent possibility of structure inaugurate a renewed conception of hegemony as bound up with the contingent sites and strategies of the rearticulation of power.

Some might say that formal logic and algebra were developed to relieve language of the task of articulating such ugly specificities, and to deny it the opportunity to pull a fast one. Not that I doubt that Butler has the real world in all its hypostatised richness in mind; however the lapse into pure abstraction has, in the eyes of some, signalled her detachment from it – and, we are told, led her into stylistic disaster. This is not just unreasonable: it betrays a foolish prejudice. A jargon's usefulness depends entirely on one's familiarity with it, since it's merely a form of in-house shorthand. For those who have learned an abstract jargon-word in its professional context, its definition is usefully narrow and precise; within its own discourse group, it can – if it needs to – invoke a synonym, or indeed an entire hypostatic set of concrete exempla along the axis of selection. The fact is that well-understood and narrowly defined abstracta assist enormously in both the rapid juggling of terms and the expression of larger, composite, nuanced ideas. The problem is that many of these words *sound* familiar to readers outside the circle – but within that circle, they are not used with the ambiguity or fuzziness others might hear, and indeed often have different senses entirely (as anyone who has encountered, say, the word 'perversity' in a critical theory context will confirm). Some read Butler as a model of lucidity, and I believe them. Other writers are less sincere, and this mode offers cover and comfort to much intellectual charlatanry and self-delusion – from undergraduate to professorial level. Its main crime is the casual hurling around of abstracta with the confidence of concrete substantives in a way that has been *insufficiently* jargonised. The test is simple: ask for a rough synonym of the word, or paraphrase of the passage. If none can be produced, you're either dealing with a chancer, or someone halfway towards a private language. Only poets are allowed say 'my immortal line can suffer no human paraphrase', and even then you should raise at least one eyebrow.

15. Music, synaesthesia and the poem

Many musicians have a touch of sound–colour synaesthesia; personally, I see/hear A major as a bit pale green, and A minor as a bit dark green. But the fact that I know another musician hears it as blue renders my association firmly 'asemic'. Relativists will also tell you that the emotional associations I ascribe here to certain harmonies are culture-specific, and by implication also asemic: they will point to the variation in the emotional interpretation of identical signs to prove the mutually exclusive musico-semantic nature of different native or folk musics. 'Minor' Indian ragas, for example, are not necessarily perceived as 'sad', any more than the microtonal intervals of Turkish music are experienced by Turkish listeners as out-of-tune. However, I think the point, while accurate, is also seriously overstated. The quality of the feeling may be culturally *shaped*, but it is very far from asemic. The extent to which musicians from any culture, whether improvisers or composers, quickly 'master' dodecaphonic tonal harmony points to it being, if not a universal system, one which can be very quickly and universally understood, as well as being a partly hardwired principle tied to the harmonic series. (There is a link to the anti-Whorfian argument here: cf. the effortless acquisition of Portuguese by the Pirahãn Amazons.) The music of Toru Takemitsu or the improvisations of Djivan Gasparayan are heavily influenced and coloured by their native musics, but the dodeca- phonic, triadic harmony on which they are often built seems close to an emotional lingua franca. The argument that all this is merely Western cultural hegemony in action is wishful thinking: the strain would show. These musicians are not speaking in any 'second language', and compose with the idiomatic fluency of any 'native speaker', while maintaining, effortlessly, their own cultural inflections. (This is setting aside the more mundane observation that they play exactly same mix of algorithmic EDM, stadium belters and what my kids call 'douche rock' on, say, Ice FM Nuuk in Greenland as they do everywhere else, with few obvious signs of cultural coercion.) At the end of the day the harmonic series is not negotiable, and has a relatively finite number of interpretations. The dominant, the fifth above the tonic, is the first 'new' non-root note in the harmonic series; whatever music we identify as being built on it has a 'tense' quality that demands resolution. (Even in the most atonal music, musicians and musically sophisticated listeners will instinctively posit a tonal centre not via a tonic, but the vestigial appearance of what sounds like dominant harmony; in such circumstances, the *existence* of a tonic is only confirmed by the appearance of dominant tension.) Since the fifth is embedded into almost all musical notes that aren't pure waveforms, it should be no surprise to find it watermarks all our human musical thinking. Basic music theory shows that once we have a tonic and dominant, some from of triadic harmony is almost a logical inevitability. If there *are* deep psychological mappings between harmony and 'meaning', the (very) vague aesthetic similarity we may sense between, say, Bach and Dickinson on the one hand, and late Schoenberg and J. H. Prynne on the other, may be more accurately defined than merely 'tonal vs atonal'; we may identify a lack of cadential resolution, for one thing, as well as an absence of the usual hierarchy of detail or scale-tone that triadic harmony provides; conversely in 'tonal' verse, one might even identify 'plagal' areas of structure which seek resolution by first moving *away* from a thematic centre (such as those typified by second quatrain of the English sonnet).

Of course, this isn't intended to suggest that other kinds of tonal organisation aren't equally legitimate – just that only one is unavoidable. There are theories as to how this situation was encouraged, though one of the simplest states that while monophonic, melodic folk music can take many forms, it is primarily an 'outdoors' or 'small space' music. It can move into an art music as it acquires complexity, but adds that sophistication horizontally in the form of intricate melodic line, especially when enhanced by improvisatory skill (Indian classical music being the prime example). When music moved into large, echoey spaces with resonant frequencies, long decays and complex reflections, triadic harmony was the inevitable, vertical product of hearing overlapping notes, whose consonance or dissonance was suddenly made unavoidable. (This is not an explanation of *polyphony*, a far older phenomenon.) Something like a universal grammar of harmony might not explain the *consistent* connection between the signs it creates and the broad emotional effects they provoke – that mechanism will remain obscure for some time – but it might at least shed some light on the stability of the relationship. By the same argument, one would be surprised not to find interlingual phenomena where identical or close tonal qualia were evoked by similar musico-semantic means; though for now these are almost wholly inscrutable.

16. Paradox and intertextuality

Forgive me for pursuing another logical quibble some small way. There are other reasons we are more conscious of the paradox of the indexical status of the ground under 'intertextual conditions'. The relationship between the p-text allusion and the a-text mimics the semiotic feedback loop that we find in the symbolic. (If you recall, this is intra-domain on the way out, inter-domain on the way back: an index is propositional of an abstract concern – the 'mirror-like sea' is a salient detail which, if we read it as an index, suggests 'peace'; that abstract concern becomes part of the thematic domain, which in turn appears to have hypostatised the *same* detail as a totem of its animus. This means that on a second reading of this poem we now *know* is about 'peace', the 'mirror-like sea' now seems less evidence proposing a theme than symbolic of a pre-existing one.) Initially the relationship between allusion and a-text appear less like V–T and more like a double subject: i.e. it looks *isologic*, where, if you like, the indexical content of the ground points in both directions. (In the example given, the Donaghy points to the Marvell, but because the sign is compound, the Marvell now seems to point us straight back to the Donaghy.) However, an isologue with one text-absent component is asymmetrical, and therefore a logical impossibility; hence my again referring to the status of the intertextual as a paradox. In a normal isologue, the indexical function of the ground is partly switched out for the active projection of shared content and family resemblance between two roughly equal domains. (In my imaginary poem 'The Final Hurdle', the fast car that crashes in l.3, say, and the sprinter in l.9 are clearly connected by their shared attributes.) The weak, two-way indexical function is largely activated by the reader. In an isologue where one subject is text-absent, the ground must *indicate* ('allude to', here) the text-absent domain for us to establish its identity; but the trade-off is that even though we discover *what* has been indicated is 'merely another subject' which might then form the basis of an isologue, it has by then effectively been upgraded to a ruling tenor. This tenor will to some extent overdetermine the meaning of the *entire* present-text in a way that inevitably renders it minimally subservient to its domain: the Marvell partly 'rules' the Donaghy. This is strongly reminiscent of the operation of symbol. Just as with the symbol, we are unconsciously gripped, I would claim, by a deep and pervasive ontologico-cultural metaphor: absent domains are *by definition* dominant (possibly because they do their work invisibly, and by unseen, ambient or mysterious means, conditions we may unconsciously associate with 'the work of God'). Despite 'intertextuality' appearing to propose a connection between two equal subjects, the asymmetric relationship created by text-absence means that the power relation between the domains is similarly one-sided, and (as with the symbol, where the animus extends its influence beyond the totemic detail which first proposed it) the influence of the a-text may be considerably more broad than just a local allusion. A-text is always the boss of p-text.

17. The burden of burdens

Repeated burdens are a problem in poetry; these often have their origin in song-forms – but if you're singing, the same words can be shaped to mean a thousand different things. In the poem, a line repeated is often just a line repeated. Poets will go to great lengths, sometimes ingenious and sometimes contrived, to put a different spin on each repetition. The villanelle is best passed over in silence, I feel; it is the S. T. Coleridge of poetic forms, and not nearly enough decent poems have been written in it to justify the discussion it has received. (Indeed its best-known example is one of the silliest poems I know, Dylan Thomas's 'Do not go gentle into that good night'. Carol Ann Duffy's perfect and regrettably long-suppressed squib 'Fuckinelle' really should have been the last we heard from the damn thing: 'The poet has tried to write a villanelle. / He's very pleased. The audience can tell.') The sestina was invented in the twelfth century by the French troubadour Arnaut Daniel. Its rules are even more tortuous than those of the villanelle. The sestina offers no repeated lines, but something even worse to test the 'inventiveness' of the poet: a fixed pattern of 'homoioteleutons' woven through six stanzas of six lines, followed by a three-line *envoi*. The six words that occur at the line endings of the one stanza have to be repeated in the next, in the precise order 615243; this procedure is then repeated with each successive stanza until six permutations have been performed. The six words must then reoccur in their original order in the *envoi*, and no-one has ever explained to me why. The result is something like the tuba solo of poetry, with the difference that in the more sensible world of music the tuba solo is more or less banned for anything but comedic effect. By the sestina's end, the poet has usually tied themselves in such wheezing, desperate knots that the envoi resembles a drunk game of Twister in a care home, with the final lines either strained beyond credibility, inexplicably surreal, total rubbish, or technically no longer in the host language. I keep a small anthology of sestina envois that I show students to make the point. I don't like sestinas. No one in the history of poetry ever fell into a swoon and was dictated a sestina by an angel. No brilliant line ever told its author it wanted to be a sestina when it grew up. The odd exceptions tend to succeed by tackling themes which tightly align with the repetitive, claustrophobic or Kafkaesque spaces the form can create. (Elizabeth's Bishop's 'Sestina' being the most obvious example, but there is a fine narrative sestina in Glyn Maxwell's long poem *The Sugar Mile*, and there are handful of blinding experiments by Paul Muldoon.) The explanatory note that accompanies Billy Collins's priceless 'Paradelle for Susan' summarises the deranged constraints of the Provençal forms: '. . . [the Paradelle] is a poem of four six-line stanzas in which the first and second lines, as well as the third and fourth lines of the first three stanzas, must be identical. The fifth and sixth lines, which traditionally resolve these stanzas, must use all the words from the preceding lines and only those words. Similarly, the final stanza must use every word from all the preceding stanzas and only those words.' The poem itself concludes: 'I always cross the highest letter, the thinnest bird. / Below the waters of my warm familiar pain, / Another hand to remember your handwriting. / The weather perched for me on the shore. / Quick, your nervous branch flew from love. / Darken the mountain, time and find was my into it was with to to.' For his trouble, Collins received some genuine, foam-flecked abuse for his failure to honour the *paradelle's* noble tradition, despite it not actually existing.

18. Love & marriage

I confess that there are very few hobbies more rewarding than winding up the radical wing of the avant-garde. Never has so little provocation met with such gloriously disproportionate response – at least from that shirty corner of *la rive gauche* who insist on the meek silence of 'the mainstream' as the price it must pay for its modest commercial success, and who will self-combust with righteous apoplexy whenever the cultural value of their own contribution is gently questioned (by adducing something as tawdry and irrelevant as, say, actual book sales). Or, I've noticed, when some hapless mainstream-ite attempts any kind of assertion about *anything*, however anodyne: one opens one's mouth and is immediately gummed alive by their hipster outriders and keyboard ninjas. But all poetic factions, my own included, are guilty of perpetuating what Michael Donaghy once called 'a knife-fight in a phone box'. What would have amounted to a little recreational cattiness over a half of mild in an upstairs room forty years ago will now, alas, take the form of a social movement. Because our lop-sided debates are now largely conducted through social media – where dissent can be blocked, and no passionate minority is small enough not to feel like a caucus – shared grievances have been refined to something like weapons-grade, though it often seems that the energy required to sustain them exceeds any being ploughed into the art they supposedly defend. (Our enemies form our characters to some extent, and perhaps that is no bad thing. I find myself at least as grateful for their advice as I am that of my mentors, as it is often the more honest. I was for years the proud owner of an indefatigable troll; behind his various cryptic *noms de théâtre* lay an otherwise clever and funny academic, a man over whom — cheeringly, if confusingly — I appeared to exercise some kind of terrible psychosexual hold. I fear the poor chap will end his days shivering at my graveside, riding out wind, rain and sleet like some tank-topped Greyfriars Bobby. But I should miss him too: he was often right.)

All the same, the mutual exclusivity of our various sects can serve a real purpose. The avant-garde remain critically important to the poetic biosphere, and contribute an alternative gene-pool that regularly saves the mainstream from death by inbreeding (the British Poetry Revival of the 1960s, for example, rescued UK poetry from a post-Movement, Americanophobe doldrums that might have rivalled the Georgians for mediocrity), as well as providing the new bacterial strains that lightly infect and then immunise the mainstream *from the avant-garde*. (One symptom of full-blown avant-gardism is the total loss of a lay readership.) They must be read and taken seriously, if not perhaps always as seriously as they take themselves. But as for those naïfs who seek nothing but the harmony of the broad church: without taking up a strong position, there can be no dialectic, and sometimes that position may involve an element of disingenuous self-caricature, as I confess it occasionally does in my own case. One follows the work of *les avants* far more closely and with far more pleasure that it sometimes suits one to admit — and it is important to: they celebrate their best writers like any other group, but their instinct is to keep them secret. (Witness the justified pride they have taken, say, in the plainly radiant talent of Veronica Forrest Thompson over the years; a pride which nonetheless has managed to do literally nothing to increase her readership, and indeed has had precisely the opposite effect.)

To finish with a more serious point: among the more extreme proponents of the avant-garde, experimental, 'innovative' postmodern, 'Cambridge', 'non-conformist' and weak-hypothesis versions of the L=A=N=G=U=A=G=E schools, there remains a lack of understanding —

a code of denial, even – over the practical consequences of discontinuous speech, the superstitious avoidance of the language of grammatical function, and what is lost when sense cannot leap the phrase boundary. Not *just* sense, but metrical impetus, phrasal rhythm, tone, style, lyric continuity, argument, narrative – all of which require larger parsable syntactic structures to provide their carriage. This is not to say there aren't other pleasures to be found besides, although 'pleasure' is perhaps not the aim. Some avants delighted in Geoffrey Hill's semi-buccolingual pronouncement 'Whatever strange relationship we have with the poem, it is not one of enjoyment'. No less celebrated was his perennial claim that 'genuinely difficult art is truly democratic'; and at this point Hill may be said to have firmly *joined* the avant-garde, whose war-cries are largely indistinguishable. Alas, this is not 'a counterintuitive truth' but a demonstrably false statement. There is nothing democratic about the business of making intelligent men and women feel stupid, decade after decade. Often the fault is the poet's, and any fool can express themselves inadequately, or provide difficulty without reward (he said, knotting his own noose). But intelligent people also have to accept that they might occasionally feel stupid because the argument or idea that the poem incarnates *is* intrinsically difficult, and its nuance is indistinguishable from its value. These poems are the products of superior intelligences. (Here we may indeed just think of Hill's best poetry; who would dare change a word of *The Mystery of the Charity of Charles Péguy?*)

BIBLIOGRAPHY

Agamben, Giorgio. *The End of the Poem: Studies in Poetics* (Stanford, CA: Stanford University Press, 1999)

Aristotle, *Politics*, ed. Benjamin Jowett (Kitchener, ON: Batoche Books, 1999)

Arnold, Matthew. *Dover Beach and Other Poems* (New York: Dover Publications, 1994)

Atkinson, R. C. and R. M. Shiffrin. 'Human Memory: A Proposed System and Its Control Processes', in *The Psychology of Learning and Motivation*, vol. 2., ed. K. W. Spence and J. T. Spence (New York: Academic Press, 1968), 89–195

Attridge, Derek. *Poetic Rhythm: An Introduction* (Cambridge: Cambridge University Press, 1995)

Attridge, Derek. *The Rhythms of English Poetry* (New York: Routledge, 2014)

Auden, W. H. *Collected Poems* (London: Faber & Faber, 2007)

Austin, J. L. *How to Do Things With Words* (Cambridge, MA: Harvard University Press, 1975)

Baddeley, A. D. and G. Hitch. 'Working Memory', in *The Psychology of Learning and Motivation: Advances in Research and Theory*, vol. 8, ed. G. H. Bower (New York: Academic Press, 1974), 47–89

Baker, Nicholson. *The Anthologist* (New York: Simon & Schuster, 2009)

Barrett Browning, Elizabeth. *Selected Poems*, ed. Marjorie Stone and Beverly Taylor (Peterborough, ON: Broadview Press, 2009)

Barrett Browning, Elizabeth. *Sonnets from the Portuguese and Other Poems* (New York: Dover Publications, 1992)

Beer, John (ed.). *Arthur Hugh Clough* (London: Orion Books, 1998)

Berkeley, George. *The Works of George Berkeley*, vol. 1 (London: Macmillan & Co., 1871)

Bishop, Elizabeth. *Poems* (New York: Farrar, Straus & Giroux, 2011)

Blake, William. *Songs of Innocence and Experience* (London: Filiquarian, 2007)

Bogan, Louise. *Body of this Death* (New York: R. M. McBride, 1923)

Borges, Jorge Luis. 'Homeric Versions', in *Selected Non-Fictions*, ed. Eliot Weinberger, trans., Esther Allen and Suzanne Jill Levine (London: Penguin, 2000)

Borges, Jorge Luis. 'The Analytical Language of John Wilkins', in *Other Inquisitions (1937–1952)*, trans. Ruth L. C. Simms (Austin, TX: University of Texas Press, 1964)

Borges, Jorge Luis. 'Pierre Menard, Author of the Quixote', in *Labyrinths*, trans. Donald A. Yates, James E. Irby (New York: New Directions, 1962)

Boroditsky, Lera. 'How Languages Construct Time', in *Space, Time and Number in the Brain*, ed. Stanislas Dehaene and Elizabeth Brannon (New York: Academic Press, 2011), 333–41

Bradley, Ian (ed.). *The Complete Annotated Gilbert and Sullivan* (Oxford: Oxford University Press, 2001)

Bredin, Hugh. 'Metonymy', *Poetics Today* 5, no. 1 (1984): 45–58; http://www.jstor.org/stable/1772425

Bridges, Robert. *The Humours of the Court, and Other Poems* (London: George Bell and Sons, 1893)

Brodsky, Joseph. *Less Than One: Selected Essays* (London: Penguin Modern Classics, 2011)

Brown, George Mackay. *The Collected Poems of George Mackay Brown* (London: John Murray, 2005)

Brown, George Mackay. *Selected Poems 1954–1992* (London: Hodder & Stoughton, 1996)

Burns, Robert. *Collected Poems of Robert Burns* (London: Wordsworth Poetry Library, 1994)

Burnside, John. *Feast Days* (London: Secker & Warburg, 1992)

Burnside, John. *The Light Trap* (London: Jonathan Cape, 2002)

Carson, Ciaran. *Until Before After* (Winston-Salem, NC: Wake Forest University Press, 2010)

Causley, Charles. *Collected Poems* (London: Picador, 2000)

Chambers Dictionary (London: Chambers Harrap, 2014)

Clare, John. *Selected Poems* (London: Penguin, 2000)

Cohen, Jean. *Structure du Langage Poétique* (Paris: Flammarion, 1966)

Coleridge, Samuel Taylor. *Coleridge's Poetry and Prose*, ed. Nicholas Halmi, Paul Magnuson and Raimonda Modiano (New York: W. W. Norton, 2004)

Collins, Billy. *The Art of Drowning* (Pittsburgh, PA: University of Pittsburgh Press, 1995)

Collins, Billy. *Questions About Angels* (Pittsburgh, PA: University of Pittsburgh Press, 1991)

Crawford, Robert. *Selected Poems* (London: Jonathan Cape, 2005)

Cureton, Richard D. 'A Disciplinary Map for Verse Study', *Versification: An Electronic Journal of Literary Prosody* 1 (1997)

Damasio, Antonio. *Looking for Spinoza: Joy, Sorrow, and the Feeling Brain* (London: Vintage, 2004)

Davtian, Stepan and Tatyana Chernigovskaya. 'Psychiatry in Free Fall: In Pursuit of a Semiotic Foothold', *Sign Systems Studies* 31, no. 2 (2003): 533–46

Dennett, Daniel, Max Bennett, Peter Hacker and John Searle. *Neuroscience and Philosophy: Brain, Mind, and Language* (New York: Columbia University Press, 2007)

Deutsch, Diana, Rachael Lapidis and Trevor Henthorn. 'The Speech to Song Illusion', invited lay language paper presented at the 156th meeting of the Acoustical Society of America, Miami, FL, *Journal of the Acoustical Society of America*, 2008

Dickinson, Emily. *The Collected Poems of Emily Dickinson*, ed. Rachel Wetzsteon (New York: Barnes & Noble, 2003)

Dickinson, Emily. *The Poems of Emily Dickinson*, ed. Thomas H. Johnson (Cambridge, MA: Harvard University Press, 1983)

Donaghy, Michael. *Collected Poems* (London: Pan Macmillan, 2014)

Donne, John. *Selected Poems* (London: Penguin, 2006)

Dunn, Douglas. *Elegies* (London: Faber & Faber, 1985)

Eliot, T. S. *Collected Poems: 1909–1962* (London: Faber & Faber, 2002)

Eliot, T. S. *Dante* (London: Faber & Faber, 1929)

Eliot, T. S. *Four Quartets* (London: Faber & Faber, 1979)

Eliot, T. S. *The Use of Poetry & The Use of Criticism* (London: Faber & Faber, 1933)

Empson, William. *Argufying* (London: Chatto & Windus, 1987)

Everett, Daniel L. 'Cultural Constraints on Grammar and Cognition in Pirahã: Another Look at the Design Features of Human Language', *Current Anthropology* 76 (2005): 621–46

Farley, Paul. *The Ice Age* (London: Picador, 2002)

Fauconnier, Gilles and Mark Turner. *The Way We Think: Conceptual Blending and the Mind's Hidden Capacities* (New York: Basic Books, 2002)

Firth, J. R. *Papers in Linguistics 1934–1951* (London: Oxford University Press, 1957)

Frost, Robert. *The Collected Poems* (London: Vintage Classics, 2013)

Frost, Robert. *The Poetry of Robert Frost: The Collected Poems, Complete and Unabridged*, ed. Edward Connery Lathem (New York: Henry Holt, 2002)

Furbank, P. N. *Reflections on the Word 'Image'* (London: Secker & Warburg, 1970)

Gershon, Karen (ed.). *We Came as Children: A Collective Autobiography* (London: Papermac, 1989)

Graham, W. S. *New Collected Poems* (London, Faber & Faber, 2004)

Hacker, Marilyn. *Love, Death, and the Changing of the Seasons* (New York: W. W. Norton, 1986)

Hardy, Florence. *The Life of Thomas Hardy* (London: Wordsworth Editions, 2007)

Harrison, Tony. *Selected Poems* (London: Penguin, 1987)

Hartmann, Charles O. *Free Verse* (Princeton, NJ: Princeton University Press, 1980)

Heaney, Seamus. *Field Work* (London: Faber & Faber, 1979)

Heaney, Seamus. *New Selected Poems 1966–1987* (London: Faber & Faber, 1990)

Heaney, Seamus. *New Selected Poems 1988–2013* (London: Faber & Faber, 2014)

Heaney, Seamus. *Seeing Things* (London: Faber & Faber, 1991)

Heaney, Seamus. *Station Island* (London: Faber & Faber, 1984)

Hecht, Anthony. *Selected Poems*, ed. J. D. McClatchy (New York: Random House, 2011)

Hejinian, Lyn. *The Language of Inquiry* (Berkeley, CA: University of California Press, 2000)

Hill, Selima. *Gloria: Selected Poems* (Newcastle upon Tyne: Bloodaxe, 2008)

Hofmann, Michael. *Acrimony* (London: Faber & Faber, 1986)

Hofstadter, Douglas. *I Am a Strange Loop* (London: Basic Books, 2007)

Houseman, A. E. *A Shropshire Lad* (New York: Dover Publications, 1990)

Hymn to Demeter, trans. Hugh G. Evelyn-White (Cambridge, MA: Harvard University Press, 1914)

Imlah, Mark. *Selected Poems*, ed. Mark Ford (London: Faber & Faber, 2010)

Jaccottet, Philippe. *Selected Poems*, trans. Derek Mahon (London: Penguin, 1988)

Jackendoff, Ray. *Semantic Structures* (Cambridge, MA: MIT Press, 1992)

Jackendoff, Ray. *The Architecture of the Language Faculty.* (Cambridge, MA: MIT Press, 1997)

Jakobson, Roman. 'Linguistics and Poetics', in *Style in Language*, ed. T. Sebeok (Cambridge, MA: MIT Press, 1960), 350–77

Jakobson, Roman. 'The Metaphoric and Metonymic Poles' (1956), in *Metaphor and Metonymy in Comparison and Contrast*, ed. René Dirven and Ralf Pörings (New York: Mouton de Gruyter, 2003), 41–8

James, William, *Principles of Psychology* (New York: Henry Holt, 1890)

Jamie, Kathleen. *Jizzen* (London: Picador, 1999)

Jamie, Kathleen. *The Tree House* (London: Picador, 2004)

Jeffers, Robinson. *The Selected Poetry of Robinson Jeffers*, ed. Tim Hunt (Stanford, CA: Stanford University Press, 2001)

Jones, Katherine Duncan (ed.). *Shakespeare's Sonnets* (London: Arden Shakespeare, 2010)

Jusczyk, Peter W., Anne Cutler and Nancy J. Redanz. 'Infants' Preference for the Predominant Stress Patterns of English Words', *Child Development* 64 (1993): 675–87

Justice, Donald. *Collected Poems* (New York: Alfred A. Knopf, 2006)

Justice, Donald. *New and Selected Poems* (New York: Alfred A. Knopf, 1997)

Kavanagh, Patrick. *Collected Poems* (London: Allen Lane, 2004)

Keats, John. *The Complete Poems*, ed. John Barnard (London: Penguin, 1988)

Kelly, M. H. and S. Martin. 'Domain-General Abilities Applied to Domain-Specific Tasks: Sensitivity to Probabilities in Perception, Cognition, and Language', *Lingua* 92 (1994): 105–40

Kiparsky, Paul. 'The Rhythmic Structure of English Verse', *Linguistic Inquiry* 8 (1977): 189–247

Kiparsky, Paul and Gilbert Youmans (eds). *Phonetics and Phonology*, vol. 1: *Rhythm and Meter* (San Diego, CA: Academic Press, 1989)

Koestler, Arthur. *The Act of Creation* (London: Hutchinson, 1964)

Kövecses, Zoltán. *Metaphor: A Practical Introduction* (Oxford: Oxford University Press, 2002)

Kristeva, Julia. 'Motherhood According to Giovanni Bellini', in *Desire in Language: A Semiotic Approach to Literature and Art*, ed. Leon S. Roudiez, trans. Thomas Gora and Alice A. Jardine (New York: Columbia University Press, 1980)

Lakoff, George. *Don't Think of an Elephant: Know Your Values and Frame the Debate* (White River Junction, VT: Chelsea Green Publishing Co., 1990)

Lakoff, George. *Whose Freedom? The Battle Over America's Most Important Idea* (New York: Farrar, Straus & Giroux, 2007)

Lakoff, George and Mark Johnson. *Metaphors We Live By* (London: University of Chicago Press, 1980)

Langacker, Ronald. *Foundations of Cognitive Grammar*, vol. 1: *Theoretical Prerequisites* (Stanford, CA: Stanford University Press, 1987)

Langer, Susanne K. *Philosophy in a New Key: A Study in the Symbolism of Reason, Rite, and Art*, 2nd edn (Cambridge, MA: Harvard University Press, 1951)

Lanham, Richard A. *A Handlist of Rhetorical Terms*, 2nd edn (San Francisco, CA: University of California Press, 2013)

Larkin, Philip. *Collected Poems*, ed. Anthony Thwaite (London: Faber & Faber, 2003)

Lawrence, D. H. *The Complete Poems of D. H. Lawrence* (Ware: Wordsworth Editions, 2002)

Liberman, Mark and Alan Prince. 'On Stress and Linguistic Rhythm', *Linguistic Inquiry* 8 (1977): 249–336

Locke, John. *An Essay Concerning Human Understanding* (London: Prometheus Books, 1995)

Longfellow, Henry Wadsworth. *Evangeline and Other Poems* (New York: Dover Publications, 1995)

Longfellow, Henry Wadsworth. *Poems and Other Writings*, ed. J. D. McClatchy (New York: Library of America, 2000)

Longley, Michael. *Collected Poems* (London: Jonathan Cape, 2006)

Loucks, James F. and Andrew M. Stauffer (eds). *Robert Browning's Poetry: Authoritative Texts, Criticism* (New York: W. W. Norton, 1979)

Lowell, Robert. *Life Studies* (London: Faber & Faber, 1959)

MacCaig, Norman. *The Many Days: Selected Poems of Norman MacCaig* (Edinburgh: Polygon, 2011)

MacDiarmid, Hugh. *The Islands of Scotland* (London: Scribner, 1939)

McGilchrist, Iain. *The Master and his Emissary: The Divided Brain and the Making of the Western World* (New Haven, CT: Yale University Press, 2009)

MacNeice, Louis. *Collected Poems*, ed. Peter Macdonald (London: Faber & Faber, 2007)

Magnus, Margaret. *Gods of the Word: Archetypes in the Consonants* (Kirksville, MO: Thomas Jefferson University Press, 1999)

Mahon, Derek. *Raw Materials* (Loughcrew: Gallery Press, 2011)

Mahon, Derek. *Collected Poems* (Oldcastle: Gallery Books, 1999)

Mahon, Derek. *Lives* (Oxford: Oxford University Press, 1972)

Mallarmé, Stéphane. *Poésies complètes* (Paris: Éditions de Cluny, 1948)

Marvell, Andrew. 'An Horatian Ode Upon Cromwell's Return From Ireland', in *The Broadview Anthology of British Literature*, 2nd edn (London: Broadview Press, 2010), 967–9

Marvell, Andrew. *The Complete Poems*, ed. Elizabeth Donno and Johnathan Bate. (London: Penguin, 2005)

Matte Blanco, Ignacio. *The Unconscious as Infinite Sets: An Essay in Bi-Logic* (London: Karnac, 1998)

Meyer, Kuno. *Selections from Ancient Irish Poetry* (London: Constable, 1911)

Millay, Edna St Vincent. *Collected Poems*, ed. Norma Millay (New York: HarperPerennial, 2011)

Miller, George A. 'The Magical Number Seven, Plus or Minus Two: Some Limits on Our Capacity for Processing Information', *Psychological Review* 63 (1956): 81–97

Miller, George A., Christiane Fellbaum and Randee Tengi. *WordNet: A Lexical Database for English* (Princeton, NJ: Princeton University, 2015), https://wordnet.princeton.edu/wordnet/

Mitchell, Roger. *Lemon Peeled the Moment Before: New & Selected Poems, 1967–2008* (Port Townsend, WA: Ausable Press, 2008)

Moore, Marianne. *Complete Poems* (London: Penguin, 1994)

Muldoon, Paul. *The Annals of Chile* (New York: Farrar, Straus & Giroux, 1995)

Muldoon, Paul. *Mules* (London: Faber & Faber, 1977)

Muldoon, Paul. *Poems 1968–1998* (London: Faber & Faber, 2011)

Muldoon, Paul. *Poems 1968–2014* (London: Faber & Faber, 2016)

Muldoon, Paul. *Quoof* (London: Faber & Faber, 2001)

O'Brien, Flann. *An Béal Bocht*, trans. Patrick C. Power (London: Dalkey Archive Press, 1971)

O'Brien, Sean. *Collected Poems* (London: Picador, 2012)

O'Brien, Sean. *HMS Glasshouse* (Oxford: Oxford University Press, 1992)

O'Hara, Frank. *The Collected Poems of Frank O'Hara*, ed. Donald Allen (Oakland, CA: University of California Press, 1995)

Olds, Sharon. *Selected Poems* (London: Jonathan Cape, 2005)

Oswald, Alice. *Falling Awake* (London: Jonathan Cape, 2016)

Oswald, Alice. *The Thing in the Gap Stone Stile* (London: Faber & Faber, 2010)

Paterson, Don. *Landing Light* (London: Faber & Faber, 2003)

Paterson, Don and Charles Simic (eds). *New British Poetry* (Minneapolis, MN: Graywolf Press, 2004)

Peirce, C. S. *The Collected Papers of Charles Sanders Peirce*, vol. 2, ed. C. Hartshorne and P. Weiss (Cambridge, MA: Harvard University Press, 1958)

Perloff, Marjorie. 'Janus-Faced Blockbuster' – Review of Cary Nelson (ed.), *Anthology of Modern American Poetry*, *Symploké* 8, nos. 1/2 (2000): 205–13

Phillips, Catherine (ed.). *Gerard Manley Hopkins: The Major Works* (Oxford: Oxford University Press, 2002)

Pinker, Steven. 'Block That Metaphor!' – Review of George Lakoff, *Whose Freedom? The Battle Over America's Most Important Idea*, *New Republic* (9 October 2006), https://newrepublic.com/article/77730/block-metaphor-steven-pinker-whose-freedom-george-lakoff)

Pinker, Steven. *The Stuff of Thought: Language as a Window into Human Nature* (London: Penguin, 2008)

Pinker, Steven. *Words and Rules: The Ingredients of Language* (1999; repr. London: HarperPerennial, 2011)

Plath, Sylvia. *The Collected Poems* (London: HarperPerennial Modern Classics, 2008)

Porchia, Antonio. *Voices*, trans. W. S. Merwin (Port Townsend, WA: Copper Canyon Press, 1994)

Pound, Ezra. 'A Few Don'ts by an Imagiste', in *Modernism: An Anthology*, ed. Lawrence Rainey (London: Blackwell, 2005)

Preminger, Alex and T. V. F. Brogan (eds). *The New Princeton Encyclopedia of Poetry and Poetics* (Princeton, NJ: Princeton University Press, 1993)

Prynne, J. H. *Poems* (Newcastle upon Tyne: Bloodaxe, 2005)

Prynne, J. H. 'Mental Ears and Poetic Work', *Chicago Review* 55, no. 1 (2010)

Quinn, Arthur. *Figures of Speech: 60 Ways to Turn a Phrase* (New York: Routledge, 1995)

Raine, Craig. *Collected Poems 1978–1998* (London: Picador, 2000)

Raine, Craig. *A Martian Sends a Postcard Home* (Oxford: Oxford University Press, 1979)

Raworth, Tom. *Collected Poems* (Manchester: Carcanet, 2003)

Richard, Ann Thompson and David Scott Kastan (eds). *The Arden Shakespeare: Complete Works* (London: Arden Shakespeare, 2001)

Richards, I. A. *The Philosophy of Rhetoric* (Oxford: Oxford University Press, 1936)

Riley, Denise. *Say Something Back* (London: Picador, 2016)

Schnackenberg, Gjertrud. *Supernatural Love: Poems 1976–2000* (Newcastle upon Tyne: Bloodaxe, 2001)

Scruton, Roger. *The Aesthetics of Music* (Oxford: Oxford University Press, 1997)

Shakespeare, William. *The Comedy of Errors*, ed. Charles Whitworth (Oxford: Oxford University Press, 2002)

Smith, Barbara Herrnstein. *Poetic Closure: A Study of How Poems End* (Chicago, IL: University of Chicago Press, 1968)

Stanford Encyclopedia of Philosophy, http://plato.stanford.edu/entries/abstract-objects/

Sutherland, Keston. *Poetical Works 1999–2015* (London: Enitharmon Press, 2016)

Sweeney, Matthew. 'In the Garden', *Poetry London* 62 (2009)

Swinburne, Algernon Charles. *Selected Poems*, ed. L. M. Findlay (New York: Routledge, 2002)

Tagg, Philip. *Music's Meanings* (Larchmont, NY: The Mass Media Music Scholar's Press, 2012)

Tate, James. *Selected Poems* (Middletown, CT: Wesleyan University Press, 1991)

Tennyson, Alfred Lord. *In Memoriam*, ed. Eric Irving Gray (New York: W. W. Norton, 2004)

Théorie analytique de la chaleur (Paris: Firmin Didot, 1822), qtd in Florence Hardy, *The Life of Thomas Hardy, 1840–1928* (New York: St. Martin's Press, 1962), 229

Vico, Giambattista. *New Science: Principles of New Science Concerning the Common Nature of Nations*, 3rd edn (London: Penguin, 1999)

Wallace, Willard M. *Sir Walter Raleigh* (Princeton, NJ: Princeton University Press, 1959)

Wilbur, Richard. *Collected Poems 1943–2004* (Palo Alto, CA: Harcourt, 2006)

Wilbur, Richard. *The Mind Reader: New Poems* (Palo Alto, CA: Harcourt, 1976)

Williams, C. K. *Collected Poems* (New York: Farrar, Straus & Giroux, 2006)

Williams, C. K. *The Vigil* (Newcastle upon Tyne: Bloodaxe, 1997)

Williams, William Carlos. *Selected Essays* (New York: New Directions, 1954)

Wimsatt, W. K. *The Verbal Icon: Studies in the Meaning of Poetry* (Lexington, KY: University of Kentucky Press, 1954)

Wittgenstein, Ludwig. *Philosophical Investigations*, trans. G. E. M. Anscombe (Boston, MA: Blackwell, 1973)

Wordsworth, William. *The Collected Poems of William Wordsworth*, ed. Antonia Till (London: Wordsworth Editions, 1994)

Wordsworth, William. *The Letters of William Wordsworth*, ed. Alan G. Hill (Oxford: Oxford University Press, 1985)

Wordsworth, William. *Selected Poems*, ed. Stephen Gill (London: Penguin, 2004)

Wright, Charles. *Chickamauga* (New York: Farrar, Straus & Giroux, 1996)

Wright, Charles. *Country Music: Selected Early Poems* (Middletown, CT: Wesleyan University Press, 1982)

Wright, James. *Above the River: The Complete Poems* (New York: Farrar, Straus & Giroux, 1992)

Yeats, W. B. *The Collected Poems of W. B. Yeats* (Ware: Wordsworth Editions, 1994)

Young, Dean. *Design with X* (Middletown, CT: Wesleyan New Poets, 1988)

INDEX

Olds, Sharon, 418
'The Daughter Goes to Camp', 418
'The Race', 416
onomatopoeia, 33, 34; *see also*
iconicity *and* phonesthemes
ontological categories, 146–7
ontologico-cultural metaphors, 113–
16, 208, 694
ontology, 194
'open'/'closed' texts, 100–1
'open'/'closed' words, 94–5
optional depth, 304–5, 310, 319
originality, 170, 191, 204, 227, 300
origo, 209
Orpheus, 8, 22, 90
Oswald, Alice, 204, 228–9
'Bike Ride on a Roman Road',
203–7, 212
'Body', 446
overdemocratisation, 669–70
overdetermination, 377, 386–97, 594,
620, 638
overinterpretation/oversignifying, 17,
110, 112, 167, 172, 226, 280, 293–
5, 328, 349, 374; *see also* meaning
overtones, 5, 244, 691
connotation and, 673–4
Owen, Wilfred, 'Strange Meeting',
60–1

p-text (present text), 304–17, 693–4
pace, 173
paeonic feet/metres, 362, 377
'page poetry', 83, 335
palindrome, 75, 682
paradigm, 135
paradox, 40, 75
intertextuality and, 693–4
rhyme and, 81–2
paragmenon, 680
parallelism, 680

paranoia, 110, 156, 173
paraphrase, 44–5, 232, 256, 528–9,
690
pararhyme, 59–61, 81, 84
degrees of, 84
parasemia, 292–3
parataxis, 99, 100, 681
parenthesis, 444, 681
Parker, Charlie, 567, 661
paronomasia, 170, 306, 430, 681
Pascal, Blaise, 16
pastiche, 669
pathemes, 6, 63, 239–59, 269–72,
432
and meaning, 257–9
music and, 243–51, 253, 256
symbols and, 256–7
pathetic fallacy, 191, 212, 223
patter-song, 552–3
pattern(ing), 48
patterning, consonantal, 88–93
pattern(ing)
counterpattern, 81–2
intonational, 253–5
template and, 355–6
variation and, 50–2, 55–6
see also form, metre *and* scansion
peak shift, 35, 66, 121
Peirce, C. S., 182, 185–6, 237, 241,
683–4
perception, 110–16, 140, 674–5
contrivance and, 56
intentionalist theories of, 38
isochrony and, 365–7
meaning and, 112–13
pitch and, 567
prelinguistic, 21, 110
screening in, 50
of speech and song, 254
of time, 21, 75–6, 363–4, 398–9,
452–3, 667